The Asian Political Dictionary

THE ASIAN POLITICAL DICTIONARY

Lawrence Ziring
C. I. Eugene Kim
Western Michigan University

ABC-CLIO

Santa Barbara, California
Oxford, England

This book is Smyth sewn and printed on acid-free paper to meet library standards.

Library of Congress Cataloging in Publication Data

Ziring, Lawrence, 1928–
    The Asian political dictionary.

    (Clio dictionaries in political science; # 10)
    Includes index.
    1. Asia—Politics and government—Dictionaries.
I. Kim, C. I. Eugene (Chong Ik Eugene), 1930—
II. Title. III. Series.
DS31.Z57   1985   950'.03'21   85-5994
ISBN 0-87436-368-3
ISBN 0-87436-369-1 (pbk.)

10 9 8 7 6 5 4 3 2 1

ABC-Clio, Inc.
Riviera Campus
2040 Alameda Padre Serra, Box 4397
Santa Barbara, California 93140-4397

Clio Press Ltd.
55 St. Thomas Street
Oxford, OX1 1JG, England

Manufactured in the United States of America

This volume is dedicated to
Jack C. Plano
a creative talent and a
good friend

Clio Dictionaries in Political Science

SERIES STATEMENT

Language precision is the primary tool of every scientific discipline. That aphorism serves as the guideline for this series of political dictionaries. Although each book in the series relates to a specific topical or regional area in the discipline of political science, entries in the dictionaries also emphasize history, geography, economics, sociology, philosophy, and religion.

This dictionary series incorporates special features designed to help the reader overcome any language barriers that may impede a full understanding of the subject matter. For example, the concepts included in each volume were selected to complement the subject matter in existing texts and other books. All but one volume utilize a subject-matter chapter arrangement that is most useful for classroom and study purposes.

Entries in all volumes include an up-to-date definition plus a paragraph of *Significance* in which the authors discuss and analyze the term's historical and current relevance. Most entries are also cross-referenced to give the reader the opportunity to seek additional information related to the subject of inquiry. A comprehensive index, found in both hard cover and paperback editions, allows the reader to locate major entries and other concepts, events, and institutions discussed within these entries.

The political and social sciences suffer more than most disciplines from semantic confusion. This is attributable, *inter alia*, to the popularization of the language, and to the focus on many diverse foreign political and social systems. This dictionary series is dedicated to overcoming some of this confusion through careful writing of thorough, accurate definitions for the central concepts, institutions, and events that comprise the basic knowledge of each of the subject fields. New titles in the series will be issued periodically, including some in related social science disciplines.

—Jack C. Plano
Series Editor

CONTENTS

A NOTE ON HOW TO USE THIS BOOK

The Asian Political Dictionary is organized so that entries and supplementary data can be located in either of two ways. First, items are arranged alphabetically within subject matter chapters. Terms like SEATO or the Colombo Plan, for example, can be found in the chapter titled "Diplomacy." When doubtful about which chapter to look up, consult the general index. Page numbers for entries appear in the index in heavy black type; subsidiary concepts discussed within entries can be found in the index identified by page numbers in regular type. For study purposes, numerous entries have also been subsumed under major topical headings in the index, giving the reader access to broad classes of related information.

The reader can also more fully explore a topic by using the extensive cross-references provided in most entries. These may lead to materials included in the same chapter or may refer him or her to the subject matter of the other chapters. Page numbers have been included in all cross-references for the convenience of the reader. A few concepts can be found as entries in more than one chapter, but in each case the definition and significance of the item is related to the subject matter of that chapter in which the entry appears.

The authors have adopted the format of this book to offer the user a variety of useful applications. These include its use as: (1) a *dictionary* and *reference guide;* (2) a *study guide;* (3) a supplement to a *textbook* or to monographs on Asia, and (4) a *social science* aid for use in government, business, and journalism.

PREFACE

Asia's diversity, its vastness and complexity, can never be captured in a single volume. That was not our objective. Indeed, our task was more modest. When we launched upon this assignment, it was with the thought that only the essential facts of contemporary Asian politics, government and foreign relations could be collected between the covers of a single book. Our assumption was based upon the satisfactory completion of other volumes in this series that focus attention on Africa, Latin America, the Soviet Union, and Eastern Europe. Moreover, one of us had earlier authored the *Middle East Political Dictionary*, and that experience reinforced our belief that an Asian political dictionary was not only possible, but necessary. We therefore immersed ourselves in this project, and the present volume is the result of our joint labor.

The Asian Political Dictionary includes twenty-seven countries and territories, spreading from South, to Southeast, to East Asia; from India and Pakistan through Indonesia, northward to China and Japan. Attention also has been given the Indian Ocean, and as a consequence, several island nations in that expansive southern sea have been added.

Like the other volumes in the series, *The Asian Political Dictionary* is divided into chapters. Each chapter groups related and comparative subject matter. The subjects or entries in each chapter are arranged alphabetically to facilitate retrieval. Each entry is divided into two parts: the first part is essentially descriptive; and the second part is primarily, but not exclusively, analytical. The book's design establishes limits for the number of possible entries. Therefore many entries will include materials and data that may not be headlined, but nevertheless represent additional items. These may be considered subsumed entries, or entries within entries. In effect, the student of political Asia will find far more than the approximately three hundred entries that form the overall outline of this book. Use of the country index found in the front matter of the volume and the general index in the back of the book will enable the reader to find these data.

The book is called a political dictionary, not an encyclopedia, because we believe the latter would be far more detailed. Although a single volume on Asia can never be judged comprehensive, *The Asian Political*

Dictionary contains descriptive information and insight which will be useful to librarians, government officials, journalists, radio and television newswriters, commentators and correspondents, and researchers. This book, like the others in the series, however, was written with the teacher and student in mind. The book is designed to help the teacher present political Asia to the class. It can be used as a supplemental text, or as the major text in a course. It should be particularly useful in survey courses focusing on Asia or the more general non-Western world courses. We hope the student will find the book stimulating as well as informative, memorable as well as manageable.

We have enjoyed writing this volume, and trust our excitement will be detected as the pages unfold. This seems the appropriate place to acknowledge our indebtedness to many contributors who have assisted us in writing this volume. We wish particularly to cite Jack C. Plano, our friend and colleague who created the format, and whose *American Political Dictionary,* the prototype for all the other political dictionaries, is now in its seventh edition. Jack Plano is more than the Series Editor, he is the inspiration and the indefatigable scholar who truly lives by the motto "the mission comes before self." Jack read the completed manuscript and shepherded its passage through the several stages of production. We are ever grateful, and in his debt.

We also wish to acknowledge the conscientious and expert efforts of Mrs. Dorothea Barr who typed repeated versions of the manuscript, who was quick to point up errors or inconsistencies, and who never lost her sense of humor.

Several of our graduate students assisted with the research, and passed long hours in the library checking sources, and identifying possible entries. They are: Joseph Veneklase, Linda Zauner, Dan Uldricks, and Sam Aga. Appreciation is also due Professor Han-kyo Kim and Professor Marjorie Ho. Professor Kim read a large portion of the manuscript and made important suggestions. Professor Ho was especially helpful in the spelling of Chinese names.

We cannot fail to cite the expert copyediting of Christine Silvestri or our delight in working with Ms. Cecelia Albert, Editor, ABC-Clio. Cecelia has always been cooperative, flexible, and patient, and she made all the difficult moments seem like minor, inconsequential events. For lightening our burden, thank you.

Finally, we must express our appreciation to our wives Raye and Hiroko, who spurred us on. And to our children, Lee and Sarah, and Margaret and Adlai, who one day, we trust, will find this book to their liking.

We alone are responsible for errors of fact or interpretation.

—Lawrence Ziring
—C. I. Eugene Kim
Western Michigan University

GUIDE TO COUNTRIES

This Guide contains references to Asian countries only. For other countries, see the Subject Index, p. 425.

The Asian Political Dictionary

1. Political Geography

Amu Darya (Oxus River)   The Amu Darya is the river originating in the Pamir Plateau in Central Asia. It is approximately 1,550 miles (2,500 kilometers) long and follows a course southwest between the Tadjik S.S.R. and Afghanistan, and then turns northwest between the Turkmen S.S.R. and the Uzbek S.S.R., until it empties into the Aral Sea in the Soviet Union. The river is only partially navigable and is more important for irrigation than commerce. The Amu Darya has had an important strategic history in the nineteenth and twentieth centuries. The river was established as a line of control between imperial Russian and British interests in the waning decades of the nineteenth century. The Russians swept into Central Asia midway through the century, conquering and absorbing the Muslim *khanates* (kingdoms) in the region. The British were concerned that the Russian advance would not end there but would continue until Afghanistan and Iran were brought within the tsar's orbit. Sensing a threat to their interests in the Persian Gulf, but especially to their empire in India, the British were determined to check the Russian drive. Such an effort, however, involved establishing Afghanistan as a buffer between the two empires, and the Amu Darya seemed the natural dividing line between the Russian domains and the Afghans. Britain went to war with Afghanistan in 1837–42, in order to establish its presence in Afghanistan, and a "Forward Policy" enunciated by Lord Lytton was eventually transformed into holy writ by Lord Curzon (both of them viceroys of India). In addition to troop maneuvers in and near Afghanistan, the British and Russians agreed on the settlement of the border between the tsarist state and Afghanistan.

Internecine conflict within Afghanistan permitted the Russians to move their Central Asian conquests to the Oxus in 1869. The British gave support to Emir Sher Ali, the Afghan king, and the Russians were encouraged to accept the Amu Darya as the northern boundary of Afghanistan in 1873. It was officially affirmed in 1887. The Bolsheviks acknowledged the Amu Darya border in 1920, and the Afghanistan-USSR Treaty of 1946 again proclaimed its significance and applied the *Thalweg* (middle channel principle in international law) to the boundary. *See also* AFGHAN-USSR CONFLICT (1979–), p. 373; WAKHAN CORRIDOR, p. 46; WARM WATER PORT POLICY, p. 47.

Significance   The Amu Darya has served as a historic dividing line, separating British and Russian imperialism in Asia. So long as Central Asia was divided between numerous rival kingdoms and tribal units, the British displayed little concern for the security of India. The elimination of these small sovereignties, by inclusion into the spreading Russian Empire, was viewed with considerable apprehension. By 1836 the Russians had almost reached the Amu Darya, and their influence had been established in Persia (Iran). Under Russian instigation, a Persian force was dispatched to Herat, and the local leaders around Kandahar were engaged in a conspiracy, with Persian-Russian assistance, to undermine the Afghan government of Dost Mohammad in Kabul. Russia, poised at the Amu Darya, was judged by the British to be a direct threat to India. Instead of supporting Dost Mohammad, however, the British also were determined to destroy him. Dost Mohammad was the only Afghan leader capable of welding the heterogeneous Afghan tribes into a unified power strong enough to stem the Russian advance, but the British incorrectly saw Dost Mohammad as serving Russian interests. The result was a costly conflict that prevented Afghanistan from assisting its Central Asian brethren in their struggle with the Russians. The British were able to get the Russians to accept the Amu Darya as the northern frontier of Afghanistan, but this did little to guarantee Afghanistan's emergence as a viable political actor in the region.

The Amu Darya border lasted through the nineteenth and well into the twentieth century. With the British withdrawal from India in 1947, however, the formidable power that had effected a balance of forces in the region was no longer available. Nor was the United States in a position to fill the vacuum left by the British. Russia, therefore, as the Soviet Union, quickly gained major influence over the Afghan scene. Between the end of World War II and the 1978 Afghan revolution, which brought a socialist government to power in Kabul, the Soviets worked to establish their preeminence in the country. When the Marxist Kabul regime was confronted by Afghan tribal and Islamic resistance, and suffering from severe internal cleavages and personality conflicts, the Soviets did what their predecessors were constrained from doing. In December 1979 the Russians moved approximately 80,000 troops across the Amu Darya. The troops fanned out over roads built earlier by the Soviets, and they attempted to bring the whole of Afghanistan under their control. Although this was not the first Russian foray into Afghan territory, this particular invasion suggested a more permanent Soviet presence in the vicinity of the Indian subcontinent and the Persian Gulf. With new bridges constructed over the Amu Darya, and with a substantial and growing Soviet force in Afghanistan, the river frontier between the two countries is no longer a geopolitical barrier.

Archipelago: Indonesia   A cluster of islands in a large body of water. Indonesia, Japan, and the Philippines are archipelago nations. Indonesia is the largest of the three and includes more than 13,000 islands stretching over an area of the South Pacific in excess of 4,000 miles, from a location to the west of Singapore as far as Papua New Guinea. The principal islands of Indonesia are Java, Sumatra, Bali, Sulawesi (Celebes), the Moluccas, the major portion of Kalimantan (Borneo) and about half of New Guinea. Indonesia is a vast region-state reflecting a high magnitude of diversity. More than 250 languages and dialects are spoken on its many islands. Although predominantly Muslim, Indonesia also has important Christian, Hindu, and Buddhist minorities. The official language of Indonesia is Bahasa Indonesia, similar to Bahasa Malaysia. Both are derived from the Malay language group. *See also* BAHASA INDONESIA, p. 57.

Significance   Indonesia's archipelagic geography and diverse population pose special problems for government. In part, because of separatist tendencies, the political system has been largely authoritarian and the country's political leaders have labored to construct a centralized unitary state. Although constitutionalism has been stressed throughout Indonesia's history, the stability of the country rests on the strength of the armed forces. Rebellious acts, whether on Java, Sumatra or the Moluccas, have been crushed by the Indonesian army. Indonesia also has aggressively pursued its interests by forcibly seizing Portuguese East Timor, which was proclaimed its 27th province in 1976. That issue remains on the agenda of the UN General Assembly, but Indonesia shows no signs of yielding to the demands of its critics, let alone to the Front for the Liberation and Independence of East Timor (*Fretilin*). The Fretilin resistance movement withdrew a key political demand in November 1984. The leftist organization dropped its claim to be the only organization representing the Timor people and called for a negotiated settlement of the conflict. Rumors circulated that the shift in guerrilla policy had come from Fretilin's leader, José Gusma. It was also believed that meetings between Fretilin, Jakarta, and Lisbon, the former colonial power, could bring a termination to the protracted conflict. Australia's apparent intention to acknowledge some form of Indonesian control over East Timor may have been a factor in the Fretilin decision to seek a diplomatic solution. Australia was more concerned with resolving a water boundary dispute with Jakarta over the oil-rich Timor Sea. Although the circumstances were different, Indonesia prevented the Dutch from sustaining their presence in West New Guinea. With UN assistance it took control of the territory, which it renamed West Irian. Indonesia also waged an unsuccessful struggle to wrest North Borneo from Malaysia. Indonesia appears determined to control all the islands of the archipelago.

Asia   The world's largest continent, 18.5 million square miles (32 million square kilometers), where more than half the human family lives (estimated in 1984 at almost 3 billion). The Asian landscape includes the tallest mountain ranges, the broadest steppe regions, the most desolate wilderness, the greatest density of population along its river basins, and a vast Arctic tundra. On one side are luxuriant tropical lands, on the other a great frozen wasteland. The world's religions have their origin in Asia. The art of cultivation began there. The oldest irrigation systems were constructed in the Asian hinterland. From Asia came the calendar, and the numeral system, medicine and music. The production of tea and wine, bricks and glass, linens and silk, gunpowder and the compass, all trace their origins to Asia. The idea of village communities and the first urban centers are identified with this great continent.

One third of the continent is more than 3,000 feet (940 meters) above sea level. The mountain ranges effectively divide Asia into southern and northern halves. They stretch from Turkish Armenia to the Georgian Kura Valley in the Caucasus, to the Elburz of Iran, and the Hindu Kush of Afghanistan. The Pamirs of the Soviet Union join with the Himalayas that form the northern border of India, Nepal, and Bhutan. From there, the great peaks extend across the expansive Tibetan plateau to the Kunlun, Tien Shan, and Altai mountains of China. Even the island nation of Japan is predominantly mountainous, forcing the population to manage its existence from an extremely thin area of habitation.

Three peninsula subcontinents project from the southern portion. In southwest Asia there is the Arabian peninsula, and in the center lies the peninsula shared principally by Pakistan, India, and Bangladesh. To the southeast lies the Malay archipelago, a remnant of what was believed to be the land bridge to Australia. Smaller peninsulas in the far eastern sector include the two Koreas and Soviet Kamchatka, which reach out to the Pacific Ocean and the earth's deepest undersea chasms, more than five miles beneath the surface. *See also* ASIAN HIGHWAY, p. 7; CENTRAL

ASIA, p. 8; HIMALAYAS, p. 16; INDIAN OCEAN, p. 22; SUBCONTINENT, p. 38.

Significance   Asia is the historic "cradle of civilization." In the area to the south and east of the central mountain ridges, a fraction of the continent's total area, reside more than nine-tenths of Asia's enormous population. The great civilizations of antiquity originated in this zone. It was also from this area that the greatest of the world's migrations and intellectual movements began their course, but because of Asia's kaleidoscopic diversity, its restless spirit, and its gigantic proportions, nothing like a unified Asian culture emerged. One need note only the differences between Arabs, Indians, and Chinese to understand this observation, or its importance. By contrast, the peoples of Europe (in a broad view, a western peninsula of the Asian continent), Africa, North and South America, as well as Oceania, exhibit varying degrees of cultural homogeneity. Similarly, Asia contains the widest variations in physical types and cultures of all the continents, in addition to a diversity of major languages equalled only by the unique circumstances encountered in the Americas.

Asian Highway   The Asian Highway project was launched in 1958 by the United Nations Economic Commission for Asia and the Far East (ECAFE). Its stated purpose was the modernization and linkage of existing roads to form a network of land communication from Turkey in the southwest, to Vietnam and Singapore in the southeastern portion of the Asian continent. The total road miles envisaged by the enterprise was 34,000 and it was meant to service an area of 2,500,000 square miles and a population well in excess of one billion. The highway traces a course over ancient caravan routes, now improved by surfaced roads capable of handling at least one lane of motorized traffic in each direction.

Although still incomplete, the Asian Highway already connects many of Asia's capital cities and seaports. Fourteen countries are covered by the project. They include: Afghanistan, Burma, India, Indonesia, Iran, Kampuchea (Cambodia), Laos, Malaysia, Nepal, Pakistan, Singapore, Sri Lanka, Thailand, and Vietnam. When completed, the Asian Highway was to be linked with the European Highway at the Iranian and Iraqi frontiers. By the end of the 1970s, it was possible to travel from Tehran in Iran to Dhaka in Bangladesh and from Vientiane in Laos to Singapore, and from there by ferry service to the island of Java, and then on to the Indonesian capital of Djakarta. By 1984, it was possible to travel the entire distance from Turkey to Vietnam, Malaysia and Indonesia, but specific areas through Nepal, northern Thailand, and southern Burma were still in need of improvement or completion. *See also* ASIA, p. 6; HO CHI MINH TRAIL, p. 19.

Significance The Asian Highway Coordinating Committee, established in 1965, was assisted by the Transport Technical Bureau, an agency designed by the United Nations. With the help of ECAFE these organs formulated plans and raised funds for the Asian Highway project. Prior to the development of the highway, overland movement throughout Asia and between Asia and Europe was difficult and heavily dependent on traditional sea routes. The Asian Highway provided a more direct, more efficient, quicker means of transportation. It was decidedly shorter and promised to make the passage of goods between the countries more economic. Moreover, feeder roads from national arterial routes were aimed at expanding agriculture and ultimately transforming Asia into a self-sufficient food producer. The highway stood to promote regional cooperation and understanding and international trade.

Although the Asian Highway offered the promise of a better future for the people of Asia, it posed political and military problems of considerable concern. Roads could be used for tactical and strategic purposes. In a hostile environment, an efficient road system could be an invitation to aggression. The Soviets built a network of roads from their Central Asian republics through Afghanistan's principal metropolitan centers, and in 1979 they proceeded to use that system to transport their army to the country's vital sectors. Prior to the invasion, the new road system placed Soviet troops only eighteen hours by road transport from Uzbekistan to the Pakistani frontier. Now thousands of Soviet troops stand astride Pakistan's frontier. In somewhat similar fashion, Nepal is now more accessible to India, and Iran to Iraq and vice versa. In the last analysis, however, the Asian Highway means that Asians are more intimately associated with one another, and beyond, with the larger world. A historic lifestyle in which people lived remote, somewhat primitive lives, is passing. Governments are destined to assume even greater authority over distant locations, and there is likely to be less tolerance of nomadic or isolated behavior.

Central Asia The broad expanse between the Gobi Desert, the Tarim Basin, the lowlands of Turan and Bukhara, the Kirghiz steppe and the high mountain ranges between them. A remote hinterland, inhabited by herdsmen and nomads, Central Asia is historically identified as the land from which the great conquerors carried their message and influence to Europe, Persia (Iran), India, and China. The more prominent among them were the Scythians, Huns, Dzungars, Mongols, and Turks. Led by personalities like Attila, Genghis Khan, and Tamerlane, they left a trail of blood and destruction from the Far East to Central Europe and the Middle East. Although absorbed by the more developed cultures and empires that they ravaged, they left behind a legacy of politico-military and administrative power that lingers to this day.

The first penetration of the region by the Caucasians is linked with the merchants of Novgorod who opened Central Asia to Russian settlers in the ninth and tenth centuries. It was not until the nineteenth century that much of the region was drawn into the Tsarist Russian empire. First, Armenia and Georgia in the Caucasus, and later the lowlands of Bukhara were absorbed by the tsar's armies. Today most of Central Asia is an integral part of the Soviet Union and, apart from the Caucasian republics, it has been divided into the republics of Kazakhstan, Turkmenistan, Uzbekistan, Kirghizistan, and Tadzhikistan. Chinese Xinjiang (Sinkiang) may be considered the eastern extension of Central Asia, and Afghanistan, the southern extension. *See also* WARM WATER PORT POLICY, p. 47.

Significance   For all its mystery and exoticism, Central Asia has acted as a geographic pivot of history. Not only is it identified with some of the more infamous personalities of European history, it has also been the landbridge between East Asia and Europe and greater Asia and the Middle East. In the nineteenth century, Great Britain saw a threat to its Indian empire in the Tsarist Russian advance toward the subcontinent and the warm water of the Persian Gulf and Indian Ocean. The contest for supremacy between Britain and Russia over Central Asia was described as "The Great Game," and the primary battleground for their confrontation was established in Afghanistan.

After the Bolshevik revolution it was believed in some circles that Lenin would permit the Muslims of Central Asia to reclaim their lost independence, but by 1926 the communists had successfully neutralized their opposition in the region and had made it an integral part of the Soviet Union. The five Soviet republics were formed during this period and a Russification program was launched to permanently tie the area to the Bolshevik state. Britain's retreat from India and the Persian Gulf following World War II left the Soviet Union alone to exploit the political and military weaknesses and rivalries in the region. Moscow drew Afghanistan within its sphere of influence during this period and was instrumental in preparing for a Marxist takeover of the Kabul government in 1978. In 1979 the Soviets invaded Afghanistan, ostensibly to save a faltering and divided Marxist government. Not to be overlooked in the campaign, however, was the Soviet Union's older quest for dominance in all Central Asia and the potential use of that dominance to press historic claims to warm water ports on the Indian Ocean.

China: Autonomous Regions   Geographical regions of China in which national minorities exercise considerable autonomy in local affairs. Mainland China's population numbers more than a billion. Although most are Han Chinese, many are members of minority groups. National minorities constitute only six percent of the population, but they inhabit almost 60 percent of China's territory, covering 16 different provinces. Divided into 50 minority groups, they are mostly concentrated in China's peripheries, bordering the Soviet Union in the north and northwest, Korea in the northeast, and India, Burma, Laos, and Vietnam in the south and southeast. China's official policy has been to permit the larger minority groups to organize their organs of self-government whenever they constitute more than 50 percent of the inhabitants of the area.

At the regional level, there are five autonomous regions: Guangxi Zhuang (Kwangsi Chung, established in September 1955); Nei Monggol (Inner Mongolia, established in May 1947); Ningxia Hui (Ningsia Hui, established in October 1958); Xinjiang Uygur (Sinkiang Uighur, established in September 1955); and Xizang (Tibet, established in September 1965). The major minority groups inhabiting these regions are: the Zhuangs (7.7 million) in Guangxi Zhung, Hui or Chinese Muslims (3.9 million) in Ningxia Hui, Mongols (1.6 million) in Nei Nonggul, Uygur (3.9 million) in Xinjiang Uygur, and Tibetan (3.2 million) in Xizang. Since 1949, the Chinese government has sought to achieve national solidarity and territorial integrity. At the same time, it has permitted the minorities to run their local governments and preserve their national identities. Although the minorities must learn Chinese, they are permitted to use their languages and dialects in their local communications. They have been systematically recruited by the Chinese Communist Party and increasingly given roles in national affairs. *See also* CHINA: MIDDLE KINGDOM, p. 11; TIBET (XIZANG), p. 42.

Significance   The autonomous regions are located in China's critical border areas. Climatically and topographically inhospitable, these areas are sparsely populated but rich in natural resources. In addition, many of the borders of these areas are disputed with neighboring states, such as the USSR, India, and Vietnam. In the past, foreign powers repeatedly sought to detach these areas from China by exploiting traditional misunderstanding, suspicion, and hatred between the Han Chinese and the minority people. Since 1949, the Chinese government has tried to integrate these states with the rest of the country, following the policy of territorial integration and cultural assimilation. It has also applied the policy of pluralism, permitting considerable local autonomy in minority areas.

From 1956 to 1968, particularly during the Great Leap period (1958–59), the policy of radical assimilation was used. Communization of the minority areas was undertaken, the Chinese spoken language was introduced in the schools, minority cadres were trained, and local nationalistic expressions were suppressed. However, minority resistance to these programs, particularly in Xizang and Xinjiang, forced the Peking government to reconsider its radical policy and introduce the policy of pluralism. Although this trend to pluralism was reversed to radicalism during the Cultural Revolution (1966–69), it has been reinstituted in the post-Cultural Revolution era. The 1982 Constitution, for example, permits the establishment of local self-government in the minority areas and allows the minority groups the right to use their languages in the conduct of their local affairs. At the same time, special efforts have been made to co-opt minority members into the Chinese Communist Party and the central government.

China: Middle Kingdom   The traditional Chinese name for their country—Zhongguo (Chungkuo)—meaning literally, Middle Kingdom, or Central Nation. The earliest evidence of civilization in China, dating from around 4000 B.C., was discovered in North China, where the Huang (Yellow) and the Wei Rivers meet. Little is known about this period. According to Chinese historic records, it was about 1766 B.C. when a warring tribe of Mongolian stock conquered the central portion of the Huang River area and established the Shang Dynasty, which was followed by many others. The Chinese people also expanded to the north and south. China's imperial expansion was greatest during the Qing (Ch'ing or Manchu) dynasty (1644–1911), extending over Mongolia, much of Central Asia, and Tibet. Its political and cultural influence extended to Korea in the northeast and to Burma, Annam (Vietnam), and Nepal in the south. Historically, China held sway over the entire area. It was rich and civilized, and its system of government was developed and stable. The Chinese produced an intricate writing system and are credited with the invention of paper, printing, the compass, and gunpowder. The Chinese came to view their country as the self-sufficient center of the universe. People along China's borders and beyond were considered less developed and barbarous. *See also* CHINA: AUTONOMOUS REGIONS, p. 10.

Significance   With a continental expanse of almost 3.7 million square miles (9.6 million square kilometers), China stretches from Manchuria in the northeast to Tibet in the southwest, and from the coast of the South China Sea northwest to Chinese Turkestan in central Asia. Its natural boundaries consist of thick forests, formidable deserts, high plateau lands, and mountains and gorges. In spite of a long coastline, China did not attract early seafarers, since real and imagined hazards of the long sea voyage were quite discouraging. In the north, where offshore water is too shallow, good ports are lacking. The southeastern seacoast is more conducive to ocean traffic, but in early days it was populated by minority races and was not under effective Chinese control. Until the era of modern travel, therefore, China had only limited contact with the outside world and developed a highly ethnocentric view of itself. The Chinese perceived their country as highly developed and civilized, and all others as inferior. This China-centered view of the world remained undisturbed until China's first serious confrontation with western nations in the nineteenth century.

Diego Garcia   A remote island in the Chagos Archipelago, located near the geographic center of the Indian Ocean, that has been transformed into a major United States military base. The United States acquired use rights on Diego Garcia, a possession of the United Kingdom, shortly after the creation of the British Indian Ocean Territory (BIOT) in December 1966. The United States action was prompted by the development of a Soviet blue water navy capable of challenging American dominance on the high seas. Although the United States navy remained the largest in the world, its role in the Indian Ocean was limited, and the Soviets were in position to fill a power vacuum. Soviet historic interests in so-called "warm water outlets" reinforced the concern of Washington strategists that Moscow would attempt dominance in the Indian Ocean. Attempts by members of the U.S. Congress to prevent the construction of a naval base in the Indian Ocean centered on their belief that the country's interests in the region could be better protected through non-military means. Although faced with staunch resistance from some members of Congress, the construction of a base on Diego Garcia was approved.

In March 1977, however, President Jimmy Carter appeared ready to reduce American military presence in the Indian Ocean and called upon the Soviet leaders to join with the United States in the "complete demilitarization" of the Indian Ocean. Negotiations between Washington and Moscow commenced against a background of Soviet activity on the Asian rimland, in the Middle East, and in sub-Saharan Africa. The discussions, therefore, failed to move beyond the preliminary stage and were in the process of dying out when the Shah was swept from power in Iran, and the Soviet Union invaded Afghanistan. These events confirmed the seriousness of U.S.-Soviet rivalry in the region, and the original base design on Diego Garcia was expanded to meet what Washington perceived as a clear threat to its most vital interests. Moreover, Washington's plan to build a global Electro Optical Deep Space Surveillance (GEODSS) system for its space strategy involves the building of ground space centers on or near the Indian Ocean. Diego Garcia is an important site for such an installation, and the island therefore has become a critical link in a vast United States communication network. Such a program goes far beyond the current use of long-range aircraft from Diego Garcia's airstrips or the conduct of routine electronic and maritime reconnaissance missions. Diego Garcia is being transformed into the principal U.S. naval and air base between the Philippines and the Mediterranean Sea, a position it is likely to hold into the 1990s. *See also* INDIAN OCEAN, p. 22; PERSIAN GULF, p. 33; WARM WATER PORT POLICY, p. 47.

Significance   Diego Garcia was a small, relatively uninhabited island before becoming a major U.S. military installation. Currently, it is perceived as Washington's response to Soviet bases at Aden in South Yemen and Cam Ranh Bay in Vietnam. The U.S. naval mission in the Indian Ocean stresses defense of sea lanes and resource access for itself as well as the western industrial states. Nowhere are those sea lanes and resources judged to be under greater threat than in the Indian Ocean. Oil supplies to Western Europe, Japan, and Australia pass from the Persian Gulf into the Indian Ocean, and the fear persists that the Soviet Union can choke off the flow if not contested. U.S. operations from Diego Garcia have been openly criticized as provocative by India, Iraq, Ethiopia, and South Yemen. Other Indian Ocean nations have expressed the need for a "zone of peace" in the Indian Ocean, but they seem to prefer American presence in the region as a counterweight to Soviet involvement.

External powers have traditionally exercised influence in the Indian Ocean, and the countries of the region are aware that in the aftermath of the British decision to move its power "east of Suez" the Soviets pressed their own interests into the area. United States operations on Diego Garcia have been geared to balance Soviet activity and there is little likelihood that either superpower will reduce its commitment. Diego Garcia, therefore, is slated to play a prominent role in the power politics of the Indian Ocean. It is also destined to remain an issue of controversy in the United States and abroad.

Ganges and Brahmaputra Rivers   Two of the major rivers of India. The Ganges is most prominent, but it shares its importance with the Brahmaputra and ultimately merges with it in Bangladesh. Both rivers have their source in the Himalayas, but the Ganges forms on the Indian side in northern Uttar Pradesh state and follows a course that takes it through the heart of northeastern India. The Brahmaputra originates in Tibet, where it is known as the Tsangpo and leaves the Himalayas to enter sparsely populated Assam state. The Ganges basin is one of the most fertile and densely populated in the world, embracing an area in excess of 390,000 square miles. The Ganges is 1,540 miles long. Beginning as a small stream from a snow cave at elevations above 10,000 feet, it drops at a rate of 350 feet per mile. At the village of Devaprayag, approximately 133 miles from its source, the stream then known as the Bhagirathi is joined by another called the Alaknanda, and together they become the Ganges.

The Ganges then descends from an elevation slightly above 9,000 feet to Hardwar and the great plain of India, at this point slightly more than 1,000 feet above sea level. From Hardwar, the Ganges winds its way through treacherous rapids to Allahabad, where it is joined by the Jumna River, and continues its steady movement until it empties into the Bay of Bengal. Branches of the Ganges form the Hooghly River on which stands the city of Calcutta, but the main channel extends into Bangladesh where it is known as the Padma, and where it merges with the principle branch of the Brahmaputra. All these great rivers then pass through the main estuary of the Meghna and create a deltaic region, the northern portion of which is fertile and intensely cultivated, and a southern section, known as the Sundarbans which is swampland and wild marshes. The Brahmaputra, by contrast, follows an easterly course through Tibet for approximately 900 miles before entering India. When the Brahmaputra reaches the Ganges Delta, it divides into several channels, the main branch becoming the Jamuna River. All channels empty into the Bay of Bengal. *See also* FARAKKA BARRAGE AGREEMENT, p. 336.

Significance   Both the Ganges and Brahmaputra are important to the people of India. The Ganges is considered by Hindus to be the holiest of rivers, and religious rites are carried out at numerous locations, such as Hardwar, Varanasi, and Allahabad. The Ganges is important for the fertility of the soil and the sustenance it provides the Indians of the great northeastern plain, often referred to as the Hindustan plain. It is also important for sustaining the vitality of Indian commerce. Calcutta's success as a financial and economic center is a result of its location on the Ganges and its accessibility from the sea.

The Ganges and Brahmaputra are also important to Bangladesh. The larger territory that comprises the nation-state of Bangladesh is the creation of these great river systems. Almost three-fourths of

Bangladesh, excepting the Chittagong Hill Tracts and the Sylhet highlands, is formed from the silt deposited over geologic time by the Ganges-Brahmaputra system. Bangladesh is an alluvial plain, rich in agricultural soil but almost devoid of other resources. The fertility of the region, however, has drawn people to it, and as a consequence Bangladesh is one of the most densely populated areas in the world. Bangladesh must be vigilant about its future. Its relations with India are influenced by the rivers that course through it. India, for example, must maintain the vitality of Calcutta. Silting of the Hooghly, however, threatens to destroy its commercial accessibility. The use of Ganges water to flush the Hooghly denies water to Bangladesh, which in the dry season is dependent on a form of irrigation. The controversy between India and Bangladesh over the diversion of Ganges water in general, and the Farraka Barrage Project in particular, predates the establishment of Bangladesh in 1971, and it is still without firm resolution. The civil war in Pakistan, which led to the establishment of an independent and sovereign Bangladesh, was sparked by a particularly severe typhoon and tidal wave in 1970 that swept in from the Bay of Bengal and inundated a vast area of low-lying East Pakistan, as the region was then called. The inability of the Pakistan government to mount an effective relief effort provided the political opposition in the province with an opportunity to rally popular support against the administration in West Pakistan. Although the calamity that struck East Pakistan (now Bangladesh) in 1970 was unprecedented, it is important to note that the area is subject to vast annual flooding as a consequence of the torrential monsoon rains, and the loss in lives and property is always substantial.

Greater East Asia Co-Prosperity Sphere   A Japanese imperial scheme aimed at bringing Northeast and Southeast Asia under Japanese hegemony. Japanese Prime Minister Konoe announced in 1938 the creation of a "New Order" in East Asia. The plan envisaged the expansion of Japan's sphere of influence over China and Manchuria, and the leadership of Japan in the military, political, economic, and cultural activities of East Asia. The expansion of the same plan to Southeast Asia was discussed as early at 1940. Seizing the opportunity offered by the war in Europe, Japan planned to establish itself in Indochina, Siam (Thailand), Burma, Malaya, and the Netherlands Indies. Japan hoped to gain control of the region's oil, tin, rubber, bauxite, and other strategic raw materials. Diplomacy was to be tried first, but the use of force was not overruled. To achieve this objective, Japan took over Indochina from the French in early 1941. With the beginning of the Pacific War, Japan quickly occupied the rest of Southeast Asia. The Greater East Asia Co-Prosperity Sphere was more than an economic and military design. It was intended to eliminate western colonialism from the area and replace it with Japanese domination. It created a network of new political alignments and engaged in a cultural crusade by teaching the Japanese language and culture. Japan's defeat in the war put an end to this imperial design. *See also* PACIFIC COMMUNITY, p. 32; PACIFIC WAR, p. 396.

Significance   In its imperial design for a Greater East Asia Co-Prosperity Sphere, Japan carried out a propaganda theme of "Asia for Asians" and planned to integrate Southeast Asia into its expanding empire to provide Japan with natural resources for its industries and markets for its products. Around 1940, the opportunity seemed ripe because the western colonial powers were losing the war in Europe. But, the United States posed a threat to Japanese expansionism. Japan's surprise attack on Pearl Harbor in December 1941 was to neutralize American interference, but its effect was only momentary. In the end, Japan lost the war against the United States and its imperial design was frustrated. Ironically, however, what Japan was not able to achieve in the war, it achieved in peace. Postwar Japanese economic expansion has come to dominate the western Pacific markets. Furthermore, the whole area of East and Southeast Asia currently represents the world's fastest growing and most viable economic zone.

Himalayas   The mountain range separating the subcontinent from larger Asia. The Himalayas are the highest mountain barrier in the world, extending approximately 1,500 miles (more than 2,400 kilometers), from the Indus river in the west to the Brahmaputra river in the east, and touching or coursing through Pakistan, India, China (Xizang), Nepal, and Bhutan. The central 500-mile portion of the Himalayas is in Nepal, where the range's tallest peaks are found. There are 250 peaks above 6,000 meters, and 22 of the 31 Himalayan peaks are above 7,600 meters, including the tallest mountain in the world, Mount Everest (8,848 meters or slightly more than 29,000 feet). The Himalayan mountain system divides into three zones. The first is the Great Himalayas, which are above 20,000 feet and perpetually covered with snow. The second zone is the Lesser Himalayas, that average between 12,000 and 15,000 feet. The third is the Outer Himalayas (2,000 to 5,000 feet), which reach out to the plains of the subcontinent and some of the most densely populated regions in the world.

The Himalayas produce wide variations in rainfall and climate, from frigid to subtropical. In some areas influenced by the Himalayas there is very little annual rainfall, and at the same time, the wettest region on earth (in northeastern India) is attributed to the unique topographical configurations of the range. The passes through the Himalayas are the highest in the world, averaging above 10,000 feet and going as high as 18,000 feet. All passes above 16,000 feet are closed between November and May. The majesty of the Himalayas has inspired poets and philosophers and influenced aspects of popular mythology. Ancient Hindus gave the Himalayas spiritual significance, and today practicing Hindus believe the Himalayan peaks to be the abode of important gods and goddesses. *See also* HINDU KUSH, p. 18; KARAKORUM HIGHWAY, p. 27; SINO-INDIAN WAR, 1962, p. 405.

Significance   The Himalayas are imposing, breathtaking, environmentally important, and the focal point for legend and folklore, and they are important in geopolitical terms. The Himalayas have given India its distinctive character. Historically, they have shielded the subcontinent from north-south penetration. The great waves of migration and invasion did not reach the subcontinent from China, primarily because of the barrier provided by the Himalayas. The numerous invaders of the subcontinent filtered through the northwestern region, through the lesser mountain chain generally referred to as the Hindu Kush. In fact, the Himalayan barrier stood the test of subcontinental defense until the post–World War II era. A major breech of the Himalayas was made by Chinese forces when they attacked Indian military positions across a broad area of northeastern India in 1962. Pakistan and China also facilitated movement through the far western region of the Himalayas when they cooperated in the building of the Karakorum Highway that links the two countries in the Gilgit-Xinjiang region of Central Asia. The Khunjerab Pass that connects the two countries is 15,000 feet above sea level (4,600 meters). The Himalayas therefore seem to be a less formidable challenge to those intent on passing through it.

British use of the Himalayas for its defense of India, particularly its "forward policy" in Tibet, is no longer valid or meaningful. Nevertheless, the Himalayan range is still a major factor in shaping the foreign policies of the states of the region. Pakistan views its intimacy with China as a major asset in its rivalry with India. India approaches the Himalayas as a dividing line between the subcontinent and the rest of Asia, providing New Delhi with a particular sphere of influence. Nepal and Bangladesh acknowledge the power of India and the ease with which it could press its influence on their respective countries. By the same token, the Himalayas do not provide these states with accessible countervailing power. Although China is a near neighbor, it is not logistically positioned to neutralize Indian power with its own. Bhutan is one case of a small Himalayan kingdom coming under the direct influence of New Delhi. Moreover, the annexation of Sikkim by India, another Himalayan state, illustrated the opportunities afforded India by its geographic position astride the Himalayas.

Hindu Kush   A mountainous region to the west of the Himalayan Mountains. The Hindu Kush extends southward, touching Pakistan and arching through Afghanistan. The range is approximately 500 miles long, beginning in the plateau region of the Pamirs on the borders of Pakistan, Afghanistan, and the Soviet Union. The mountain passes in the initial 100 miles from the Pamirs are found at elevations ranging between 12,000 and 17,500 feet. These high regions are the source of the Amu Darya (Oxus River), the Helmand, Kabul, and Kunar of Afghanistan. Several of the Indus tributaries also have their beginning in the Hindu Kush. The Durand Line, drawn by Sir Mortimer Durand in 1893 and still the official frontier between Afghanistan and Pakistan, attempts to trace the course of the Hindu Kush.

The Hindu Kush gives Afghanistan its physical and human character. It is considered the natural frontier between Central and Southern Asia, and invaders who penetrated the mountain barrier entered the subcontinent through the rugged but relatively low-lying passes of the lesser Sulaiman and Kirthar ranges. Among these celebrated passes are the Khyber, the Gomal, and the Bolan. The Wakhan corridor on Afghanistan's northeastern extremity is also a feature of these mountain ranges. Nestled in the high terrain where the Hindu Kush, the Pamirs, and Himalayas appear to converge are the mountain states of Gilgit, Hunza, Chitral, Dir, and Swat. All these states are located in contemporary Pakistan. *See also* CENTRAL ASIA, p. 8; HIMALAYAS, p. 16; KARAKORUM HIGHWAY, p. 27; WAKHAN CORRIDOR, p. 46.

Significance   The "Great Game" of the nineteenth century was the contest between Imperial Britain and Tsarist Russia in Central Asia. Britain sought to protect its empire in India, as well as its influence in the vicinity of the Persian Gulf, from a relentlessly expansive Tsarist empire that had subdued and annexed the Central Asian Muslim *khanates,* or local kingdoms, and continued to press its influence south to the warm water of the Indian Ocean. Britain's objective was to hold the tsars' armies at the Amu Darya and prevent their penetrating the Hindu Kush in Afghanistan. The Durand Line was drawn with this purpose in mind, as was the Amu Darya border with Afghanistan. The Wakhan corridor, a curious finger of territory in Afghanistan's extreme northeast, was given to Kabul in order to prevent tsarist territory from touching British India. Afghanistan became the true buffer state between the two rival empires and Britain fought two wars with Afghanistan in the nineteenth and one in the early twentieth century in order to safeguard this arrangement.

Britain's withdrawal from the region in the post-World War II period left two sovereign states in its place. Pakistan assumed the strategic position formerly filled by the British, and India appeared dependent on Pakistani defensive capabilities for its own security. But Pakistan's dependence on Afghanistan, and India's dependence on Pakistan, only made sense if the three countries proved compatible and shared the same geostrategic and political interests. History has shown that neither was prepared to support the other. Afghanistan repudiated the Durand boundary with Pakistan and was more an enemy than a friend to its brother Muslim state. Pakistan struggled with India over another border territory in Kashmir, and the two countries were bitter foes from the moment they achieved their independent status.

Given such divisions in so vital a region, the Soviet Union, the successor state to the tsars, perpetuated tsarist policy and, in the absence of the British, gained a sphere of influence in Afghanistan and developed amicable relations with India. Pakistan looked to the United States, but the U.S. could not play the role abandoned by the British. Rivalry and war between India and Pakistan and continuing difficulties with Afghanistan provided Moscow with the leverage it required to cross the Amu Darya and gain control of the Hindu Kush. The Soviet invasion of Afghanistan in 1979 was a continuation of an historical movement which once again opened the subcontinent, as well as the Persian Gulf, to northern influences. Although the Afghan resistance to the Soviet invasion sought to take advantage of the rugged Hindu Kush terrain, the Kremlin showed little inclination to give up its quest to bring the Hindu Kush and Afghanistan within its sphere of influence. In the 1980s, Pakistan was exposed to threats from both India and the Soviet Union, and natural defenses were absent in each case.

Ho Chi Minh Trail   A complex series of roads and trails running from North Vietnam through Laos to South Vietnam. The trail was constructed by Vietnamese forces under the direction of their leader, Ho Chi Minh. The principal access system was known in the outer world as the Ho Chi Minh trail, and by the mid-1960s it consisted of several, often-changing road, trail, and path complexes. Hanoi was the starting point for the trail, which moved in a southward arc, crossing the border of Laos by way of the Mu Gia pass, north of the seventeenth parallel separating North Vietnam from South Vietnam.

In Laos, the Ho Chi Minh Trail divided into three main branches and several lesser paths, which cut through mountainous terrain where monsoon rains produced dense forest. Several of these roads curved eastward into southern Vietnam. The development of this road network was made even more complex with the addition of the Sihanouk Trail, named for the last monarchical ruler of Cambodia, which branched into Cambodia, and thus provided northerners with direct access to the Mekong Delta region of southern Vietnam. *See also* MEKONG RIVER, p. 30; RED RIVER DELTA, p. 35; SEVENTEENTH PARALLEL, p. 37.

Significance   The Ho Chi Minh Trail became the primary supply route to the south for North Vietnamese insurgents during the Indochina War of the 1960s and early 1970s. The guerrillas, or Viet Cong, used the trail to mobilize their struggle against the American-supported government in Saigon. Soldiers and materiel passed through this network in an unending stream. Efforts by United States forces to destroy the trail proved futile. Massive and repeated bombing runs and a costly defoliation program could not stem the flow of troops and equipment. American programs aimed at enlisting Laotian forces and tribesmen were geared to interdicting the trail and sustaining a pro-Washington government in Laos. This too failed, and the northwestern region of Laos was transformed by the Vietnamese into a staging area for Laotian insurgents, the Pathet Lao. In the 1960s, with help from China, the Vietnamese and their Laotian allies developed an even more elaborate network of roads, which gave them absolute control of this vital northern region and access to the main road system of northern Thailand.

The United States had attempted to maintain a friendly government in Cambodia and was instrumental in ousting Prince Sihanouk, who seemed to vacillate on the matter of insurgent use of his country. The United States used its air force against the North Vietnamese bases in Cambodia and even sent an invasion force into the country with orders to clean out the insurgents, but this tactic, like those in Laos, failed. Although the U.S. objective was to stop the flow of Vietnamese forces and supplies to South Vietnam, American actions in Laos and Cambodia appeared to spread and intensify the conflict. The Saigon government and the pro-western governments in Laos and Cambodia were brought under increasing pressure. With the force of North Vietnamese arms, and the United States decision to withdraw its troops, South Vietnam was overrun and unified with the North, Laos came under the influence of Hanoi, and Cambodia was opened to the Marxist Khmer Rouge, who eventually formed the new government in Phnom Penh. The rule of the Khmer Rouge was short-lived, however, when Vietnamese forces invaded the country, deposed the Khmer Rouge administration of Pol Pot, and installed a puppet regime.

Hong Kong   Great Britain occupied the island of Hong Kong (approximately 29 square miles) and converted it into a naval base during the Opium War with China. At the conclusion of that war,

Britain and China signed the Treaty of Nanking in 1842, and Hong Kong was ceded to the British in perpetuity. After the Second Opium War in 1860, Britain added the peninsula of Kowloon (approximately 3 square miles, 4.83 kilometers), and Stonecutters island to its possessions. In 1898, Britain acquired the New Territories (approximately 365 square miles, 10,969.83 kilometers) on the Chinese mainland under a 99-year lease that also included Hong Kong, which was scheduled to revert to Chinese sovereignty in 1997.

Hong Kong is located at the mouth of the Pearl River, 90 miles southeast of the important Chinese city of Canton. The Japanese seized Hong Kong and the extended territories in December 1941, and Britain did not regain possession until Japan's surrender on August 14, 1945. The Chinese Communist victory over the Kuomintang Nationalists in 1949 did not directly affect Hong Kong. Beijing (Peking) was content to leave the colony in British hands until the lease expired, in order to reap advantages from Hong Kong's role as an economic and financial center in the Far East. Nevertheless, the Chinese indicated they had every intention of reacquiring the territories when the lease expired. After long, sometimes strained negotiations, Britain and China entered into a Draft Agreement on the future of Hong Kong on September 26, 1984. The Draft Agreement was not open to amendment or revision and had to be accepted by the people of Hong Kong in its entirety or not at all. The British noted that the territory would either revert to China with the negotiated agreement or without one. London argued that great care had been taken to consult the people of Hong Kong prior to and during the negotiations. The Draft Agreement therefore was final and unalterable. Prime Minister Margaret Thatcher and Premier Zhao Ziyang signed the agreement in the Great Hall of the People in Beijing on December 19, 1984. Under its terms, Britain would pass full sovereignty over the territory to China in 1997, and in return Beijing pledged to guarantee a 50-year extension of Hong Kong's capitalist economic system. Britain's parliament had already ratified the accord, but China's National People's Congress waited for the formal ceremony before taking similar action.

As a formal British dependency, Hong Kong is governed by a British governor, who is the paramount civil and military authority in the colony. Sir Edward Youde, the present governor, is assisted by an executive council and a legislative assembly. Guidance in the administration of the colony comes directly from London. *See also* OPIUM WAR, 1839–42; CHINA, p. 394.

Significance   The most critical question for the people of Hong Kong was the reversion of the territory to Chinese sovereignty. Negotiations on the eventual transfer opened in Beijing in September

1982 at British request, but serious discussions did not begin until July 1983. In preparation for the transfer, the new Chinese constitution of 1982 specifies in article 31 that Hong Kong, Macao, and Taiwan will be identified as "special administrative regions."

Negotiations, therefore, were even less successful than those held earlier, and negotiators were forced to adjourn the proceedings on a pessimistic note. Hong Kong's only hope of avoiding the imposition of a harsh ideology seemed to be the health of the colony's economy. The island's prosperity had been a boon for China, and Beijing hesitated before threatening a very important source of national wealth. Nevertheless, fear of the eventual Chinese changeover caused investors to hesitate, and deficits began to escalate. Banking institutions were strained, and unemployment increased markedly in a region where work had been available to almost all comers. China, meanwhile, extended its hand to influential Hong Kong residents. It continued to hold out the possibility of improved trade opportunities, and it even appointed some Hong Kong dignitaries to the National People's Congress and the Chinese People's Political Consultative Conference. Beijing also agreed to renew the negotiations and signalled its willingness to find a compromise formula acceptable to all parties.

These efforts were followed by a dramatic change in Chinese economic policy in mid-1984. China began the dismantling of some of its prominent Maoist institutions and surprising emphasis was placed on a mixed economy, especially in the agricultural sector where free landholders were promoted and the commune system was drastically modified. These internal changes had their impact on the negotiations concerned with the status of Hong Kong. An agreement to allow Hong Kong to retain its capitalist system was said to be the brainchild of Deng Xiaoping, China's preeminent leader. It was also the key to the success of the negotiations with Great Britain. London believed legal understandings would be respected by Beijing, and the Draft Agreement was completed. But howsoever the agreement was created, it was heralded as a showcase for Deng's domestic policy of encouraging market forces and foreign investment. Deng publicly stated China's dependence on Hong Kong's vigorous economy and how it was linked with the country's general modernization program.

Indian Ocean   The vast body of water that washes the shores of Asia, Africa, Australia, and Antarctica. The total area of the Indian Ocean is approximately 28,350,500 square miles. The ocean is partially divided by the Indian peninsula with the Bay of Bengal on its eastern side and the Arabian Sea on its western shore. From the Arabian Sea there are two northward extensions, the Persian or Arabian Gulf and the Red Sea. The Indian Ocean is, on average, slightly deeper than the Atlantic, but not as deep as the Pacific. Some of the celebrated rivers of Asia empty into the Indian Ocean. They are the Ganges, Brahmaputra, Irrawaddy, Indus, and the Shatt al Arab. Sri Lanka is the largest Asian island in the Indian Ocean. Lesser islands include the Maldives and Mauritius.

Just as the Middle East and Southwest Asia connect Europe with the people of eastern Asia, the Indian Ocean is the connecting link between the Atlantic and Pacific oceans. Trade and commerce has followed these traditional routes and the Indian Ocean has been the most international of waterways. More countries border on the Indian Ocean than either the Atlantic or Pacific. The United States has established a military presence in the Indian Ocean, making it a "third" strategic theater. American policy centers on the Persian Gulf and rests on contingency access and prepositioning arrangements; less so on permanent bases. A major new geographic unified command, the U.S. Central Command (CENTCOM) headquartered at McDill Air Force Base in Florida, with forward operations located with the U.S. Navy's Middle East Force, has institutionalized the Rapid Deployment Force. The Indian Ocean deployment involves a carrier battle group near the North Arabian Sea and a Marine Amphibious Unit (MAU) for possible land action. Approximately seventeen logistics ships were deployed near Diego Garcia in 1985, capable of ferrying supplies for a heavy-mechanized Marine Amphibious Brigade and for highly mobile American Army and Air Force units. Navy land-based surveillance and AWACS aircraft also operate in the region, the latter from bases in Saudi Arabia. All these deployments highlight American strategic interests beyond the needed protection for friendly governments and the safeguarding of important petroleum supplies. Minerals such as chrome, manganese, cobalt, and copper are also deemed to require protection. The difficulty in protecting resource access and Indian Ocean sealanes ultimately requires managing five geopolitical areas: the Cape of Good Hope and the Mozambique Channel; the Horn of Africa, the Red Sea, and Suez Canal; the Persian Gulf and Strait of Hormuz; the Malacca, Sunda, and Lombok Straits; and Australia. Therefore, while United States attention is largely in the northern sector, it is important to note that planners must consider the total region and its linkages to American Atlantic and Pacific military postures. *See also* DIEGO GARCIA, p. 12; PERSIAN GULF, p. 33.

Significance   The Indian Ocean has become a major region of competition between the United States and the Soviet Union. Before World War II, Great Britain was the only genuine naval power in the Indian Ocean. The British dominated strategic points on the ocean's perimeter.

The naval installations at Aden, the Trucial States on the Persian Gulf, the Indian and Ceylonese facilities, as well as its position at Singapore, appeared to assure Great Britain's mastery of the Indian Ocean. During the post-World War II period, however, Britain relinquished its empire and decided to pull back its forces "East of Suez."

The necessity for maintaining open sea lanes and resource access next fell upon American shoulders, and the United States found itself without adequate base facilities in this crucial environment. The U.S. was prompted to remedy the situation when it became evident that the Soviet Union was intent on building a substantial blue water navy and merchant fleet. The Soviets had long displayed interest in the Asian rimland that blocked its access to the warm water of the Indian Ocean. Its actions all along this territorial expanse seemed to dovetail with its naval and maritime pursuits in the Indian Ocean, and the United States was galvanized to thwart what was perceived as a Soviet drive to bring the Indian Ocean within its sphere of influence. Therefore, in 1966 the United States entered into negotiations with the British for the development of a major naval base on the small Indian Ocean island of Diego Garcia. Diego Garcia was centrally located near the middle of the Indian Ocean, approximately 1,500 miles from the southern tip of India. Britain held undisputed sovereignty over the island, but United States intentions to transform it into a major military installation angered New Delhi and frightened the government of Sri Lanka. In 1971 Colombo (the capital of Sri Lanka) publicized the need to make the Indian Ocean a "zone of peace" and New Delhi added its voice to the UN resolution. Since that time Indian Ocean states have tried to pressure the United States and the Soviet Union into withdrawing their naval forces from the area. Discussions between United States and Soviet negotiators, however, have only served to intensify the rivalry.

The Soviets have established a major presence at Aden, now under Marxist control, and on the South Yemen island of Socotra. They have also been welcomed in Ethiopia, where they have a functioning base at Massawa. Iraq has offered the Soviets use of its facilities at Um al Qasr, and India permits servicing of Soviet ships at its naval facility in Vishakhapatnam. The United States has attempted to offset these operations by branching out from Diego Garcia to arrange for the use of the Somali port of Berbera, the Omani island of Masirah, and the Kenya installation at Mombasa. The collapse of the Shah's regime in Iran, and the threat that the ensuing Iranian revolution posed to Persian Gulf oil, caused the United States to increase the size of its Indian Ocean fleet, the bulk apparently posted in the vicinity of the Gulf and the vital Strait of Hormuz. Given this United States presence there was little doubt the Soviets would seek to match it, or indeed to manifest a still larger role in the region.

Indus River   One of the three rivers most associated with the development of civilizations outside China, along with the Nile and the Tigris-Euphrates. The Indus, which flows through the northwestern sector of the subcontinent, is unique among the great rivers of South Asia. It originates amid the snow-capped peaks of western Tibet, flows from the Himalayas through Jammu and Kashmir in India, touches the mountain ranges of the Hindu Kush, and levels off in Pakistan. The Indus' course in Pakistan follows a north-south direction and after a journey of 1,700 miles it finally empties into the Arabian Sea.

The major tributaries of the Indus are the Sutlej, Ravi, Chenab, and Jhelum. These four tributaries, along with the mother river, give the Punjab its name, derived from the Sanskrit word "panch" or five, hence the land of the five rivers. The Punjab is Pakistan's most populated and influential province. The Indus actually enters the Indian Punjab before it reaches Pakistan. It is only navigable in Pakistan, however, where it is joined by the Kabul river. The Indus and its tributaries provide the water for the most extensive irrigation system in the world. The Punjab's high agricultural yields are a consequence of this man-made hydraulic system. Hydroelectric projects on the Indus and its tributaries have contributed to high output of farm products, improved flood control, and generated electricity. *See also* HINDU KUSH, p. 18; ASIA, p. 6.

Significance   The Indus valley shares with Egypt and Mesopotamia the role of "cradle of civilization." Indus civilization dates from 2500–1700 B.C.. It is reputed to be the greatest, most advanced example of Bronze Age civilizations. The principal archaeological sites are Mohenjo-Daro and Harappa, north and northeast of Karachi in Pakistan. There is sufficient evidence to indicate that this civilization extended along the Makran coast, across the Indus delta to the Kathiawar peninsula and the Gulf of Cambay in present-day India.

For all its historical significance, the Indus is a powerful contemporary phenomenon. The Indus makes it possible for Pakistan to survive, and it is as vital to that country as the Nile is to Egypt. Just as Egypt does not control the source of the Nile, Pakistan does not control the source of the Indus. Indeed, after independence, India sought to take advantage of the water from the Indus as it passed through its territory. These efforts further strained relations between India and Pakistan, and only international intervention prevented a major confrontation. The division of the Punjab into an Indian and Pakistani half left some of the important Indus barrages in India. Precious water could therefore be diverted from Pakistan and an equitable solution became more urgent than ever.

The United States played an important role in mediating the dispute, and the Indus Waters Agreement was signed between India and

Pakistan in 1960. Under the terms of the agreement, enormous financial and technical assistance was earmarked for Pakistan by the World Bank. The larger portion of this money was used to build two major storage reservoirs. The Mangla Dam on the Jhelum was the first of these, completed in 1968. The second was the Tarbela Dam on the Indus. Both Mangla and Tarbela were fully operational in 1985. Mangla returned Pakistan to the position it held prior to the agreement. Tarbela permitted broad expansion, and promised more successful development. Both dams, however, had limited life-spans. Silting problems reduced their utility appreciably, particularly in Tarbela. Although conflict between India and Pakistan over the use of Indus water had been avoided, future problems seemed likely.

Irrawaddy and Salween Rivers   Two great rivers of the Asian rimland that give character to the land and its people. In China the Salween is called Lujiang. It flows from its source in Tibet, to Yunnan Province, before entering northeastern Burma. The Irrawaddy is Burma's most important river, running through the middle of the country to the sea in a north-south direction. The Irrawaddy can be considered an indigenous river because its source lies in Burma at the confluence of the Mali and Nmai rivers. It cuts a swath approximately 1,250 miles long from Myitkyina in Kachin state to the Andaman Sea. Burma can be divided into three geographical zones. In the north are the mountain ranges, some of which have peaks as high as 12,000 feet. The next zone is densely forested hill country, with elevations from 3,000 to 5,000 feet. The Irrawaddy, the Salween, and their many tributaries have cut deep gorges in the terrain, and passage through the country is tedious at best. The southern, or third, zone is a vast alluvial lowland created by the Irrawaddy. This is the most intense rice-growing area of Burma.

The Irrawaddy is navigable year-round from a point at Bhamo approximately 870 miles from the sea. The Irrawaddy is Burma's principal artery of communication, linking the capital of Rangoon with cities and towns to the north such as Katha, Shwebo, Mandalay, and Henzada. The Salween passes into Burma from China and flows south on the eastern side of the country. Measuring from its source in Tibet, the Salween is about 1,750 miles long and before emptying into the Gulf of Martaban it forms a small portion of Burma's border with Thailand. Unlike the Irrawaddy, navigation on the Salween is limited to the area near its mouth.

Significance   The Irrawaddy and Salween have helped the independent tribes of Burma and Thailand to sustain their individual status.

The terrain is difficult to traverse and has prevented the building of a modern transportation system. Controlling rebellious behavior among the tribes or limiting the sale and transfer of narcotics or other criminal acts is a major dilemma for the Rangoon government. Indeed, the remoteness of specific Burmese regions provided some isolated contingents from the Chinese Nationalist army with a relatively safe haven, but Burmese authorities were hard-pressed to deal effectively with this force. Eventually, an agreement with the Nationalist government on Taiwan brought about their peaceful removal. Nevertheless, Chinese communist forces were still capable of penetrating the country's northern sector.

The Irrawaddy has aided Burma's economy. The British established the wet-rice industry in the Irrawaddy delta, which transformed the region into a rice bowl, and the country into a significant exporter. The rivers provide the main means of transport, and the Salween is important for the shipment of timber, especially teak logs. Thailand's three natural inland boundaries are the Mekong River, the watershed of the Bilauktaung Range, and the Salween River. Like Burma, northern Thailand is still undeveloped, and political dissidents go there seeking sanctuary and aid from other government foes.

Karakorum Highway   Connects Pakistan with the People's Republic of China. Described by some observers as the "eighth wonder of the world," the Karakorum Highway was constructed amid the Himalayan Mountains, "The Roof of the World." It passes from Abbottabad in the Northwest Frontier Province of Pakistan, through the mountain states Gilgit and Hunza, to the Khunjerab Pass on the Chinese side of the frontier. From there it links Kashi and Ürümqi in Chinese Xinjiang Province. The Highway is approximately 500 miles (800 kilometers) in length. It was started on the Pakistan side in 1959, and after the 1963 border agreement between Islamabad and Beijing it was decided to transform the road into a two-lane highway following the historic silk route of Marco Polo. The Chinese constructed 24 bridges through the mountainous terrain. Although the Highway was formally inaugurated in June 1978, the Khunjerab Pass, 15,000 feet (4,600 meters) above sea level, was not opened until August 1982. *See also* KASHMIR DISPUTE, p. 386; WAKHAN CORRIDOR, p. 46.

Significance   The Karakorum Highway links Pakistan and China by an all-weather road and is of particular interest to military tacticians. Although a potential boon to trade and tourism between the two countries, its immediate importance lies in its strategic role. China is brought into near proximity to Pakistan's northwestern frontier through the use of the highway. Chinese military supplies can be moved more rapidly to Pakistani forces. Moreover, given Soviet occupation of the Wakhan corridor, Afghanistan's border with China has been sealed. If China wishes to supply weapons to the Afghan mujahiddin resisting the Soviet invasion, the Karakorum Highway offers the most direct route. The Soviet Union has registered its concern over the use of the Karakorum Highway, believing it to be a threat to its Central Asian interests.

India also protested the building of the highway. It did so again when the Khunjerab Pass was opened. New Delhi argues that the territory through which the highway passes is in dispute, and furthermore, that Pakistan had no legal right to settle the Himalayan border with China without taking India's claim into account. Islamabad rejects India's argument and sees no basis for it in international law. The Chinese also repudiated the Indian protest, declaring that the Chinese section of the highway is not subject to Indian complaint. India's fear involves the ongoing dispute in Kashmir, through which the highway travels. Although India controls the Vale of Kashmir and Jammu, it does not dominate the entire region. Pakistan's intimacy with China, and the possibility that the Indian positions in Kashmir could be assaulted by combined Pakistan-Chinese forces, remain troublesome issues. Therefore the Karakorum Highway may link Pakistan and China geographically, but it also brings India and the Soviet Union into close embrace.

Kuril Islands   A chain of approximately fifty islands, seized by the Soviet Union from Japan in the waning days of World War II. The islands extend from the tip of Hokkaido in a northeastern direction for approximately 700 miles to the Kamchatka peninsula. The Kurils have been historically Japanese, but the Russian advance to the Pacific in the nineteenth century caused rivalry to develop between the two countries. In 1875, Japan agreed to cede the island of Sakhalin to the Tsarist Empire, who in turn recognized Japan's sovereignty over all the Kurils.

The Soviet claim to the Kurils is that they were uninhabited until Russian forces occupied the islands in the nineteenth century and that the tsarist state acknowledged Tokyo's sovereignty under pressure. The Japanese, on the other hand, insist that the islands are an integral part of Japan and that the Soviet Union took advantage of their weakness to press its peculiar national objectives. Moreover, the islands of Habomai and Shikotan were always Japanese and were administered as part of the Hokkaido prefecture. The Russians insisted that these islands were part of the Kuril chain, over both Japanese and American objections. When the Soviets demanded a presence on Hokkaido too, the United States held its ground but yielded on the matter of the offshore islands. The dominant population of the islands has been Ainu, but Sovietization has also led to "Russification." The establishment of a major Russian presence in the islands, the nearest only three miles from Hokkaido, suggests demographic changes. The islands are administered as an extension of Sakhalin Oblast and their combined area is approximately 6,020 square miles (9,686.18 kilometers). *See also* SAKHALIN, p. 36.

Significance   The Kuril Islands are an abrasive point in Soviet-Japanese relations. The Japanese have never acquiesced in the Soviet annexation of the Kurils, and a formal peace treaty terminating their hostile interaction in World War II has never been agreed upon. The Japanese have consistently argued their claim to sovereignty over the Kurils. The Soviets, however, have been equally insistent on retaining the islands as legitimate Soviet territory. Moreover, the Kurils are part of a broad network of interlocking military bases that the Soviets have erected in the northeastern corner of their vast Eurasian state. In the 1980s the Soviets increased their force levels on the islands and appeared poised to strike directly at Japan's heartland in the event of hostilities.

The Soviets have publicized their concern that Japan is a base for United States nuclear forces. They are also troubled by Sino-Japanese reconciliation, which promises more cooperation between the two East Asian neighbors. Soviet suspicions and national security interests intertwine to make peaceful change a remote possibility.

In December 1984 Soviet suspicions were intensified when two American aircraft carriers were detected operating within fifty miles of the Soviet base at Vladivostok. Washington insisted the naval action was simply part of regular maneuvers in the Sea of Japan. Nevertheless, Moscow scrambled more than 100 jet fighters, bombers, and reconnaissance aircraft to track the U.S. vessels. Vladivostok is the Soviet fleet's Far Eastern headquarters and the center for a complex of naval and air bases that stretch north to Sakhalin Island, the Kuril Islands, and Kamchatka. Some observers speculated an American naval presence close to Soviet territorial waters was a signal to the Kremlin that the United States stands by its treaty commitments to Japan. Soviet violations of Japanese airspace in 1984 had been reported on the increase, and the U.S. Defense Department may have attempted its own brand of intimidation. The Tokyo government nevertheless registered its official concern with Washington. But U.S. authorities simply noted that the Soviet fleet is not reluctant to demonstrate a presence in the Caribbean. The Soviets were not pacified, however, and the Beijing announcement in November 1984 that American warships would be allowed to make goodwill visits to Chinese ports seemed to raise new defense questions in the Kremlin. This announcement by the general secretary of the Chinese Communist Party was made following a decision to purchase American military equipment. Earlier, China had granted similar rights to Britain,

Canada, and Australia, and naval courtesy calls had already been made by those countries. Given these military maneuvers in the region, there was every reason to believe the Soviets would continue to bolster its defenses and forces in the Kurils.

Malacca Strait   The body of water that separates the Indonesian island of Sumatra from the Malay peninsula. The Malacca Strait is approximately 500 miles long and varies in width from about 30 to 200 miles. The Andaman Sea, an extension of the Indian Ocean, is tied to the South China Sea by this waterway. The British built the island port of Singapore in order to facilitate the use of, as well as to protect, the Strait of Malacca. The growth of the British Empire resulted in large part from the control it exerted over this vital waterway. Even today, most international shipping uses the Strait of Malacca, and it is a focal point for rivalry between the United States and the Soviet Union. The United States maintains advance naval bases in the Philippines, and the Soviets have the use of the American-built installations at Cam Ranh Bay in Vietnam. Each superpower seeks to protect its interests by positioning forces far from home, but in close proximity to important trade routes. The United States, however, is more dependent on international commerce, and Soviet power astride these sea lanes is seen as an opportunity for Moscow to interdict western shipping. Malacca has become the acknowledged key to Soviet influence at Sunda, Lombok, Wetar, and Taiwan, as well as the Bashi Channel enroute to the Ryukyus and Japan from the Indian Ocean. *See also* INDIAN OCEAN, p. 22; TAIWAN STRAIT, p. 39.

Significance   One of the main factors in the rivalry between the United States and the Soviet Union centers on the western world's need for resource access and open sea lanes and a potential Soviet capability to disrupt that need. The development of the Soviet blue water navy, as well as a vast submarine fleet in the post–World War II period, has given the Kremlin global interests, as well as global reach. The Soviets are no longer simply concerned with continental defense. Importantly, Soviet penetration of traditional western spheres of influence has placed Moscow astride the world's principal shipping lanes, and it seeks to consolidate its positions not only in Vietnam, but in India, South Yemen, Ethiopia, and Cuba.

Mekong River   A major Asian river that has had a great impact on the history of its riparian nations. Rivers like the Mekong play a dominant role in the lives of people everywhere. Indeed, civilizations have risen, flourished, and disappeared due to the vagaries of the river systems upon which they depend. The Mekong River has its origin in Tibet and flows in a southerly direction through South China, forming the border of Burma and Laos and most of the border between Laos and Thailand. From there it passes through Cambodia (Kampuchea) and the southern part of Vietnam, emptying into the South China Sea.

The journey of the Mekong to the sea is approximately 2,600 miles, although it is navigable only from a point south of Luang Prabang in Laos. Seasons are a major factor in determining navigability, however, and approximately 900 miles of the Mekong are suitable for shipping during the rainy season, while less than 400 miles are manageable in the dry period. Cambodia and Vietnam derive the greatest benefits from the river. The port of Phnom Penh in Cambodia was built because of the Mekong and is able to accommodate ships of 5,000 tons during the dry season. The Mekong also gives Cambodia a major connection with the outside world through neighboring Vietnam. But relations between the two countries are traditionally poor, and the Mekong River has been used by Vietnam to exploit rather than assist its smaller, weaker neighbor. *See also* ASIAN HIGHWAY, p. 7; HO CHI MINH TRAIL, p. 19; RED RIVER DELTA, p. 35.

Significance   The lower Mekong River Basin held out great promise for Cambodia and Vietnam. Laos and Thailand were also expected to benefit from this development project initiated by the Economic Commission for Asia and the Far East (ECAFE) in the 1950s. Conflict and war, however, interfered, and by the 1980s nothing had been done. The International Bank for Reconstruction and Development (World Bank) had issued a preliminary study which was known as the "Wheeler Report," and by the early 1960s approximately 12 countries and a number of UN agencies and private organizations had displayed a willingness to join in the effort of harnessing the resources of the Mekong.

North Vietnam, by this time under the rule of Ho Chi Minh, was intent on moving its revolution south, however. The attack on the South Vietnamese government by the Viet Cong and North Vietnamese escalated the fighting and development projects were difficult and sometimes impossible to pursue. Moreover, with American involvement in the conflict, Cambodia could not remain totally neutral and it was caught up in the greater struggle that had begun to engulf Laos and South Vietnam. Cambodia had even attempted to reduce its dependence on South Vietnam by building the new port of Sihanoukville on the Gulf of Siam in 1960. Even this effort proved futile.

In the late 1960s and early 1970s, the whole region was consumed in conflict. The withdrawal of U.S. forces in 1973 was followed by the collapse of South Vietnam in 1975 and its integration with the north. Laos became a satellite of Vietnam. The pro-United States Cambodian government, which had been overthrown by the Marxist Khmer Rouge in this same period, was attacked by the Vietnamese before it could consolidate its victory. The ensuing war between the Khmer Rouge and the Vietnamese communist army forced the former to lose control of the country, and Vietnam established a puppet government in its place. Cambodian refugees fled to Thailand, which was also caught up in episodic attacks by Vietnamese troops. Finally, guerrilla war between the Khmer Rouge and the Vietnamese continued to take a heavy toll on lives and property in the 1980s, and the Mekong development schemes have had to wait for more tranquil times and possible other sponsors. One fact was evident, however: the Mekong had interwoven the lives and destinies of the people that it touched, and there was no escaping its influence.

Pacific Community   An idea which has been advanced by nations around the Pacific Ocean emphasizing a need for closer political, economic, and cultural cooperation. Since 1965, various proposals have been advanced to organize a Pacific Community in order to capitalize on the following advantages: (1) the fastest growing economies among the newly industrialized nations, such as South Korea, Taiwan, and Singapore; (2) rich natural resources such as uranium, coal, petroleum, iron ores, nonferrous metals, and lumber; (3) major food exporting countries such as the United States, Australia, Canada, and Thailand; (4) the world's most dynamic economies, such as the United States and Japan; (5) increasing economic exchanges in trade and investment; and (6) rapid improvement in communication and transportation.

The nations often included in these proposals are: (1) the United States, Japan, Australia, Canada, and New Zealand among the advanced, industrialized nations; (2) Indonesia, Malaysia, the Philippines, Singapore, and Thailand of the ASEAN nations; and (3) South Korea, Taiwan, and Hong Kong in Northeast Asia. Community implies not only shared needs but also shared minds. Although the idea of a Pacific Community has increasingly become a topic of study and discussion, its prospective institutionalization has encountered a great deal of skepticism. *See also* GREATER EAST ASIA CO-PROSPERITY SPHERE, p. 15.

Significance   The concept of Pacific Community is one of the latest ideas discussed for regional cooperation among the Pacific nations. Earlier efforts included the United Nations' Economic and Social Commission for Asia and the Pacific (ESCAP), which includes nearly all of the Asian Pacific countries; Asia Development Bank (ADB), which was established to promote and finance investment in the ESCAP region; the Association of Southeast Asian Nations (ASEAN) for promotion of economic growth, cooperation in agriculture and industry, and expansion of trade and cultural exchanges among its members; and the Pacific Basin Economic Council (PBEC) of the five advanced Pacific nations, to further their economic interests in the region. These organizations were established at different times for specific purposes. However, geographical propinquity, use of the world's greatest ocean, and increasing interchanges within the Pacific region resulting from remarkable economic vitality in recent years in the area have contributed to a new community awareness among the Pacific Rim nations.

To realize such a community, many obstacles must be overcome. Thus far, there is no agreement on membership requirements. Some would like to include all nations in the region—not only the nations with market economies, but also nations with non-market Communist economies, such as the People's Republic of China and Vietnam. Others would like to limit membership to the market-economy nations. Furthermore, the Pacific Rim nations vary as to their levels of economic development and power status. Many newly independent nations in Asia, particularly those of ASEAN, are suspicious of any scheme initiated by the advanced nations in the region, which would undermine their independence and make them subservient to the international power struggle.

European integration in NATO and the European Community serves as a model for the Pacific nations. Unlike Europe, however, the countries along the Pacific Ocean are extremely diverse in their historical, ethnic, and cultural backgrounds and, thus far, their new common identity has not developed sufficiently to overcome their differences and suspicions. Emphasis currently is on incremental and non-governmental cooperation among the fast-growing market-economy nations of Asia, in order to sustain and maximize their growth. Leaders are skeptical as to whether the building of a Pacific Community would have a positive or negative impact on their nations' futures.

Persian Gulf   Identified as the Arabian Gulf by the Arabs on its western littoral, it is almost an inland sea covering an area of approximately 90,000 square miles (235,000 square kilometers). It is 180 miles (290 kilometers) across at its widest and only 35 miles (57 kilometers) at its narrowest points. The distance from the mouth of the Shatt al-Arab river at the uppermost extension of the Gulf to the Strait of Hormuz, where it empties into the Gulf of Oman and the Indian Ocean, is over 500 miles (800 kilometers).

The countries bordering the Gulf are: Iran, Iraq, Kuwait, Saudi Arabia, Qatar, the United Arab Emirates, and Oman. The island nation of Bahrein lies midway in the Gulf close to Saudi Arabia and Qatar. There are numerous other small islands in the vital waterway. Some are little more than sand or mud banks, rising only a foot or two above the water. Even the larger ones are devoid of any vegetation. Established settlements on these islands are very limited, and most are visited by migratory inhabitants during certain seasons. Several islands in the Gulf have attained considerable importance, however. The town of Abu Dhabi is built on a triangular-shaped island. Das Island is an important ocean terminal for off-shore oil drilling. Similar facilities have been built on Halat at Mubarras. Dalma Island is the center for pearl fishing. Sadiyat Island is being used to experiment with controlled environmental agriculture. Um an Nar has archeological digs of interest to the scholarly community.

Perhaps the most famous islands in the Gulf are Abu Musa, which is legally a possession of Sharjah (a member of the UAE), and the Greater and Lesser Tumbs (claimed by Ras al Khaimah, also of the UAE). These islands were seized by Iran in 1971, when the UAE was being formed. The islands are strategically placed near the Strait of Hormuz, and the Shah of Iran feared they could fall under the influence of Iran's enemies, particularly Iraq. Although Iran developed an agreement with Sharjah, Ras al Khaimah never countenanced the Iranian occupation of the Tumbs. After the demise of the Shah, Ras al Khaimah had reason to believe the dispute would be resolved, but the revolutionary government in Tehran showed no more willingness to evacuate the islands than the previous Iranian regime. Iran has sovereignty over many other islands in the Gulf, closer to its frontier. By far the most important of these is Kharg Island off the coast of Iranian Khuzistan. Kharg is the principal petroleum refining facility and major transit point for the shipment of Iranian oil from the Persian Gulf. Efforts by Iraq to prevent the flow of Iranian oil to the industrial world in 1984 increased international tensions across the globe. *See also* DIEGO GARCIA, p. 12; INDIAN OCEAN, p. 22.

Significance   In the context of contemporary international politics, the Persian (Arabian) Gulf is the most important waterway in the late twentieth century world. It is from the Gulf that approximately two-thirds of the world's exportable oil flows into the principal commercial sea lanes. If an unfriendly power were to gain control over the Strait of Hormuz, the Gulf could be effectively closed, the oil would cease flowing, and other countries beyond the littoral states would be affected. The world economy is dependent on the steady movement of Gulf petroleum, and chaos would prevail if it became impossible to move it to the consuming nations. The protracted Iraq-Iran war threatens to choke off that supply of oil, and attacks on neutral vessels by the warring states in 1984 provoked Washington to improve the defenses of Saudi Arabia and Kuwait, as well as increase its naval readiness near the mouth of the Gulf. United States bases in Oman and on the Omani island of Masirah in the Indian Ocean are evidence of Washington's great concern. The United States is also mindful of Soviet treaty commitments to Iraq, and Marxist South Yemen, where Moscow has developed a major naval and air station in Aden and on the island of Socotra. All United States and Soviet activities in the region point to the Persian Gulf, which is clearly a centerpiece for superpower rivalry.

Red River Delta   The lowlands bordering the Gulf of Tonkin in northern Vietnam. Reputed to be the natural homeland of the Vietnamese people, the Red River Delta region is flat, fertile, intensely cultivated, and thickly populated. Triangular in shape, it is criss-crossed by numerous waterways. From the Tonkin Gulf it extends 130 miles in a northwesterly direction before it runs into the mountain gorges north of Hanoi. In the south, the Delta is linked to a coastal plain that runs on for 250 miles. Approximately 90 percent of Vietnam's population north of the seventeenth parallel live in this fertile zone.

The Red River is crucial to the productivity of the Delta and its sudden rise in summer has necessitated the building of numerous dikes, canals, dams, and ditches. This intricate hydraulic system makes it possible to cultivate two rice crops each year and the region has been noted for its high output. Moreover, the peasants have long had an obligation to maintain the system, and from earliest times, almost one-third of a cultivator's annual work period was spent keeping the Delta viable. During French colonial rule, efforts were made to improve flood control. The French also established agricultural and hydrological research stations and introduced large-scale production of rubber, coffee, and tea, which reduced the area under rice cultivation. The unification of Vietnam in 1975 and the dominance of the north over the south in no way diminished the importance of the Delta. In fact, the Delta has taken on even greater significance as efforts are made to reclaim many of the cash crop areas for foodgrain production. *See also* DIEN BIEN PHU, p. 380; HO CHI MINH TRAIL, p. 19; MEKONG RIVER, p. 30.

Significance   The Red River Delta was transformed into a battleground during the Vietnamese struggle against French colonialism. Many major hydraulic installations were destroyed during that period and several hundred rice-growing acres were transformed into barbed-wire strongholds and minefields. Villages and livestock were also destroyed in large numbers and the Vietnamese were forced to exist on minimum rations. The departure of the French in 1954 gave the Hanoi government the opportunity to rebuild the Delta's hydraulic systems and to step up its productivity.

Throughout the second Indochina War, this time involving the Americans, the battle was brought south, and the Delta was relatively safe from enemy attack. The United States weighed the advantages of destroying the rebuilt facilities in the Delta, especially the elaborate dike system, but it decided not to unleash its bombers against this target. All through the war the United States argued it was not interested in defeating, let alone occupying, North Vietnam. Its principal purpose remained the preservation of a sovereign, independent South Vietnam. Moreover, the French destruction of Delta facilities did not provide Paris with victory. On the contrary, the world viewed the French action as an act against humanity, and it seemed to underline their selfish motives. The United States did not want to be tarred by the same brush and consciously decided to leave the Red River Delta intact. The farmers of the Delta thus were permitted to conduct a relatively normal routine during the 1964–73 hostilities and to provide the North Vietnamese forces and population with the nutrition vital to their survival.

Sakhalin The island which is the far eastern extension of the Russian Soviet Federated Socialist Republic, the largest and most important Republic in the Soviet Union. Sakhalin is located in the Sea of Okhotsk and is separated from the mainland by the Tatar Strait. It is also close to the northernmost Japanese island of Hokkaido across the La Perouse or Soya Strait. The island has a mountain chain that runs from north to south along its full length. Sakhalin is 600 miles long, ranges from 15 to 100 miles wide, and is fairly rich in natural resources, particularly oil, coal, and lumber. In 1855 the Tsarist Empire and the Empire of Japan agreed to establish a joint condominium over the island. In 1875, however, Japan recognized Russian sovereignty over the whole island in return for Tokyo's claim to all the Kuril islands. As a consequence of the Russo-Japanese War in 1905, Japan assumed control of southern Sakhalin. In the aftermath of World War II, Japanese rule was removed from Sakhalin, and the Soviet Union reasserted its authority over it, as well as all the Kurils which it now claimed for itself. *See also* KURIL ISLANDS, p. 28.

Significance The Soviet Union has established a major military complex at Sakhalin, and with the annexation of the Kurils, Moscow asserts the Sea of Okhotsk has become an inland sea, entirely subject to its jurisdiction. The Russian/Soviet quest for total control over the islands and seas between Kamchatka and Japan required almost a century of effort but it was finally realized in 1945 with Japan's defeat in World War

II. Since then the Soviets have been engaged in a vast program aimed at transforming the region into an impregnable frontier.

Sakhalin is the key to this defense posture. It protects the Soviet mainland, especially the port areas to the north, and south to Vladivostok. The sensitivity with which the Soviets view this region was tragically demonstrated in September 1983 when Soviet air defense forces were ordered to destroy a South Korean commercial airliner that had unknowingly strayed off course and had flown over the Sea of Okhotsk and Sakhalin. The South Korean plane was on the verge of departing Soviet airspace when it was shot down. Although first denying it had deliberately destroyed the airliner with its innocent cargo, the Soviets later justified their action, arguing that the plane was on a spy mission.

Seventeenth Parallel   The temporary boundary line that divided North Vietnam from South Vietnam between 1954 and 1975. Following the French defeat at Dien Bien Phu in 1953, Ho Chi Minh's victorious forces agreed to settle the matter of Vietnam's independence at a peace conference in Geneva. The Vietnamese Communists and the French, however, were not the only actors in the scenario. The country was already divided between the Communist-dominated north in Hanoi, and the non-Communist south in Saigon. Moreover, numerous small groups organized para-governments, and they were determined to rule their portion of the country. A majority of them were anti-Communist Buddhist organizations, such as the Cao Dai, Hoa Hao, and Binh Xuyen, and they anticipated giving their support to Saigon. Therefore, the Communists went to Geneva with the understanding that they still were some distance from their goal of national unification.

Ho Chi Minh's delegation in Geneva proved to be both reasonable and flexible. When the question arose about drawing a line between the communist north and the non-Communist south, Ho Chi Minh first insisted on the thirteenth or fourteenth parallel. Later, however, he agreed to yield territory gained in the war against the French, and the seventeenth parallel was adopted by all the major parties. The seventeenth parallel became the official frontier between North and South Vietnam until the South was overrun and forcibly merged with the North in 1975. *See also* GENEVA ACCORDS (1954), p. 339; PARIS ACCORDS (1973), p. 351; THIRTY-EIGHTH PARALLEL, p. 41.

Significance   The seventeenth parallel was never conceived as a permanent frontier between North and South Vietnam. Both sides at Geneva interpreted it to be no more than a temporary line of military demarcation. General elections, scheduled for 1956, were supposed to complete the process of national unification, but these were never held. After Geneva, the South Vietnamese government came under the influence of the United States, and the Americans concluded there was no way Ho Chi Minh could be defeated at the polls. Washington began to view the seventeenth parallel as a legal and fixed frontier between the two Vietnams, and the South Vietnam government of Ngo Dinh Diem received massive American assistance. U.S. advisors literally hand-crafted military, police, and economic institutions in the country. All efforts were aimed at establishing a viable counterforce against the North. This strategy required a consolidation of the Saigon government's authority and influence, and Ngo Dinh Diem launched campaigns to destroy the Buddhist sects in the south. The destruction of the Cao Dai, Hoa Hao, and Binh Xuyen, however, removed a phalanx of anti-Communist organizations and provided Ho Chi Minh and his generals with the opening they sought in penetrating below the seventeenth parallel.

Ngo Dinh Diem, a Catholic in a Buddhist country, had little popular appeal. Whatever his attributes, he could not rally the South Vietnamese in the manner that Ho could the northerners. Once the Communist (Viet Cong) insurgency in the South began in earnest, Diem's policies and actions appeared designed for self-aggrandizement, more than national preservation. His assassination in 1963 signalled the futility of building a nation-state below the seventeenth parallel. Deprived of direct American military support in 1973, the South Vietnamese forces disintegrated. Within two years the two Vietnams became one under Hanoi's leadership.

Subcontinent   The great peninsula that extends to the south of the Asian continent, and points to the heart of the Indian Ocean. Known as South Asia, the subcontinent is dominated by India, but also includes Pakistan, Bangladesh, Nepal, and Bhutan. This region is called the subcontinent because of its size, importance, and unique characteristics. Geographically, the subcontinent—sometimes referred to as the Indian subcontinent, or the Pak-India subcontinent—is separated from larger Asia by the Himalayan Mountains to the north, rugged terrain in the northwest, and dense jungles in the northeast. Culturally, the subcontinent is the home of Hinduism, a religion followed by more than half a billion people, almost all residing within this area. *See also* HIMALAYAS, p. 16; HINDU KUSH, p. 18; MILITANT HINDUISM, p. 103.

Significance   The subcontinent is sometimes perceived as a self-contained entity. India dominates the region and tends to isolate it from the mainstream of international life. Geography and Hindu culture blend to create a mind-set among Indians which reinforces their distinctiveness and behavior. Hindus emphasize the oneness of the subcontinent. Its "partition" in 1947 between India and Pakistan was difficult to accept for these stalwarts. Mahatma Gandhi was assassinated because some radical groups held him responsible for the breakup of the territory. These and other organizations would support a more aggressive posture toward Pakistan. "Akhand Bharat" or United India is a dream of Hindu extremists that seems to imply the destruction of Pakistan and the annexation of its territory to India. Pakistan-Indian enmity revolves around this issue, and no amount of explanation can convince Pakistanis that India's goal is not the unification of the entire subcontinent. After the Indo-Pakistani War of 1971, Pakistan reoriented itself toward the Muslim Middle East and particularly toward Southwest Asia. This posture confirmed in some Indian minds that Pakistanis were alien to the subcontinent. It also led Indians to conclude that they were a "small" island in a "Muslim sea."

Taiwan Strait   The body of water that separates the Chinese mainland from the island of Taiwan and helps to sustain the reality as well as the notion of "two Chinas." The Taiwan or Formosan Strait is approximately 100 miles wide. There are other islands in the strait, such as the Penghu or Pescadores. The Nationalist government on the island of Taiwan also maintains control over the Quemoy islands near the mainland city of Amoy and the Matsu group in the vicinity of Fuzhou. Taiwan has been the home of the Nationalist Chinese regime since 1949 when Mao Zedong's Communist armies took control of continental China. The Nationalists also held the Tachen Islands but in 1955 the Chinese Communists attacked these positions near Zhejiang province. The United States was compelled to assist the Nationalists, but in return for an American guarantee to defend Taiwan and the Pescadores, they were called upon to yield the Tachens to the Communists. The Nationalists withdrew from the Tachens in February 1955, and the United States commitment to safeguard the integrity of the Nationalist Regime has been sustained into the 1980s. *See also* USSURI RIVER, p. 45.

Significance   The Taiwan Strait has served as a defensive barrier for the Nationalist Chinese since 1949. Until 1971, the United States supported the Nationalist Chinese contention that they were the true representatives of all the Chinese people. The United States refused to recognize the Communist government in Beijing (Peking), and during the Korean war (1950–53), American and Communist Chinese forces clashed in largescale battles that produced tens of thousands of casualties. The Taiwan Strait, with American support, proved to be a significant moat which the Communist Chinese could not cross without sustaining enormous losses. Beijing therefore decided to avoid an all-out struggle for the island. The United States, however, because the Nationalists were secure in their fortress island, sustained the myth of their legal right to govern the whole Chinese nation.

The United States was late in seizing the opportunity provided by the Sino-Soviet schism, but the intensification of that dispute pointed the American government toward a new reality. The "two China" policy was a belated but natural response for the United States. It enabled Washington to maintain support of the Nationalists while also opening a window on communist China. The Nationalists were displeased with American policy but powerless to prevent it from being implemented. The Chinese Communists insisted on their eventual acquisition of Taiwan and emphatically rejected the notion of two Chinas, but they were unprepared to break their new ties to the West, especially to the United States.

Third World   A concept used to distinguish the more than one hundred underdeveloped countries of Africa, Asia, Latin America, and Oceania from the First World of modern capitalistic democracies of Europe, North America, Japan, Israel, and South Africa, and from the Second World of economically advanced communist nations, such as the Soviet Union and much of Eastern Europe. The Third World is a phrase initially derived from the French *tiers monde* and originally used to describe those nations that are neither communist nor western. Since most of these countries are poor compared to the western democracies and advanced communist nations, poverty is also used as a common denominator. The Third World is often referred to as "the South," because most of its members are located south of Western Europe, North America, and Eastern Europe. *See also* BANDUNG CONFERENCE, p. 328; MODERNIZATION, p. 313; NON-ALIGNED MOVEMENT, p. 348.

Significance   Some Third World nations are European in terms of their ancestries, as in Latin America, and some are communist states, such as China, North Korea, Vietnam, Cuba, Nicaragua, Afghanistan, and Ethiopia. The United Nations has identified a Fourth World of those nations with exceptionally small per capita incomes, which can be distinguished from relatively high per capita income nations, such as South Korea, Taiwan, Malaysia, and Singapore. Although the Third World as a concept has many shortcomings, it has been used widely by the developing bloc of nations to build their political and economic strength through unity. In a world dominated by the two superpowers and by giant economic powers, such as Japan and many European nations, the Third World has sought to develop a common group identity among the poor nations of the world, as they compete with the First and the Second Worlds for their share of the world's wealth. The Group of Seventy-Seven (G-77), functioning as a massive caucusing group, has been an effective voice for the Third World nations, especially in United Nations decision making. Most Third World nations have also been active in the non-aligned movement.

Thirty-Eighth Parallel   The *de facto* boundary line initially drawn by the Allied Powers in World War II, dividing the Korean peninsula into the Soviet and the American zones of occupation for accepting Japanese surrender and disarming Japanese troops in Korea. The origin of the division is still a mystery, but it may be traced to the Yalta Conference of February 1945 when President Franklin D. Roosevelt of the United States, Prime Minister Winston S. Churchill of Great Britain, and Marshal Josef Stalin of the Soviet Union agreed upon Soviet entry into the Pacific war. The Soviet Union was to enter the war against Japan within three months following the surrender of Germany, which came on May 8, 1945. On August 8, 1945, the Soviet Union declared war against Japan and its troops quickly overran Manchuria and initiated the penetration of the Korean peninsula. When Japan surrendered on August 15, 1945, Soviet troops were already in North Korea and had started to move south.

In order to stop Soviet occupation of the whole of Korea, a hasty decision had to be made in Washington to draw a line of demarcation dividing the Korean peninsula into respective zones of occupation by Soviet and American forces. This line was intended to be temporary, since Allied leaders at the Cairo summit conference of October 1943 had promised Korean independence "in due course." However, following the Japanese surrender, the Soviet Union and the United States were unable to decide on the type of government to be installed in Korea. When the United Nations was called upon to help solve the problem, the Soviet Union objected to its Commission on Korea operating in North Korea. In the end, two separate governments were established in Korea—the Democratic People's Republic of Korea (DPRK) in the north, sponsored by the Soviet Union; and the Republic of Korea (CROK) in the south, sponsored by the United Nations. Several attempts have been made to reunite these two Koreas but the country remains divided. *See also* KOREAN WAR, p. 388; UNIFICATION PROPOSALS: KOREA, p. 368; WARTIME CONFERENCES: ALLIED POWERS, p. 370.

Significance   The Korean division at the thirty-eighth parallel was one of the most tragic consequences of World War II in the Pacific theater and of subsequent Cold War development. Ethnically, the Korean people are among the most homogeneous in the world. They have existed as one nation since 688 A.D. when the Silla kingdom (57 B.C.–936 A.D.) established a unified Korea throughout the peninsula. Geographically, it was an artificial boundary. Politically, there were no factions divided into north and south to justify it. Economically, the north was more industrial and the south more agricultural, one complementing the other. The division caused dislocation of the fragile Korean economy at the outset. In addition, it compounded the chaotic situation that followed Japanese colonialism. Furthermore, the division was a direct cause of the Korean War (1950–53), which ended only in a truce. Following the war, the Demilitarized Zone (DMZ) was established, running from points south of the thirty-eighth parallel in the west to those north of the original line in the east. A state of war still exists between the two Koreas. Divided and hostile, both Koreas symbolize a discordant world. The DMZ remains one of the most heavily guarded areas in the world.

Tibet (Xizang): China   One of the autonomous regions of the People's Republic of China (PRC), bordering Nepal and India, and inhabited mostly by some three million Tibetans who constitute one of the largest national minority groups in China. Following the establishment of the PRC in 1949, the People's Liberation Army (PLA) marched into Tibet (Xizang) in a move designed to consolidate its outlying borders. In 1951, the PRC government concluded an agreement with the Tibetan Buddhist ruler, the Dalai Lama, to keep him under Chinese control while allowing him to continue the existing local political arrangement. In an apparent move to reorganize Tibet as an autonomous region of China and assimilate the Tibetans into China proper, a preparatory committee was established in 1956, and some radical reforms were introduced in line with the Great Leap Forward movement of 1958. Opposing these measures, however, Tibetans revolted in March 1959. The rebellion was easily suppressed, yet it generated sympathy for the Tibetan cause for independence in the international community. When the rebellion failed, the Dalai Lama and several thousand Tibetans fled to India. They continue to provide a challenge to the legitimacy and acceptability of Chinese Communist rule in Tibet. *See also* CHINA: AUTONOMOUS REGIONS, p. 10.

Significance   China's national minorities (non-Han Chinese) number some 52 million people. Of these, the biggest problem relates particularly to Tibet and Inner Mongolia (Nei Monggol), where the minority people constitute the local majority. In these regions, any effort to develop an independence movement is always regarded by the Chinese government as a definite threat. The PRC's relentless suppression of the Tibetan rebellion in 1959 must be viewed in this light. In its treatment of minority groups, the PRC has generally oscillated between the policies of assimilation and pluralism. During periods of radical politics, such as the Great Leap Forward (1958–59) and the Cultural Revolution (1966–69), the policy of assimilation was emphasized. At times, however, pluralism was encouraged by making accommodations to the cultural differences and special needs of minority groups. For example, all autonomous regional governments are permitted, in the 1982 constitution, to make regulations unique to the areas and to employ their own languages in the performance of their duties. It appears that these constitutional guarantees have been honored.

Tonkin Gulf   The strategic waters adjacent to the coast of Vietnam. The northern region of Vietnam is also known by its historic name, Tonkin. It is bounded on the east by the Tonkin Gulf. The Vietnamese capital of Hanoi as well as the industrial center and chief port of Haiphong are located in Tonkin, making the area vital to the Vietnamese government and people. The Tonkin Gulf is remembered in the outside world because of the incident that occurred there in August of 1964. North Vietnamese patrol boats attacked U.S. naval destroyers, allegedly in international waters. In retaliation, President Lyndon B. Johnson ordered air strikes against North Vietnamese installations. The American president also requested and obtained a Joint Resolution from the Congress empowering him "to take all necessary measures to repel any armed attacks against forces of the United States (and) all necessary steps, including the use of armed force" in defense of South Vietnam and Southeast Asian Treaty members. The Tonkin Gulf incident in effect brought the United States directly into the Vietnamese civil war, and Washington was determined to sustain the South Vietnamese government. *See also* GENEVA ACCORDS (1954), p. 339; PARIS ACCORDS (1973), p. 351; SEVENTEENTH PARALLEL, p. 37; SINO-VIETNAM CONFLICT, 1979, p. 409.

Significance   The Tonkin Gulf incident was a minor military engagement, but it precipitated a long and grueling struggle. North Vietnam had no intention of drawing the Americans into a wider conflict in Vietnam, but they demonstrated a resolute will in defending their interests, and particularly their territory, from foreign penetration. At the time of the "incident" South Vietnam was in disarray. Ngo Dinh Diem had been assassinated in November 1963 and the South Vietnamese military leaders could not fill the political vacuum. Rebellious elements attacked the Saigon government and Viet Cong insurgents escalated their operations against American-trained Vietnamese forces. The United States government seemed to be faced with two choices: to abandon South Vietnam or to introduce American forces, which, unlike the French earlier, were expected to achieve their military objectives. Although the Soviet Union suggested taking the Tonkin Gulf question to the UN, the Chinese declared their brotherhood with North Vietnam and offered to provide assistance to a "fraternal" socialist country. Aggressive American behavior in Vietnam, noted the Chinese, was aggression against China and the "Chinese people will absolutely not sit idly by without lending a helping hand."

This declaration from the Chinese government confirmed in the minds of American leaders that the Vietnamese problem was inextricably intertwined with "Red" China's ambition to spread Marxist revolution throughout Asia. The United States, therefore, was not only seeking to neutralize North Vietnam, it was also responsible for containing the Chinese People's Republic. By contrast with Chinese statements and actions, the Soviets appeared conciliatory. Washington, therefore, saw itself warding off the "Yellow Peril." The Soviets encouraged this American perception and although it repeatedly called for the United States to withdraw its forces from Indochina, it drew strength from the realization that its major adversary was bogged down in a war that it could not win. It is important to note that since the unification of Vietnam in 1975, the Soviet Union, not China, was the major foreign influence in Vietnam. Indeed, China and Vietnam engaged in a major border conflict in 1979, which remained unresolved in the mid-1980s.

Union Territories: India   Ten special political units that, along with twenty-two states, form the Republic of India. The Union Territories are: the capital city and area of Delhi; Chandigarh (the joint capital of the states of Hariana and the Punjab); the Andaman and Nicobar Islands; Dadra and Nagar Haveli; Pondicherry; Arunachal Pradesh (NEFA); Lakshadweep Islands; Goa and Daman; Diu; and Mizoram. Many Union Territories were under non-British control before they were brought under Indian sovereignty. Union Territories are administered by the central government but the method of rule varies from place to place. Some territories may be considered too small for statehood. A few, however, may achieve that status in the future, while others could be absorbed by prevailing states.

Significance   The controversial nature of some of the Union Territories, the manner in which they were formed, or their strategic importance suggests they will continue to be administered by the central government. Such is certainly the case with Arunachal Pradesh which has been claimed by China, and which witnessed sporadic conflict in the 1960s and 1970s. Arunachal Pradesh shares a long border with China and links with the homeland of the Nagas to the south. The Nagas, a non-Hindu tribal people, fought ferocious battles with the Indian army in a desperate effort to separate themselves from New Delhi's control. The determination of the central government to hold the territory produced a costly internal war which India argued was aided and abetted by Beijing. The post-Mao era that brought a new administration to China also reduced Beijing's commitment to the Nagas. Nevertheless, the integration into Indian society of the tribal peoples of what was formerly called the North East Frontier Agency (NEFA), as well as the Assam Hills and Mizoram, in proximity to the Chittagong Hill Tracts, is a great test of the Indian system. Local insurrections such as those generated by the Nagas and Mizos could be more threatening to Indian security if they were to occur in Arunachal Pradesh.

Ussuri River   Rising in the Sikhote-Alin range in the southeastern portion of the Russian Soviet Federated Socialist Republic, it flows approximately 500 miles to join the Amur River and form a section of the border between China and the Soviet Union. These countries share a long, controversial frontier, but it is in the most distant eastern sector that differences produced violent interaction. The Ussuri River is part of the natural border between Manchuria and the Soviet state. Just to the southeast is the port city of Vladivostok, the Soviet Union's most important metropolitan center in the Far East. Chinese claims to the region cannot be ignored and the tenuous nature of the territory is documented by the large army that each country has assembled on their side of the Ussuri. *See also* KURIL ISLANDS, p. 28; SAKHALIN, p. 36; SINO-SOVIET SPLIT, p. 356.

Significance   The Ussuri River was the setting for a physical confrontation between the world's largest communist states. Sino-Soviet relations began to deteriorate in the late 1950s, but it was not until March 1969 that their differences degenerated to the point of open conflict. The Soviets claimed sovereignty over a small island in the Ussuri River, and the Chinese sought to deny their claim. Fighting erupted between Chinese and Soviet border guards and it is alleged that thirty-one of the latter died before the skirmish abated. The Soviets seized the incident to propagandize the awakening of the "Yellow Peril." The Kremlin's spokesmen communicated a message to the Soviet people that reminded them of the Mongol invasions, centuries earlier. The Chinese, according to Soviet Premier Leonid Brezhnev, were collaborating with the American imperialists, and Mao Zedong had shown himself to be a "traitor" to socialism and the anti-capitalist crusade. The Chinese were deemed to be a military threat as well as ideological deviants.

For their part, the Chinese described the Soviet leaders as "worse than the tsars" but neither side was prepared to spread the combat. The Chinese, however, had signalled the United States that it was time to begin a process of reconciliation. The United States began to wind down its involvement in Indochina in the first months of 1971, and later that year, President Richard M. Nixon's National Security Advisor, Henry Kissinger, made his secret journey to Beijing where he met with Mao and the other Chinese leaders. Détente with China began to emerge as President Nixon visited China in 1972 and a diplomatic program was launched which, in the 1980s, promised to draw the largest Communist state and the world's most successful capitalist nation into an even more intimate embrace.

Wakhan Corridor   A thin finger of Afghan territory that separates the Soviet Union from India and Pakistan in the Pamir region of Central Asia. The Wakhan Corridor is approximately 150 miles (240 kilometers) long and 50 miles (80 kilometers) wide. At the far eastern extreme of the Wakhan Corridor, Afghanistan shares a 40-mile border with China. To the north is the Soviet Union, and to the south, the northernmost extension of the Indian-Pakistani subcontinent. Given its mountainous terrain, there are few inhabitants in the Wakhan region. The Corridor was demarcated for Afghanistan by the British and Russians in the nineteenth century, the latter intent on pressing its influence south toward India, and the former determined to thwart such ambition.

This competition between Russia and Britain, known as the "Great Game," led the British to draw the frontier between their Indian colony and Afghanistan in 1893. The Wakhan was part of this larger program of boundary delineation. As early as 1873 the Russians and British had agreed that the Wakhan territory from Badakshan to the Pamirs would remain part of Afghanistan, thus physically separating the two empires. This understanding was affirmed in 1887, but the Russians continued to send expeditions into the area. In 1891 one such exploratory mission attempted to claim the Wakhan Corridor for the czar. The British were duly provoked, and after indicating their concern, the Russians agreed to participate in a joint boundary commission. The Pamir Convention of 1895–96 settled the question, and the Wakhan was to remain under Afghan sovereignty until the Soviet invasion of Afghanistan in December 1979. *See also* AMU DARYA (OXUS RIVER), p. 3; HINDU KUSH, p. 18; INDIAN OCEAN, p. 22; PERSIAN GULF, p. 33; WARM WATER PORT POLICY, p. 47.

Significance   The Wakhan Corridor is a geopolitical contrivance. Rivalry between the British and Russians placed the area under Afghan sovereignty. China refused to accept the delimitation, arguing that the Russians and British were pressing their expansion at the expense of the local inhabitants as well as China's. China also disputed the British-imposed McMahon Line, drawn in 1910 to separate the subcontinent from Tibet and Chinese influence. It was not until 1963 that China finally recognized Afghanistan's control over the Wakhan Corridor. It is interesting to note that China's penetration of the McMahon Line in its border war with India in 1962 raised anew the question of the legal boundary between the two Asian giants.

The Soviet thrust into Afghanistan in 1979 and the *de facto* annexation of the Wakhan Corridor effectively sealed off the only border between Afghanistan and China. The Soviets justify their action with the explanation that the Wakhan had been controlled by a local warlord who refused to acknowledge Kabul's sovereignty in the region. The flight of the warlord to Turkey, according to Moscow sources, necessitated a Soviet takeover of the region. Moreover, control of the Wakhan provides the Soviet Union with a common border with Kashmir. It also presents Pakistan with a new neighbor in its sensitive northwest frontier region. The Durand Line, separating eastern Afghanistan from Pakistan, has also become a Soviet staging area. For the Soviet Union, dominance of the Wakhan provides total control of the Pamir mountain range and facilitates management of the Hindu Kush. It also projects Soviet power closer to the open water of the Indian Ocean.

Warm Water Port Policy   The Warm Water Port Policy is attributed to the Soviet Union. Before the Bolshevik revolution of 1917, Imperial Russia expanded its empire in the direction of the Indian Ocean, as well as toward the Pacific. In the nineteenth century, the Russians invaded Central Asia, destroying established Muslim kingdoms and absorbing the region. The Bolsheviks, who brought an end to the tsarist system, however, had no serious intention of releasing the nationalities from Russian control. With the formal emergence of the Soviet Union in 1924, the marginal territories on the southern periphery of the Russian state were again forcibly brought within the Russian/Soviet fold.

The Soviets, like the Russian imperial forces earlier, paused at the Iranian frontier on the one side, and Afghanistan and British India on the other. The position of British power in India, and Great Britain's interest in Iran and the Persian Gulf area, perpetuated that border and prevented the Soviets from pressing toward the open sea. During World War I, the British-French Sykes-Picot Treaty of 1916 divided the Ottoman territories in the Arab world among themselves. In return for

Russian services, Moscow had been promised control over the Turkish straits, but the Bolshevik revolution cancelled that understanding. The Soviets did not give up their quest for total control over the Black Sea and dominance of the Turkish straits, and for an outlet to the Indian Ocean.

Prior to World War II, Hitler, through Foreign Minister Ribbentrop, and Stalin, through Foreign Minister Molotov, entered into the Nazi-Soviet Pact. The Germans encouraged the Soviets to press their southward expansion in the direction of the Indian Ocean, which they described as Russia's "natural tendency." The Soviets displayed keen interest in "the area south of Batum and Baku in the general direction of the Persian Gulf," but they were also insistent on being compensated in Poland, the Balkans, Finland, and the Turkish straits. In the aftermath of World War II, Britain retreated from India and no longer pressed its "Forward Policy" against Russian encroachment in Afghanistan. Neither India, the major power in the area, nor the United States, which sought to contain the Soviet Union, was in a position to assume the role vacated by the British.

Shortly after the War, the Soviet Union attempted to establish two socialist republics in northwestern Iran and in proximity to the Persian Gulf. The Soviets also applied pressure on Turkey to share control of the straits with Moscow. Because of this, as well as Soviet assistance for Greek Communists in their struggle against the Athens monarchy, President Harry Truman announced a "Containment Policy," known as the Truman Doctrine. The Soviets were frustrated in Greece and Turkey and compelled to evacuate their forces from Iran, and they did not press their expansion toward the Indian Ocean until December 1979. In the wake of the collapse of the Shah's political system in Iran, and the widespread anti-Americanism of both the Iranians and the Pakistanis (the American embassy in Islamabad was burned by Pakistani students shortly after another American embassy and its personnel were seized in Tehran), the Soviets invaded Afghanistan and moved their forces within a few hundred miles of the Persian Gulf and the Indian Ocean. Despite international pressure, there was little likelihood that the Soviets would withdraw from Afghanistan, and some political analysts sensed that a final drive for warm water ports was a distinct possibility. *See also* AMU DARYA, p. 3; INDIAN OCEAN, p. 22; PERSIAN GULF, p. 33.

Significance   The Soviet Union's interest in warm water ports is strong because of the landlocked nature of the Soviet state. Although it is spread over one-sixth of the land surface of the globe, the Soviet Union does not have adequate access to the sea. As a superpower with major political, military, economic, and ideological interests and commitments across the planet, the Soviet Union's great power status appears to demand ready access to the open seas. Moreover, Soviet defenses would be enhanced by control of Indian Ocean ports. Offensively, it would be in a more advantageous position from which to utilize its naval arm and to defend against the stationing of hostile American forces, especially long-range missile firing submarines, in the Indian Ocean.

Interdicting western supply lines and denying the industrial states access to vital raw materials would provide Moscow with considerable leverage in the ever-present international power game. Dominance in the Persian Gulf would bring Iran within the Soviet sphere of influence, and it is doubtful whether Iraq, Saudi Arabia, or the other oil-producing Gulf states could long resist Soviet influence. Although some scholars argue that the Soviet Union is not seriously concerned with a warm water port strategy, the Kremlin's invasion of Afghanistan, its efforts to influence the Iranian revolution, and its treaties with Iraq (1972), Syria (1980), and the People's Democratic Republic of Yemen (1979), as well as continuing friendship and support for Libya and India, suggest that the Soviets would not be adverse to permanently positioning their forces on the Indian Ocean littoral.

Yalu River   The river, also known as the Amnok, that forms the boundary between the Korean Peninsula (North Korea), and the People's Republic of China. The Yalu river is approximately 490 miles (788.4 kilometers) long, rising in the Zhangbai Mountains and flowing in a south and southwesterly direction to Korea Bay, an extension of the Yellow Sea. The river is too swift for navigation, but is nonetheless an important source of hydroelectric power. It is also used for transporting lumber. The Yalu is a natural dividing line between Korean and Chinese civilization and has given the former a degree of security from the latter, which has permitted the development of a unique Korean culture and heritage. *See also* KOREAN WAR, 1950–53, p. 388; THIRTY-EIGHTH PARALLEL, p. 41.

Significance   The Yalu River provided the Koreans with the opportunity to develop their distinct lifestyle, relatively free from the actions of their giant neighbor. The hydroelectric power generated by the waters of the Yalu transformed the northern part of the peninsula into an industrial zone. But the Yalu frontier also pointed Korea toward Japan, and that island nation's interest in the peninsula finally brought it to conquer and dominate the Korean people in the early decades of the twentieth century. (The Yalu was also a strategic body of water during the Sino-Japanese War of 1894 and the Russo-Japanese War of 1905–06.)

Japan's defeat in World War II caused Korea to be occupied by Soviet and United States forces. Korea could not avoid becoming an arena for superpower rivalry, and its partition at the thirty-eighth parallel was the consequence of a developing Soviet-U.S. struggle. The Korean War of 1950–53 was fought with the objective of unifying the two Koreas. After the Communist North Korean drive to the south was repulsed, the combined force under UN auspices drove to the Yalu, routing the North Korean armies. Instead of ending the war, it entered another more complicated and protracted phase because China sensed a threat to its security. The Chinese had warned the U.N. commander, General Douglas MacArthur, that the Chinese would enter the war if the forces under his command attempted to establish a presence on the Yalu. General MacArthur chose to ignore the warning, and the war entered a new, more intense period. Despite a ceasefire in 1953, the state of belligerence continued into the 1980s. North Korea's separate existence had been saved by the Chinese intervention, but in subsequent years the Soviet Union became its primary supporter. Nevertheless, the two Koreas assumed a reality not contemplated during most of Korea's history.

Yangtze River (Changjiang)   The longest river in Asia. The Yangtze follows a course approximately 3,400 miles in length, beginning in the Kunlun Mountains in the southwestern region of Ginghai Province. From there, it flows through Sichuan and Yunnan where it turns northeast, passing through China's central region and several more provinces before emptying into the East China Sea north of Shanghai. Oceangoing vessels can navigate the river as far as Hankou, approximately 600 miles inland. The Yangtze allows smaller craft to pass from the open sea to a point almost 1,000 miles into the country. Although originating in elevations as high as 16,000 feet, the Yangtze runs at sea level for its final 200 miles. The Yangtze has many tributaries and drains a vast region of central China. The Grand Canal, celebrated in the development of early China, connects the Yangtze to another of China's great rivers, the Huanghe. The Yangtze is straddled by some of China's great cities, and the delta formed at its mouth is the country's principal rice-growing region. *See also* ASIA, p. 6; SINO-JAPANESE WAR, 1894–95, p. 407; SINO-JAPANESE WAR, 1937–45, p. 407.

Significance   The Yangtze is the cradle of Chinese civilization. The vast territory drained by the river has provided fertile soil for the development of agriculture, and the density of human habitation is extreme. The Yangtze endowed China with an elaborate and highly functional transportation network, and Chinese culture and history is rich in the region. The Yangtze also offered an opportunity for foreigners to penetrate Chinese society and to spread their influence. Nineteenth century and early twentieth century adventurers and colonialists sent their ships up the Yangtze and established stations of opportunity in China. Given China's weakness in the late decades of the nineteenth century, the country was exploited by Europeans and Japanese. Special privileges were obtained from the Chinese court which enabled the Europeans to operate in China almost without restriction. These privileges were enshrined in grants of authority known as the "capitulations," and they permitted those obtaining them to avoid Chinese laws and pursue their commerce unencumbered by the host country. The United States became the beneficiary of such arrangements, and Washington did not renounce them until mid-way through World War II. During World War II, the Japanese armies occupied the navigable portion of the Yangtze and from there sought to strangle Chinese society. Chinese resilience, however, and their capacity to dwell in the country's more rugged hinterland, has been another response to the conditions that the Yangtze imposes upon China.

2. Political Culture and Ideology

Ahmediya   The followers of Mirza Ghulam Ahmed (1835–1908). Ahmed, a member of a Punjabi Moghul family, claimed revelation and attracted a broad following in his town of Qadian in the Indian Punjab. (Ahmediyas are sometimes referred to as Qadianis.) From there, he and his disciples spread their beliefs to other parts of the subcontinent and beyond. Ahmediyas still look to their spiritual center in the subcontinent, but they are found in growing numbers in Sri Lanka, Burma, Malaysia, Iran, Iraq, Saudi Arabia, and Syria. Ahmediya missionary activity has also spread to Africa where they have made significant inroads in Nigeria, Ghana, and Tanzania, as well as other black African countries. Persecuted in their day, and subsequently in Pakistan, the Ahmediyas claim to be Muslims. Their break with orthodox or Sunni Islam, however, derives from a fundamental belief of convential Islam that Mohammad was the last or Seal of the Prophets (Khatm-i-Nabuwaat). Ghulam Ahmed claimed prophethood and his followers portray their founder as a Muslim spiritual guide to the present day.

Significance   The Ahmediyas are considered heretics by most Pakistani Muslims. Approximately four million Ahmediyas reside in Pakistan, although their spiritual center is in the Indian Punjab. A closely related community, Ahmediyas have protected their own and tended to flourish during the colonial period. Accepting western education, the Ahmediyas moved into the army, business, and politics, and at the time of partition were relatively influential. Pakistan's first foreign minister, Mohammad Zafrullah Khan, an Ahmediya, had been knighted by the British crown and later served Pakistan with distinction as President of the United Nations General Assembly and Justice of the International Court in the Hague.

In 1953, however, riots coursed through the Punjab over the status of the Ahmediyas. Islamic fundamentalists demanded the removal of all Ahmediyas from the government and the declaration that the Ahmediyas were non-Muslims. The Pakistan government collapsed as a consequence of those demonstrations. It was not until the administration of Zulfikar Ali Bhutto, however, that the Ahmediyas were declared non-Muslims by the Pakistani legislature, and an amendment to the constitution made it official. This action in 1974 was also a response to riots against the Ahmediya community. During the administration of General Mohammad Zia ul-Haq, agitation reached a new peak of intensity. Zia's emphasis on the construction of an Islamic state in Pakistan whetted the appetite of the fundamentalists. The Ahmediyas were again their target in 1984, and the government was persuaded to pass an ordinance preventing the Ahmediyas from identifying themselves as Muslims, preaching to Muslims, or using the terminology of Muslims. The Muslim word for mosque or house of worship is *masjid*, and Ahmediyas were prohibited from using that term, as well as *azan*, the traditional call to prayer. They were also forbidden from making any public display of their religion.

The most extreme fundamentalists were not placated by these measures, however. They urged the government to ban Ahmediya use of Muslim surnames that glorify Allah and to destroy the minarets of Ahmediya "mosques." They also called for the death penalty against Muslims committing apostasy. If complied with, an Ahmediya who still claimed to be a Muslim could be put to death. The fundamentalist organization, Tahaffuz Khatm Nabuwaat, dormant since the government's suppression of the 1953 rioting, resurfaced in the 1970s and expanded its ranks during Zia's rule. It now was determined to destroy the Ahmediya power base, to deny their access to education, to seek the removal of all Ahmediya military and bureaucratic personnel from government service, in addition to undermining the practice of the Ahmediya faith.

Asian Communism   Communist doctrines and practices in Asia. Asian communism stands for the application of communism in the underdeveloped, peasant Asian societies, contrary to Marxist predictions. To Marx, communism was a post-industrial, post-capitalist development, but the most powerful ideological centers claiming allegiance to Marxism are found today in Asia and Latin America. Thus Asian communism has been closely identified with national liberation and has become a motive force for nationalistic development and modernization. Theoretically, the critical question for Asian leaders is how to translate the Euro-centered Marxist ideas to the peasant masses of Asia. In the

Chinese context, Mao solved this problem by his concept of pro-letarianization: the peasant masses could be proletarianized through ideological indoctrination and mobilization. The peasants could be made to think like factory workers through ideological inculcation. Furthermore, though the peasants and workers differ in their economic activities, they are alike at least in one sense—both are the exploited classes.

As prescribed by Marx, Asian communism means the revolution of the exploited class against the exploiting class, but in Asia this means the mobilization of the peasants against the landlords for the creation of a society that is without exploiters. In terms of organization, however, it is much like the Soviet and East European Communist states in that the Communist party rules in a totalitarian fashion, and economic socialism, planned and centrally operated, governs the economic life of the people. Furthermore, among the Asian Communist states, the personality cult of one ruler appears prevalent. Mao Zedong (Mao Tse-tung), Kim Il-Sung (Kim Il-sŏng), and Ho Chi Minh are examples of fostering the cult of the individual, contrary to Marx's call for collective rule. *See also* COMMUNISM, p. 74; KIMILSUNGISM, p. 95; MAOISM, p. 101.

Significance   Asian communism is a radical deviation from the Euro-centered Communist development. As an indigenous movement, it has triumphed in China, Vietnam, Laos, and Kampuchea (Cambodia). It has appealed to many intellectuals and dissident groups in Asia and has been closely identified with the anti-colonial, nationalistic expressions of the Asian people. Indebtedness to Karl Marx and his theoretical propo-sitions for the future is acknowledged, but the Asian people wish to be the masters of their own destiny. Communism has proven to be a useful vehicle to many Asians for revolutionary change.

Asian Races   The majority of Asians are Mongoliforms who occupy most of the northern, central, and eastern parts of the continent. The Mongoliform races of Asia are (1) Mongolian, which divide into Aralian, Tungusian, Sinian, and Pareoean subgroups; (2) Himalayan; and (3) Indonesian. Another classification are the Europiform races such as the Uralic between the Urals and the Ob basin; the Ainu in Sakhalin, Hokkaido, and one of the Kurils; the Pamirian that inhabit a region from Anatolia to Xinjiang; the Mediterranean of the Levant, Arabia, Caspian Iran, Afghanistan, Pakistan, and the Indo-Gangetic plain; and the Dravidian of India and Sri Lanka. The Veddian or pre-Dravidian are proto-Australoid and the only Australiform race of Asia. They are found among the Veddas of Sri Lanka and the Kadirs, Kurum-bas, Paniyans, Irulas, Bhils, Gonds, and Chenchus of southern and north central India. Smaller groups of Veddoids are located in Baluchistan, southern Arabia (Hadramaut) and the two Yemens. Asian Negriforms are the Negrito of the Andaman islands, the Semang of the Malayan jungles, and the mountain people of Aeta of the Philippines. Southern India also displays some Negrito characteristics in the Kadars and the Pulayas. Traces of Negritoid people are also found in Sumatra.

It is generally believed that the Mediterranean type with characteristically long head structure, brown skin, and wavy hair were the earliest inhabitants of southwest Asia. Different varieties of Mediterranean types range from the small-boned, Eurafrican stock of Arabia to the tall, long-faced variety of the Iranian plateau. The Indian subcontinent, however, has the largest concentration of Mediterranean types, and approximately one-fifth of the world's total population. Pre-Dravidian types in the same area generally represent the lower strata of Hindu as well as Muslim society. Furthermore, the culture and languages of southern India are more ancient than those of the north. Pre-Dravidian and Dravidian peoples were imposed upon by the Aryans who descended on them from northwest, as well as some Mongolian penetrations from the north and northeast.

Southeast Asia experienced the largest inundation of Mongoloid types, with the Negrito surviving in remote Philippine forests. Tribes of proto-Malayan origin can be found in the highlands of Burma, Thailand, and the countries of Indochina. The Chinese are Mongoliform, but their origin remains clouded in mystery. Some theory persists that they may have come from Egypt and Babylon. Others refute such speculation. Differences between Cantonese and Mandarins, for example, suggest a variety of places of origin. In general, however, most Chinese possess the common characteristics of straight black hair, broad face and nose, and the Mongolian fold of the eyelid. The Japanese are believed to have come from Malaya, the islands of Indonesia, and the Korean peninsula. Indeed, there is considerable archaeological evidence that the Korean peninsula was the first nesting ground of the Japanese. *See also* ASIA, p. 6; ASIAN HIGHWAY, p. 7.

Significance   The racial landscape of Asia is a kaleidoscope of colors, culture, features, and history. The notion of Asianism, an Asian consciousness, showed signs of stirring only in the aftermath of World War II. The postwar period marks the independence of states and peoples heretofore under distant, alien rule. It also brought peoples and states together in international organizations that promised cooperation and the pooling of resources. But Asia's diversity does not yield easily to new arrangements suggesting conformity, no matter how well-intentioned the desired union. The Asian village is still a paramount institution in the lives of the people. The Japanese "buraku," the Philippine "barrio," the Indian "panchayat," the Pakistani "mohalla," and the Chinese "hsien," remain important in the lives of the majority of people and the growth, spread, and concentration of power in centralized political systems has altered traditional lifestyles very little. In many regions of Asia, government officials are still considered outsiders and national consciousness is circumscribed or limited.

Contrasted with other sectors of the continent there is greater awareness of nationhood among the people of East Asia. In the broadest context, the people of Asia still address themselves to local headmen, and tribal or family leaders. In such atomistic circumstances, it is no wonder that people saw their primary objective in life in personal and local terms. The first duty of the knowledgeable and influential leader, whether schooled in the teachings of the Muslim Qur'an, the Hindu sutras, or the Chinese analects, was service to the immediate family and himself. In people long accustomed to serving their own needs, it is immensely difficult to engender a sense of abstract identity, to stimulate political consciousness beyond their familiar circumstances.

Although Japan is the great exception, and China, the Koreas, and Vietnam appear to have managed favorably the question of national integration, the numerous other entities of Asia have not been so successful. Many countries display deep internal cleavages, usually the result of ethnic/linguistic or religious differences, and their quest for nationhood is still an elusive goal. With such internal questions unanswered, it is not surprising that Asianism or something akin to an "Asian mind" is absent. Nevertheless, it is important to note Asia's current emphasis on modernization, and that the physical world of the Asian people is being altered by technological, economic, and organizational change. The impact of these changes on the social structure and political character of Asians everywhere is destined to be profound.

Bahasa Indonesia   Javanese is spoken by a majority of Indonesians, but the official language is Bahasa Indonesia, which is a modern form of Malay. This policy was adopted despite the fact that Malay was the mother language of a relatively small number of Indonesians. Javanese was rejected because it could not generate the unity required to keep the archipelago nation together. Fear of the more numerous, more influential and prosperous Javanese gave rise to centrifugal forces which threatened the new country. Indonesian leaders discarded the idea of a federation and adopted the unitary model for those same reasons. Although the Javanese considered Malay an inferior language to their own Javanese, it has been adopted as the language of inter-regional communication. At home, in their own islands and regions, therefore, Indonesians speak their mother tongue. Javanese and Chinese continue to flourish, along with a wide variety of other languages. *See also* BAHASA MALAYSIA, p. 58; COLONIALISM: NETHERLANDS, p. 67; JAVANISM, p. 94; PANTASILA: INDONESIA, p. 110.

Significance Indonesian nationalists adopted Malay as the *lingua franca* and their national language at least two decades before independence. Malay had long been the language of communication. In fact, the use of Malay in Indonesia can be traced back centuries. It was most important in commerce and trade and thus was cosmopolitan in content as well as flexible in structure. Chinese, Indian, and Dutch settlers used Malay in dealing with the indigenous people of the archipelago. It was the language in vogue during the colonial period, and it was also the preference of those who did not speak, or found it difficult to learn Javanese. The choice of Malay or Bahasa Indonesia proved to be a wise one. It underlines the pragmatic character of Indonesian leadership. It also says something about a government of civil-military administrators who are determined to dampen tribal or regional sentiment and contain personal and group passion.

Bahasa Malaysia A national language developed by Malaysia's leaders to deal with the problem of national integration. Malaysia is a multiethnic, multilingual country, divided between racial and cultural barriers that do not respond easily to national pleas for unity. The dominant Malay community, as well as the minority Chinese and Indian communities, has generally accepted the use of Bahasa Malaysia, and the policy implementing its official employment has been largely successful. But this surface acceptance cannot conceal underlying problems. Clearly, the adoption of Bahasa Malaysia is a political move aimed at sustaining Malaysia's traditional elite in positions of high authority. The ruling elite requires grassroots support to remain in power, and the language policy has taken some of the sting out of the Malay opposition's bite, while satisfying the important elements in the non-Malay communities who do not want to see a change in the country's pattern of rule. The non-Malay groups do not want to arouse the Malays' reputed volatility, and the elite's manipulation of cultural symbols, such as language, is recognized as necessary to sustain equilibrium and progress. *See also* FEDERALISM: MALAYSIA, p. 226; UNITED MALAYS NATIONAL ORGANIZATION (UMNO), p. 204.

Significance Bahasa Malaysia aims at promoting national integration, and at the same time it helps to sustain the prevailing political system. The need to placate the majority Malay population has become more apparent, given their increasing political consciousness and tendency toward radical organization. Islamic fundamentalism is also on the increase, primed by external events in the larger Islamic world and adopted and adapted by the increasingly better educated, younger generation. Furthermore, Malaysian youth have gained considerable influence among the poor, often backward peasantry. Together, they represent the greatest challenge to Malaysia's traditional leaders. Opposition political parties, organized along Islamic lines, and stressing religious principles, have grown in popularity.

It is suggested that religion and Islamic revival have superseded language as the principal national issue facing the Malaysian elite in the 1980s. The government, therefore, has run with the tide and implemented legislation that calls for restrictions on gambling. Dress codes, suggesting an Islamic character, have also been established for government personnel. The Islamic Youth Movement of Malaysia, an organ of the dominant United Malays National Organization (UMNO), has gained influence among rank and file UMNO members and is considered a potent force in Malaysian politics. Anwar Ibrahim, leader of the Islamic Youth Movement, was brought into UMNO when it became obvious he was the sentimental favorite of a significant portion of the Malay population. Observers believe he is now the third most important figure in the ruling organization, just behind the prime minister and deputy prime minister. It is important to note that Prime Minister Datuk Seri Mahatir bin Mohammad was similarly co-opted by UMNO when he was a leader of the Bahasa Malaysia language movement in the 1960s. Bahasa Malaysia, therefore, is but one of many tactics employed by the Malaysian elite to promote national unity and sustain the integrity of the dominant party.

Buddhism   The name the western world has ascribed to the teachings of Gautama Buddha, a wise man or sage of the Sakya clan, whose work spread from India to other lands but especially to China, Japan, Korea, and the countries of Southeast Asia. In the time of the Buddha, a little more than 2,500 years ago, his teachings were identified as *dharma* —that which is right and that which is as it ought to be. This doctrine was also called *Buddha-vacana*, the word or speech of the Buddha; and *Buddha-sasana*, the message, instruction, or dispensation of the Buddha. The purpose of Buddhist teaching, then and now, is the pursuit of inner and outer peace, the harmony of man and nature, man and man, and man with himself. Buddhism has been described as more philosophy than religion because it neither speaks of god, nor worships godheads. Unlike Hinduism there is no *Isvara,* or Brahman in the tradition of the Upanishads. For the Buddhist, the essential objective is not preparation for life in the hereafter but for the instilling of discipline and balance to a life that is to be lived. If the teachings of the Buddha are scrupulously followed, it is believed they will lead to what is correct and best, to the highest good. Ultimately, the goal of the practicing Buddhist is to find true contentment, an inner peace that opens the path to super-consciousness, the merging of self with the elements and the attainment of *Nirvana,* the Buddhist conception of salvation. The epitome of freedom for the Buddhist, therefore, is the capacity of the individual to become so absorbed in meditation that all material things and desires are transcended.

The Buddha was born around 563 B.C. in present-day Nepal. He was a scion of the Sakya clan who were warriors and nobles of the *kshatriya* caste. A man of wealth and prestige, he lived ostentatiously and pursued those activities associated with his rank. But the Buddha was seized by the urge to break with the pattern of his existence and in so doing, escape the cycle of life and the scheme of birth and rebirth associated with his Hindu beliefs. He therefore renounced all his worldly possessions and position and began his journey in search of "true enlightenment." He lived in total austerity in the years that followed and one night, while sitting beneath a botree, he sensed the wisdom that he had been seeking. After a period in which he questioned his attainment, the Buddha felt the necessity for spreading his discovery to those willing to learn of it. Disciples flocked around him, and the yellow robe of the order of monks was adopted to identify those who walked in the path of the Buddha. Four centuries passed, however, before the teachings of the Buddha were written down, and responsibility for spreading his message rested on the monks who verbalized his doctrine.

Buddhism generally divides into two principal schools. Mahayana Buddhism, or the Greater Vehicle, refers to those who emphasize the Buddha's later life and thought. The use of the term "vehicle" is deliberate, in that it is the Buddha's *dharma* that is transmitted to his followers; and that *dharma* is believed to be a float or boat that carries the believers across life's ocean of suffering to salvation and *Nirvana.* Mahayana Buddhism can be compared with Hinayana Buddhism, the Lesser Vehicle, which is more narrowly defined and ritualized. Mahayana is determined to have universal character, and its tenets and purpose are judged suited for all times and conditions. Currently, Mahayana Buddhism predominates in Nepal, Tibet, China, Korea, and Japan. Hinayana Buddhism, dominated by a school known as the Theravadins (one of eighteen traditional sects of the Hinayana), is the national religion of Sri Lanka, Burma, and Thailand. Tantric Buddhism in the Himalayan states blends the message of the Buddha with animistic spells and rituals, whereas the Zen Buddhism of Japan is heavily dependent on the wisdom of the learned monks.

Chinese Buddhism reveals the flexibility of the teachings of Buddha. China was influenced by Indian culture between 150 and 1000 A.D. and the Hindu sutras that included the teachings of the Buddha were translated into Chinese. The result was the intermingling of Chinese Taoism with Buddhism to an extent that one could hardly be distinguished from the other. As a consequence, the devotees of Chinese Buddhism adopted a variety of positions in explaining the teachings of the Buddha. In this way, Chinese Buddhism became the most distinguished offshoot of Indian Buddhism, and it spread to Vietnam, Korea, and Japan. It is interesting to note, however, that Hindu India was not nearly so tolerant, and Buddhism was virtually eliminated there. *See also* HINDUISM, p. 83; THERAVEDA BUDDHISM, p. 121.

Significance Buddhism is a philosophy/religion that emphasizes inner peace, tranquility, and nonviolence. In reality, Buddhist societies are no more free from violent expression than societies holding other religious beliefs. Burma, Thailand, Vietnam, Kampuchea (Cambodia), some of the principal Buddhist states, have all experienced long periods of violence. Moreover, much of the violence was self-generated and not always directly related to external factors. Internal power struggles were seldom avoided or even moderated by the Buddhist character of society. Any notion that suggests Buddhist societies were incapable of adopting violent measures in the pursuit of worldly power is negated by the historic Vietnamese struggle against the Chinese, Cambodians, French, and Americans.

Hostility between Buddhist states is not uncommon. Antagonism between Vietnam and Cambodia, and between Thailand and Cambodia is well-chronicled. Burma's government was violently seized by its military establishment in the early years following its independence, and the country has never been celebrated as an island of Buddhist calm. During the post-World War II struggle for the unification of Vietnam, Buddhist monks in South Vietnam played an important role in destroying the United States-supported government of Ngo Dinh Diem, a Catholic. Buddhist organizations were assaulted by the Diem government, and Buddhist expression was often circumscribed. In a public display of protest against the heavy-handed tactics of the Diem government, Buddhist monks ritually immolated themselves. These acts of self-sacrifice caused American support for Diem to falter and galvanized the opposition against his administration, providing the Communist North Vietnamese and Viet Cong with the opportunity to establish deep roots in the south.

The genocide committed against the people of Cambodia by the Kampuchean Khmer Rouge between 1975 and 1977 further illustrates how violence can overwhelm a Buddhist country. The western world tends to view Buddhism as passive, because Buddhists are symbolized by asceticism and the apparent rejection of material things. The historic record reveals that they are motivated by many of the same desires that characterize other people, and that they are not reluctant to use violence in the pursuit of their objectives.

Caste   Caste is the hierarchical arrangement of society into groups as a consequence of birth. Although transcendence of or change in caste has occurred, it is quite limited and often concealed. In India, caste has provided the nucleus around which most institutions governing human relationships have been developed. Caste is therefore imbedded in Indian culture and pervades the Indian political world. It would not be an exaggeration to assert that caste is the single most important consideration in daily individual decision making. At the political level, caste associations and groups play an active role in pressuring government, and political parties have adapted their programs to accommodate particular caste interests. In most societies, the term "class" is used to distinguish one group from another by socio-economic ordering, so that higher, middle, and lower classes describe income capabilities, from which flow social status, influence, and power. Unlike "class" which permits mobility, "caste" tends to be ascriptive, and persons identified with a particular caste usually cannot move from one category to another despite their accomplishments, skills, and utility. Roles tend to be frozen. This is especially true in Hindu societies. *See also* HARIJANS, p. 82; HINDUISM, p. 83.

Significance   India's stability is largely dependent on the effectiveness of the caste system. In the voting booth, all Indians, irrespective of caste, are permitted one vote. Moreover, India's constitution specifies that caste cannot be used to deprive lower castes or outcastes from full participation in the political process. Nevertheless, caste is a dominant feature of Indian political life and its social and economic life. Caste organizations interpret issues to their members. These organizations try to establish positions that enhance the role of specific castes in Indian society. The mobilization of voters is a function of caste associations and political coalitions cannot ignore the voting power of a significant caste organization. Generally speaking, caste politics is more obvious and hence more significant at the local level where concentrations of caste interest can be realized. But India's recent political history reveals opportunities for lower as well as higher castes to influence national policies and leadership. It is important to note that although the caste system is directly related to Hinduism, other religious groups have found themselves caught up in the socio-economic web woven by the dominant community. It is therefore not unusual to find Indian Muslims and Christians represented by caste. Although the Muslim and Christian adoption of caste designations is divorced from their religious beliefs, caste plays a significant role in their socio-economic activities. Some aspects of this form of socio-economic caste are, in fact, found in Bangladesh, Pakistan, and Sri Lanka, where Hindus are a distinct minority.

Colonialism   A practice whereby a stronger state subjugates, occupies, and/or exploits a weaker society for its own benefits and advancement. Colonialism is basically a superior-inferior relationship, although it may also refer to a new settlement by emigrants from the mother country to form a new political entity. In either case, the purpose of colonialism is to promote military security, economic advantage, and international prestige of the imperial power. In Asia, colonialism has been identified with western domination and exploitation of the native people and resources; thus, it has become a focal, rallying point of nationalistic and anti-western agitations. *See also* COLONIALISM: FRANCE, p. 64; COLONIALISM: GREAT BRITAIN, p. 65; COLONIALISM: JAPAN, p. 66; COLONIALISM: NETHERLANDS, p. 67; COLONIALISM: UNITED STATES, p. 69; NATIONALISM, p. 104; NEOCOLONIALISM, p. 315.

Significance   At the height of colonial expansionism in the eighteenth and nineteenth centuries, most Asian countries came under the imperial control of the United States, Great Britain, the Netherlands, France, Japan, the USSR, Spain, or Portugal. The Philippines was initially colonized by Spain, but following the Spanish-American war (1898), it was transferred to U.S. control. The only exception to western colonization of Asia is perhaps that of Japan. Following the Meiji Restoration (1868), Japan was able to modernize successfully, to escape western colonial subjugation, and become a colonial power, colonizing neighboring states such as Taiwan and Korea.

The Japanese colonial design for these areas was to assimilate the people as second-class citizens, yet make them integral to further Japanese imperial expansionism throughout Asia. The western colonial practices in Asia varied. While some represented direct control, others functioned through indirect control. Because of the rivalry of the imperial powers, for example, China remained technically independent but indirectly subservient to the interests of these powers. But direct or indirect, serving the interests of the colonial people was not a common practice. Whatever development they experienced under the colonial metropolitan powers was a by-product of exploitation. The colonies often found themselves ill-prepared to assume statehood when the metropolitan powers withdrew from their territories in the period following World War II. While the anticolonial revolution of self-determination has largely run its course, freeing Asians from western political control, many Asians believe they are now victims of a form of neo-colonialism that places them in a subservient economic posture.

Colonialism: France   Overseas possessions ruled from Paris. European imperialists in the nineteenth century justified their seizure of overseas peoples as an act of civilization, but no country had a more explicit doctrine on the subject than France. Jules Ferry, a prominent French journalist, became Prime Minister of France in 1880 and again in 1883–85, and during those tenures France occupied Tunisia in North Africa, the island of Madagascar in the Indian Ocean, and Tonkin in Indochina. Ferry's name is associated with the phrase *mission civilisatrice,* the civilizing mission. The slogan represents a creed which holds that: the industrial state needs raw materials and colonial markets; the Europeans, especially the French, are a higher form of humanity with a responsibility to bring civilization to primitive people; a great nation needs and is entitled to coaling stations for its navy and merchant fleet. France, it was argued, could not refrain from imperialism while the other European states were so deeply committed to the activity. Moreover, France had a better message for the backward people of the earth. Colonization was propagandized as a matter of life and death for the French nation. "The future of France," it was said, "is in her colonies." *See also* DIEN BIEN PHU, p. 380; GENEVA ACCORDS (1954), p. 339.

Significance   A nation can be led to believe that it has a holy mission, irrespective of the harm that mission may impose on innocent and often defenseless people. Such was the case with French colonialism. France had fallen from its eighteenth century position as Europe's most formidable power. The industrial revolution was late in coming to France, and by the last half of the nineteenth century the French saw themselves surrounded by aggressive, hostile foes, particularly Germany and Great Britain. The unification of Germany following the Franco-Prussian War of 1871 was a telltale sign that France needed to revitalize its spirit and especially its military might. It had to compete with the principal European powers if it was to remain a first rank nation. Paris saw its destiny in the colonization of Asia and Africa. In Southeast Asia, France occupied Vietnam, Laos, and Cambodia. In Southwest Asia, it dominated Syria and Lebanon. France also exerted influence over Thailand, but that country managed to retain its independence by exploiting the rivalry between London and Paris.

France clung desperately to the belief that its role in the world was inextricably linked to its retention of empire. Despite grievous losses in World War I and humiliating defeat in World War II, Paris clung to its colonies. Old ideas are never easily discarded by nations, and national self-deception is a common phenomenon. Unlike the British, the French continued to believe in their civilizing mission long after it had lost its meaning. Thus the end of World War II saw France again attempt to resurrect its past glory by restoring its empire. Indochina was not the only place where France planned to forcibly reimpose its authority, but it was the most celebrated. Despite French efforts to instill harmony between themselves and their charges, the indigenous folk were determined to remove the alien yoke that sapped their pride and denied their integrity. France, the home of contemporary nationalism, failed to understand the meaning of nationalism in its own colonies. The French were destined to pay a high price for their myopia. The First Indochina War, 1946–54, ended with the French defeat at Dien Bien Phu.

Colonialism: Great Britain   Overseas possessions ruled from London. Rudyard Kipling's phrase, "the White Man's Burden," symbolized the British quest for colonies and empire. The English told themselves and the world that their purpose in extending their power throughout the planet was humanitarian, not economic or political gain. British colonialism can be divided into two periods: (1) the age of discovery that commenced in earnest in the fifteenth and sixteenth centuries; and (2) the "new imperialism," that period which was fueled by the industrial revolution, from 1870 to the outbreak of World War I. The first significant British settlements in Asia were notably established by the English East India Company, which was founded in 1600. Commerce and power were primary considerations and the company, on charter from the Crown, assumed the role of governor of the vast Indian colony until the Mutiny of 1857 demanded direct control by the political authority in London.

In addition to India, Britain's colonial Asian empire included present-day Sri Lanka, Burma, Pakistan, Bangladesh, Malaysia, Singapore, and Hong Kong in the southeast and east, and Iraq, Jordan, Palestine, the United Arab Emirates, and the Egyptian Sinai peninsula in the southwest. Furthermore, special privileges, as well as commercial opportunities and mining concessions, were obtained in Iran, China, Nepal, and the Arabian peninsula. *See also* INDIAN CIVIL SERVICE (ICS), p. 230; MUTINY OF 1857, p. 392.

Significance   The far-flung British empire made the English the dominant world power in the nineteenth century. The *Pax Britannica* or

"British Peace" made possible a century of relative tranquility, from the Conference of Vienna in 1815, to the outbreak of the First World War in 1914. This period also provided the impetus for a more dynamic form of colonialism/imperialism. The British brought law and order and efficient administration to their colonies, but control of the colonies provided the mother country with ready markets for its manufactured goods. British factories were assured a steady flow of needed raw materials. Alien authority, however, was never accepted by the indigenous populations, and their political consciousness was provoked and stimulated by the foreign presence. Socio-political reforms were slow in developing in the British colonies, but they were sufficient to stoke the fires of Asian nationalisms. Asian demands for more autonomy and self-government escalated into cries of self-determination and independence, but freedom was not realized until World War II weakened British capacity to rule their possessions. The British withdrawal from empire, however, was relatively peaceful and the newly independent Asian states retained an association with the British throne and thus helped form the contemporary Commonwealth of Nations.

Colonialism: Japan   Overseas possessions ruled from Tokyo. After the Meiji Restoration (1868), Japan reversed her long-standing, self-imposed isolation policy and opened her doors to foreign intercourse as a means of modernizing herself. Japan's modernization was to assure national survival in a world dominated by the West. It also generated national assertiveness. Like the Western nations, Japan strove for international power and influence and acquired colonies at the slightest opportunity. It acquired the Ryukyus, a chain of islands between Kyushu and Taiwan (Formosa) unilaterally in the 1870s. It obtained Taiwan and adjacent islands following the first Sino-Japanese war (1894–95); and the southern part of the Sakhalin Island in the north of Hokkaido after the Russo-Japanese War (1904–05). Japan annexed Korea as a colony in 1910. Before World War II, the Japanese imperial expanse also covered Manchuria and North China.

In many ways, Japanese colonialism differed from western colonialism. First, the Japanese empire-building came late in the history of modern colonialism. Second, it extended only over neighboring states and was regional in scope. Third, it was primarily over the people who were ethnically and culturally similar to its own. Fourth, it was over well populated areas like Taiwan, Korea, and Manchuria. Fifth, it was acquired usually at a higher price than the price which the western powers paid for their colonies. Sixth, it involved a systematic government effort from the outset. Seventh, it rested on the ready availability of military and police power for its security. These differences contributed to some other unique features. Japanese colonialism in Asia, for example, emphasized cultural assimilation. The Japanese language and culture were taught systematically. The concepts of Asia for Asians and of anti-westernism were widely propagated. Economically, Japan was better able than the western colonial powers to integrate colonial economies into its metropolitan economy. *See also* COLONIALISM, p. 63; GREATER EAST ASIA CO-PROSPERITY SPHERE, p. 15; KOREA: MARCH FIRST MOVEMENT, p. 390.

Significance   The practice of Japanese colonialism in Asia had some local variations. The Korean people were highly nationalistic and resisted Japanese colonialism more than the others within the Japanese empire. However, the Japanese government did not permit any nationalistic expressions by the Korean people and used force to suppress them. The Japanese colonial design was to integrate all the colonies into the Japanese metropolis, and a systematic policy of assimilation was used to teach the ways of Japan to colonial people.

The colonial people were brought closely into the Japanese development scheme in that they were exposed to modern education and socioeconomic development. Still, the development which the Japanese colonies experienced was Japanese in content and skewed to serve Japanese interests. The Japanese maintained their superior position in all development efforts. They never accepted the colonial people as their equals, but only as second-class Japanese citizens. No preparation was made for future independence. Furthermore, the Japanese departed from their colonies as a defeated enemy nation. The liberation was sudden and dramatic, and a great deal of confusion followed the dismantling of Japanese institutions and practices. Sudden involvement with the West, which had been denied by Japanese colonialism, involved major culture shock, as the former Japanese colonies in Asia strove for independent nationhood.

Colonialism: Netherlands   Overseas possessions ruled from Amsterdam. The Dutch were among the earliest colonizers. Commercial contacts between Dutch and Portuguese seafarers produced cooperative ventures and the Portuguese followed the Dutch to Asia by way of the high seas. The Dutch were pioneers in map-making, and their scientific charting of the sea routes to the Indies rewarded them with spices, silks, carpets, calicoes, ivories, pearls, and more. Dutch commercial success endowed them with the name "waggoners of the seas," and the British insisted on following their lead. Indeed, the Dutch East India Company was founded in 1602, two years after the English had established a similar company in India.

Dutch activity centered on the Moluccas in present-day Indonesia. The Dutch erected fortified settlements in the East Indies, and their power extended over areas of Sri Lanka, India, and the Persian Gulf states, until the British forced their withdrawal. Thereafter, the Netherlands concentrated its efforts in the East Indies, where the government had taken over following the collapse of the East India Company in 1798. The British replaced Dutch rule in the Indies (often referred to as Netherlands India) during the Napoleonic wars but returned the possession to Holland in 1818. Modern Dutch imperialism in the nineteenth century centered on the exploitation of the native population. Unlike the British in India, the Dutch did not introduce administrative or educational reforms, nor were they concerned with the protection of indigenous labor. The Dutch centered their attention on the construction of sugar, coffee, tobacco, tea, and cacao plantations, and they built the roads necessary to transport these commodities. Above all, they were determined to draw as much product from the land as the peasant could generate.

In the 1830s the Dutch introduced the "Culture System" which specified that one-fifth of the native's land would be set aside for the government. The peasant was required to work one-fifth of his time on this "government land" without compensation. Moreover, the government specified the crops to be grown on this land, usually sugar, coffee, tea, and cinnamon. Because the indigenous peoples resisted this harsh imposition, the Dutch later let up on their demands, but Dutch rule remained repressive. Eventually the Dutch substituted a free or hired labor arrangement for the "Culture System," and the government plantation economy was replaced by an entrepreneurial, free enterprise system that turned Indonesia into an economic playground for adventurous Europeans. A new "Ethical Policy" was introduced by the Dutch which aimed at providing some educational and administrative opportunities for the native population. The new program also sparked the formation of political organizations, and in the 1920s and 1930s a new, politically conscious and cosmopolitan elite began to form. This was the overall condition when the Japanese occupied the Indies during World War II, and promoted Indonesian nationalism. *See also* ARCHIPELAGO, p. 5; GUIDED DEMOCRACY, p. 228; POLITICAL PARTIES: INDONESIA, p. 180.

Significance   The Dutch reluctantly ended their colonial rule and gave Indonesia its independence after World War II. The Netherlands had failed to introduce meaningful political reforms in the region, opting to continue the rule of local chieftains and headmen. National leadership, therefore, emerged as a consequence of indigenous effort and Japanese actions. Indonesians had been denied a role in the government. There were no Indonesian governors, and there was only one department head up to World War II. Although there were more than 3,000 higher civil service positions, only slightly more than 200 were open to Indonesians. Few Indonesians were recruited for the armed forces prior to the Japanese invasion, and none were allowed to attain high rank. Overall, the Dutch did little to prepare the islands for self-government. Thus, when the demand for independence was made after the war, the Dutch refused to treat it with the seriousness it deserved. The result was a bloody encounter, interspersed with broken promises. Finally, after suffering considerable losses, with opposition to the colonial policy on the increase at home, and with pressure from abroad—especially from the United States—demanding that they yield the colony, the Dutch government agreed to relinquish its imperial possession in 1949.

Colonialism: United States Overseas possessions ruled from Washington. The United States modified European imperialism to suit its needs and purposes. The Declaration of Independence, the establishment of the first modern republic, and the Monroe Doctrine did not leave room for chaste colonial ventures. The American version of colonialism became a mixture of "manifest destiny" and "international paternalism," and it remained forever ambiguous. The United States was influenced to compete with the great powers of the nineteenth century, but it also wished to distance itself from their techniques and methods. The United States perceived its role as a vanguard nation in a new and unfolding era that would put an end to monarchy and aristocracy. Americans emphasized "government of the people, for the people and by the people," and their outward expansion became intertwined with their views concerning the spread of democratic institutions. The United States moralized a policy of self-determination at the same time that it engaged in activities to benefit specific national private interests. Indeed, the enhancement of private interests was considered the purpose of popular government.

United States expansion, like that of the Soviet/Russian state, was initially over land and continents. The Russian colonization of Siberia, for example, is comparable to the American conquest and absorption of much of North America, west of the Mississippi. The United States purchase of Alaska from Russia in 1867 was linked to their parallel but separate endeavors at continental expansion. The United States began to expand overseas only after its frontier reached the Pacific Ocean. The Spanish-American War of 1898 was the most dramatic display of European-type colonialism. The United States obtained a foothold in the Caribbean, occupied the Hawaiian islands, and imposed its mandate on the Philippines. It also gained control of the Pacific islands of Guam, Wake, and Midway, jockeyed for position in the Samoan group, and sought and gained extra-territorial privileges in China. The Philippines became the test case for the American experiment in Asia. After crushing local resistance to its rule, the United States government announced its intention to prepare the Philippines for independence. That promise was fulfilled in 1946, although the United States held to its Pacific acquisitions, and indeed, added the islands formerly occupied by Japan. *See also* SECOND INDOCHINA WAR, p. 401; TYDINGS-MCDUFFIE ACT, 1934, p. 367.

Significance   The United States did not launch an aggressive campaign of imperialism, nor did it publicize an insatiable appetite for colonies. Washington, however, did seek to improve its security, and it was eager to assist banking and commercial interests in pursuit of profitable enterprises. "Dollar Diplomacy" and "Gunboat Diplomacy" were synonymous slogans, signifying American government support for national business interests. Although its "colonial" policies were concentrated in the western hemisphere, the United States became deeply involved in the Far East, and its "Open Door Policy" of 1900 publicized an interest in China.

Washington claimed it wanted to protect China from rapacious imperialist states like Britain, Japan, France, and Germany who were carving out spheres of influence and establishing treaty ports in the Middle Kingdom. In fact, the United States was concerned that the Chinese market could be closed to its entrepreneurs, and it acted to enhance their bargaining power. Nevertheless, the United States came to see China as its ward, and it was the last nation to give up its extra-territorial privileges in the country. The United States convinced itself that its "colonial" mission was noble and promoted the cause of democracy and progress. The Philippines was the site for its most serious experiment.

Americans drew considerable pride from the idea that they were more interested in the welfare of the native population than in their own profit. They believed that their experience in the Philippines would stand as a model for other states and would influence Europe and Japan to follow their lead. For this reason, the United States refused to assume the role of a mandatory power after World War I. It criticized the Mandate System as little more than a cover for imperialist activity, and it demanded an accelerated transfer of authority to indigenous leaders. The United States continued to represent the forces opposed to imperialism, when President Franklin D. Roosevelt and Prime Minister Winston Churchill agreed to the Atlantic Charter in 1942. That agreement specified that the Allied powers would not seek territorial gain as a consequence of World War II. The United States position remained ambiguous, however. After the war, Washington impressed upon the British the need to quit India. It also pressured the Dutch to vacate their empire in Indonesia, but it provided the French with substantial military aid in their war against the Viet Minh in Indochina. That war was judged a struggle to prevent the spread of international communism, and the French were considered the best defense against a communist takeover. The Viet Minh victory over the French in 1954 was grudgingly accepted by the United States, but at the same time, Washington prepared to continue the struggle. As they had done in the Philippines earlier, the Americans moralized the cause of democracy and endeavored to establish a government for the Vietnamese that they, not the Vietnamese, thought would be more popular.

Colonialism: USSR Territories incorporated into the Soviet Union and overseas possessions ruled from Moscow. Soviet/Russian colonialism was different in technique and substance from that of the western Europeans. It also proved to be more durable. The Soviet Union, the successor state to the Tsarist Russian empire, continues to denounce European imperialism long after its demise, but it gives no sign of freeing territories bequeathed to it by the tsars of all the Russias. Soviet/Russian imperialism, an ever-expanding phenomenon, began before the era of great European conquests and was spread by land, not by sea. It dealt more subtly with racial differences, given the intermingling of Eurasians in the vast, continental steppe region of Asia. There were no "shocking" interactions between the white and black races such as those the western Europeans encountered in Africa. Moreover, racial distinctions were less apparent among people coinhabiting the same general region.

Commerce and profits were not objectives of Soviet/Russian imperialism. Therefore, Soviet/Russian colonization tended to be political and permanent, and justification for the activity was and continues to be manifested in strategic behavior, not public statements. Russian occupation and annexation of the Central Asian Muslim *khanates* (kingdoms) in the last half of the nineteenth century (currently the territories of Kazakhistan, Turkmenistan, Kirghizistan, Tajikistan, and Uzbekistan), the seizure of territory from Iran (Azerbaijan and Georgia), and its advance to the shores of the Pacific Ocean where it clashed with Japanese imperial ambitions in 1905, symbolize the pace and scope of Soviet Russian colonialism prior to World War I. *See also* AFGHAN-USSR CONFLICT, p. 373; AMU DARYA, p. 3; KURIL ISLANDS, p. 28; RUSSO-JAPANESE WAR, p. 400; WAKHAN CORRIDOR, p. 46; WARM WATER PORT POLICY, p. 47.

Significance   Geographically, the Soviet Union is more an Asian state than a European state. Covering approximately one-sixth the land area of the earth, it has taken more than five hundred years of relentless pressure and conquest for the Soviet Union/Imperial Russia to achieve its current status, and there is no indication that the Soviet/Russian appetite has been sated. The post-World War II annexation of the Japanese Kuril islands and the 1979 Soviet invasion of Afghanistan hint at future thrusts toward the open seas and an improved security perimeter.

Soviet efforts to carve out socialist republics in northwestern Iran following World War II did not succeed, but there is little reason to conclude they will not try again. The Soviet invasion of Afghanistan, after a one-hundred-year pause at the Amu Darya, suggests a new phase of colonialism. The establishment of Soviet autonomous republics for the Asian Bashkir, Buryat, Mongolian, Kalmyk, Tatar, Tuva, and Yakut indicates the multiethnic character of Soviet colonialism. Dominance over Outer Mongolia, putatively independent, is another demonstration of contemporary Soviet imperialism. Ideological truth (Marxism-Leninism), rather than sentimental hyperbole ("White Man's Burden"), supposedly motivates Soviet actions. Moreover, the Kremlin insists it is merely assisting wars of national liberation when it encourages revolution against established authorities in noncommunist Third World nations, and that Marxist-Leninist dialectics have predetermined the course of history and consecrated the Soviet Union's revolutionary role.

Communalism: Sri Lanka

Communalism: Sri Lanka   The population of Sri Lanka is divided between its majority Sinhalese (approximately 73 percent) and Tamils (20 percent). Moors, Dutch Burghers, Malays, Eurasians, and other Europeans make up the remainder. Sharp cleavage exists between the Sinhalese and Tamils and the historic bitterness between the two communities has often degenerated into broadscale bloodletting and destruction of property. The lesser communities are essentially placid and for purposes of survival they have attempted to steer a neutral course between the major combatants. Differences are essentially socio-cultural and economic but in recent times they have also developed political dimensions. The Sinhalese are Buddhist, whereas the Tamils are Hindu. The Sinhalese also represent the more historically established social group. The Tamils owe their large numbers on the island in part to the British who brought them from India to work on their plantations. The larger community of Tamils, however, migrated to Sri Lanka before the arrival of the British. The Sinhalese viewed the Tamils as extensions of British power. Moreover, the British cultivated the Tamils and often provided them with opportunities in disproportion to their numbers. No serious assimilation of Tamils into the larger Sin-halese society was possible and few Tamils indicated a desire to draw closer to the Sinhalese. Most Tamils thought in terms of separatism and the Tamil United Liberation Front (TULF), formed after the independence of Sri Lanka, was committed to secession.

Britain's divide and rule policy may have sustained the empire but its legacy proved a terrible burden for the Sri Lankans. It made national integration virtually impossible and threatened the country's territorial integrity. Severe rioting shook the island nation in 1983–84 and hundreds were reported killed in the communal conflict. The disturbances centered on a Tamil claim to the northern sections of Sri Lanka, to deny Colombo's sovereignty over the region, and to insist on full autonomy. Bands of Tamil guerrillas ambushed and killed Sinhalese soldiers, precipitating Sinhalese counter-attacks. On July 30, 1983 the government banned the Communist Party and two other Marxist organizations for allegedly instigating the riots. The seriousness of the disorder also caused the government to force a sixth amendment to the constitution through the parliament. All parliamentary members were required to swear their loyalty to an indivisible Sri Lanka. Members of TULF, however, did not participate in the proceedings and given their continued absence from the assembly were declared to have lost their seats.

The United National Party sustained its hold over the country despite the escalation in communal violence. President J. R. Jayewardene assembled a conference of national reconciliation in 1984, which was attended by all the opposition parties including the TULF. But after months of deliberation nothing substantial was resolved, even though the government pledged to turn district administration over to local management. The Tamil parties continued to insist on direct control over the northern and eastern provinces of the country, and the government was just as adamant in refusing their demand. In the meantime, the country experienced spreading disorder, and the administration promised to liquidate the "terrorists." The Tamils, however, found support, supplies, and sanctuary in the Indian state of Tamil Nadu. They also found an ally in Amnesty International, which condemned the Sri Lankan government's aggressive counter-insurgency program. The International Commission of Jurists similarly chastised the Jayewardene regime for its alleged acts of repression. Moreover, India-Sri Lanka relations worsened dramatically. New Delhi could not turn its back on the Tamils, and it put pressure on Colombo to arrive at a political settlement. New Delhi was also angered by Sri Lanka's appeal to Washington and the arrival in Colombo of Israeli counter-terrorist specialists. Although the Israelis were supposedly withdrawn in September 1984, observers believed they still played a role in developing tactics against the Tamil insurgents. By 1985 the Sri Lankan communal problem had reached a critical stage, and students of the condition suggested three possible scenarios. First, they spoke of genocide being committed against the Tamil community, followed by Indian intervention and the formal division of the island into two political entities. The second scenario addressed the question of intensified violence leading to a coup d'état and then to Indian intervention. New Delhi would be left to determine the future political setup on the island, and forced political fusion was not ruled out. The third scenario spoke of a repentent Jayewardene government and its capacity to find a moderate solution satisfactory to both communities, with India guaranteeing the final arrangement. *See also* BUDDHISM, p. 59; HINDUISM, p. 83; MILITANT HINDUISM, p. 103; TROTSKYISM: SRI LANKA, p. 203.

Significance   Despite the periodic clashes between Sinhalese and Tamil communities, Sri Lanka is still perceived to be a democracy. Its most recent constitution, promulgated in 1978, and the work of Julius R. Jayewardene, the country's president, combines aspects of both the parliamentary and presidential systems. The country's leading political party in 1983–84, the United National Party (UNP), sought a middle course between the somewhat leftist Sri Lanka Freedom Party of Sirimavo Bandaranaike and the communal party of the Tamils, the Tamil United Liberation Front (TULF). The Jaffna Tamils who preceded the British presence in the country have been more disturbed by Sinhalese dominance than their brethren who arrived later. Predominantly Hindu and well-educated, these Tamils resent the cultural chauvinism exemplified by the Sinhala majority.

Tamils have difficulty finding employment, and in desperation some of the younger, educated members of the minority community have taken to violent extremes. The rioting which shook Sri Lanka in the 1980s was allegedly initiated by the Tamil Liberation Tigers, a renegade movement which opposed the 1981 settlement worked out between Jayewardene's UNP and the TULF. That agreement had followed an earlier round of large scale disturbances and it promised to raise the status of the Tamil language as well as offer more local self-government. It was obvious that sizeable elements within the Tamil community wanted little to do with that understanding, however, and they were even more determined to take direct action in pursuit of their objectives, irrespective of the difficulties involved or the cost in lives and national treasure.

Communism   In the modern context, an ideology based on the concepts articulated by Karl Marx and Friedrich Engels for the establishment of a socialist society. To Marx and Engels, communism is the final stage of human development in which there are no class differences, no exploiters and exploited, no suppressive agents and suppressed, and where there is an equitable distribution, "From each according to his ability, to each according to his needs."

According to Marx and Engels, communism is founded on scientific truth as revealed by the development of human societies governed by economic determinism and class struggle. The productive forces and their productive relations determine the nature of the prevailing class struggle. In the capitalistic stage of development, it is a struggle between the bourgeoisie and the proletariat. In this struggle, the victory of the proletariat is predetermined by the unfolding of history toward the next highest stage of socialism, in which the victorious proletariat establish a dictatorship of the proletariat, devoid of the exploiting class. Ultimately, socialism will, according to Marx and Engels, evolve into the final state of pure communism.

The ideas put forward by Marx and Engels have been subjected to modifications through varied interpretations and applications by different societies. Today, they are readily identified with a totalitarian socialism where the Communist party reigns supreme over a collective society in which land and capital are socially owned, and private property and entrepreneurship are not permitted, or are rigidly controlled by the state. *See also* ASIAN COMMUNISM, p. 54; KIMILSUNGISM, p. 95; MAOISM, p. 101.

Significance The doctrine of communism has had different interpretations and applications. To its true believers, communism is the wave of the future. To its western critics, it represents totalitarian rule by the Communist party bureaucracy, either led by one man or by an oligarchy. To non-western people, it stands for anti-colonialism and anti-capitalistic exploitation. It also means to them a short-cut to industrialization and economic and political independence. It was in the name of communism that Mao Zedong (Mao Tse-tung) mobilized the peasant masses of China for "national liberation" and prepared for their subsequent development. Mao's success has become a motive force for revolutionary development in a number of backward, peasant societies. Successful Communist revolutions in the Third World have defied Marx's dogma that such upheavals could occur only in mature capitalist societies, such as those of Western Europe.

Confucianism A code of ethics for the Chinese people, attributed to the teachings of Confucius (Kung Fu Tzu or Kong Fuxi), who lived from 551 B.C. to 479 B.C. The main tenets of Confucianism are peace and social harmony. The basis of harmonious living is for all to follow *Tao*

(Dao) (moral principles). All social roles, duties, and obligations are to be prescribed in accordance with Tao. Confucianism is a vision of cooperative living in which people strive to perfect their social relationships and thereby remove all traces of antagonism and suffering. The last years of the Chou (Zhou) dynasty (1027–256 B.C.) in China were characterized by confusion and inept leadership. As a way out of this ineptitude and moral bankruptcy, Confucius emphasized the institutionalization of high ethical principles in the management of public affairs. He likened politics to ethics and argued that social improvement and justice were matters which required decisive collective action. Knowledge, he argued, is virtue. A virtuous style of life on the part of public administrators would set the moral tone for the rest of society and provide the necessary political climate conducive to progress and development. He stressed *Li*, which is role performance. Because of his belief in good and virtuous leadership, he stressed that the governors be rigorously educated to ensure the internalization of these leadership qualities.

According to Confucius, society is made up of rulers and ruled. The rulers were to rule, and the followers were to follow. All social relations were conceived in this superior-inferior relationship, except when friends interacted among themselves as equals. Thus, a wife was subordinate to her husband; children to their parents; a younger brother to his older brother; and a subject to the ruler. But, Confucius was humanistic enough to uphold *Jen (Ren)* as the governing principle of any subordination and superordination relationship. Variously translated as benevolence, love, compassion, and sympathy towards others, Jen is the cardinal principle of Confucianism. Confucius believed that the writings of ancient philosophers were valuable guides to virtuous behavior, and that China's golden age was to be sought in the past. *See also* BUDDHISM, p. 59; NEO-CONFUCIANISM, p. 105; TAOISM, p. 121.

Significance   Throughout China's long history, Confucianism has been the most influential, dominant philosophy of the people. Much about Confucius and his influence during his lifetime are not well known, but he had many faithful followers and advocates. His greatest successor was perhaps Mencius (Meng Tzu or Meng Zi, ca. 371–289 B.C.), who traveled widely offering advice to rulers for moral leadership and government. When Confucius' teachings were incorporated into the state creed of the Han dynasty (202 B.C.–220 A.D.), Confucianism became widespread as the code of ethics for every Chinese. The essential principles of Confucian teachings are found in the so-called Five Classics and Four Books.

The *Analects*, a collection of pithy Confucian "sayings," is well known. In it, Confucius dealt with the everyday world of social problems and individual relationships. He was less interested in religion and theory, than in immediate human problems. The family was the basic social unit and the state was the family writ large. The family taught respect for authority and deference to superiors. It practiced ancestor worship. Filial piety meant loyalty to the state. In the state, the emperor was like the father. He was at the apex of the traditional Confucian Chinese statecraft, and his legitimacy was sanctioned by the "mandate of heaven." His councilors and officials were Confucian scholars. Any aspirant to office in traditional China was obligated to study Confucian writings.

The sustained, unifying qualities of traditional Confucian Chinese government over so many centuries and through a succession of dynasties resulted from the socializing influence of the family and the monopoly of Confucian learning and political power by the self-perpetuating gentry and scholar-official class. Merchants and artisans were despised. The sedentary Chinese masses were family-centered and lived simply, avoiding conflict as much as possible. Later subjected to various interpretations and emphases, orthodox Confucianism eventually merged with elements of popular beliefs and religions such as Taoism (Daoism) and Buddhism under the leadership of Chu Hsi (1130–1200), thus presenting a broader concept of the universe and the human relationship to it. It was this Chu Hsi Confucianism or neo-Confucianism that spread widely to Korea and other parts of Asia. If Confucianism emphasized virtuous rule and the status quo, the new China of Communism stresses struggle, change, and development. The basic tenets of Confucianism and Communism are in this way antithetical and the new China of Communism implies the wholesale change of the traditional Chinese value and belief systems.

Consensus Politics: Japan   A decision-making process by which general agreement is reached through informal interactions, without a majority-minority division. Consensus politics is particularly common in Japanese political culture. Political interactions in Japan are generally more diffuse than specific. The Japanese people are unwilling to humiliate their opponents. The result is a conscious effort to arrive at a consensus decision within the group. Japanese decision-makers are likely to talk together rather informally—*hanashiai*—for many hours, and often in a casual atmosphere to arrive at a unanimous decision. *See also* DEMOCRACY, p. 78; JAPAN: DEMOCRACY, p. 220.

Significance   The old and new are intricately mixed in the Japanese political process. Outwardly, many Japanese political structures are modern, but internally, traditional, informal, paternalistic orientations govern decision making. Traditionally, being correct in form in interpersonal relations is important, but substantive decisions are often made through informal consensus building. Drastic decisions are unlikely in this situation, and even if such a decision is made, it is made under the guise of outward calm. Consensus politics is a time-consuming process that produces incremental and evolutionary change.

Democracy   A form of government in which the sovereign power resides in and is exercised by the entire body of free citizens. Democracy is distinguished from monarchy, aristocracy, or oligarchy by its broad distribution of power and authority, its emphasis on fundamental rights, and its stress on legal-institutional remedies that apply equally to the governors as well as the governed. According to theory, in a democracy every citizen should participate directly in the business of government, and the legislature should reflect the interests of the total population. Unlimited information and free choice are absolutely essential.

Democracies are often described as "representative democracies," with special importance given to constitutions of both the written and unwritten variety. Democracy replaces hereditary and arbitrary systems and allows for maximum predictability and accountability. Popular sovereignty and the power of the electorate to choose its leaders are hallmarks of democratic expression. Constitutions are contracts between the people and their governors and are meant to limit, not confer power upon authority. Democratic systems, therefore, maximize individual expression and protect the citizen from the tyranny of the group, whether elite or mass. The opportunity for individual growth and development stimulates achievement criteria and makes it possible for the humble to share power with the mighty. Egalitarianism and the rule of law safeguard the interests of all and neutralize the influence of the few. *See also* DEMOCRATIC CENTRALISM, p. 219; GUIDED DEMOCRACY, p. 228; ORIENTAL DESPOTISM, p. 107.

Significance   Democracy is a complex form of political order. It is also fragile and vulnerable. Democracy in practice is less an idealized political arrangement, and more what people deem it to be, or what people say it is. Democracy, therefore, comes in a variety of forms. Decentralized as well as centralized political systems claim to be democratic. Marxist people's democracies are highly integrated ideological units that allow the few to make decisions for the many. Obedience is a function of democratic centralism, and popular dissent becomes a criminal offense.

Societies described as people's democracies are characteristically highly mobilized, devote themselves to collective endeavor, and revere leadership as infallible. Control is the central theme in such "democracies," and justification is found in ideological dogma and group security. Asian countries like China, North Korea, Vietnam, Laos, Kampuchea (Cambodia), Afghanistan, and South Yemen fit the category of communist people's democracies. India, Sri Lanka, and Burma, on the other hand, although emphasizing socialism, see themselves in a different context. Despite the heavy hand of authority, they are relatively less centralized. They are also nationally inspired rather than ideologically motivated. They judge themselves to be closer to the democratic norm, while recognizing that the desired goal is still distant. Japan, more than India, seems to reflect democratic principles.

Although the Liberal Democratic Party has controlled Japanese political life since its establishment in 1955 in postwar Japan, the relative homogeneity of the Japanese nation has minimized authoritarian expression. A successful industrial system and a prosperous economy have also contributed to the development of Japanese democracy. India, by contrast, continues to be plagued by divisive religious, ethnic, and cultural questions. Burma and Sri Lanka suffer similar problems. Government, therefore, must frequently resort to strenuous methods in order to prevent the unraveling of the delicate socio-political fabric. The difficulty of implementing democratic theory in Asian countries has produced aberrations such as "Basic Democracy," "Guided Democracy," and "Emergency" democracy. Generally speaking, Asian leaders do not believe their people are prepared for full-blown experiments in democracy. Moreover, expressions of "democracy" that reject individual expression and exaggerate the importance of collective responsibility tend to pave the way for centralized forms of government that are often associated with aspects of Marxism.

Dynastic System   A traditional, authoritarian system of government run by a ruling family, whose position of ultimate power is determined generation after generation through inheritance. Within the dynastic system, a new ruling family may come into power replacing the previous dynasty, usually by force, but this dynastic change rarely involves revolutionary transformation of the society or change in the basic pattern of ruler-subject relationship. Instead, the same traditional system of unequal power and superordination-subordination is maintained, and the passive role of the sedentary masses remains unaltered. The dynastic system was the prevalent form of government in Asia until replaced, for instance, in China in 1911 by republican forces. *See also* TRADITIONAL SOCIETY, p. 322.

Significance   The dynastic system was one of the most prevalent governing features of traditional Asian societies. Associated with this system were the concepts of "mandate of heaven," and the cyclical notion of history. The "mandate of heaven" legitimized dynastic rule. The ruler was conceived as possessing powers beyond those of the commoner. He was perceived as a heavenly messenger. He would be forced to forfeit his heavenly mandate, however, if he failed to govern as a proper heavenly messenger by ignoring the welfare of the people and the state, and replaced by a new ruler. Thus, no ruling family was considered to be perpetual. The concept of history, allied closely with the observance of natural phenomena, justified the ephemeral nature of political fortune in traditional Asian societies. Natural phenomena were perceived as cyclical—life and death, rise and fall, summer and winter. The traditional cyclical concept of history has not changed, but increasingly in Asia, the traditional dynastic system of government has been replaced by republicanism.

Gandhian Nationalism   Many figures are responsible for the development of Indian nationalism, but its character and representation can be attributed to Mahatma Gandhi. Gandhi's strength was his unusual capacity for personal sacrifice. He led by example and he built a mass base that gave the Indian National Congress a sense of unity and purpose. Gandhi was no orthodox politician. His nonviolent demonstrations and insistence on non-cooperation frustrated the British, while galvanizing his countrymen into political activity.

Gandhi pricked the conscience of India's alien rulers and forced them to weigh their paternalistic behavior alongside their declarations of justice and equity. Gandhi's mass protest movements began in earnest in 1921 and continued through the early 1930s. Even when in prison, his refusal to accept amenities and his long, debilitating fasts symbolized Indian will and determination and helped to build the spirit of nationalism. Gandhi's saintly performance was transformed into legend, and the Indian population endowed him with unprecedented adoration, which Gandhi returned.

Gandhi's practical goals were to revive village India and reclaim its legacy of social harmony and economic self-sufficiency. To this end, he rejuvenated handicraft industries. His own spinning of *khadi*, or homespun cloth, was no idle activity. By his example he instilled a new confidence and self-respect in the peasantry. He was never dissuaded from the belief that India's future depended upon the viability of the rural sector. Progress for him would not be found in the expansion of industrial centers or the development of urban communities, but in a renaissance of village tradition. Human development, not economic development, was his principal objective. This is amply illustrated by his criticism of the caste system, his efforts at removing the stigma of untouchability, as well as his call for Hindu-Muslim amity. *See also*

CABINET MISSION, p. 329; HARIJANS, p. 82; LAHORE RESOLUTION, p. 97; SWARAJ AND DYARCHY, p. 255.

Significance   India's nationalism was transformed by Gandhi into a program of action that ordinary people could perform. Gandhi brought disparate and competing factions together, and the Congress hierarchy was drawn closer to the masses. Village India received special consideration, and the British were compelled to question their own legitimacy. Gandhi symbolized India's quest for freedom. The masses that emulated his performance addressed him as *netaji* (great leader), or *bapu* (father).

For all Gandhi's mystique and charisma, he was a practical politician. Although he never became an official member of the Congress Working Committee, he was its chief decision maker. Gandhi's dictatorial powers angered many within the Congress, but his general popularity thwarted challenges from well-known personalities, such as Subas Chandra Bose, the Hindu Bengali leader. Gandhi's style also disturbed Mohammad Ali Jinnah, leader of the Muslim League. Like Gandhi, Jinnah was a lawyer, yet far more committed to the profession and more successful at his craft. Jinnah had played an important role in attempting to bridge Hindu-Muslim differences before Gandhi's return from South Africa. He believed minority rights could only be assured within a framework of constitutionalism, and he was disturbed by Gandhi's appeal to the illiterate masses. Jinnah was appalled by Gandhi's tactics because they exploited the sentiments and aroused the passions of the multitude. He was convinced that such activity would undermine established institutions and destroy respect for the rule of law. This fundamental difference in tactics between himself and Gandhi forced Jinnah to press for the creation of an independent, sovereign Pakistan. Thus Gandhi's actions provoked two separate, but also antagonistic nationalisms. Gandhi inspired his countrymen to join with him in forcing the British to yield their Indian colony. He also convinced Muslim separatists that their aspirations could only be fulfilled in an independent Pakistan.

Gentry   In its narrow and traditional Chinese definition, the individuals who, having passed the examinations conducted by the state for official recruitment, held various degrees and constituted the most powerful elite class. The gentry in imperial China were Confucian scholars. Not all degree holders were officials, but they constituted a reservoir from which officials were recruited. In imperial China, gentry status usually meant landed wealth, and the gentry class and the landowning class were often synonymous. Even though, theoretically, every person could become a scholar and an official in imperial China, it was

very unusual for a peasant's son to master enough Confucian scholarship to pass the highly competitive and rigorous state-run examinations for official degrees. In reality, this meant the perpetuation of the
gentry and their stability, which contributed greatly to the continuation
of China's traditional imperial system. Even those who were not officials
constituted the local elite and served as intermediary between the peasant masses and the officials. *See also* CONFUCIANISM, p. 75; NEO-CONFU-
CIANISM, p. 105; YANGBAN, p. 130.

Significance   The Chinese gentry class was not only a distinct social
group, but also the most powerful stratum of traditional imperial China.
Initial entry into this group was based on attaining an official degree,
following the successful passage of the state-run examination on Confucian scholarship. Elevation to this status included the whole family. Since
only a wealthy family could afford the education demanded of a successful candidate, the gentry class was able to perpetuate itself through
continually producing Confucian scholars and officials. Gentry families
were usually large, extended families, and their family centers survived
for more than a thousand years. They lived in the walled towns rather
than in the villages and had their own compounds of many courtyards,
replete with servants and hoarded supplies. The powerful local elite,
through their ideological leadership and wealth, kept peace and order
in their regions. They were held in awe by the peasantry and served as
functionaries for the officials. Perpetuation of the gentry class allowed
both stability in the imperial Confucian state system and maintenance
of the status quo of imperial Chinese civilization. In Communist China
the party bureaucracy plays as powerful a role as the traditional Chinese
gentry class has.

Harijans   A term Gandhi used to describe India's "untouchables."
India's caste system includes four general classifications. Omitted from
the system and known historically as outcastes or "untouchables" are
more than 100 million Indian citizens who, as a consequence of birth,
are judged by the caste members to be unclean and unworthy. These
members of Indian society are Hindus who during the British period in
India were given the title "scheduled castes." The Indian constitution of
1950 sought to protect outcastes from social and economic as well as
political deprivation, and the scheduled caste was officially outlawed.
Nevertheless, untouchability is deeply ingrained in the Indian mind.

   Religious tradition prevents revolutionary tampering, and caste discrimination persists, especially in rural areas that house the mass of
Indian society. The Indian political system, however, is designed to
safeguard the interests of the scheduled castes. Most important,

Mahatma Gandhi, the prime force behind the Indian independence movement, demanded an end to caste discrimination and intolerance. Although judged a pious Hindu, Gandhi rejected the ancient institution of untouchability and he insisted on referring to the outcastes as "Harijans" or "children of God." Such designation aimed at social uplift, but even Gandhi could not expect to change a system in place for more than two millenia without first achieving wide and deep behavioral change. *See also* CASTE, p. 62; HINDUISM, p. 83.

Significance   The Harijans today remain among the poorest, least educated members of Indian society. Because of Mahatma Gandhi's efforts, the Harijans or scheduled castes tend to identify with the Congress party, and particularly the Congress organization that was dominated by Prime Minister Indira Gandhi. This association goes back to the pre-independence period when the most influential member of the scheduled caste, Dr. B. R. Ambedkar, a close associate of the Mahatma, founded the Scheduled Caste Federation in 1942. Ambedkar played a vital role in the struggle for independence, was named the chairman of the Drafting Committee of the Indian Constitution, and was India's first Minister of Law in the administration of Jawaharlal Nehru, a high caste Brahmin. In 1956, the Scheduled Caste Federation became the Republican Party of India, but its strength was isolated to northwestern India, and by the 1960s it had lost its vigor and political leverage.

In the vacuum created by the demise of the Scheduled Caste organization a militant group known as the Dalit Panthers gained some prominence, but its activities were localized to the northwestern region around Maharashtra state. Another organization called the All-India Backward and Minority Communities Employees Federation has sought to spread scheduled caste organization throughout the country. It is centered on members of the oppressed castes who hold government civil service positions, guaranteed to them in law. It was hoped such an organization could reestablish the once prominent voice of the scheduled castes and other deprived minorities of India. Finally, it is important to cite the activity of Jagjivan Ram and his splinter Congress party. Jagjivan Ram, an untouchable, has served in more cabinet posts than any other Indian. His break with Mrs. Gandhi in 1977 was designed to gain him the role of India's prime minister, but he was frustrated in that pursuit by other political personalities who apparently were not yet ready to work under the leadership of a Harijan.

Hinduism   The predominant religion of India. There are more than 500 million Hindus in the world today, the overwhelming majority residing within India. Unlike Judaism, Christianity, Islam, or Buddhism, there is no central figure around which to explain the Hindu faith, and the institution of prophethood is virtually unknown. Hinduism is the intertwining of spiritual and practical expressions of belief and performance. It associates social structure, patterns of relationship, and mundane affairs with philosophical complexity and cosmological uncertainty.

Hinduism is organic to the Indian subcontinent, having developed there over three millennia. At the core of the Hindu belief system is the idea that all living things are possessed of souls, that all souls have equal merit, but are nonetheless differentiated by the accumulation of previous deeds. This is the notion of *karma,* the law of moral consequences, which conditions and influences the development or passage of the souls as they move from one life form to another. Hinduism includes the concept of birth and rebirth, in which the soul wanders from one expression to another by reincarnation, or as it is better known, the transmigration of the soul between many different types of bodies. The purpose of this passage from birth to rebirth is to fulfill the law of karma by the strict observance of *dharma,* or moral duty, thus breaking the cycle of rebirth. The release of the soul from all bodily restrictions is the ultimate quest, and it is achieved by the final passage of the soul from its earthbound condition to its cosmological resting place. This release from reality is usually associated with salvation, the Hindu *moksha,* when the soul is merged with the essential order of the universe and finds true peace. The doctrine of birth and rebirth is known as *samsara* and it has provided Hinduism with its distinctive thought, philosophy, and cultural expression.

Hinduism centers on a number of texts, but there is no single bible. Among the more important literary tracts are the Upanishads (ca. 600 B.C.), which are a record of the teachings and discussions of ancient mendicants who gave up worldly possessions and bodily concerns to immerse themselves in meditation and thereby endeavored to break the cycle of birth and rebirth. The thematic substance of the Upanishads is the unity of the individual soul "*atman,*" with the world-soul, "*Brahman.*" The unity of all things in one Absolute Being, and the escape from samsara, birth and rebirth, is equivalent to denying the value or significance of personality.

Hindus are required to observe their moral duty, *dharma,* performing their religious acts wherever they find themselves. Hindu temples venerate the deities of Hindu cosmology, but they are not churches, or mosques, or synagogues. They are more-or-less sacred, but not crucial to the expression or performance of faith. By the same token, there are no congregational prayers similar to those found in Judaism, Christianity, or Islam. Hindus see themselves as members of a vast society which for all its anarchic outward appearances is ordered cosmologically, and within which each member is a part of the whole. This notion of totality, collectivity, and order in Hinduism elevates the concept of family over self and reinforces the institution of caste to which Hindus are inextricably bound. *See also* CASTE, p. 62; HARIJANS, p. 82.

Significance   Politically, Hinduism is best expressed in the institution of caste. The Indian constitution of 1950 sought to terminate discrimination between castes but the caste system persists despite all efforts to bypass it. Caste is related to the Hindu belief in cosmological unity and the ultimate quest of the individual soul to achieve oneness with the eternal. To attain this goal Hindus are obligated to follow the dictates of their karma and its expression of moral duty. Thus caste is a matter of accepting the consequences of the birth and rebirth cycle. The believing Hindu cannot avoid that status which makes him a part of the universal order. This philosophical/social system is attributed to the Aryans who invaded and conquered the subcontinent approximately three thousand years ago. They are believed to have divided society into four castes, but the arrangement is also deemed to have existed from the time of creation.

At the apex of the four castes is the *Brahman*, the priest whose life is devoted to teaching and study. The next order is that of the *Kshatriya*, the warrior or nobleman who maintains law and order and acts as the protector of society. The third caste is that of the *Vaisya*, the merchants and cultivators who provide for the sustenance and well-being of the community. The lower caste is the *Sudra*, providing the menial labor in the service of the other three higher castes. The stratified nature of the caste system has persisted over time, but it has not prevented power from being expressed by lower caste personalities. In fact, there are examples of caste changes having taken place, thus enabling lower caste groups to move into higher classifications. Nevertheless, the ascriptive order of the caste system prevails and the castes remain distinct and exclusive, neither intermarrying, nor sharing meals together.

Changes that have been introduced during the colonial and postcolonial periods in India, however, have done away with such older rituals as the immolation of the widow, female infanticide, child marriage, and temple prostitution. Animal sacrifice still obtains but it is no longer considered common practice. Untouchability, the belief that persons denied position in the caste order are *malecca*, unclean, and thus to be ignored, has also been modified by legal enactment and contemporary political reality. Untouchability remains, however, and caste Hindus have not tempered their perception of these outcastes. Divorce and widow remarriage have been legalized, and polygamy has been forbidden. Indeed, the caste system in its traditional sense has been outlawed but it continues to manifest itself in the form of *jatis,* or subcastes, which are more occupational than religiously inspired. There are literally thousands of subcastes in modern Hinduism and their interrelationships establish the fabric of modern Hindu society.

Islam   A major world religion in the Judeo-Christian tradition. The word "Islam" is derived from the Arabic root "salima," which can be interpreted as meaning peace, submission, and obedience. In religious usage, Islam means submission to the will of God and obedience to His law. Muslims, believers in Islam, adhere to the understanding that only by submitting to the will of God and by obeying God's law can one achieve true peace and enjoy lasting purity now and in the hereafter. *See also* ISLAM (SHIITE), p. 86; ISLAM, (SUNNI), p. 89; MUSLIM, p. 104.

Significance   Non-Muslims have often referred to Islam as Mohammadanism. Muslims both reject and protest such description of their faith. Mohammad is revered as a prophet of God, one of many to whom God revealed himself. Mohammad's special significance is his role as the last, or Seal of the Prophets, in Arabic, *Khatm-i-Nabawaat.* Nevertheless, Mohammad is accepted as a mortal human being. He is not worshipped, nor did he create the Islamic religion. Mohammad was commissioned by God to bring his word to the world. He is best viewed as a model of piety and perfection and the leader of the Muslim community (*umma*). The only founder of Islam, however, is God himself. The Islamic religion spread from the Arabian peninsula in the seventh century A.D., and today its devotees extend around the globe, totaling approximately 700 million. In addition to the countries of the Middle East, North and East Africa, as well as Nigeria, predominantly Muslim nations are: Pakistan, Bangladesh, Malaysia, and Indonesia. India has a Muslim population estimated to exceed seventy million, and Muslims live in considerable number in Soviet Central Asia, China, and the Philippines.

Islam: Shiite   The lesser of the two major sects of Islam. Shiite Islam differs from orthodox Islam in that it narrows the qualifications of the candidate for the *imamate* (the equivalent of the Sunni caliphate) and hence the leadership of the Muslim community. These qualifications are limited to members of the Prophet Mohammad's tribe of Quraysh, and further, descendants of the Prophet's son-in-law, Ali, and his daughter, Fatima. Shiites insist that the legitimate right to the Prophet's mantle is through Ali and his descendants. Although there is no record of any such designation, Shiites believe that Ali was selected by the Prophet to succeed him, and after him, his descendants in direct line. Thus Ali is believed to have been endowed with divine authority, with the secret knowledge to interpret the *Qur'an*. This knowledge Ali is believed to have passed on to his male descendants. Ali, therefore, is perceived by Shiites to be the repository of Islamic truth, and special powers are ascribed to his person. So total is this belief in the divine ordination of Ali that even Mohammad is sometimes considered a lesser messenger of God.

According to Shiite tradition, Ali and his descendants were infallible leaders. This devotion to Ali is further heightened by his martyrdom and that of his son and would-be successor, Husain. Shiite Islam is not monolithic, however. Sects abound. Differing opinions on the role and nature of the *imamate* produced numerous factions and splits. Although Shiite Islam is defined as the "partisans of Ali," his followers have proven to be divisive. On the one side there are the *Zaydis*, who argue for the election of the *iman*, or spiritual leader, from among Ali's descendants. On the other side there are the more familiar forms of Shiite Islam known as the *Ithna Ashari* or Twelvers, and the *Ismailis* or Seveners. The Twelvers and the Seveners are separated by controversy over the death of the sixth imam, Jafar al-Sadiq, who died in 765 A.D. The Twelvers argue that Sadiq's son, Musa al-Kazim, succeeded to the imamate. The Seveners differ, giving their support to the elder brother, Ismail. The descendants of Ismail are identified with the Fatimid Caliphate of Egypt. The Ismailis of today are found in India, Pakistan, Soviet Central Asia, Syria, Iraq, and East Africa. A socioeconomically successful community, the Ismailis are led by their spiritual leader, the Aga Khan, who today is a cosmopolitan, Harvard-educated, international civil servant concerned with the worldwide refugee problem. The Ismailis are also found in different tribal groups such as the ruling Alawites of Syria or the commercially successful Khoja community of Pakistan. The Druze of the Middle East are also an offshoot of Ismaili Islam.

The principal form of Shiite Islam, however, is that of the Twelvers. They follow the line of Musa al-Kazim and his descendants until the disappearance of the Twelfth Imam, Mohammad ibn Hasan al-Askari, who is believed to have gone into occultation in 874 A.D. Until the reappearance of the Twelfth Imam, his role is to be filled by *mujtahids* (secular and religious divines), essentially the mullahs and ayatollahs. Until the return of the Twelfth Imam as the *Mahdi* (messiah), the mullahs and ayatollahs serve in his place. Their dominance in the Shiite sect explains the political dualism always latent in Iran, where Shiite Islam has been a state religion since the Safid dynasty's proclamation in the sixteenth century. In Iran, any temporal political figure is a mere pretender and an illegitimate usurper of authority. This challenge to authority posed by Shiite belief, as well as the insistence on following a wholly different course from that of the Sunni Muslims, has put the

Shiite community under considerable pressure. Persecution and death stalked the Shiites as successive Sunni caliphs sought to destroy their faith. The Shiite response was to practice dissimulation (*taqiyah*), to hide their beliefs. Other Shiites, however, risked martyrdom in the tradition of Ali and Husain, and in time martyrdom became the core of the Shiite belief system. Shiites are more mystical in the performance of their faith than their Sunni counterparts, and martyrdom aroused deep emotions and passions, which helped sustain the partisans of Ali. Observers have often described Shiite ceremonies as fanatical representations of religious expression. Few, however, doubt the depth of Shiite faith. Shiite conceptions of law and politics are strictly authoritarian. Obedience to the *imam* is far stronger than the relationship between adherents of Sunni Islam and their temporal rulers. In Shiite Islam, the *imam* has the final interpretation of legal doctrine. Such is not the case in Sunni Islam. By the same token, although both Sunnis and Shiites never question the *Qur'an*, the *hadiths* (traditions of the Prophet Mohammad) are not accepted unless the *imam* legitimates them. Also, the Muslim Sunni practice of *Ijma*, judgment by consensus of the learned community, is unacceptable to Shiites if the *imam* has not participated in the decision-making process. *Qiyas*, or reasoning by analogy, is discounted almost totally in Shiite Islam. The result is a far more rigid system of Islamic jurisprudence and procedure than that found in the larger Sunni world. *See also* ISLAM, p. 86; ISLAM (SUNNI), p. 89.

Significance   Shiite Islam is especially strong in Iran, where the vast majority of the population follow the Twelver tradition. Iraq's population is split between Sunni and Shiite Muslims, but the Shiites are thought to be more numerous. They are scattered through every Muslim country, but their numbers are a smaller percentage of those populations. Shiites have their own rituals and special occasions; they also share a long and bloody history with their Sunni brethren. As it has in the past, controversy swells around these two major Islamic communities. Periodic displays of brutality by one community against the other occur, but tolerance and cooperation are also evident, and mutual assistance, if not compatibility, has been demonstrated. Conflict continues, however. For example, the ruling Shiite Alawites of Syria have been opposed by the Muslim Brotherhood which disapproves of their un-Islamic behavior. The physical destruction of the Brotherhood along with their sympathizers in Syria in 1982 allegedly caused 20,000 deaths. Although little attention was given to this massacre, the course of the Iranian revolution was keenly watched.

    The Ayatollah Khomeini's call to Shiite Muslims, as well as Sunni Muslims, to overthrow their current leaders and join with him in the resurrection of an Islamic state, was considered a significant threat in countries like Saudi Arabia, Kuwait, and Iraq. The Ayatollah believed that the Iranian revolution was but one phase of an all-embracing Islamic revolution, and he saw his role as that of a leader for all Muslims. Claiming divine ordination, Khomeini insisted that his judgment was unerring and must be heeded by Muslims everywhere. Khomeini ordered his followers to martyr themselves in resisting Iraqi aggression against Iran in 1980. His call to service of all able-bodied Shiite Iranians ultimately turned the tide of battle and drove the Iraqis from Iranian soil. Although Iraq signalled its desire to terminate the hostilities, Iran's clergy was determined to continue their holy war. Iraq's leaders, notably Saddam Husayn, did not accurately judge the depth of Shiite faith or its management by Iran's theologians. Iranians proved again they were prepared to sacrifice themselves for their beliefs. The Iran-Iraq conflict, generated and perpetuated by Shiite faith, and in human terms already the most costly in the Middle East since the end of World War II, reached new levels of intensity in 1984–85.

Islam: Sunni   The dominant Islamic group. Sunni Islam refers to the majority of Muslims who follow the orthodox (as contrasted with the nondoctrinal Shiite) tradition. Sunni Muslims identify with the *sunna,* a body of legal and moral principles that predates the Islamic era. The *sunna* represented Arabian customary law and in its earliest expression was pagan in character. Idolatry and political fragmentation were key features of pre-Islamic Arab society. The tribal chief or *sayyid* was selected on the basis of age, experience, and intelligence, and he held office because of the loyalty demonstrated by his supporters. The most important role played by the chief was the adjudication of disputes by referral to tribal custom. In this context, the *sunna,* or primitive law of the tribal folk, reinforced the authority of the personal ruler. Idol worship was an integral feature of tribal law and tended to legitimate authority.

The rise of Islam did not replace the *sunna,* but it did drastically modify it. The Prophet Mohammad was primarily concerned with warning people against idolatry and impressing upon them the Oneness of God (*Allah*). Although there was some resistance to Mohammad's plea, the idols were smashed and God's law was declared supreme over idolatrous law. The ancient *sunna,* however, remained as a foundation for the new Islamic way of life. Sunni Muslims identify themselves with a highly developed juridical order that regulates the totality of the believer's activities and thoughts. The *sunna* of the Islamic era has been described as an ideal system because it is derived from a divine source and embodies God's will and justice. Thus, in the Sunni tradition, only God is the source of ultimate authority. Sovereignty can only belong to

God and is therefore held in trust by men who act according to God's intentions and will. The caliphs of Islam were considered God's vice-regents on earth, required by law to protect the Muslim community (*umma*), but always recognized to be fallible mortals. Contemporary reference to the Islamic state, as in Pakistan, emphasizes the sovereignty of God and the governors as His servants.

For Sunni Muslims, Islamic law was the ideal legal system; it was divine, perfect, eternal, and just. Moreover, it applied to all people, everywhere. Sunni Muslims insist that divine law takes precedence over society and state, hence the declarations in Muslim countries that laws that are repugnant to Islam are invalid. In other words, governments that fail to enforce Islamic law are often judged to be beyond the pale and without legitimacy. Even when governments stood in clear violation of it, believers were obliged to observe Islamic law.

The Sunni Muslim's understanding of the correct course to follow, irrespective of his circumstances, is assisted by the *shari'a* or right path. It is incumbent on Sunni Muslims to fulfill their duties according to the *sunna* and *shari'a* despite existing conditions. The fulfillment of one's obligations, the adoption of the *shari'a* (the right path), is the single most important objective in life. Happiness in this life and salvation are the rewards of all believers. God's law was revealed to humankind through his messenger, Mohammad, a verse at a time in the *Qur'an*. In fact, the *Qur'an* was assembled some two decades after Mohammad's death. Its teachings are judged to have universal value and application for all Muslims. The path established by the *Qur'an*, however, is often narrow and limited. Believers are told what is required (*fard*) and what is forbidden (*haram*), what is recommended (*mandub*), and that which is objectionable but not forbidden (*makruh*). In areas where the law appears to be indifferent, the Sunni Muslim is judged to have wide latitude (*jaiz*). For example: daily prayers are fard; adultery is haram; extra prayers are mandub; eating certain flesh is makruh (pork is specifically forbidden and considered to be haram). Selling goods, to be distinguished from usury or interest-taking, which is forbidden, is jaiz.

Thus, the divine law as revealed to the Prophet Mohammad provided a system of all-embracing legal codes and commands, and it has been noted by Islamic scholars that Islamic law has the character of religious obligation and also provides a political sanction of religion, thus representing a total way of life. As a result, it also imposes a form of authoritarianism, and some would argue, totalitarianism, on all Muslims. In Sunni Islam, however, this is a self-imposed authority. There is no church hierarchy or clergy as in Shiite Islam, and each Sunni Muslim may choose to perform the rituals prescribed by God's teachings. *See also* AHMEDIYA, p. 53; ISLAM, p. 86; ISLAM (SHIITE), p. 86.

Significance   Sunni Muslims are the dominant sect in contemporary Islam, comprising approximately 80 percent of the total Muslim world. The division between Sunni and Shiite developed over the successorship to the Prophet Mohammad. Since that time the Islamic sects have never reconciled their positions, and each order has been embellished with its own dogma and rituals. In a larger sense, the Muslim community was the inheritor of God's revelations to Mohammad and the ancient customs and traditions of the Arabian peninsula. This blending of experiences also occurred in lands conquered by the Arab armies in their seventh and eighth century surge across North Africa to Western Europe, through the Fertile Crescent, skirting Asia Minor (Byzantium) to Iran, Central Asia, and India. The Iranians quickly Persianized the Islamic experience, and the Turks, although a bit more resistant, also adapted their traditions to Islam.

Similar interactions occurred wherever Islam gained a foothold, as in Malaysia, Indonesia, Nigeria, and among the Berbers of North Africa. Given its great geographic expansion, the Muslim community (*umma*) was forced to find ways to deal with life as it existed in the Arabian peninsula. Syria, Iraq, Egypt, and Iran had been the sites for sophisticated, developed civilizations, and adaptations to the new austere, demanding, and disciplined life-style of Arabian Islam required patience and innovation. The early caliphs of Islam therefore used personal opinion (*ra'y*) to supplement Islamic teachings. The second caliph, Umar, declared that the *Qur'an*, the *sunna* (largely Arabian customs at this time, but also some traditions of the Prophet), and reason (*ijtihad*) were to be used in addressing the needs of different populations and cultures. Others, however, contested this view, insisting that the application of reason violated the notion of divine law and permitted man-made legislation.

Controversies such as this produced the four schools of Islamic jurisprudence, which are still in vogue in contemporary Sunni Islam. The Hanafite school (Abu Hanifa, 699–768) is considered the most liberal of these four schools. Hanifa argued that reasoning by analogy (*qiyas*) was a proper source of law when neither the *Qur'an* nor the *hadith* (traditions of the Prophet) were helpful in answering a question or solving a problem. Abu Hanifa's logic especially appealed to non-Arabs who wished to sustain their own characteristic methods and culture. Hanafite tradition is found in modern Turkey and Pakistan. The Malikite (Malik ibn Anas, 718–96) is another Sunni Muslim school of Islamic Law, known for its stress on the *hadith*. The activities of the Prophet as well as the local *sunna* were presented in the form of *ijma* (consensus of the learned community), which Malik is believed to have spawned. Learned theologians or religious jurists were made responsible for determining the correct path whenever the *Qur'an* was not explicit. The Malikites, however, had their detractors. The opposition argued that *ijma* was a form of man-made law and thus in violation of divine prescription. Nevertheless, Malikite interpretation of Islamic law held special importance for Iraqis, Syrians, Egyptians, and North Africans, and it was incorporated in their rituals.

The third school of Islamic jurisprudence is the Shafite (Shaf'i, 768–820). Reputed to be the most systematic of early Muslim legal theorists, Shaf'i was critical of local *ijma* but adopted it whenever broad community agreement was possible. Shaf'i also rejected that part of the *sunna* which did not deal directly with, or reflect on, Islamic tradition. He emphasized that only that *sunna* could be followed which dealt with the utterances of the Prophet. Shafite doctrine proved to be weak despite its erudition. The inability to arrive at broad consensus was a key failing, and controversy has followed this school of jurisprudence to the present day. The Shafite school of Islamic law, however, is prominent in Muslim Indonesia and elsewhere in Southeast Asia. Shafite scholarship gave rise to the term *madhhab*, meaning school of law, which was applied to the work of Hanifa and Malik as well as Shaf'i. The fourth school of Islamic jurisprudence is the Hanbalite (Ahmed ibn Hanbal, a ninth century student of Shaf'i). The most rigid and conservative of the Sunni Muslim schools, Hanbal's work was given significance by Taqi-al-Din Ahmed bin Taymiah (1263–1318). Taymiah insisted that only the *Qur'an* and the *hadith*, or traditions of the Prophet, were acceptable. He condemned any kind of innovation, mystical expression (*sufism*), or saint-worship. The Hanbalite school as developed by Taymiah ultimately gave rise to Wahhabism, the Islamic practice that permeates Saudi Arabia.

These four schools of Islamic jurisprudence were well established by the eleventh century, and *ijtehad* (discretion or reason) gave way to *taqlid* (imitation), or acceptance of the four schools. The period is known as the *Bab al-Ijtihad*, the closing of the door to reason. Sunni Islam assumed its unchanging character during this period. Subsequent efforts to challenge prevailing doctrine were met with stiff resistance, and those who attempted to modify the precepts of Islamic tradition were charged with heresy. In Pakistan, for example, the Ahmediya community (followers of the nineteenth century religious leader Ghulam Ahmed) were officially designated non-Muslim because of their heretical beliefs.

Sunnis and Shiites are bitter rivals. Attempts to placate the opposed communities in Lebanon led to a distribution of offices in the government so that a Sunni would be the prime minister, and a Shiite would be the speaker of the assembly. Conflicts abound between the Shiite leadership (Alawite) in Syria and the majority Sunni population of that country. The reverse is true in Iraq, where Sunnis have governed a nation in which Shiites are in the majority. Shiite-Sunni clashes are not unusual occurrences in Pakistan, although many Shiite factions have achieved status and influence in the predominantly Sunni state. Discussions about Muslim unity must take into account basic divisions within Sunni Islam and between Sunni and Shiite Muslims. Historic cleavages run deep, and calls to the Muslim *umma* to respond with one will to dilemmas afflicting the Islamic world have yet to be answered.

The rigidity of Islam and Muslim practices is clear when compared with other religious and religious-cum-philosophical orders, such as Hinduism and Buddhism. Islam resists any tampering that could dilute its role and purpose. Muslims are cautioned not to deviate from a narrowly conceived path. Although efforts have been made to adopt non-Muslim tradition, particularly education and technology, only a small fraction of the Muslim *umma* have been affected. In times of extreme tension, Muslims with such alien experience are often judged to be a threat to the larger Islamic society. The repudiation of foreign ideas, methods, and institutions, therefore, involves the condemnation of so-called modern cosmopolitan Muslim elites.

Jainism   An indigenous Indian religion, practiced by a relatively small group located mainly in northwestern India. This Indian religion emerged from the same area, at about the same time, as Buddhism. Unlike Buddhism, however, it did not spread outside the subcontinent and, although still practiced there, it is judged a minor religion. The founder of Jainism is Vardhamana Mahavira (Great Hero), a contemporary of Buddha. Mahavira is reported in legend to have entered an ascetic life at an early age in order to find salvation. Finding salvation by conquering his own soul, he established an order of naked monks who pursued lives of absolute simplicity. The term "Jain" is derived from the sanskrit word "jina" or conqueror. Jainism became prominent a century after the death of Mahavira when the Maurya emperor adopted Jainism. But by this time a controversy had split Jainism into a more austere group that continued to practice monkist nudity and another that wore white robes. The latter became dominant and remains the principal order of Jains. *See also* BUDDHISM, p. 59; HINDUISM, p. 83.

Significance   Jainism describes an age of decline in which there is need for authority. The state, for the Jains, protects the social fabric and therefore is a necessary aspect of human activity. Although the Jains advocated benign authoritarianism, they did not threaten Hinduism. Thus, unlike the Buddhists, the Jains were permitted to follow their doctrines. At the same time, their lack of dynamism, their total immersion in material order, and their profound atheism had only minimal popular appeal. Jainism has remained in its present form for more than two thousand years.

Javanism   The indigenous culture of a majority of Indonesians. Islam spread to Indonesia toward the end of the thirteenth century and followed the trade routes as far as the spice islands of the Moluccas. Initially influencing the people of the coastal areas, it moved inland, often supplanting the prevailing order. Islamic law intertwined with the Muslim faith and the latter was locked in a struggle with *adat*, or local custom, which continued through the twentieth century. As a consequence, most Javan Indonesians are Muslims, but their Islamic expression is heavily influenced by indigenous custom, animistic performance, and mystical beliefs. Indonesians commemorate special periods of the year, such as the planting season and the harvest, with a commensal religious meal, known as *slametans*. Dutch overseers in Indonesia before independence spoke of the "pagan" in many Indonesian Muslims, but this did not imply they were nominal Muslims. What the Dutch and other observers wished to convey was that historic Javanism was more obvious than chaste, orthodox Islam. *See also* ARCHIPELAGO, p. 5; HINDUISM, p. 83; PANTASILA, p. 110.

Significance   Understanding Indonesian culture demands insight into the life of the Javans. They value historic Javanism more than traditional Islam. The majority of Javan villagers, for example, practice "Agama Java," or Javanese way of life. These same villagers describe practicing, devout Muslims as "Islam." The latter are linked with the "Muhammadijah," which spawned the Muslim Masjumi political party. They are also found in the Nahdaltul Ulama and the Himpunan Mahasiswa Islam. The unique character of Javan Islam is believed related to the influences of the Indian occupation and the importation of Hinduism. Indianization preceded Islamization and one influenced the other; they did not replace one another. The *wayang*, or Indonesian shadow play, illustrates this phenomenon. The heroes and heroines of these plays, deeply embedded in Javanese Indonesian culture, are drawn from Hindu epic literature, including the *Mahabharata* and the *Ramayana*. These recitations form the basis for Javan thought, especially in ethical matters. Indonesian leaders like Sukarno and Suharto have been known to seek understanding in these mystical performances, as well as through the traditional observance of Islamic ritual.

Kautiliya   The reputed author of the oldest surviving Hindu texts concerned with statecraft, known as the "Arthasastras" or Treatise on Material Gain. Believed to be the work of Kautiliya, a minister of Chandragupta Maurya, who was a contemporary of Alexander the Great, the Arthasastras provide deep insight into the political machinations of ancient Indian rulers as well as the socio-political forces prevailing in the subcontinent at that time. Alexander invaded India in 326–325 B.C. and impressed Indian leaders with the necessity of mobilizing their scattered units into a unified military and political force. Kautiliya, the Machiavelli of Hinduism, instructed his king to reorganize the polity of India in order to meet the challenge of marauding Hellenes. The Arthasastras are guides to successful administration and government. Kautiliya glorified the role of the king and offered a pragmatic series of lessons for those aspiring to be rulers. He stressed the paternalistic character of the king, compassion for his supporters, and a ferocious, unforgiving nature in combat with the enemy. Rulers, noted Kautiliya, were free to use all means in defense of their realm. Deceit and cunning, plot and subterfuge were legitimate actions in defense of the kingdom. Punishment for crimes against the state was severe and meted out by a substantial bureaucratic structure that imposed a tight rein on human activity. Hints of rebellion were ruthlessly suppressed. Kautiliya counselled the creation of a vast spy network capable of ferreting out subversives. Effective government was deemed the only counter to anarchy. *See also* HINDUISM, p. 83; MILITANT HINDUISM, p. 103; SIKHISM, p. 117.

Significance   Kautiliya is frequently cited by political analysts of the contemporary Indian scene, just as Machiavelli's medieval writings are applied to modern European behavior. Kautiliya describes a realistic view of political life and addresses the question of amorality in the affairs of states. Power is the watchword, and the ruler prevails not because he is wise and humane, but because he understands his enemies and is not afraid to act ruthlessly in defense of his realm. India's leaders today, judged by the writings of Kautiliya, are no more righteous, compassionate, or selfless than their counterparts in other countries. The Indian government's international posture as a peacemaker is juxtaposed with its domestic performance as a determined enforcer of law and order. India is also prepared to ally itself with nations that maximize its advantages, irrespective of differences in outlook or expression. Expediency, not morality, guides public policy, and India, no less than other states, unashamedly expresses itself in terms defining its national interests.

Kimilsungism   A set of ideas attributed to North Korean leader Kim Il Sung (Kim, Il-sŏng) and propagated in North Korea as a new revolutionary world view that is Kim's theoretical contribution to Marxism and Leninism. Kimilsungism is founded on the idea of *chuch'e* (*juche*) which is variously translated as independence, self-reliance, and being able to manage one's own affairs on the basis of his or her own needs and available resources. It is the opposite of the traditional Confucian notion of depending on the stronger. Since it was first expounded by Kim Il Sung in 1955, North Korea has made Kimilsungism its guiding spirit, and much scholarship in North Korea has worked to apply it on a global scale. In the philosophical system of North Korea, nationalism means the affirmation of self, development means the fulfillment of self, and is all accomplished in the spirit of chuch'e. North Korea's foreign relations are conducted and guided by this spirit. According to their revised Constitution of 1972, "The Democratic People's Republic of Korea is guided in its activity by the Chuch'e idea of the Workers' Party of Korea, which is a creative adaptation of Marxism-Leninism to our country's reality." *See also* ASIAN COMMUNISM, p. 54; COMMUNISM, p. 74; JUCHE, p. 308; MAOISM, p. 101.

Significance   By Kim's own admission, the idea of chuch'e is not new. Its real antecedents are found in both the nationalistic expression of the colonial people and the revolutionary strategies of Mao Zedong. However, Kim gave it a special emphasis and identified it with his brand of nationalistic communism. While consolidating his power in North Korea, Kim insisted, "Some advocated the Soviet way and others the Chinese, but is it not high time to work out our own?" Faced with the Sino-Soviet dispute, Kim refused to take sides and insisted on North Korea's chuch'e. It is also in the name of chuch'e that North Korea has insisted on the withdrawal of American troops from South Korea, and maintained the position that the reunification of North and South Korea must be consummated by the Korean people themselves. To the North Korean people, chuch'e is a new, revolutionary world view, and Kim Il Sung is its founder. Kim is believed to be the world's greatest contemporary thinker, whose historical contributions exceed those of Karl Marx and Mao Zedong. According to North Korean accounts, Kim's idea of chuch'e is studied by many in the Third World. In fact, North Korea has been generously funding various international study centers of chuch'e and Kimilsungism and has systematically propagated the writings attributed to Kim Il Sung in many countries.

Kokutai   The concept which has been translated as national entity, or national unity, meaning the undiluted sense of oneness of Japan as a nation. The concept of *kokutai* was not new in pre-war Japan, but for the first time it was codified in *Kokutai no Hongi* (Principles of the National Entity or Polity) which was published by the Ministry of Education in 1937. The book became the main text for the course in "ethics" offered throughout the Japanese school system. The basic emphases in the book were: rejection of western ideas and values, particularly individualism, socialism, anarchism, and communism; articulation of the unique historical experience of the Japanese people; glorification of the emperor; and an invocation of the consciousness of the Japanese people. Also emphasized were loyalty (willingness to offer oneself for the sake of the emperor) and filial piety (serving one's parents). According to *Kokutai no Hongi*, these two values were intimately related, since filial piety in the home meant loyalty to the nation. In other words, the book stated that filial piety directly had for its object one's parents, but in its relationship toward the emperor found a place within loyalty. *See also* CONFUCIANISM, p. 75; MILITARISM: JAPAN, p. 284; NEO-CONFUCIANISM, p. 105; SHINTOISM, p. 115.

Significance   The publication of *Kokutai no Hongi* in 1937 was one of the most important events in the development of modern Japan following the Meiji Restoration of 1868. The concept of kokutai which it enunciated served as the backbone of military expansionism abroad and mobilization of the people within Japan in the 1930s. The power of the military was clearly ascending on the Japanese political scene, following the so-called Mukden Incident of September 18, 1931, which led to the conquest of Manchuria by the Japanese Kwantung Army. From Manchuria, Japanese military expansionism advanced to North China. Its goal was to establish Japan as the unrivaled, dominant power in East Asia. It was willing to go to war against the United States and the USSR to achieve what was regarded as Japan's historic mission. The most radical exponents of this military expansionism were found among junior officers and their ultra-nationalist civilian collaborators. They were strongly antiwest and were disappointed with Japan's democratic parliamentary interlude in the 1920s.

According to *Kokutai no Hongi:* "The various ideological and social evils of present-day Japan are the fruits of ignoring the fundamentals and of running into the trivial, of lack in sound judgment, and of failure to digest the things thoroughly; and that this is due to the fact that since the days of Meiji so many aspects of European and American culture, systems, and learning have been imported, and that, too rapidly." In other words, *Kokutai no Hongi* strove to rediscover the essence of Japan as founded on the sovereignty of the sacred personage of the emperor and as manifested in history. The concept of kokutai as revealed in *Kokutai no Hongi* was highly nationalistic and patriotic. It emphasized the oneness of the Japanese people with the emperor.

Lahore Resolution   Today known as the "Pakistan Resolution," it called for the establishment of a Muslim state or states in those areas of British India where the Muslim community was in the majority. It was

proposed and carried in a session of the Muslim League, convened in
Lahore (the most important city in the Punjab), on March 23, 1940. It
was moved by the Bengali, Fazlul Huq and seconded by Choudhury
Khaliquzzaman, who in subsequent years was to become president of
the Muslim League. This resolution was ten years in the making. At a
similar session of the Muslim League in 1930, Mohammad Iqbal, the
poet laureate of Pakistan, and then the president of the Muslim League,
said he would like to see the Punjab, Northwest Frontier Province, Sind,
and Baluchistan formed into one sovereign Muslim state. In 1933,
Chaudhry Rehmat Ali, a Muslim student studying in England, developed the name Pakistan as an acronym specifying P for Punjab, A for
Afghania, S for Sind, etc. The word "Pakistan" is also translated as
"Land of the Pure." Whatever the derivation or origin, Pakistan became
the objective of many Muslim League leaders and they instructed their
followers to adopt the name and cause.

World War II erupted in Europe in September 1939, and the Muslim
League leaders wanted to communicate to the British colonial authority
in India that the Muslim community was prepared to join with them in
the war effort, but that a free, independent Pakistan was their ultimate
goal. The Lahore Resolution followed, and although the British were
reluctant to partition India into separate Hindu-dominant and Muslim-
dominant states, they eventually complied with the Muslim League
demand. The Lahore Resolution became the Pakistan Resolution after
Pakistan was established on August 14, 1947. *See also* CABINET MISSION,
p. 329; KASHMIR DISPUTE, p. 386; TWO NATION THEORY, p. 128.

Significance   The Lahore or Pakistan Resolution is the most important date on the Pakistan national calendar after the date of independence. It is a day of celebration throughout the nation, and the country's
three formal constitutions (1956, 1962, and 1973) were all promulgated
on that day. The Lahore Resolution forecast the division of British India
into two sovereign states, and Congress leaders, instead of compromis-
ing, reinforced Muslim fears by condemning and ridiculing the Muslim
League action. Although the Muslim League seemed determined to
create an independent state, some of its most important leaders, including Mohammad Ali Jinnah, were ready to negotiate another arrangement. Intransigence and bitterness on both sides made compromise
impossible.

Another important aspect of the Lahore Resolution was its ambiguous
call for one or more Muslim states. Indeed, some Muslim thinkers in the
subcontinent entertained the notion of several Muslim states, with a
commonwealth drawing them together but not necessarily reducing, or
eliminating their individual, sovereign status. Therefore the creation of
a single Muslim state from those areas in the northwestern and eastern

parts of the subcontinent where the Muslims were in a majority was only one of several possibilities. As Pakistan took form, divided in two parts and separated by one thousand miles of hostile Indian territory, questions were raised about Pakistan's viability. The division of Bengal and the Punjab between India and Pakistan produced even more difficult geopolitical surgery and even greater pain. The Kashmir question symbolized the confusion in determining whether one or more Muslim states would result from the decision to partition what had been British India. Given the British role in the days leading up to independence, it was not clear if they wished to see two or more states carved out of their once formidable colony. On the one hand, they appeared to turn a deaf ear to other groups demanding national independence, such as the Sikhs. On the other hand, they agreed to transfer power to the several hundred royal potentates that ruled over various regions of the subcontinent, and, more significantly, to the Indian National Congress and the Muslim League.

Lamaism: Bhutan   A theocratic state in the Himalayas that is ruled by lamas or priests. Bhutan is derived from the Indian name "Bhotana," meaning the end of "Bhot" or Tibet. Of the more than one million people residing within the country, the vast majority are Bhotias from Tibet. The major language is a dialect of Tibetan and their religious philosophy is similar to that practiced in Tibet. Nepalese immigrants are extremely industrious, and they have managed to convert wasteland to productive soil, while becoming a significant political voice in the kingdom.

The political changes taking place in Bhutan can in part be attributed to the juxtaposition of the Bhotias and the Nepalese (approximately 25 percent of the population). This also helps to explain how Bhutan has been transformed into an independent kingdom dominated by a national assembly known as the Tshongdu. Up to 1969 Bhutan was an absolute monarchy, but the Tshongdu, which was created in 1953, assumed the power to select and remove the monarch, and now it has the power to control the monarch's position and behavior as well as his legislative authority. In effect the monarch has become a figurehead with the Royal Advisory Council (established in 1965) initiating most legislation. In addition to this body the Bhutanese government has a Council of Ministers responsible to the Tshongdu, although nominated by the king.

The Tshongdu has 150 members, 100 representing the country's 17 districts, 10 the regional monastic orders, and 40 appointed by the monarch. The king in 1984 was Jigme Singye Wangchuk, who assumed the throne in 1972. His father, Jigme Dorji Wangchuk (1953–72) saw his power ebb away, but his progressive attitude led him to abolish slavery and the caste system, declare land reforms, emancipate women, and introduce secular education. All of this did little to offset the power of the monastic orders that continue to wield political power.

The lamas, or priests, possess both spiritual and temporal power and are regarded with reverence by the larger population. Their monasteries are citadels of worldly power, as well as religious expression. The most successful political organization in Bhutan is the Drupka monastic order, led by a high priest, the *Je Khempo,* whose status rivals that of the king and who exhibits more formidable power. The 6,000 monks that make up the order are found throughout the government. The success of the order is often attributed to its unity and discipline, something the other organizations have not been able to emulate. The legal system of Bhutan grows out of its Lamaist teachings and Buddhist precepts. Bhutan has displayed political flexibility and a capacity for change, while sustaining its traditional way of life. *See also* BUDDHISM, p. 59; TIBET (XIZANG): CHINA, p. 42.

Significance   Bhutan's history before the sixteenth or seventeenth centuries is almost impossible to ascertain. The mountain kingdom tucked away in the Himalayas comprises 18,000 square miles, much of it unsuitable for human habitation. Central authority disintegrated when the country was divided by warring factions in the seventeenth century. British power penetrated the state in 1772 in search of a road that would be accessible from India to Lhasa in Tibet. Expeditions followed, and Britain ultimately brought Bhutan under its protection. Treaties in 1865 and 1910 gave the British viceroy in India control of the kingdom's external affairs. But the British pledged to respect the country's internal system and gave an annual allowance to the monarch. Britain in effect interposed itself between Bhutan and its primary enemy, China. Chinese claims to Bhutan were ended by the British action. Moreover, China was too weak to resist, and the relationship forged between the British and the Bhutanese remained intact until Britain granted India its independence. The Indian government sustained the relationship with Bhutan, and the British legacy there was perpetuated by subsequent Indian governments.

In 1949, India entered into its own treaty with Bhutan and took control of its external affairs but increased the size of the annual allowance and ceded a stretch of territory known as Dewangiri. In 1970, the first visit of an Indian president to Bhutan brought an agreement from India to sponsor Bhutan's admission to the United Nations, thus emphasizing Bhutan's sovereign status. Bhutan was admitted to the world body in 1971. India, however, remained a formidable power in Bhutan. The Indian Border Roads Commission completed hundreds of miles of roads throughout the kingdom and primary access to the country was from India. Chinese intentions toward Bhutan were more aggressive in the 1950s and early 1960s than in the 1970s and 1980s, but India maintained a strong armed force in the country and assisted the Bhutanese defense forces.

Continuing Indian-Chinese antagonism suggests India's intention to remain a dominant presence in Bhutan. India has retired its own princes and royal potentates and there can be little doubt that it seeks an end to kingship in Bhutan and possibly even in neighboring Nepal. Indeed, India played a significant role in promoting the displacement of the king of Sikkim, another Himalayan kingdom which was absorbed within the Indian Union in 1975.

Mandarins   High ranking government officials within the traditional imperial Chinese bureaucracy. The mandarins were all Confucian scholar-officials and represented the ruling gentry class in traditional China. Though limited in number, they were the powerful officials who manned the central government and were strategically positioned throughout the country to oversee government operations. The mandarins in traditional China were important decision makers and administrators. *See also* CONFUCIANISM, p. 75; GENTRY, p. 81; NEO-CONFUCIANISM, p. 105.

Significance   The Chinese people have been historically credited with the introduction of bureaucratic institutions. The mandarins were high government bureaucrats who were responsible for government operations. In modern democracies, elected politicians and political appointees in government are held responsible for the increasing scope and complexity of government activity. However, these individuals often lack technical expertise, knowledge, and the time needed to monitor government activities. The result has been an increasing reliance on the high ranking civil servants for decision making. This development has been referred to as the "mandarin" phenomenon. In contemporary China, party members who function as bureaucrats are sometimes referred to as mandarins.

Maoism   A collection of ideas developed by Mao Zedong (Mao Tse-tung). Mao's numerous writings have been collected in the *Selected Works of Mao Tse-tung*, but Maoism is not an integrated system of thought. Rather, it is a collection of ideas that Mao advanced to mobilize the peasants and to guide his followers in his revolutionary struggle for control of China. As a Communist revolutionary, Mao's theoretical indebtedness to Marxism and Leninism was undoubtedly great, but he was a nationalist before he became a Communist revolutionary. His primary revolutionary motivation was the recovery of China's lost glory, and he was willing to adapt Marxism-Leninism to the Chinese reality. The end product of this adaptation was some unique theoretical contributions to Marxism-Leninism.

Maoism stands for the mobilization of the peasants in the countryside and their transformation into a formidable revolutionary force. At the heart of Mao's thought is the concept of "mass-line," which means that all the policy decisions must follow the dictate of the masses and serve their interests, "from the masses, to the masses." To Mao, theory without practice is not only useless but also dangerous, because undue reliance on ideas produces dogmatism. For this reason, Mao emphasizes policy experimentation, flexibility, and useful knowledge. Mao's ideas of "contradiction" and "permanent revolution" are especially noteworthy. To Mao, life is full of contradictions: life/death, sun/moon, darkness/lightness, black/white, and individual/collective. Mao's indebtedness to Hegelian dialectics and Marxian dialectical materialism is clear, but his natural inclination to think in terms of harmony of opposites could be traced to the traditional Chinese concept of *yin* and *yang*. To Mao, these opposite forces of life are in constant struggle, but there are two different kinds of opposite forces: "antagonistic contradiction" and "non-antagonistic contradiction." In antagonistic contradiction, the one side must give way to the other, as in a struggle between "ourselves" and the enemy. In non-antagonistic contradiction, the struggle is within ourselves, and should be encouraged, in order to discover a harmonious whole. The continuous class struggle (permanent revolution) is to reach a higher level of proletarian consciousness and create the "new socialist man." *See also* ASIAN COMMUNISM, p. 54; COMMUNISM, p. 74.

Significance   The extent of Mao's theoretical contributions to Marxism and Leninism has been much debated. Mao was more a practical national revolutionary than a theoretician. He was neither scholar nor philosopher, but he understood Marxism and Leninism enough to speak the language of a Communist revolutionary. Hence, his theoretical task was to determine how to adapt Marxism/Leninism to the peasant Chinese society and mobilize the masses in its name. The resolution of this dilemma was the so-called Sinification of Marxism and Leninism. Through various revolutionary encounters, Mao enunciated practical solutions with some far-reaching impact. He demonstrated how the traditional peasant masses could be mobilized for a revolutionary cause, and he guided a successful revolutionary guerrilla war. His example has been emulated by others in the Third World.

Mao's mass-line idea has a democratic connotation. His idea of theory and practice accords with the writings of American pragmatists, such as John Dewey and William James. However, the core of Maoism is in the theory of contradiction and permanent revolution. As a revolutionary practitioner, Mao was realistic enough to acknowledge the permanence of contradiction in life and to emphasize a continuous struggle for human betterment, thus parting from the Marxian notion of the "struggleless utopia."

Militant Hinduism   An extreme form of contemporary Hinduism. Since the assassination of Indira Gandhi by Sikh extremists, Hinduism had been observed shifting to greater orthodoxy, verging on (if not wedded to) violence. Organizations like the Hindu Mahasabha and Jan Sangh have been notable for their ultraconservative platforms and programs. Mahatma Gandhi was felled by an R.S.S. militant shortly after independence. But the tide of Hindu fundamentalism apparently reached new intensity with the death of Mrs. Gandhi. Religious sectarianism is a more significant challenge to Indian secularism in 1985 than it was in 1947. Few nations in the contemporary world have religion so directly and so centrally intertwined with the lives of their citizens as does India. And although tensions between Indian religious communities can be traced to a period preceding independence, they have never been more serious. The growth of Hindu fanaticism is noted in the growing strength of the R.S.S. despite government crackdowns. Moreover, Mrs. Gandhi's party often sought the "Hindu" vote. By contrast, she was prepared to sacrifice the "Sikh" vote in attacking the Golden Temple. Furthermore, the sacking of the Kashmiri Chief Minister in 1984 seemed to imply she could also do without the "Muslim" vote. It is believed these actions reinforced the extremists, strengthened their determination, and convinced them of the righteousness of their cause. *See also* ELECTIONS: INDIA, p. 224; COMMUNALISM: SRI LANKA, p. 72; HINDUISM, p. 83; INDIAN NATIONAL CONGRESS, p. 159; INDIAN PEOPLE'S PARTY, p. 163; SIKHISM, p. 117; SUBCONTINENT, p. 38.

Significance   It is argued that Hindu militancy is a consequence of the disintegration of the old Congress party. Hindu fanaticism remained in check so long as the Congress party sustained a functioning coalition of otherwise disparate elements. Congress' collapse gave rise to personalized factions, the most prominent being that identified with the line of Jawaharlal Nehru and perpetuated by his daughter Indira. Indira's desire to see her son Sanjay succeed her, and following his premature death, her surviving nonpolitical son Rajiv, illustrates the personalized character of the dominant Congress (I). Moreover, the Indian (Hindu) electorate responded in the overwhelming affirmative to Rajiv's ascension of authority following the death of his mother at the hands of Sikh assassins. Hindu militants have as their raison d'être the belief that internal and external forces threaten the breakup of Hindustan. Despite Rajiv Gandhi's declarations that communalism will destroy India, there is little likelihood he will anatagonize those Hindu fundamentalists who have become some of his closest supporters.

Muslim   One who submits to the will of God, who believes that Mohammad is God's messenger, and who accepts the legal principles and obligations of the faith. *See also* AHMEDIYA, p. 53; ISLAM, p. 86; ISLAM (SHIITE), p. 86; ISLAM (SUNNI), p. 89; JAVANISM, p. 94.

Significance   Muslims are found in every part of the world. All Muslims believe in One God, Allah, but their practices vary. The two major groups of Muslims are identified by the words "Sunni" and "Shiite," with Sunni Muslims the more numerous. Sunni Muslims and Shiite Muslims are further divided into different groups, and strains exist between Sunni and Shiite Muslims, as well as within each classification. Although Islam preaches community, and Muslims are called upon to practice unity and brotherhood, violent divisions have characterized the Muslim world from its inception to contemporary times.

Nationalism   The desire of a people to be united as an independent, sovereign state for the betterment of their lives. Nationalism has been one of the great forces that has helped shape the modern world, uniting people in the name of their nation-state, but it defies any precise definition. Nationalism is loosely equated with the concept of self-determination and is identified historically with the search for linguistic and ethnic self-determination. The expression of nationhood is essentially a product of the modern era and has been associated with the rise of modern nation-states, initially in England and then in Europe from the sixteenth and seventeenth centuries. Subsequently, it has spread to the rest of the world. It has had particularly great impact on colonial and semi-colonial Asia. Asian nationalism is anti-colonial but not necessarily anti-western. The Asian people, in order to determine their own destiny, seek to build independent, sovereign states. *See also* COLONIALISM, p. 63; DEVELOPMENT, p. 297; MODERNIZATION, p. 313.

Significance   Nationalism has been a powerful force in Asia since about the turn of the century. In one sense, this has meant rediscovery and renaissance of self-identity. In another sense, nationalism has meant rejection of western dominance. It has been identified with anti-colonial and anti-imperial movements and has become a powerful motivating force for modernization and development. Nationalism in Asia has emerged in a complex global environment characterized by western colonialism and dominance, as a response to inequities in the division of the world's wealth and power.

Neo-Confucianism   A synthesis of Confucianism with Buddhism and Taoism during the Sung (Song) (960–1279 A.D.) dynasty. Neo-Confucianism is also known as Chu Hsi (Zhu Xi) (1130–1200 A.D.) Confucianism. Many schools flourished in the revival and reinterpretation of Confucianism during the late T'ang (Tang) and Sung periods, but the Chu Hsi school became most influential and replaced all the others as the orthodox school of Confucianism. Chu Hsi elevated the impersonal, ethical, and social doctrines of Confucianism to the realm of metaphysics. According to Chu Hsi, every natural object has an essence, or *Li,* which is an aspect of Supreme Ultimate. This Ultimate is manifested in *Ch'i* (Qi), that is, matter. While matter changes, the Ultimate remains unaltered. All material things go through a cycle of creation and decay but not the Ultimate. In the field of ethics, Chu Hsi followed Mencius' interpretation of Confucian teachings and held that Li, or the essence of humankind, was intrinsically good. However, Li must be cultivated through formal education and self-enlightenment. Chu Hsi emphasized the importance of the family and stressed the state as an extension of the family. He also emphasized the importance of government by the enlightened and benevolent ruler. *See also* BUDDHISM, p. 59; CONFUCIANISM, p. 75; TAOISM, p. 121.

Significance   Confucianism became the state creed of the Chinese Han dynasty (206 B.C.–220 A.D.). After the collapse of the Han dynasty, however, its influence declined and people increasingly turned to Buddhism and Taoism (Daoism) for personal salvation. Many Confucian scholars became Buddhists and Taoists (Daoists). Under the T'ang and the Sung dynasty, the appeal of Confucianism to Chinese intellectuals revived, and the popularity of Buddhism and Taoism declined. The serious study of Confucian classics, however, caused many different interpretations. Chu Hsi was regarded as the greatest synthesizer of the different schools of Confucianism at the time and his commentaries on the Confucian teachings became the neo-Confucian orthodoxy which lasted until modern times. It was this neo-Confucianism that became widespread in other parts of East Asia such as Korea, Japan, and Vietnam. Neo-Confucianism concerned itself more with the metaphysical state than did the original teachings of Confucius. Its interpretation of Li, the essence of all things, was influenced by Buddhism and the Indian religion in general. Given its metaphysical depth, Confucianism became more than a code of ethics; it became a philosophy and was widely accepted by religiously oriented people. It underwent several different interpretations which led to irreconcilable disputes, as well as division among the Confucian scholar-officials.

Nomads and Hill People   The hills of Southeast Asia between the Irrawaddy, Salween, Ping, and Mekong rivers to the northern mountain peaks of the Himalayas and through northern India, Tibet, and southern China is the setting for a variety of nomadic, tribal orders. The major groups are the Chin, Kachin, Karen, Meo, Yao, Lahu, Lsu, and Akha who inhabit territories in Thailand, Burma, and Laos. Although often described as "tribal minorities," the nomads and hill people of these countries are far more prominent than the term suggests. Forty percent of the population of Burma is made up of tribal hill people, and Laos is primarily populated by uplanders. Thailand may be only 5 percent tribal, but those tribes inhabit approximately 60 percent of the northern area of the country. Until recent times these people were seldom known to leave their remote hills. They are easily distinguished by their dress but not their physical characteristics from the lowland Thai, Burmese, and Laotians in whose proximity they dwell. The nomads and hill people of this region live on land too difficult for paddy cultivation and along non-navigable streams. Their activities are therefore isolated from the major communities and they commune primarily with the nature that surrounds them. As a consequence of their isolation, the languages of the hill people are different from those of the Thai, Burmese, and Lao, although relationships can be discerned.

In the bamboo villages of the nomads and hill people of Southeast Asia, little attention is given to the ornate temples of the more settled populations. There is a hint of Hindu belief among the tribal folk but Buddhism is almost ignored. The monkist life of the general region is not found among these numerous tribes. The hill people practice a different form of cultivation than that of the larger population. Slash and burn techniques and a shifting agricultural setting are more in keeping with the terrain, despite the criticism that they destroy the land and accelerate erosion. The destruction of forests has caused the loss of topsoil and hence soil nutrients. This, coupled with an expanding population, has compounded the problems of the hill people and has caused worry in the more settled regions of the country, which are also affected by these pronounced changes in the ecology. *See also* ASIAN RACES, p. 55; TRIBALISM, p. 125.

Significance   It is argued that the hills are so densely populated that patterns of migration are no longer feasible. The lowlands are also overcrowded and offer virtually no opportunity for the resettlement of the tribal people. The separation between the hill people and the lowland settlers is therefore likely to be permanent. The essential dilemma is that the lowlands depend on the highlands, and the increasing impoverishment of the hill people does not promise a better relationship with the lowlanders. The one significant cash crop open to the hill people is the opium poppy which they grow on ridges 3,500 to 5,000 feet above sea level. This is the region known as the "Golden Triangle," and it yields raw opium in excess of 1,000 tons a year. Although illegal in Thailand, prevention is almost impossible given the inaccessibility of the hills. Moreover, there are lowlanders who eagerly await the shipments of opium, and they are not about to discourage the hill people from growing the plant.

The entire economy of Laos could collapse if the opium trade were terminated. The Burmese government is in a weak position to deal with the problem, again because the terrain that must be patrolled is too difficult for adequate management. The Meo and Yao of Thailand, like the other tribes of the area, receive only the smallest fraction of the profits from this trade, but it is far more than the tribesmen could expect to receive from other commodities, and they are reluctant to change their practices. Opium addiction is pervasive among the tribes and causes debilitation and a variety of ailments. Nevertheless, the hill people have maintained a significant warrior character, although not considered a warlike folk. Where they can no longer retreat into a deeper part of the jungle, they have been known to fight for the maintenance of their way of life. They have played a significant role in the history of their region. Representing about 40 percent of the population of Burma, the hill people have subdued more elaborate kingdoms in the lowlands.

In the aftermath of World War II, Karen forces almost seized the Burmese capital of Rangoon. The Meo tribesmen were recruited by the United States Central Intelligence Agency during the Indochina War. Some Meo also fought with the North Vietnamese against the Americans and their South Vietnamese allies. The Naga hill people of northeastern India fought a costly war against the regular Indian army in the 1950s and 1960s, finally succumbing to the greater firepower of the government forces.

Oriental Despotism   A theory of total power and control that relates to the mode of production in a society. This concept was publicized by Karl Wittfogel in a book titled *Oriental Despotism* (1957). Wittfogel's treatise explores the subject of total power. Another term for

"Oriental Despotism," according to the author, is "hydraulic society," by which he means societies absolutely dependent on irrigated agriculture. Wittfogel deemphasizes geographic Asia in order to describe an Asian mode of production. Hydraulic societies can be compared with feudal societies and industrial societies. Thus the Asian mode of production, or hydraulic societies, can be found in other areas of the world, not simply Asia. Wittfogel's assumption, however, is that hydraulic societies have their origin in Asia and were most developed there. Such societies require centralized, highly bureaucratized power structures to build, operate, and maintain the essential waterworks. The mobilization of large numbers of people, and their direction by powerful administrators, gives rise to managerial systems of enormous power, as in China, India, and Egypt.

Society's dependence on abundant agriculture, coupled with peasant weakness, explains the existence of agrodespotic states, which Wittfogel insists, are different from the feudal states of European experience. He associates medieval European feudalism with rain-fed agriculture, which is described as a system of decentralized agrarian units, each relatively self-sufficient and characterized by countervailing and complementary powers. Bureaucracies are not found in European feudalism, but in Asian hydraulic societies they monopolize power and its uses. Wittfogel believes private property emerged in institutional form in Europe because climatic and topographic conditions influenced a unique form of ecological development. The Asian experience demanded a strategic approach to the question of agricultural production, and the result was government dominance over the land, the people, and the product of their labor.

Significance   Wittfogel applies his thesis to contemporary times, and argues that the Soviet Union is a marginal hydraulic society and that its use of power is more clearly a function of oriental despotism than Marxist socialism or communism. The Chinese example is perhaps more obvious, but Wittfogel is intent on destroying Moscow's claim to being the citadel of Marxist revolution. In the pursuit of this argument, Wittfogel revives Marx's fear of an "Asian Restoration," so-called communist revolutions that occur out of phase, that is, before they have passed through specific stages of pre-revolutionary activity. Communist revolution in the still "backward" states of Asia, Marx warned, would only play into the hands of entrenched authority. The institution of bureaucracy may be altered in nomenclature and personnel by changes in leadership, but the historically functional bureaucrats will remain and so will their powers.

Following Marx, Wittfogel rejects the Soviet Union's "communist revolution" and cites the strengthening of autocratic power in the post-tsarist state. Soviet ideologists, almost thirty years before the publication of the Wittfogel thesis (1957), rejected the concept of oriental society. But as late as 1950, Soviet scholars were still agitated by the theory and seized the appropriate moment to declare "the rout of the notorious theory of the Asiatic mode of production." Nevertheless even this proclamation could not erase Lenin's published statement in 1906–07 that the next Russian revolution may well produce an Asian Restoration rather than the anticipated socialist society. Lenin considered the thought that the Soviet Union was an Asian country and was influenced by East Asian experiences (notably the Mongols who dominated Russia between the thirteenth and fifteenth centuries), long before it began to borrow and adapt western ideas and institutions. On this point, western scholars seem to agree. They further suggest that in 1917 Russia had the choice of opting for its adopted European experience, or continuing its Asian tradition.

Panch Sila: India   The Five Principles of Peaceful Coexistence around which early Sino-Indian relations were developed. *Panch Sila* or *Panch Sheel* signifies (1) mutual respect for each other's territorial integrity; (2) mutual nonaggression; (3) mutual noninterference in each other's internal affairs; (4) equality and mutual benefit; and (5) peaceful coexistence. Although a fundamental aspect of proclaimed Indian foreign policy, Panch Sila can be traced to clauses in the United Nations Charter as well as Chinese and Soviet statements of mutual friendship and cooperation to Asian nations. Indian leaders have referred to Panch Sila as though it were part of ancient Hindu and Buddhist tradition. Whatever its origin, Asian governments have come to look upon Panch Sila as the cornerstone of their countries' foreign policies. Repeated use of the term in official government communiques, treaties, and other documents has given a certain sanctity to the concept. Violations of the principles have not altered the reverence which some Asian nations pay to the term. Panch Sila is more a guideline for interstate behavior than a prescription for amicable and cooperative relations. *See also* BANDUNG CONFERENCE, p. 328; NONALIGNED MOVEMENT, p. 348.

Significance   *Panch Sila* has been the central theme of Indian foreign policy from independence to the present. It provided moral justification for India'a decision to avoid direct involvement in disputes engaging the superpowers. The policy of nonalignment which India has helped develop into a worldwide phenomenon, and which prompted the creation of the Nonaligned Movement, can be attributed in major part to the efforts of India's leaders from Nehru to his daughter, Indira Gandhi. India sought to lead the Third World away from superpower-sponsored military alliances and toward a more neutral role in international politics. In large measure, India was guided in its actions by the spirit of Mahatma Gandhi and his movement of nonviolence. India's overall purpose was to influence the developing nations to follow a course emphasizing cooperation and accommodation rather than rivalry and conflict. Panch Sila was considered realistic policy-making and in the nonaligned country's national interest. Neither India nor the other Third World nations that joined it in proclaiming the importance of Panch Sila could steer away from conflict. Panch Sila could not insulate India from a Chinese invasion in 1962. However, the doctrine of Panch Sila, despite numerous lapses, continued to stand as moral doctrine as well as a test of good relations between Third World states.

Pantasila: Indonesia   Principles of Indonesian self-government. Japan's conquest of the Dutch East Indies during World War II provided the Indonesians with their first serious governmental responsibilities. In 1944, under pressure to evacuate the East Indies, the Japanese announced their intention to declare Indonesia's full independence. The Japanese organized a small Indonesian army (*Peta*), which they placed under indigenous command. The purpose of Peta was internal security, but it soon became the nucleus for a revolutionary Indonesian army which ultimately fought the Japanese, the British, and finally the Dutch, before the country acquired its independence in 1949. Sukarno, an officer in the Peta, led the Japanese-sponsored assembly of religious, ethnic, and social groups which convened in Madura on the island of Java in March 1945. Sukarno sought to bridge differences between the religious and secular factions in the Indonesian nationalist movement. It was Sukarno who put forth the Pantasila, or five principles of reconciliation and national unity. The five principles were adopted as the philosophical foundation for the Indonesian revolution and specified the following: nationalism, humanitarianism, representative government, social justice, and belief in God (with emphasis on religious freedom). Sukarno's vision of a free Indonesia included all the islands of the Dutch East Indies. He noted Indonesia's diversity but insisted that the concepts of representative government and social justice were broad enough to provide all groups with a voice, as well as the means, to satisfy their aspirations. The emphasis on religious freedom was meant to neutralize Muslim nationalists whose demand for an Islamic state terrified the minorities. *See also* ARCHIPELAGO, p. 5; COLONIALISM: NETHERLANDS, p. 67; CONFRONTATION STRATEGIES, p. 378.

Significance   Pantasila was put into operation on August 7, 1945 when the Japanese established an All-Indonesia Preparatory Committee and made Sukarno its chairman. The Sumatran leader, Mohammad Hatta, was named vice-chairman. The imminent defeat of the Japanese, however, short-circuited plans to transfer power to the Indonesians. Realizing the need to act, Sukarno and Hatta decided to declare the independence of Indonesia on August 17, 1945. Following the declaration, fighting erupted between the Peta and the Japanese occupiers. Sukarno was determined to control Java and Sumatra before the allied forces landed on the islands and the Dutch demanded the restoration of their former colony. The British were the first to arrive, and after finding the Sukarno administration in charge, they pressured the Dutch to negotiate a settlement with their former wards.

In 1946, the Netherlands and Sukarno's government signed the Linggadjati Agreement which acknowledged the *de facto* independence of Java and Sumatra. In July 1947, however, the Dutch violated the treaty by attacking Indonesian forces. The Dutch intended to reestablish control over the East Indies but the Indonesians put up an effective resistance and the United States was forced to intervene. Through the good offices of the United States, the two sides entered into the Renville Agreement which called for a ceasefire and the later holding of a plebiscite to determine the future rulers of the islands. The Dutch had no intention of keeping this agreement, and their actions drove many Indonesians to support the Indonesian Communist Party (PKI). The Communists claimed they could better insure Indonesia's independence. Sukarno fought the PKI and the Dutch simultaneously, but there were no decisive battles. After several inconclusive but costly campaigns, the Dutch finally realized that contining the struggle was futile. On November 2, 1949, Indonesia's independence was recognized in return for guarantees protecting Dutch economic interests. The PKI, however, was a strong adversary, and Sukarno's attack on the Islamic religious parties gave it the opportunity to make a future play for power. For the foreseeable future, Pantasila seemed a better guide to action for the Marxists than the nationalists.

Parsis Originating in Persia (Iran), these followers of Zoroaster are the Aryan cousins of the Indo-Aryans. Zoroastrianism teaches a qualified dualism in which Ahrumazda (God) is in conflict with Ahriman (Satan). Although both God and Satan coexist, Parsis believe that God ultimately triumphs over Satan at the end of time. Humankind is caught up in this struggle, and human suffering is inevitable, indeed fully justified in order to defeat Satan. The Parsis follow fixed rituals and are often described as "fire worshippers." Most prominent in India and Pakistan where they number less than half a million, they arrived from Persia (Iran) in the eighth century A.D., seeking to avoid persecution and conversion to Islam. In their social customs they are neither Indian nor European, preferring to live in close-knit communities and adhering to strict inbreeding. Because proselytism is not practiced, Parsis avoid the anger of the majority communities and adequately protect the welfare of their members.

Significance   The Parsis are prominent in India, and to a lesser extent in Pakistan, far beyond their numbers. Given their emphasis on education, their care for one another, and their peculiar industry, the Parsis wield economic power and display a public spirit of unusual dimension. The Parsis are credited with the construction of the Jamshedpur-Asansol industrial zone in Indian Bengal. They were central to the development of Bombay. In Pakistan they helped transform Karachi from a minor sea resort to a major banking and industrial center. Shipbuilding, steel, chemicals, jute, and banking, as well as general commerce, are associated with the Parsis.

Patron-Client Relationship   An informal system of interaction between two parties unequal in status, wealth, and influence, based on reciprocity in the exchange of goods and services. The patron-client relationship depends on personal favor. Patrons possess the goods and services to be distributed, and the clients who receive these goods and services are expected to satisfy the patrons' needs. Patrons and clients cooperate in order to maximize their mutual benefits in the utilization of their assets. Asian countries make effective use of the patron-client relationship in domestic and foreign policy. *See also* DEMOCRACY: JAPAN, p. 220; PRISMATIC SOCIETY, p. 316; TRADITIONAL SOCIETY, p. 332.

Significance   Patron-client relationships exist in all human interactions, but the political systems of developing nations particularly depend on this relationship in which entrepreneurs, political leaders, and bureaucrats play a major role. In the developing nations, job security and political and bureaucratic positions are largely based on a special relationship between those who bestow favors and those who receive them in exchange for their services and loyalty. At the top of the pyramid in this relationship there exists a set of major networks that include the presidency, the bureaucracy, the military, and the business leaders. The developing political system has the necessary number of sinecures to ensure the political support which the ruling elites need in order to sustain their economic and political control of the country. In the developed political system, however, a job or promotion is largely based on what one does for the organization, not necessarily for one's immediate superior. The distribution of favors or punishments is likewise based on set rules and regulations, not on personal relationships or favors. The enduring quality of patron-client interpersonal relationships in the Asian context is manifest in contemporary Japan, which is highly developed and modern, but where personal favors, support, and loyalty are still highly valued.

Political Culture: Indonesia   The blend of historical tradition, values, and practices that underpin and continue to influence the political thought and behavior of the people of Indonesia. Indonesian political culture centers on the self-contained village, a microcosm of the ordered universe. The idea of *mana* has been the driving ancestral force behind the community and sustained by ritual and ceremony providing the village with meaning and protection. Here, political life is intertwined with economic needs and performance, religious expression, and magical incantations and spells. The synergistic relationship between the parts projects a totality that is both reassuring and uplifting. Everything has its place and each component interacts with and relates to the others.

This elaborate belief system required a hierarchy of spiritual divines, the *shaman*, who wielded great temporal as well as spiritual powers. The shamans were the perceived link to the village's ancestral spirits, the ultimate holders of the community's mana and destiny. The dominance of the shamans was affirmed in cultural practices and expression. The fixing of inferior-superior relationships was perpetuated in a body of customs and legal arrangements known as *adat*. Adat was the traditional law guiding the people and it included a broad variety of activities, such as ceremonies at birth, marriage, and death, how and when to plant and harvest rice, construct homes, or prepare food. Virtually nothing escaped ritualization, neither politics, commerce, nor religion. The power of the local leader, the continuing importance of mana, and the always present adat influence Indonesian life to the present day, despite the overlaying of other cultures in subsequent centuries. *See also* BAHASA INDONESIA, p. 57; JAVANISM, p. 94.

Significance   The Indonesians have been slow to change from within. The power of *adat*, customary law, sustained a way of thinking and a mode or life in which innovation was frowned upon, and internal change was limited. Alien forces therefore monopolized the process of change. In the first century A.D., Indian traders and missionaries superimposed Hinduism on the indigenous population. Indonesian beliefs were systematized and more securely structured by Hindu practices.

The *shaman* became an even more potent figure, similar to the Indonesian *mana* and the Hindu *karma*. The hierarchical character of the

Hindu system suited the shaman, whose power swelled with the broadening of the political base. The Hindu traders, however, held sway over the larger region, forming aristocracies and feudal kingdoms that drew the scattered villages into a network of relationships. The Hindu rulers were careful not to interfere with local tradition or disturb the functioning of adat. During this period, Buddhism also established a foothold in the Indonesian archipelago, and a Buddhist university was erected at Palembang that drew scholars from all over Southeast Asia. The most successful Hindu kingdom in Indonesia was the Majapahit which flourished from the thirteenth century to the sixteenth century until Muslim invaders overwhelmed it. Hindu feudalism came to an end with this event, and the highly ascriptive and stratified Hindu order was replaced by the comparatively more progressive teachings of Islam.

When the Europeans brought Christianity to the islands in the seventeenth century the archipelago was firmly in Muslim hands, and only Bali retained the Hindu traditions of its past. Islam broke the hold of the traditional leaders, and to a large extent, even that of the village shaman. Nevertheless, the resiliency of adat spoke to the people in terms of headmen, and local leaders continued their guardianship of the village community. Neither Islamic order nor subsequent Dutch European rule could do more than modify a way of life that had been nurtured through the ages. Adat remained a part of Indonesian political culture despite the influence of external borrowings and practices.

Samurai   The warriors who constituted the military ruling class in feudal Japan. The *samurai* class evolved from the practice of traditional landowning clan chiefs recruiting armed retainers to protect their domains. The samurais sometimes held their own land, but more often, they helped to oversee the estates of their lords in peacetime and fought as warriors in times of strife. In return they received their lord's protection and patronage. Eventually evolving into a distinct class, they were known for their swordsmanship, strict code of behavior, and loyalty to their lords. Once samurai status was attained, it became hereditary.

The samurai class wielded unrestricted power over the rest of the population. They maintained law and order and sustained the status quo in feudal Japan. Their traditional code of behavior, later called *bushido* or "the way of the warrior," stressed honor, justice, faithfulness and loyalty to their lords, and the simplicity of life. In feudal Japan, the samurai's ascendancy to power coincided with the decline of Chinese influence and, given their place in traditional Japanese society, they made Japan unique in the history of East Asia. *See also* MEIJI RESTORATION, p. 310; TOKUGAWA FEUDALISM: JAPAN, p. 123.

Significance   In feudal Japan, competition for power was strong, and contestants for power were many. Especially after 1333, Japan plunged into a civil war until the country was unified first by Oda Nobunaga, then by Toyotomi Hideyoshi, and lastly, by Tokugawa Ieyasu. It was under Hideyoshi that samurai was made a distinct class. In 1586, Hideyoshi froze everyone in his profession by decree; thereby creating the four distinct classes: (1) samurai; (2) peasants; (3) artisans; and (4) merchants. It was also Hideyoshi who drew a distinct line between the privileged samurai class and the rest of the population, or commoners, by carrying out a "sword hunt" (1587) to disarm the commoners. Only the samurai were permitted to wear swords, and they were feared by the commoners. In peacetime, however, the samurais were more than warriors; they became the hereditary ruling class performing many governing functions, while honoring their strict code of behavior. It was this samurai governing class that brought about the Meiji Restoration in 1868 and guided Japan's modernization process.

Shintoism   A religion which has been identified, in its origin and development, with the Japanese people. Shintoists worship the way of *kami* (spirits or deities) who are believed to have helped create the land and the people of Japan and who have themselves been manifest in many natural and human forms. The *Kojiki* (Record of Ancient Things, 712 A.D.) and the *Nihonshoki* (Chronicles of Japan, 720 A.D.), both written in Chinese characters, are the two principal written sources of information about early Japanese beliefs and customs. Both are full of myths, legends, and events which tend to buttress the legitimacy and prestige of the ruling king and his clan as descendants of the divine founders who created the land and people of Japan. Prominent among these divine ancestors of Japan is the sun goddess, *Amaterasu-o-mi-kami*. In Shintoism, Kami, which are present in humans as well as in natural objects, are awe-inspiring and outside the ordinary. They signify the deities of heaven and earth. They are present in birds, beasts, trees, plants, seas, mountains, and rocks. They are also present in good and evil. Among the kami are the successive generations of emperors, who have been regarded as sacred and awe-inspiring personages.

The Shinto worship of nature and the imperial family existed in ancient Japan. In the course of development, however, its rituals and institutions have been strongly influenced by Buddhism and Confucianism. The central focus in Shintoism, however, has remained the direct appreciation of nature rather than the development of a complicated doctrine and abstract philosophy. Shinto is a way of life for the Japanese people who believe in the omnipresence of kami as the source of life and blessings and as the object of thanksgiving. In prewar Japan, Shinto was blended into an authoritarian political system, and it became Japan's state religion. In order to differentiate Shinto as Japan's state religion from the Shinto practice in everyday life, Shinto was divided in

1882 into Shrine Shinto, often refered to as State Shinto, and Sect Shinto, the traditional native religion. In prewar Japan, State Shinto became the official cult sponsored by the government for the purpose of inspiring in the Japanese people single-minded obedience and loyalty to the emperor, and through him, to the state. The Meiji constitution of 1889, which was superseded only by the present post-World War II constitution, stated in its preamble that the emperor, "Having, by virtue of the glories of Our Ancestors, ascended the Throne of a lineal succession unbroken for ages eternal. . . ." When Japan was defeated in World War II, Shinto was disestablished as Japan's state religion. *See also* CON-FUCIANISM, p. 75; MEIJI RESTORATION, p. 310; NEO-CONFUCIANISM, p. 105.

Significance   Shinto has grown out of prehistoric Japanese animistic beliefs and practices, but its unique institutional expressions may be regarded as a major contribution to the history of religion by the Japanese people. It is indebted to Buddhism and Confucianism, but its distinctive contribution has been in the blending of native Japanese religion with foreign elements, creating one great national tradition. Particularly since the Meiji Restoration (1868), which established Japan as a modern state, abandoning the traditional feudal system and incorporating the characteristics of the modern western political systems of the time, Shintoism merged with the Japanese state system as the state religion.

The fusion of Shintoism with the Meiji political system resulted in state support of Shintoism and the glorification of the imperial family as the head of the Japanese people. Under this system, the people became imperial subjects. The emperor, sacred and inviolable, was "kami." He was to govern the people with care and love, as head of the empire. In the educational rescript of 1890, the Japanese people were asked to "be filial to your parents, affectionate to your brothers and sisters; as husbands and wives be harmonious, as friends true; bear yourselves in modesty and moderation; extend your benevolence to all; pursue learning and cultivate arts, and thereby develop your intellectual faculties and perfect your moral powers; furthermore, advance the public good and promote common interest; always respect the Constitution and observe the laws; should any emergency arise, offer yourselves courageously to the State; and thus guard and maintain the prosperity of Our Imperial Throne, coeval with heaven and earth." The effect of this kind of educational emphasis was shown in part in the nationalistic frenzy of the Japanese people in the pre–World War II years and in the Japanese soldiers who were willing to die for their emperor. Although Shinto was disestablished as the state religion following Japan's defeat in World War II, it still has followers who practice the beliefs and rituals traditionally associated with it.

Sikhism   A major religion of India. Sikhism is a consequence of the interaction between Hinduism and Islam in South Asia. Its origins may be identified in the *Bhakti,* or new faith movement, with its emphasis on monotheism that passed through the subcontinent from the eleventh to the sixteenth century. The founder of Sikhism, Guru Nanak, a fifteenth-century figure of the Punjab, was influenced by Bhakti. The Punjab had already experienced a long period of Muslim rule. Muslim *Sufi* or mystical orders, such as the Chisti, Suhrawardy, Qadiri, and Naqshbandi had established their presence in the region. Their saintly ways impacted on the Hindus of the Punjab as well as on the Muslims. Sufism and Bhakti each brought the individual worshipper into closer personal association with God. But it was Guru Nanak (1469–1538) who became the founder of Sikhism. Nanak was born a Hindu of the *Kshatriya* caste but adopted the wandering life of an ascetic at the prompting of a Muslim sufi. Leaving his family behind, he moved through the length of India to Ceylon and is believed to have visited the Muslim holy sites in Mecca and Medina on the Arabian peninsula. His final years were spent in the Punjab where he founded a "Sikh" village, in which his teachings laid the foundation for the Sikh faith. God is at the center of Nanak's teaching, and his work forms the heart of the Sikh faith today. He taught that humankind is of little consequence and is nothing unless identified with the Eternal.

Sikhism developed as an offshoot of Hinduism but soon became a blend of Islam and Hinduism, and in its ultimate expression was neither of them. Nanak called upon his disciples and followers to reject the ascetic life in favor of active involvement, and Sikhism from his day to the present describes a distinctive way of life and worship that emphasizes personal achievement, as well as societal development. Caste and other Hindu rituals and institutions ceased to have meaning for Sikhs as they went about creating a common lifestyle and emphasized cooperative and shared endeavor. The holy scripture of the Sikhs is the Granth, and the Adi Granth, or first book, is a compilation of the hymns and sayings of Nanak and his successors. Sikhs revere the Granth with the same intensity that Muslims show the Qur'an. Sikhism developed a distinctive language, scripture, ritual, and collective society or community. It therefore developed characteristics that separated it from both Hinduism and Islam. Most scholars have argued, however, that the separation from Islam was more complete than that from Hinduism. The conversion of Hindus to Sikhism was also far greater than from Islam. Moreover, given Muslim Moghul power that held sway over the subcontinent in this period, the Sikhs often found themselves in coalition with Hindus against the reigning power.

The Sikhs assumed a warrior role in the latter part of the seventeenth century. In 1699 the *Sikh Khalsa,* or brotherhood of fighting Sikhs, was established and the five signs distinguishing Sikhs from Hindus and

Muslims was institutionalized. They are to this day (1) the uncut hair and beard; (2) the turban; (3) the ceremonial dagger; (4) the wearing of undershorts; and (5) the arm bracelet. The fighting Sikhs were given the name Singh. They drank from the same bowl and were promised entry into paradise by dying in the cause of their faith and community. Sikhs have been taught to recognize the *Khalsa* in the *Guru* or spiritual leader. Thus the principal institutions of Sikhism were: the institution of the Guru, the *Granth Sahib* or holy book, and the brotherhood of Sikhs. The intertwining of the three institutions places great importance on the dominant gurus who lead, protect, and provide wisdom to the larger community through succeeding generations. *See also* AKALI DAL, p. 133; HINDUISM, p. 83; MILITANT HINDUISM, p. 103.

Significance   The solidarity of the Sikh community and its demonstrative militancy was illustrated during the rule of Ranjit Singh (1780–1839), the founder of a Sikh empire. Ranjit Singh credited God with his success and stressed the collective personality, the *Khalsa* or commonwealth of all Sikhs. Religious belief was inextricably linked with political power, the one reinforcing the other. Although thwarted in pressing his Pan-Sikhism objectives by the British, the institutions established in an earlier period remained strong, especially the preservation and strengthening of the community of believers. The British military recruitment policy in India sustained the esprit of the Sikh Khalsa. The Sikhs were a significant element in the British Indian Army and proved to be a formidable instrument of British rule, especially during the Mutiny of 1857. The British did their utmost to preserve the Sikh character and distinctiveness, and Sikh traditions and conventions were an asset rather than a hindrance in promoting discipline in the colonial forces.

The Sikh Akali Movement, which sought to purify Sikh customs and redefine Sikh power in the late nineteenth and early part of the twentieth century, was also aided by the British, in part because the Sikhs proved to be loyal subjects. The Sikhs provided the British with needed leverage in dealing with the Hindus on one side, and the Muslims on the other. The Akali Movement, apart from establishing its right to control the Sikh temples, was a political organization. And in the context of the political struggle for independence between World Wars I and II, the Akali Sikhs sought to represent the Sikhs of the Punjab, and they insisted on the creation of a separate Sikh state or *Khalistan*. Although this demand was denied the Sikhs when India and Pakistan achieved statehood in 1947, the idea of Sikh separateness remained. In subsequent years, Sikh militancy resurfaced, and the leaders of independent India were called upon to answer Sikh demands for a separate *suba* or assembly. Demands for greater Sikh autonomy finally caused the Indian government to divide the Indian Punjab into a separate Sikh state and another Hindu dominant state which was named Hariana. This gesture did not satisfy the more militant Sikhs who continued to dream of a separate homeland. Discontent among the Sikhs burst through the surface calm in 1981 when extremists seized an Indian commercial airliner and forced it to fly to Lahore in Pakistan. Although the Pakistan government foiled the hijackers, the event dramatized the Sikh cause and it grew in intensity in 1982–83.

In 1984, terrorists, allegedly Sikh militants, committed acts of arson, sabotage, and assassination. Operating from Amritsar's Golden Temple, the centerpiece of Sikhism, numerous attacks were made on Indian government installations and personnel, and members of the Hindu community. With the intensification of violence in 1984 the Gandhi government lost patience with the Sikh militants. On June 6, 1984 special units of the Indian army invaded the compound of the Golden Temple as well as other religious sanctuaries throughout Punjab state. The Akali Dal contingents resisted the invasion and in the ensuing battles, hundreds, possibly more than one thousand, were killed. Several weeks earlier, Sikh protestors publicly burned a section of the Indian constitution which grouped Sikhs with Hindus. Sikh condemnation of idolatry, their distinctive religion and appearance, it was argued, entitled them to a separate existence, free from Hindu threats. The Akali Dal, the Sikh political organization, used that occasion to demand even greater autonomy for the state government. In addition, the Akali Dal wanted a more substantial distribution of the river water for the Sikh state, the transfer of Chandigarh, the joint capital of the Punjab and Hariana, to the Punjab alone, and a declaration by the New Delhi government that Amritsar was a holy city and therefore off-limits to central government authority. The June 1984 attack on the Akali Dal in their sacred and holiest shrines added new dimensions to Hindu-Sikh antagonism.

Sikh extremists at home and abroad publicized their anger and promised to destroy Prime Minister Gandhi. On October 31, 1984 this pledge was fulfilled when Mrs. Gandhi was shot in her own compound by Sikh guards who had been entrusted with her safety. Her assassination ignited an explosion in numerous areas of the country, but nowhere was it so destructive as in the Indian capital. Dispossessed communities of Hindus like the Gujjars, Chamars, and farmers, finding the administration on their side, joined with elements of the Youth Congress (I), and together they unleashed a campaign of terror and revenge against the New Delhi Sikhs. Murder, torture, and arson could not be quelled without the support of the army, and hundreds perished in the carnage before law and order was restored. Sikh anguish was deep and possibly irreversible. In more than 300 years the Sikh community had never experienced such direct assault by Hindus upon its faithful or its way of life. As Indian commentators pointed out, "for the first time the Sikhs have seen that the Hindus can riot not only against Muslims, but against them as well. Suddenly they feel that they are a minority of only two percent in the country.... Therefore the faith of the Sikhs in the Hindus has been lost."

Socialism   A general term that describes economic doctrines favoring the collective well-being of society over that of private property and individual entrepreneurship. Applied socialism covers a wide spectrum of programs, from the mixed economy in which free enterprise remains dominant, to total collectivization in which the state controls all economic endeavor. Socialism developed in reaction to the excesses of capitalism during the industrial revolution of the late eighteenth and nineteenth centuries. Communism emerged during the same period, and although related to socialism, the former is distinguished by its more radical doctrine. Socialism can coexist with capitalism, both in theory and in practice. Theoretical communism leaves no room for capitalism. Pragmatic communism, an expression of Marxism-Leninism, assumes a condition of peaceful coexistence with capitalism during the gestation of dialectical forces. *See also* COMMUNISM, p. 74; MILITARY AUTHORITARIANISM, p. 289.

Significance   Socialism has been verbalized in most Asian countries, but policy making skirts the central goal of socialism, that is, closing the gap between haves and have-nots. Socialism describes the need for public ownership of utilities and industries critical to the development of society, and to some extent that objective has been realized in socialist countries. Social welfare, the providing of material assistance to the needy and deprived, and a key objective of socialist programs, has not enjoyed the same success. Public corporations and national planning, the pragmatic aspects of socialism, have also gained importance. Asian nations, however, have yet to examine the corrosion of personality or the limitations of bureaucracy in the socialist state. This failure to come to grips with entrenched historical institutions that insulate the few against the many, reduces the effectiveness of socialist programs.

Nevertheless, the multidimensional nature of socialism, and particularly its broad adaptability, permit its merger with more traditional conceptions of human belief and organization. In the course of modernizing and updating cultures, several Asian states have adopted "Islamic socialism" or "Buddhist socialism." Even India's emphasis on "secularism" and "socialism" reveals efforts at bridging convention with modernity. Such linkages with traditional cultures stress the importance of cooperation in building integrated national communities. They also suggest ideological variants that seek to limit commitment to alien ideas.

Taoism (Daoism)   A philosophical and religious system of China, second only to Confucianism in importance. Taoism is named after its central idea, Tao (Dao), or "The Way," which according to Taoism is the basic principle of the universe, the Ground of Being. It asserts that a person who grasps the meaning of tao accepts the doctrine of *wu-wei* or "doing nothing," of not interfering with nature. According to Taoism, through gentleness, humility, and nonstruggle, a person gains nobility of soul, serenity of mind, harmony of emotions, and freedom of spirit. All corruption in the world comes when people act contrary to nature. The basic source of corruption is civilization. People should withdraw from the formalities and ceremonies dictated by civilization, return to nature, and fit into its great pattern.

Taoism preaches realizing and attaining everything by doing nothing. This simplistic mysticism is Taoism's attraction. Its origins are shrouded in mystery. According to one tradition, a certain Lao Tzu (Lao Zi) (Old Master) was the author of the *Tao Te Ching* (*Dao de Jing*) (Classic of the Way and of Virtue) which has provided the basic source of Taoist teaching. Lao Tzu was for many years keeper of the Imperial Archives at Loyang (Luoyang). Upon giving up his post, he left everything behind and headed west to Central Asia. As he was passing through the Great Wall, the gatekeeper urged him to put down on paper what he knew as an old man. In response, Lao Tzu composed the *Tao Te Ching*, a 5,000-character text. *See also* BUDDHISM, p. 59; CONFUCIANISM, p. 75; NEO-CONFUCIANISM, p. 105.

Significance   In many ways, Taoism is contradictory to Confucianism, yet they have complemented each other in molding the Chinese mind. While Confucianism taught the Chinese to be virtuous, moralistic, and hardworking, Taoism provided them with the value of relaxed enjoyment and of inner peace. Together they have appealed to the opposite sides of the Chinese character and provided spiritual inspiration and moral standards. Taoism has influenced Chinese landscape painting and other art forms through its love of nature and sense of serenity. The Taoist ruler was expected to shun pomp and ceremony, warfare, or interference in his subjects' lives.

Theraveda Buddhism   The main body of Buddhist teaching, known as the "Teaching of the Elders." *Theraveda* came into prominence approximately 100 years after the death of Buddha, following controversy over monastic discipline and doctrine. Given a schism which spun off the more doctrinaire Mahayana school, the Theravedan Buddhists practiced a more popular ritual. Buddhism teaches "Four Noble Truths": (1) all life must be sad; (2) sadness comes from desire; (3) sadness can only be managed by reducing desire; and (4) life demands discipline, moral performance, and ultimately, meditation. The goal of all Buddhists, the attainment of *Nirvana* or salvation, signifying the total extinction of ego and self, is also the doctrine of the Theravedans. The idea that it is possible for ordinary persons to achieve the goal of Nirvana is fundamental to Theravedan Buddhism, and it is the only Buddhist school identified with what is called the "Lesser Vehicle," that survives. Theravedan Buddhism is found today in Sri Lanka, Burma, Thailand, Kampuchea (Cambodia), and Laos. *See also* BUDDHISM, p. 59.

Significance   Buddhist literature says very little about the political and social lives of human beings. Buddhism, generally speaking, is perceived by outsiders as less a popular religion and more a monkish philosophy. The virtual disappearance of Buddhism from India is sometimes attributed to its lack of pragmatic content. It was no match for Hinduism with its more aggressive and fundamental control over society. By its very nature, Buddhism challenged the preeminence of Hindu kings and sought to modify their prerogatives. The ideal ruler was a compassionate governor and a virtuous leader. Among all the Hindu kings, only Ashoka (268–233 B.C.) adopted Buddhism in serious fashion. The spread of Theravedan Buddhism outside India is, in part, a consequence of its distance from Hindu power. It is also testimony to a simplicity of doctrine that captured the imagination of common folk.

Three People's Principles (San Min Chu I)   The principles of nationalism, democracy, and people's livelihood, which Dr. Sun Yat-sen, father of republican China, put forth in 1924 as the three major goals of his Nationalist Party (*Kuomintang*) and promoted as the ideological foundation of Nationalist China. To Sun Yat-sen (1) the principle of nationalism meant exerting China's independent nationhood by driving the foreigners (including the Manchu or Ch'ing [Qing] dynasty) and their dominant political and economic influences out of China; (2) the principle of democracy meant instituting a parliamentary system with the representatives popularly elected by the people; and (3) the principle of people's livelihood meant providing for the general welfare of the people by more equitably distributing wealth, creating nationally owned basic industries, and encouraging small-scale privately owned businesses. These principles were expounded by Sun Yat-sen in 1924 in a series of lectures and have been promoted by the Nationalists as the basic guide to the building of a nation and as the principles to be observed by the Nationalist Party. *See also* REPUBLICAN REVOLUTION: CHINA, p. 196; NATIONALIST PARTY (KUOMINTANG): CHINA, p. 176.

Significance   *San Min Chu I* is a synthesis of Sun Yat-sen's various ideological indebtedness and revolutionary motivations. Born in 1866 on a farm near Canton, Sun Yat-sen was exposed to the West from an early age. When he was 13 years old, he was sent to Hawaii to live with his older brother who had migrated there. While in Hawaii, he attended an Anglican school. Sun's association with Christianity came from this experience. Later, assisted by a British missionary, he studied medicine in Hong Kong. Disappointed by limited prospects for practicing medicine successfully in Macao and other places, he became an active revolutionary.

Sun wanted to overthrow the Ch'ing (Qing) dynasty and chase foreign domination out of China. He traveled widely in the United States, Japan, and other places to raise funds and recruit followers. In 1911, the Ch'ing dynasty was finally overthrown, but Sun was faced with a politically divided country. Unable to unify the country under his leadership against Yuan Shikai's (Yüan Shih-k'ai) government in Beijing (Peking) and the warlords, he was forced to set up his revolutionary government in Canton in 1917. He sought help from the West in vain. When the Soviet Union and the Comintern offered to help restructure and strengthen his Nationalist Party, he was willing to accept their offer.

In the "Three Principles of the People," Sun envisioned a democratic, parliamentary system for China, which could be accomplished in three stages ending with a general election. His principle of the people's livelihood emphasized a strong central government actively promoting economic development and reallocating the wealth so that the peasants' lot could be improved. He died in 1925.

Although Sun's Nationalist Party under the leadership of Chiang Kai-shek lost to the Communists in the ensuing civil war in the mainland and was forced into exile into Taiwan (Formosa) in 1949, Sun's Three People's Principles have been promoted by the nationalists as the principles to be observed by all the Chinese people and they are studied in all schools in Taiwan under Nationalist control. The Nationalist Government is, however, not the only heir to Sun's Nationalistic and democratic legacies as the Chinese Communist Party also claims that it is their heir.

Tokugawa Feudalism   The period from the twelfth to the nineteenth century in Japan was the feudal period, which is further divided into the following three sub-periods: (1) the Kamakura (Minamoto) period (1185–1333); (2) the Ashikaga period (1333–1568); and (3) the Tokugawa period (1603–1868). The ruling houses of these periods assumed the title of *Shogun* (Military Governor). No shogun usurped imperial power, but each wielded the actual power of government. In the Tokugawa period, the house of Tokugawa with its headquarters in Edo (present-day Tokyo) was the most powerful. It held the largest estates and the greatest wealth. Wanting to control the other lords, particularly their former enemies, including the lords of Satsuma and Choshu in south and southwest Japan, the Tokugawa also established a complicated network of surveillance and helped unify the country, much more than their predecessors had done.

The Tokugawa, however, isolated the country from foreign influence. They wanted the feudal status quo and maintained a rigid class system headed by the *samurai* (warriors), who were followed by peasants, artisans, and merchants. They nurtured the neo-Confucian ideas aimed at conditioning people to believe in the ethical state, benevolent rulers, and obedient subjects. In the end, however, the United States, in its expeditions to Japan of 1853 and 1854, led by Commodore Matthew C. Perry, succeeded in ending the Tokugawa's long-standing policy of isolation. By its Treaty of 1854 with the United States, Japan was forced to open her ports to friendly intercourse and to protect American ships sailing past Japanese shores enroute to China, or frequenting Japanese coastal waters in search of whales. Soon thereafter, in 1868, the Meiji Restoration terminated the Tokugawa shogunate and Japan's feudal period. *See also* CONFUCIANISM, p. 75; MEIJI RESTORATION, p. 310; NEO-CONFUCIANISM, p. 105; SAMURAI, p. 114; SHINTOISM, p. 115.

Significance   Before the Meiji Restoration, Japan was a feudal state controlled by a military governor. Neo-Confucianism was fostered during this period, but unlike traditional China or Korea, the hereditary samurai class remained powerful. The ruling Tokugawa family preserved the formal feudal status quo. However, a culture is never completely static, no matter how isolated. Within Tokugawa Japan, changes occurred making continued feudal controls impossible. After two centuries of peace, for example, the lower-class merchants gained power, while the samurai and feudal lords lost it. Many towns and cities developed. The emphasis on Confucianism and the relative peace that prevailed encouraged samurai scholarship.

Some samurai scholars, engaged in the study of the Japanese gods, began to question the legitimacy of Tokugawa rule and feared the spread of Buddhism as a popular religion. There was, at the same time, a growing interest in European culture, despite Tokugawa's long-standing policy of isolation. A small but intellectually vigorous group of students informed in the European sciences emerged, particularly in southwestern Japan. These scholars worked through the medium of the Dutch language, which they learned from the Dutch at Nagasaki, the only Japanese port open at the time. Thus, they became keenly aware of the technological prowess of the West. The demise of Tokugawa feudalism and the emergence of a new Japan in 1868 resulted from the convergence of many forces.

Tribalism   The frontier areas of Pakistan, Afghanistan, and Iran contain some of the world's largest concentrations of tribal folk. The political conflict that challenges these countries can, in major part, be attributed to these oldest of human organizations. The Iranian revolution of 1978–79 brought several tribes to world attention, such as the Kurds, Azerbaijanis, and Turkomen.

The most notable expression of militant tribalism is found on the frontier between Afghanistan and Pakistan and between the USSR and Afghanistan. The two principal tribal divisions of Baluch and Pathan are found in Pakistan and Afghanistan. The Baluch also spill over into Iran. They are predominantly Sunni Muslim, but some Shiite tribes inhabit the region. The Baluch occupy a desolate, dry, mountainous landscape south and southwest of the Hindu Kush mountains and southward to the Arabian Sea. The largest branch of Baluch tribes is found in Pakistan. Afghanistan has a smaller number of Baluch than Iran. Baluch also reside in other, more settled parts of Iran and Pakistan. Iranian Baluch are found in more congenial Kerman province, and more Baluch live in Pakistani Punjab and Sind provinces than in Baluchistan. Baluch in Pakistan and Iran share their native homeland with other ethnic and tribal groups such as the Seistanis in Iran and Pathans, Punjabs, and Brahuis in Pakistan. Baluch also work and live in the Persian Gulf shaykhdoms of Abu Dhabi, Dubai, and Oman. Oman has recruited Pakistani Baluch for service in its armed forces.

This intermingling has diversified the ethnolinguistic character of the Baluch and variations of life-style have resulted. Iranian Baluch have been largely Persianized, and many Afghan Baluch speak a form of Afghan Persian called Dari. Others speak Pashtu, the language of their Pathan neighbors. There are wide differences in custom and tradition between the nomadic Baluch of Iran's Sarhad Steppe and the more agricultural tribes of southern Baluchistan. The Brahui (a Dravidian-speaking tribe) live on the Kalat plateau of Pakistani Baluchistan, thus separating the Suleimani from the Makrani Baluch. Because of centuries of interaction between Brahui and Baluch, there is little to distinguish them from one another. Brahui tribes have identified with Baluch nationalism, and some of their leaders have been prominent in the ranks of the Baluch opposition to central Pakistani control. Irrespective of these divisions, variations, and often scattered existence, the Baluch are a recognizable political force. Approximately 75 percent of the Baluch population have Pakistan citizenship. Their total is about three million. The Brahuis represent another 800,000; whereas the Baluch of Afghanistan are approximately 100,000 and the Brahui Afghan about 200,000. If a separate Baluchistan state is a conceivable development, it could cover an area from the Strait of Hormuz on the Persian Gulf to the Indus River in the interior of Pakistan, some 700 miles (1,100 kilometers) from west to east, and 400 miles (640 Kilometers) from the Arabian coast inland to the Afghan city of Kandahar.

The Pathan tribes are more numerous than those of the Baluch and historically more active. Almost one-third of Afghanistan and less than one-sixth of Pakistan comprise the land of the Pathans. Framed by the Indus river in the east and the deserts of the Iranian-Afghan frontier in the west, the Hindu Kush in the north and the Baluchistan desert to the south, approximately 400 miles (640 kilometers) from the Wakhan Corridor to Quetta (the capital of Pakistani Baluchistan), and approximately 300 miles (480 kilometers) from the Indus south of Kabul to Afghanistan's central interior near Delaram, but including Kandahar, the region has long been noted for its remoteness.

The Pakistani Pathan region is one of Pakistan's four provinces. Established as the Northwest Frontier Province (NWFP) by the British, it continues to bear that name despite Pathan efforts to change it to *Pakhtunistan.* The NWFP was divided into eleven districts and six Tribal Agencies in 1972. There are four centrally administered Tribal Areas located adjacent to regular districts. The Tribal Agencies lie next to the Durand Line separating Pakistan from Afghanistan. Among the settled districts are Amb, Chitral, Dir, and Swat. The word "Pathan" is the plural form of Pushtun, also Pastun, Pakhtun, and Pukhtun. The words are interchangeable, although geographic differences give rise to the usage of one over the other. The language of the Pathan is Pashtu or Pushtu among the Persian-influenced speakers in the southwest, and Pakhtu or Pukhtu in the northeast along the Pakistani-Afghan frontier. Most Pathans, even those residing in Pakistan, describe themselves as Afghans. Indeed, when Pakistan was first conceived in the early 1930s, the northwest border area of British India was known as Afghania by many Muslims. Pathans identified as Afghans, however, must be distinguished from those residing in Afghanistan who are also Afghan citizens.

The tribal orientation of the frontier Pathans has been exploited by elements bent on undermining, if not destroying, the Pakistani state. The tribal Pathans, after all, have little if any national consciousness, and they are inclined to think in terms of narrow tribalism. Pathans have been divided into three groups: (1) western Afghans, Persian-influenced like the Durranis who ruled Afghanistan from the middle of the eighteenth century until 1973; and their rivals, the Ghilzais; (2) the eastern Afghans of Pakistan living on the Trans-Indus plain, such as the numerous Yusufzais; and (3) the mountain tribes, the most independent grouping, who seem to be more loyal to their personal codes than to national union. Such Pathans are more readily identified as genuine Pathans, given their self-contained lifestyle. Among them are the Afridi, Wazir, Mohmand, Mahsud, and others. These highlanders are free-wheeling, semi-nomadic, not given to the sedentary life. They are poorer than their agricultural counterparts and often associated with brigandage, female kidnapping, and violent interactions. They are more closely identified with their brethren in Pakistan than those on the Afghan side of the frontier. *See also* AFGHAN-USSR CONFLICT, 1979– , p. 373; HINDU KUSH, p. 18; JIRGAH, p. 231; PERSIAN GULF, p. 33.

Significance   The border between Pakistan and Afghanistan slices the Pathan tribes into two segments. This artificial division, from the Pathan standpoint, is a nuisance. For Pakistan and Afghanistan it has long been a point of contention and sometimes of conflict. The border has been impossible to police, and no government has ever brought the highland Pathans under effective control. The Pushtu-speaking population of Pakistan is estimated to be about 12 million, approximately 15 percent of the total population. This figure includes more than a million Pathans living and working in the port city and industrial capital of Karachi. Pathans, more so than Baluch, also comprise a sizable component of the Pakistani armed forces. Afghanistan was home for about 7 million Pathans prior to the Soviet invasion of 1979. The flight of more than 20 percent of the Afghan population to Pakistan, the majority of them Pathans, however, makes an accurate estimate impossible. The Pathans have put up the staunchest resistance and have paid the highest price in dead and wounded.

The tribes of the Iran-Afghanistan-Pakistan triangle are the last heavy concentration of nomadic and semi-nomadic people in the modern world. These tribes inhabit a geostrategic zone of great contemporary significance. The Baluch stand astride the geopolitically important Persian Gulf and in near proximity to the Strait of Hormuz. The Pathans are the gatekeepers to the subcontinent and the key to the survival of Pakistan. Demands by both the Pathan and Baluch tribes for greater autonomy, and sometimes for independence, have caused problems for the central governments in the countries where they reside. Pathans demonstrated political consciousness earlier than the Baluch. A nationalist movement was launched against the British during their rule in India, but the Pathans lacked the unity to press their objective. The Afghan government picked up the Pathan battlecry for a separate homeland, and since the creation of Pakistan in 1947, it has championed the movement to separate the Northwest Frontier Province from Pakistani sovereignty. This is dramatized in the Pathan/Afghan call for the creation of an independent *Pakhtunistan.*

The Baluch were restive in the 1970s. A major insurgency pitting Baluch tribes against the Pakistan army produced several thousand casualties but was eventually brought under control. The invasion of Afghanistan by the Soviet Union adds variables to the unfolding scenario. The Soviet Union is determined to stabilize the Marxist regime in Kabul and to spread socialism throughout the country. The principal resistance to this Soviet maneuver comes from the Pathan tribes that remain devoted to Islam and their ethnocentric life-style, both of which are endangered by the Soviet penetration of their traditional strongholds. The Soviets are convinced that tribalism is no longer appropriate, and they perceive the Pathans as antisocial, backward, and essentially indolent. The Soviets, therefore, are bent on destroying the tribes, much as they did in their Central Asian republics, before recreating Afghanistan as a modern, progressive, political entity, friendly to, and in harmony with Soviet policies and aspirations. The Soviets would like to establish a preeminent position in the vicinity of the Persian Gulf and the Indian Ocean. The Kremlin has assisted the Baluch in their struggle with Pakistan, and the Soviets are in a strategic position in Afghanistan to further so-called Baluch independence movements. Moreover, the Soviet presence in Afghanistan may yet involve geographic engineering that could reshape the Afghan territory, as well as that of Iran and Pakistan. Whatever the outcome, there is no mistaking the sledgehammer blows falling upon the tribal populations. Their future is subject to considerable speculation.

Two Nation Theory: Pakistan   The justification adopted by the Indian Muslim League for demanding the establishment of a Muslim state within the subcontinent. Under the leadership of Mohammad Ali Jinnah, the Muslim League insisted that there were two major nations within British India, the Hindu and the Muslim. The Muslims, the Muslim League leaders argued, were so numerous (approximately 100 million in 1946) that they constituted a force that could not be ignored. In addition, the Muslims publicized their great differences with the Hindus. Religion, dress, diet, customs, and philosophy were at significant variance. Associations between Hindus and Muslims were extremely limited. Religious orders and practices were in total opposition. Historically, the Muslims judged themselves the supreme conquerors and rulers of India (as in the Moghul period), only to be displaced by British power in the nineteenth century.

Muslims believed they were superior in every way to the more numerous Hindus. With the anticipated withdrawal of the British in the immediate aftermath of World War II, many Muslims feared that the Hindus would gain political control of the country. The Muslim League, in particular, was reluctant to submit itself to the whims of the Indian National Congress, led by Mahatma Gandhi and Jawaharlal Nehru. The only recourse seemed to be the creation of a separate state for the Muslims of India. The Two Nation Theory became a persistent theme of Indian Muslim nationalists, and they finally convinced the British government that only the partition of the Asian subcontinent into two independent, sovereign states would suffice. Pakistan, the creation of the Indian Muslim League, was established on August 14, 1947. *See also* LAHORE RESOLUTION, p. 97.

Significance   The Two Nation Theory was at the heart of the demand for an independent Pakistan. It asserted that the two major religious communities within British India were essentially incompatible, and that each ought to be permitted the right of self-determination. Although Pakistan was formed on the basis of religion, it is important to note that tens of millions of Muslims remained in India and never considered shifting to Pakistan. Nevertheless, approximately ten million Muslims did move from India to Pakistan, and about the same number of Hindus transferred their allegiance to the Indian Union.

In the 1980s, the Muslim population of India is estimated to be roughly comparable with the population of Pakistan. Of course this does not account for the Muslims of Bangladesh, who before 1971 were also considered Pakistanis. Moreover, the creation of Bangladesh, with assistance provided by India, appeared to make a mockery of the Two Nation Theory. The Indians argued that the Two Nation Theory was dead, given the determination of the Muslim Bengalis to break with Pakistan and form their own independent state. Critics of the Two Nation Theory wished to emphasize the inability of Islam to hold Pakistan together. Bengali nationalism proved to be stronger than the Islamic connection, and the Muslims of East Pakistan were prepared to accept Hindu help in fighting the Muslims of West Pakistan. Despite this development, however, the Two Nation Theory is still considered vital to the people of Pakistan. Given their bitter relations with India and their fear that India seeks to destroy Pakistan and annex the territory within a greater India, commonly referred to as Akhand Bharat (United India), the Muslims of Pakistan continue to give credence to the Two Nation Theory.

Vertical Society   A hierarchical grouping of people in Japan, on the basis of firm personal ties. This characterization of Japanese society owes to Chie Nakane, who used the term "*tate*" meaning "vertical" in Japanese to identify the peculiarity of Japanese social structure. It is basically a two-person interactional model with the following distinguishing features: (1) it is based on individual ties rather than on shared characteristics; (2) it involves direct social exchange of favors; and (3) it emphasizes bonds of friendship and loyalty. Dyads can be fanned out and the person in the superior position could command many subgroups which are again organized in a similar dyadic manner. In Japan, a myriad of vertical or dyadic groups exist, and every individual belongs to, and is devoted to, at least one of these groups. Through group membership, the individual seeks identity and meets emotional and affective needs. Individual distinction is deemphasized in this kind of social setting, and group solidarity is emphasized. *See also* DEMOCRACY: JAPAN, p. 220; PATRON-CLIENT RELATIONSHIP, p. 112.

Significance   A myriad of groups make up Japanese society. Feudal in origin, the Japanese informal and personal pattern of interaction in intimate groups persists, and the Japanese people identify themselves with the group to which they feel most devoted. These groups vary in size, but each group is organized vertically in a delicate ranking system. A leader who holds the highest rank in a group leads on the basis of personal and emotional ties. He or she relates to subordinates in a paternalistic manner. Leaders and followers, employers and employees, join together to promote their group interests. They develop strong in-group feelings. The obverse of such group orientation of the Japanese people is indifference to or even rejection of outsiders. On the whole, the Japanese people find it difficult to relate to strangers. Voluntary organizations, where people of diverse backgrounds join together in pursuit of a common goal, tend to fragment into smaller, more intimate groups in Japan. In other words, these organizations become factionalized and their common goals become a collection of the diffuse interests of factional leaders.

Yangban   The traditional Korean ruling class. The origin of *yangban* may be traced to the Koryo dynasty (935–1392). When founded in 935, the Koryo dynasty created a new ruling class consolidating the royal clan, the families who had singularly contributed to the founding of the new dynasty, and the powerful local magnates who were descended from the previous dynasty. This ruling class was divided into two groups, civil and military, and it was collectively called yangban. Following the Koryo dynasty, the Yi dynasty (1392–1510) continued to call its ruling class yangban. Since the title of yangban was hereditary and extended to all of the legitimate heirs, the yangban family proliferated. Still, the yangban class in traditional Korea constituted only about three percent of the total population at the end of Korea's dynastic period in 1910. Similar to traditional China's gentry class, the yangban class in traditional Korea enjoyed power and wealth. Not all the yangban families were officials, but it was generally from this class that the Yi dynasty officials were recruited, based on successful examination in Confucian classics. *See also* CONFUCIANISM, p. 75; GENTRY, p. 81; NEO-CONFUCIANISM, p. 105.

Significance   The yangban enjoyed both power and wealth. It monopolized Confucian learning and supplied government officials. It also constituted a large segment of the landlord class in traditional Korea. The rigid Confucian code of behavior to which the Yi dynasty strictly subscribed made this class special in the eyes of the common people who were taught to be subservient to it. The yangban class jealously guarded its privileged status within traditional Korea. Rigidly separated from this class was *chungin* meaning middlemen. This class consisted of the practitioners of various skilled professions such as medicine, painting, and astronomy. The common people, a majority of whom were farmers, were called *sangmin*. Sangmin also included merchants, artisans, fishermen, and various other occupational groups. Slavery was also practiced in traditional Korea. In the declining years of the Yi dynasty, however, the rigid class system which favored yangban, declined. Many well-to-do commoners married into the yangban family. The yangban status could also be bought and sold. The demise of yangban was especially precipitated by Japanese colonialism in Korea, which purposely attempted to eliminate it. Today, yangban does not exist in Korea as a separate class, but it has generally come to mean anyone who is well-bred.

3. Political Parties and Movements

Akali Dal   The Sikh nationalist party that has deep roots in north-western India. The Akali Dal is the contemporary representation of extreme Sikh nationalism. The party pre-dates India's independence, and it played a major role in the communal warfare that ravaged the Punjab in the wake of the British withdrawal from the region. The Akali Dal pressed for the creation of Khalistan, a separate homeland for the Sikhs. Denied this goal by the British in 1947, the Akali Dal immersed itself in Indian politics after independence and began to agitate for greater autonomy for the Sikh population. Given the intensity of the Sikh demand, the New Delhi government finally agreed to split the Punjab into two states in 1966. What remained of the Punjab was established for the Sikhs. Hariana, a new state, was created for the majority Hindu population. The Akali Dal expressed dissatisfaction with this division, however, and they continued their agitation for still larger concessions from the Congress government. The central government's inclination to oppose these later demands exacerbated an already desperate situation and between 1981 and 1984 acts of political terror rose dramatically. Moreover, the often indiscriminant killing of Hindus by Sikhs was traced to members of the Akali Dal or its supporters. The militant Akali Dal leaders were Harchand Singh Longowal and Jarnail Singh Bhindranwale. Bhindranwale, however, was killed by Indian forces when they stormed the Golden Temple complex in June 1984. *See also* MILITANT HINDUISM, p. 103; SIKHISM, p. 117.

Significance   The Akali Dal movement presents India with one of its greatest challenges. The Indian Punjab borders on Pakistan, and New Delhi suspects that Islamabad seeks to exploit Sikh separatism, just as the New Delhi government took advantage of Bengali separatism in

133

Pakistan in 1970–71. Both countries have accused each other of assisting terrorist organizations, and New Delhi considered the Akali Dal such a body. But independent of these cross-border problems, the Akali Dal represented a frontal attack on the soul of Congress policy. The theme of Indian secularism as projected and interpreted by the ruling Congress party argues that all Indian religious, ethnic, and linguistic communities can live in social harmony and political unity irrespective of regional differences, cultural diversity, or political persuasion. Sikh Akali Dal demands, from New Delhi's vantage point, were a denial of this ideology and the actions of the group threatened to lead to secession. In fact, the increasing militancy of the Akali Dal movement and the violence attributed to it tore at the ethos of the Indian union. New Delhi believed it had to stand firm against the Akali Dal. If it failed to do so, it would only invite other would-be separatists in Kashmir, Bengal, Karnataka, or Tamil Nadu to begin dismantling the country's unity. Thus, after a considerable increase in the level of violence between Sikhs and Hindus in the Punjab, Prime Minister Gandhi in 1984 ordered her troops to neutralize the Akali Dal fortress-shrines in the province. The decision to invade the Golden Temple in Amritsar, the holiest shrine in Sikhism, however, was a bold and fateful step. The death of hundreds, possibly more than one thousand, in the Golden Temple action and the arrest or detention of several thousand Akali Dal members, in addition to the desecration of sacred property, did not end the problem, let alone promote Indian secularism or democracy.

The assassination of Indira Gandhi on October 31, 1984 was traced to the decision to invade the Golden Temple. Sikh extremists, some identified with the Akali Dal, had predicted the violent death of Mrs. Gandhi, and there were ample displays of approval in India and abroad to suggest that they believed justice had been done. Akali demands, therefore, are even more suspect. This does not mean that Akali demands are all anti-India. Chandigarh, for example, belongs to the Punjab. In the same framework, river water could be fairly distributed. The Indian government of Rajiv Gandhi has the task of discussing with Akali leaders the possibility of a political solution. No less is New Delhi's demand to the Sinhalese government in Sri Lanka with regard to the minority Tamils. The postponement of the 1984 elections in the Punjab (in Assam too) while the remainder of India was free to choose their representatives, cannot be protracted without causing further alienation among the Sikh community. The Hindu population of India, and especially its leaders, realize that the Sikh population identifies with and supports the Akali Dal, more so since the Golden Temple incident and its aftermath. If the Sikh community is again to consider itself an integral part of the nation, Hindu chauvinism will have to be brought under control. Moreover, this may be the only way to neutralize Sikh extremism.

Awami League: Bangladesh The political group that provided the inspiration, leadership, and organization for the founding of the new sovereign state of Bangladesh. Bangladesh was created from the former province of East Pakistan in 1971. The Awami League was organized in 1949 in opposition to the ruling Muslim League party that dominated Pakistan in the years immediately following its independence from the British Indian Empire. Although established as an all-Pakistan party, the Awami League was strong only in East Pakistan. Nevertheless, it played a key role in the destruction of the Muslim League and paradoxically contributed to the events which accelerated the military takeover of Pakistan's political life in 1958.

The Awami League was formed by H. S. Suhrawardy and Maulana Abdul Hamid Khan Bhashani. Both leaders had been members of the Muslim League but broke with that party after the establishment of Pakistan. Suhrawardy was a national figure, the last chief minister of undivided Bengal before independence, and a politician committed to the formation of Pakistan as a secular, democratic state. Bhashani was a provincial leader, sensitive to the needs of the impoverished millions of East Bengal (East Pakistan), and determined to protect their interests against the power represented in West Pakistan. Suhrawardy became prime minister of Pakistan for a brief period in 1956–57. Bhashani never assumed a governmental office. In 1957, Bhashani broke with the Awami League and Suhrawardy, and with the help of other prominent provincialists in the Punjab, Sind, Baluchistan, and the North West Frontier Province, he built the National Awami Party (NAP). With the declaration of martial law in Pakistan in 1958, the Awami League assumed an exclusive provincial character and came under the leadership of Shaykh Mujibur Rahman, a young disciple of both Suhrawardy and Bhashani. Mujib had strong ties to Bengali students, intellectuals, professional people, and businessmen. His party was the best organized and the most experienced in provincial matters, and after Field Marshal-President Ayub Khan was forced to relinquish power in 1969, Mujib pressured his successor, General Yahya Khan, to call general elections and to transfer power to civilian control. In the first-ever general elections of 1970, Mujib's party won almost every parliamentary seat in East Pakistan. Zulfikar Ali Bhutto, a prominent personality in West Pakistan, proved to be the big winner in Sind and the Punjab.

As the principal vote-getters, Bhutto and Mujib were called upon to find a formula for the transfer of power from military to civilian hands. Their failure caused the Pakistan army to take direct action against the Awami League and its supporters, whom the military accused of separatist acts. The civil war in Pakistan began in earnest in March 1971. Mujib was arrested and jailed in West Pakistan, but the Awami League continued to represent Bengali aspirations. India assisted the party and helped arm and train the Mukti Bahini or Bengali Liberation Army. India also internationalized the civil war in December 1971 by invading East Pakistan. New Delhi recognized the Bangladesh government in exile on its soil and ordered its troops to assist Awami League leaders in forming the new administration. After the surrender of Pakistani forces, Bangladesh was officially established with the Awami League at the center of the state's affairs. Mujib was released from his prison in West Pakistan and allowed to return to Bangladesh where he assumed the role of president, and later prime minister. The Awami League, however, was forced to contend with and often suppress numerous factions and political organizations as well as paramilitary groups that had sprung up during the civil war. Unable to reconcile the competing interests in the country, Mujib fell back upon his family and personal supporters. He organized his own militia, the Rakhi Bahini, but this dramatized Mujib's weakness more than his strength. In 1975, Mujib attempted to eliminate his opposition by transforming Bangladesh into a one-party state or BAKSAL system, but it was too late to save him or the Awami League. In August 1975, he and many family members were murdered by elements of the Bangladesh army.

In subsequent years the Awami League split into two major factions, one led by the organization's secretary-general Abdur Razzaq, the other by Mujib's daughter, Shaykh Hasina. Razzaq's faction stood for the establishment of the one-party BAKSAL system, while Shaykh Hasina stressed the need to develop parliamentary democracy. Still another splinter of the old Awami League was the Jatiyo Samajtantric Dal or National Socialist Party, organized in 1972 by student militants and radicals. The program of this former wing of the Awami League was leftist, emphasizing scientific socialism, Marxism, and revolution. *See also* BANGLADESH NATIONALIST PARTY, p. 137; NATIONAL SOCIALIST PARTY: BANGLADESH, p. 175.

Significance   The Awami League is a case study in negative politics. Despite noble and profound intentions, it could neither develop coherent organization, nor provide consistent, stable leadership. H. S. Suhrawardy envisaged the party assuming the role rejected by the Pakistan Muslim League. He wanted a party which represented the interests of all sectors of society in every part of the country. Suhrawardy's dream, however, could not be translated into reality by him or those who succeeded him. Suhrawardy died before the dismemberment of Pakistan and the creation of an independent and sovereign Bangladesh. His successors proved to be men of limited vision. More importantly, they were leaders in name and sentiment, but not in fact. Bhashani and Mujib were carried along by forces they could not control.

Neither left a legacy of constructive development. They may have symbolized the emergence of independent Bangladesh, but they could not take credit for its formation. The violent death of Mujibur Rahman demonstrates the strength of this analysis. By the same token, the Awami League never fulfilled its promise. It did not cohere before Bangladesh, and it continued to splinter afterwards. The role of the military in Bangladeshi politics and government is a consequence of political party failure, for which the Awami League bears primary responsibility.

Bangladesh Nationalist Party (BNP)   After the assassination of Shaykh Mujibur Rahman in 1975, the military maneuvered itself into a position of political responsibility. The politicians had failed to galvanize the nation following independence, and disparate groups and organizations threatened to plunge the country into anarchy. When General Ziaur Rahman (no relation to Mujib) became the military president of Bangladesh, the need for a new political organization seemed obvious. In 1978, Zia brought together the six parties supporting his candidacy and thus created the Bangladesh Nationalist Party (BNP). The BNP was constructed around a civil-military nucleus and included socialists from Maulana Bhashani's National Awami Party (NAP) as well as Islamic fundamentalists and Hindu secularists. The BNP also appealed to the student population and a BNP youth wing known as the Jatijotabadi Chhatra Dal attempted to syphon off some of the highly politicized students from the Awami League. General Ziaur Rahman was the key to the success of the coalition. His personality and driving enthusiasm sustained the party. Without him the BNP was simply a loose collection of individuals and groups that had seldom cooperated with one another.

The assassination of General Ziaur Rahman in 1981, therefore, caused the unraveling of the delicate organizational fabric. His army successor, General H. M. Ershad, tried to sustain the unity of the BNP with the help of Abdus Sattar who won a five-year presidential term in November 1981. Ershad, however, organized a ten-member National Security Council in January 1982 and insisted that the military establishment's political role be written into the constitution. Sattar rejected this assault on his civilian power and he tried to use the BNP to block the creation of a military supercabinet. In March 1982, negotiations between Sattar and Ershad broke down and the former was forced to vacate the presidency for the latter. Ershad ordered the banning of political parties as well as the abrogation of the constitution and the dissolution of the legislature. The BNP had failed to prevent the military from dominating Bangladesh political life and the party soon splintered. *See also* AWAMI LEAGUE: BANGLADESH, p. 135; NATIONAL SOCIALIST PARTY: BANGLADESH, p. 175.

Significance   The Bangladesh Nationalist Party is another example of personality politics in Bangladesh. These political parties have yet to develop institutional roots that offer the organizations a chance of surviving without their creators and prominent leaders. The Awami League was never the same after the death of Shaykh Mujibur Rahman. Similarly, the Bengali Krishak Sramik Party of Fazlul Huq remained an important political organization only until his passing. Pakistan has shared this experience. The death of Jinnah and the assassination of Liaquat Ali Khan proved the undoing of the Muslim League in the 1950s, as much as the execution of Zulfikar Ali Bhutto signaled the disintegration of the Pakistan People's Party in the 1980s.

Bangladesh in the 1980s was the home for approximately 72 political parties. In 1983, 32 of the most active political organizations were grouped in three alliances. The most prominent were the 15-party alliance led by the Awami League and a 7-party alliance led by Sattar's Bangladesh Nationalist Party. All the parties and alliances, however, stressed a common theme: the withdrawal of martial law and the restoration of representative civilian government. To this end, the politicians have sustained pressure on the Ershad government by organizing protest meetings and labor strikes. And just as the daughter of Shaykh Mujibur Rahman, Shaykh Hasina, has become politically active, so too, the wife of the late General Ziaur Rahman, Begum Khalida Zia, has joined the opposition movement. General Ershad's defiant reaction to their demands was the amending of the Martial Law Proclamation of 1982 permitting him to retain the office of chief martial law administrator after becoming president of Bangladesh. Ershad assumed the presidency in December 1983 and set himself the task of civilianizing his administration. There was little evidence, however, that the Bangladesh Nationalist Party would ever again achieve the distinction it enjoyed under Ziaur Rahman. Ershad seemed to turn a deaf ear to the established parties, but he did publicly associate himself with a new organization called Janadal which was said to be created by elected nonpartisan members, and chairmen of union councils at the lowest level of administration.

After repeated attempts to calm the political atmosphere and gain the support of the political opposition, General Ershad concluded that they were only concerned with his destruction. Thus in October 1984 he ordered the indefinite postponement of national elections and the continuance of martial law. By the end of the year the opposition had organized its sixteenth general strike against the military regime, but even this pressure did not change the character of rule in the country. Muslim fundamentalists, on the rise in Bangladesh as elsewhere, defied martial law and held public rallies to denounce the regime. The secular opposition followed their example, but when the government threatened the use of force, they yielded to an array of military power. Later, however, the students, long a political force in the country, took to the streets and clashes could not be avoided. Nevertheless, the government prevailed, and in January 1985 Ershad indicated he would sustain military rule until the politicians learned to use the established political institutions.

Bharatiya Lok Dal: India   Former Prime Minister Charan Singh organized the Lok Dal in 1975 to give vent to his frustrations, as well as representation to the Jat community of northern India. The organization absorbed seven political parties including the Swatantra Party with its focus on free enterprise. In 1977 the Lok Dal joined the Janata coalition which defeated Mrs. Gandhi's Congress at the polls. Its withdrawal from the Janata also caused the collapse of the government and paved the way for Mrs. Gandhi's return to power in 1980. Although the Lok Dal won more than forty seats in the Lok Sabha elections of 1980, its role continues to be either that of a catalyst or spoiler. *See also* DEMOCRATIC SOCIALIST PARTY: INDIA, p. 152; ELECTIONS: INDIA, p. 224.

Significance   The Lok Dal has its support among the relatively wealthy agriculturists and landowners of northern India. These persons are drawn from castes that have improved their standard of living as a consequence of improved agricultural techniques, especially those introduced through the "Green Revolution." The Lok Dal, however, has no chance of becoming a national party. It has no appeal for the landless, the city-dwellers, or the higher castes. Its success must be attributed in part to the resources it is able to draw from its prosperous constituents. It is interesting to note, however, that the leadership of the Lok Dal and the possible successors to Charan Singh are generally described as socialist. It is a matter of some conjecture whether the party can survive Swaran Singh, and if it does survive, whether it can sustain its current, narrow program. Charan Singh's chairmanship of the new National Democratic Alliance, which includes Atal Bihari Vajpayee's Indian People's Party, may be aimed at shoring up weaknesses in the party and improving its position in future polls.

Burma Socialist Program Party (BSPP)   General Ne Win is chiefly responsible for the creation and operation of the Burma Socialist Program Party. The BSPP was organized in July 1962 following the coup d'état that terminated the civilian rule of U Nu. The party is known as Lanzin in Burmese and its establishment was the pretext for government action declaring all other parties illegal. The Law to Protect National Solidarity confirmed the military establishment's determination to disallow all other forms of political organization. Under this law, members of the intelligentsia, Buddhist monks, and university students who opposed the military takeover were suppressed, and many were arrested for actions that were deemed anti-state.

Ne Win attempted a different path from that of other Third World nations. He argued that a policy of strict neutrality was not enough and that the country could only avoid big power entanglement by closing itself off from the larger world. The BSPP emphasized Burma's intention to internalize its programs and to minimize foreign assistance, even if it meant a slower pace of development. By following such a policy the martial law government sought to prevent the emergence of organizations whose support base lay outside the country. Ne Win's policies also signaled Burma's powerful neighbors, including India, China, and to some extent the Soviet Union, that the country in no way intended to join forces with its adversaries. While Burma attempted to "identify" with the other socialist states in the region, it showed no inclination to associate with them. The BSPP brand of socialism was Buddhist, not Marxist, in character. Philosophically it ascribed to the tenets of Buddhist belief, not Marxist class struggle. Structurally, however, it focused on the creation of a highly centralized governmental apparatus and thus borrowed heavily from the other Marxist parties.

In recent years the BSPP has moved from a semi-elitist to a mass party. In 1984 almost two million Burmese, more than 10 percent of the adult population, were estimated to have joined the party. The leadership of the party is controlled by its chairman and the Central Executive Committee. The first BSPP chairman was Ne Win. Born in 1911, he was educated at Rangoon University and received military experience during World War II. After the British withdrawal from Burma, Ne Win held several high military positions in the new Burmese army. He served as both prime minister and defense minister during 1958–60 and was the major force behind the coup of 1962. He presided over the Revolutionary Council before becoming president of Burma in 1974. He was instrumental in the selection of Brigadier General San Yu to succeed him as president in 1981. The younger San Yu is judged to be first in line to assume the chairmanship of the BSPP when Ne Win retires. Thus it appears that the party will remain firmly in the hands of the military establishment. *See also* COUP D'ÉTAT: BURMA, p. 272; ONE-PARTY STATE: BURMA, p. 240.

Significance   Although the armed forces are prominent in the building and sustaining of the BSPP, the roots of the organization lie in ground prepared by the nationalist "Dobama Asiayone," a civilian organization that pressed the British to grant independence to the Burmese in the 1930s. The leader of the group was Aung San, who was assassinated in 1947. Ne Win and U Nu were also members of the organization and they assisted Japan in establishing a quasi-independent Burma during the Japanese occupation of the country between 1942 and 1945. Japan's defeat in World War II permitted the British to return to Burma but colonial rule was ended in January 1948. Britain left behind a form of parliamentary system and an inchoate party system. Neither, however, seemed suited to Burmese conditions and in an atmosphere of unabated lawlessness, the armed forces finally assumed full power in the 1962 coup.

The BSPP was the military's answer to the party system. The officers that were engaged in the coup saw themselves as civilians in uniform. Above all they considered themselves nationalists, and they were determined to maintain the integrity of Burmese territory and society. The BSPP therefore reflected their values and concerns. It claimed to represent all the people and groups of Burma. It saw no purpose served in competitive politics which exaggerated tribal and historic differences. National unity and mobilization for development were the fundamental goals of government and the officers believed they could best be pursued through the efforts of a single, all-embracing national party. Burma traditionally was plagued by bandit groups, and following World War II, by insurgency movements. The Burmese army was called upon to neutralize the Burma Communist Party, a more realizable task since the death of Mao Zedong (Mao Tse-tung) and the shift in China's external policies. The army had to contend with the Karen Liberation Army, and the Kachin Independence Army. As a result, Burma has remained a garrison state. These factors, and the overriding desire to keep Burma free and independent, help to explain the importance of the Burmese armed forces, and they illustrate why Ne Win has had so long and fruitful a career. His work is likely to be sustained even when he can no longer play an active role.

Chinese Communist Movement: Long March   A strategic retreat of the Chinese Communists in 1934 and 1935, from the Jiangxi (Kiangsi) base area in central China (Ruijin [Juichin], the provincial capital) to Shaanxi (Shensi) province (Yan'an [Yenan], the provincial capital), to escape from the encirclement of the Chinese Nationalist forces under Chiang Kai-shek. In the Communist-Nationalist struggle for power in China, Chiang Kai-shek was determined to crush the Communists through his combined strategies of economic blockades and military attacks against the Communist soviet districts in central China. To avoid total collapse, the Communists decided to break the

Nationalist encirclement and started the long march. The Long March lasted 368 days and covered some 6,000 miles on foot through the most rugged part of China. Participating in this March were about 120,000 to 130,000 men, including Mao Zedong (Mao Tse-tung) and other leaders who later constituted the core of the post-1949 Chinese Communist leadership, the so-called Long March cadres. Pursued by the Nationalists and often forced to engage in encounters with them, many died on the way, many were lost, and many dropped out. According to one classic account of the March, the survivors dwindled to a tenth of their initial strength.

It was during this March that Mao took control of the Chinese Communist Party. After reaching the Shaanxi province, the Chinese communists under Mao's leadership regrouped and formed a united front with the nationalists to fight Japan. They were able to spread their influence throughout the country during their war against Japan (Sino-Japanese War, 1937–45), thus setting the stage for the final conquest of the Chinese mainland in 1949. *See also* NATIONALIST PARTY: CHINA, p. 176; MAOISM, p. 101.

Significance   The Long March was not an ordinary ordeal. A great deal of camaraderie developed among its survivors and remained strong enough for the marchers to stay united with dedication to their cause of transforming China into a Communist society. Furthermore, the Long March was a critical catalyst for the emergence of Mao as the most powerful leader in the Chinese Communist movement. At the Zunyi (Tsunyi) conference of 1935, which was held during the Long March, Mao successfully challenged the Party leadership and gained control of the Party and its powerful Military Affairs Committee.

The Long March was an invaluable experience for the Chinese Communists in other ways. It showed the strength and value of party discipline and ideological commitment, developed the guerrilla warfare skills of the Communists, helped Mao to consolidate his leadership, and reduced the Party's reliance on advice and legitimation from the Soviet Union and the Comintern. Once in Yan'an, away from Nationalist harassment, the Party effectively ruled its so-called "border area." In so doing, it experimented by governing a large territory with meager resources to emphasize the need for mass support and dedicated, ideologically correct Party workers. Mao was productive during this period, writing essays about wide-ranging topics such as *On Protracted Warfare, On New Democracy, On Contradiction, On Practice, On Liberalism,* and *Talks at the Yan'an Forum on Literature and Art.* From their position in Yan'an, the Chinese Communists were able to insist on a united front with the Nationalists against Japan. Moreover, during the Second Sino-Japanese War (1937–45), they were able to expand their areas of control throughout China fighting as anti-Japanese guerrillas and insisting on reforms in areas under their control.

Chinese Communist Party: Rectification Campaigns   A major device, *zheng-feng* (cheng-feng), rectification in Chinese, used by Mao Zedong (Mao Tse-tung), leader of the Chinese Communist Party, to maintain a high degree of ideological purity and revolutionary discipline within the Party. The first large-scale rectification campaign occurred during China's anti-Japanese war years (1937–45) and is usually dated 1942–44. The campaign began in earnest after two speeches by Mao Zedong in early February 1942, when he attacked subjectivism in study, sectarianism in Party work, and dogmatism of the intellectuals as a graver danger than the empiricism of practical workers. At the same time, the campaign emphasized the mass-line principle throughout the Party and a flexible understanding of Marxism-Leninism among new members.

As the campaign spread, it increasingly stressed Party purification and anti-subversion. The initial success of the campaign made it a powerful weapon of the Party to be used from time to time particularly under the leadership of Mao Zedong. Rectification campaigns differ from regular Party study programs in two aspects. First, rectification campaigns are not regular campaigns; they occur only when special needs are felt. Second, rectification campaigns emphasize a thorough study of participants' own errors and attitudes through intensive group interaction, whereas regular theoretical studies do not. *See also* GREAT PROLETARIAN CULTURAL REVOLUTION, p. 156; MAOISM, p. 101; MASS LINE, p. 309.

Significance   The initial rectification campaign followed the rapid growth in Party membership from about 20,000 in 1936 to 800,000 in 1940. It was caused by lack of sufficient progress in Party education work from 1938. Once in Yan'an, following the Long March, Party officials studied documents by Mao Zedong and other Chinese and non-Chinese leaders including Marx and Lenin. Later, as the rectification program spread to other places, it gained importance as a technique for thought reform and political socialization. Since 1942, several major campaigns have been undertaken in special political situations or as a result of changes in Party policy. They include (1) the campaigns of 1947 and 1950 for the political education of new Party recruits of various backgrounds; (2) the Three Anti-Campaign of 1952 against "waste, corruption and bureaucratism"; (3) the Hundred Flowers Blossom Campaign of 1957 against "bureaucratism, sectarianism, and subjectivism"; (4) the campaign of 1960 to chastise many Party members in responsible positions for the failure of the Great Leap Forward movement of 1958–59; (5) the Socialist Education Campaign of 1962; and (6) the most widespread and famous of them all, the Great Proletarian Cultural Revolution of 1966–69.

Communist Party (CCP): China   The ruling party of the People's Republic of China. Initially organized in 1921 among a few students and intellectuals, the Chinese Communist Party was later able to broaden its mass base incorporating a large number of peasants and workers, particularly under the leadership of Mao Zedong (Mao Tsetung); fought successfully in the civil war against the Chinese Nationalist Government, and established itself in power on the Chinese mainland in 1949. Despite many difficulties which the party encountered in its development, membership grew rapidly, particularly among peasants. Membership numbered more than one million by the time of Japan's surrender to the Allied Powers and her termination of war in China in 1945. Thereafter, party membership continued to grow and was reported to be 4.5 million in 1949, with some 90 percent representing peasant families. In 1984, membership was estimated at more than 40 million. In spite of its large membership, however, the Chinese Communist Party is still considered an elite party, as its membership constitutes only about 5 percent of the total population.

As a ruling Communist party, it is organized hierarchically, paralleling the government and administrative structure to the lowest level in order to oversee and guide their operations. It is organized in factories, mines, enterprises, streets, government offices, schools, military units, and production teams. The party's lowest level organizations are joined in the district commune, county, or city organizations, which in turn become the basis of the provincial, regional, or special municipal organizations. At the apex of this pyramidal organization are the national organs.

According to the party constitution (which has been periodically rewritten with the latest revision in 1982), the National Party Congress is the highest organ whose members are elected indirectly for a term of five years. While not in session, however, its business is conducted by a Central Committee which is also elected for a five-year term. The Central Committee is headed by the General Secretary of the Central Committee of the Party, which in the 1982 Party constitution constitutes the highest elective office of the Party. It is the General Secretary of the Central Committee who is responsible for convening the meetings of the Political Bureau and its Standing Committee and presides over the work of the Secretariat of the Party. The Political Bureau and its Standing Committee elected by the Central Committee to conduct business while it is not in session constitute the core of decision making in China, and they are composed of the most powerful figures in the party and government. The Party's Secretariat, organized throughout the country, is headed by the party's general secretary of the Central Committee. Its organization is parallel to the administrative structure of the government, and its functional departments usually correspond to the various departments of the government. Mao Zedong remained the chairman of the Party from the time he assumed leadership in 1935 until he died in 1976 and was succeeded by Hua Guofeng (Hua Kuo-feng) from 1976 to 1980. Since 1980, Hu Yaobang (Hu Yao-pang) assumed the post of general secretary of the Central Committee of the Party (the post of chairmanship of the party has been abolished), but Deng Xiaoping (Teng Hsiao-ping) remains elder statesman of the party and most powerful. *See also* CHINESE COMMUNIST PARTY: LONG MARCH, p. 141; COMMUNIST REGIME: CHINA, p. 212; MAOISM, p. 101.

Significance   The Chinese Communist Party is the largest Communist party in the world with some 40 million members. Phenomenal success in its quest for power has made it a highly assertive and united group. Until Mao assumed leadership in 1935, the party was by no means united as to which revolutionary course to pursue and how to achieve revolutionary success. It was small and powerless, relying on instructions from the Comintern. Given Mao's guiding role throughout the successful struggle for power, however, the party has been undoubtedly marked by the qualities of his strength and leadership. Mao's Communist party was based on the mass following of peasants; even its leadership was largely of peasant background. Following their revolutionary success in 1949, however, many of them died or became too old to participate actively in party affairs. There were also disagreements on policy matters.

The old leadership was replaced by a new group of leaders who have emerged since 1949. The path to party leadership is not easy in Communist China. First, one must become a member of the party. Constitutionally, anyone who is 18 years old or older, working, and who accepts the party program can become a member. The first requirement, however, is recommendation for membership by other party members. Any candidate must show complete loyalty to the party and excel in his or her tasks. Usually, the Young Communist League, Red Guard units (during the Cultural Revolution), and increasingly the PLA (People's Liberation Army) are regarded as the best channels for achieving party membership, but intellectuals and professionals are also recruited into the party. The proper political socialization for new recruits of the party remains a critical task of the party, and the party subjects its members to a rigorous system of discipline, self-denial, and service. Furthermore, given the enormous task of modernization, the party experiences constant need of readjustment, and its relationship with government and society remains in flux.

Communist Party: Japan (JCP)   A major Japanese political party. The Japan Communist Party (JCP) was first organized in 1922 recruiting its members among the intellectuals and laborers. The Koreans in Japan, constituting the largest minority, alienated and discriminated against, were also active in it. Soon after its founding, however, the party was suppressed by the Japanese government and forced underground. Many of its leaders were in jail at the end of World War II. Following Japan's surrender in 1945, its leaders were released from jail and the party was reorganized with the blessing of the American occupation authorities. During the Korean conflict, however (1950–53), its leaders were forced underground temporarily because of their support of Communist North Korea's invasion of South Korea and SCAP's concern about their possible subversive activities in Japan. Becoming active again following the Korean War, the party has been diligent in propagandizing its policies and programs, recruiting its followers and running its candidates in the elections.

Although the JCP has never enjoyed popularity among the Japanese voters, the result of its efforts has been some noted electoral successes as in 1976, 1979, 1980, and 1983 general (lower house) elections, when it polled about 10 percent of total votes cast. The JCP has been drawing its support from the metropolitan and large urban areas, appealing to a particular segment of the Japanese voters. Although ideologically rather dogmatic, the JCP has recently emphasized appeals for a peaceful, nonmilitary Japan insisting on the abrogation of the Security Treaty between Japan and the United States, the immediate elimination of American bases in Japan, and the neutralization of the country. Under the leadership of its elder statesman, Nozaka Sanzo, the party has emphasized making it a "lovely Communist party," renouncing a revolutionary means of achieving power. It has also insisted that it is a Japanese, not an international, institution.

The split between the USSR and Communist China has been troublesome for the party, as it caused the division of the party into two bitter factions. Although they have been able to mend their differences, their extreme followers of either Soviet or Chinese lines have set up their own independent Communist parties—the pro-Soviet Voice of Japan Party and the pro-Chinese Japan Communist Party. The lovely JCP opposes violence and radical leftist groups such as the *Sekigun* (Red Army) and the *Rengo Sekigun* (United Red Army). Organizationally, it claims some 300,000 card-carrying members. Its highest decision-making organs include a Central Committee, a Presidium (elected by the Central Committee), and a Standing Committee of the Presidium. The party secretariat is charged with the general administration of the party. *See also* POLITICAL PARTIES: JAPAN, p. 183; SINO-SOVIET SPLIT, p. 356.

Significance   The Japan Communist Party (JCP) is one of the major Japanese political parties. Although its chance of assuming power in Japan is slim, it is politically active in electing its candidates to the Diet. Since the 1972 general Diet elections, it has been consistently polling about 10 percent of the total votes. It has not had any consolidated union support such as the Japan Socialist Party has from the General Council of Japanese Trade Unions (*Sohyo*). Instead, it has had its support from the intellectuals and the urban underprivileged segment of the Japanese people alienated from the postwar Japanese recovery and development.

Recently, it has been active in rural areas and claims to be a mass party. It has mended internal rifts between the USSR and the Chinese Communist factions and now insists on an independent course of action, seeking a peaceful revolution in Japan through parliamentary means. The JCP's ideological stance has been too divergent from the other left-wing forces in Japanese politics to organize a "democratic" united front. Instead, it seeks to attain its goals through various mass and organizational appeals. It publishes a daily newspaper, *Akahata* (Red Flag), and is active in various peace movements. It plays a leading role in the Japan Council against Atomic and Hydrogen Bombs (*Gensuikyo*), and sponsors international friendship associations such as the Japan-Korea (North Korea), the Japan-Soviet, and the Japan-China (Communist China) Associations. It also operates various fronts, the best known of which is the Democratic Youth Organization (*Minseido*).

Communist Party of India (CPI)   A major political party in India. Indian Communists were well organized prior to the withdrawal of British authority from South Asia. The Communist Party of India has its roots in the international movement that was managed by the Moscow Comintern through much of World War II. It was also loosely tied to the British Communist Party. The CPI was organized in 1925 and attempted to work with the Congress party, especially with the leftist elements of that dominant organization. During World War II, however, the CPI broke with the Congress party over the country's belligerence. The CPI identified with the Soviet Union, and when Nazi Germany launched its invasion of the Bolshevik state, the CPI supported the allied war effort. The Congress party continued to oppose India's involvement in the war.

After the war, the CPI favored dividing British India into the independent states of India and Pakistan, which infuriated the Congress Party. But CPI leaders believed a divided Indian subcontinent would be a weak subcontinent and would give the party greater influence. After independence, therefore, the CPI continued to press for more state autonomy. The CPI was implicated in the rebellion in Andhra Pradesh in 1948. Because of its aggressive posture, the CPI lost stature as a credible political organization. The Nehru government arrested many Communist leaders, and a number were accused of engineering the uprising. Nevertheless, the CPI remained viable, and when the Congress developed amicable relations with the Soviet Union in 1955, the Indian Communists were given another opportunity to establish their bona fides in the country. In 1957 the southern Indian state of Kerala voted into office a coalition opposed to the Congress and led by the CPI. The Kerala government was headed by E. M. S. Namboodiripad, a colorful and popular personality. The central government's dissatisfaction with Namboodiripad's policies, however, provoked New Delhi to impose President's Rule in Kerala in 1959, and the CPI-dominated government was ousted. In 1962 the CPI faced an even greater crisis. The border war between China and India produced a split in the party. One segment of the CPI sided with Moscow, while another identified with Beijing. As a consequence of this schism, the pro-Chinese faction formed its own communist organization in 1964. It has been known as the Communist Party of India (Marxist) or CPM ever since.

Differences in the party were deep, however. The traditional CPI followed Moscow's policy of providing support for the Congress-dominated government in all matters that did not threaten the integrity of the party. Moscow encouraged Congress in its "anti-imperialist" attacks on the United States. The CPM, meanwhile, was inclined to minimize the Chinese threat to India and emphasize the Congress party's heavy-handed tactics in states like Kerala. The CPI assisted Mrs. Gandhi in the 1969 election and was rewarded for its efforts. By contrast, the CPM has always been treated with contempt. During the emergency of 1975–77, elements within the CPI leadership refused to support the prime minister's policies, and this caused still another split in CPI ranks. In 1981 the CPI subdivided again. CPI leader S. A. Dange broke with the parent organization that he had led and formed the All-India Communist Party (AICP). He and his followers in the AICP continued to aid Mrs. Gandhi. *See also* COMMUNIST PARTY OF INDIA (MARXIST-LENINIST), p. 149; ELECTIONS: INDIA, p. 224.

Significance   The schisms in the Communist Party of India (CPI) have weakened its general performance, but it still plays an important role in Indian politics. By attaching itself to the Congress party led by

Mrs. Gandhi, the CPI maintained position, integrity, and a large following. Moreover, the CPI was instrumental in helping Mrs. Gandhi cling to the prime minister's office in 1969. In return, Mrs. Gandhi indirectly assisted CPI candidates by not putting up her own candidates for the contested seats. Although hostility developed between Mrs. Gandhi and CPI General Secretary C. Rajeswara Rao in 1980–81, S. A. Dange's efforts to build the All-India Communist Party appeared to leave the bulk of CPI membership in Mrs. Gandhi's "camp." Moreover, CPI publications like "Link" and "New Age" are read by a broad cross-section of the attentive Indian public, and despite divisions within the parent organization, there is little indication that the Communists have been irreparably harmed.

The CPI's close association with the Soviet Union and the intimate relations developed between New Delhi and Moscow seemed to assure the CPI a strong future. Philosophically, the CPI and the Congress Party share a common interest in promoting secularism, industrialization, and land reform. CPI emphasis on the nationalization of industrial holdings and collectivization of farms, however, was not adopted by the Gandhi administration, despite its stress on building a socialist state. Generally speaking, the CPI supported Mrs. Gandhi's foreign policy, especially in its criticism of the United States, and its support for a variety of Third World causes. The CPI, however, is in a period of transition, and new leaders are surfacing. That leadership may find a way to heal the rifts in the organization. Given its strength in West Bengal, Kerala, Andhra Pradesh, Uttar Pradesh, and Bihar, and its affinities with political dissidents in the Punjab, Karnataka, Madras, and Kashmir, the CPI may have an important future, but its failure in the December 1984 polls illustrate the importance of personality over ideology or policy in post-Indira India. There is also sufficient evidence that the CPI and the CPM will have to struggle against the forces of Hindu fundamentalism and a rising tide of political conservatism.

Communist Party of India (Marxist-Leninist: CPML)   The Communist Party of India (Marxist-Leninist), distinguished from the Communist Party of India (CPI), the Communist Party (Marxist: CPM) or the All-India Communist Party (AICP). The CPML has its origin in a 1967 uprising in a hinterland of West Bengal, known as the Naxalbari district. For a considerable time, this rebellious group was known by the term "Naxalites." The Naxalites committed acts of sabotage and assassination and at several points they seemed capable of igniting a larger conflict. Indeed, Naxalites spread their violence to Bihar and Andhra Pradesh and the New Delhi government decided that the movement had to be physically crushed. The Indian army was given the task of eliminating the movement. Although successful, the army could not prevent its transformation into a political organization. In 1969, what remained of the Naxalite factions were merged into the CPML. *See also* NAXALITES, p. 393.

Significance The CPML has never been a potent force in Indian politics. Its violent origin was never fully overcome and its several factions have been at loggerheads over whether to operate through the parliamentary process or resort again to violence. In the 1960s and early 1970s the Naxalites could lean somewhat on Beijing's support. In the 1980s, however, the People's Republic of China was disinclined to assist such clandestine movements. Moreover, China's relations with India had improved, and neither government wished to seriously disturb the other. The CPML as a pro-Mao organization, therefore, had failed to find an external mentor.

Communist Party of Thailand (CPT) The oldest political party in Thailand, organized in 1925. The CPT has never been permitted to run candidates for public office and is technically, as well as officially, outlawed. The Communist Party of Thailand operates as a subversive organization, using terror and acts of violence to press its purposes. The CPT has assisted and led guerrilla movements in northeastern Thailand. It has also been active among the student population of Bangkok. Despite aggressive action by the Thai army and government, the CPT remains relatively vital in the villages and among the rural population. Its activities in Bangkok have not fared well due to the conflict between Vietnamese and Kampuchean (Cambodian) Communists, the flight of Kampuchean refugees to Thailand, and the threat posed to Thailand's border area by the Vietnamese army.

The student and intellectual community of Bangkok displayed considerable interest in the Communist victory in Vietnam and Kampuchea between 1973 and 1976. By 1978, however, the Vietnamese ouster of Pol Pot, and the subsequent Chinese incursion into Vietnam, disillusioned impressionable Thais. Division within the CPT over whether to support Beijing or Hanoi, or Beijing and Moscow, caused dissension and defections. *See also* THAI CITIZENS PARTY, p. 201.

Significance The Communist Party of Thailand has never had independent roots. Its ties have usually developed from Moscow or Beijing, and as a consequence of their long and continuing rift, the CPT has had difficulty in following a consistent program of action. Although Thai students and intellectuals were attracted to the Communist Party, it was more from frustration than conviction. The Thai left desperately seeks a change in the political order which sustains the military and business community in high positions, but since 1978 they have become more aware of the need to domesticize their organization and operations. As of 1984, it appeared that the Communist Party of Thailand had entered another phase in its history. Under considerable pressure from the right, it seemed more inclined to reorder its own house and to join with other groups opposed to the prevailing power structure. The CPT appeared to aim for a United Front posture in the last half of the 1980s.

Democratic Party: Thailand   A major political party of Thailand. Formed in 1946 as the Progressive Party, the political organization of Thai aristocracy, the Progressives evolved into the Democratic Party in 1948. It was not until 1975, however, that the party assumed a prominent position in Thai politics. The liberal program of the Democrats raised suspicions in conservative circles, and it was ousted soon after its leader, Seni Pramoj, became prime minister. The Democratic Party fought back, and in 1976 Seni was able to form a new coalition-government with the assistance of army-supported political parties. Again, because of its somewhat socialist orientation it was attacked from the far right and this time a coup destroyed the young government. The party was torn by right-left factions and the more conservative branch broke away and became the Thai People's Party (TPP) in 1978. The Democratic Party suffered substantial losses in the 1979 election, but made a comeback in 1983 and regained its prominence in Bangkok. *See also* SOCIAL ACTION PARTY (SAP): THAILAND, p. 198.

Significance   The Democratic Party is described as the only truly national party in Thailand because it has a network of organizations that spreads across the country and reaches down into the villages. Its strength, however, rests in the southern portion of the country, especially in the capital of Bangkok. The Democrats are the most senior politicians in Thailand, and although respected, they have not been able to capitalize on their broad experience and reputation. The Democrats seem more content to serve the government in power, and ministers are often drawn from their ranks by the military elite. The Democratic Party should not be confused with the National Democracy Party which is the organizational extension of General Kriangsak Chomanan. Like the New Force Party (organized in 1974 by intellectuals, teachers, and students in opposition to the Thai military), the Kriangsak organization cannot operate without support from the more developed parties. The National Democracy Party, however, has limited its chances even more by its seemingly pro-left program and its insistence that U.S. presence in the country be eliminated. It is a primary target of the Thai Citizen's Party.

Democratic-Republican Party: South Korea   A political party created by the leaders of the 1961 military coup in South Korea. The formation of the Democratic-Republican Party was officially announced on February 26, 1963 with General Park Chung Hee (Pak, Chŏng-hui), leader of the 1961 military coup, as its president. The party later nominated him as its standard bearer for the October 15, 1963 presidential election. As a political arm of General Park and his junta, the party succeeded in keeping them in power, but in the course of its development, the party's original plans were greatly modified due to division within the junta and other diverse pressures. The party was initially created to address many ills of South Korea's fragile party system. It was to be hierarchically organized, to be a party of principle and of identifiable programs, to be organized on the basis of continuity of party activity, and to be staffed by permanent, well-trained party cadres and integrated into the national power structure. However, it suffered from internal division and factional strife as well as from relegation to an insignificant position in national decision making which was increasingly dominated by the central executive. In the end, the Democratic-Republican Party was unable to outlive its founder, and it died with President Park in 1979 when he was assassinated. *See also* COUP D'ÉTAT: SOUTH KOREA, p. 277; POLITICAL PARTIES: SOUTH KOREA, p. 194.

Significance   The birth of the Democratic-Republican Party of South Korea is a clear case of modern institution-building in a developing context. A new political party was meticulously planned and organized to overcome various maladies associated with political parties and their workings in the Third World. In South Korea, the military revolutionaries spearheaded such institution-building, assisted by the nation's leading political figures and academicians. In the end, however, the party increasingly became a mere mechanism of electoral mobilization for those who were in power. It was unable to develop into a true interest-aggregating device and policy-formulating instrument. Because it was too closely identified with a single personality and his power, it was unable to generate genuine popular support. For this reason, when President Park was assassinated in 1979, his Democratic-Republican Party could not survive as an institution. The Democratic-Republic Party came to share the same political fate as other ruling political parties in South Korea had experienced, such as the Liberal Party of President Syngman Rhee (Yi, Sung-man) (1948–60) and the Democratic Party of Prime Minister Chang Myon (Chang, Myŏn) (1960–61).

Democratic Socialist Party: India   An opportunistic leftist party. Many of India's politicians were members of the Indian National

Congress. Differences with Congress leadership, however, have caused numerous ruptures and defections. H. N. Bahaguna was such a member who broke with the party prior to the elections of 1977. Bahaguna claims to represent the poorer classes and his appeals are somewhat Marxist in character. Some observers describe Bahaguna as a communist. After initially joining with Jagjivan Ram in the organization of the Congress for Democracy, he celebrated the defeat of Mrs. Gandhi's forces at the polls in 1977. He then became a member of the Janata coalition, but when it began to fall apart he returned to the Gandhi fold. This union was of brief duration, because Mrs. Gandhi depended heavily on her son, Sanjay, a foe of Bahaguna. Bahaguna therefore organized his own Democratic Socialist Party and with help from the Indian left, particularly the Lok Dal, he won a by-election in Uttar Pradesh state (where he had earlier been its chief minister) in 1982. Given the importance of Uttar Pradesh in Indian politics, observers expect that Bahaguna is a personality who will loom large on the Indian horizon in years to come in spite of his failure in the December 1984 polls.

Significance   Bahaguna is currently more important than his Democratic Socialist Party in Indian politics. Nevertheless, he has shown himself adept at forming coalitions, and given a future climate of political disarray it is reasonable to suggest that an organization under his command will be an important actor in Indian political life. Bahaguna may use the Democratic Socialist Party to maneuver himself into a position of broader leadership. That party may well give way to another that more nearly embraces the multiple demands of India's many publics, especially those on the left seeking to replace Congress (I) rule.

Bahaguna's withdrawal of support from the Jagjivan Ram government brought the demise of the Janata in 1979 and laid the groundwork for Mrs. Gandhi's triumphant return. Given the passing of Indira Gandhi and the elevation of her son Rajiv, Bahaguna will have to contend with new and still developing forces.

Dravida Munnetra Kazhagam (DMK): India   An important regional Indian party that represents the Tamils of southern India. The Tamils have sought to sustain their distinctive character and historic differences with the descendants of Aryan ancestry in the northern part of the country by forming the Dravida Munnetra Kazhagam or DMK. The DMK was formed in 1949 to act as the spokesman for the dominant Dravidian-speaking people of southern India, as distinct from the preeminent Hindi-speaking Indian National Congress. Over the years, the DMK has come to represent the Tamils of Madras state, the most influential state in southern India. The strength of the DMK enabled it to change the name of Madras state to Tamil Nadu and to take control of that state government in 1967.

The political success of the DMK tempered its call for secession from the Indian union, but cultural and linguistic parochialism have been hallmarks of DMK policy. The party, however, has not been free of internal squabbling. The death of the party's founder, C. N. Annadurai, in 1969, caused a struggle for a successor and in 1972 the party split into two factions. A group led by M. Karunanidhi held sway over the DMK and it managed to govern Tamil Nadu until 1976. Another group organized by M. G. Ramachandran identified itself as the All India Anna DMK or AIADMK. The AIADMK gained control of the state government in 1977. Through such in-fighting, the Dravidian movement isolated itself to Tamil Nadu. *See also* ELECTIONS: INDIA, p. 224; TELEGU DESAM, p. 200.

Significance   The DMK is a reaction to the dominance of the non-Dravidian elite that have dominated the Congress Party and India's government since independence. It is a reminder to the non-Dravidian leaders that the people of southern India are a force to be reckoned with and cannot be ignored. The language controversy of 1964 is a case in point. Efforts by the New Delhi government to make Hindi the only national language of the country precipitated bloody riots in southern India, especially in Tamil Nadu (then identified as Madras state). The central government was forced to yield in its quest for a *lingua franca* and, indeed, the controversy sustained the English language in official dealings between north and south.

States rights remain the primary concern of the DMK and AIADMK, and attempts by the federal government to impose its will have been resisted in the economic and political spheres as well as in the cultural. The Tamils of southern India are therefore uncomfortable with those who would mix Hinduism with politics. Tamils have opposed the Hindu extreme right, such as the Hindu Mahasabha and Jan Sangh, and appear to stress greater toleration of religious belief. Nevertheless, the DMK, as an ethnic-linguistic organization, is deeply interested in political matters that touch the Dravidian community wherever they are. Thus the DMK and other Dravidian organizations have been identified with the Tamil secessionists in Sri Lanka. The Tamils of Tamil Nadu are reported to be in direct support of the insurgents opposed to the Sinhalese government in Colombo, much to the embarrassment of New Delhi. The latter, however, is not eager to enflame Dravidian passions and the central government has tended to refrain from direct efforts aimed at breaking the connection.

Golkar (Golongan Karya): Indonesia The principle of the unity of all Indonesians, no matter how scattered their domicile, or diverse their livelihood and position. Indonesian political life is organized around functional rather than competitive activities. This scheme was introduced during Sukarno's tenure and was expanded and made more sophisticated by his successors. Golkar tries to remove controversy from politics by mobilizing society and channeling mass energies into projects of broad national value. Golkar is, therefore, designed to transcend divisiveness, to avoid debate, and to maximize unity. Golkar is also the primary instrument of military rule, and it has sustained Sukarno's successor, Suharto, since 1966.

Indonesia gained its independence from the Dutch in 1949. Since that date, the country has had only two national leaders, and both emerged from military backgrounds. It would not be a misreading to assert that Golkar is the political party as well as the institutional core of the governing military apparatus. A creation of the Suharto administration, Golkar established the supremacy of the army and civil bureaucracy over the political parties. Golkar traces its public posture to 1964 when senior officers in the army and air force attempted to beat back a Communist challenge. The Indonesian Communist Party, or PKI, had developed into the largest Communist Party in Asia, outside the People's Republic of China. The Muslim religious parties, prominent in the first years after independence, failed to attract elements among the population who could have helped expand their memberships. This task was assumed by the PKI, and they succeeded to the degree that even Sukarno came under their influence.

The military establishment, especially the army, was the only Indonesian institution with the resources to stem the Communist tide. Golkar was only one response, however. The Communist "putsch" of 1965 was aimed at destroying the inner circle of commanding officers before they could enact Golkar. This violent maneuver, however, provided the army with the opportunity to strike back, and it did not cease its aggressive counterattack until hundreds of thousands of PKI followers, sympathizers, and suspected or potential sympathizers, were brutally murdered. The physical destruction of the PKI gave the green light to Golkar, and the army leaders spread a broad net, enlisting the support of labor unions, retired soldiers' organizations, women's groups, professional, business and student associations, etc. In 1969, Golkar was declared a political party and it has totally dominated the government and parliament (Dewan Perwakilan Rakyat) since the 1971 elections. *See also* COUP D'ÉTAT: INDONESIA, p. 273; POLITICAL PARTIES: INDONESIA, p. 180.

Significance   Golkar minimizes the importance of political action. It symbolizes national unity and economic development, and it seeks to provide institutional support for these objectives. The alliance between the armed forces and the bureaucracy, and their role in the distribution of patronage, gives Golkar an advantage that the political opposition cannot approach. Moreover, Golkar has substantial appeal in those provinces (islands) outside Java, and this leverage is important in counterbalancing Muslim fundamentalists, as well as Communist subversion. Golkar dominates the cabinet positions and ministries and is sustained by public funds. General and President Suharto was elected by the Majlis Permusyarawatan Rakyat (People's Consultative Assembly) to a fourth, five-year term in 1983. It is important to note that this Assembly meets once every five years for the sole purpose of electing a president and vice-president. Assembly membership includes the members of the parliament (Dewan Perwakilan Rakyat) and a like number appointed by the president and provincial governors. Suharto's power therefore can only be challenged from within Golkar or the armed forces.

Great Proletarian Cultural Revolution: China   A nation-wide political campaign waged by Mao Zedong (Mao Tse-tung) (1966–69), mobilizing the Red Guards to rectify Communist China of deviation from his prescription for development and to purge his opponents. The Great Proletarian Cultural Revolution, also called the Cultural Revolution, began with attacks on writers and party officials responsible for the control of cultural expression. Primary targets were the educational system, which was becoming increasingly inaccessible to ordinary workers and peasants, and the lifestyle of the people who were imbued with the "four olds" (old ideas, culture, customs, and habits). At a September 1965 meeting of the Central Committee of the Chinese Communist Party, Mao also attacked revisionist influences in the Party and set up a Central Committee Cultural Revolution Group to direct the campaign.

Public attack by Red Guard activists (also identified as revolutionary young people) had been initiated, and it quickly spread throughout the country bringing millions of young people, mostly students, into the streets demonstrating support for Mao, denouncing "revisionist" leaders on the wall papers and by the use of other media, destroying various symbols of "bourgeois or reactionary culture," and seizing local party organizations. In the course of this development, the Party organization was dismantled. Organized in its place was the "Revolutionary Committee" based on a "three-way alliance of leaders of revolutionary mass organizations, PLA (People's Liberation Army) representatives, and revolutionary leading cadres." The government was momentarily unable to keep law and order, and ultimately in 1967 the PLA was called in. When order was restored, Mao purged his opponents, but at great cost. The Cultural Revolution helped to discredit the Party and the government, and it contributed to the rise of the PLA as the most powerful group in the country. Minister of Defense Lin Biao was named heir-apparent to Mao at the Ninth Party Congress of April 1969. The power struggle continued, however, into the 1970s, even after the death of Mao in 1976, until the emergence of a new power structure headed by Deng Xiaoping (Teng Hsiao-ping). By then, Lin Biao (Lin Piao) had died in a plane crash, according to an official explanation, while escaping from China after an unsuccessful attempt to assassinate Mao and stage a coup. The so-called Gang of Four, who were led by Mao's wife, Jing Qing (Chiang Ching), had been arrested and put into jail, and Hua Guofeng (Hua Kuo-feng), who had succeeded Mao, had been demoted from his position of power in the Party and government. *See also* CHINESE COMMUNIST PARTY: RECTIFICATION CAMPAIGNS, p. 143; MAOISM, p. 101; GREAT PROLETARIAN CULTURAL REVOLUTION: RED GUARDS, p. 158.

Significance   The Great Proletarian Cultural Revolution was probably the most significant mass political movement since the establishment of the People's Republic of China in 1949. It has left a lasting impact on the history and development of Communist China. In the Cultural Revolution, Mao suppressed, momentarily at least, most of his long-time colleagues whom he thought were increasingly ignoring him and had degenerated into the "privileged" stratum. In the campaign, Mao set out to prevent his Communist China from abandoning the class struggle. He was determined to train a new generation of totally dedicated revolutionary successors, whose world views would be genuinely Marxist-Leninist. There is a certain historical continuity in this revolutionary emphasis.

The phrase "cultural revolution," often found in communist terminology, has its historical antecedents in China's non-communist cultural reform efforts such as the May Fourth and the "New Culture" movements of the 1910s. China's emphasis on cultural transformation is a continuous, on-going process of modernization. Although it witnessed a power struggle and was closely identified with Mao, the Cultural Revolution reflects the complexity of China's historical development. Following the Cultural Revolution, bureaucratic organizations became simplified and their personnel were periodically sent to May Seven Cadre Schools for a mixture of manual labor and ideological study. Educational reforms were instituted, universalizing primary education, and emphasizing applied and practical studies and political education throughout the whole educational system. Revolutionary themes were widely used in cultural expressions and performing arts. Rural areas were especially targeted for development, and local initiatives for greater productivity were encouraged.

Following Mao's death in 1976, the new leadership headed by Deng Xiaoping emphasized a new set of development priorities demanding accelerated advancement of the Four Modernizations of agriculture, industry, national defense, and science and technology with help from former enemies, if necessary. In this connection, China's leadership has found its new friendship with the United States and Japan useful.

Great Proletarian Cultural Revolution: Red Guards   Students who were mobilized during the Great Proletarian Cultural Revolution in China. The first group mobilized in the Cultural Revolution were the students of Beijing's (Peking's) colleges and universities, and they used such symbolic names as "The Eagles," "Red Flag," and "Revolutionary Rebels." One group at Qinghua (Chinghua) University was known as "Red Guards." The name was soon adopted by all the others and attained a national and worldwide reputation. Following the Central Committee's Eleventh Plenum of the Chinese Communist Party, which met in August 1966 and approved Mao Zedong's (Mao Tse-tung's) call for the Cultural Revolution, the students were told by the Party hierarchy to organize in Red Guard units and wage a nationwide campaign to fight recurrence of old habits and to revitalize the Chinese Communist revolution. Later, high school students joined in the movement, holding rallies and demonstrations. As a result, all the schools were closed. The students started attacking government and party officials. Violence was reported in many places. Nearly 11 million Red Guards visited Beijing hoping to see Chairman Mao personally and proclaim their affection for the leader. Because of many excesses, the movement was halted in August 1968. Mao disbanded the Red Guards and organized the Worker-Peasant Mao Zedong Thought Propaganda Teams. *See also* GREAT PROLETARIAN CULTURAL REVOLUTION, p. 156; MAOISM, p. 101.

Significance   The Red Guard movement showed the magnetic power of Mao's charismatic mass appeal. In the name of Mao, the young students were stimulated, encouraged, and mobilized not only to attack the increasingly bureaucratic establishments in Communist China but to relive the revolution that brought the Communists into power. They were to strengthen their commitment to the building of a strong China in Mao's own image. When the movement became extreme, however, it lost Mao's favor. The students became unwieldy and violent, and their disruptions caused a long period of chaos in China. They put up wall papers charging many in authority with crime. The destruction of the "four olds" (old ideas, old culture, old customs, and old habits) meant indiscriminate destruction of valuable cultural properties and the dismantling of educational institutions. Eventually, Mao had to call in the military (PLA) to restore order and force the students to return to school. Many urban students were even sent to the countryside to work with the peasants in the fields.

Indian National Congress, Congress (I)   The major organization that provided leadership for India both prior to and following its independence. Organized in 1885 under British auspices, the Congress Party was more a debating society than a true political movement. The Indianization of the party, however, provided a platform for a number of articulate indigenous leaders who were determined to reorient the organization. Dominant figures like B. G. Tilak (1856–1920) and G. K. Gokhale (1866–1915) laid the foundation for India's most formidable political organization. Tilak took a more radical position and stressed Hindu tradition, whereas Gokhale proved to be a genuine liberal, deeply committed to religious and ethnic integration as well as to the adoption of European ideas and institutions. Thus, the Congress became a haven for a wide spectrum of thought and behavior but the Gokhale views on secularism and moderation gained the upper hand.

Nevertheless, the Congress had been and continued to be an elitist organization, dominated by a few magnetic leaders. Mohandas K. Ghandi, later known as Mahatma Gandhi ("Great Soul"), assumed the leadership of the party in the 1920s, following the deaths of Tilak and Gokhale. Gandhi was assisted by a number of able personalities in restructuring the Congress, notably Sardar Vallabhai Patel and Jawaharlal Nehru. Together they directed a political movement which awakened the masses and led to the independence of India from British rule in 1947. Gandhi was the saint of Indian politics. His campaign against the British is renowned for its emphasis on non-violence (*ahimsa*) and soul force, or passive resistance (*satyagraha*). He was also committed to the Gokhale school of secularism, and the melding of diverse communities into a unified political society. Gandhi labored against discrimination in all forms, both traditional and functional, but he could not calm the fears of the Muslims who organized and followed the Muslim League party (organized in 1906). Despite strenuous efforts to maintain the unity of India, Gandhi acknowledged the claim of the Muslim League to partition India. When the British transferred power to the Congress leaders, therefore, they performed the same act with the leaders of the Muslim League. As a consequence, two dominions, India and Pakistan, were carved out of British India. Gandhi was assassinated by a member of the Hindu extremist R.S.S. organization in 1948, allegedly over the role the Mahatma played in the division of the subcontinent. Gandhi had not aspired to political office, and after India gained independence, the Congress Party was led by his disciple, Jawaharlal Nehru.

Nehru became India's first prime minister, a post he held until his death in 1964. He dominated the Congress party, and under his leadership the party dominated national government. The individual states, however, were more difficult to control. Mrs. Gandhi's first tenure as prime minister (1966–77) exaggerated this division of power. Although no opposition party could challenge the Congress in the Lok Sabha, the central parliament, several states charted courses independent of the Congress party. Congress suffered a substantial decline in the state elections of 1967 and 1977. But in 1980 it regained control over most of the states. And in the 1982 state contests, the party added to its leverage. Disturbances in Assam, Punjab, Karnataka, and Kashmir in 1983–84, however, pointed to renewed Congress difficulties at the grassroots. Congress had overcome numerous factional splits since 1947. Its most lasting division to date occurred in 1969 when members of the Congress elite, known as the "Syndicate," broke with Mrs. Gandhi.

The "Syndicate" had selected Mrs. Gandhi to be prime minister in 1966, following the sudden death of Lal Bahadur Shastri, Nehru's successor. But after assuming the office, Mrs. Gandhi proved to be a determined figure and she stubbornly refused to yield to the older Syndicate members. Mrs. Gandhi's victory at the polls in 1971 eliminated her opposition within the elite body and she dominated the Congress thereafter. In the 1977 election, Morarji Desai, a former member of the "Syndicate," and a follower of Gandhi and Nehru, exploited popular opposition to the state of emergency that had been imposed in 1975. He led the Janata coalition which defeated the Congress and turned Mrs. Gandhi out of office. Janata's ties to the old Congress party, however, perpetuated the policies and programs of the previous administration. The defection of important groups within the coalition forced new elections in 1980, and Mrs. Gandhi and her wing of the Congress party, the Congress (I), were returned to power.

Mrs. Gandhi ruled India with something akin to a personal coterie, perhaps altering the Congress party irreversibly. Observers commented on the party's minimal institutional base and the exaggerated importance given to Indira's personal qualities. "Indira is India" was a common cry as well as lament and it seemed to sum up the demise of the old party as well as the crystallization of personal rule. Mrs. Gandhi's death at the hands of Sikh assassins in October 1984 put the Congress to new test. Her son Rajiv was immediately sworn in as her successor and India's prime minister despite his limited political experience. A family tradition had been transformed into a national symbol, and in the country's trying hour no other personality was judged to have the support of India's disparate multitudes. The wisdom of this choice was borne out in the elections which were hurriedly organized between December 24–27, 1984. Rajiv and the Congress (I) that he now led won a stunning victory, vanquishing almost all of the older opposition. Despite electoral gains that eluded his grandfather and mother, the skeptics doubted that the old Congress party could or would be revived. *See also* ELECTIONS: INDIA, p. 224; MILITANT HINDUISM, p. 103.

Significance   The Indian National Congress is one of the great political success stories of modern Asia. Despite many setbacks and distractions, the Congress remains the only genuine national party in India and its preeminence has neither undermined the Indian experiment in democracy, nor prevented other organizations from pressing their programs and interests. Congress has its strength in its overall organization from the village to the federal capital. Its annual conferences and state and district organs maintain the integrity of the party and promote political awareness. No other party has the personnel, the resources, or the experience demonstrated by the Congress. Power is wielded by the Congress Working Committee which is comprised of approximately twenty members, the majority of whom are appointed by the Congress president. The Congress president is appointed by the prime minister, thus bringing the party into intimate embrace with the government.

Prime Minister Nehru was president of the party in the early 1950s, and his daughter Indira assumed that role in 1980. Faced with opposition from other Congress parties, Mrs. Gandhi's faction was designated the Congress (I). Observers have commented that between the tenures of Nehru and Mrs. Gandhi, India has been governed by one family for all the years of its existence, except brief periods between 1964–65 and 1977–79. They have cited Mrs. Gandhi's desire to pass the mantle of leadership to her son Sanjay. His accidental death in 1980 seemed to end that dream, but the political role designed for her older son, Rajiv Gandhi, renewed such speculation. Moreover, Rajiv's chance to perpetuate the "dynasty" came sooner than anyone believed possible. His mother's death left the country stunned and divided as it had not been since independence was achieved. The surfacing of Hindu fanaticism and the lethal assaults on defenseless Sikhs in New Delhi, aboard railway cars, and elsewhere in the country, seemed to threaten India's tenuous unity. Rajiv was the heir to the "crown" and the Congress leaders were quick to press him into service, making him India's new prime minister. Rajiv received the loyalty of government administrators and police and especially the Indian armed forces, and with their assistance law and order was restored within a week of the murder. The country remained in desperate straits, however, and when the elections were called for December 1984 it was obvious a large majority would bolster Rajiv's hand. Nevertheless, the victory of the Congress (I) surprised Rajiv's most ardent supporters and humbled other political luminaries. The defeat of many of the latter hinted at a new course in Indian politics. Rajiv's youth (he was only 40 on assuming the prime minister's office), and the selection of young people for his cabinet, addressed a question that many had been posing before the October tragedy. Can a new generation govern India? That question was now about to be answered.

Indian National Congress (J)   An Indian splinter party. This party owes its existence to Jagjivan Ram, a leader of India's untouchables and the man who holds the record for serving in more Indian governments than any other personality. His break with Mrs. Gandhi in 1977 contributed to her electoral defeat, and he played a prominent role in the Janata coalition party that governed India from 1977 to 1979. Jagjivan Ram wanted to become India's prime minister but he was thwarted in these efforts by other coalition leaders. Failure to rally behind him proved the undoing of the Janata. Disillusioned after Mrs. Gandhi's electoral success, Jagjivan Ram organized his own Indian National Congress, but it was not expected to receive much support. Moreover, Jagjivan Ram's age and the personal character of the organization seemed to suggest a short life for the party. *See also* INDIAN NATIONAL CONGRESS, CONGRESS (I), p. 159.

Significance   India's multiple-party system has made it possible for personalities to form political organizations, but the proliferation of parties also helps to explain the staying power of the Indian National Congress. Although the Congress has witnessed many spin-off organizations, under the leadership of Indira Gandhi it sustained the continuity of the original Congress rule, somewhat modified. All other Congress parties appear to be fringe organizations except, perhaps, the Indian National Congress (S), the more radical of the operational Congress parties.

Indian National Congress (S)   An Indian splinter party. Personalities are a vital part of the Indian political scene and Mrs. Gandhi's power was often a subject of complaint from those who have steadfastly clung to Congress values. The formation of the Indian National Congress (S) was the outcome of a 1978 struggle among those formerly associated with Mrs. Gandhi. The party was originally organized by Bramananda Reddy. Later, it came under the leadership of Swaran Singh who had served as Mrs. Gandhi's foreign minister. Swaran Singh was followed by Devraj Urs. It is of some importance to note that the Congress was distinguished by the letter "S" during the tenure of

Swaran Singh, whereas during that of Urs it was known as the Congress "U." Mrs. Gandhi's Congress has been known as the Congress "I" which again underlines the importance of personalities. The Indian National Congress "S" was restored following the 1980 elections in which Mrs. Gandhi was returned to power. The Congress "S" stood for the concepts of "secularism" and "socialism" in its latest metamorphosis. Younger leadership has attempted to revitalize this segment of the old Congress, which incidentally insists on laying claim to the original Congress organization. A. K. Anthony of Kerala is alleged to be one of its principal spokesmen. Charan Singh, however, was active in 1983 in attempting to form a new coalition called the National Democratic Alliance and the Congress "S" was apparently torn between those advocating a more radical leftist program and those calling for a right of center approach. *See also* INDIAN NATIONAL CONGRESS, CONGRESS (I), p. 159.

Significance   The Congress "S" was an outspoken critic of Mrs. Gandhi's authoritarian practices and apparently sought to play a role similar to that of the Congress "O" (for opposition) which gained considerable leverage during the early 1970s. To a large extent it was the Congress "O" which formed the nucleus of the successful Janata coalition in 1977. The Congress "S" claims to represent the genuine Congress. Its central argument was against Mrs. Gandhi's manner of governing, with the criticism that she was too much inclined toward autocratic rule. It is interesting to note that Maneka Gandhi, the widow of the prime minister's late son, joined the National Democratic Alliance in 1983 in opposition to what she characterized as her mother-in-law's propensity for dictatorial powers. Maneka remained with the oppositon following her mother-in-law's death, but ran against Rajiv in the December 1984 elections, losing by a wide margin.

Indian People's Party   A conservative Indian party that represents Hindu extremism. This political party emerged in 1980 from the breakup of the Janata party which was a coalition of right and left wing parties that had combined to defeat Indira Gandhi's Congress party in the 1977 elections. The Indian People's Party, or Bharatiya Janata Party (BJP) is the current designation given to the Jan Sangh Party, a long-time, ultra-conservative organization that has represented Hindu extremism. The Indian People's Party is related to both the Rashtriya Swayamsevak Sangh (R.S.S.) or National Volunteer Organization which was implicated in the assassination of Mahatma Gandhi in 1948 and the Hindu Mahasabha, a militant Hindu organization that predated the independence of India. Both organizations were associated with the Jan Sangh in the early 1950s. The Hindu Mahasabha was absorbed by the

Jan Sangh, but the R.S.S. was reestablished in the 1970s, and in the 1980s it stood with other chauvinist Hindu organizations in defying both the Sikh Akali Dal and the Muslim Jamaat-e-Islami and the Majlis-e-Ittehadul Muslims. The Jan Sangh drew its support from the Hindi-speaking areas of northern India and was prominent in the federal capital of New Delhi.

The Jan Sangh's emphasis on Hindu culture and its politicization always aroused the concern of the ruling Congress party which has constantly stressed secularism and pluralism in Indian political life. Many Congress leaders believe the country will experience even more horrifying displays of communal warfare if the forces of Hindu militancy achieve their political objectives. The suspension of fundamental guarantees and the declaration of a state of emergency between 1975 and 1977 was attributed in part to Jan Sangh activities. During the emergency, the leaders of the Jan Sangh, as well as many rank and file members, were imprisoned by the Gandhi government. Even more drastic measures were taken against the R.S.S., which was banned again. The Jan Sangh joined in coalition with the Janata in 1977 and helped defeat the Gandhi government in the general elections. The Janata failed to sustain this unity, because like the Congress, it emphasized secularism and moderation. When the coalition fell apart, the Jan Sangh and R.S.S. members returned to their more exclusive pursuits. When Mrs. Gandhi won the 1980 elections, the Jan Sangh underwent reorganization and emerged as the Indian People's Party, or BJP, under the leadership of Atal Bihari Vajpayee. In 1983, Vajpayee attempted to give greater voice to his party by convincing former Prime Minister Swaran Singh to add his organization, the Lok Dal, to the Indian People's Party, in what was described as a National Democratic Alliance. Maneka Gandhi, the widow of Sanjay Gandhi (Indira Gandhi's son) also put her limited political forces, the Rashtriya Sanjay Manch, behind the NDA. *See also* HINDUISM, p. 83; MILITANT HINDUISM, p. 103.

Significance   The Indian People's Party has remained dedicated to the objective of preserving Hindu traditional values and practices but it has proved remarkably flexible in matters of public policy. Formerly known as the Jan Sangh, it allied itself with the Swatantra Party and heavily emphasized free enterprise. Since its reformation as the BJP it has shifted to socialist ideas and pronouncements. This move reveals some frustrations in party ranks, due to an inability to wean the entrepreneurial class from its support for the Congress. In the area of foreign policy, however, BJP leaders were critical of Indira Gandhi's intimacy with the Soviet Union.

During Vaypayee's tenure as foreign minister in the Janata coalition government, he worked toward improving relations with the United

States. He has continued to exert pressure for a more even-handed policy since joining the ranks of the opposition. The Indian People's Party, however, remains outspoken in its opposition to Pakistan and many of its adherents continue to talk of one day absorbing Pakistan. The concept of "Akhand Bharat" or "United India" implies the dissolution of Pakistan and the merger of its territories in a greater Indian union. The Indian People's Party has called for a strong defense establishment and has promoted India's role among the major nuclear powers. Because it has a dedicated and militant cadre and has never broken its ties to the R.S.S., the BJP is considered a powerful party in India. In view of its political organization, the communal warfare between Hindus and Muslims in and around Bombay in 1984, as well as attacks on the Sikh Akali Dal, must be considered ominous signs. Renewed emphasis on religious revival among Hindus, Muslims, and Sikhs is not aimed at encouraging a peaceful, let alone a democratic, India. The popular Vishwa Hindu Parishad, an R.S.S. sub-group, continues to organize Hindu soul union pilgrimages throughout India. Indira Gandhi spoke of the deepening religious cleavages in Indian society and the "rabid communal forces" loose in the country. It is now her successors who must deal with those forces.

Janata Party: India   A major coalition of opposition forces to Indira Gandhi, that governed India from 1977 to 1979. The forces of the opposition were aroused and galvanized into a winning combination by Prime Minister Indira Gandhi's heavy-handed tactics during the 1975–77 state of emergency. During that period Mrs. Gandhi virtually suspended all fundamental guarantees of free speech and assembly, and opposition leaders were imprisoned wholesale. The Janata was a response to this crisis by the politically active from a broad spectrum of Indian political life. At the heart of Janata, however, were old-line Congress politicians who argued that Mrs. Gandhi was thinking less about the nation and more of her personal aspirations. The original Janata consisted of the Congress "O," the Jan Sangh, the Bharatiya Lok Dal, the Congress for Democracy, and the Socialists. The Janata proved to be an organization only good for the elections of 1977. After an astonishing victory, it had enormous difficulty in welding its disparate parts into a coherent political organization. When it came undone, therefore, it resembled a vestige of the old Congress organization, but little more. The Janata government went through several permutations between 1977 and 1979, to collapse in total despair. Mrs. Gandhi was the obvious beneficiary and her electoral victory in 1980 was testimony to the failure of India's political coalitions to sustain their integrity or uniform posture. The December 1984 elections that followed her death proved the Janata Party was too weak to be revived. Moreover, the opposition found it impossible to organize an effective coalition under its leadership. *See also* ELECTIONS: INDIA, p. 224; INDIAN NATIONAL CONGRESS, CONGRESS (I), p. 159.

Significance   The post-1979 Janata is little more than a minor political organization led by Chandrasekhar. Morarji Desai, an old Congressite and long-time foe of Mrs. Gandhi, provides the organization with a degree of legitimacy. Desai, who was prime minister of India when the Janata took power in 1977, will never again assume active political leadership. If the Janata remains a feature of Indian political life, it will be more as a reminder of the past than as a part of a vital future. It will at least remind some Indians of their heritage and the spirit of Mahatama Gandhi and Jaya Prakash Narayan who both preached a form of indigenous socialism.

Khmer Rouge: Cambodia   The political organization which defeated the American-supported government of Lon Nol and Sirik Matak in 1975. The Khmer Rouge leader, Pol Pot, enlisted the services of Cambodian intellectuals like Khieu Samphan, Hou Youn, and Hu Nim who helped recruit a sizeable portion of student and intellectual leaders from Phnom Penh. The rural masses followed in the thousands, given their disenchantment with the central government. The Khmer Rouge fought an ostensibly independent war against the established government. Recalling historic Vietnamese attempts to control Cambodia, the Khmer Rouge avoided dependence on Hanoi. This solitary Khmer Rouge effort was obscured by local propaganda that described them as an arm of the Vietcong and North Vietnamese. Khmer Rouge bases were actually remote from Vietnamese border areas.

Prince Sihanouk, forced to leave Cambodia when Lon Nol perpetrated his coup, also identified with the Khmer Rouge resistance and thus further legitimized the movement. Although the Khmer Rouge professed a version of Marxism, Khmer nationalism was more significant. In fact, the Lon Nol government faced a spontaneous, popular uprising, and thousands of American-trained Cambodian troops deserted their units for service with the Khmer Rouge after 1970. Although the government prevailed in Phnom Penh until 1975, the Khmer Rouge moved freely in the countryside. Moreover, it provided the bridge between Cambodia's intellectuals and peasants. *See also* ONE-PARTY VASSAL STATE: KAMPUCHEA (CAMBODIA), p. 242.

Significance   It is important to distinguish between the Khmer Rouge and the Khmer Viet Minh. The latter are a relatively small group of

Cambodians who were part of the Vietnamese-sponsored Khmer Issarak (Free Khmer), a group that fought the French between 1945 and 1954. These insurgents did not return to Cambodia until 1970 and were highly suspect among the Khmer Rouge of Pol Pot. The survivors of this group became the leaders of Khmer Rouge deserters who fled the killing, torture, and repression of the Pol Pot regime in 1977–78. The Khmer Viet Minh and Khmer Rouge defectors under the leadership of Heng Samrin, boosted by the Vietnamese army and Communist party, forced Pol Pot and his depleted Khmer Rouge to flee Phnom Penh and seek refuge in the jungles along the Thai border. Heng Samrin proclaimed the People's Republic of Kampuchea on January 10, 1979. Prince Sihanouk, however, refused to recognize the regime, and except for the Soviet Union and its client states, all other states continued to acknowledge the authority of the Pol Pot Khmer Rouge, despite reports that approximately three million Cambodians had been victimized during its reign from 1975 to 1979.

Kilusang Bagong Lipunan (KBL): Philippines　　A political movement led by President Ferdinand E. Marcos. The Philippines were introduced to political parties during United States occupation of the islands from 1898 to 1946. The Americans left behind a multi-party system, and a U.S.-styled democracy operated in the country until September 23, 1972 when President Ferdinand E. Marcos abrogated the constitution and declared martial law. Political parties were banned, and the National Assembly dissolved. Personal freedoms were suspended and the President, with assistance from the army ruled by decree. Although political parties were permitted to resume activity in 1978, and martial law was lifted in 1981, there was little evidence that arbitrary methods of rule had been discarded. The assassination of opposition leader Benigno Aquino in 1983 was cause for a major display of public bitterness and frustration by a broad cross-section of Filipino society. Marcos was accused of ordering the murder and his denial was treated with considerable skepticism by the politically conscious and aroused population in Manila.

The Kilusang Bagong Lipunan (KBL), or New Society Movement, was conceived by Marcos and his followers in 1978. The purposes of the party were several; Marcos wanted a government party to "compete" with the other reinstated political organizations, the lifting of martial law made elections inevitable, and the government party anticipated playing an active role. Marcos had been pressured to civilianize his administration and reduce his dependence on the military establishment. Although KBL remained a shadow organization without coherent structure or headquarters, it was the clear victor in the 1978 elections and in May 1984 managed to eke out another win. In both instances, however, the opposition had good reason to believe the results were rigged. The large vote garnered by the opposition in 1984 was interpreted differently by the opposed sides. The opposition declared it had demonstrated its growing strength against a despotic regime, whereas Marcos pointed to the close nature of the contest and argued it was a genuine indication of the vitality of Filipino democracy. *See also* POLITICAL PARTIES: PHILIPPINES, p. 192.

Significance   The Kilusang Bagong Lipunan is not expected to survive the passing of Ferdinand Marcos. The party is identified with him and his wife, Imelda, and there is little permanent structure or substance in the organization. Filipino parties prior to 1972 were aggressive actors in a political process dominated by Liberals and Nationalists. The vitality of these organizations has been sapped by a decade of martial law and a repressive regime that has not hesitated to arrest and incarcerate politicians or muzzle the press. The formation of the "Justice for Aquino, Justice for All" movement, as well as the Nationalist Alliance, are signs of increasing political radicalism and can be attributed to years of repressive rule. The United States cannot escape criticism in this context. The extension of U.S. base rights in the Philippines in 1983 was grist for the opposition mills. Washington is accused of imposing Marcos on the Filipino nation and of sustaining his adminstration. The liquidation of American bases and the banning of multinational corporations are considered essential for defeating Marcos.

Korean Workers' Party: North Korea   The Communist Party of North Korea, organized in June 1949. The Korean Workers' Party is an elite body of one-and-a-half million members. It is a monolithic organization under the absolute leadership of Kim Il Sung (Kim, Il-sŏng). According to the party constitution, the National Party Congress is "the highest decision-making organ of the Party" and its Central Committee directs the affairs of the Party during the four-year intervals between congresses. The Central Committee then elects a standing committee to serve while it is not in session. This committee is called the Political Committee (Politburo), and it is the highest decision-making body under the chairmanship of Kim Il Sung. The Party Congress also provides a Party Secretariat. The secretariat was abolished in 1966 for some unknown reason but was revived in 1970 with Kim Il Sung as General Secretary. The Secretariat supervises the various party executive departments which are charged with the supervision of the corresponding government departments.

The bulk of the Party's organizational efforts are concentraed on mass organizations, placing everyone, whether residing in the urban area or in the countryside, in an organized group. The Party strives for ideological purity and the training of youth along ideological lines receives top priority. The educational system and performing arts are also mobilized for this purpose. The Young Pioneers and the Socialist Working Youth League are the two major youth groups forming an integral part in this united and monolithic Communist system. *See also* COMMUNISM, p. 74; KIMILSUNGISM, p. 95.

Significance   On October 10, 1945, the Soviet Command, in occupation of North Korea following Japanese surrender in World War II, called for a meeting of the leaders of various local Communist groups to form a "North Korean Branch" of the Korean Communist Party. In December 1945, it was renamed the North Korean Communist Party. In July 1946, it was merged with the New People's Party which was organized by returnees from China. Following the establishment of the Democratic People's Republic of Korea in September 1948, the North Korean Workers' Party merged with the South Korean Workers' Party to organize the Korean Workers' Party in June 1949. Through these maneuvers, Kim Il Sung, leader of North Korea since its inception as an independent Communist state, was able to place himself at the helm of North Korea's Communist Party.

Competition for power continued throughout the Korean War period (1950–53), but Kim was able to purge such power rivals as Mu Chŏng, the military leader of distinction who was identified with the Korean Communist returnees from China following the Korean liberation and Pak Hŏn-yong, the leader of the domestic Communists from South Korea. By the time of the Fourth Party Congress in 1961, Kim was able to announce that the Party had been purged of dissident factions, the army solidified under his leadership, the economy totally socialized, the working-class enlarged, and the people indoctrinated in his ideology. Today, the Korean Workers' Party constitutes a huge bureaucracy which is ubiquitous throughout North Korean society. It is considered the body and soul of its chief, Kim Il Sung, whom it serves with unquestioned loyalty.

Liberal Democratic Party (LDP): Japan   The dominant political party in Japan since it was organized in 1955 by merging the post-war conservative Liberal and Democratic parties. The LDP is more than a single party. It is a collection of various factional parties. Each faction is headed by a leader, is stable and institutionalized, and lasts until the leader is no longer politically active. All the factions work together, however, because of their shared views on a number of issues. They are all anti-Marxist and anti-Communist, they all uphold democratic principles, advocate a sound capitalist economy, and desire close cooperation with the United States. They are closely allied with the Japanese business community, drawing most of their funds from it, but they also have strong local bases of support.

The LDP maintains headquarters in Tokyo. The formal system of decision making consists of the Party Conference, the Assembly of the Members of Both Houses of the Diet (parliament), and the Executive Council. Other important organs of the party include the Policy Affairs Research Council, Organization Committee, Party Discipline Committee, and Election Policy Committee. The secretary-general is the chief administrator of party affairs, whereas the party president, elected by the Party Conference for a three-year term, is the highest executive officer. The party president also assumes premiership as head of the dominant party in the Diet. The party president together with the Executive Council are the most important policy-making organs of the party. Appointed by the party president, the membership of the Executive Council includes most of the influential figures in the party, representing various factional interests. The Policy Affairs Research Council usually makes major policy recommendations to the Executive Council. The national organization of the LDP includes the prefectural (provincial) federations and local branches. The Central Academy of Politics is an auxiliary institution of the party, which was established for the purpose of systematically training party cadres (workers) and activists. Attempts have also been made to transform the party into a mass-based party, but they have been without much success. The LDP remains a cadre party. Its strength is not in its mass organization, but in the success of the individual candidates in the elections and the generally conservative orientation of the Japanese people, particularly in rural areas. *See also* JAPAN: ELECTORAL SYSTEM, p. 222; JAPAN: POLITICAL PARTIES, p. 183.

Significance   The conservatives have been continuously in power in postwar Japan. They were organized into the LDP in 1955. Having one party so dominant, as it is in Japan, is almost unprecedented in a democracy, but it is not without explanation. First, the Japanese are on the whole politically conservative and pragmatic. Radical ideological appeals have not sunk too deep with them. Second, the conservatives have been identified with the postwar Japanese recovery. Third, the conservatives are conservative by Japanese, not American, standards. The government of the LDP has promoted various social welfare measures. Fourth, the LDP is a flexible, pragmatic party, coalescing into it various ideological strands and policy orientations. Fifth, the LDP's decision-making process, as is typical in Japan, is consensual, catering to divergent interests. Sixth, the LDP is supported by the business community, which exerts an enormous influence over the voting public. Seventh, the LDP is supported by the rural voters who are favored in the Japanese electoral process. Eighth, the LDP as a party in power has been able to recruit capable leaders. Ninth, the LDP has been able to cash in on the Japanese electoral system which favors individual candidates rather than party labels. Tenth, the LDP's opposition has been weak and ideologically too divided to organize a united front.

Despite these advantages, popular support for the LDP has been declining. Some of the factors usually cited to explain the decline are (1) general apathy among the Japanese voters; (2) the feeling of many that the LDP has been in power too long; (3) the involvement of high-ranking LDP leaders in national scandals and corruption; and (4) changes in partisan support patterns in Japan. Recently, some dissident LDP members have organized into the New Liberal Club and are competing against LDP members in the elections.

May Fourth Movement: China   A Chinese intellectual and political movement, named after a demonstration in Beijing (Peking) on May 4, 1919. In the May Fourth Movement, students protested the decision of the Big Powers at the Versailles Peace Conference that ended World War I hostilities and assigned to Japan Germany's rights in China's Shandong (Shantung) province, instead of returning them to China following German defeat. Police suppression and arrests caused demonstrations and strikes to spread further into other cities, intensifying the spirit of nationalism and popularizing a "new culture" movement already under way. At the time of the May Fourth Movement, Beijing was recognized as an important intellectual center. Under the dynamic leadership of Cai Yuanpei (Ts'ai Yuan-p'ei) (1868–1940), Beijing University had a brilliant faculty, most of whose members, such as Hu Shih (Hu Shi) and Chen Duxiu (Ch'en Tu-hsiu), had received advanced education abroad. They inspired their students with liberal reformist ideals.

The *New Youth Magazine,* founded by Chen, emphasized intellectual inquiry and instilled a sense of iconoclasm towards traditional Chinese culture. Intellectuals searched for the underlying causes of China's backwardness; many concluded that the culture itself needed drastic reform. Interest in anarchism and socialism revived, and the Soviet Union became a popular model. In a number of cities, young intellectuals created new anarchist and socialist study groups, producing reformist journals and creating workers' organizations. The May Fourth Movement inspired a new generation of leaders in many fields. It led to a revival of support for China's Nationalist Party (Kuomintang). It also

led to the founding of the Chinese Communist Party in 1921. *See also*
COMMUNIST PARTY: CHINA, p. 144; NATIONALIST PARTY: CHINA, p. 176;
REPUBLICAN REVOLUTION: CHINA, p. 196.

Significance   China's Ch'ing (Qing) dynasty was overthrown, and its
age-old dynastic system was discarded in 1911 in favor of a republican
system of government with Yuan Shihkai (Yüan Shih-k'ai) as president.
Yuan's presidency was his reward for having supported Sun Yat-sen's
revolutionaries in forcing the abdication of the last emperor of the
Ch'ing dynasty. A traditionalist by heart, Yuan had no illusions about
China's republican future. His real dream was to create his own dynasty.
He was declared Emperor in 1915 by a national congress he convened to
give the aura of legitimacy to his imperial ambition, but died the
following year.
      Thereafter, China plunged into the chaotic period during which
powerful regional figures shifted alliances for control of the central
government. In this so-called warlord period from 1916 to 1928, hundreds of sub-national figures dominated the country. They enjoyed
virtual territorial autonomy since their military forces owed them personal allegiance. In addition to this internal disunity, the nation was
threatened from without by the Japanese. When World War I broke out
in 1914, Japan fought on the Allied side and seized German holdings in
China's Shandong province. In 1915, the Japanese presented the Beijing
government with the so-called Twenty-one Demands, which would have
reduced China to the status of Japan's protectorate. With U.S. support,
China rejected some of these demands but had to yield to the Japanese
insistence that they keep the Shandong territory already in their possession. In 1917, through secret notes, Britain, France, and Italy confirmed
the Japanese claim in exchange for the latter's naval action against
Germany. China's belated declaration of war against Germany in 1917
was not enough to recover Shandong. In the end, the Chinese government accepted a secret deal with Japan in 1918, granting the claim to
Shandong. When the Paris Peace Conference of 1919 confirmed the
Japanese claim and the Beijing government's putative sellout became
public, domestic reactions were shattering. On May 4, 1919, there were
massive student protest demonstrations against the Beijing government
and Japan. The student activism and the iconoclastic and reformist
intellectual currents which were set in motion by patriotic student
protesters developed into a national awakening known as the May
Fourth Movement, the intellectual derivative of which was known as the
New Culture Movement. Moreover, anti-Western and anti-Japanese feelings heightened. Many of the activist leaders in the May Fourth Movement including Chen Duxiu (Ch'en Tu-hsiu), and Li Dazhao (Li Tao-
chao), later accepted an offer of help from the Soviet Union and the

Comintern and participated in the organization of the Chinese Communist Party in 1921.

Muslim League: India   The Muslims of India reacted to the formation of the Indian National Congress by organizing their communal party in 1906. Open only to Muslims, the Muslim League was inaugurated in Dhaka, East Bengal. The Congress party, from its beginning in 1885, was by contrast open to all persons irrespective of religious, ethnic, or other distinctions. The Muslim League, however, understood that the Congress would come under the sway of the Hindus and they therefore held to the exclusive nature of their organization. It is important to note that neither the Congress nor the Muslim League prevented Muslims from holding simultaneous membership in both parties. Mohammad Ali Jinnah, for example, the man credited with winning an independent Pakistan, was a member of both parties in the years prior to World War I. The Muslim League was moved to Delhi in 1912 in order to make it more central to Muslim needs. Delhi had also become the political capital of British India and the League believed it necessary to have its headquarters close to the sinews of colonial government. In this way the All-India Muslim League was formed. The party was eventually to receive the transfer of power from the British, which established the independent state of Pakistan in 1947. With the creation of Pakistan, the Muslim League of India quickly withered and disappeared. It remained somewhat vital in the southern Indian state of Kerala, by dint of its alliance with the Christian community there. Although it has had no influence in national policy, the Muslim League does an adequate job of representing the interests of Kerala Muslims. *See also* INDIAN NATIONAL CONGRESS, CONGRESS (I), p. 159; LAHORE RESOLUTION, p. 97; TWO NATION THEORY, p. 128.

Significance   India has a very large Muslim minority, estimated at between 70 and 100 million. Nevertheless, the Muslims of India failed to keep the Muslim League intact. In part, this was due to the movement of most Muslim League leaders to Pakistan. Another explanation, however, might be the realization that the Muslim League was more a movement than a political organization. As a movement, its principal objective was the creation of an independent Pakistan. The fact that the Muslim League quickly disintegrated in Pakistan seems to support this explanation. If it could not survive in Pakistan, how could it be expected to flourish in India? The future of a communal party such as the Muslim League is questionable given India's emphasis on being a secular state. Most Muslims find their interests enhanced by membership in secular organizations and they are more likely to identify with the Congress or the other left of center organizations.

National Conference: India A Kashmir political movement. Kashmir has been a troubled region since India gained independence. The National Conference developed from the Muslim Conference and held its first session in October 1939. It was founded by Shaykh Mohammad Abdullah (the Lion of Kashmir) to give voice to the particular demands of the region's Muslim majority. First concerned with gaining greater political freedom from British rule, Shaykh Abdullah turned his attention to limiting Congress power in the post-1947 period. Overall, the National Conference symbolized Muslim distinctiveness and the community's desire to remain free from Hindu influence. Shaykh Abdullah was incarcerated by Indian authorities on numerous occasions, but in the early 1970s he entered into a working arrangement with Mrs. Gandhi and finally became Chief Minister of the state. In 1981, shortly before his death, Shaykh Abdullah transferred responsibility for managing the National Conference to his son, Farooq Abdullah, despite opposition from Ghulam Mohammad Shah and his supporters within the National Conference. This controversy remained unresolved when Shaykh Abdullah died in August 1982.

In 1983, the National Conference won the state-wide elections, defeating the powerful Congress Party of Mrs. Gandhi, and Farooq Abdullah became the state's Chief Minister. The quarrel between Farooq and Mohammad Shah continued, however, and in July 1984, Farooq was summarily dismissed by Mrs. Gandhi, following the defection of twelve Conference legislators, followers of Mohammad Shah. Mrs. Gandhi had accused Farooq of permitting Sikh terrorists to train in Kashmir. She had feared an intensification of the Kashmiri problem while she was preoccupied with the Punjab. Despite criticism that the prime minister had acted unconstitutionally, and street demonstrations in behalf of Farooq, Mrs. Gandhi appointed Mohammad Shah as Kashmir's chief minister. *See also* KASHMIR DISPUTE, p. 386; KAUTILIYA, p. 94.

Significance The state of Kashmir is approximately 75 percent Muslim and has been a bone of contention between India and Pakistan since the British withdrawal from India. The National Conference has become the vehicle through which the Muslims of Kashmir have attempted to steer a middle course between India and Pakistan. The National Conference has learned to work with the Congress party while at the same time avoiding its close embrace. The National Conference therefore has supported Congress' foreign policy and accepts the idea of India as a secular state, which has allowed the Kashmiri Muslims to affirm their separate identity and safeguard their traditions and interests, while minimizing friction between themselves and the powers in New Delhi. At the same time, New Delhi has a deep and abiding interest in Kashmiri affairs, and it will not permit the National Conference to drift too far from its control. Fear that Pakistan might still seek to exploit Muslim sentiment in the state is a primary reason for federal government concern over developments there. All indicators, however, point to New Delhi placating the National Conference, much as it does the regional parties in Tamil Nadu (Madras). Nevertheless, Farooq Abdullah's dismissal reveals how short term the relationships between India's politicians can be. Coalitions, alliances, and associations are made for immediate advantage and just as quickly abandoned. Manipulation remains the name of the game, the purpose being to stay on top. Kautiliyan rules set the tone and character of political interaction.

National Socialist Party: Bangladesh   The National Socialist Party, or Jatiya Samajtantrik Dal, was assembled as a front organization for the variety of leftist elements in Bangladesh. Its leader was M. A. Jalil, a prominent figure in the liberation struggle against Pakistan. Also joining the coalition was Abu Taher, another hero of the civil war. Taher's role was the creation of the Revolutionary People's Army, a secret cell within the Bangladesh army. Taher and his loyal forces were instrumental in bringing Ziaur Rahman to power, but the military president later accused Taher of treason and he was hanged in July 1976. The National Socialist Party was banned in 1977 but permitted to operate again in 1978. Radicals in Bangladesh have struggled against government bans and repressive policies in an effort to sustain their organizations and programs. The Bangladesh Communist League was organized in 1972 by Serajul Alam, and it drew recruits from the Awami League's student, labor, and peasant branches. *See also* BANGLADESH NATIONALIST PARTY, p. 137.

Significance   The National Socialist Party of Bangladesh is a Marxist organization, and its allegiance is split between Beijing and Moscow. General H. M. Ershad's program of Islamization was launched in an effort to control the spread of Marxist radicalism in the country. In 1983, riots raged through some of the important municipalities over the government's proposal making Arabic and the Qur'an mandatory in the nation's schools. As in Pakistan, Bangladesh's military rulers concluded that the ideology of Islam was the only counter to the ideology of Marxism. But the Marxists and their supporters among the other secular organizations sought to contest this government program, and the arrest of numerous politicians and the closing of the universities was a predictable outcome. Ershad also initiated a dialogue with the leaders of the political organizations in order to isolate the leftists. This tactic, however, was not more successful than those tried earlier. Frustrated by the opposition's intransigence, but still seeking broader support, Ershad, like his counterpart in Pakistan, promised to restore constitutional government and hold elections by March 1985. Few political leaders responded affirmatively to his call for patience and cooperation, however. Bangladesh's military governors concluded that their work was made more difficult by the Soviet Union's support of the radicals, especially the Nationalist Socialist Party. In 1983, Ershad ordered the expulsion of 14 Soviet diplomats who were allegedly engaged in antigovernment activities. The oversized Soviet Cultural Center in Dhaka and the Soviet Consulate in Chittagong were closed for the same reason.

The opposition organized numerous demonstrations in 1984, all focusing on one theme—the termination of martial law and the return to civilian government. Frustrated, Ershad announced the indefinite postponement of the elections in October 1984 and seemed inclined to strengthen his new Jana Dal Party whose members now filled his cabinet.

Nationalist Party (Kuomintang): China   The ruling party of China from 1928 to 1949 and thereafter of Taiwan. The Nationalist Party in China is called *Chung-kuo Kuo-min Tang* (Chinese People's Party), or *Kuomintang* (Nationalist Party) for short. The triumphant rebels overthrew the Ch'ing (Qing) dynasty in China, proclaimed the Chinese Republic on January 3, 1912 and named Dr. Sun Yat-sen as the first president of China. Later in 1920, Sun Yat-sen founded the Nationalist Party and held its First National Congress in 1924. However, the origin of the Nationalist Party can be traced to several short-lived preceding organizations, beginning in 1894. Sun Yat-sen founded the Society to Restore China's Prosperity in Hawaii and Hong Kong between 1894 and 1895; the Revolution Alliance in Tokyo in 1905; the National People's Party as a parliamentary party in China in 1912, and the Chinese Revolutionary Party in Tokyo in 1914. The Nationalist Party of 1920 was first established in Shanghai against the Beijing (Peking) government, which at the time was under the control of warlords.

In his efforts to strengthen the party, Sun Yat-sen welcomed aid from the Soviet Union and the Comintern. From 1922 to 1924 he was assisted by Michael Borodin who was sent to China as the agent of the Comintern. Following the Soviet model, the Nationalist Party adopted the principle of "democratic centralism," but Sun Yat-sen insisted on his ideology of the Three People's Principles—Nationalism, Democracy and People's Livelihood. With help from the Soviet Union, the

Nationalist Party also established the Whampoa Military Academy in June 1924 to train and indoctrinate officers. Out of this development a close alliance emerged between the Party and the military in Nationalist China. The Party was organized hierarchically, with branches established throughout the country. Under the leadership of Chiang Kai-shek, who eventually succeeded Sun Yat-sen, the Party set out to unify the country militarily. Chiang's initial military efforts (his so-called Northern Expedition) were successful, but he was unable to defeat the Communist movement in China under the leadership of Mao Zedong (Mao Tse-tung). In the civil war between Chiang's forces and the Communists, Chiang's forces lost control of the Chinese mainland and were forced to evacuate to Taiwan where they established an exile government in 1949. In Taiwan, the Nationalist Party remains the ruling party. *See also* CHINESE NATIONALIST GOVERNMENT: TAIWAN, p. 238; THREE PEOPLE'S PRINCIPLES, p. 122.

Significance　　Sun Yat-sen died in 1925. Under his leadership, the Nationalist Party had permitted Communists to become members. However, his successor, Chiang Kai-shek, became increasingly apprehensive over Communist influence in the Party and openly challenged them. Chiang was supported by China's banking interests and big business in his anti-Communist move. On April 12, 1927, his forces marched into Shanghai in an extended military campaign against the warlords. Chiang ordered a round-up of Communist-led labor union members in the so-called "White Terror." Following the success of this operation, Chiang's suppression of the Communists spread to other cities. By spring of 1928, Chiang was the unchallenged leader of the Nationalist Party. His military expedition against the warlords in the north was momentarily successful, and in June 1928 he completed the military unification of the country.

The warlords, however, were never completely defeated. Some of them, especially in southwest and northwest China, remained in effective control of their territories. It was an uneasy alliance that made the warlords subservient to Chiang, and only nominal unification was possible in 1928. The Communists, still at large, were able to set up various soviets under their control. Chiang's military conquest of the warlords and their subsequent alliance were only the beginning of China's nation-building efforts. The peace that prevailed between 1928 and 1937 was deceptive. Besides the warlords, Chiang had to contend with persistent Communist movements. The Japanese imperial ambition in China also intimidated Chiang's legitimacy since he was unwilling to confront Japan in the midst of his Communist extermination campaign. However, following his kidnapping at Xian in December 1936 by the former Manchurian warlord Chang Hseuh-liang (Zhang Xueliang),

Chiang was forced to abandon his anti-communist campaign and join them in opposing Japan.

In the Second Sino-Japanese War (1937–45), Chiang's troops were forced to retreat to the wartime capital of Chongqing (Chungking), while the Communists were able to operate as guerrillas, extending their areas of control and fighting Japanese troops. At the war's end, the Communists were in control of a large area of China. A coalition effort between the Nationalists and the Communists to set up a unified government with help from the United States failed, plunging the country into a full-scale civil war. This time it was the Communists who prevailed and Chiang's forces were eventually forced to withdraw from the Chinese mainland to Taiwan in 1949. In the Chinese mainland, the Nationalist party was never effective in generating mass followings like those of the Communists. This was in part due to preoccupation with military unification of the country, but even more so to a lack of time and resources necessary to effectively carry out a socio-economic revolution, which was drastically needed in China. Chiang started a "new life" movement in February 1934 and established New Life Promotion Associations in several provinces throughout the country in order to boost public morale and encourage disciplined behavior along with nation-building efforts. Like so many other movements, however, Chiang failed to generate popular support in his anti-Communist campaign.

People's Action Party (PAP): Singapore   The most vital political organization in Singapore. Singapore was established as an independent and sovereign parliamentary republic in 1965. The People's Action Party (PAP) has never experienced meaningful opposition. More than three-quarters of Singapore's population is Chinese, which explains Malaysia's willingness to separate the island from the Malaysian federation. PAP's leader, Lee Kuan Yew, tried to minimize ethnic and racial differences and believed it possible to develop the Malaysian federation for the benefit of all communities. Difficulties with the United Malays National Organization, however, brought a final and permanent divorce. Lee has therefore devoted his life to creating in Singapore what he could not achieve in Malaysia. PAP was organized in 1954 by a group of intellectuals and professionals who wished to establish democratic institutions in the region. Seeking to isolate no one from their movement, the PAP leaders attracted recruits across a broad spectrum of political thought and behavior. In recent years, however, the party has been more identified with moderate and sometimes conservative rather than radical views. As a consequence, the leftists have abandoned PAP in order to form their own organizations. Nevertheless, PAP is still socialist in program and philosophy.

The structure of PAP places particular emphasis on its Central Executive Committee which is a policy-making organ. No less important is PAP's Central Political Bureau which maintains the discipline of party members and disseminates information on party and state matters. The Central Executive Committee has long been judged the real government of Singapore because it sets the pattern for decision making, identifies priorities, and allocates resources. PAP leadership flows from the center to district and sub-district operators, to "liaison stations." Citizens' Consultative Committees ensure that party directives are carried through to the grassroots. Tight-knit organization is possible in so small a country, but the perils posed to the nation can never be underestimated. PAP is therefore ever-vigilant. Assisting the party and government is the Internal Security Department which oversees the activities of the opposition. Anything deemed to be subversive or divisive is dealt with swiftly and severely. For all its power, PAP is not a mass party. Its membership is reported to be less than 50,000 and no effort is made to expand it. The members are divided into two groups, the regulars and the elite. The latter are said to be no more than several hundred men who are pledged to secrecy. But Lee Kuan Yew is the recognized head of PAP and, although he is still relatively young (he was born in 1923), he is concerned with the matter of succession and has made serious efforts to bring young disciples into the party's inner circle. In August 1984 Lee declared his desire to retire at age 65, that is, in 1988. He called for an elected president rather than the prevailing traditional one and influenced older leaders in the PAP to resign their positions on the party's Central Committee so that younger members could be appointed. He also encouraged his son, Lee Hsien Loong, a brigadier general in the army, to enter politics as a parliamentary candidate. Lee Hsien was not only the second ranking officer in the army, he was also the first high ranking military figure to enter politics in Singapore. The president defended his son's new role, insisting it was not his intention to create a family dynasty. By January 1985 Prime Minister Lee Kuan Yew had organized a new cabinet consolidating the power of the young leaders. Goh Chok Tong, defense minister in the previous cabinet, also assumed the role of first deputy prime minister and thus became the likely successor to Lee. His son, Lee Hsien, was made a junior minister. With the exception of the prime minister, only two members of the governing party's traditional elite remained in the 13-member cabinet. *See also* FEDERALISM: MALAYSIA, p. 226.

Significance   Singapore's People's Action Party has held center stage since the nation's independence. Nevertheless, other political parties have emerged and observers believe a multiple party system could be in the offing if PAP leaders are serious about building democratic institutions and processes. The so-called opposition parties are the Malay National Organization of Singapore, originally a branch of Malaysia's dominant UMNO; the Worker's Party, the first opposition party to win a seat in the parliament; the United National Front, seeking reunion with Malaysia; the People's Front, organized as a permanent critic of Lee's dictatorial practices; and the Socialist Front (SF), or Barisan Sosialis, a splinter organization of the PAP.

SF members abandoned their parliamentary seats in 1966 and the party adopted violence in pursuit of its objectives. The government came down hard on the organization and it was constrained from participating in active politics. Among all the parties noted above, only the Worker's Party seems to have found leverage to deal with the PAP. The Worker's Party is a non-communist, liberal organization, primarily Chinese, that is concerned with social and economic issues. Where there is need for another spokesman, the people of Singapore might find the Worker's Party a useful instrument. Nevertheless, there is no significant challenge to the PAP or Lee Kuan Yew, and barring the unforeseen, Singapore appears likely to maintain a relatively steady course.

Political Parties: Indonesia   The political parties of Indonesia owe their role and importance to the effectiveness of the Suharto administration. Indonesia has been relatively stable since the chaos and bloodshed of the mid-1960s. General-President Suharto won a fourth five-year term in 1983 but has been the preeminent ruler, with assistance from the armed forces, since 1966. In the 1980s Indonesia had a modified three-party system. These parties were gleaned from the literally dozens of political parties that took part in the first parliamentary elections of 1955. President Suharto officially assumed the presidency in 1968 after banishing Sukarno, the country's first president. In 1969 Suharto proclaimed a broad set of policies called the "New Order." The "New Order" specified the need to hold elections in order to legitimate the new administration. Nine parties were then active and expected to compete for votes.

The Suharto government, however, was intent on organizing its own party which it labeled *Golkar*, an acronym derived from *golongan karya*, or functional groups. The Golkar, or functional groups, were divided into seven categories or *kino*, all coming under a central joint secretariat which was identified as the *Sekber* Golkar. Although free from conventional political activity, the Golkar was permitted to run candidates in the 1971 election and thus became a political party. Each kino or group among labor, women, the peasants, army, and intelligentsia, etc., was provided with a leader by the government, usually a retired military officer. The entire Sekber Golkar was lodged in the Ministry of Interior, ensuring its role as a pillar of the administration. Golkar cut across ideological, racial, ethnic, religious, and economic differences. It stressed authoritarian organization and military discipline. It has provided Suharto with popular acceptance as well as legitimacy and has assisted in giving the country a degree of harmony absent in other areas of Asia. Moreover, the functional groups interact in a productive manner and consensus is a working norm. Golkar's seven-point working program, the *Sapta-Krida,* is as follows: (1) promotion of political stability; (2) economic stability; (3) security and stability; (4) development; (5) public welfare; (6) measures to improve the state apparatus; and (7) general elections. With such organization and programs, it is not surprising that Golkar has been the overwhelming winner in elections to date.

Golkar and the other major parties, the Development Unity Party (*Partai Persatuan Pembangunan*) and the Indonesian Democracy Party (*Partai Demokrasi Indonesia*), are regulated by a 1975 law which forbids the formation of other political organizations. The government provides funds to the three parties, pays salaries to political figures, and generally makes it possible for them to serve in the parliament. Parties are prevented from appealing to the public except when election campaigns are conducted. This program is known as the "floating mass" concept. Parties are provided with central offices in Jakarta as well as at the provincial and district levels. Golkar and Development Unity are both associations of groups, but the latter has more of an Islamic bias. It also incorporates the ideas and objectives of the older *Masjumi Nahdatul Ulama* and *Partai Muslimin Indonesia* parties. Development Unity, however, was not permitted to adopt a Muslim name. Nevertheless, it controls the *Gerakan Pemuda Ansor,* or Youth Group, and the *Muslimat NU,* a women's group. On the other hand, Golkar requires all civil administrators and government officials to join the organization or leave the party. Development Unity attracts the more devout elements of the population and is successful in reaching the rural population. By contrast, the Indonesian Democracy Party, which is secular, is also almost exclusively urban. Indonesian Democracy, formerly the prominent Indonesian Nationalist Party, is a poor third to Golkar and Development Unity. Its roots are found in the Sukarno era when most government officials supported the nationalist organization and it dominated Javan politics. Separated from influential members of the government, it is now an insignificant organization, with minor standing in the parliament. *See also* GOLKAR, p. 155; PANTASILA, p. 110.

Significance   Indonesian political parties are currently the handiwork of the armed forces. The military was the only institution standing in the way of a radical takeover of the government in 1965 when the *Gestapu*

Gerakan September Tigu Puluh (September 30 Movement) attacked Indonesia's senior military officers, killing six of the nation's highest ranking generals. The perpetrators were associated with the Indonesian Communist Party (PKI), and when the army regrouped under General Nasution and General Suharto, a broad net was spread over those believed to be involved with or sympathetic to the leftists. In the counteroffensive that followed, several hundred thousand people are estimated to have perished. President Sukarno was implicated in the conspiracy and although he remained in the presidency for a time afterward, he was forced to transfer his responsibilities to General Suharto in 1966. The New Order has its origin in this period, although its development has been incremental and methodical.

The political parties were not reduced to three until 1975, but at each step along the way the government has stressed unity, cooperation, and progress. The New Order therefore involved the establishment of several government institutions, most important being Pertamina, the national oil company; Kopkamtib, Operations Command for the Restoration of Security and Order; and Bappenas, national economic planning. Golkar is geared to the efficient operation of these institutions and it is not far removed from *Gotong Royong,* or mutual aid, and NASAKOM, Sukarno's acronym for the unity of nationalist, religious groups, and Communists. The Suharto administration has eliminated Communists and other Marxists from public life, but has left a substantial base for the intermingling of secular and religious groups, out-island provincialists, Javan centralists, and nationalists and ideologists. Nevertheless, Indonesia was not immune to acts of political dissent and terrorism. A number of Muslim fundamentalist leaders were arrested in September 1984 because of their perceived complicity in fomenting unrest. Members of the "Petition-of-Fifty" group of antigovernment intellectuals, professionals, and retired army generals were barred from preaching in mosques. Nevertheless, their young disciples continued to defy the government and in one incident almost 2,000 demonstrators attacked a military district headquarters. In October, an explosion in an ammunition dump rocked the outskirts of Jakarta and artillery rounds and rockets were sent hurtling into residential areas killing and injuring nearby inhabitants. Terrorists also attacked banks and shops, and set factories ablaze, seeking to dramatize the government's inability to restrain them.

Indonesia in the mid-1980s was guided by Suharto, the armed forces, Golkar, and the state ideology of *Pantasila,* or five principles that proclaim belief in One God, sovereignty, unity, social justice, and humanity. Pantasila is reputed to be the foundation for all social and political organizations. Suharto and the generals rejected demands by Muslim fundamentalists for an Islamic foundation. Military justice was in vogue, and action against accused criminals was swift and severe. Secret trials and almost-as-secret executions were carried out. Competitive politics was something Indonesia had had little experience with, and the military establishment continued to demonstrate that the country was ill-prepared for the give and take of party activity. The armed forces derived its legitimacy from the doctrine of *dwi-fungsi*, the military's dual role, managing the nation's defense while playing a central and constructive role in Indonesia's political, social, and economic life.

Political Parties: Japan   Following the Japanese surrender to the Allied Powers in World War II, many old-line party politicians became active again, regrouping themselves, as political parties proliferated. Out of these emerged Japan's major political parties; the Liberal-Democratic Party, the Japan Socialist Party, the Japan Communist Party, and the Democratic Socialist Party. The Clean Government Party (*Komeito*) was organized in 1964. In 1976, dissident Diet members of the Liberal Democratic Party organized the New Liberal Club.

The Liberal-Democratic Party (LDP) is the ruling party in Japan. It was organized in 1955 by merging the postwar conservative Liberal and Democratic parties. Its dominant position in the Diet has declined in recent years, but it still controls the personnel and policy-making of the central government. Its formal decision-making organizations include the Party Conference, the Assembly of the Members of Both Houses of the Diet, and the Executive Council. Other important organs of the party include the Policy Affairs Research Council, the Organization Committee, the Party Discipline Committee, and the Election Policy Committee. The secretary-general is the chief administrator of party affairs, whereas the party president, elected by the Party Conference, is the highest executive officer. The LDP is closely allied with the Japanese business community, drawing most of its funds from it. Its electoral support comes from traditionally conservative, particularly rural, voters. Ideologically, the LDP is anti-Marxist and anti-Communist. It publicly upholds democratic principles, advocates a sound capitalistic economy, and represents close alliance with the United States. As the enduring ruling party in Japan, however, it has a strongly pragmatic orientation. It is a conservative party by Japanese, not American, standards. The government of the LDP promotes legislation of various social welfare measures.

The Japan Socialist Party (JSP) was organized in its present form in 1955 and holds the second largest party status in the Diet. Theoretically, the Party Congress is the highest governing body, and it elects members of the Central Committee, the Central Executive Committee and its chairman, and a general secretary. The real decision-making power of the party, however, resides with the top executive officials headed by the chairman of the Central Executive Committee. The chief administrative officer of the party is the general secretary. The party's main support comes from the General Council of the Japanese Labor Union (*Sohyo*). Ideologically, the JSP opposes the pro-American attitude of the LDP and Japan's Security Treaty with the United States. It advocates a "peaceful revolution" to a socialist Japan.

The Democratic Socialist Party (DSP) was organized in 1960 as a splinter party of the JSP. The perennial controversies between the ideological left and right factions within the JSP resulted in the establishment of the DSP as a separate socialist party. Organized much like the JSP, it espouses a middle-of-the-road policy within the Japanese political spectrum. The DSP's main support comes from the Japanese Federation of Trade Unions (*Domei*), a politically moderate labor federation, as compared with the Sohyo. Furthermore, its moderate program includes rejection of the policy of neutralism for Japan, but promotion of cooperation with the free world through the United Nations, anti-Communism, the gradual modification of Japan's Security Treaty with the United States, and the eventual withdrawal of American troops from Japan. It has only a minor party status in the Diet.

The Japan Communist Party (JCP) was revived as a political party with the blessing of occupation authorities following Japan's surrender to the Allied Powers in World War II. As soon as it was organized in 1922, the party was forced to operate underground due to government oppression, and at the time of Japan's surrender, most of its leaders were in prison. As a full-fledged Communist party, it is organized like the Communist party of the Soviet Union. Its Party Congress is structurally the highest party organ, but its Central Committee and Presidium are the most powerful decision-making bodies. The party's following has been among the ideologically committed and those alienated from the mainstream of Japanese post-war recovery and development. Although traditionally small, it forms a vocal minority in the Diet. Since the open estrangement of relations between the USSR and China (PRC), the party has suffered from an intense, factional struggle between the Soviet and Chinese factions, but it has recently insisted on an independent and neutral course of action. It has also moderated its former militancy and seeks to control the Diet in cooperation with other "democratic forces" through parliamentary means.

The Clean Government Party (*Komeito*) was organized as a political arm of the Value Creation Society (*Sokagakkai*), a Buddhist religious organization. Known as the Clean Government League before 1964, it was active in local elections. It also ran its candidates in the 1962 election for the House of Councilors. The political party designation was finally adopted in 1964 as the League planned active campaigning for its candidates in the 1967 election for the House of Representatives. The party drew its main support from members of the Value Creation Society. In 1970, however, the Value Creation Society officially dissociated itself from the party. The party draws its main support from alienated or unsuccessful segments of the rapidly changing Japanese society and it successfully competes with the Japanese Communist Party for support in the urban centers. Ideologically, the party is anti-Communist. It favors a democratic system of government and a capitalistic economy. However, it advocates greater welfare payments for people in need and opposes the rearmament of Japan, atomic testing, and the docking of American nuclear warships in Japan. *See also* COMMUNIST PARTY: JAPAN, p. 146; DEMOCRACY: JAPAN, p. 220; LIBERAL DEMOCRATIC PARTY: JAPAN, p. 169.

Significance   Japan as a democracy presents a multiplicity of political parties representing various political ideologies and programs. However, due to the conservative dominance of the LDP, the Japanese party system has been dubbed by some critics as a "one-and-one half party system." Opposition parties have been relatively weak and unable to organize a viable coalition alternative. Their ideologies are too divergent for compromise, appealing to different constituencies and support groups. The Japanese voting public, particularly in rural areas, is less influenced by ideological appeals than by pragamatic considerations. They are persuaded less by formal organizational appeals than by traditional group norms and personal loyalty.

The LDP, as a conservative party in power, appeals most successfully to the conservative Japanese voters, who are still traditional in their political orientation. In order to stay in power, however, the LDP makes concessions and adjustments to meet the demands of the increasingly articulate populace, and it identifies itself with much progressive social legislation. As a matter of fact, various factions within the LDP are really parties within a party. They cater to different groups and interests in the country, thus contributing to the policy adjustment and the longevity of the LDP's power. The formation of the New Liberal Club in 1976 showed some basic weaknesses of the LDP, which the youthful members of the Club denounced as "a gerontocracy bent on back-room power struggles."

Political Parties: Malaysia   Malaysia's ethnic diversity is reflected in its political organizations. Only the United Malays National Organization (UMNO) can be described as a truly national organization, but apart from coalition-building activities, even that body confines itself to Malay affairs and concerns. The other organizations of note are the

Malayan Chinese Association (established in 1949); Gerakan, a predominantly Chinese party founded in 1968 to promote communal harmony; the Malayan Indian Congress (origin 1946), a weak party because of its minority status and the scattering of its constituents; the Sabah People's Union (origin 1975); the United Sabah National Organization (origin 1976); the Sarawak Dayak Party (origin 1983); the Sarawak United People's Party (origin 1959); the Sarawak National Party (origin 1961); the United People Party (Sarawak-based, origin 1973); the People's Progressive Party of Malaysia, appealing to economically backward Chinese in Perak state (origin 1961 as the Perak Progressive Party); and the Berjaya or Barisan Jama Islamia Semalaysia (origin 1977).

All of the above parties are more or less identified with the ruling National Front and hence are generally influenced by UMNO. Opposition parties tend to be few. The more important are as follows: (1) the Democratic Action Party (origin 1966), which emerged after the separation of Singapore from the Malaysian union. This party was associated with Lee Kuan Yew's People's Action Party and like that organization it emphasizes social justice, economic opportunity, and aspects of socialism. It is largely a party for the cosmopolitan element, and it seeks to deemphasize ethnic differences and communal competition in the country; (2) the Pan Malaysian Islamic Party (origin 1953), a fundamentalist Islamic organization that broke with UMNO in 1955 because the larger organization sought the cooperation of non-Malay communities. It appeals to the rural poor among the Malay population. UMNO underwent significant change in 1984. Party elections reinforced the power of its president, Mahathir, and a cabinet reshuffle brought his closest supporters into the inner circle. By contrast, the second largest party, the Malaysian Chinese Association, was wracked by interpersonal conflict, and the party was unable to mobilize an effective program. The United Sabah National Organization was also separated from the National Front coalition. Of the lesser parties, only the Parti Bansa Dayak Sarawak, a new organization, achieved notable success. Its acquisition of seats in both the state and federal National Front governments received onsiderable attention. *See also* UNITED MALAYS NATIONAL ORGANIZATION (UMNO), p. 204.

Significance   The political parties of Malaysia, with few exceptions, manage to interact with one another at official levels. This interaction has provided Malaysia with a unique form of stability. The parties associated with the National Front have representatives in the federal cabinet, and the government tends to be a reflection of the larger society. Malay domination is a fact that the minorities must contend with, however, and they have determined that their interests lie in the direction of cooperation rather than confrontation.

Difficulties arise in attempting to establish coherent organization. Patronage is a sine qua non of successful politics, but it is also an invitation to corruption and inefficiency. The scandal created by the government-supported Bank Bumiputra's unethical dealings with its Hong Kong subsidary in 1983 was a case in point. Individual ministers and other government officials have exploited the loosely organized political system for personal gain, and only in celebrated instances were elicit acts uncovered, or were the perpetrators prosecuted. The 1981 amendment to the Societies Act prevents political activity by organizations not listed as political. This requirement places limitations on those wishing to reform political party practices or to make them more accountable. Nevertheless, there are hints of change from the younger, more educated generation. A modern, foreign-educated, new elite is taking form and traditional ties and conventional politics are becoming less appealing.

Political Parties: Mauritius   Mauritius is a relatively large island in the southwestern portion of the Indian Ocean, east of Madagascar. It gained its independence in 1968 and established a parliamentary form of government which it has sustained into the 1980s. The election campaign of 1982 pitted the Mauritia Militant Movement (MMM), a leftist organization, and the Mauritius Socialist Party against the traditional ruling organization, the Mauritius Labor Party and its allies among middle class Muslims and lower-caste Hindus. The MMM totally demolished its opposition, winning all the elected seats in the Mauritius parliament. Following this victory, the new Prime Minister, Aneerood Jugnauth, sought political changes that would enable him to deal more effectively with the multi-ethnic island country. High on his list of priorities was a desire to separate Mauritius from its continuing ties to the British crown. The majority of Mauritius' population is Hindu, but Muslims, Europeans, Chinese, Africans, and Creoles make up slightly less than half the total. Given the ideological character of the MMM, it set itself the task of weaving these historically competitive groups into a social pattern in harmony with the regime's Marxist program. *See also* DIEGO GARCIA, p. 12; INDIAN OCEAN, p. 22.

Significance   The primary goal of the Mauritia Militant Movement centered on preventing a resurgence of middle class or bourgeois power on the island. Aware of the ties that the middle class maintained with the West European community, the MMM was determined to discredit western influence on Mauritius and in the larger region. The MMM was vehemently opposed to British and United States activities on the nearby Indian Ocean island of Diego Garcia in the Chagos archipelago.

Mauritius had been part of the Chagos until Britain detached it in 1965. Mauritian claims to the Chagos are ambiguous but the Jugnauth government has joined India in condemning Britain and the United States for building military installations on Diego Garcia. Speculation persists, however, that the Marxist government might strike a deal with Moscow for the use of its naval facilities at Port Louis. But such an action would intensify, not reduce, superpower rivalry in the Indian Ocean.

The MMM had an active ally in India. Indian President Zail Singh visited the island on October 16, 1984 and reaffirmed his government's support to the people of Mauritius in their "legitimate" efforts to regain Diego Garcia and the whole of the Chagos archipelago. India also agreed to establish 24 projects in diverse fields, ranging from agriculture to small industries and social services. In addition, it pledged substantial credits for the purchase of goods and services from New Delhi. India's assistance to Mauritius was deemed cooperative, but Zail Singh was moved to explain his government had no intention of establishing a sphere of influence in the region. Indeed, the foreign policy of the MMM was an almost perfect replica of New Delhi's. Mauritius, like India, was convinced that its population had been drawn into the vortex of superpower rivalry by American naval presence in the Indian Ocean and that Washington's actions were a threat to all littoral nations as well as the small island states. There was no indication that the MMM felt the same way about Soviet maneuvers in the region.

Political Parties: Pakistan   The martial law government of President (General) Mohammad Zia ul-Haq officially banned all political party activity in 1981. Although neutralized, the parties continued to represent the most formal challenge to the military junta that took power following the coup of July 1977 and the ouster of the civilian government of Zulfikar Ali Bhutto. In August 1983 President Zia announced the formation of a "new" political system and declared his intention to hold nationwide elections by March 1985. Zia was reluctant to reinstate the political parties, however, and he expressed his desire for partyless elections. A true Islamic State, he argued, had no need for partisan politics or diverse political organizations.

The politicians reacted much as anticipated. They denounced the junta's program and called for demonstrations to pressure the government to reconsider its plan. Disturbances erupted in Sind province only days after the president's declaration, and they were not brought under control until the army intervened. The toll in lives and property was high. Arrests were also substantial, estimates running to several thousand. Although the conflict was confined to Sind, the Zia administration sensed the need to mend fences, and the president met with leaders of many of the political parties. Members of his inner staff met with others, all in an effort to find an acceptable formula for the holding of elections. After considerable speculation in the press that he might change his mind, Zia stuck to his decision not to permit the parties to play a role in the elections. Under the threat of more agitation, in March 1984, Zia announced a ban on newspaper coverage of political party activities or statements. Recalcitrant politicians were arrested and held without being charged. The junta was clearly determined to have things done its own way. Although personnel changes in the cabinet hinted at difficulties among the decision makers, all actions pointed to a hardening of the government's resolve. In December 1984 Zia announced and held a national referendum in which the population was called upon to declare their support or disapproval of the government's Islamization program. Zia noted that a favorable response would also be interpreted as a vote of confidence in his leadership and that he would be justified in sustaining his rule for an additional five years. Despite opposition efforts to influence a boycott of the referendum, Pakistanis cast their ballots in large numbers, the overwhelming proportion registering their acceptance of government policy. Subsequent elections in March 1985 further strengthened Zia's hand.

There are three principal parties in Pakistan. Pakistan People's Party (PPP) was founded in 1967 by Zulfikar Ali Bhutto. Since his execution in April 1979, the PPP has been led by his wife Nusrat and his daughter Benazir. Both women were kept under house arrest. Nusrat was permitted to leave the country for medical treatment in 1982 and Benazir was permitted to go abroad in 1984. In their absence, the PPP is managed by its secretary general, Farooq Mohammad Laghari and several other Bhutto stalwarts. The PPP has fractured, however, and a splinter group has been identified with Mustafa Khar, a former Punjabi chief minister in the Bhutto government. Although perceived as the most popular party in Pakistan, the real strength of the PPP is unclear. Ideologically, the PPP emphasizes secularism and socialism. The Tehriq-e-istiqlal party was the creation of Air Marshal (ret.) Mohammad Asghar Khan. The Tehriq is somewhat left of center and is the only demonstrably democratic party in Pakistan. It holds regular elections for party office and it encourages parliamentary debate. The Tehriq tends to attract moderate intellectuals but it has been less successful in enlisting popular support. Asghar Khan also played an important role in the founding of the Movement for the Restoration of Democracy (MRD) in 1968–69, and the MRD has continued as the umbrella organization for many of the otherwise disparate political parties. The Jamaat-e-Islami party was led by Tufail Mohammad, following the death of its founder, Maulana Ala Maudoodi. A fundamentalist organization, the Jamaat is very well organized. Its members are carefully selected, highly disciplined, and dedicated to the proposition of building Pakistan into a formidable

Islamic State. General Zia has been identified with the Jamaat, although differences on the degree and manner of Islamization caused strains to develop in the relationship. The activities of the Jamaat's student wing, the Jamiat-e-Tulaba, were curtailed by the army and police, and this too caused strains between the government and the party.

The other parties of some prominence in Pakistan are the Jamiat-e-Ulema-e-Pakistan of Maulana Shah Ahmed Noorani; the Jamiatul Ulema-e-Islam of Maulana Abdullah Darkhwasti; the Pakistan Muslim League (Pagaro Group) of Pir Saheb of Pagaro; the National Democratic Party of Wali Khan; the Pakistan Muslim League (Khwaja Khairuddin Group), led by Khwaja Khairuddin; the Pakistan National Party of Mir Ghaus Bux Bizenjo; the Pakistan Democratic Party of Nawabzada Nasrullah Kahn; the Pashtoonkhwa of Mahmud Khan Achakzai; the Pakistan Awami Tehriq of Rasool Bux Palejo, and the Awami Jamhoori Ittehad of Afzal Bangash. All the above mentioned parties focus on personalities and regions. None were considered national parties in 1985. *See also* COUP D'ÉTAT: PAKISTAN, p. 274; MAJLIS-E-SHURA, p. 236.

Significance   Pakistan's political parties have failed to meet the needs of the larger society, and the armed forces have had a long history of interposition between the population and the politicians. When the British withdrew from the subcontinent in 1947, they transferred power to the Congress Party in India and the Muslim League in Pakistan. The Muslim League could not sustain its preeminence and in 1954 began a precipitous decline that finally resulted in the establishment of martial law and the banning of political party activity in 1958. Although political parties were reinstated in 1962, the country remained under military supervision until December 1971. The loss of East Pakistan and the independence of Bangladesh returned government to civilian hands and political parties again became active. The July 1977 coup, however, nullified political activity and martial law was reimposed.

Given an inability to exercise their role, traditional parties have focused on narrow issues, and the result has been political atrophy, not growth. The political field therefore seems open to the more radical, extremist organizations, whether of the right or left. The Pakistan Awami Tehriq, for example, was implicated in the 1983 riots in Sind along with the PPP. The former, however, is reputed to be a revolutionary party. Its leader, Rasool Bux Palejo, was arrested by the martial law authorities in 1979 and has been detained without trial. Although his release has been sought on grounds of ill health, the Zia government believes his freedom will spark even more widespread disturbances. Palejo, Bizenjo, and Bangash are reputed to be pro-Moscow communists, and in the absence of Palejo, there is some concern that the radical left will link up behind Bizenjo. There was also speculation that Bizenjo, a Baluchi leader, and Wali Khan, a Pathan leader, could form a new coalition and recruit dissidents in Sind for a concerted drive against the Punjabi-dominated government of Zia-ul-Haq. Pakistani politics remain chaotic. There is little indication that the country is prepared for meaningful political give-and-take, and in all likelihood the army will remain a prominent, if not the dominant, actor.

Political Parties: Papua New Guinea   Papua New Guinea and the Bismark Archipelago in the Southwest Pacific Ocean, formerly under Australian administration, gained their full independence in 1975. The country is a parliamentary democracy, with a single house of 109 elected representatives. In the election of 1982 there was a noticeable increase of trained, educated members, and a number of European origin were also added. The political parties of Papua were organized to give meaning to the parliamentary system. They are generally representative of local concerns and tend to develop around strong personalities and families.

The five principal parties represented in the parliament in 1984 were (1) Pangu Pati, or the Papua New Guinea Party of Prime Minister Michael Somare; (2) the National Party of Iambakey Okuk, Somare's archrival; (3) the People's Progressive Party of Julius Chan who served as prime minister for a brief period and whose party has coalesced with Pangu Pati; (4) the Papua Besana, a weak secessionist group; and (5) the Alliance for Progress and Regional Development, or Melanesian Alliance, more often than not a supporter of Somare and Chan. Another political organization of some prominence but outside the parliamentary setting is the Free Papua Movement which aims to prevent Indonesia from seizing all of New Guinea. The Free Papua Movement has attacked Indonesian installations in West New Guinea despite government efforts at preventing such forays. Considerable tension exists between Papua and Indonesia over refugees from the territory which Indonesia controls. The flight of the refugees has been attributed to several factors, including Indonesian military action, a drought in West New Guinea, and Indonesia's policy of settling Javanese migrants in the territory. The latter has been especially disturbing to the Papuans who suspect an Indonesian plot to destroy their independent existence. Prime Minister Somare struggled to reduce tensions between his government and Jakarta and agreed to repatriate more than 10,000 Melanesian refugees from Indonesian New Guinea (Jaya Irian). He also dismissed his defense minister for verbally abusing the Indonesian government. On October 31, 1984 Jakarta and Papua New Guinea signed a five-year border agreement setting up a joint border security committee to mediate disputes between the two governments. But the Indonesian Foreign Minister, Dr. Mochtar Kusumaatmadja, also said his government would not tolerate the activities of Irian Jaya rebels operating from bases inside Papua New Guinea. The Papuan Foreign Minister, Rabbie Namaliu, however, was invited to open a consulate in Irian Jaya and Prime Minister Somare was inclined to accept the offer as a gesture of good will. *See also* ANZUS, p. 325.

Significance   Papua New Guinea was granted independence despite Indonesia's feverish efforts to absorb it. Jakarta used the same argument against Australia (the mandatory power before independence) as it had against the Dutch who administered West New Guinea as part of their colonial empire. Although the United Nations acknowledged Indonesian sovereignty over territory formerly under Dutch rule, it rejected Jakarta's claim to the Australian managed eastern half.

Papua New Guinea's politicians are familiar with this history and cognizant of the need to limit their attacks on one another. They have reason to believe that any issue which produces internal cleavage could be exploited by the Indonesians. Therefore, they can ill-afford petty divisions that may destabilize the government. Papuan politics are heated and hard-fought, as was evidenced by Somare's return to power in 1982, but thus far passions have been controlled and the country enjoys a modicum of stability. Australia has been a major ally for the young nation. Financial dislocation and high unemployment threatened the country's equilibrium in 1982, but an increase in aid from Australia buttressed the economy long enough for Papua's copper market to improve.

Political Parties: Philippines   The established political parties are opposed to the continuance of Ferdinand E. Marcos in office. These parties include the following: the Social Democratic Party (organized in 1981), a weak organization led by Francisco Tatad; and the United Democratic Organization (assembled in 1981), a moderate party that brings together five small parties. It reflects the tradition of the early Nationalists and Liberals who emphasized constitutionalism and open elections. The Mindanao Alliance (organized in 1978) seeks to emphasize regional objectives.

The Philippines has two communist parties. The Philippine Communist Party, or Partido Kommunista ng Pilipinas (PKP), gave birth to the Hukbalahaps (Huks) who resisted Japanese occupation during World War II. After the war, the Huks attacked the new Filipino government and were repulsed and eventually destroyed by troops under the command of Ramon Magsaysay who later became president of the Philippines. The PKP returned to notoriety in 1974, when its leaders agreed to work with the Marcos government and were given amnesty. The party has been associated with the Soviet Union. The other Communist party is the Communist Party of the Philippines (CPP) organized in 1968 and identified with Beijing. The party has been outlawed by the government but it operates clandestine cells and engages in sporadic acts of violence. The CPP attracts university students and intellectuals but seeks to appeal to a broad segment of poor peasants. It supports front organizations like the National Democratic Front which appeals to labor, as well as to the very poor. It also sustains the New People's Army which it claims operates in all key areas of the country.

Another organization engaged in violent behavior is the Moro National Liberation Front (MNLF). The MNLF was organized in 1970 in Malaysia and represents Muslim separatism in the Philippines. Only approximately 5 percent of the Filipino population is Muslim, whereas more than 90 percent is Christian. Comprised mainly of Tausug and Maguindanao Muslims, they seek to represent the Islamic community of Mindanao island and the Sulu archipelago. The MNLF has its primary benefactor in Colonel Muammar Qaddafi, the military ruler of Libya, and a headquarters unit is maintained in that North African nation. It is estimated MNLF violence and government countermeasures have cost more than fifty thousand lives since martial law was imposed in 1972. Many more have been wounded or forced to leave their homes, but there is no indication that the movement has been defeated or is about to curtail its activities. *See also* HUKBALAHAP UPRISING, p. 384. KILUSANG BAGONG LIPUNAN (KBL), p. 167.

Significance   The political parties of the Philippines have been restricted for so long that the traditional party seems to have lost its meaning. Parties are either representative of personalities or prone to violent acts. There is little indication that any of the current political organizations could operate in an open, competitive environment. Marcos scrapped the original Philippines constitution for his own in 1973, and even that has never been properly, let alone fully, implemented. Filipino affairs are conducted by a handful of individuals, operating in semi-secret conditions. The National Assembly is recognized as the handmaiden of Ferdinand Marcos and his wife Imelda. The judiciary is likewise at the president's mercy, and corruption has further sullied its reputation.

Given this background it is highly unlikely that an accountable and responsible political party system can emerge in the foreseeable future. Moreover, in the absence of popular and coherent institutions, the Filipino armed forces will continue to play a dominant role. The military establishment has been reasonably successful in beating back the Muslim rebellion in the south, but the ranks of the Communist New People's Army are alleged to have increased from 6,000 in 1981 to 10,000 in 1984. While ill-equipped to ignite a popular revolution, the guerrillas have taken a toll in blood and treasure. Their continued aggressiveness guarantees a prominent role for the Filipino armed forces. In summary, the Philippines political parties do less to aggregate and more to fragment the body politic. After approximately twenty years of dictatorial Marcos rule, the Philippines remains a divided nation.

Those divisions were especially pronounced following the August 1983 assassination of Benigno Aquino, Marcos' primary antagonist. Although the government insisted Aquino's slayer had been hired by Communists, massive demonstrations forced a judicial enquiry. In October 1984 the board of enquiry issued its report and dramatically implicated the armed forces, including its chief of staff, General Fabian C. Ver. General Ver was also a cousin and confidant of President Marcos. Although Ver was permitted to take leave, a number of other officers were subpoenaed by a newly created tribunal. Marcos therefore continued to draw fire. An election conducted in May placated the United Nationalist Democratic Organization, and the opposition parties won almost 40 percent of the assembly seats, despite criticism of numerous voting irregularities. But Marcos was still the target of popular condemnation. Demonstrations calling for his resignation persisted, and in November and December rumors circulated that he was severely ill. Marcos appeared on television in order to dispel such beliefs. Moreover, the government announced he intended to run for reelection in 1987, thereby seeking to reinforce the official view of his continued good health. And in January 1985 General Ver was formally charged as an accessory to a military coverup in the murder of Aquino.

Political Parties: South Korea   When Korea was liberated from Japanese colonialism in 1945, the political situation was confused. No preparation was made for Korea's independence. No one group was able to inherit the political power vacated by the Japanese colonial government. Korea was divided into north and south along the thirty-eighth parallel, occupied by the Soviet Union and the United States, respectively. In North Korea, the Soviet Union was ready to install a Communist government, while in South Korea, the United States was reluctant to support any one group and allowed the emergence of various individuals and groups, all competing for access to power. The result of this American policy was confusion and a proliferation of political parties. Some parties claimed legitimacy as nationalists, some were big landlords, and some were ideologically inspired.

When the American Occupation authorities decreed that political parties must register, some 134 registered by March 1946. Leftists were eventually suppressed. When South Korea was established as an independent republic, the rightists, headed by Syngman Rhee (Yi, Sungman), took control of political power. The ascendency of the right was accentuated by the onset of the Cold War and South Korea's confrontation with Communist North Korea. During South Korea's First Republic (1948–60), the rightists competed for power within a narrow ideological spectrum. The *Chayu Tang* (Liberal Party) was organized in support of President Rhee and his government, and it was opposed by the *Minju Tang* (Democratic Party). Both of these parties were loose coalitions of various rightist interests. The major issues in party competition were concerned with the basic structure of government—whether it should be a presidential system or a parliamentary system—and with the abuse of power by President Rhee and his government. When President Rhee was forced to resign as a result of massive student uprisings in 1960, his Liberal Party also ceased to exist, and his opposition, the Democratic Party, came into power with the creation of South Korea's Second Republic. The new constitution established a parliamentary system of government with the prime minister as chief executive. However, the Democratic Party was split into two factions by the followers of Prime Minister Chang Myon (Chang, Myŏn) (new faction) and President Yun Po-son (Yun, Po-sŏn) (old faction), frustrating the fragile attempt at democracy. The Chang Myon government, furthermore, suffered from political uncertainty following the overthrow of President Rhee's First Republic. Student demonstrations continued making various demands. Discipline within the military seemed to be breaking down.

Within less than a year of its establishment, this government was overthrown by a military coup in May 1961, led by Major General Park Chung Hee (Pak, Chŏng-hui). General Park's junta government then ruled until December 1963, when a civilian government was reconstituted. In the new civilian government, General Park was elected president as head of his own party, the *Minju Kongwha Tang* (Democratic Republican Party). The opposition coalesced into the *Sin Min Tang* (New Democratic Party), but the dominance of the Democratic Republican Party as the government party remained unshaken during Park's presidency. When President Park was assassinated in 1979, his party failed to survive his death. General Chun Doo Hwan (Chŏn, Tu-hwan) assumed power in 1980, and created his own party, *Min Chŏng Tang* (Democratic Justice Party). *See also* COLONIALISM: JAPAN, p. 66; DEMOCRATIC REPUBLICAN PARTY: KOREA, p. 152; PARTY SYSTEMS, p. 247.

Significance   Political parties in South Korea are post-independence phenomena. When Korea was liberated in 1945, political parties proliferated. What has emerged out of South Korea's experience with political parties and party politics, however, is a one-party dominant system. Each new government creates its own party. Opposition parties are present, but they are unable to unseat the party in power. The dominant party and its oppositions operate within a narrow ideological spectrum. No leftist parties are permitted. No major policy differences exist between them. The main issue of party politics is power—who is in power and who is out. The dominant party contrives to stay in power at any cost. The opposition parties exist to oppose the dominant party as a matter of principle, and the voting public are mobilized to support the dominant party. Studies on South Korean political parties have characterized the South Korean party system as follows: (1) there is no peaceful transition of power from one party to another because the ruling party manages to perpetuate its rule; (2) there is a tendency to suppress opposition parties by the party in power and the government; (3) the ruling party tends to lose its subsystem autonomy and becomes subservient to the executive branch of government; (4) there is a tendency toward illegal and corrupt election practices and government mobilization of bureaucratic instruments (such as the police) to benefit the ruling party and the government in the electoral process; (5) there is a tendency toward bifurcation of party strength between the party in parliament and the party outside parliament; (6) political parties tend to become identified with leadership personalities at the expense of party ideology or programs; and (7) there is a resulting instability and lack of continuous party support by the mass public.

Republican Revolution of 1911: China   A series of uprisings throughout China, which were instigated by the followers of Dr. Sun Yat-sen for the purpose of establishing a republican system of government and overthrowing the Ch'ing (Qing) (Manchu) dynasty. Known also as the Wuchang Uprising, or the Double Tenth (the Tenth Day of the Tenth Month), the first in the series of uprisings took place on October 10, 1911 at Wuchang, the seat of the Huguang Viceroyalty, and the center of a planned railway network. The influx of foreign capital into the country created a great upsurge of activity in railway constructon, participated in by many enterprising Chinese. Suddenly, the Ch'ing government proclaimed that it would nationalize all main railway lines. Private shares were to be bought under inequitable conditions. Many shareholders and others were dissatisfied.

When unrest began, the government used indiscriminate repression. On October 9, a bomb exploded in a house in the Russian section of Hankou, opposite Wuchang on the bank of the Yangtze (Changjiang) River. An investigation of the explosion found that the premises were used as a secret arsenal by Dr. Sun's followers, many of whom were officers at the garrison in Wuchang. Preempting a possible wholesale arrest, the revolutionary officers revolted during the next day, October

10, and occupied Hanyang and Hankow. They also declared the establishment of an independent government in the province of Hubei (Hupeh). The news spread quickly and similar revolts occurred throughout China. On Christmas Day, the rebels set up their government in Nanjing (Nanking) and elected their leader, Dr. Sun Yat-sen as their temporary president. The Double Ten is still celebrated by the Chinese, particularly by the nationalist government which has been in exile in Taiwan since the Communist victory in the mainland in 1949. *See also* NATIONALIST PARTY: CHINA, p. 176.

Significance   Sun Yat-sen, a medical doctor by training, and a Christian by faith, started organizing his followers as early as 1894. He was determined that the archaic system of the Ch'ing (Manchu) dynasty be overthrown. It was foreign to the Han Chinese and was decaying and becoming weak. The Manchu was originally a Manchurian tribe that had successfully invaded China south of the Great Wall and established its own dynasty in 1644. After establishing their dynasty, the Manchu practiced discrimination against the Han Chinese. Dr. Sun decried western exploitation in China. Organizing the Alliance Society in 1905 among the Chinese students in Japan, he continued his revolutionary activities, attracting followers both in China and abroad. In Wuchang, many of the officers at the garrison were his followers. The revolt there on Double Ten was accidental, but its spread attested to the dilapidated state of the Ch'ing dynasty.

The rebels lacked central leadership and coordination, when they were faced with government troops under the leadership of Yuan Shihkai (Yüan Shih-k'ai) who was appointed by the Ch'ing court as the viceroy of Hubei and Hunan to retake Hanyang and Hankow from the revolutionary forces. Yuan became the most powerful man in China. Seeking alliance with Yuan, the revolutionary forces promised him the presidency. With this understanding, Yuan substituted the palace guards in Beijing with soldiers loyal to him and forced Ch'ing to abdicate. The edict of imperial abdication was finally issued on February 12, 1912, and Yuan was elected president of the Chinese Republic by the Republican Council in Nanjing on February 15, 1912. Dr. Sun resigned his temporary presidency and thus began China's experiment with republicanism. However, a traditionalist by heart, Yuan had no illusion about China's republican future. He desired to set up his own dynasty. In 1915, he had himself declared Emperor, but when he died in the following year the power vacuum created ushered in profound political confusion in China. Dr. Sun's forces were still too weak and scattered to assume national leadership. Regional military powers (warlords) became dominant throughout the country. China plunged into a long civil war, which did not end until the establishment of the people's Republic of China in 1949.

Social Action Party (SAP): Thailand   The most popular of
Thailand's many political parties. Organized in 1974 by Kukrit Pramoj,
the Social Action Party has posed as a reformist party and thus captured
the imagination of the country's senior intelligentsia. It demanded strict
control of rice pricing, medical assistance to the impoverished, and free
schooling. It also promoted improvement in wage scales for labor and
stressed the need for public housing. Kukrit became prime minister
with the help of several smaller parties and in 1976 shepherded his
reform program through the Thai parliament. SAP created and supervised the Tambon Development Funds and distributed large sums of
money to local tambons (a council of villages) for the construction of
schools, dispensaries, roads, irrigation works, etc. Kukrit's success and
popularity, however, was not enough to sustain him in office. Opposition
among the business community of Bangkok, and especially from within
the army, was overwhelming and he was forced to yield his position to
the Thai generals. SAP continued to gain in popularity because of its
opposition to the military, and in 1983 it won another electoral victory,
taking more seats in the parliament than any other organization. Nevertheless, military domination could not be overcome. Indeed, the
army's political role was enhanced by the fragmented nature of Thai
politics. No party appeared capable of winning an absolute majority and
government coalitions were usually weak and therefore easily manipu-
lated by the army high command. *See also* DEMOCRATIC PARTY:
THAILAND, p. 151; THAI CITIZENS PARTY, p. 201; THAI NATION PARTY,
p. 202.

Significance   The leaders of Thailand's Social Action Party understand that the country's political system has been controlled by the army
since the 1932 coup that destroyed the absolute monarchy. Political
parties, therefore, have had to form and operate in an environment
heavily influenced by the military establishment. Political parties did not
exist before 1932, and only since World War II have parties become
popular. The Thai military has grown accustomed to its role in the
political system. For the high ranking officers such activity is not a
deviation from responsibility or professional calling. In Thailand politicians, not army officers, must demonstrate their ability to govern. The
Social Action Party is as close as Thai society has come to developing a
coherent political organization, but it lacks adequate organization and
national identity. In the meantime, the army sets the rules. The 1975
constitution, for example, called for legally registered political parties,
and the army screens all applications. The role of the army impairs
cooperation between the parties. In 1983, the parties were unable to
agree on a coalition government and the SAP was prevented from
harvesting the fruits of its electoral victory. General Prem Tinsulanond

had announced his intention to retire from politics following the elections, but faced with political party paralysis, he decided to remain prime minister for another four-year term. In May 1983, General Prem established a new government which included ten high-ranking military officers. Prem's poor health, however, activated General Arthit Kamlangek, promoted to command of the army in 1982, to assert his authority over government decision making. Arthit's term was in fact extended beyond his scheduled retirement in 1985. He also continued to pressure the Thai parliament to amend the constitution so that a serving military officer could hold cabinet office. In the meantime the parliament moved to enhance the power of General Pichit Kullavanich by giving him command of the First Regional Army. Despite rumors of an impending coup, these tactics temporarily protracted Prem's role as prime minister, a condition favored by Kukrit Pramoj and his Social Action Party. However, few observers doubted that Arthit was destined to succeed Prem.

Sokagakkai: Japan   The Value Creation Society, the most energetic, militant, highly organized, and widely discussed new religious movement in Japan. The *Sokagakkai* was established by Makiguchi Tsunesaburo in about 1930 and experienced phenomenal growth in the 1950s. The Sokagakkai was initially identified as an organization of lay believers in a traditionally nationalistic Buddhist sect, *Nichiren Shoshu* (orthodox Nichiren Sect). Its sudden growth following Japan's defeat in World War II, however, is regarded as a new national phenomenon, giving cause for concern to those wanting stable, democratic political growth in Japan. It is known for its fanatical, nationalistic, and millenarian orientation. It draws membership from among the uneducated, poor, urban lower class people. Its vertical organization has *kumi* (group), of up to ten families, at the lowest level. Members of each kumi get together often, worship together, and help each other. In the political realm, Sokagakkai created the League for Clean Government (*Komei Seiji Renmei*) in January 1962. In 1964, the League was transformed into the Clean Government Party (*Komeito*) as an official political party of the Sokagakkai. *See also* BUDDHISM, p. 59; POLITICAL PARTIES: JAPAN, p. 183.

Significance   Many new religions have developed in postwar Japan, but the Sokagakkai is the most successful. The sudden growth in the Sokagakkai membership in the 1950s was regarded as a new Japanese phenomenon. Highly nationalistic, it drew its membership from the urban poor and those alienated from the growth process of postwar Japan. Furthermore, its cell-like organization at the grassroots level and the fanaticism and cohesion of its members created a militant image of the Society in the minds of many. However, its growth has slowed and its militant image has been tempered. Its political expressions concentrate on the improvement of the quality of life for the poor. In foreign affairs, although it advocates a neutral, non-nuclear foreign policy for Japan, it is also pro-West. Moreover, the Sokagakkai was forced to sever its ties with the Clean Government Party in 1970. The Society's use of undemocratic tactics silencing its critics and intimidating writers and publishers of anti-Sokagakkai books has negatively affected the image of the Clean Government Party.

Telegu Desam Party   An Indian political organization founded in January 1983 by former movie idol N. T. Rama Rao to challenge Congress (I) rule in the state of Andhra Pradesh. The Telegu Desam Party was an instant success, winning 200 of the state's 295 assembly seats, and Rama Rao became a rallying point for the country's disgruntled politicians and their followers. Disturbed over Prime Minister Indira Gandhi's apparent determination to centralize authority, Rama Rao struck a chord in the voting public of Andhra Pradesh and successfully exploited regional sentiment. Not insignificant in his party's popularity was the support the Telegu Desam received from an upward mobile Hindu caste. This contrasted with traditional Congress influence among an older caste of small businessmen. Mrs. Gandhi judged Rama Rao to be another potential regional threat, and she was already consumed by critical issues in the Punjab, Assam, and Kashmir. Local Andhra congressmen, however, were more provoked by Rama Rao's popularity and how it affected their personal fortunes. Therefore, in the summer of 1984 following the Golden Temple incident, Rama Rao and his government were forced from power despite claims that they were still the majority political force in the legislature. The imposition of a Congress (I) government in the state, however, further enflamed the situation, and widespread rioting ensued, causing numerous deaths and considerable destruction of property. Moreover, the demonstrations could not be stifled, and they threatened to ignite similar disturbances in neighboring states. The political opposition used the event for its own purposes and rumors began to circulate about the formation of a new political coalition. Faced with a difficult set of choices, Mrs. Gandhi insisted she had not urged Rama Rao's ouster. Nevertheless, she could not ignore the consequences by pretending to remain aloof, and in September she ordered Rama Rao's reinstatement as chief minister of Andhra Pradesh despite her obvious embarrassment. The success of the Telegu Desam in the countrywide balloting of December 1984 underlined the strength of the party under Rama Rao's leadership. Indeed, the final election results revealed the party had bucked the tide of Rajiv Gandhi's landslide electoral victory in the wake of his mother's assassination. The Telegu Desam had the distinction of being the most prominent opposition party in the Lok Sabha when it convened in January 1985. *See also* ELECTIONS: INDIA, p. 224.

Significance The success of the Telegu Desam in Andhra Pradesh must be examined against a background of regional assertiveness that has been a principle feature of the Indian political scene since independence. It can also be understood in the context of Center-State conflict, particularly during the administration of Indira Gandhi. That conflict seems destined to remain unchanged during the rule of Rajiv Gandhi. The reappointment of Rama Rao was judged a severe blow against the power and prestige of the late prime minister. Although Mrs. Gandhi's death nullified the electoral consequences of the Rama Rao affair, Rajiv Gandhi also played a role in its development. He was the Congress (I) general secretary during that period and allegedly handpicked the politicians who challenged the movie idol's popularity. His failure to overcome Rama Rao's influence in the state impacted on his mother, and it is also likely to shadow his activities in the region. The continued success of the Telegu Desam in the December 1984 polls might be interpreted as a personal defeat for Rajiv. All the same, it is unlikely that Rama Rao or his party entertains wider political gains. The Gandhi dynasty remains intact. It will be important therefore to observe how the latest member of the Nehru line relates to regional and sectional opposition now that he is the chief decision maker. It will also be interesting to note how regional figures like Rama Rao seek to transcend simplistic anti-Gandhi tactics and assume more constructive postures and programs.

Thai Citizens Party: Thailand The Prachakorn Thai Party, established in 1979 by Samak Sandaravej, a gifted orator and extreme rightist. The Thai Citizens Party was an immediate success. In its first election it won enough seats to make it the third most popular political organization in the country. In the 1983 elections it held its own, and even slightly increased its number of seats in the assembly. Although a critic of the Prem Tinsulanonda governments, it received considerable backing from the military establishment. The Prachakorn party is intimately associated with militant, right-wing youth organizations and all are involved in rooting out leftist activity among university students. These para-military groups have assisted the army in combating communist insurgency and have been successful in helping to gain the surrender of Thai, Karen, and Hamong tribesmen in the northern and southern parts of the country. *See also* DEMOCRATIC PARTY: THAILAND, p. 151; SOCIAL ACTION PARTY (SAP): THAILAND, p. 198.

Significance   The Thai right has become more aggressive and more successful in countering the left movements in the country. In part, this assertion of ultraconservative activity can be traced to the Vietnamese threat on the Kampuchean (Cambodian)/Thailand border. Vietnamese attacks on Thai forces provoked a large counterassault in 1983. It also provided the Thai army with justification for ferreting out insurgents and left dissidents. Para-military forces from the Nawapon and the Village Scouts, and aided by the Prachakorn Thai party, have played an important role in neutralizing the violent as well as the nonviolent opposition. Moreover, the Prachakorn or Citizen's Party appears to have become the favorite political group of the armed forces and vice versa. Citizen Party leader, Samak Sundaravej, was an influential figure in Thai politics even before the formation of his party. Close to the royal family, he has helped to make and unmake governments over a ten-year span. As interior minister in the 1976 Thanin Kraivichien government, Samak unleashed a wave of terror not experienced in Thailand since the end of World War II. Observers view Samak and his party as the contemporary torchbearers of Thai fascism.

Thai Nation Party: Thailand   Organized in 1974 by members of the Thai army, this party has consistently sponsored and supported civilian candidates since the 1975 Thai elections. The Thai Nation Party's leader, Major General Praman Adireksan, is known as an outspoken critic of the Thai left and he has not hesitated in the use of extreme measures to defeat his opposition. The Thai Nation Party played an important role in destroying the liberal government of Seni Pramoj of the Democratic Party. It performed a similar role in breaking the back of Kukrit Pramoj's Social Action Party. The return of staunch conservatives to power, especially from the army, did not mean an immediate role for the Nation Party. The party was denied key positions in the governments of Thanin Kraivichien in 1976 and General Kriangsak Chomanan, 1977–80. When General Prem Tinsulanonda took office, however, the Thai Nation Party was given ample representation in the cabinet. In the 1983 election, the Nation Party made considerable gains, moving from 38 seats in the national assembly to 73, second highest in the country behind the Social Action Party. *See also* DEMOCRATIC PARTY: THAILAND, p. 151; SOCIAL ACTION PARTY, p. 198.

Significance   The Thai Nation Party is the most successful of the four army-sponsored political parties. The others are Social Justice, Social Nationalist, and Social Agrarian. Its success provides considerable leverage among the more conservative elements and attracts sizeable financial support. It is reputed to be the wealthiest political organization in the country. It has considerable influence over Thai media, both the electronic and printing establishments. Combining army and business support, the Nation Party is a force to be reckoned with. Nevertheless, it has acted more as a spoiler than a constructive political alternative, and it has usually paved the way for military control of the government. General Praman, the Nation Party's leader, was made a deputy prime minister in the Prem cabinet. Other dominant personalities in the party are Major General Chatichai Choonhawan and Major General Siri Siriyothin.

Trotskyism: Sri Lanka   The only mass Trotskyite party in the world today is found in Sri Lanka. The country's Marxist roots go back to the 1930s when young intellectuals from affluent families joined together in political organization to pressure the British for socio-political reform. Their party was known as the Lanka Samasamaja Pakshaya (LSSP), and it set itself apart from the Soviet Comintern. After independence was achieved in 1947, the LSSP was absorbed by the Sri Lanka Freedom Party (SLFP). Virtually all the country's politicians, however, come from the same upper strata of society. Efforts by less fortunate elements to assume leadership roles have thus far been blunted by the heavy influence of the country's elites. Trotskyism, therefore, is not the ideology of the lower classes. Moreover, Marxism is not the doctrinaire variety found in most other countries. The Sri Lankans have been more keen to press their personal rivalries and engage in pragmatic interaction than to challenge one another on the basis of ideological purity.

This behavior also explains Sri Lanka's experiment with democracy. Despite serious ethnic and religious divisions, the country has sustained a political process that is essentially open and forward-looking. The SLFP, an offshoot of the Sinhala Maha Sabha of S. W. R. D. Bandaranaike, was founded in 1951. In 1956 the party captured the elections and its leader became prime minister. A benign Marxist, essentially a Trotskyite, Bandaranaike was assassinated by a Buddhist monk in 1959. Mrs. Sirimavo Bandaranaike, his wife, assumed leadership of the party and was prime minister from 1960 to 1964 and again from 1970 to 1977. She and her party were driven from power by the United National Party in the elections of 1977. *See also* COMMUNALISM: SRI LANKA, p. 72.

Significance   After the death of S. W. R. D. Bandaranaike, his wife and successor found it expedient to join with more radical organizations, and a series of reforms followed that disturbed the other political factions. On the one side, Mrs. Bandaranaike pushed through nationalization programs and land reforms that threatened the traditional elites. On the other, she sought to placate the Sinhala Buddhist movement, which exacerbated relations between the Sinhalese and Tamil communities. Tamil demands for autonomy, as well as violent struggles for secession, intensified during this period. The extreme left also expanded its influence. Moderate J. R. Jayewardene rallied the disenchanted elements in the leadership, and through them the population was mobilized, and an electoral victory was achieved over Mrs. Bandaranaike's coalition in 1977. In an effort to restore pragmatic Sri Lankan Trotskyism in the country, a new constitution was drafted and promulgated in 1978. Jayewardene struggled to reduce antagonism between the major religious and ethnic communities and to revitalize the country's mixed economy. These efforts did not appease the radicalized elements on the right or left, however, and the fragile nature of the democratic experiment was all too apparent with the Tamil-Sinhalese riots that ravaged much of the country in 1983.

United Malays National Organization (UMNO)   Malaysia's parties are rooted in communalism. The Malays are approximately half the population, whereas one-third is Chinese, and one-tenth Indian. The United Malays National Organization was organized in 1946 in order to give political voice to the majority, but economically deprived Malay community. UMNO's first president was Dato Onn bin Jafar. His efforts at opening the party to non-Malays were strenuously resisted and UMNO held to its exclusive character. UMNO was officially established as a political party in 1950, before the independence of the Malayan Federation in 1957. Malaya was transformed into Malaysia in 1963 with the addition of Sarawak, Sabah, and Singapore to the Federation. In 1965, however, Singapore was permitted to separate from Malaysia and establish an independent existence. All Malaya/Malaysia's prime ministers since 1957 have been drawn from UMNO. They are; Tunku Abdul Rahman, Tun Abdul Razak, Datuk Hussayn Onn, and Mahatir Mohammad.

UMNO faced a crisis of confidence in the 1950s which led to the formation of an "alliance" with the Malayan Indian Congress. By 1969, however, the Alliance faltered, did poorly in the elections, and was ill-prepared to confront the communal rioting that threatened the country's democratic experiment. After the government declared a state of emergency and suspended the work of the parliament, UMNO leaders built a more positive and broader coalition known as the National Front. The Front was registered as a national party in 1974 but it did not bring about the dissolution of UMNO. The nine parties associated with the National Front maintained their individual identities. UMNO was continually challenged by forces of internal change. Leftists and Marxists attempted to gain control of the party but were beaten back. Accusations of corruption were legion, and they imposed a heavy burden on the government as well as the party.

In 1983, the Malaysian parliament, dominated by the National Front and UMNO, labored to amend the Malaysian constitution in order to reduce the power of the king. They intended to strip the king of his authority to approve legislation or call a state of emergency. They also sought to terminate the Privy Council's right to hear appeals in civil cases. All amendments, however, required the assent of the king and he was reluctant to allow a reduction of his power. Supporting the king were the nine hereditary state rulers and sultans who elect the presiding king for a five-year term. They, too, were strongly opposed to constitutional changes that would limit their prerogatives. UMNO members were divided on whether to proceed with the program, and their reaction to the monarchs' delaying tactics also varied. A compromise solution was found by permitting the parliament to reconsider a bill if the king has not given his assent within thirty days. If parliament passes the bill a second time it automatically becomes law within another thirty-day period. UMNO was strained by this struggle, but the party leader Mahathir used the divisions within the organization to consolidate his power. The UMNO-dominated government also took the opportunity to clamp tighter restrictions on journalists and publishers. Items deemed offensive to the government were cause for banning the publications. Arrests for repeated offenses were threatened. The official national news service, Bernama, was also given sole authority for all foreign news distribution. Articles deemed unfavorable to the government were denied circulation in the country. *See also* FEDERALISM: MALAYSIA, p. 226; POLITICAL PARTIES: MALAYSIA, p. 185.

Significance UMNO remains the spokesman for the Malay community. It has displayed remarkable acumen in coalescing with a variety of other political organizations, but coalitions are tenuous arrangements and only successful when there are indications of positive payoffs. The National Front's difficulties compound those of UMNO and make their operations more complex, and hence less coherent. The struggle within UMNO over leadership of the party is important because whoever prevails will be the next prime minister. The prime minister controls patronage and would-be job-seekers must satisy the prime minister if they hope for higher, more lucrative appointments. The failure to satisfy coalition members also threatens the organization.

In 1983, the Sarawak National Party broke with the National Front. This dispute led to the convening of a new party, the Sarawak Dayak Party, which joined the National Front. UMNO's success is not so much a measure of its internal strength or organization, or even of its leadership. Rather, UMNO seems to prevail because the other parties have limited constituencies, are divided on issues over regions and personalities and are frustrated by Malay ethnocentrism. UMNO is reported to have one million members in a country of approximately fourteen million people. It is the most well-organized party on a nation-wide basis. The attack on the monarchs of Malaysia dramatizes the discontent among the new intellectuals in Malaysian society, but it is unlikely that the leaders of UMNO seriously contemplate reducing the countervailing power of the royal rulers. Malaysia is a mix of modern and traditional politics in delicate balance, and UMNO not only straddles both, it is the glue that holds the multi-ethnic and multinational country together.

Vietnam Communist Party (VCP)   Known in Vietnam as the Dang Cong San Viet-Nam, this is the most sophisticated, highly structured communist party outside the Soviet Union and China. The Vietnam Communist Party was organized in 1930, and shortly thereafter, on instructions from Moscow's Comintern, assumed the name Indochinese Communist Party. The broader responsibility of the party was therefore established long before its rise to prominence. The actual work of the party in the pre-World War II period was limited to some isolated rural areas. During this period, the leaders of the VCP underwent training in the Soviet Union and developed their strategy of revolution. That strategy moved from a passive to an active stage in World War II with the formation of the League for the Independence of Vietnam (Viet Minh). Operating as a guerrilla force against Japanese occupation of Indochina, the Viet Minh rallied the Vietnamese people and inspired them with the notion of freedom. French administration had been preserved by the Japanese; therefore assaults on the Japanese also affected the French.

By the time the leader of the Viet Minh, Ho Chi Minh, declared Vietnam to be an independent sovereign republic in September 1945, the Japanese were no longer concerned. The French, however, refused to acknowledge the declaration and Paris publicized its intention to reestablish colonial rule over the region. In December 1946 the Viet Minh initiated a war against the French which did not end until France was beaten on the battlefield at Dien Bien Phu in 1953. During the war with France the VCP assumed the name of Lao Dong or Worker's Party and left Kampuchea (Cambodia) and Laos to organize their independent communist organizations. At a peace conference convened in Geneva in 1954, the French agreed to withdraw from Indochina, but at

United States insistence the region south of the seventeenth parallel continued to operate under a separate, non-Communist government. Independent North Vietnam, therefore, devoted itself to the unification of the two Vietnams under its command. When this could not be achieved through electoral means, the VCP organized, trained, equipped, and supported the Viet Cong, the southern version of the Viet Minh, for war against the government in Saigon.

United States entry into this war developed slowly between 1954 and 1964 but escalated dramatically between 1964 and 1971. After a costly involvement in lives and national treasure, American enthusiasm for the struggle quickly dissipated and a peace treaty was entered into between the parties in 1973. In 1975, following the American withdrawal from South Vietnam, the North Vietnamese opened a full-scale attack that quickly crushed South Vietnamese resistance. The two halves of Vietnam were reunited, and the Vietnam Communist Party was officially proclaimed in December 1976. Le Duan, party secretary general since 1956, was reelected to that position and in 1985 he remained the country's preeminent personality. Ho Chi Minh died during the war. *See also* COMMUNIST REGIME: VIETNAM, p. 215; DIEN BIEN PHU, p. 380; SEVENTEENTH PARALLEL, p. 37.

Significance   The VCP has a membership in excess of two million. The years of struggle and sacrifice shaped not only the character of the party, but also that of the population. Although resistance to Marxist-Leninist doctrine is still active in the southern part of the country, the peasant masses are responsive to the demands of party and government leaders. The VCP is extremely demanding on its membership, and since the unification of Vietnam it has been restructured to serve the needs of an emerging industrial community. Current emphasis is on the transformation of the party from an agrarian to a workers' organization, and recruitment is directed at the better educated, urban-based, factory population. Because it must compete with the industrialized states, and obtain advanced technology, inner party discussion centers on modifying the party's peasant image. The VCP wishes to appear less doctrinaire, and a program of economic liberalization was inaugurated in 1982 and accelerated in 1983–84.

The VCP, however, has been careful not to promote capitalist endeavor while pushing these reforms. Ethnic Chinese, Buddhist clergy, and former members of the South Vietnam administration remain suspect. Moreover, decisions have been implemented which open possibilities for limited private economic activity in the north but not in the south. The VCP leaders were ambivalent on the subject of Kampuchea and Laos. The creation of an expanded federation, or a more decentralized confederation, is not yet apparent, but the VCP has maintained approximately 250,000 armed men in Laos and Kampuchea, and despite the cost and continuing burden, there is no indication that they will be withdrawn. The Hanoi decision to resettle Vietnamese in eastern Kampuchea was aimed at relieving population congestion. It was also an effort to exploit the resources of the neighboring state and to advance the process of Vietnamization.

4. Political Institutions and Processes

Cadre   *Kanbu* in Chinese, a bureaucratic leader. In its broadest usage, cadre includes all those who are both party and non-party functionaries in the bureaucratic hierarchies. The term originally meant leadership and authority, but over the years it has come to mean anyone with any degree of authority including those in low level posts. China (PRC) provides different types of cadres, and each has its own salary classification system with ranks and grades. Three important distinctions are state, local, and military cadres. The state cadres belong to the state hierarchy and draw their salary from the state, whereas the local cadres are leaders at the commune level and below. They draw their salary from their local collective institutions. The military cadres draw their salary from the military. The term cadre is widely used; thus, there are party cadres, administrative cadres, Long March cadres, Civil War cadres, veteran cadres, and leading cadres. *See also* COMMUNISM, p. 74; MAOISM, p. 101.

Significance   The term "cadre" is used throughout Communist party systems. Although each usage is somewhat different from the others, it means in general those bureaucratic functionaries who occupy key positions in the party and the government of a Communist state and who are distinguished from the masses. In other words, all cadres belong to the ruling elite group in the country, and a great gap exists between cadres and ordinary people. The cadres hold power and authority. According to one study, the ratio between the number of state cadres (not including local and military) and ordinary people in China is 1 to 80. This means a central leadership of between 50 and 60 million cadres for one billion people in China.

209

Charisma   Personal magnetism that draws people into blind obedience. Charisma is identified with widespread, popular, and emotional support. A person who is able to elicit such support because of his real or perceived personal qualities is called a charismatic leader. Charismatic leaders, as conceived by Max Weber, represent a specific leadership style which legitimizes personal rule, and commands willing and emotional support from the masses. Furthermore, charismatic leaders are usually identified with a crisis and revolutionary situation. In Asia, they are regarded as heroes, unifiers, and modernizers. They stand for personal sacrifice for the sake of national independence and development. Examples are Mao, Gandhi, Nehru, Nasser, Sukarno, and Ho. They are transitory phenonema, and many have been forced out of power in the declining years of their popularity.

Significance   Charismatic leadership is personal. It stands above conflicting interests. It elicits mass followings on the basis of personal, emotional appeals. In the new, developing nations of Asia, charismatic leadership has often proven functional, helping to unify the nation and mobilize the masses for development. As these nations become more institutionalized and their problems of development more complex, charismatic leadership is replaced by party politicians and military and civilian bureaucrats. The political excesses associated with charismatic leadership have proven counterproductive and politically destabilizing for a long-term, durable process of national development.

Communes   The primary production and/or administrative units within the Communist system, emphasizing joint, cooperative efforts for production, management, and administration. The communes are not all alike throughout the Communist systems. However, they share common characteristics in that they are used as basic production and/or administrative units, particularly in rural areas. Organized into a commune, the people apply a collective effort towards production and administration. No private enterprises are allowed. Instead, the common needs of the people are met collectively under collective management, establishing and managing their own schools, nurseries, mass halls, and militia units. Generally speaking, all available manpower is deployed for common production efforts. Although largely discarded in the post-Mao reforms, the rural communes in China were to have "six benefits and one convenience," namely, the benefits of cooperation, production, transportation, communication, forestation, culture, and education; and convenience for the advancement of socialism. *See also*

COMMUNIST REGIME: CHINA, p. 212; DEVELOPMENT STRATEGY: GREAT LEAP FORWARD, p. 303; MAOISM, p. 101.

Significance   The Chinese commune movement was a major aspect of the Great Leap Forward movement (1958–59) for the rapid indus-trialization and development of China. By the end of September 1958 there were more than 23,000 communes established in the rural areas, representing some 90 percent of the total number of peasant house-holds in the country. In creating these communes, the existing agri-culture producers' cooperatives were combined into a group to form a new farming unit coterminous with the *xiang* (township), the lowest level of public administration, usually embracing a population of about 20,000. The commune was then given responsibility for farming, as well as agricultural construction and development of local industry. The commune was merged with the xiang political administration to become an all-embracing social unit providing for education, welfare, health care, and security. It also served as the unit of capital accumulation and investment. From the practical point of view, the commune was designed to be large enough to allow effective deployment of local resources but small enough to be responsive to democratic control. In the course of this movement, the peasants were forced to give all their material posses-sions to the communal organization. Their public kitchens, dormitories, and nurseries were designed to do away with traditional parochial orientation, familism, and inefficient production methods. The peas-antry was to become an integral part of the total mobilization towards social construction. They were to develop a new technical and scientific orientation. They were to be self-supporting and self-producing. Finally, their sources of energy were to be more effectively channeled into useful agricultural and industrial tasks, under the management of party cadres.

However, the initial Chinese communization program suffered many setbacks because of its excesses, and as a consequence, it proved ineffec-tive. The result was a significant modification of the commune system. For example, the size of the commune was reduced with the production team becoming the main unit of ownership and income distribution. Furthermore, the role of the commune administrative agency was reduced to such tasks as management of political responsibilities, invest-ment in infrastructure, and development of some local industries which had survived the debacle of the Great Leap Forward. The peasants were allowed personal plots for cultivation, and various incentive systems were introduced to entice the people to increase productivity.

From the late 1970s to the present, further dramatic changes have been introduced in the function of the commune. Increasingly, the system of household production (*boa-chan-dao-hu*) and contracts are being employed. The policies of Deng Xiaoping (Teng Hsiao-Ping) have meant a decreasing economic role for commune leadership and increasing economic decision making for the individual peasant household. This responsibility system (*ze-ren-zhi*) has become the hallmark of Deng's economic policy in the countryside and has produced a political economy distinct from the pervasive relationship of politics and economics during Mao's time.

Communist Regime: China   The People's Republic of China (PRC), with Beijing (Peking) as its capital, established on October 1, 1949 by the victorious Communist forces under the leadership of Mao Zedong (Mao Tse-tung). The first formal constitution of the PRC was adopted in September 1954. Earlier, on September 21, 1949, the Chinese People's Political Consultative Conference (CPPCC) convened in Beijing to consider Mao's guidelines for the "People's Democratic Dictatorship." The new state was to be an alliance of four classes: workers, peasants, petty, and national bourgeoisie, who would exercise dictatorship over the "reactionaries" and govern democratically in the interest of all. In the constitution, the concept of the People's Democratic Dictatorship and united front are underlined (Preamble and Chapter One).

China is designated as a unitary state, not a federal state as in the Soviet Union. The constitution does not allow secession rights for any particular group. It promises rapid social change and economic development. Chapter Two of the constitution deals with the organization of the government, whereas Chapter Three discusses the rights and duties of citizens. This constitution has been revised in 1975, 1978, and again in 1982, legitimating major political and leadership changes. The last revision in 1982 corresponded with the emergence of Deng Xiaoping as the most powerful man in the Party and the government.

In the latest revision, the basic framework of government remains the same as before. The PRC is a Communist state, controlled by the Communist Party of China, organized on the basis of democratic centralism and dedicated to the socialist construction of the nation through mass mobilization. Constitutionally, the highese organ of this government is the National People's Congress, which has wide-ranging power to elect key government officials such as the president and the vice-president (newly provided in the 1982 constitution), the premier and the vice-premiers, and members of the Supreme People's Procurate, the Supreme People's Court, and the Central Military Commission. When not in session, its affairs are administered by a Standing Committee. In the day-to-day national administration, the State Council headed by the premier is the most important center of decision making. For local administration, the country is divided into three special municipalities (Beijing, Shanghai, and Tianjin), twenty-one provinces, and five autonomous regions. Each province is subdivided into counties and cities; each county into townships and villages. The autonomous region is divided into prefectures and each prefecture is like a province and follows the pattern of provincial subdivisions. Furthermore, each local unit has a people's congress. These local government units are the creations of the central government and owe their existence to it. They exist in hierarchical order as administrative units to facilitate political communication between different levels of government. The party is present at all levels, but increasingly local management and initiatives are encouraged. *See also* DEMOCRATIC CENTRALISM, p. 219; GREAT PROLETARIAN CULTURAL REVOLUTION, p. 156; MAOISM, p. 101.

Significance   To govern the most populous nation in the world spread over the continental expanse of some 3.7 million square miles, and to develop it as a viable nation has posed many problems for the PRC, as it had for previous regimes, and experiments with new policies and institution building continue. Mao Zedong's emphasis was on the ideological mobilization of the masses for socialist construction, as demonstrated in his Great Leap Forward movement (1958–59). In this movement, Mao carried out the massive and speedy communization of the country for increased productivity through local self-help initiatives. Mao was fearful of Chinese bureaucratic obsessions, fearful that all revolutionary fervor and initiative would be lost in the bureaucratic routine. The alternative approach to Mao's revolutionary emphasis was to emphasize technocratic and pragmatic orientations, opting for planned development, central direction, and a willingness to learn from the West, while accepting foreign trade and investment. Following the death of Mao, particularly under the leadership of Deng Xiaoping (Teng Hsiao-Ping), China has been emphasizing the latter course of action. It established diplomatic relations with the United States in 1979 and has pursued economic, technical, educational, and cultural exchange programs with those countries who were earlier regarded as enemies. Purposefully discarding the excesses associated with Mao's scheme of mass mobilization and reorienting the course of China's development, Deng has carried out a massive reorganization of the country. The commune system has been dismantled as an administrative system. It has also been modified as an organizational unit for production efforts. Instead, the system of responsibility has been instituted linking more closely the task that is performed and the income that is received. Under this system, each household has increasingly become a contracting unit and it has become the primary unit of account and accumulation. The only socialist aspect of this system is the collective ownership of land;

peasants do not own the land and can use it only in order to fulfill the contract.

Communist Regime: North Korea (DPRK)   North Korea was proclaimed an independent state on September 9, 1948, under the constitution which had been drawn up as early as November 1947, while North Korea was still under Soviet occupation in the wake of World War II. This constitution, under which Kim Il Sung (Kim, Il-sŏng), one time anti-Japanese guerrilla leader in Manchuria, became premier, legitimized the existing system which was modeled after the Soviet Union. In 1972, the constitution was revised and Kim Il Sung became president, formalizing his supreme position. The new constitution declares that North Korea is "an independent socialist state. . .guided in its activity by the *juche* (chuch'e) (independence or self-reliance) idea" of the Korean Workers' Party. According to this constitution, the sovereignty of the nation belongs to "the workers, peasants, soldiers, and working intellectuals," who elect their representatives to manage the affairs of state.

The highest organ of government is the Supreme People's Assembly, which consists of delegates elected indirectly for a four-year term. Its impressive array of powers includes the election of a Presidium to serve while it is not in session, the election of a president, a procurate-general, and judges of a Supreme Court. However, these powers are seldom exercised independently, as the Supreme People's Assembly is subservient to the will of the Party and its supreme leader, Kim Il Sung. The constitution also provides the Central People's Committee and the State Administrative Council as the highest governing bodies.

The Central People's Committee is perhaps the most powerful of the two super-governing bodies as it is headed by the President himself and is charged with overall policy-making and government supervision. The State Administrative Council is headed by the premier, and is charged with the general administration and the implementation of national economic policies. In North Korea, the relationship between the national, provincial, and local governments is unitary, comprising a highly centralized system. Each local unit of government (such as province, city, county, town, village, and workers' settlement) has its own people's assemblies, but it serves as an agent of the state. The deputies of the local assemblies are periodically elected by the voters and they are to perform functions similar to those of the Supreme People's Assembly at the national level. These local organs are not autonomous bodies, however. They are created by the central government, and their decisions may be repealed or changed by the higher organs of government. *See also* COMMUNISM, p. 74; KIMILSUNGISM, p. 95; KOREAN WORKERS' PARTY: NORTH KOREA, p. 168; THIRTY-EIGHTH PARALLEL, p. 41.

Significance   The North Korean regime represents a monolithic Communist system. It emphasizes *juche* (chuch'e) (independence or self-reliance) as its guiding philosophy. Kim Il Sung, president of the Democratic People's Republic of Korea, general secretary of the Workers' Party of Korea, and the sole generalissimo of the People's Army, is the supreme and undisputed leader. With the cult of his personality practiced in the most pervasive manner, the whole country appears to be his personal domain. His personal quotations, portraits, busts, and statues, as well as buildings, museums, and monuments dedicated to him, are found throughout North Korea. Not only is Kim Il Sung himself the target of this unadulterated admiration, but his whole family has been given a special place in history. Kim's eldest son, Jong-il (Chŏng-il), has been designated to inherit his father's mantle of power. If this plan is fulfilled, North Korea may prove to be the first successful Communist dynasty.

The 1972 revision of the constitution was intended to legitimize Kim Il Sung's total control over North Korea, by placing him above the government. The Central People's Committee further strengthens central decision making. The Committee is chaired by Kim Il Sung and includes practically all members of the ruling Communist party politburo and the Standing Committee of the Supreme People's Assembly.

Communist Regime: Vietnam   The Vietnam Communist Party (VCP) dominates Vietnam's government and society. Political institutions are subordinated to the VCP and receive all directions from it. Organized on the Leninist model, the VCP is managed by the Political Bureau, which contains the highest ranking leaders in the state. The Central Committee selects the Political Bureau members and also elects the party's secretary general, who oversees the organization's secretariat. Technically, the National Party Congress, which is supposed to convene every five years, is the highest authority in the VCP. However, the Congress has met infrequently, assembling only three times between 1935 and 1976. The work of the party therefore has been conducted by a small circle of personalities led by Le Duan, the party chief.

As in other communist states, the government of Vietnam administers the policies of the VCP. In this "proletarian dictatorship," (the words drawn from the new constitution of 1980), executive and administrative authority resides in the Council of Ministers. The Council is elected by the National Assembly and is responsible for drafting legislation, managing foreign affairs, and administering economic plans. Pham Van Dong, Vietnamese premier since 1955 and a member of the VCP inner circle, was selected chairman of the Council of Ministers in 1981. The Council of State is the equivalent of a collective presidency. It oversees the work of the National Assembly and examines the activities of the Council of Ministers. The first chairman of the Council of State was Truong Chinh, elected to that post in 1981. *See also* ONE PARTY VASSAL STATE: KAMPUCHEA, p. 242; SINO-VIETNAMESE CONFLICT, 1979– , p. 409; VIETNAM COMMUNIST PARTY (VCP), p. 206.

Significance　　　The Vietnam Communist Party has been dominated by the triumvirate of Le Duan, Pham Van Dong, and Truong Chinh. All are in their late 70s and have carried the burden of state from the days of the First Indochina War to the present. Their passing, however, is not likely to alter the course that the party has established over the last 30 years, and it is not likely that younger men (in their 40s and 50s) will rise to prominence. Those in the wings are in their early 70s and late 60s and they have patiently waited their turn at the helm. Younger members of the Political Bureau are likely to be much older when their turn at succession arrives. The advanced age of the Vietnamese leadership suggests a degree of conservatism in policy matters. There is little likelihood that Vietnam will entertain innovative programs, and the new institutions developed by the 1980 constitution will require a period of trial and error. With the political system firmly in place, the Communist regime in Vietnam can be expected to consolidate its gains and begin the long-postponed program of modernizing the country's industrial and agricultural sectors.

However, a severe drawback to Vietnam's economic program was the perceived need to sustain a high level of mobilization in the Vietnamese armed forces. The continuing border "war" with China and Hanoi's expansionist adventure in Kampuchea necessitated the syphoning of needed resources from the development sector. Moreover, foreign assistance for economic and technical projects was affected by a decision of the Association for Southeast Asian Nations (ASEAN) to link aid to Vietnam's withdrawal from Kampuchea.

Constitutional Secularism: India　　　India achieved independence on August 15, 1947 when Great Britain transferred power to the leaders of the Indian National Congress. From the outset, India was a federal parliamentary state. Initially it functioned under the terms of the India Independence Act, passed by the British parliament in 1947. On January 26, 1950, India promulgated a constitution which transformed the country's dominion status to that of a republic. Parliamentary federalism was reaffirmed, but no less important was the nation's commitment to secularism. The subcontinent had been partitioned by the British, and the new state of Pakistan had emerged in August 1947. The demand for a separate, independent, and sovereign state by a large and relatively well-organized segment of the Muslim community of British India could not be ignored by the departing colonial rulers. The creation of Pakistan did not signify the transfer of all the Muslims to Pakistan, or all the Hindus to India. In fact, India retained a huge Muslim minority which in subsequent years continued to expand. Indian leaders therefore had to come to grips with the country's multi-religious, multinational, and multilinguistic makeup.

The decision to emphasize the secular nature of Indian democracy was aimed at calming the fear of the minorities, not only the Muslims, but Sikhs, Christians, Jains, and others. The constitution of 1950 promised to protect the minorities from the majority. At the same time, the constitution empowered the government to adopt emergency measures if political stability could not be sustained, or if national unity was threatened. *See also* ASSAM MASSACRE, p. 375; KASHMIR DISPUTE, p. 386; NAXALITES, p. 393; SIKHISM, p. 117; TELEGU DESAM, p. 200.

Significance India's democracy depends on the workability of the 1950 constitution, one of the longest and most elaborate of its kind. That constitution is constantly under stress from the many glaring divisions in Indian society. Provincialism, religious differences, cultural controversies, the sharp juxtaposition of rich and poor, contemporary and traditional complexities, ideological versus nationalist appeals, all tear at the fabric of Indian society. Nevertheless, India seeks to sustain its constitutional and democratic experiment. The declaration of a state of emergency by Prime Minister Indira Gandhi in 1975 was finally lifted in March 1977. Constitutional guarantees were suspended during that period, but the opposition, despite severe constraints, continued to remind the government that its actions were unacceptable. When the people were given an opportunity to express their preferences, the constitution was sustained.

Another event which threatened to undermine the constitutional order was the Sikh affair in India's Punjab state. The invasion of the Sikh's holiest shrine at Amritsar by elements of the Indian army in June 1984, and the more than a thousand deaths that resulted from that fateful decision of the Indian government, produced a wave of disturbances in many areas of the country. The assassination of Indira Gandhi in October 1984 was directly attributed to this action. The slaughter of Sikhs by Hindus in the wake of her death further undermined India's constitutional tradition. Moreover, continuing atrocities in Assam and persistent Hindu-Muslim clashes were additional indicators of the fragile nature of the constitutional experiment. The need to often resort to emergency rules, although sanctioned by the constitution, also brings into question the genuineness of the democratic experiment.

Constitutionalism: Singapore   Singapore's constitution is a unique arrangement of several documents. The constitution in force when Singapore separated from Malaysia is the key document, and sections of the Malaysian constitution have also been adapted. The 1965 Independence Act and the Constitution Amendment Act round out the legal arrangements. The routine that had existed prior to independence was retained as much as possible. Thus, the governor became the president, and the legislature was transformed into the parliament. Singapore's president is elected by the parliament for a four-year term. The first president was Inche Yusof bin Ishak. He was followed in 1970 by Dr. Benjamin Henry Sheares who died in office in 1981 and was replaced by the present incumbent Devan Nair.

Parliament controls the president, whom it may decide to reelect, or to remove from office by a two-thirds vote. The president has considerable power on paper, but in actuality is outside the political decision-making process and fills a purely ceremonial role. The president supposedly officiates over a Presidential Council of Minority Rights which scrutinizes legislation and appoints the Public Service Commission. Real power, however, rests with the prime minister, who heads the cabinet and all government ministries. In effect, the powers of the president have been exercised by Prime Minister Lee Kuan Yew since the independence of Singapore. Singapore has a one-house parliament of 75 members. The Speaker presides over the parliament and bills are passed by simple majority and approved by the president. The country has a multilingual policy and parliamentary activity can be conducted in English, Chinese, Malay, or Tamil. Parliament has a five-year life, but new elections can be called at any time. The People's Action Party (PAP) won all the seats in parliament in the 1968, 1972, 1976, and 1980 elections. The majority of PAP candidates have run unopposed. Singapore follows the British system of jurisprudence and the highest court of appeal is the Privy Council in London. *See also* PEOPLE'S ACTION PARTY (PAP), p. 178.

Significance   For all intents and purposes, Singapore has been a one-party state. The dominant position of the PAP has given it carte blanche in assembling the institutions and developing and executing the policies necessary for Singapore's safety, satisfaction, and development, although the task of leadership has not been simple. Singapore is a multi-racial society, crowded into a small area which cannot be increased. The population is therefore burdened by the knowledge that growth and prosperity, if not survival, depends on maintaining workable ratios of people and space. The Lee government has been very strict in implementing family planning programs, and although there is ample recognition of the problem, not everyone is content with the measures taken to keep Singapore's population in balance. Lee, however, has been direct in such matters. His often swift and decisive response to incidents which threaten to disrupt the equilibrium of the island state has earned him the epithet of "dictator." He has brushed aside such criticism, insisting that his interests are one with those of the nation.

In recent years Lee has emphasized the need for a more educated elite and has even suggested that the more educated might be induced to have more children, implying that the less educated could forego such luxuries. Despite growing criticism, Lee initiated a program for "gifted children" in 1984. The general concern in Singapore was that Lee was not only circumventing the constitution but also personalizing the office of the prime minister. Lee, however, believed he was personally responsible for protecting the constitutional order, to ensure that it would be passed on to a new generation of leaders. Having reached his 60th birthday in 1983, the philosophical prime minister and leader of the PAP sensed his final responsibility would be to ensure the preservation of what had been created, and he believed that this would require even more astute leadership than he or his colleagues were capable of manifesting.

Democratic Centralism   Lenin's principle of organization and decision making incorporating both democratic and centralistic advantages. The principle of democratic centralism has been identified with the Russian revolutionary leader Vladimir I. Lenin, and the Communist party organization. In the organization of the Communist party, Lenin attempted to meet two contradictory demands: (1) the demand for mass participation in decision making by his revolutionary followers, and (2) the demand for a tightly organized and disciplined party for the unified and efficient execution of policy. Under democratic procedures, the rank-and-file participates in decision making at the primary level of organization and selects representatives to a higher body. This process is repeated throughout the different levels of organization until representatives are elected to the highest decision-making body (National Party Congress). Once the decisions are made at the center, they are related to the lower bodies for explanatory discussion. Then, they must be followed and executed without dissent. *See also* COMMUNIST REGIME: CHINA, p. 212; COMMUNISM, p. 74; MAOISM, p. 101.

Significance   Although the principle of democratic centralism was advanced by Lenin for the organization of the Communist party, it has found wider applicability in the context of development among Third World nations. While it is intended to appeal to the democratic aspirations of the people and provide them with a sense of participation in decision making, it also stresses the need for unity among the people and for central planning and administration. In practice, however, centralism has been emphasized more than democracy and a true synthesis of the advantages of both has been rare. For example, the constitution of the Chinese Communist Party (CCP) declares that "solidarity and unity are the very life of the party and the source of strength," and it provides that the party organization at a higher level has the power to veto decisions reached at the lower level. It may also appoint, dismiss, or transfer responsible officials at the lower level when the Party congresses at that level are in recess.

Democracy: Japan   Japan's parliamentary cabinet system of government and its participatory political process based on the post–World War II constitution. The post–World War II Japanese constitution was drafted by the Occupation authorities (Supreme Command for the Allied Powers, or SCAP) and put into effect on May 3, 1947. This constitution is Anglo-American in spirit, and it includes some of the most democratic features found anywhere. It is based on the principle of popular sovereignty, and it guarantees the right to vote for all citizens who are twenty years or older and who have established residency in the district for three or more months. Much of the constitution is devoted to the guarantee of fundamental human rights. It stipulates in its Article 9 that the Japanese people are "forever" to renounce "war as a sovereign right of the nation and the threat of use of force as means of settling international disputes." Under this provision, the Japanese people are forbidden to maintain "land, sea, and air forces, as well as other war potential."

Within the national government, the two house legislature (Diet)— the House of Representatives and the House of Councilors—is the highest organ of state power. The other branches of government, the executive and judicial branches, are responsible to it. The prime minister is head of the cabinet in the executive branch, and he is chosen by the Diet. The Supreme Court judges are appointed by the prime minister, but they must be approved by the electorate. Under this constitution, national and local relations are unitary. As such, all local units of government are created by the national government and exercise only the powers delegated to them. However, local autonomy is encouraged, and the constitution stipulates the direct popular election of local officials such as governors and mayors. The constitution can be amended on the initiative of a two-thirds vote of all the members of each House of the Diet. Once initiated by the Diet, a proposed amendment must be ratified by a majority of votes cast at a special referendum. *See also* DIET: JAPAN, p. 221; POLITICAL PARTIES: JAPAN, p. 183; SCAP REFORMS, p. 318.

Significance   Japan today has one of the most democratic constitutions in the world. Although it was drafted by the Occupation authorities (SCAP), the Japanese people have not only accepted it, but have also applied it successfully without major modifications. Alien to the Japanese political heritage are the concepts and practices of democracy, but they have been adopted with passion in postwar Japan. Political contestants representing various parties and ideologies freely compete for public offices. Voters show a remarkable degree of political awareness and turn out in a large number to participate in the electoral process. For the national election, the voter turnout rate is about 70 percent; for local elections, it is higher. The major parties represented in the Diet in recent years are the Liberal-Democratic Party, the Democratic Socialist Party, the Clean Government Party, the Japan Socialist Party, and the Japan Communist Party. However, party label and ideology are less important than personal relationships as a voting determinant in Japan. Informal interaction is more influential in Japanese decision making than formal requirements and qualifications. Paternalism is a powerful political force in Japan and various small politicical groups or factions are formed on the basis of it. In this way, democracy in Japan has many features which may be regarded as uniquely Japanese.

Diet: Japan   Japan has a parliamentary system of government. The National Diet (Parliament) is directly responsible to the people and is the highest organ of state power and the sole law-making organ of the state. It consists of the House of Representatives (lower house) and the House of Councilors (upper house). Of the two, the lower house is more powerful, as it selects the prime minister. The prime minister selects his cabinet members, usually drawing them from the membership of the lower house.

The lower house consists of 511 members, who are elected from 130 electoral districts, plus Okinawa, for a term of four years. It is usually dissolved before the expiration of its term. The organization of the lower house includes a speaker who is normally elected by the majority party in the House, and a vice-speaker, who at times comes from an opposition party. The lower house meets in full sessions, but increasingly the standing committees of the House perform the major deliberative functions.

The upper house consists of 252 members elected for six-year terms by the electorates organized in two different constituencies. The local constituencies consist of 47 electoral districts (each prefecture constituting a district); 152 councilors are elected in these districts. The remaining 100 councilors are elected from the nation as a whole and represent the national constituency. The people vote separately for these two different constituencies. Half the membership stand for election for every three years—76 from the local constituencies and 50 from the national constituency. Each voter, then, casts two votes—one for a local representative and the other for a national representative. Since 1982, the electoral system for the national constituency has been changed to a proportional representation system. In the 1983 election, for instance, votes in the national constituency race were cast for a party rather than for an individual candidate and the seats were apportioned to each party on the basis of the proportion of the votes the party won.

In the legislative process, party discipline is strictly followed. On the whole, the Japanese legislators are political professionals. Many incumbents are reelected. Many legislators are ex-bureaucrats, particularly those of the ruling conservative party (LDP), or group officials, such as labor union officials. They are usually organized into small factions, but a consensus is sought in major decision making. *See also* DEMOCRACY: JAPAN, p. 220.

Significance   The Meiji constitution (1889) provided for the House of Representatives and the House of Peers. Before the introduction of the postwar constitution, however, legislature was never regarded as the highest organ of state power and the sole law-making body. The emperor was sovereign in prewar Japan. The concept of legislative supremacy provided in the postwar Japanese constitution is, therefore, new, but the Japanese people have been able to put it into practice with remarkable success. In the relationship between the executive and the legislature, however, the executive has become increasingly dominant, enjoying greater resources in personnel and technical expertise. The cabinet's Bureau of Legislation either drafts or reviews all public bills. The cabinet originates all important legislation, and cabinet-sponsored bills invariably pass the legislature, which is controlled by the party in power.

Electoral System: Japan   A set of arrangements used for the selection of officials or representatives by the voters in Japan. The electoral system exists in various forms, which reflect different political expressions and emphases. In the occupation of Japan, the Allied Powers were determined to democratize the former enemy nation. They expanded the franchise so that all men and women of twenty years and older could vote, and they instituted several electoral devices, including (1) the House of Representatives; (2) the House of Councilors; (3) the governors and assemblies of prefectures; (4) the mayors and assemblies of cities, towns, and villages; (5) referendums on the holders of Supreme

Court justiceships; (6) referendums on proposed constitutional amendments; and (7) referendums for initiative and recall measures.

Politically the most important election is for the House of Representatives. The country is divided into 130 electoral districts (since the 1976 general election) from which 511 representatives (the membership size set as of July 4, 1975) are chosen for a four-year term.

Each voter is entitled to vote for one candidate, but each district is assigned three to five seats, except for the special district of the Amami Islands, which is assigned only one seat. The system does not allow multiple voting. It is a multi-member constituency, single-vote system. The official campaign period is limited to 30 days.

For the House of Councilors (252 seats), the Councilors are elected by two different constituencies. The local constituencies consist of 47 electoral districts (each prefecture constitutes a district) and they elect 152 councilors, 2 to 8 councilors from each district. The remaining 100 councilors are elected from the nation as a whole, on a system of proportional representation since 1982, and represent the national constituency. Voting for these two different constituencies is separate. Unlike the House of Representatives, the House of Councilors cannot be dissolved. The councilors serve a term of six years, with elections staggered at three-year intervals. *See also* DEMOCRACY: JAPAN, p. 220; DIET: JAPAN, p. 221; SCAP REFORMS, p. 318.

Significance   Elections were held in pre–World War II Japan, and the present Japanese electoral practices, based on the Public Offices Election Law of April 1950, incorporate some earlier laws. Still, elections carry different meaning today than they did in Japan's past. They are more significant, they are noisier, they are more competitive, and they are more expensive. Since the House of Representatives plays the most powerful role in decision making in Japan's parliamentary system of government, its general elections are fought bitterly. For practical politicians and political strategists, however, they pose rather exotic problems, unfamiliar in the West. Each electoral district is small, but it has three to five seats assigned to it. The strategic problem for a major party is to decide on the number of candidates to run from the same party. Running only one candidate may be the safest strategy. Running too many may scatter the party support. However, to opt for the safest strategy means yielding seats to other parties. Running more than one candidate from the same party results in bitter fraternal competition, as usually each candidate represents a different faction within the party. Once the candidacy is secured, the problem then becomes financing the campaign. Although fixed at a normal level, campaign expenses have become enormously high. *Go-to yon-raku,* a slogan which has been much publicized in the Japanese press in recent elections, means literally "500 million ($1.6 million) wins, 400 million ($1.3 million) loses." These figures may be exaggerations, but they underline the high cost of winning an election. Each candidate is, therefore, hard pressed to come up with adequate funding. Although funding sources vary with parties, if unable to draw from their family resources or personal connections, candidates must rely on their parties, factional leaders, and business, labor, and other group contributions. Businesses have traditionally supported conservative candidates, but they usually make their contributions to the party headquarters and to selected factional leaders as opposed to individual candidates. The labor unions actively support their socialist candidates, and the *Sokagakkai,* a Buddhist sect, their Clean Government Party candidates. In support of its candidates, the Communist Party has been raising funds from its publications, dues, and the like.

Elections: India   Often described as the largest democracy in the world, India has managed to hold elections for national and statewide offices despite turbulent events. Such was demonstrated in December 1984 when elections were conducted less than two months after the assassination of Prime Minister Indira Gandhi. Moreover, the electoral support given Mrs. Gandhi's son and successor, Rajiv and his party, was more dramatic than anything achieved by his grandfather, Jawaharlal Nehru, or his mother. With 508 of the 542 seats in the Lok Sabha under contention (law and order problems prevented the holding of elections in the Punjab and Assam), Rajiv's party won nearly 80 percent, or 401 seats. As of January 1, 1985, Rajiv's Congress (I) controlled approximately 73 percent of all the seats in the lower house of parliament, including the seats reserved for the Punjab and Assam. Only two opposition parties improved their position in the Lok Sabha—the Telegu Desam (organized in 1983) and the All India Anna Dravida Munnetra Kazhagam. Among the biggest losers were the Communist Party of India (Marxist), which dropped from 36 seats to 22, and 2 national parties, the Bharatiya Janata Party (BJP) and the Dalit Mazdoor Kisan Party (DMKP). The BJP slipped from a strength of 16 seats in the old Lok Sabha to only 2 in the new one. The Congress (I) also won in 16 Indian states, the exceptions being Kashmir, West Bengal, Andhra Pradesh, and Tripura. *See also* INDIAN PEOPLE'S PARTY, p. 163; TELEGU DESAM PARTY, p. 200; SIKHISM, p. 117.

Significance   The Congress (I) victory was in large measure a vote of confidence in Rajiv Gandhi. The timing of the election was slated to draw a heavy sympathy vote, but officals and observers were surprised at the magnitude of support demonstrated by the electorate. Most commentators believed the vote displayed a decided shift to the right, and it seemed to emphasize the need for Hindu unity in the face of perceived internal and external threats. The elections also displayed voter dissatisfaction with the opposition parties who were unwilling or unable to orchestrate a manageable coalition. R. K. Hegde, a former chief minister of Karnataka, summed up voter reaction by noting that the theory of coalition government at the Center did not carry conviction with the people. "People must have wondered how the opposition parties could unite to form a government if they could not come together even on seat adjustments. In many places, the opposition parties were contesting against each other."

Prominent opposition leaders such as the BJP president Atal Bihari Vajpayee, and DMKP leader H. N. Bahaguna, as well as Janata leaders Chandrasekhar and Georges Fernandes, and CPI(M) leader Samar Mukherjee were defeated. Only the regional Telegu Desam made significant gains—28 seats—in the Lok Sabha. Indeed, even the 2 major communist parties of India claimed only a combined total of 28 seats in the Lok Sabha. Rajiv's success, therefore, was instantly translated into a "mandate." India's sixth prime minister streamlined the cabinet, cutting it to half of its previous membership, thereby "retiring" a number of heretofore influential politicians. Rajiv's appointments to high positions reflected upon his own youth, many being in their 30s and 40s. The appointments revealed Rajiv's intentions to control provincial party leaders by naming their opponents to key positions in the government. Rajiv also drew from among family members, much as his grandfather and mother had before him. Arun Nehru, the party's general secretary and a cousin of the prime minister, was made a junior minister for power. Rajiv also surrounded himself with former schoolmates such as Arun Singh. Arun Singh's importance in the Rajiv Gandhi administration was illustrated in January 1985 by his appointment to a special commission whose task it was to uncover a vast network of government officials allegedly engaged in the sale of defense secrets to foreign powers. However, the new prime minister's attention was riveted on the dilemmas of communalism that plagued the country. Only days after he assumed power, he appointed a special cabinet group to address the separatist question in the Punjab. He also gave special priority to the 5 years of agitation and turmoil in Assam which had taken an estimated 6,000 lives. Only time will tell if Rajiv had the capacity to manage India's centrifugal forces.

Emperor: Japan The symbolic head of state of Japan, whose throne is inherited but whose power is limited by the constitution. Before 1945, the Japanese people were led to believe that the Emperor was a divine figure who descended in direct and unbroken line from their founding sun goddess. He was supposed to be all-powerful, sacred, inviolable, and sovereign. Following Japan's defeat in World War II the Emperor denounced his divinity and Japan was restructured as a democracy. Redefining the Emperor and the Imperial Throne, the postwar constitution states: "Article 1. The Emperor shall be the symbol of the state and of the unity of the people, deriving his position from the will of the people, with whom reside sovereign power"; and "Article 4. The Emperor shall perform only such acts in matters of state as are provided for in this Constitution and he shall not have powers related to government." *See also* DEMOCRACY: JAPAN, p. 220; KOKUTAI, p. 96; SCAP, p. 318.

Significance   In postwar Japan, the Emperor is relegated to a symbol of the state and of the unity of the people, and he performs only ritual and ceremonial functions. He does not have any power related to government, and his official acts are limited to ceremonially legitimating the political actions already taken, as in the appointment of the prime minister and chief judge of the Supreme Court, and in the promulgation of laws, cabinet orders, treaties, and amendments to the constitution. His ceremonial functions also include convoking the Diet (Parliament) and dissolving the House of Representatives; attesting certain official appointments; awarding honors; receiving ambassadors and ministers; and performing certain other ceremonial functions. The imperial position in the Japanese political system has been radically transformed. Officially, the Japanese Emperor's position is far weaker than that of the British monarch. The way the Japanese people readily accepted the change is amazing. The Emperor today is regarded more fondly than fearfully. He is undoubtedly considered a special person, but not a divine figure. Historically, the Japanese imperial family is the oldest reigning family in the world and its direct ancestors may be traced at least to the early sixth century A.D. The laws that govern the imperial family are strict, and no adoption is permitted within it. Succession is by the eldest son of an Emperor, followed by the eldest son of the eldest son.

Federalism: Malaysia   The joining together, or comprehensive union, of nations or political units who, although maintaining a distinctive character, nonetheless share a common political structure and thus acknowledge the primacy of the central authority. The range of authority of the central government may vary from federal state to federal state, with the constituent states retaining more or less residual authority. In other words, federal unions describe powers designated to the central authority, those reserved for the constituent parts, and those managed concurrently. The broad tendency in all federations is for power to move toward the center, but some are more highly centralized, such as the Soviet Union, whereas others are less so, such as the United States. Ethnic and geographic diversity have made federalism an absolute necessity in Malaysia. The federation was established in 1957 when the British transferred power to indigenous authority, but it assumed a more complex status in 1963 when the eleven states of the Malay peninsula were joined by the East Malaysia territories of Sabah and Sarawak and the island of Singapore. Singapore withdrew from the federation in 1965 and became an independent state with encouragement from the Malaysian government. Kuala Lumpur, the capital of Malaysia, was declared a federal territory in 1974. The constitution of Malaysia was adopted in 1957, the year the country achieved its independence, and it has remained in force despite subsequent changes in the federal structure. *See also* PEOPLE'S ACTION PARTY: SINGAPORE, p. 178; POLITICAL PARTIES: MALAYSIA, p. 185; UNITED MALAYS NATIONAL ORGANIZATION (UMNO), p. 204.

Significance   Malaysia has a parliamentary form of government, and a cabinet system responsible to the legislature. Its federal structure is reflected in the makeup of the parliament, but it is even more pronounced in the unique Conference of Rulers (Majlis Raja Raja). This body, made up of the country's 13 rulers of the states of the federation, acts as a third house of parliament. The nine most prominent rulers also take turns in a five-year rotation which determines the head of state or king. This process is confirmed by an election engaged in by the nine rulers and thus seems to guarantee a form of democratic monarchism as well as representative federalism. In such a system the king's powers are constitutionally limited and the real power resides in a prime minister (Perdana Mentri) who is appointed by the king from the dominant party in the parliament. The prime minister's cabinet is also formally appointed by the king but its members are responsible to the Perdana Mentri and the parliament. The two houses of parliament are the Senate and the House of Representatives. The Senate includes 2 representatives from each of the 13 states, but the king appoints an even greater number (42) on the advice of the prime minister. The lower house has 154 members who are elected from single member constituencies on a national basis.

Genro: Japan   A small, informal decision-making body within the Meiji constitutional system (1889–1945) in Japan. The *genro* served as the Imperial mind, particularly after 1900, wielding the decision-making powers of the emperor, and coordinating all of the official organs such as the Cabinet, Diet (Parliament), Imperial Household Ministry, Privy Council, and Supreme Command. The genro, literally meaning "Elder Statesman," included Yamagata Aritomo, Ito Hirobumi, Inouye Tsuyoshi, Oyama Iwao, Matsukata Masayoshi, and eventually Katsura Taro and Saionji Kimmochi. All of these leaders, except Saionji, were of samurai (feudal Japanese warrior class) background and the original five were leaders of the Meiji Restoration (1868), playing a lead role in the formative years of the modern Meiji government. They were also former prime ministers and constituted an informal group which intimately advised the emperor, often exercising his decision-making powers. The genro was a unique Japanese political institution within the Meiji constitutional system. Its members were never replaced. *See also* MEIJI RESTORATION, p. 310; SAMURAI, p. 114.

Significance   The genro as an institution was not provided for anywhere in the Meiji constitution. As such, it was an informal body, but it exercised more power and influence in the operation of the Meiji constitution than any organ in the government. The power of informal government in Japan has been deeply imbedded in the tradition of genro. The Meiji constitution was not a well synthesized document, leaving many loopholes and providing no institutional checks and balances in the government. It prescribed imperial sovereignty, but the emperor was made a sacred personage. The emperor was given all the decision-making powers but he was out of touch with political realities. The genros became constant personal counselors to the emperor, coordinating government operations, serving as the "king-maker" in the selection of prime ministers, and choosing leading government officials. Very often they alternated as prime ministers. Though some policy differences existed among them, they contributed significantly to the continuity and stability of the Meiji constitutional system.

Guided Democracy   The rebellion on the Indonesian island of Sumatra in 1957 convinced Sukarno that the country was not ready for a full-blown experiment in parliamentary democracy. He put forth the idea that Indonesia needed a period of "guided democracy" in which national leaders would attempt to bridge differences between the islands, while promoting economic development and social uplift. Indonesia's 1950 constitution was abandoned and Sukarno turned toward China and the lessons of Mao Zedong. All political factions were to be united in a creation called the National Front, consisting of functional groups rather than political parties. Political activity was deemed wasteful and had no place in an emerging nation. General A. H. Nasution was sympathetic with Sukarno's plan because it offered the possibility of controlling the Communist Party of Indonesia (PKI). But the army's struggle with the PKI prevented full implementation of the guided democracy program.

Despite the lack of a formal parliament, Indonesia's political parties continued to organize, some openly, such as the PKI, and others clandestinely. The National Front of functional groups was postponed as Sukarno tried to balance the PKI on the one side and the army on the other. The PKI had become the largest Asian Communist party outside Communist China, and given American complicity in the Sumatran rebellion, Sukarno seemed to favor the Communists. Dutch economic holdings were seized by the government and the Europeans were compelled to leave the country. Sukarno seemed poised to throw in his lot with the Soviet Union and Communist China, both of whom became Indonesia's chief weapons suppliers. Dependence on the Communist giants raised the credibility of the PKI and tended to diminish the pro-western orientation of the Indonesian army high command. Sukanro's political manifesto, "MANIPOL," outlining guided democracy, was adopted by the PKI. But guided democracy, the PKI declared, would be successful only after the destruction of vested interests, both foreign and domestic. The PKI improved their political leverage by adopting the notion of guided democracy, and they used Sukarno as a buffer between themselves and the army. *See also* GOLKAR, p. 155; PANTASILA, p. 110; POLITICAL CULTURE: INDONESIA, p. 113; POLITICAL PARTIES: INDONESIA, p. 180.

Significance Guided democracy permitted Sukarno to check his opposition, but it also gave the PKI exceptional status. When the army attempted to limit PKI activities, Sukarno blocked its path. Moreover, the PKI stood to gain from Indonesia's confrontation with Malaysia over northern Borneo in the 1960s. The army had counseled Sukarno against the adventure, but flushed with victory over the Dutch in West New Guinea, Sukarno could not be restrained. Northern Borneo, however, presented different problems. International pressure prevented the Dutch from retaining West New Guinea. Britain was determined to assist the Malaysians in the defense of Northern Borneo, but Indonesian army leaders did not want a wasteful war over Northern Borneo, especially one that was bound to weaken their position at home. They had already concluded that only the PKI could benefit from the confrontation with Malaysia. The confrontation proceeded, nevertheless, and as predicted, Indonesia's economy suffered markedly. Guided democracy was lost in an avalanche of slogans and symbols. National planning was transformed into "guided economy," but it too proved to be bankrupt. Although the media and all government officials were required to repeat the slogans of the Sukarno revolution, no amount of repetition could obscure the fact that the country was badly run, and that the continuing struggle between the PKI and the army now involved Sukarno directly.

Indian Civil Service (ICS)   The men who governed India in the British colonial period were members of an elite civil service. After the mutiny of 1857, the British restructured the governing apparatus in the subcontinent. The Indian Civil Service Act of 1861 reaffirmed the Charter Act of 1833 which introduced a series of competitive examinations for those aspiring to a career in colonial administration. Indians as well as Englishmen were legally encouraged to apply for the Indian Civil Service, but the indigenous recruits had to overcome obstacles of prejudice. Nevertheless, more and more Indians joined the Indian Civil Service (ICS), and although sometimes condemned as handmaidens of imperialism or accused of becoming "Brown Englishmen," they, like their European counterparts, developed a reputation for stability and efficiency. In time, the ICS became known as the "Steel Frame" of government in the subcontinent. ICS members, therefore, provided the needed expertise in the organization and operation of formal administrative structures when India and Pakistan achieved their independence in 1947. ICS officials became the nucleus of the newly constituted Indian Administrative Service (IAS) and the Civil Service of Pakistan (CSP). These post-independence services carried the burden of daily administration, and, in the case of Pakistan, dabbled in politics. *See also* BUREAUCRATIC POLITY, p. 295; MILITARY: CIVIL-MILITARY RELATIONS, p. 286.

Significance   Members of the Indian Civil Service were considered among the most privileged and powerful persons in British India. This reputation carried over into the Indian Administrative Service (IAS) and the Civil Service of Pakistan (CSP) after independence. In India, however, given the importance of the parliamentary system and the power of the Indian National Congress, IAS members were restrained, and generally depoliticized. Moreover, the centrality of the service was eliminated with provincialization.

Pakistan was another story, however. There, the CSP became the dominant institution in the governing process. The weakness of the Muslim League exposed the party to political attacks that it could not counter. As a consequence of League preoccupation with its political opposition, the CSP managed the ministries as well as the field services, and five years after independence made a play for power. The CSP joined with ambitious political figures, especially the landlords of the Punjab, to form a ruling coalition in the name of national stability.

Actually, the coalition negated the role of the political parties and prepared the ground for the army coup of 1958. Pakistan's political life has been dominated by an armed forces-civil bureaucracy coalition since that time. Although the CSP was dissolved in 1973 by an interim civilian government led by Zulfikar Ali Bhutto and a "nonpolitical" All-Pakistan Unified Services took its place, the higher bureaucrats remained powerful agents of government. The overthrow of Bhutto and the army takeover of 1977 emphasized the continuing importance of the civil servants. While no longer identified by the CSP designation, they remained in policymaking as well as administrative positions, close to the military junta of General Mohammad Zia ul-Haq.

Jirgah   The Jirgah, or tribal council, is the institution through which the Pathan population of Afghanistan and Pakistan administer tribal codes and customs and dispenses justice. As a collective body of senior tribesmen, it is revered and respected. In cases where blood feuds still predominate, the local jirgah plays a prominent role in moderating interpersonal and intergroup behavior. Efforts by the Pakistan and Afghanistan government to replace the tribal system were unsuccessful. However, when government proved sensitive to tribal ways and sought to blend national and parochial institutions, greater headway was achieved. The jirgah has persisted as an important institution in all legal and political matters. Given the Pathan's pride of independent life-style and tribe, the only truly legitimate decision-making body was the tribal jirgah, comprised of strong headmen, saintly figures, and wise patriarchs.

Afghanistan's 1965 constitution created a representative form of government in the parliament, or Shura, with a directly elected *Wolesi Jirgah* (House of the People) and a more or less appointed body called the *Meshrano Jirgah* (House of Elders). Above these two houses was the Loya Jirgah, or Great Council, made up of members drawn from both houses of the Shura as well as the chairmen of elected provincial jirgahs. The Loya Jirgah's functions were more traditional in that it followed older patterns of organization. Historically, the Loya Jirgah was assembled in time of emergency. Its meetings were always informal in atmosphere but defined by custom and usage. The 1965 Afghan constitution attempted to institutionalize the Loya Jirgah and bring it into the service of the Kabul government. Such a body should have been able to reflect public opinion and counsel government in times of crisis. Pakistan did not experiment with such a system. The tribal jirgah was not interfered with, and it continued to administer local questions such as disputes, grievances, and material need.

The tribal jirgah utilizes a legal system known as *Pakhtunwali* that combines both tribal and personal law. Pakhtunwali governs the relations within the tribes and of one tribe with another. In theory, the system of tribal law is complete. Future lawmaking is unnecessary. Where doubts arise concerning interpretations, such as intertribal disputes or disputes between individuals within a tribe, affairs are either resolved violently or by the tribal jirgah. The jirgah, with the assistance of a respected theologian, will prescribe the law. Enforcement of a jirgah decree is also handled informally. The tribes are their own police agency. Law enforcement comes in the form of the *lashkar*, the tribal use of force. The lashkar has also been associated with tribal warfare. Before 1947, lashkars were ordered by the tribal jirgahs against the British. Most recently they have been authorized against the troops of the Soviet Union in Afghanistan. *See also* TRIBALISM, p. 125.

Significance   The jirgah is an important tribal institution among the Pathans. The Pathans (often referred to as Pakhtuns or Pushtuns) are characterized by disunity and fragmentation. Tribes jealously guard their native habitat and seldom cooperate in the absence of high emergency. Left to themselves, the Pathans focus their attention on day-to-day concerns. Local jirgahs address mundane questions that threaten to disrupt conventional ways of life. Local jirgahs are highly respected and decisions taken by them are seldom ignored. Violations of directives are judged antisocial, and violators are subject to heavy penalty. In this manner the tribes police their individual communities.

The jirgah represents all the government a Pathan normally requires. In the republican atmosphere of the tribes, tribesmen do as they please so long as tribal codes are observed. Calls for the Loya Jirgah have been rare. In Afghanistan they have been assembled when a king has been deposed or murdered, and the new authority seeks the allegiance or support of the tribes. The Loya Jirgah therefore is a form of legitimating institution. Loya Jirgahs are also called when the tribal area has been penetrated by alien aggressors. A Loya Jirgah was assembled to confront the Soviet invasion of Afghanistan in 1979. Although the tribes fought the Red Army in small, often self-contained tribal units, the Loya Jirgah provided a semblance of unity to the resistance.

Koenkai: Japan   A Japanese word for support association or support group, which is organized and cultivated by a Japanese politician as a power base, particularly for an election campaign. In rural areas, *koenkai* is organized around *jiban*, a geographically defined bailiwick, and it relies on the politician's local attachment and family connections. In urban areas, however, it is based on a more diffuse support and is created by aggregating the interest groups with which the politician can readily identify. In any case, the politician maintains a close personal relationship with his support group, much as a patron does with his clients. In this sort of relationship, the clients' support of their patron is also loyal and dependable, and koenkai performs many electoral and other functions for its leaders. *See also* DEMOCRACY: JAPAN, p. 220; ELECTORAL SYSTEMS: JAPAN, p. 222; PATRON-CLIENT RELATIONSHIP, p. 112.

Significance   No successful politician in Japan is without his personal support group, and no successful candidate can ignore it. Electoral politics in Japan is waged at the local level and it caters to local and personal needs. The emergence of koenkai, particularly in the Japanese electoral process, is inherent in Japanese political style. To maintain it, however, the politician must exercise constant personal care, attending to the personal needs of its members. Politics in Japan is personal, but it is also elaborately structured and costly.

Labor Unions: Japan   Organizations of industrial workers for collective bargaining. Labor unions existed in pre–World War II Japan, but they remained weak and ineffectual, often suppressed by the government. The highest prewar level of union organization was in 1931 and it attained only 7.9 percent of the industrial labor force. However, labor unions, encouraged by the Occupation authorities (SCAP), mushroomed in postwar Japan and today they claim a total membership of about 12 million, 27 percent of the Japanese labor force. By American standards, these labor unions are unusual, because they are organized on the basis of enterprises and not by craft or industrial lines. These enterprise unions are then aggregated into national unions. Many national unions are further joined into larger national federations or councils of unions, of which the most important are: the General Council of Japanese Trade Unions (*Sohyo*), the Japanese Confederation of Labor (*Domei*), the Federation of Independent Unions (*Churitsuroren*), and the National Federation of Industrial Organizations (*Shinsanbetsu*).

These four labor federations claim a total membership of over 8 million, which represents about 67 percent of all unionized labor or about 15 percent of the total Japanese labor force. The largest and the most politically active is the General Council of Japanese Trade Unions. Made up mostly of unions of governmental or public corporation employees, it is a federation of some 22 thousand unions, and its individual membership totals 4.3 million. Its political program is manifestly socialist and militant, and its close association with the Japan Socialist Party is unwavering. The second largest is the Japanese Confederation of Labor. Its membership is drawn almost entirely from private industry.

It is less politically active than the General Council, however. The political party with which the Confederation is principally identified is the Democratic Socialist Party. The other two are much smaller, and they have no formal association with a political party, although they consistently maintain anti-Conservative Party stands. *See also* POLITICAL PARTIES: JAPAN, p. 183; SCAP, p. 318.

Significance   Political interest groups play a well-established role in the postwar Japanese political system. Of these groups, labor unions are most active organizing demonstrations, struggles, and strikes. They also actively oppose the ruling Liberal-Democratic Party and support the socialist cause. However, these unions have been politically less effective than their numerical strength would indicate, mainly because of the unusual nature of union structure in Japan. Because Japanese unions are enterprise unions and each enterprise is organized as a unified group, workers tend to suffer from divided loyalties. Workers' welfare is as much dependent on union activities as on the continued prosperity of their employers. Furthermore, the paternalism of Japanese business and the practice of permanent employment in Japan tend to moderate anti-enterprise union agitations. Not all enterprise workers are union members either, and any union activity involves less than a total effort of the workers within the enterprise. The largest of the unions are also ideologically dogmatic and militant. For instance, the General Council is not only the principal supporter of the Japan Socialist Party, but its leadership is also unyieldingly socialist. Very often, therefore, ideological considerations outweigh economic benefit in labor union activities.

Legitimacy   The quality of being accepted as lawful and authoritative. Legitimacy implies support of the superior by the inferior in any power relationship and compliance with rules and regulations. Legitimacy reflects an underlying consensus in a system and acceptance of leaders, institutions, and prescribed behavioral norms and sanctions. Legitimacy may be based, singularly or in combination, on tradition, ideology, citizen participation or specific policies, and these bases often determine the kind of exchange possible between citizens and authorities in the political system. The extent of legitimacy has an important bearing on the efficiency and stability of the political system.

Significance   The level and basis of legitimacy of the government have important implications for system propensities. The level of legitimacy may be high or low. The basis of it may be consent or coercion. If the government is widely supported by the people, it is easier for it to seek compliance. If not, coercion may be applied. It is easier to get compliance when citizens accept the government as legitimate. Therefore, virtually all governments, even more coercive ones, seek legitimacy and try to make citizens believe they are lawful and have the right to use force against those who violate their rules and regulations. In the Third World nations of Asia, the lack of legitimacy bestowed on those who are in power has been a major cause of endemic political instability.

Lok Sabha: India   The Hindi term for the lower house of the Indian parliament. It means "People's Assembly" and it is designed to be the dominant body in a bicameral legislature which also includes the Rajya Sabha or State Assembly. The Lok Sabha has 542 members who are directly elected from single-member district constituencies of near equal population. Members serve five year terms and can be reelected. (The five year term was stretched during the emergency of 1975 when the parliament was extended for a sixth year and would have remained for another if elections had not been called in 1977.) Although parliamentary elections are conducted every five years, the president is empowered, on advice of the prime minister, to call elections earlier. Elections were conducted before the normal five-year period in 1971 and 1980.

The Lok Sabha customarily meets three times each year, but it is constitutionally directed to assemble only twice. It includes members from many of the communities comprising the Indian nation, and special efforts have been taken to provide adequate representation for those groups whose voices might otherwise be weak or even silent. A significant number of seats, 79, have been reserved for the Scheduled Castes, the untouchables in the Hindu caste system. Forty seats are also reserved for the Scheduled Tribes, the less sophisticated of India's vast society. In addition, two Anglo-Indians can be appointed to the Lok Sabha if it is determined this small community is without representation. The presiding officer in the Lok Sabha is the Speaker who is elected from among the membership and possesses wide-ranging powers in organizing the work of the Assembly. By passing a no-confidence motion the Lok Sabha can bring down a government and force the creation of another. It could also cause the presidnt to call for new elections. The Lok Sabha shares responsibility for the passage of legislation with the upper house, but money bills can only originate in the lower body. The upper house can reject a money bill, but the Lok Sabha need only pass the bill again in order for it to become law. *See also* CONSTITUTIONAL SECULARISM, p. 216; ELECTIONS: INDIA, p. 224; RAJYA SABHA, p. 252.

Significance   The Lok Sabha is the Indian equivalent of the British House of Commons. As such it is the central institution in the constitutional system. The Indian National Congress has dominated the work of the Lok Sabha since independence, but party schisms provide the forum with lively debate. During the Shastri administration (1964–66) there was a noticeable increase in the independence of the Lok Sabha. The same could be said for the Janata interregnum (1977–79). During Prime Minister Gandhi's extended tenure, however, parliamentary expression had been more constrained. During the emergency of 1975–77, the parliament was little more than a rubber stamp for administration policy. Nevertheless, the Lok Sabha is a key institution in India's democratic experiment and its preservation is deemed essential by the variety of elites that make up the country's political scene. Although opposition politics are a feature of Indian life, failure to control at least 50 seats in the Lok Sabha leaves India without an official opposition in the body.

Majlis-e-Shura: Pakistan   Also known as the Federal Council, it was Pakistan's temporary answer to the creation of a "genuine" Islamic State. The Majlis was publicly proclaimed by President Mohammad Zia-ul-Haq on December 24, 1981. It called for the creation of a 350-member body, filled by appointment of the president and drawn from a cross-section of society. The Majlis was given responsibility for bringing Pakistan's suspended 1973 constitution into harmony with the tenets of Islam. The power of the Majlis was described as consultative and advisory. It could recommend the enactment of laws, discuss the annual budget and developmental plans, and ask for information from the various ministries or other agencies and divisions of government, but it was not permitted to make laws.

The first session of the body was convened on January 11, 1982, and it has met at least three times each year since that initial meeting. Members represented such groups as women's associations, farmers, peasants, landlords, and minorities. Approximately one-third of the original members selected had central government experience, and many others were members or former members of defunct parties. The parties, however, denounced the Majlis as an instrument of the military junta. The Majlis-e-Shura dovetailed with government efforts to modify the judicial system, so as to bring it into conformity with Islamic requirements. The military government created *Shari'a*, or Islamic courts, and special courses were developed to train judges in the dispensing of Islamic justice. *Qazi* courts, a lower order of Islamic courts, were also forecast. After the December 1984 referendum "legitimized" the Islamization program and reinforced Zia's authority, elections were held in March 1985 for a 237-seat National Assembly and a 63-seat Senate.

With 11 opposition parties calling for a boycott of the polls, Zia's supporters won a majority of seats.

Significance   Despite strong interest among Pakistanis in the establishment of a state in harmony with Muslim tradition and performance, the Islamic program was not greeted with total enthusiasm. Informed and sophisticated Pakistanis, although practicing Muslims, would have preferred to retain the parliamentary political system inherited from Great Britain and modified by the country's political culture. They perceived the junta's Islamic program as self-serving, contending that the military was exploiting Muslim sentiment for its own purposes. The destruction of the established political institutions, the neutralization of political parties, the controlled press, the management of the country by decree and ordinance, were all aimed at eliminating competitive politics.

The military establishment made no attempt to conceal its belief that political organizations were disruptive and counterproductive. The larger population, it argued, wanted nothing to do with political parties, nor did they want a political system alien to their way of life. According to the junta, the masses were with them, and they wanted to recreate the Pakistani nation by bringing Pakistan's political institutions into conformity with Islamic ideology. The Majlis, and the new National Assembly and Senate in 1985, were said to represent the interests of the Muslim population. The military held firmly to the conviction that Pakistan's fundamental unity, its territorial integrity, could only be protected through the application of Islamic prescription. The secular western approach had been tried and had failed. The junta, therefore, concluded that the country had no other recourse than to follow the path laid down by the martial law regime.

Majlis Raja Raja: Malaysia   Malaysia's assembly of kings. Malaysia has developed a unique executive or head of state from their nine hereditary royal rulers. None of the Malaysian kings is considered dominant over the others. While considered supreme within their own states, their influence seldom extends to the larger nation. Monarchy was considered an institution worth preserving, albeit in a restricted national context. Thus, for purposes of national unity, it was deemed essential to design a system that would sustain the traditional socioeconomic fabric, while encouraging the development of contemporary representative government. The king of Malaysia is "elected" by the nine hereditary rulers for a five-year term, but his assumption of the office is determined by a prescribed list that specifies the order to be followed. The king shares membership in the Majlis Raja Raja, or

Conference of Rulers, with the other royal figures; but they are also joined by the governors of Penang, Malacca, Sabah, and Sarawak. This 13-person body has quasi-legislative functions and shares lawmaking responsibilities with the Malaysian parliament, which is comprised of the Diwan Nigara (Senate) and the Diwan Rayat (House of Representatives). *See also* FEDERALISM: MALAYSIA, p. 226.

Significance   Although the younger generation of educated Malaysians generally believes monarchy in general, and the Majlis Raja Raja in particular, are outdated institutions and ought to be abolished, they have played a unifying and hence stabilizing role in a country of ethnic, religious, and ideological divisions. Controversy over the power and influence of the rulers has been keen, however, and in 1983–84 the Malaysian parliament considered a series of amendments aimed at reducing the authority of the kings in national affairs. The reigning monarch refused to give his assent to the amendments, and their implementation was unlikely.

Nationalist Government: Taiwan   The government of the Chinese Nationalist Party (*Kuomintang*) which evacuated from the Chinese mainland to Taiwan in 1949 and which has persisted as the legitimate government of the Chinese people. The Nationalist government still professes its goal of returning to the mainland, and martial law, though very mild and limited, is enforced in Taiwan, ever-vigilant against possible subversion from mainland China (PRC). When exiled to Taiwan, the Nationalist government maintained the façade of its legitimacy over all of China and superimposed its authority over the Taiwanese provincial government.

Constitutionally, the highest organ of this national government is the National Assembly which is popularly elected and charged with the election and recall of the president and vice-president, in addition to the amendment of the constitution. The president and the vice-president are placed above the regular branches of government which consist of five *yuans* (branches)—executive, legislative, judicial, control, and examination. Like the National Assembly, the legislative yuan is popularly elected. However, the Control yuan (constitutional supervisory organ) is indirectly elected. The rest of the yuan are appointed. By far the most powerful office of the Nationalist government is the presidency which Generalissimo Chiang Kai-shek held until he died in 1975. After his death, he was briefly succeeded by his vice-president, Yen Chia-kan, but in 1978, his son, Chiang Ching-kuo, who had long been groomed to succeed his father, was elected president. Though minor parties have been permitted in Taiwan, control of the government by the Nationalist Party has always been secure. *See also* REPUBLICAN REVOLUTION: CHINA, p. 196; NATIONALIST PARTY: CHINA, p. 176.

Significance   Following the withdrawal of Chiang Kai-shek and his remnant forces to the island province of Taiwan in 1949 and the establishment of their government in exile, there has emerged two sets of government in Taiwan: (1) the Nationalist government controlled by Nationalist refugees from the mainland, and (2) the provincial administration left to the native Taiwanese, who were mostly descendants of seventeenth-century Chinese immigrants. The native Taiwanese are dissatisfied with this arrangement and aspire to their independence. The exiled Nationalist government, assisted by a security arrangement with the United States (1954 defense treaty between the United States and the Republic of China abrogated in 1979), however, has proven effective in the control and administration of the island.

The highly disciplined Nationalist Party, together with its armed forces and police, effectively control the political processes of the island. The Nationalist government has also broadened the electoral participation of Taiwanese citizens, tolerating a considerable amount of political liberty particularly on local issues. The Taiwanese citizens may now elect (1) members of the provincial assembly; (2) members of the county or municipal councils; (3) magistrates, mayors (excepting the mayor of Taipei, the capital city, who is appointed by the president on the recommendation of the premier), and chiefs of rural and urban districts, townships, and villages; and (4) local administrators not appointed by the mayors. Taiwanese leaders have recently been co-opted into the Nationalist Party leadership structure, and the Nationalist government has been trying to dispel its image as an occupying force. Mainlander and Taiwanese mutual cooperation has been further encouraged by the recent economic success of the island. The Nationalist administration has been responsible for the successful implementation of land reform, and its close association with the United States, Japan, and other allies has proven economically advantageous. Taiwan's impressive record of economic growth in recent years tends to legitimate separate existence in direct competition with the mainland. Since the establishment of diplomatic relations with the mainland government, the United States has withdrawn its diplomatic and security relations with the Nationalist government, but its economic and other ties with Taiwan have remained strong. Continued relations between the United States and the Nationalist government are among the most troublesome problems in the furtherance of more promising U.S. relations with the People's Republic of China.

One Party State: Burma   Burma achieved independence when the British transferred power to the Anti-Fascist People's Freedom League (AFPFL) on January 4, 1948. U Nu, an AFPFL leader, became the country's first prime minister under a form of parliamentary government modeled on the British experience. In 1958 U Nu asked the army commander, General Ne Win, to crush rebellious elements and form a caretaker government until law and order could be restored. In 1960 U Nu won an election and reassumed the prime minister's role. Instability and violent outbreaks, however, could not be managed by the civilian government and Ne Win removed it, placing the country under martial law on March 2, 1962. U Nu was never again permitted to rule, and the military establishment took up the task of defining a political system for the Burmese nation. In force since 1948, the constitution was cast aside, and in July 1962 the military council announced the formation of the Burma Socialist Program Party (BSPP). All other political parties were declared illegal in March 1964. Another constitution was drafted and promulgated by the BSPP in 1973 and it went into force the following year. The name of the country was altered from the Union of Burma to the Socialist Republic of the Union of Burma.

The new constitution established a Council of State and a Council of Ministers, each organized by a People's Assembly. The chairman of the Council of State was made the president of the country and thus performed functions reserved for the head of state. Both the president and members of the People's Assembly serve four-year terms. In 1984 the president was General San Yu. The Council of State, overseen by the army, has been granted significant powers over foreign affairs, military activities, and emergency conditions. It can declare martial law and suspend political activities. Although Ne Win retired from the presidency in 1981, he continued to run the BSPP as party chairman, and he and the armed forces remained the real power in Burma. For all intents and purposes, the BSPP was the party of the armed forces. *See also* BUDDHISM, p. 59; BURMA SOCIALIST PROGRAM PARTY, p. 139.

Significance   The BSPP foundation documents are "The Burmese Way to Socialism" and "The System of Correlation of Man and His Environment." These publications emphasize the need for both unity and socialist organization. The form socialism takes in Burma, however, is more Buddhist than Marxist. Emphasis is not on class struggle but rather on the transitory nature of life and the inevitability of change. BSPP organization, however, is similar to Marxist parties in other countries. The Central Committee is linked to party congresses, and the party has its branches in all units and at all levels of government. A central Secretariat administers to the party faithful and it continues to be dominated by Ne Win. The BSPP has also mobilized the party in functional organizations like peasant's councils, worker's councils, and youth groups. These latter bodies are hierarchically structured similarly to those in the Soviet Union, and they provide a constant stream of new recruits for the party. One of the principal friction points between the BSPP and the Burmese people is the requirement that all farmers sell their harvest to the government at a fixed price. This program has reduced the incentive of farmers to expand their production, and the result has been a decline in farm products.

The BSPP has always stood for strict neutrality in foreign affairs and for many years the Burmese closed their country to most outsiders. More recently, Burma again displayed its desire to remain aloof from world affairs by resigning its place in the Nonaligned Movement. The Burmese have endeavored to avoid foreign manipulation by this self-imposed isolation, but in October 1983, they could not avoid becoming embroiled in disputes between other nations. A visit by leaders of the South Korean government precipitated a terrorist action that took the lives of many in the delegation as well as a number of Burmese. North Korea was implicated when members of the terrorist team were apprehended. Identified as members of the North Korean armed forces, they reportedly were sent on their mission by high-ranking members of the army. The BSPP's delicate balancing act was affected by the incident but there was little indication the party's leaders would consider altering the country's unique foreign policy.

One-Party State: Republic of the Seychelles   The Seychelles obtained their independence from Great Britain in 1976. The islands occupy an area of the Indian Ocean to the northeast of Madagascar. Sparsely populated, the Seychelles were a French possession before they fell to the British in 1814. French culture remained, however, and the prevailing Creole features intensified during the period of British rule. Political consciousness was slow in coming to the Seychelles, and the inhabitants seemed reluctant to break with the British Empire. When political parties were organized in the 1960s, political personalities, not organizations, became the center of attention. James Mancham represented the cause of conservatism, and France Albert Rene assumed a somewhat radical posture. After independence was achieved, Mancham became president and Rene was named prime minister. But in 1977, Rene took advantage of Mancham's absence from the country and deposed him. Assuming dictatorial powers, Rene reshaped the island's political character, and in 1979 his new constitution was approved in a popular referendum. Rene became the Seychelles new president.

Mancham's party, the Seychelles Democratic Party, had been outlawed earlier, but Rene used the occasion to announce the formation of the Seychelles People's Progressive Front, the only acceptable political party on the islands. In keeping with Marxist tradition, Rene assembled a youth group, a labor union, a women's organization, and integrated them with his People's Progressive Front. Mancham's loyalists were suppressed and their voice in political affairs silenced.

Significance   The establishment of a one-party state in the Seychelles awakened the lethargic conservatives to a fate they had not envisaged. Their leader, James Mancham, was forced into exile and they did not have the resources or the acumen to regain their lost position. Although an attempt was made to overthrow the Rene regime in 1979, it failed and its leaders were either arrested or expelled. In November 1981 an even more daring assault was planned. Forty-eight European mercenaries, allegedly hired by Mancham and assisted by South Africa, arrived at the Seychelles airport. The authorities were apparently waiting and opened fire on the group before they could launch their campaign. Leaving five of their members behind, the mercenaries seized an Air India plane and made a hasty retreat to South Africa.

Another plot failed in August 1982 when units of the Seychelles army mutinied and were forcibly subdued by loyal Rene troops. Rene's success in beating back the opposition has added to his stature. These violent threats to his revolution have mellowed his ideological disposition. Although fiercely critical of the capitalist West, he has welcomed the flow of European investment capital and tourists to the Seychelles. The French retain use of the naval facility at Port Victoria. At the same time, Rene and especially some of his ministers are gracious hosts to Soviet visitors. The Soviet navy makes port calls and Moscow has provided the Seychelles with material aid.

One-Party Vassal State: Kampuchea (Cambodia)   The People's Republic of Kampuchea was established in January 1979 by the Vietnamese army. It was the successor state to the communist Kampuchean state headed by Pol Pot (1975–79). The new Kampuchean government was led by Heng Samrin who had defected from the Khmer Rouge of Pol Pot, but the real power in Kampuchea was in Vietnamese hands. A Vietnamese army remained in Kampuchea in pursuit of Pol Pot and remnants of his forces who were secreted in the jungle border region with Thailand. In 1983 reports circulated throughout Kampuchea that Vietnamese settlers were moving into the eastern portion of the country. Hanoi later confirmed these reports, insisting that Kampuchea would derive economic benefits from the settlements. The

Kampcheans sensed the permanence of the Vietnamese presence, and although it disturbed them, their resistance was feeble.

The only legal party in Kampuchea was the Kampuchean People's Revolutionary Party (KPRP). The KPRP was intertwined with the government in 1981 when a new constitution was drafted and put into force. Leaders of the government were also leaders of the KPRP, but the party was slow to establish itself. The 1979 Congress of the Communist Party of Kampuchea decided to scrap the organization's older name in order to divorce it from the Khmer Rouge of Pol Pot. The Kampuchean People's Revolutionary Party was adopted in its place and the party's ties to Vietnam were reiterated. The Congress elected the KPRP Central Committee and Political Bureau, and after a brief period in which Pen Sovann acted as general secretary of the party, Heng Samrin was selected to replace him. Heng Samrin was intimately associated with the Vietnamese, and with their help he tightened his control over the party, the government, and the nation. The Kampuchean leader curtailed activities of the Buddhist community, and religious instruction was declared illegal. Public purges were launched to isolate and eliminate supporters of counter-revolutionary groups, and Kampuchean officials were replaced by Vietnamese or Kampuchean members of the Khmer Viet Minh, a Marxist-Leninist group trained and supported by Vietnam. *See also* COMMUNIST REGIME: VIETNAM, p. 215; KHMER ROUGE, p. 166; ONE-PARTY VASSAL STATE: LAOS, p. 244; SINO-VIETNAMESE CONFLICT, 1979– , p. 409.

Significance   Vietnam was determined to prevent Kampuchea from establishing an independent existence. The alliance between Kampuchea and China was supposed to protect the former from Vietnam, but Hanoi was not intimidated, and it moved to prevent Beijing from weakening its position in the Mekong Delta or surrounding area. The KPRP was engineered specifically with the objective of making Kampuchea a vassal state of Vietnam. The war against the Pol Pot regime was described as a humanitarian effort that sought to destroy a hideous, savage regime that had taken an estimated three million Kampuchean lives since 1975.

Although there was little doubt about the carnage inflicted on Kampuchea by Pol Pot's administration, the Vietnamese were more interested in reducing Chinese influence in the country than in rescuing a desperate segment of humanity. A case in point was the character of the resistance groups holding out against Vietnamese occupation. There were three of them, including the Communist Khmer Rouge of Pol Pot, the non-Communist Khmer People's Liberation Front (KNPLF or Moulinaka), and Prince Norodom Sihanouk's National United Front. All resistance groups indicated an interest in joining their forces in common struggle against the Vietnamese. Prince Sihanouk, who was forced into exile in China in 1970–71 by a U.S.-engineered coup and who had lost numerous members of his personal family in the slaughter perpetrated by Pol Pot, agreed to join hands with the resistance, and even with Pol Pot, in order to dislodge the Vietnamese from his country. The futility of this exercise, however, was underlined when the Vietnamese mounted a massive campaign against the opposition in 1983. That campaign destroyed important resistance bases and caused the flight of additional tens of thousands of Kampuchean refugees to Thailand.

Barring a protracted war with China, there was little likelihood that the Vietnamese could be coaxed into leaving Kampuchea. Undaunted, Prince Sihanouk tried to repair and cement his beleaguered and divided coalition. At a ceremony on the Thai-Kampuchean frontier in 1983, the prince received the credentials of the ambassadors of China, North Korea, Malaysia, Bangladesh, and Mauritania. Later, he was greeted in Paris as a head of state. Outside the Communist world, the fiction of an independent Kampuchea prevailed.

Hanoi, however, was determined to crush all resistance to its management of Kampuchea. In April 1984 it opened a more aggressive campaign against the Kampuchean guerrillas. By the end of the year it launched a major assault against the remaining bases of the resistance along the Thailand frontier. Six of eight Khmer People's Liberation Front camps were overrun by mid-November. By January 1985 Rithisen and Ampil, two of the largest guerrilla bases inside Kampuchea, also fell to the Vietnamese. In addition, Thailand's frontier forces skirmished with Vietnamese troops, and artillery rounds and air strikes hit refugee villages in the would-be neutral country. Although the resistance leaders insisted they would continue the fight, the heavily equipped Vietnamese army was equally determined to destroy all opposition to their Heng Samrin puppet government.

One-Party Vassal State: Laos   The People's Democratic Republic of Laos was established in December 1975. Its contemporary destiny was shaped by the Indochina War that raged throughout the region from World War II until 1973. The American withdrawal from Indochina in 1973 left the weaker states exposed to Vietnamese ambition, and in quick sequence, South Vietnam was overrun by the troops of the Communist north and absorbed into a unified Vietnamese Socialist People's Republic. Laos' monarchy was terminated by the intruders from Hanoi during this same period. King Savang Vatthana vacated a throne that his family had occupied for more than 500 years, and the Lao People's Revolutionary Party (LPRP) assumed control of the government under Vietnamese supervision. Laos had traded one colonial master, the French, for another, the Vietnamese. The head of the LPRP in 1984 was Kaysone Phomvihan. He was also chairman of the Council of Ministers and prime minister of the country. Prince Souphanouvong, the creator (1951) and leader of the Pathet Lao or Lao People's Liberation Army, a Marxist as well as a relative of the former king, was given the ceremonial office of president of the Republic. (Phomvihan and the Vietnamese assumed effective control of the Pathet Lao in 1955.)

Laos, like other Communist states, was governed by the party, which made rules and policy. The government was an extension of this structure, responsible for the implementation of decisions made by the supreme leaders of the LPRP and approved by Hanoi. Thus, the chairman and his five vice-chairmen passed directives to the ministers, who transformed them into functional responsibilities for transmittal to deputy ministers. The deputy ministers had the responsibility of translating programs into actual tasks. Because of Laos' primitive condition, government programs focused attention on agriculture and forestry. Government officials, along with their Vietnamese supervisors, encouraged the development of communication and transportation networks which would more intimately connect Laos with Vietnam and with Vietnam-occupied Kampuchea. *See also* HO CHI MINH TRAIL, p. 19; ONE-PARTY VASSAL STATE: KAMPUCHEA (CAMBODIA), p. 242.

Significance   Laos is a landlocked, underdeveloped country surrounded by traditional foes. The North Vietnamese exploited Laos' geopolitical location by secretly constructing a network of roads, trails, and paths from Hanoi through Laos to South Vietnam and Kampuchea (Cambodia). The United States attempted to cut this supply route and bolster the independence of the Laotian monarchy and government. As a consequence, Laos could not avoid being plunged into the Indochina War. Although the United States provided military support, attempted to improve the Royal Laotian Army, and mobilized fierce, tribal warriors for combat against the Vietnamese-supported Pathet Lao, the latter could not be defeated.

Thus, when the Americans signed a peace treaty with the North Vietnamese in Paris in 1973, the fate of the Laotians, as well as the South Vietnamese and Kampucheans (Cambodians), was sealed. Communist China was too blinded by its distrust of the United States to take advantage of the situation. Events therefore favored the Vietnamese and their allies, the Soviets. When the dust of the Indochina war settled, Moscow, through its client Vietnam, not Beijing, established a sphere of influence over the region. The Chinese role in Kampuchea was quickly nullified by the Soviet-encouraged Vietnamese invasion of the Communist Khmer Rouge state. Laos, like Kampuchea, was compelled to accept Vietnamese *diktat*.

Resistance to the Marxist-Leninist takeover in Laos has been minimal and sporadic. The Hmong or Meo tribesmen, who fought alongside U.S. forces during the Indochina War, are a potential source of difficulty for the Communist regime, but without major external assistance it is doubtful they can again be drawn into battle. Thailand, although totally dependent on the West, and especially the United States, appears determined to establish cordial relations with the Laotian government. Bangkok is not likely to act as a conduit for supplies to Laotian resistance, although it seems destined to provide sanctuary for refugees fleeing the excesses of the revolutionary government. As with Kampuchea, there is little likelihood of change in the Laotian relationship with Vietnam. Only a major clash with China could reverse the current course of events, and even in such an instance, Laos would merely trade one master, Vietnam, for another, the People's Republic of China.

Panchayat System: Nepal   A celebrated institution of self-government in subcontinent history. The original *panchayats* were local councils of five elders, learned in the traditions of their people, and responsible for the dissemination of justice. In the nineteenth century, the British formally introduced something akin to a panchayat system in rural India with the Ripon reforms. The modern panchayats of Nepal were supposed to be a throwback to a classical period of local government, but the real reason for their reestablishment was the king's fear of political parties. Nepal is ruled by an absolute monarch. The country's brief exposure to a form of parliamentary government was inaugurated in 1959 and terminated in 1960. In 1961 King Mahendra substituted a panchayat system for the erstwhile parliament, with the explanation that it was more appropriate for the Nepalese nation.

Nepal's short experience with parliamentary government had centered on the activities of the political parties. The parties were aggregations of opinion that were, more often than not, critical of the monarchy. The king, therefore, argued for a partyless political system and the panchayat system appeared to be the best answer to a need for popular representation on the one side and the monarch's wish to be free of organized political pressure on the other. Thus, the panchayat system was designed to assist the king and his followers in overseeing the political life of the nation, unencumbered by opposition politicians.

Nepal's panchayat system was conceived as a four-tiered structure with its roots in the villages. At the apex of the panchayat system was the National Assembly, the ultimate expression of the councils at the lower levels. Later, the system was reduced to three tiers but the original design remained. The National Assembly also has been modified since its establishment in 1961. Currently it is firmly under the control of King

Birendra Bir Bikram Shah Dev who ascended the throne in 1972 and who oversees virtually all legislative selections and actions. The political parties have never accepted their demise, however, and a 1979 demonstration in the capital of Kathmandu, provoked in major part by frustrated students and politicians, forced the king to hold a countrywide referendum to determine if the parties should be reinstated, or if the panchayat system should remain partyless. The referendum was held in 1980 and the majority of voters opted for sustaining the partyless system. Nevertheless, the politicians continued to press their demands and they found many supporters among the urban intelligentsia, small business community, and students. *See also* PARTYLESS GOVERNMENT: NEPAL, p. 249; PARTY SYSTEMS, p. 247.

Significance   The panchayat system is tailor-made to the monarch's needs in governing the country. The king cannot avoid being the central figure in the country's political life, nor can he avoid being made the target of opposition criticism. Many in the attentive public think that political change is possible only after the monarchy has been eliminated, or the king has been transformed into a figurehead. Nevertheless, Nepal is far from being a doctrinaire police state. The monarchy has emphasized liberal reforms, and the Nepalese are relatively open in their general criticism.

Others find fault with the monarch, but they are convinced that the institution is vital to Nepal's ethos, and that it provides the essential stability and continuity crucial to the maintenance of an independent country. These elements view the king as a barrier to Indian ambitions in their region and they have urged patience and acceptance of the political order, even if it seems to postpone democratic innovations. The most significant opposition in Nepal therefore is found among the radical left which has broad acceptance among university and college students. The volatility of the Nepalese student community remains a potent threat to the king's panchayat system. It is also dramatic evidence that the Nepali Panchayet System possesses little sentimental or historical significance for the country's political elites.

Party Systems   Patterned interactions of groups organized for the purpose of aggregating various interests and translating them into public policies, by controlling the personnel of the decision-making apparatus of government through election or other selection devices. Various party systems exist. Epistemologically, a system implies component parts and a party system connotes two or more parties. However, a one-party system is also discussed as a party system because of its importance in Asia. Besides the one-party system, other party systems commonly identified are a two-party system and a multiparty system. However, a finer classification includes

(1) The Party-State System, which is epitomized by the Communist party state. The Communist party is the ruling party and its leadership position is constitutionally prescribed. For example, it is stated in the Constitution of the People's Republic of China: "The Communist Party of China is the core of leadership of the whole Chinese people. The working class exercises leadership over the state through its vanguard, the Communist Party of China." In the Party-State System, then, not only does party leadership overlap with state leadership, but also it is placed in the controlling, guiding, and supervisory position over the state. No competition among groups for power is permitted. Such groups are unconstitutional in the Party-State System.

(2) The Competitive Single Party System, of which the Congress Party of India provides the best example. In India, various parties exist and a multiparty system is constitutionally guaranteed, but the ruling Congress Party has been in power since independence, and it has been identified with political power and privilege. Organized nationally, the Congress position has never been threatened in India. The Congress has also organized a broad coalition of diverse groups and parochial interests within the loose confines of its party framework.

(3) The Competitive One-Party Dominant System. South Korea (ROK) best represents this system. The ROK has experienced violent regime changes, each change ushering in a new controlling party. Because the constitution guarantees a multiparty system, opposition parties are always present. However, they are successfully controlled and never strong enough to undermine the legitimacy of the ruling party. The ruling party has never been able to organize a broad coalition of diverse interests and parochial loyalties and has never been long enough in power in the Competitive One-Party Dominant System to develop a durable national organization and followings.

(4) The Competitive Two-Party System. The United States, England, Australia, and New Zealand are prime examples of this system. These nations represent the world's most stable democracies and they have become the models of democracy and stable party systems. No Asian nations have been able to experiment with this system successfully. Under this system, as in the United States, each of the two major parties, which are rooted in history, relies on voluntary mass support and coalition formation of a broad spectrum of social and economic interests. Furthermore, both parties are able to compete freely for power and the party in power is often voted out by the electorates in a peaceful transition of power.

(5) The Competitive Limited Multiparty System, of which Japan is a prime example. Two or more major political parties exist in Japan and

each is organized nationally and shows a stable following. However, the ruling Liberal-Democratic Party (LDP), successfully coalescing various factional leaders and their followers, has stayed continuously in power. The other parties may be dominant locally at times, but given their ideological adherence and particularism, they are unable to organize a successful united front against the LDP. The LDP's parliamentary strength has never been too dominant to ignore the other parties, however, and special efforts to generate broader support for decision making are always in demand.

(6) The Competitive Extreme Multiparty System. The governments of postwar France and Italy at times exemplified this system. Various parties freely compete for electoral support, but none is able to attain a majority status. Each party runs on specific issues or programs and each appeals to a limited group that may be either ideologically cohesive, or regionally and parochially based. The government that results from the Competitive Extreme Multiparty System is necessarily a coalition government. In the development of Third World nations of Asia, this party system has been eschewed as unstable. *See also* DEVELOPMENT, p. 297; MODERNIZATION, p. 313; MODERN SOCIETIES, p. 312; TRANSITIONAL SOCIETIES, p. 323.

Significance   Great diversity characterizes party systems in the independent states of Asia. However, political parties play a substantially less important role in national decision making in the Third World non-Communist nations of Asia than in the western, developed nations. As modern political institutions, political parties perform the function of interest aggregation and control policy making by supplying personnel to the government. In the Third World non-Communist nations of Asia, however, leaders organize political parties to aggrandize their own interests and to mobilize mass support for their causes. Political stability is created, therefore, not through a coalition of various interests, but through force and repression. The government creates its own ruling party that successfully mobilizes and exploits the electoral support necessary for it to stay in power, and it tolerates a limited opposition. The most prevalent party system in the non-Communist Third World nations of Asia is a Competitive One-Party Dominant System. All the Asian Communist states (the PRC, North Korea, Mongolia, Vietnam, Laos, and Kampuchea) practice the Party-State System.

Partyless Government: Nepal   Political parties were introduced into Nepal in the aftermath of World War II. Because of Nepal's near proximity to and intimacy with India, its party system resembled that of its larger neighbor. Nepal was dominated by the Rana family from 1846 until 1951. The initial objective of the political parties was the destruction of the family's political monopoly, and the establishment of a democratic system in the country. This goal, however, was thwarted by Nepal's monarchical history and the reinvigoration of the Shah dynasty which predated the Rana usurpers.

A revolution against the Ranas in 1950–51 was led by King Tribhuvan with the active support of the then Crown Prince, who was later to assume the throne as King Mahendra. King Mahendra was a reformer who intended to usher Nepal into the twentieth century without weakening the authority of the monarchy. Thus in December 1960 King Mahendra introduced the partyless Panchayat System in Nepal. The political parties condemned the action, declaring it to be a royal coup. But the majority were in no position to resist the royal decree. The majority of Nepal's parties were little more than personal followings and the personalities dominating them were able to negotiate with the throne for a place in the government without the necessity for formal organization. The Congress Party, the Communist Party, and the politicized students, however, were less malleable. The Congress Party was organized along socialist lines and was successful in winning the general election of 1959. B. P. Koirala, the leader of the Congress, became Nepal's prime minister and the country's most outstanding statesman, but even he could not prevent the monarchy from establishing the partyless panchayats. His death in 1982 left the Congress and the politicians at large without an active voice. A number of prominent Congressites shifted their support to the Panchayat System and the Congress split into factions making its role even more nebulous.

The picture was little different for the Communist Party, which broke into pro-Moscow and pro-Beijing factions. The ineffectiveness of the political parties is reflected in the absence of politicians with broad popular support. Nevertheless, the 1980 referendum and the 1981 election indicated a trend toward liberalizing the Panchayat System so that it might better represent the interests of the Nepali nation. Although the evolution toward a political party system may still be in the future, the sophisticated population clearly yearns for a more competitive arrangement. *See also* PANCHAYAT SYSTEM: NEPAL, p. 246.

Significance　　The development of a more responsible political process in Nepal was signaled by the 1983 resignation of Prime Minister Surya Bahadur Thapa. His failure to maintain the confidence of the National Panchayat (National Assembly) represented the first time that a Nepali head of government had been forced from office by an elected body rather than by royal decree. The new government of Lokendra Bahadur Chand was placed on notice that its activities would be thoroughly scrutinized, and that abuses of power would be dealt with in the open. It is notable that the king's representatives all voted against Thapa, and alliances between the throne and the politicians seemed to have been strengthened by the action. The Panchayat System was thus given more credibility without weakening the monarchy. There was, at the same time, an effort on the part of politicians to reassert their particular interests. Although political parties had been banned in 1960, they began to represent themselves unofficially in the National Panchayat, and the Congress Party became more bold in publicizing its activities. The Communist parties were also more active in the colleges and Tribhuvan University, where they recruited students for what were described as progressive tasks.

Presidential Power: India   The president of India is head-of-state and supreme commander of the armed forces, but still a ceremonial figure. The president is expected to act on advice from the prime minister, the head of government and the leader of the federal cabinet. Because concern has periodically surfaced over the president's potential power, amendments to the constitution in 1976 (number 42), and 1978 (number 44), reiterated the requirement that acts of the president must be related to advice received from the cabinet. Real power, therefore, is lodged in the office of prime minister.

The president is indirectly elected by an electoral college comprised of the Rajya Sabha (upper house) and Lok Sabha (lower house) of the Indian parliament, as well as the lower houses of the state legislatures. Presidents serve five-year terms and may be reelected. Historically, they have been persons acceptable, if not sponsored, by the prime minister. In fact, the president has been more the "appointment" of the prime minister than the prime minister is an appointment of the president. In constitutional terms, however, the president is an elected official who calls upon the political leader with the most effective power in the Lok Sabha, or lower house of the Indian parliament, to form the government. The president also appoints other members of the cabinet on recommendation of the prime minister. They are removed in roughly the same manner. Since the promulgation of the Constitution of 1950, India has had six presidents: Rajendra Prasad, Sarvapalli Radhakrishnan, Zakir Husain, V. V. Giri, Fakhruddin Ali Ahmed, and Zail Singh. India has also had six prime ministers since 1947 and two of them, Jawaharlal Nehru (1947–64), and his daughter, Indira Gandhi (1966–77, 1980–84), governed the country for almost 32 years. Rajiv Gandhi succeeded to the post following his mother's assassination. The others were Lal Bahadur Shastri (1964–66), Morarji Desai (1977–79), and Charan Singh (1979). *See also* CONSTITUTIONAL SECULARISM: INDIA, p. 216; LOK SABHA, p. 235; RAJYA SABHA, p. 252.

Significance   The strength of the prime minister over the Indian president was reflected in the decisions made during the state of emergency (1975–77). Although the powers utilized in suspending constitutional guarantees fell within the constitutional purview of the president, it was the prime minister who wielded the ruling instrument. The prime minister was also the officer who called upon the president to impose presidential rule on states that seemed unable to manage their parliamentary affairs, or that faced a condition of near anarchy. The frequent use of such prerogative to suspend the regular functions of local government has added to the power of the prime minister, but not the president. Emergency has become a permanent condition in India and the Indian executive, namely the prime minister, has assumed maximum power, often unencumbered by legal practices. This condition helps to explain the longevity of Indira Gandhi and her triumphal return in the 1980 elections. It also explains the succession of her son, Rajiv. Despite efforts to construct impersonal political institutions based on solid democratic traditions, the popular need for a "great leader" remains dominant.

Rajya Sabha: India   The upper house or Assembly of States in the Indian parliament. The Rajya Sabha has 250 members, 12 nominated by the president, and the remainder coming from the 22 states in the Indian Union. The number of seats allocated to each state is determined by the size of their population, with special allowances given states with smaller populations. Members of the Rajya Sabha are elected by their respective state assemblies and serve six year terms. Unlike the Lok Sabha, the Rajya Sabha cannot be dissolved. The Rajya Sabha theoretically safeguards the constitutional prerogatives of the states. It enjoys equal power with the Lok Sabha in amending the constitution, which is managed by a simple majority in both houses of parliament, followed by ratification by a majority of the Indian states and the president's automatic assent. The Rajya Sabha, however, is inferior to the lower house in that it can delay an appropriation bill but cannot initiate one, nor can it impede the operation of Cabinet government. Ordinary legislation, however, is handled by the Rajya Sabha in the same fashion as the Lok Sabha, and both houses are required to pass a bill before it is sent to the president. *See also* LOK SABHA, p. 235.

Significance   The Rajya Sabha is not the equivalent of the British House of Lords. It was designed to represent the interests of the states within the Indian Union and thereby reduce the parochial tendencies of the different regions. The Rajya Sabha, therefore, is a critical component in the operation of Indian democracy. India had little experience with parliamentary democracy in 1947. A borrowed institution, the parliamentary system seeks to provide stability to a society that seems perennially poised at the edge of chaos. Mrs. Gandhi has often commented that India is a vast territory with incredibly complex problems. The fact that India is determined to achieve democratic goals and has adopted democratic procedures and institutions in pursuit of that quest is no small accomplishment. The Indian parliament attempts to represent the population at large, as well as the states and regions. The Rajya Sabha has not reduced tension in the Punjab, Kashmir, Assam, Karnataka, Tamil Nadu, and other areas, but it remains with the Lok Sabha, an important forum for competing ideas and cultural groups.

Sultanate: Brunei   A small country (only 2,226 square miles, 5,900 square kilometers) which achieved its independence on December 31, 1983 when its status as a British protectorate was legally terminated. The country is formally described as Brunei Darussalam, which translates to "Brunei Abode of Peace" in official circles. Brunei has a population of almost 250,000 and consists of two enclaves within the Malaysian state of Sarawak, but it is totally free of Malaysian control. (Both Brunei and Sarawak are located on the northern perimeter of the Indonesian island of Borneo [Kalimantan]). The decision not to join Malaysia was taken in 1963, but Brunei must still resist efforts to be absorbed by both Malaysia and Indonesia. It therefore maintains a small defense establishment comprised mainly of Gurkha troops that were brought to the region by the British. The early history of Brunei is sketchy but there are indications it was a vassal state of China before it came under the influence of the Hindus of Java.

By the sixteenth century, however, Brunei had developed into a formidable power and extended its authority over all of Borneo as well as other lesser islands of the Malay archipelago. By the nineteenth century it had lost most of this territory, but continued to hold sway over Sarawak and a portion of Sabah (located on the northeastern tip of the island of Borneo). The British penetration of the area forced the sultan of Brunei to cede Sarawak in 1841. The sultan entered into a formal treaty with Britain in which the latter helped to promote Brunei's commercial activity and suppress piracy.

In 1888 Brunei was formally made a protectorate of Great Britain, and its foreign affairs and defense came under English control. In 1906 the sultan agreed to accept a British Resident, and European presence in the country was magnified. Oil was discovered in Brunei in 1929, and the economy of the sultanate began its contemporary metamorphosis. Interrupted during World War II by the Japanese occupation of the region, the exploitation of oil accelerated in later years.

Brunei's separation from Sarawak, under whose administration it had fallen, was proclaimed in 1959. A British high commissioner was appointed that same year and the country's first constitution was drafted and proclaimed. Political parties became active, and in 1962 the Partai Ra'ayat (People's Party) was given responsibility for forming the government. A revolt led by the Tentera Nasional Kalimantan Utara (TNKU) caused serious disturbances, however, and British forces were called to restore law and order. With tranquility somewhat restored, Brunei experienced its first genuine election in 1965. In 1968 the People's United Party (Pekara) was organized to represent the interests of the government and the Partai Ra'ayat was destroyed. Political parties were legally banned, but Pekara was permitted to maintain a presence as has the People's Independence Party which continues to press for more constitutional guarantees.

The sultanate is ruled by Sultan Hassanal Bolkiah Mu'izzadin Waddaulah, the 29th sultan of Brunei. The sultan, officially crowned in 1968, succeeded his father, Sir Omar Ali Saifuddin, who abdicated in 1967. Despite British efforts at "democratizing" Brunei, the sultan, his brothers, and the Malay aristocracy retain direct rule over the country. The sultan is president of the Council of Ministers (formerly the Executive Council) which is the governing body under the constitution. The Mentri Besar, or chief minister, is appointed by and responsible to the sultan. The members of the Legislative Council are likewise appointed by the sultan, as are the chief administrators of the country's four districts and four municipalities. *See also* FEDERALISM: MALAYSIA, p. 226.

Significance The Sultanate of Brunei is governed by a relatively worldly and enlightened ruler, who is both a devout Muslim and a former cadet from the British military academy at Sandhurst. He shows respect for the elders in the Brunei hierarchy while mixing freely with the general population. Although interested in the modernization of the country, the sultan remains a traditional, feudal potentate. Administrative integrity has deteriorated since the phasing out of British control, and corruption and inefficiency have escalated. The aristocrats are reluctant to change with the times, and their fear of politicians has tended to generate considerable bitterness in the country. They have tried to influence the sultan to slow his reform program. The Partai Ra'ayat led by A. M. Azahari has thus seen its leadership imprisoned or forced to flee the country because of its radical views. Indeed, Azahari is considered something of a Marxist.

What seems to concern the traditional rulers of the country is the opposition's interest in establishing closer ties with Malaysia or Indonesia. If opposition programs were implemented, it would most certainly mean the liquidation of the historic Brunei feudal order. Brunei is therefore divided between its traditional ruling elements, supported by a large portion of the peasant and tribal population which is wedded to the sultan, and the political intelligentsia who have successfully infiltrated the ranks of the intellectuals, as well as industrial labor, particularly in the oil industry.

Burnei's population is approximately 55 percent Malay and Muslim, 30 percent Chinese and Buddhist, 12 percent tribal (primarily Dayak), and 3 percent Indian European, mostly Dutch and English. As in Malaysia and Vietnam, the Chinese population lives under considerable pressure, and many have chosen or been forced to leave the country, in part because the country is no longer under strict British protection. The Chinese of Brunei have been associated with those political parties emphasizing change in the traditional ruling patterns of society. They are found almost exclusively in the urban areas.

In spite of this sociopolitical strife, Brunei is something like a welfare state, made possible by the sale of natural gas and petroleum. It has one of the highest standards of living in Southeast Asia. There are no income taxes, medical care is free to all, pensions for government service are handsome, and the government provides free education to the masses. Brunei's future, however, seems to lie with the sultan, who must address the questions of continued modernization while seeking to retain the country's independence and traditional lifestyle. It remains to be seen if the two objectives are compatible. On September 21, 1984, Brunei became the 159th member state of the United Nations.

Swaraj and Dyarchy: India   Aspects of colonial rule in India. The loss of indigenous authority was a blow to the subcontinent's politically conscious elites. After the Mutiny of 1857 the British sensed a need to bring Indians closer to the ruling circle and some were added to the Viceroy's legislative council. It was not until the 1909 Indian Councils Act that serious effort was made to enlist their services. This token beginning whetted the Indian appetite for greater representation, and a "home rule" movement developed prior to the outbreak of World War I. The Indian National Congress (organized in 1885) and the Muslim League (organized in 1906) assumed important roles during this period. Their call for self-government, or *swaraj*, pressured the British to consider broader and deeper reforms. The Montagu-Chelmsford Reforms of 1917 led to the Government of India Act, 1919, which in turn introduced a form of parliamentary government. The latter operated under the concept of *dyarchy*, which meant certain specified powers were reserved for the Viceroy and colonial governors. The British were reluctant to share power with the indigenous elites, and the method of self-government contrived for the situation was a form of "basic democracy." *See also* MUTINY OF 1857, p. 392.

Significance Swaraj, though somewhat negated by Dyarchy, was a cause that would not go away, and Dyarchy was stronger only in the short term. The Indians were too well organized to relent in their efforts, and the indigenous intelligentsia felt justified in spreading their dissatisfaction to the illiterate masses. The *Swadeshi* or Freedom Movement, which involved a boycott on imported textiles and other European manufactures, stressed the revitalization of village handicrafts and cottage industries, especially home-spun cloth. Street demonstrations supported the boycott, and the use of repressive measures by colonial authorities only inspired larger displays of civil disobedience.

The Indian national elite was formed in these circumstances. Another consequence of these activities was the mass mobilization of India's many publics, and the shaping of their political consciousness. The Swadeshi Movement brought together diverse interests with a single objective. The British were accused of moral pretension and heavy-handed action, and their publicized humanitarian purposes could not be reconciled with their police-state tactics. Tutored by their European conquerors, the Indians let it be known they were prepared for Swaraj. A more genuine experiment in self-government occurred with the Government of India Act, 1935, which terminated Dyarchy.

Traditional Politics: Maldives The Republic of the Maldives achieved its independence in 1965. The Maldives are several hundred small islands located in the central Indian Ocean. For centuries they acted as way stations for Arab seafarers and were ruled by a hereditary Muslim sultanate dominated by the Didi family. The British established a protectorate over the Maldives in 1870 and it remained in force until 1947. Sri Lanka assumed limited responsibility for the Maldives between 1947 and 1965 while the islands were prepared for statehood. Although the republic replaced the traditional Maldives sultanate, the character of political rule on the islands was little changed. Family relationships shaped patterns of political behavior and each patriarch protected the interests of his particular clan. Sinhalese, Dravidian, Arab, and African races intermingled, but the dominant organizing principle was still found in Sunni Islam. Moreover, the legal system in the Maldives follows the principles of Islamic jurisprudence as expressed in Shafite doctrine. The language of communication, however, is Divehi Sinhalese, reflecting the islands' earlier association with Buddhism. *See also* INDIAN OCEAN, p. 22; ISLAM (SUNNI), p. 89.

Significance   The Maldives would perhaps go unnoticed were it not for the importance of the Indian Ocean in contemporary international relations. The Maldives have pursued a policy of nonalignment in order to escape superpower rivalries in the region. The British-built airbase on Gan island was abandoned in 1976 and the Maldives' need for hard currency led to leasing the facility to the highest bidder. The Soviet Union displayed keen interest in the base and offered a lucrative reward to the Maldives government. Under pressure, however, the government decided to reject the offer and convert Gan into a haven for tourists.

Yushin (Revitalization) Reforms: South Korea   A wholesale revision of South Korea's Third Republican Constitution in 1972, which broadened the power of the president, eliminated the limit on the presidential term, and created indirect presidential election by the National Conference of Unification. Following the 1961 military coup in South Korea, its leader, General Park Chung Hee (Pak, Chŏng-hui), was elected president in 1963 under the Third Republican Constitution and reelected in 1967. To circumvent the two-term limitation of the presidency, the Constitution was amended in 1969 and President Park was elected again for a third term in 1971.

In 1972, this constitution was discarded *in toto* by a coup in office, and a new constitution called *Yushin*, meaning revitalization, replaced it. This constitution appears to have been designed to (1) discourage the institutional growth of political parties, allowing independents to be candidates for political office; (2) further restrict the rights and liberties of the people by broadening the emergency power of the president; and (3) insulate the presidency from popular politics by indirect election for an unrestricted term by an electoral college of not less than 2,000 or more than 5,000 popularly elected deputies, who comprise the National Conference of Unification. These and other changes in the constitution were advocated as a means of better preparing the country for negotiating an eventual, peaceful reunification of the divided land with North Korea, and of better coping with national economic and security problems. *See also* COUP D'ÉTAT: SOUTH KOREA, p. 276; MILITARY AUTHORITARIANISM, p. 289; UNIFICATION PROPOSALS: KOREA, p. 368.

Significance   The 1972 transition from the Third Republic to the Fourth Republic in South Korea was most propitious for President Park. The national economy was suffering, largely due to the world oil crisis. The Guam Declaration of U.S. President Richard M. Nixon in 1969 created uncertainty regarding U.S. commitment to its allies in Asia. In 1972, North and South Korea began a dialogue for the peaceful reunification of their divided country. The Fourth Republic was created as a way to cope with these unsettling and critical domestic and international problems. When the new constitution was proclaimed, despite its politically restrictive nature, there was relatively little opposition to it. The country was under martial law at that time. A national referendum on the new constitution was held on November 21, 1972, and it was approved by 91.5 percent out of 91.9 percent of the voters participating. The *yushin* reforms created a yushin political system, which deemphasized popular politics, discouraged the institutional growth of political parties, restricted civil rights and liberties, and made the central executive dominant in decision making. This type of political system was advocated as a way to cope with both domestic and international crises and to promote national development and reunification.

Zaibatsu: Japan   A powerful financial clique, giant business family or great business magnate. *Zaibatsu* wielded enormous economic power in prewar Japan, an economic empire which included various business activities such as manufacturing, shipping, banking, trading, mining, insurance, real estate, and colonial undertakings. These conglomerates were usually identified by the founders' family names. Among the biggest and most widely known were Mitsui, Mitsubishi, Sumitomo, and Yasuda. The founders of some of these conglomerates were traced back to the feudal merchant class of the Tokugawa period, but most were the products of modern Japan, their development closely coinciding with Japan's modernization and colonial expansion.

The government of modern Japan favored a few big businesses and nurtured their growth with favors. For instance, following the Meiji Restoration (1868), the modern government of Japan pursued a policy of economic development, and financed various industries and industrial infrastructure building. Many of these projects were later sold at very reduced rates to favored business and government leaders, thus laying the business foundations of many zaibatsu. The result of such practice was an unusually close tie between business and government in Japan's economic development during the pre-war period. This practice, regarded by the Allied Powers as responsible for Japan's imperial expansionism, became one of the first targets of postwar reform. *See also* LIBERAL DEMOCRATIC PARTY: JAPAN, p. 169; ZAIKAI: JAPAN, p. 259; MEIJI RESTORATION, p. 310.

Significance   Prewar zaibatsu of Japan was a unique institution, peculiar to Japan's development financing. The zaibatsu grew with assistance from the government. As a huge business conglomerate, the zaibatsu had its own bank to finance capital investment and the introduction of modern technology. However, its alliance with politicians and govern-

ment officials, and its support of Japan's authoritarian, militaristic government, and imperialistic foreign policy made it vulnerable to attack by
social and political reformers. Following Japan's defeat in World War II,
the zaibatsu institution became one of the first targets of reform by the
United States.

Although it was not historically proven, the American occupation
authorities (SCAP) theorized that Japan's aggressive prewar imperialism
was mainly caused by an excessive concentration of industrial wealth and
power in the hands of the zaibatsu. The great zaibatsu firms were
therefore disbanded, and their leaders were purged from their positions. This reform soon proved impractical. As the American authorities
began to emphasize Japanese economic recovery, the further implementation of the zaibatsu reform was terminated, and prewar zaibatsu were
revived. Mitsui, Mitsubishi, Sumitomo, and Yasuda are still powerful
economic combines in Japan today, though they have lost many of their
leading personnel, and much of their prewar economic dominance in
the country. They are no longer controlled by a single family and its
members, and they operate more like big U.S. corporations. However,
the new zaibatsu system retains many of the traditional features of
Japanese business practices, such as government-business cooperation,
lifetime executive careers, lifetime employment of labor, and the paternalistic relationship between employer and employed.

Zaikai: Japan   The financial world's collective designation of business interests that are politically relevant. The *zaikai* is often referred to
as a single, powerful business and political entity in Japan, particularly
in the mass media. Japan is described as "Japan, Incorporated," and its
political system as a tripartite division of power among organized business, the Liberal-Democratic Party in power, and the professional
bureaucracy. However, the zaikai defies simple definition. Its most con-
spicuous leaders include the so-called "Big Four Economic Groups"—
the Federation of Economic Organizations (*Keidanren*), the Committee
for Economic Development (*Keizai Doyukai*), the Federation of Employers' Organizations (*Nikkeiren*), and the Japan Chamber of Commerce
(*Nissho*). Of these, the Federation of Economic Organizations is the most
powerful. It is composed of big businesses—Japan's largest corporations—and industrial, financial, and commercial associations of business interests.

The Committee for Economic Development was originally formed by
a group of young business leaders interested in Japanese business development. It is somewhat liberal in its political orientation, even seeking
reforms in the Liberal-Democratic party and in the system of political
campaign financing. The Federation of Employer's Organizations is

mostly concerned with problems of business-labor relations. The Japan Chamber of Commerce is known for its diffuse membership representing both large and small businesses. The Federation of Medium and Small Enterprises more actively represents small business interests, but it is not so influential as the other big business organizations. *See also* LIBERAL-DEMOCRATIC PARTY: JAPAN, p. 169; ZAIBATSU: JAPAN, p. 258.

Significance   Various voluntary organizations and interest groups exist in Japan, but business organizations are politically most influential. Business organizations actively support the ruling Liberal-Democratic Party. The Federation of Economic Organizations in particular maintains routine and frequent communication with the government, and its input to the Ministry of International Trade and Industry is always regarded as significant. Its support sometimes plays a crucial role in the selection of prime minister, as in the case of Ikeda Hayato in 1960. However, the premiership of Tanaka Kakuei demonstrates that its support is not the sole determining factor in the selection of prime minister. Despite the Federation's support of Fukuda Takeo in 1972, Tanaka was chosen. Fukuda had to wait for his turn until 1976. Although business interests are politically influential in Japan, their influence is more strongly felt when they speak with one voice, and when they concern themselves with the areas of their special interests.

Zengakuren: Japan   An abbreviation of *Zen Nihon Gakusei Jichikai Sorengo,* or "All-Japan Federation of Student Self-Governing Associations," a national organization of Japanese students, founded in September 1948. As the name indicates, the *Zengakuren* is a national federation of separate *jichikai,* or student governments, which are organized within each university. All students are automatically members of the jichikai, and compulsory dues are collected along with their tuition. Although the number of politically active students may be small, the Zengakuren enjoys a hugh membership and a sizeable amount of activities funds.

     When the Zengakuren was founded, student members of the Japan Communist Party (JCP) controlled it, and for a decade it functioned as an integral part of JCP politics. When this group lost control to the Communist League (*Kyosan Shugisha Domei,* nicknamed the "*Bunto*" from the English word "bund"), a group opposed to the JCP, the pro-JCP elements organized a new Zengakuren (July 1960) which since 1964 has been known as the *Minsei Zengakuren.* The anti-JCP New Left forces were then split into the *Kakumaru* faction and an alliance of other factions that had at one time been known as the "*Sampa*" (Three Faction) *Zengakuren.* The alliance broke up in July 1968 into four or five

Zengakuren groupings. The pro-JCP Minsei has been strongest, however, and it has consistently controlled more jichikai than all other groups combined. Despite a continued history of factionalism and schism, the name Zengakuren has become widely identified in Japan and abroad as a powerful left-wing student movement in post–World War II Japan. *See also* COMMUNIST PARTY: JAPAN, p. 146; JAPAN-UNITED STATES SECURITY TREATY, p. 343.

Significance Students of the Third World nations of Asia and elsewhere are highly political. Japanese students are no exception, having a long history of political activism. The Zengakuren are most powerful in contemporary Japan. Although various factions exist, almost all the leaders and activists of the Zengakuren consider themselves Marxists or are Marxist sympathizers. Zengakuren students have been active waging strikes and demonstrations against the university authorities and their policies. They have supported JCP policies and played a leading role in protests against the U.S. occupation policy of suppression of the JCP in the early 1950s and in opposition to the U.S. military presence in Japan under the terms of the United States-Japan Security Treaty of 1952. Active protestors of the revision of the United States-Japan Mutual Security Treaty in 1960, they caused the so-called *Ampo* (Security Treaty) crisis and established the "Ampo 70" movement. Their increasingly militant confrontation with the police has become known as *geba*—short for *gebaruto*, from the German *gewalt* meaning "force." The *Sekigunha*, or Red Army Faction, is an extreme faction of the Zengakuren. Its international wing, the *Nihon Sekigun* (Japanese Red Army), has been known for a series of international terrorist attacks and hijackings waged in the 1970s.

5. Militarism and the Armed Forces

Armed Forces: Chinese People's Liberation Army (PLA)

China's (PRC) military forces, which probably number some 4 million, making it the largest armed force in the world. Over 3 million troops are committed as ground forces with the remainder divided among the other service arms—air force, navy, armor artillery, second artillery (strategic missiles), engineers, railway engineers, and telecommunications. The PLA is largely a ground army, divided into main force units and regional forces. The main forces are under a direct central command, whereas the regional forces are controlled through the national system of 11 military regions (subdivided into 28 military districts). The main forces are responsible for the PLA's national defense and strategic missions; the regional forces are responsible for internal and border security, for the provision of garrisons for local defense and a reserve pool for training, and for recruitment to the main forces. Regional forces are also responsible for providing direction to the militia and the Production and Construction Corps.

Founded in the late 1920s when the Chinese Communist Party (CCP) was struggling against Chinese Nationalist forces, the PLA was organized as an integral part of the CCP, and performed a variety of non-military functions, including party recruitment and training, economic construction, and education. Furthermore, it shared leadership with the CCP and was close to the center of many policy debates. This PLA and CCP relationship has persisted since the establishment of the PRC in 1949, but the Party has controlled the military through ideological indoctrination and various organizational devices. The PLA ideologically supports the central leadership in which many military leaders are also found. The organizational devices for control of the military are (1) the Party's Military Commission (previously called the Military Affairs

263

Committee), usually headed by the most powerful leader of the Party (previously party chairman); and (2) the system of political departments within the military, which places political officers down to the platoon level. According to the 1982 state constitution, the PLA is to be directed by the Central Military Commission in the government. The National People's Congress elects the chairman of the Central Military Commission and, upon his nomination, chooses the other members of the Commission. Within the State Council, the Ministry of Defense (headed by a minister of defense) is the central administrative organ of military affairs in the country. *See also* MAOISM, p. 101; RED-EXPERT CONTRO-VERSY, p. 317; SINO-SOVIET SPLIT, p. 356.

Significance		Bred in the CCP's revolutionary tradition, the PLA has maintained an inseparable relationship with the CCP and its role has been perceived as the military arm of the CCP. In a national emergency, such as the Cultural Revolution, it has readily assumed important administrative powers. Throughout history, particularly under the leadership of Mao Zedong (Mao Tse-tung), the political demands made on the PLA have outweighed professional military demands. Increasingly, however, the PLA has perceived itself as a professional group requiring specialized training and modern weapons. Although it is technologically unsophisticated, and its weapons systems are far from modern, the PLA is the largest army in the world and remains a formidable force. It fought in the Korean War on the side of Communist North Korea, and it has fought border wars with the USSR, India, and Vietnam. It stands ready to oppose any military action by Chinese Nationalist forces from Taiwan, or by Soviet forces on the long border which mainland China shares with the Soviet Union.

Armed Forces: Japanese Self-Defense Forces		The Japanese army, navy, and air forces, maintained for the purpose of self-defense in accordance with the post–World War II constitution. The constitution states under Article 9 that "the Japanese people forever renounce war as a sovereign right of the nation and the threat or use of force as means of settling international disputes." Article 9 also states that "In order to accomplish the aim of the preceding paragraph, land, sea, and air forces, as well as other war potential, will never be maintained. The right of belligerency of the state will not be recognized." According to the latter provision, Japan is precluded from maintaining any armed forces, but this has been interpreted to apply only to offensive forces. By the time the Treaty of San Francisco was signed in 1951, terminating the postwar American occupation of Japan, the United States increasingly regarded Japan as an important ally in Asia against the threat of world communism, and helped form the first contingent of Japan's present armed forces.

Despite U.S. hopes for an increase in Japanese forces, the Japanese government has been satisfied with the limited size of its armed forces. The Ministries of Army and Navy had been disbanded following Japan's defeat in World War II, and were replaced by the integrated National Defense Agency. The Agency is headed by a director, and has about 235,000 men and women in all branches, less than the total authorized strength of 266,000 (180,000 for the ground, 41,000 for the maritime, and 45,000 for the air defense forces). Despite pressure from the United States for Japan's assumption of a larger share in the maintenance of security in Northeast Asia, Japan's military and military-related annual budget is less than seven percent of all government expenditures, and less than one percent of the gross national product. These are the lowest figures for any major state in the world. *See also* JAPAN-UNITED STATES SECURITY TREATY, p. 343; SCAP, p. 318.

Significance   Following World War II, Japan's demilitarization was carried out most expeditiously, and Article 9 of the postwar Japanese constitution stated categorically that Japan was never to maintain "land, sea, and air forces, as well as other war potential." The spirit of Article 9 may have been punitive in nature, but it acquired widespread public support in Japan.

The American change of mind about the need for a Japanese military, however, came about during the Korean War (1950–53). When American forces in Japan were deployed to meet the North Korean attack on South Korea in 1950, the United States authorized the creation of a National Police Reserve in Japan as a security measure against the possibility of Communist-inspired subversion. At the time of the San Francisco Peace Treaty (1953), the United States allowed Japan to establish a National Safety Force of about 110,000 men and an 8,900-member Maritime Safety Force. These troops became the basis of Japan's Self-Defense Forces. Japan has been reluctant to increase the size of its forces and the amount of its military expenditures beyond one percent of GNP, despite American insistence that Japan share more of the burden for its own defense and for the security of Northeast Asia. Japan is one of the great economic powers in the world, but the size and capability of its armed forces are insignificant. Article 9 of the constitution, furthermore, forbids Japan to assign its forces to any overseas peacekeeping services.

Armed Forces: North and South Korea   The Korean peninsula is one of the most heavily armed regions of the world. The Korean War

(1950–53) ended in a condition of tactical stalemate under the armistice of 1953. An armistice is a bilateral agreement for the cessation of military operations. An armistice is not a treaty of peace; the two Koreas are still in a technical state of war. A Demilitarized Zone (DMZ) dividing North and South Korea is, in reality, a no-man's-land, demarcating two hostile states.

North Korea's People's Army. Before Korea was liberated in 1945, Korean guerrilla forces fought Japanese troops, both in Manchuria and in the border areas between Manchuria and North Korea. These Korean forces were small in number, but they persisted in their resistance throughout the Japanese colonial period. When hard pressed by the Japanese forces, the Korean guerrillas found sanctuaries in Siberia. These units later joined with the Soviet Red Army in the occupation of North Korea at the close of World War II. Other Korean guerrilla units joined Chinese Communist forces operating in China, and fought Japan during the Second Sino-Japanese War (1937–45). Under the tutelage of the Soviet Union, these Korean forces were built into North Korea's post-1945 army.

The official date of establishment of the Korean People's Army (KPA) is February 8, 1948. At the time of the Korean War, the KPA numbered about 200,000, armed with tanks and other Soviet-built heavy weapons. Although destroyed as a fighting force during the Korean War, it was quickly rebuilt with the help of the USSR and PRC. Currently, its estimated strength runs at 678,000, with about 90 percent (or 600,000) in ground forces, 47,000 in air forces, and 31,000 in naval forces. North Korea has been spending from 15 to 20 percent of GNP (South Korea estimates 20 to 25 percent) on the military. North Korean defense industries, once dependent on USSR or PRC supplies and technology, have been manufacturing many of their own weapons, including submarines. Although closely modeled after Soviet armed forces, the military of North Korea are much more politicized than those of the Soviet Union. The Communist party rules in North Korea, but the North Korean People's Army is fused into the leadership structure of the state under the supreme, perennial leader, Kim Il Sung (Kim, Il-sŏng), who is the president of the Republic, the general secretary of the Party (Korean Worker's Party), and the only generalissimo of the KPA. He also chairs the Party's Politburo, its Standing Committee, and several other powerful committees, including the Party's Military Commission.

South Korea's Armed Forces. The inception of South Korea's armed forces began during the American occupation period (1945–48). The initial recruits came from varied backgrounds and, unlike the initial recruits of North Korea's KPA, no one group monopolized them—no one group controlled the incipient South Korean military organization. Swelled by refugees from North Korea and displaced young men from rural areas, the composite army suffered from haphazard American involvement. The officer corps reflected internal conflicts: some were Korean nationalists who had fought with Chinese Nationalist troops against the Japanese; others were officers trained by the Japanese for colonial service; many had no prior military experience at all. The United States created the first officer's training school and called it the Military English Language School. Soon after the establishment of the Republic of Korea (ROK) in August 1948, South Korea enacted the Armed Forces Organization Act. This provided for the standard military advisory command (a cadre of American advisors), who, by the time of the Korean War, had built up an armed force of 100,000. Poorly equipped with rudimentary weapons, the South Korean Armed Forces proved little match for the Soviet-equipped North Korean invaders.

During and after the war, ROK's armed forces were hurriedly increased, reflecting the sense of national crisis, and, by 1954, the forces reached a level of 600,000. From 1950 to 1979, U.S. military aid to South Korea (grants-in-aid, sale of excess defense articles, foreign military sales credits, and military education and training programs) accounted for nearly U.S. $6 billion. Furthermore, as concern for eventual U.S. troop withdrawal from South Korea rose in the late 1970s, the ROK government undertook a large scale modernization program for its defense establishment (Force Improvement Plan).

South Korea's defense expenditure currently amounts to 6 percent of GNP. The largest branch of service is the army, with about 520,000 troops. The air force has 32,000 on active duty; the navy, 25,000 sailors and 23,000 marines. Most heavy weapons are U.S.-made; however, South Korea has been developing its own defense industries. Since the coup d'état of 1961, the military has become the most powerful political actor. Following the U.S. model, the constitution mandates civilian controls over the armed forces. Military professionalism is emphasized, but the military remains a highly political group, resulting in an ambivalent civil-military relationship. *See also* KOREAN WAR, p. 388; KOREA-U.S. MUTUAL ASSISTANCE AGREEMENT, p. 344; THIRTY-EIGHTH PARALLEL, p. 41.

Significance   The Korean peninsula is one of the danger spots of the world. The Korean War (1950–53) ended in a limited truce, and both Koreas have maintained a hostile and acrimonious relationship. Both sustain huge military establishments, increasingly equipped with modern, expensive, and sophisticated weaponry. Not content with reliance on the regular armed forces, ordinary citizens are mobilized into reserve forces, militias, and homeland self-defense forces. The adversaries are on constant alert against each other's movements, political or military. This state of permanent tension, fueled by an escalating arms race, bodes a future of violence and war. Any violent soluton of the Korean question may lead to a greater Asian conflict involving the big powers surrounding the Korean peninsula—the USSR, PRC, Japan, and the United States. To offset this potential for theater or global conflict, the United States maintains a major military force commitment in South Korea.

Armed Forces: South Asia   Expenditures for defense in South Asia (the subcontinent) average 2.9 percent. This is comparatively lower than in other regions of the world. Only Latin America spends less, at 1.2 percent. By contrast, countries in the Far East expend 3.2 percent and the Middle East nations, 10.9 percent. Because of the heavy expenditure on weapons in the Middle East, Third World nations overall spend 4.3 percent of GNP on defense. Within South Asia, India and Pakistan are the major procurers of military paraphernalia. Bangladesh, Nepal, and Sri Lanka have comparatively tiny military establishments compared to India and Pakistan. These smaller countries spend less than 1 percent of GNP for military purposes.

The contest over arms, therefore, is essentially confined to India and Pakistan. Pakistan expends approximately 5 percent of GNP, and India approximately 3 percent for defense and defense-related purposes. Although Pakistan's soldiers per capita number 6.3 per 1,000 as against India's 1.9 per 1,000, India's armed forces were almost 3 times the size of Pakistan's. In 1984 India had an estimated 1.2 million men under arms, whereas Pakistan had less than half a million. By contrast, Bangladesh had 81,000, Nepal, 25,000, and Sri Lanka, approximately 17,000. In fact, India possessed the third largest standing army in the world, the fifth largest air force, and the eighth largest navy. More important, India had the only indigenous armament industry in South Asia. Described as the largest of its kind among noncommunist Third World countries, it had a reputation for volume production, diversity of manufactures, as well as research and development. Moreover, India had the most developed nuclear and space program in the Third World, and the detonation of a nuclear device in May 1974 placed it in the exclusive nuclear club with the United States, the Soviet Union, Britain, France, and China.

Pakistan has been provoked to emulate India's nuclear capability, and although it denies intentions to produce atomic weapons, most observers believe that objective is within reach. Pakistan, however, cannot compete with India's industrial base (the tenth largest in the world), or its supply of skilled and technical manpower. Furthermore, India is more closely identified with the Soviet Union, than Pakistan is with the United States. Since 1966, the Soviet Union has become India's major weapons supplier. Between 1965 and 1975 the United States embargoed sales of weapons to Pakistan. By contrast, the Soviet Union entered into an agreement with New Delhi in 1968 which allowed the manufacture of sophisticated weapons of Soviet design in Indian factories. No similar arrangement exists between Pakistan and the United States. India has purchased several billion dollars of additional defense items from Great Britain, West Germany, and France. Pakistan cannot approach, let alone match, these levels of procurement. *See also* DEPENDENCY RELATIONS: INDIA, p. 335; FARAKKA BARRAGE AGREEMENT, p. 336; INDO-SOVIET TREATY, 1971, p. 340; KASHMIR DISPUTE, p. 386; PAKISTAN-UNITED STATES MUTUAL DEFENSE AGREEMENTS, p. 349; PAKISTAN-INDIA WARS, 1947–48, 1965, 1971, p. 398; PANCH SILA, p. 109; SOUTH ASIAN REGIONAL COOPERATION (SARC), p. 358.

Significance   India is now the preeminent power in South Asia, and its military emphasis is designed to reinforce that status, but it was not always that way. In the years immediately following independence, Pakistan insisted on "equality" with India, and its military program following its 1953–54 agreements with the United States, was geared to demonstrating Pakistani prowess. India-Pakistan rivalry, especially their conflict over Kashmir, prompted antagonistic defense postures. As a consequence, the two neighboring states perceived each other as mortal enemies, and made war on one another in 1947–48, 1965, and 1971. In the first two encounters, there was no clear victory. In the 1971 affair, however, India humiliated Pakistan, and dismembered it as a nation. This Indian action forced Pakistan to recognize India's preponderance of power, but it did not make living with New Delhi easier. Although diplomatic relations were restored following the 1971 war, the two countries remained bitter adversaries. Internal problems such as political agitation in Sind in 1983 were in part attributed to Indian machinations. New Delhi's difficulties with the Sikhs of the Punjab and the Muslims of Kashmir in 1984 were blamed on "foreign," (Pakistani) meddling in India's domestic life.

Since the Sino-Indian border war of 1962, New Delhi has also considered Beijing its sworn enemy. That conflict brought to a close a diplomatic effort begun in 1950 which sought to publicize the common interests of the two Asian giants. "Hindi Chini Bhai Bhai," (Indians and Chinese are Brothers) and "Panch Sila" (Five Principles of Peaceful Co-existence) were the touchstones for cooperative Indian-Chinese relations. These slogans proved to be empty of meaning, however, when the Indians discovered the Chinese encroaching on territory it believed to be within its sovereign control. Chinese arguments that the territory in question had been taken from them by the British during a period of Chinese weakness did not impress the Indians. New Delhi's offer of sanctuary to the Tibetan Dalai Lama in 1959 was considered a hostile act by Beijing. The failure of Indian arms in the 1962 border war awakened New Delhi to its military deficiencies. Although the United States rushed weapons to India following the Chinese incursion, New Delhi believed its best defense lay in concert with the Soviet Union. Military transfers from the Soviet Union to New Delhi began in earnest in 1964 and have accelerated since that date. Pakistan never confronted the Soviets as India had the Chinese. Nevertheless, Islamabad's pro-American posture provoked Moscow, and caused anxiety in India. Pakistani-American relations have been influenced by the sentimental more than the practical, and periodic ruptures have weakened the association. The Soviet invasion of Afghanistan in 1979 brought the Red Army to the Pakistani frontier, and although Islamabad was agreeable to a new Washington-sponsored arms buildup, there was little indication that the Pakistanis intended to use their recently acquired American arms against the Soviets. Islamabad denied having any intention to join in a new alliance with the United States or to provide the Americans with bases in the country.

The military establishments of India and Pakistan, as well as those of Nepal, Bangladesh, and Sri Lanka, have been important instruments of internal control. Each South Asian nation has seen fit to use its armed forces to control centrifugal sociopolitical forces. Political and social unrest have usually required the imposition of martial law, or at the very least, the suspension of constitutional guarantees. India has employed its army in the forcible integration of the Indian states. The seizure of Hyderabad and Goa are notable examples. Pakistan and Bangladesh, however, are the only South Asian countries to experience long periods of direct military rule. Nevertheless, the political opposition in all South Asian nations believe defense expenditures are directed at them, not at external threats.

India's dominance in the subcontinent frightens not only Pakistan, but Nepal, Bangladesh, and Sri Lanka as well. All India's immediate neighbors believe New Delhi's ultimate aim is to absorb them into a greater union. Whereas Pakistan has attempted to challenge India on the battlefield or in an arms race, Nepal, Bangladesh, and Sri Lanka appear more inclined to use diplomacy to neutralize Indian military prowess.

Coup d'état (coup)   Seizure of government power with a swift, decisive action made usually by a small group of military personnel from within the existing system. Coup d'état can be waged by civilian groups, but almost all the coups in Asia, both successful and unsuccessful, have been waged by the military. In the military coup d'état, a small group of military officers, defying the military command structure, lead their men and strike at major centers of government power, capturing key government personnel. The coup leaders then suspend the constitution, enforce martial law throughout the country, and rule the country by decree. For the coup to be successful, any counter-coup must be prevented. The coup is usually justified as a surgical operation needed by the country in order to remedy its ills. *See also* JUNTA, p. 280; MILITARY REGIME, p. 290; PRAETORIANISM, p. 292.

Significance   The military of the Third World nations of Asia have become some of the most powerful of political actors, and a military coup d'état has become the main means of transferring government power from one group to another. The Asian nations (east of Afghanistan) that have experienced successful military coups include: South Korea, Indonesia, South Vietnam (before takeover by North Vietnam), Laos, Kampuchea, Thailand, Burma, Bangladesh, and Pakistan. The coup d'état is obviously the most overt form of participation by the military in politics. Seizing the reins of government is by no means the only, nor the most important, way in which military groups influence politics. The military is able to exert political influence because it possesses enormous political resources, such as size, organization, and discipline, and because of the general weakness of civilian government, and the lack of civilian control of the military. Even in the Philippines, Malaysia, India, and Sri Lanka, where there have been no successful military coups, no civilian government can last without military support. In the Communist countries of Asia, the military occupies an equally dominant power position.

Coup d'état: Bangladesh   A series of military takeovers of the government since the country seceded from Pakistan and became independent in 1972. The first coup, on August 15, 1975, was against the government of Prime Minister Shaykh Mujibur Rahman, the "father" of Bangladesh. The creation of Bangladesh had been preceded by much violence in the war for independence against Pakistan. Bangladesh ultimately needed India's help to defeat Pakistan (the India-Pakistan War of 1972). As an independent nation, the country had not yet recovered from the damages of the revolutionary war. The economy was in a shambles, and the charisma of Mujibur Rahman did not prevent popular dissatisfaction with the state of affairs in the country. Mujib became increasingly intolerant of oppositions, and exhibited dictatorial behavior. He formed an inner circle of government by his immediate family members and close relatives. Fearing for his life, he also fostered his own personal militia, called the Rakkhi Bahini.

When militant radicals stepped up their campaign of terror, a state of emergency was declared in December 1974. On August 15, 1975, elements of the Bangladesh Army attacked the home of Mujib, killing him and most of his immediate family (two of his daughters were abroad and escaped the massacre). The Army also assassinated Mujib's powerful relatives and close supporters and attacked the headquarters of the Rakkhi Bahini. Once Mujib's power was destroyed, the coup leaders set up Khondakar Mushtaque Ahmed as president. When he subsequently tried to consolidate his own power, the dissatisfied faction within the military overthrew his government on November 6, 1975, and installed the Chief Justice of the Bangladesh Supreme Court, Abu Sadat Mohammed Sayem, as president. To advise this new president, the coup leaders established a military council drawn from the two service branches: General Ziaur Rahman, Army and Vice-Marshal G. M. Tawab, Air Force. When President Sayem resigned in April 1977 for health reasons, he named General Ziaur Rahman his successor.

The government of General Ziaur Rahman reintroduced normal political processes in the country and organized the Bangladesh Nationalist Party. It conducted presidential and parliamentary elections in 1978, overwhelmingly electing General Ziaur Rahman and his followers to power. President Ziaur Rahman was, however, assassinated on May 30, 1981, and his vice-president, Abdus Sattar, became Acting President. Elections were held in November in order to legitimize the transition. The government of President Abdus Sattar was itself overthrown by another coup on March 4, 1982, led by Lt. General M. H. Ershad. New elections were promised, but the country was placed under martial law with Ershad as the Chief Martial Law Administrator. *See also* COUP D'ÉTAT, p. 270; PAKISTAN-INDIA WARS, p. 398.

Significance   Since the first military takeover of the government in August 1975 and the assassination of Mujib, civil disorder has persisted in Bangladesh in a cycle of coups d'état. The political void left by the death of Mujib has not yet been filled. The military has emerged as the most powerful political group in the country, but suffers from internal factionalism, hence civil disorder and military disorder prevail. No military leader has been able to command loyalty from the various factions within the military. As a result, any move to consolidate the military in favor of one group suffers the wrath of the other groups. Furthermore, the bitter taste of Mujib's rule (which degenerated into a personal, dictatorial government) has contributed to the military's negative image of politicians and civilian government. Bangladesh remains a praetorian state and its frequent military intervention in politics has been violent.

Coup d'état: Burma   Control of the government of General Ne Win in 1962 and the establishment of military rule under the Union Revolutionary Council. Burma became independent on January 4, 1948, but the country was unprepared to cope with a myriad of problems. Despite high expectations, the government lacked trained personnel. The government called for *pyidawtha*, or a Burmese welfare state, but had no money to pay for it. Furthermore, Burma's diverse ethnic groups (Burmans, Karens, Shans, and Kachins) and many political factions were constantly at war, with the indigenous military constantly deployed for internal peacekeeping roles.

When the country became independent, the AFPFL (Anti-Fascist People's Freedom League), as the most active nationalist group, inherited power. The AFPFL soon split into two groups, rendering the government unable to function. As a result, Prime Minister U Nu resigned in 1958 and asked General Ne Win, Commander-in-Chief of the Army, to replace him. U Nu had wanted a working majority in parliament and so elections were held under General Ne Win in 1960. Victorious in this effort, U Nu, still highly popular, returned to office as prime minister. This new U Nu government was soon overthrown by General Ne Win, who, in contrast to his earlier caretaker role, assumed power and introduced sweeping changes in the government. He abolished the existing political parties, imprisoned a number of political leaders, including U Nu, and established a Revolutionary Council manned by his followers in the military. He declared his intent to make Burma a socialist, not communist state, controlled by the Burma Socialist Program Party which he himself headed. *See also* COUP D'ÉTAT, p. 270.

Significance   General Ne Win's 1962 coup was no surprise. In 1958 he had replaced Prime Minister U Nu, his close friend, as requested and in his caretaker role, prepared the country for new elections by keeping peace and order and modernizing and improving the administration. The expectation was that he would remain in power, yet he supervised elections as promised and handed over the government to a new administration again headed by U Nu. General Ne Win had become convinced that the civilian government was too divided and weak to govern and that the country was at the verge of splitting apart, each ethnic group fighting for its own self-government. To prevent what was regarded as an impending calamity, General Ne Win affected a change of government which the people accepted. General Ne Win's Burmese Way to Socialism contains aspects of the preindependence nationalist movement of Burma, and anticolonialist and anticapitalist ideology, and government by a small governing elite under a single political party, based on authoritarian rule. Ne Win had taken an active part in this movement along with U Nu and Aung San (the leader of the movement, assassinated in 1947).

Coup d'état: Indonesia   A successful counter-coup of military leaders against the coup instigated by the Communist Party of Indonesia (PKI) to take over the government and reduce the powerful influence of the military in the government. On September 30, 1965, six of Indonesia's senior army generals were murdered by followers of an order called the *Gestapu* (Gerakan September Tiga Puluh or the September 30 Movement). The commander of President Sukarno's palace guard, Lieutenant Colonel Untung, led the movement and justified his acts by insisting that the generals had been plotting to overthrow the government. General Nasution, who had been marked for death, escaped and rallied his loyal troops. Joined by General Suharto (who had not been targeted by Gestapu), they led the successful counterattack and soon crushed the revolt. President Sukarno was perceived as having been sympathetic to the Untung coup and was placed under house arrest while those who were responsible for the revolt were summarily executed. Leaders of the PKI were seized and executed and all PKI operations were closed down. When President Sukarno tried to defy the military, he was forced to resign and eventually sent into exile in a remote village in Java. Meantime, General Suharto was appointed acting president on March 12, 1967 by the country's Consultative Assembly. A year later on March 27, 1968 General Suharto was appointed president. *See also* COUP D'ÉTAT, p. 270; GUIDED DEMOCRACY, p. 228.

Significance   Sukarno, the father of independent Indonesia, had been designated president-for-life, but events were beginning to overtake him by 1965. He had permitted himself considerable flexibility in dealing with his diverse polity, but was increasingly compelled to support one side against the other. However, when he favored the leftist (including the PKI), this precarious equilibrium was destroyed. The Untung coup was designed to prevent the military's takeover of the government, and had the support of President Sukarno. When the coup failed, Sukarno was discredited, paving the way for the military's assumption of power. The military then acted swiftly to destroy its power rival, the PKI, seizing their leaders and closing down their operations throughout the country. Indonesia's traditional anti-Chinese sentiment also exploded during the chaotic cycle of coup and counter-coup, and many Chinese were killed. As president, General Suharto has maintained a low profile. His government has been more of a working government than his predecessor's, and he has been able to maintain political stability and improve the economic position of the country. Internationally, Indonesia has moved closer to the west, particularly to the United States. It has also ended its confrontation with Malaysia, and rejoined the United Nations, thus "de-Sukarnoizing" Indonesia's radical foreign policy.

Coup d'état: Pakistan   President Iskander Mirza proclaimed martial law on October 7, 1958, and named General Mohammad Ayub

Khan, the commander-in-chief of the Pakistan army, as chief martial law administrator to lead the country out of disaster. Pakistan had been faced with general economic breakdown, as well as political chaos, and militant and separatist movements in its eastern and western regions. The martial law proclamation suspended the constitution which had been put into effect in 1956, following a long and bitter struggle. All the ministers were dismissed, and the country was placed under the direction of General Ayub Khan. On October 27, 1958, President Mirza resigned from office at the "request" of the generals, and General Ayub Khan, chief martial law administrator, became president.

This pattern of military coup has been repeated in Pakistan in 1969 and 1977; that is, the general in charge of the administration of martial law eventually takes over control of the government. On March 25, 1969, President Ayub Khan asked the army to restore tranquility to his troubled land and announced his resignation from the presidency. He named his Commander-in-Chief of the Army, General Agha Mohammad Yahya Khan, to replace him and reimpose martial law. Following the secession of East Pakistan and the establishment of the independent state of Bangladesh, in 1971, President Yahya Khan resigned from the presidency and named as his successor Zulfikar Ali Bhutto, leader of the Pakistan People's Party (PPP), who had been prominent among the ranks of leaders opposed to military rule.

With Pakistan's armed forces humiliated in the India-Pakistan War of 1971, Bhutto, a civilian leader, basked in initial popularity. Bhutto's design was to create a new Pakistan. He introduced many reforms. He ordered the retirement of a score of top army and navy officers. He inaugurated a new constitution which called for a parliamentary system of government with a prime minister as the chief executive. Bhutto became the prime minister. Opposition against his regime grew steadily. Economic difficulties created general dissatisfaction, and in the 1977 elections Bhutto's government was accused of fraud. Opposition forces were strong enough to make their charges credible, and as Bhutto's popularity declined riots and demonstrations became widespread. To restore order, martial law was once again declared. Army Chief-of-Staff General Muhammad Zia-ul-Haq, acting as chief martial law administrator, led a coup on July 14, 1977, arresting Bhutto, members of the cabinet, and opposition leaders. According to Zia, the purpose of the coup was to save democracy in Pakistan. New elections were promised in October, but the promise was not honored. When the five-year term of the elected president, Fazal Elahi Chaudhri, expired in August 1978, General Zia-ul-Haq declared himself president while continuing as chief martial law administrator. *See also* COUP D'ÉTAT, p. 270; MAJLIS-E-SHURA: PAKISTAN, p. 236.

Significance   The military assumption of power in Pakistan has followed the pattern which was initially established by General Ayub Khan. With the declaration of martial law as a signal, the chief martial law administrator has assumed power. In the cases of Generals Ayub Khan and Yahya Khan, the transfer of power was orderly, expected, and nonviolent. In the case of General Zia-ul-Haq, however, a large scale arrest of political and government leaders was involved. The execution of Bhutto was unprecedented. Compared with the two previous periods of military rule, General Zia-ul-Haq's administration has been less popular and harsher in dealing with opposition.

Coup d'état: South Korea (1961)   A military coup of May 16, 1961, which was carried out by a small group of military officers headed by Major General Park Chung Hee (Pak, Chŏng-hui) against the government of the constitutionally established Second Republic of Korea. The coup was executed swiftly and almost without bloodshed. Out of South Korea's 600,000-member armed forces, the personnel mobilized for the coup numbered about 2,000. The success of the coup is all the more surprising given the fact that all South Korean armed forces were still under the United Nations Command, in place since the Korean War. In spite of this, neither the UN Command nor the Second Republic of Korea (1960–61) of Prime Minister Chang Myon (Chang, Myŏn) were effective enough to prevent the coup. The coup leadership, headed by General Park, quickly established a junta government, promising to turn the government over to civilian leaders once they had achieved their goal of revitalizing the country. A new constitution was drawn up and, to implement it, elections were held. Typically, the coup leaders did not return to the barracks. Instead, they retired from active service and ran for public offices, taking important government positions. They created their own political party, the Democratic-Republican Party. General Park, as the standard bearer of this party, was elected president in October 1963. The new government of General Park was inaugurated in December 1963. Park was reelected president and stayed in office until assassinated by his KCIA (Korean CIA) director in October 1979. *See also* COUP D'ÉTAT, p. 270; MILITARY REGIME: CIVILIANIZED, p. 291.

Significance   The 1961 coup in South Korea has transformed the South Korean political system. Since the coup, the military has become the most powerful political group in the country, and many retired military leaders have been recruited into government. Together with a new breed of mostly western-educated technocrats, they constituted the core of leadership in the government. The Park regime in this way represented a new Third World political style. Given South Korea's oversized military (about 600,000 strong), the support of the military is critical for the survival of any government. Yet, the Park regime depended on more than just military support, and many civilian politicians and technocrats were members of the regime. The result was a fused military and civilian leadership structure which successfully served Park and generated industrialization and export-oriented economic developments for South Korea. The Park regime was also credited with South Korea's rural development. The regime was politically durable, lasting more than 15 years, but opposition was never quiescent.

Coup d'état: South Korea (1979)　　　A military coup of December 12, 1979, in South Korea, by younger generals headed by Major General Chun Doo Hwan (Chŏn, Tu-hwan), against their senior generals, including General Chung Seung-hwa (Chŏng, Sŏng-hwa) (the army chief of staff and martial law commander following South Korean President Park's assassination), who were suspected of complicity in the assassination of their president. The coup was swift, placing the real power of South Korea in the hands of its leaders. The coup leaders represented a new generation in the Korean military as the first products of the regular four-year South Korean Military Academy. Known for their loyalty to President Park, they had been extensively politicized by his authoritarian system. They were to become a mainstay of his "Koreanization" of the South Korean military, a response to the perceived reduction of American military presence in Asia. To the young generals, any move to dismantle President Parks' system following his assassination seemed threatening to their own security. The coup was inspired in part by these considerations, and it effectively stifled any further move to liberalize President Park's authoritarian system. General Chun, leader of the December 12 coup, eventually assumed power as president of the Fifth Republic of Korea in 1980. *See also* COUP D'ÉTAT: SOUTH KOREA (1961), p. 276; YUSHIN (REVITALIZATION) REFORMS: SOUTH KOREA, p. 257.

Significance　　　The December 12 coup reaffirmed the powerful role of the military in the South Korean political process. Following the assassination of President Park, the forces of democracy in South Korea proved too fragmented to carry out a peaceful transition to liberal democracy. Within the military, younger generals were against any revolutionary dismantling of President Park's authoritarian system. Furthermore, they felt their security threatened if any anti-Park forces assumed power. Once the coup succeeded, coup leaders forced the retirement of many senior generals, carried out a purge of many high-ranking government officials and business leaders, and dictated the direction of post-Park political change in the country. Headed by General Chun Doo-hwan, they were willing to use force for the effective imposition of martial law, and to frustrate any unauthorized demonstrations. In one instance, the blatant use of force marked an incident surrounding the city of Kwangju, the capital of South Cholla province. The city was taken over and controlled by anti-government demonstrators from May 18th to 27th. The military authorities dispatched special forces to reestablish order within the city, which was accomplished with great loss of life. This incident has become known as the Kwangju massacre. General Chun's rise to power has been identified with the Kwangju incident and other unsavory developments in South Korean politics.

Coup d'état (1932): Thailand   Forceful overthrow of Thailand's longstanding absolute monarchical system and the establishment of a constitutional, monarchical, quasi-parliamentary form of government. The coup leaders, both civilians and military, represented the new breed of young, western-educated intellectuals in the country. The ideological leader of the coup was Nai Pridi, a Doctor of Law from the University of Paris. Colonel Phraya Phahon Phomphayuhasena, who represented the older generation among the coup leaders, had received advanced military education in Germany. Field Marshall Philbunsongkhram, a younger generation coup leader, had studied in France. The revolution, however, was never intended as a popular or radical movement, and the aristocratic nature of traditional Thai politics was very obvious. An appointive Supreme Council, created by the first constitution following the coup, was comprised of princes, princely bureaucrats, and military leaders. By abolishing the traditional monarchical system, the coup broadened the oligarchical circle of government to include not only members of the royal family but also civilian and military leaders. Subsequently, different groups of these oligarchs have vied for supremacy, alternating power among themselves, but with no single group achieving enough strength to institutionalize durable control. Since the first coup in 1932, Thailand has experienced a recurrence of coups with military and civilian governments alternating in power. *See also* BUREAUCRACY POLITY, p. 295; COUP D'ÉTAT, p. 270.

Significance   The coup of 1932 brought about a void in a Thai political system which had been traditionally controlled by an absolute monarchy. Following the coup, the initial system of power alliance in the government between the civilian and military coup leaders had precluded the emergence of a strongman to fill the void. Both military and civilian leaders have been strong enough to prevent either side from discarding totally the power of the other; thus, when the military is in power, the civilian leadership clamours for constitutional government, and when civilian rule is instituted, the military is always ready to intervene at the first available opportunity. The coups in Thailand have on the whole been bloodless, and have not affected the government bureaucracy. The people, mostly rural, have been excluded from the government change of hands. The Thai military remains the most powerful political group in the country, highly nationalistic but also protective of their own power base from erosion by any civilian government.

Garrison State   A nation which is in preparation for a total war and which gives military considerations top priority in national decision making. The garrison state is a crisis phenomenon. In the garrison state, the specialists of violence become powerful and dictate to civilian leaders the appropriate national decisions. Lasswell, in his pioneering work on the concept of garrison state, was concerned with events in Germany and Japan of the 1930s, warning against the emergence of garrison states among western democracies (Harold D. Laswell, "The Garrison State." *American Journal of Sociology* XLIV [January 1941], pp. 455–468). In a garrison state, military leaders dominate their civilian counterparts, seeking popular followings for their cause through the use of war scares and by forcing the government to spend more on military personnel and hardware, such as the production of "gadgets" specialized for acts of violence. *See also* MILITARISM, p. 283; MILITARISM: JAPAN, p. 284.

Significance   In the garrison state, the military becomes politically dominant and powerful, but is not interested in assuming political power. Instead, it seeks to influence civilian leaders with war scares, and succeeds in preparing the country for total war through manpower mobilization and maximum expenditures on military hardware. The concept of garrison state argues that the instinctive institutional interest of the military is in preparing for war and providing for national security. Once the military assumes power, therefore, it is most likely to urge total war concepts on the nation, and develop a regimented state. Japan in the 1930s is often cited as a prime example of the phenomenon.

Guerrilla Warfare   Irregular warfare by small bands in an unconventional manner largely utilizing hit-and-run tactics. *Guerrilla* is a Spanish word which was first used to identify those civilians in Spain who were resisting the Napoleonic invasion between 1808 and 1813.

Mostly peasants, they fought to protect their lands, religion, and way of life without the externally imposed discipline of a regular army. Their objective was basically defensive. In Asia, however, guerrilla warfare has been identified with revolution, as a systematic effort to undermine the legitimacy of a political order or to overthrow an established government. The Chinese Communists used this technique successfully against the Chinese Nationalist government. In Vietnam, the Communist Vietminh duplicated the technique, first against the French and then against South Vietnamese and American forces. To be successful, guerrillas need popular support, terrain which is amenable to their operation, and the dedicated leadership of a binding cause and ideology. *See also* GUERRILLA WARFARE IN MALAYA, p. 381; HAKBALAHAP UPRISING, p. 384; MAOISM, p. 101.

Significance   Regarding guerrilla warfare, Karl von Clausewitz is a leading theoretician and Mao Zedong (Mao Tse-tung) a most successful tactician. Clausewitz lists general conditions for the successful pursuit of guerrilla warfare as follows: (1) it must be carried on in the interior of the country; (2) it must extend over a considerable area; (3) it must be supported by the people; (4) it must be fought in terrain that is irregular, difficult, and inaccessible to regular forces; and (5) it must not rely on a single decisive battle. All these conditions existed in Mao's success with his guerrilla war against the Nationalist government. However, Mao's emphasis was especially on the element of the people. To Mao, guerrilla war starts with the people and is for the people. The Chinese Communist guerrilla fighters were instructed to behave not as conquerors or bandits, but as reformers and disciplined representatives of a new social and economic order.

Junta   A Spanish word which means (1) a committee; or (2) an administrative council or board. A military *junta* is usually established following a military coup d'état. Following the coup, the coup leaders set up a junta as a supreme governing body, suspend the constitution, ban political activities, and imprison and/or execute key personnel of the previous administration. When they are not top ranking armed forces officers (as in the case of the so-called "young Turks"), they usually set up a cabinet, drawing into it the three main service chiefs-of-staff of the army, navy, and air force. The junta needs the united support of the military to avoid a counter-coup and stay in power. *See also* COUP D'ÉTAT, p. 270; MILITARY REGIME, p. 290.

Significance   The word *junta* has become widely used in the Third World nations of Asia where many countries have experienced recurrent coups d'état. Following a successful coup, the leaders de facto constitute a junta. However, the junta is usually a temporary arrangement. Without a strong leader, the junta often becomes fragmented into factions due to differences regarding future courses of action. The resultant power struggles usually produce a "strongman." If this does not occur, the junta may find itself too weak to govern.

Martial Law   A temporary rule by military authority in time of an emergency when the civil authorities are unable to function. Martial law is usually declared by the chief executive who also designates the chief martial law administrator. It becomes effective when military authorities supplant civil authorities. It is distinguished from military law, which is the law governing those in the military service. It is also distinguished from situations in which military forces are called upon to assist the civil authorities in maintaining law and order, such as disaster relief or civil defense. In the latter case, the civil courts continue to function and administer the civil law. But under martial law, the normal administration of the law is vacated and the military authorities maintain law and order by summary methods. *See also* COUP D'ÉTAT, p. 270.

Significance   The U.S. constitution does not contain any provision regarding martial law, but the constitutions of many Third World nations include a martial law provision. Martial law implies a stage intermediate between law and anarchy. Imposition assumes that civil authorities are unable to function, whereupon the chief executive is empowered to declare martial law and call upon the military for enforcement. During a period of martial law, the constitution is usually suspended and no political activities are permitted; the authority of the martial law administrator becomes almost supreme. The office of the chief executive is maintained under martial law, and the chief executive is authorized to lift the declaration when the situation returns to normal. Martial law may be applied either nationally, or to a limited area and/or for a limited purpose.

Martial Law Regime   A government that operates under martial law for an extended period of time. Martial law is usually declared by a civilian government for a limited period of time (usually denoted as "National Emergency") to restore law and order with the help of the military. Usually of brief duration, a state of martial law may last longer, as has been the case in Taiwan since 1949; in the Philippines, 1972–81; and in India, 1975–77. Martial law regimes are distinguished from military regimes because the former do not supplant civilian chief executives. Martial law regimes suspend, but do not abolish, the constitution. As such, a military martial law administrator operates under a civilian chief executive. No military coup d'état has taken place in a martial law regime. *See also* MILITARY REGIME, p. 290.

Significance   Under martial law, the military authorities assume civil powers and are charged with the maintenance of law and order, either nationally, or in a selective, limited area where a state of emergency has been declared. Martial law decrees may be absolute or limited in degree of authority. In Taiwan, for instance, a limited martial law has been in force since the Chinese Nationalist government-in-exile was established in 1949. The Nationalist martial law prohibits (1) Communist party activities; (2) Taiwanese independence movements; (3) criticism of Nationalist control of Taiwan; and (4) criticism of security measures against the mainland Communists. This is tempered, however, by a great deal of personal freedom and encouragement of Taiwanese local self-government. In the Philippines, President Marcos remained effective during the martial law period. Although his martial law administration was politically repressive, the regime has succeeded in carrying out land reforms and other measures for its plan of a "New Society." In India, Prime Minister Indira Gandhi used almost dictatorial powers to silence her vociferous opposition during the martial law period. She was, however, able to control rampant inflation, improve the national economy, and emphasize order and discipline in the national life. On lifting martial law in 1977, after two years of administration, Mrs. Gandhi announced new elections for the *Lok Sabha* (lower legislative body). Her party lost its majority status in the Lok Sabha in the elections, and Mrs. Gandhi was thus forced to resign her premiership.

Military   A professional organization provided for national (or group) defense and security, entrusted with the instruments of violence, and trained and organized to wage war. The military assumes the existence of an external or internal enemy. The military as a specialized group dates back to 1700 B.C., in the Babylon of Hammurabi, where this group remained organized at all times, stood ready for action, and was rewarded for its specialized skills. However, the term "standing army" is of relatively recent usage. The standing army means professional forces. As such, their personnel, particularly the officers corps, are permanent career persons, specifically trained and rewarded for the performance of their duties and responsibilities. In this sense, professional military are like other professionals.

Since providing for national defense and security is one of the primary concerns of the government, it becomes a government responsibility. The military is, therefore, provided by the government, and its personnel become government employees. Mercenaries hire themselves out to the highest bidder and they are not attached to any state. Military service is often regarded as a citizenship requirement and made compulsory. Voluntary military service does not require every citizen to become a soldier for a specified period of time. The modern military is usually organized in three branches—army, navy, and air force—and it is trained and organized to make use of increasingly sophisticated weaponry. *See also* MILITARISM, p. 283; MILITARY REGIME, p. 290.

Significance National security and defense is a primary concern of any state, and each state maintains some form of military organization. In Asia, China's People's Liberation Army and the Indian Army are among the largest in the world. Japan's Self-Defense Forces are small in size but technologically sophisticated. North and South Korea maintain the most heavily armed forces per capita in Asia. Although they vary in size, the newly independent states of Asia have quickly provided for the protection of their independence. Some inherited their forces from the colonial period, and modeled them after the metropolitan powers. Some created their forces immediately following independence, assisted by the Big Powers in the post–World War II/Cold War environment. In either case, the modern armed forces of the advanced states became models and the indigenous forces were organized into modern forces and provided with a relatively generous allocation of scarce national resources. As a modern force, the military is characterized by command structure, hierarchical organization, discipline, personnel selection on the basis of merit, technical orientation, nationalistic outlook, and corporate feeling. These characteristics of the modern military make indigenous military forces distinct from the rest of the society, and politically powerful through the exercise of their influence over traditional society.

Militarism A condition of dominance by the military, and the prevalence of military considerations in both the lives of the people and the national decision-making process. In the liberal and democratic political tradition, the military is conceived as a nonpolitical, professional institution charged with responsibility for national defense, yet subordinate to general civilian control. The rise of militarism is almost always equated with political decay. However, within the Third World, the military has increasingly become the dominant political group through its concurrent assumption of power and rule by force over the people. This development is, to a great extent, due to the weakness of the civilian government, and the military's possession of various critical political resources, among which the dominant elements are size,

organization, training, a puritanical or national outlook, and the possession of weaponry.

Other factors which may encourage or cause a military coup include
(1) factional strife within the military; (2) protection of the military's own
corporate interests; (3) presence of political instability resulting from
ineffective government; (4) perceived opportunities for the removal of
corruption in government; (5) desire for intervention in, or prevention
of, the rise of radical elements to power; and, (6) desire for rapid
economic modernization. The coup is the most extreme and violent
political expression of the military. Given its political resources, the
military may also dominate the policy of a civilian government and
exercise veto over the actions and personnel of the government. *See also*
GARRISON STATE, p. 274; PRAETORIANISM, p. 292.

Significance   Militarism is not a new phenomenon. Any group controlling the means of force and violence exercises inordinate influence in
decision making. The more valued the existence of such a group is in the
lives of the people, the more influential it becomes in decision making.
Renewed interest in militarism in recent years results from both the
generalized East-West conflict and arms race of the post–World War II
era, and the frequent occurrence of military coups among Third World
nations. In Asia, most of the non-communist states have experienced a
military coup, including South Korea, Indonesia, Thailand, Pakistan,
Burma, Bangladesh, and South Vietnam. The military has also been
influential in the national power equation of other Asian states. Given
these developments, scholarly analysis has concentrated on militarism in
Asia less as a deviant phenomenon than as a symptom of development.
Increasingly, emergent political systems among the Third World nations
of Asia are characterized by a condition of shared power between
military and civilian leaders.

Militarism: Japan   The control of government by the military in
Japan during the 1930s, which mobilized the people for Japan's expansionist foreign policy in China and Southeast Asia and for war with the
United States in World War II. Japanese militarism has deep historical
roots. Before the Meiji Restoration (1868) and the beginning of Japan as
a modern state, Japan was a feudal society where the *samurai* (warrior)
class ruled supreme, deeply imbedding their code of behavior in Japanese culture. They also constituted the forces behind the Meiji Restoration movement, advocating a richer and stronger Japan. As leaders of
the Meiji Restoration, it was samurai who held important positions in the
post-Restoration government and society.

The military was organized as a modern institution with universal
conscription in 1872, and placed directly under the emperor and his

personal counselors. There was no tradition of civilian control of the military in prewar Japan; therefore the military was able to freely exert its political influence in the government and society at large. It became the guardian of Japan's modern imperial system; the inheriter of Japan's feudal samurai virtues which emphasized honor, justice, loyalty, discipline, and the simplicity of life. Once in power in the 1930s, the Japanese military was able to mobilize the entire society for its expansionist foreign policy, extending Japan's influence into China and Southeast Asia only to encounter American and western opposition. *See also* MEIJI RESTORATION, p. 310; MUKDEN INCIDENT, p. 391; SAMURAI, p. 114.

Significance   The pre–World War II Japanese government, which was founded by the Meiji constitution of 1889, had no built-in mechanism to legitimate civilian control of the powerful, military. Instead, the government helped extol the foreign exploits of the military. Japan's victories in the Sino-Japanese War (1894–95) and Russo-Japanese War (1904–05) became highly publicized affairs, and the myth of an invincible military, highly loyal to the emperor, was purposely cultivated. During World War I, Japan was on the side of the Allied Powers and the Japanese military took over the German possession of Shandong in China. Japan also presented a set of demands to China (the so-called Twenty-One Demands) in order to maintain Shandong permanently in the Japanese sphere of influence, and to seek other rights and privileges in China.

The Japanese military supported these aggressive foreign policies, envisioning Japan's future in further expansionism. Any deviation from their expansionist outlook was regarded as defeatism. When the government supported peace abroad and liberalization at home, many ultranationalistic imperial officers, most of them junior in rank, rebelled and took matters into their own hands. On September 18, 1931, the Japanese Army (Kwantung Army), which had been stationed in Manchuria since the Russo-Japanese War to guard its Southern Manchurian Railway System, initiated an attack on Chinese troops without prior consultation with the Tokyo government and overran Manchuria. The Tokyo government, powerless to intervene, eventually came out in defense of the Kwantung Army. When the League of Nations condemned the Japanese military action in Manchuria, Japan simply walked out of the League. In February 1936, young army officers mobilized their troops, occupied part of downtown Tokyo, and killed a number of government leaders. They threatened the assassination of "evil leaders" around the throne and advocated the "Showa Restoration." Subsequently, they were suppressed and their leaders executed, but this incident deterred any chance of further democratic growth in Japan in the pre-war years. In 1937, an army general was named as prime minister and organized his cabinet excluding all party leaders. From the second Sino-Japanese War (1937–45) to Japan's defeat in World War II in 1945, the military was in total control of the Japanese government and increasingly mobilized the Japanese people to fight the war in the Chinese and Pacific theaters. When Japan surrendered to the Allied Powers in World War II, she was forced to totally demilitarize.

Military: Civil-Military Relations   Various models of civil-military relations exist which attempt to explain military intervention, particularly in the Third World. Variables often considered in the effort to explain different modes of civil-military relations include (1) the extent and nature of political participation in the populace (high, medium, or low); (2) the strength of civil institutions in the civil or praetorian polity (high, medium, or low); (3) the extent of military strength through its coercive, political, and organizational resources (high, medium, or low); and (4) the nature of military institutional boundaries (either integral or fragmented). (See Claude E. Welch, Jr. and Arthur K. Smith, *Military Role and Rule: Perspectives on Civil-Military Relations.* North Scituate: Duxbury Press, 1974, Chapter 3.)

The matrix of these variables produce 36 cells, allowing for all possible combinations. Cases in each cell are not static and may develop or degenerate into another cell. According to the above classification, for example (1) Japan is a civic polity which ranks high on the extent of political participation and low on the political strength of the military, with an integral institutional boundary between the military and civic sectors of the government; (2) South Korea is a praetorian polity which ranks medium on the extent of political participation and high on the political strength of the military, with a fragmented institutional boundary between the military and civic sectors of the government; (3) India is a civic polity which ranks medium on the extent of political participation and medium on the political strength of the military, with an integral institutional boundary between the military and civic sectors of the government; and (4) The People's Republic of China is a civic polity which ranks low on the extent of political participation and high on the political strength of the military, with a fragmented institutional boundary between the military and civil sectors of government. *See also* MILITARISM, p. 283; MILITARY: PROFESSIONALISM, p. 289; PRAETORIANISM, p. 292.

Significance   The complex nature of civil-military relations defies a simple classification and any classification model is still not rigorous enough for empirical testing. The high, medium, and low rankings are subjective, as are the integral or fragmented classification of the civil-military institutional boundaries. The study of civil-military relations continues and many ill-founded, often simplistic, hypotheses and theories have been disputed, since each instance of civil-military relations displays unique features. The dichotomous treatment of military and civil sectors of Third World societies may be unrealistic, because national development becomes a total effort by the people of various power groups, including the military, to participate in the process.

Military: Civic Action The use of indigenous military forces on projects useful to the local population. Military civic actions are widely used in the Third World. Given inherent military resources such as manpower, organization, discipline, and technical expertise, the military in peace, war, and national emergency is a preferred method for achieving projects in education, training, agriculture, transportation, communications, health, sanitation, and other public works. Not only do these projects contribute to general economic and social development, they also help to create closer ties between the military and civilians, and to improve the standing of the military with the population. Whether a civic action is successful or not depends on the nature of its program and its acceptance by the local populace. *See also* GUERRILLA WARFARE, p. 279; MILITARY, p. 282; MILITARY: PROFESSIONALISM, p. 289.

Significance In modern Asia, military civic action has become part of the repertoire of insurgency/counterinsurgency actors. The Chinese Communist insurgents, in their long guerrilla war against the Nationalist government before 1949, were successful in introducing much-awaited reforms in civilian areas held under their military control and thereby winning the popular support. In the Philippines, President Magasaysay was successful in the use of the military in his counterinsurgency campaign against the Huk rebellion of the 1950s and for the pacification of the countryside. During the war in South Vietnam, however, the massive civic action programs, assisted by the U.S. Armed Forces, were unable to win the support of the people for the South Vietnamese government. Military civic action programs are also used for social and economic development. The resources of the military are readily tapped for civilian construction and development purposes. The effectiveness of the military for civic action programs during peacetime has not always been reliable. Since the military is not specifically trained for many developmental construction works and social programs, its efforts can be costly and wasteful. Military civic action programs tend to politicize the military and undermine professional concerns. The military may also antagonize the local populace by achieving program results through the use of force.

Military: Civilian Control   Various models exist for the civilian control of the military, whereby the military accepts a subordinate position to the civilian leader, be he president, prime minister, party chairman, or monarch. According to Eric A. Nordlinger (Nordlinger, Eric A. *Soldier in Politics—Military Coups and Governments.* Englewood Cliffs, NJ: Prentice-Hall, 1977, Chapter 1), they are: the traditional model, the liberal model, and the penetration model.

The Traditional Model: No differences exist between civilians and soldiers and no opposing beliefs or conflicting interests are in open competition. No military intervention is necessary because of the absence of civilian-military differences, and because of shared personnel in the civil and military sectors of the society. In other words, the same people wear both hat and helmet as in feudal society.

The Liberal Model: Differences exist between civilian and military personnel because of their different areas of expertise and responsibility. The military is specifically trained and responsible for the maintenance of external and internal security, and entrusted with control of the means of violence, that is, weaponry. In this model, the military is specifically placed under civilian control and treated as a professional group. The duty of the soldier is not to criticize or interfere in any way with the political affairs of the country. This model is associated with modern liberal democracies.

The Penetration Model: Differences exist between the civilian and military sectors of government, but civilian governors seek loyalty and obedience from the military by penetrating it through the use of political indoctrination and surveillance personnel (political officers in the military). Any deviation from orthodox political ideas is punished. This model is most fully developed among the Communist regimes. *See also* MILITARY: PROFESSIONALISM, p. 289; PRAETORIANISM, p. 292.

Significance   The military commands enormous political resources, and civilian leaders, particularly those surrounded by unstable political situations, are constantly faced with the question of how to control the military. The traditional, liberal, and penetration models are simplistic, historical characterizations and none of them adequately fits the civil-military relations that exist among Third World developing nations of Asia. The real situation is more fluid than these models delineate. The traditional model may be effective for civilian control of the military, but it does not truly apply to contemporary Asia, since the military is organized as a separate institution and away from the civilian sector of government. The liberal model has been tried in the developing nations of Asia, but it has proven generally unsuccessful. The penetration model has been successful only in a Communist system where a Communist party rules dictatorially. In the developing nations of Asia, the model of a civil-military coalition may be more realistic and useful than other models. In the civil-military coalition model, once the military is in power, it co-opts both civilian politicians and technocrats and establishes a unified, durable regime that undertakes national development projects.

Military: Professionalism   Technical orientation of the military as an institution, specifically created to perform the assigned responsibilities for national defense and security. Military professionalism is characterized by expertise, social responsibility, and a sense of corporate identity. Military officers are professionals who pursue their careers as occupations in military science, with advancement on the basis of merit rather than political or family connection. Ideally, the professional military, either in the commissioned or non-commissioned officer corps, maintains a disciplined and structured relationship with all personnel on the basis of the doctrine of the lawful order. *See also* MILITARISM, p. 283; PRAETORIANISM, p. 292.

Significance   The theory of military professionalism has been widely discussed in the developing nations of Asia as a way of depoliticizing the military and preventing the occurrence of military intervention in politics. The theory maintains that the more professional the military becomes, the less likely it is to intervene in politics. In other words, as the professionals are trained to be experts in their chosen fields, they are likely to stay within their institutional boundaries. This theory, often identified with Samuel P. Huntington's (Samuel P. Huntington, *The Soldier and the State: The Theory and Politics of Civil-Military Relations.* Cambridge: Harvard University Press, 1957), has been widely challenged in the context of the Third World. A more realistic theory posits the military and civil spheres as interactive, and partially overlapping (see Morris Janowitz. *The Military in the Political Development of New Nations.* Chicago: The University of Chicago Press, 1965). Some also maintain that Third World development is a total national effort which requires total societal participation by those who may have different skills, but share common national goals and aspirations. In the fluid and transitional situation of development in Third World nations, the military's increased professionalism has not precluded it from political intervention, as in South Korea, Pakistan, and elsewhere.

Military Authoritarianism   A form of bureaucratic authoritarianism, which is staffed and controlled by the military leaders who have come into power through a coup. Among the main characteristics of military authoritarianism are (1) key government positions are either directly held or controlled by military leaders; (2) political control is exercised vertically and opposition forces are minimally tolerated; (3) aspirations to economic participation by the popular sector are reduced and compromised; (4) "excessive" politics are deemphasized and social and political problems are reduced to the level of technical or administrative routine; and, (5) economic development is conceived in terms of an industrialization process, with the state playing an active role. Given its prevalence among the Third World nations of Asia, Africa, and Latin America, military authoritarianism must be regarded as a particularly distinguishing characteristic of the Third World political dynamic. *See also* MILITARISM, p. 283; MILITARY REGIME, p. 290.

Significance   In the Third World nations of Asia, military authoritarian systems have been not only prevalent, but also enduring. Once the military acts in a *de facto* assumption of power, it must make some hard decisions as to how that power will be exercised. Possible scenarios include (1) Direct rule; (2) "Proxy" rule, where the military return to the barracks and turn the government over to selected civilian leaders; (3) Conjoint rule, where the military organize a coalition with civilian leaders and jointly govern the nation. The last option has often been followed by authoritarian regimes in Asia, although the extent of the "mix" of military and civilian leaders has varied. Such conjoint, military authoritarian governments in Asia have been politically durable and have contributed to the creation of conditions necessary for economic growth through industrialization and social accommodation. Military authoritarianism is clearly antagonistic to communism. Although its economic orientation is capitalistic, it takes an active part in the economic lives of the people by directing the course of national economic development. Politically, it maintains a conditional tolerance towards opposition, exercising close surveillance over opposition activities, and selectively using force against chronic dissidents.

Military Regime   A government established by military coup d'état and subsequently controlled by leaders either remaining in uniform or in civilian cloth as officers retired from active service. Military officers first wage a coup against the government in power; then directly assume leadership and control of the successor government. Such a government requires continued military support to maintain itself in power, and the military becomes a critical political actor in the national power equation. Except when a government is run directly by a military junta in the aftermath of a coup, however, its leadership is seldom all military, and usually consists of a variable mixture of military and civilian leaders. Following a coup, the military leaders draw up a new constitution and establish a new government. In this newly founded government, they retain control of the critical position of chief executive and recruit prominent military leaders, civilian politicians and technocrats for cabinet and other high-level positions. The result is a mixed military and civilian political system. *See also* COUP D'ÉTAT, p. 270; MILITARY AUTHORITARIANISM, p. 289.

Significance   In most of the Third World nations, the military has become a powerful political actor, but its degree of political influence varies. The military regime is characterized by military dominance in the government, with the chief executive position controlled by a coup leader. Most of the military regime is a combination of military and civilian leaders. Emerging out of this political experience is a new political modality, characterized by a fused military and civilian leadership structure. It is this newly emergent political modality that has increasingly come to represent the Third World political systems found in Asia, Africa, and Latin America. The viability of this military and civilian mixed system is shown by its ability to successfully provide political stability and promote economic development.

Military Regime: Civilianized

A government which is established by military coup leaders who have become civilianized through retirement from active service, followed by subsequent election or appointment as officials or leaders of a newly instituted government. The civilianized military regime has both military and civilian components. Following a coup, coup leaders provide a new constitution; to implement it, they organize their own political party and control the newly instituted government in the guise of civilian leaders. They often co-opt many retired military personnel, civilian politicians and technocrats, and organize a military-civilian coalition government. Most of the Third World military regimes are of this type. *See also* MILITARY AUTHORITARIANISM, p. 289; MILITARY REGIME, p. 290.

Significance   The so-called Third World military regimes are seldom all military. In the reconstituted civilian government following a military coup d'état, the coup leaders, instead of returning to the barracks, retire from active military service and control the personnel and policies of the new government in their civilian role. They are also likely to co-opt civilian politicians and technocrats. This type of military-civilian coalition is more likely to be formed by the military than by the traditional civilian politicians and technocrats, who have an antimilitary orientation. In civil-military relations, this type of coalition is also most likely to be formed when the power of the civilian sector within the society is relatively developed, but weak compared to that of the military sector.

Military Regime: Modernization   Identification of a military regime with the modernization strategy. The modern military is often characterized by technical training, disciplined organization, and the rational approach to problem solving. The military as a modern institution of developing society is also regarded as a modernizing agent, responsible for promoting and guiding socioeconomic development. Once a military regime is established, military leaders deemphasize politics and use coercion, if necessary, to induce political stability and undertake planned socioeconomic development programs. Priorities in these programs vary with regimes, according to determining factors that are often found in either the socioeconomic backgrounds and personal idiosyncracies of military leaders, or the national level of development. Not all military regimes are alike, of course, but those that have identified with modernization have used daring and innovative methods for national development. *See also* MILITARY AUTHORITARIANISM, p. 289; MILITARY REGIME, p. 290.

Significance   The Asian nations that may be classified as having military regimes at one time or another include South Korea, Indonesia, Thailand, Bangladesh, and Pakistan. Of these, South Korea, under the late President Park, recorded the most impressive achievements of socioeconomic development. It successfully implemented the first Five Year Plan (1962–66), achieving an annual average growth rate of real gross domestic product (GDP) of 5 percent. During the second Five Year Plan (1967–71), the GDP growth rate was 9 percent. Emphasis was placed on heavy industrial development and construction of modern infrastructures, with export-oriented industries given special consideration. With initiation of the third Five Year Plan (1972–76), however, increasing attention was given to rural development, such as the promotion of the New Community Movement (*Saemaul Undong*). South Korea's per capita income stood at about $100 in 1961, rising to about $2,000 in 1984. Coincident to such economic growth has been increased political centralization, curtailments of human rights, increased control of oppositions and a spreading abuse and corruption of official power.

Praetorianism   A recurrent development in which military officers or groups maintain control over government by virtue of their actual or threatened use of force. The term, "praetorianism," is taken from one of the earliest and most famous instances of military intervention in the political process by the Roman Praetorian Guard, a special military unit that acted as the bodyguard of the Roman emperor. The Guard became powerful and controlled the selection of the emperor by the Roman Senate. In its contemporary application, the term refers to a practice in which military officers or groups frequently threaten or use force in order to enter or dominate the political process, influence governmental decisions, or occupy the seat of government by themselves. *See also* COUP D'ÉTAT, p. 270; GARRISON STATE, p. 274; MILITARISM, p. 283.

Significance   Praetorianism is one of the most prevalent forms of military intervention in the political processes of the Third World nations of Asia, where the military has come to play a dominant political role. Among the Third World nations of Asia, the military has become a powerful political force because of its size, organization, and discipline and because of its control of the instruments of violence—guns, tanks, planes, and the like. The practices of praetorianism may be identified with any of the following occurrences: (1) when military officers or groups threaten to carry out a coup d'état unless their demands are met; (2) when they wage a coup, either successful or unsuccessful; (3) when they dictate the choice of civilian government personnel; and, (4) when they take over the government by themselves. According to Rossi and Plano (Rossi, Ernest E. and Jack C. Plano. *The Latin American Political Dictionary.* Santa Barbara: ABC-Clio, 1980, p. 138), these practices of praetorianism make it distinct from (1) *caudillismo,* the rule of traditional chieftains; (2) *caesarism,* the dictatorship of a charismatic personality who is usually a former military leader; and, (3) the garrison state, a nation in which the military enjoys much decision-making power within the constitutionary established government because of an acute national security crisis.

6. Modernization and Development

Bureaucratic Polity   A system of government in which public officials exercise all political powers, not only rule execution but also rule making and rule adjudication. The bureaucratic polity flourishes in a political environment where political institutions outside of government bureaucracy are not sufficiently developed to exercise effective control over bureaucrats. The bureaucrats are trained for specific jobs. They are not only powerful in the discharge of their responsibilities, but they also control decision making in the government. No control mechanism exists within the political system to check their activities. They hold the power to seek compliance to their rule by the people. Bureaucratic polity is a nontraditional system because its public bureaucracy is relatively well developed as a functionally specific group. It is also a nonmodern system because no groups outside of the government bureaucracy, such as political parties, have been able to develop to check and control government officials. In a bureaucratic polity, power changes hands within the powerful bureaucratic circle, and ordinary people are excluded from this process. *See also* COUP D'ÉTAT: THAILAND, p. 278; MILITARY AUTHORITARIANISM, p. 289.

Significance   The concept of bureaucratic polity emphasizes the fact that public bureaucrats are in power and no control and checks over them exist within the political system. This concept is helpful in identifying military polities or Communist party polities. In these polities a special group rules, and no political institutions exist to check and control them. Fred Riggs uses the concept of bureaucratic polity in his discussion of the modernization process of Thailand (Riggs, Fred. *Thailand: The Modernization of a Bureaucratic Polity.* Honolulu: University of Hawaii, Eastwest Center Press, 1966). According to him, Thailand has evolved a bureaucratic polity since the military coup of 1932. The coup abolished the traditional absolute monarchy system of Thailand, but failed to modernize Thailand's political system. It is, therefore, neither traditional nor modern but still in a transitional phase. Modernization is sought in Thailand, but the coup promoters and their supporters in the government have jealously guarded their prerogatives and perpetuated themselves and their followers in power. They have failed to develop political institutions outside of the government bureaucracy.

Civic Polity   A political system in which the political processes are highly institutionalized, particularly in relation to political participation, and in which political rules and regulations are usually obeyed and constitutional order is maintained, despite increasing levels of political demand and participation. A civic polity is contrasted with a praetorian polity, which is characterized by a high political participation to political institutionalization ratio, and therefore is politically unstable due to various social forces acting directly in the political sphere. A civic polity, on the other hand, is politically stable because political-institutionalization and political-participation are in a proper relationship. According to Huntington (Samuel P. Huntington, *Political Order in Changing Societies.* New Haven: Yale University Press, 1968, pp. 78–80), a civic polity must constantly increase the complexity, autonomy, adaptability, and coherence of its political institutions as political participation increases. It is possible for a political system which is highly institutionalized to become politically unstable if political demands and participation exceed the level of political institutionalization. *See also* DEMOCRACY, p. 78; MODERN SOCIETIES, p. 312; MODERNIZATION, p. 313.

Significance   Rapid social mobilization and increasing demands on the political system are characteristics of many newly independent states. However, the political institutions of these states are inadequate to accommodate such change. The result has been political instability and the forceful overthrow of constitutionally established governments. For political stability and the orderly process of development, the expansion of political participation must be accompanied by the development of strong, complex, and autonomous political institutions such as political parties and interest groups. The developing nations of Asia have been characterized by the underdevelopment of these institutions despite rising expectations and increasing political demands. As Huntington maintains, the result is very often "a loss of community and decay of political institutions during the most intense phase of modernization." (Huntington, 1968, pp. 99–100).

Dependency Theory   A theory that explains the continued under-development of Third World nations as the result of a persisting quasi-colonial exploitation of inferior nations by the superior, powerful, and economically developed nations. Although many variations of the dependency theory exist, it is primarily based on a historical analysis of colonialism and a persistence of colonial practice in the relationships between economically developed and underdeveloped nations. On the basis of his analysis of the historical experience of Latin America, Andre Gunder Frank, one of the most articulate spokesmen for dependency theory, maintains that development and underdevelopment are two aspects of the same process; i.e., developed nations have been able to develop by exploiting the resources of those countries which have become underdeveloped. *See also* FOREIGN AID, p. 306; JUCHE, p. 308; MULTINATIONAL CORPORATION, p. 314; NEOCOLONIALISM, p. 315.

Significance   The dependency theory has its major followings among Latin American scholars who attempt to explain the continuing economic development problems Latin American countries have had, despite their close economic relationship with the United States. According to Latin American dependency theorists, the overpowering presence of the United States in Latin America has not contributed to the overall development of countries. Instead, what has emerged out of their historical relationship with the United States has been the internal destruction of their traditional way of life and exploitation of their economic, social, and political assets by external actors. In place of a balanced equilibrium, a new relationship of dependency is created between metropolis and satellite. Internationally, the metropolis is the developed nation, and the satellite is the economically dependent nation. Domestically, such a relationship has usually created a single, rich, metropolitan region existing upon the large, or satellite, under-developed region. As long as the rich remain rich, and the poor remain poor in the world, and as long as the rich become richer and the poor become poorer, the dependency theory will find many sympathizers among Asian and other Third World areas.

Development   A concept which, in its simplest form, means better-ment. Development is, in essence, achievement of desired goals and aspirations. For poor states of the Third World, development is the attainment of a standard of life, and of the corollary enjoyment of a higher level of available goods and services already achieved by the industrialized states. Development is often measured in terms of various indexes, such as per capita income, energy consumption, number of schools, literacy rate, use of communication media and transportation facilities, availability of health care, and extent of urbanization. The countries clustering near the top of development include the United States, Great Britain, France, Germany, the Low Countries, Scandinavia, Japan, Canada, and the Soviet Union. While political development is closely related to social and economic development, it is highlighted by the attainment of a government that is not only effective and efficient in meeting both domestic and international problems, but also legitimate and stable. In such a government, people are free to express their political views and take part voluntarily in the political decision-making process, whether selecting their government representatives or applying pressures against decision-making authorities to protect and/or promote their interests. *See also* DEMOCRACY, p. 78; MODERN SOCIETIES, p. 312; MODERNIZATION, p. 313; TRANSITIONAL SOCIETIES, p. 323.

Significance   Expressed in terms of the overall development of a society, the role of the political system appears to be crucial. First of all, it must be in a position to control the population and the resources of the state effectively, because civil disorder correlates poorly with long term investment and economic growth. Second, it must be able to mobilize necessary human and material resources in support of objectives of economic and social modernization. Third, it must be able to success-fully meet the demands generated by social and economic mobilization, and lessen the stress increasingly imposed on it, without force and repression. Many Third World nations are clearly in the development phase today as they move from a pre-modern society to a modern one. However, in coping with the strain of social, economic, and political change, they have frequently opted for a non-democratic, authoritarian, or Communist system. Democracy remains a universal aspiration, but as a political system, it is limited to a few nations in the Third World.

Development Strategies   General plans for development pursued by Third World nations. Identified by Gabriel A. Almond and G. Bingham Powell, Jr. (Gabriel A. Almond and G. Bingham Powell, Jr. *Comparative Politics.* Boston: Little, Brown & Co., 1978, 2nd ed., pp. 372 ff.), they are (1) the Democratic Populist Strategy; (2) Authoritarian-Technocratic Strategy; (3) Authoritarian-Technocratic-Equalitarian Strategy; (4) Authoritarian-Technocratic-Mobilizational Strategy; and, (5) Neo-Traditional Strategy. These and other classifications are neces-sarily ideal types, with the real or operational strategies often defying classification. The Third World nations of Asia are in search of their own identities. They are in the process of discovering the most efficacious mix of old and new which will satisfy their aspirations for a better life, and a promising and dignified future.

The Democratic-Populist Strategy has been tried by many nations, usually supported in their endeavors by the United States and other western nations. However, the performance of this strategy has led to many disappointments since it calls for a parliamentary form of democracy utilizing universal suffrage, and it introduces a market economy. Reasons for the failure of this strategy include (1) the country's low level of modernization; (2) the abuse and exploitation of democratic privileges by those who possess political resources and skills; and, (3) the sudden explosion of political participation by a large segment of the population who seek both political power and scarce economic resources. The Democratic Populist Strategy has been equated with low governmental capacity, poor socioeconomic growth, and political instability.

The Authoritarian-Technocratic Strategy emphasizes the maintenance of political order and stability, and the generation of economic growth under government and technocratic leadership. This strategy shuns competitive popular participation in decision making and permits only controlled opposition. Economically, it calls for a planned market economy which favors big and export oriented businesses and heavy industrial development. By offering tax and other advantages, this strategy also creates attractive opportunities for foreign investment.

The Authoritarian-Technocratic-Equalitarian Strategy is a variation of the Authoritarian-Technocratic Strategy. As in the case of the Authoritarian-Technocratic Strategy, it is politically repressive and concentrates political power in the executive and bureaucracy. Its leadership is often more reform oriented, and is likely to pursue a distributive economic policy. South Korea, Taiwan, and Singapore are examples of the successful use of this strategy.

The Authoritarian-Technocratic-Mobilization Strategy is exemplified by the Communist states such as China (PRC), North Korea (DPRK), Vietnam, Laos, Kampuchea, and Mongolia. In these states, Communist parties rule and mobilize the people for social construction. They permit no political opposition. Economically, they pursue thorough-going distributive policies, emphasizing the equal distribution of the various services and necessities of life. However, their economic growth has shown only a mixed record of achievement.

The Neo-Traditional Strategy is essentially a status quo orientation. It is pursued by traditional systems, such as Nepal, which has survived into the modern era with its social structures and culture largely unchanged. The regimes pursuing this strategy tend to have a low economic growth rate, low urbanization-industrialization, and low literacy. They are low in governmental capacity and maintain their stability through elite cohesion created by a system of shared privileges. *See also* DEMOCRACY, p. 78; KIMILSUNGISM, p. 95; MAOISM, p. 101; MILITARY AUTHORITAR-IANISM, p. 289; POLITICAL ECONOMY, p. 316.

Significance   The development strategies pursued by the Third World nations of Asia defy classification. The strategies identified are ideal types, useful for analytic and comparative convenience. Any strategy in use is a mixed type, which is dictated by the imperatives of resources available for development, and colored by elite perceptions of developmental needs and constraints. Among the ideal types identified, however, the most prevalent strategies increasingly pursued by the Third World nations of Asia are either the Authoritarian-Technocratic model or the Authoritarian-Technocratic-Equalitarian model. The latter model seems particularly characteristic of a regime sponsored by reform-oriented modern military leaders and highly trained civilian technocrats. In this newly emergent model, developmental priorities are placed on economic growth and political stability. Participatory politics are discouraged, if not totally banned, but the government works for distributive justice within the structure of a controlled market economy.

Development Strategy: Ch'ŏllima Undong   A mass mobilization movement by North Korea to attain the "revolutionary high tide of socialist construction" at an accelerated speed. *Ch'ŏllima* means "a horse capable of running one thousand *li* a day." It was defined in North Korea as "the revolutionary spirit of rebirth through our own power." The Ch'ŏllima Movement was initiated by the December 1956 Workers' Party Central Committee of North Korea "in order to overcome difficulties which have arisen in the domestic and international spheres. . . ." At the time, North Korea was threatened by diminishing aid from Communist bloc nations for use in further recovery from Korean War (1950–53) damages. As a consequence, long-term economic development and the ambitious five-year plan (1957–61) were thought to be compromised. However, North Korea stubbornly proceeded with its five-year plan by mobilizing all available human and material resources. The plan stressed heavy industrial development and further collectivization of agriculture. It also emphasized the cultural revolution of the countryside, and the technological revolution of industry as prerequisites for the successful construction of socialism in North Korea. The success of the Ch'ŏllima Movement was highly extolled. According to the North Korean account, it caused the completion of the 1957–61 five-year plan far ahead of schedule, in fact, within only two and one-half years. In North Korea, the Ch'ŏllima Movement has come to mean, in general, a speedy and dedicated working spirit, and ch'ŏllima work teams, active throughout North Korea, are to embody such a spirit in North Korea's socialist construction. *See also* DEVELOPMENT STRATEGY: CH'ŎNGSANRI METHOD, p. 301; DEVELOPMENT STRATEGY: GREAT LEAP FORWARD, p. 303; KIMILSUNGISM, p. 95.

Significance The Ch'ŏllima Undong was initiated as a mass mobilization scheme for the fulfillment of the five-year plan (1957–61) and its success, unlike the Great Leap Forward Movement in the People's Republic of China, has transformed it into a lasting feature in North Korea's continuous efforts for socialist construction. Since the initiation of the movement, industry and agriculture have been reorganized. The people have been constantly exhorted to make personal sacrifices. The first priority in the Ch'ŏllima Movement was given to the ideological indoctrination and transformation of workers into dedicated, selfless, and patriotic members of the socialist society. This cultural revolution preceded the technological revolution in North Korea, and stressed the efficient production and management of agricultural and industrial work. In conjunction with the Ch'ŏllima Movement, the so-called Ch'ŏngsan-ri method was introduced in 1960 to improve agricultural production while the Taean system was introduced in 1961 and applied as a solution to industrial management problems.

In both cases, Kim Il Sung (Kim, Il-sŏng) was credited with having provided personal, on-the-spot guidance. Ch'ŏngsan-ri had been a poor agricultural cooperative. According to a North Korean account, Kim Il Sung personally demonstrated in Ch'ŏngsan-ri a better organization and production method that would incorporate a material incentive system for harder work and more productive efforts. Faithfully following the instructions given by Kim Il Sung, Ch'ŏngsan-ri was able to transform itself into a prosperous agricultural cooperative. Kim Il Sung's guidance in Taean (a huge, modern electrical machinery factory) provided a way to achieve greater cooperative production efforts and efficiency through worker participation in management. At both Ch'ŏngsan-ri and Taean, teamwork among workers, managers, and party leadership was emphasized. Together, the Ch'ŏllima Movement, the Ch'ŏngsan-ri method, and the Taean method constitute the core of North Korea's socialistic development strategies.

Development Strategy: Ch'ŏngsanri Method

A method of rural development in North Korea, which has been attributed to President Kim Il Sung (Kim, Il-sŏng) and the on-the-spot guidance and instruction he provided in 1960 which has been credited with turning a poor farm cooperative into a rich, model farm cooperative. The Ch'ŏngsanri cooperative farm is located about 20 kilometers (12.5

miles) from Pyongyang, the capital city of North Korea. President Kim's instructions, as later reported, were (1) to apply hard work and not waste even an inch of land; (2) to increase production through improved interaction between the administrators of the cooperative and ordinary farmers; and, (3) to heighten political consciousness and cultivate self-sacrificing spirit among the farmers. Each cooperative in North Korea is organized as a commune, which is not only an agricultural production unit but also a political and administrative unit. The farmers in each cooperative work together to fill the production quota for which they are paid by the state. Extra production is distributed among them according to their classifications and the merit points that they have accumulated during the year. In each cooperative, the farmers also run their own social, educational, and health facilities. *See also* COMMUNES, p. 210; DEVELOPMENT STRATEGIES, p. 298; KIMILSUNGISM, p. 95; DEVELOPMENT STRATEGY: SAEMAUL UNDONG, p. 305.

Significance   Since his initial visit, President Kim has frequented the Ch'ŏngsanri cooperative and the success of the Ch'ŏngsanri cooperative has been propagated as a model to follow, not only for agricultural development in North Korea, but also in other Third World nations. According to a North Korean account, "The path traversed by Ch'ŏngsan-ri, its history of change and prosperity, constitutes a history of scrupulous guidance and warm love shown all the time by the beloved leader; it is an epitome of the proud course of development of our rural areas after liberation." North Korea has attained self-sufficiency with its own grain production, and much credit for North Korea's agricultural development is given to Kim Il Sung and his Ch'ŏngsanri method.

Development Strategy: Foreign Trade Regime   A government that stresses international economic competition and import and export business as strategies to follow for industrialization and economic development. Foreign trade regimes favor export businesses and nurture them. For these countries, export business is a way of life. They have predicated their economic growth on increasing exports. They are, on the whole, small in territory and poor in the endowment of natural resources, but rich in their skilled workforce. They have used foreign loans and welcomed foreign investments to build their industries. Once built, these industries are manned by skilled and industrious workers who are willing to work at a cheaper wage than their counterparts in the more industrialized nations. The result has been the production of quality products that are internationally competitive. To operationalize this sort of development strategy, the country must be politically stable and the government must be efficient and staffed by trained economic strategists. Furthermore, the foreign trade regimes need the world of free trade to continue to prosper. *See also* DEVELOPMENT STRATEGY: IMPORT SUBSTITUTION, p. 304; JUCHE, p. 308.

Significance   The foreign trade regimes of Asia have proven to be some of the fastest growing economies in the world. Japan's rate of economic growth in the 1950s and 1960s was most impressive, with the average annual GNP growth rate of 10 percent. Following Japan's example has been the policy of other foreign trade regimes in Asia. In many ways, however, the pattern of Japanese growth and development has been exceptional. Japan is the only fully operational democracy in Asia. South Korea, Taiwan, and Singapore are capitalistic in economy, but not free politically. Political repression exists in these countries. Their performance in the area of human rights and in labor policy is poor, although it has been tempered to some extent by the favorable effects of income distribution and paternalistic employer relations with employees. Inasmuch as the economies of foreign trade regimes are dependent on free trade, any worldwide protectionism may adversely affect them.

Development Strategy: Great Leap Forward (1958–59)   A revolutionary, accelerated effort to carry out socialist development in Communist China, thus building an industrialized, developed state in one "great leap." According to an official pronouncement, the Great Leap Forward was to "build socialism by exerting our utmost efforts and pressing ahead consistently to achieve greater, faster, better and more economical results." In 1957, Mao Zedong (Mao Tse-tung), as chairman of the Chinese Communist Party, was able to get support from a majority of the Party's Central Committee for radical departures from the orthodox Soviet organization of production and investment which had required extensive purchases of heavy machinery from the Soviet Union.

In the Great Leap Forward, the peasant communities were rapidly reorganized into communes and were encouraged to contribute jointly to socialist development by using their own surplus labor, savings, and local resources. Surplus rural labor would be used to construct water conservancy projects and set up small industrial establishments to process crops, manufacture farm tools, and provide consumer goods. These projects would create the funds which agriculture itself could not sufficiently generate. The Great Leap Forward as carried out initially was a disastrous failure. Instead of community self-help and self-management, excessive coercion was used. Inexperienced leadership at the local level resulted in a gross waste of investment. Furthermore, in 1959, bad weather struck the over-extended, exhausted, and demoralized labor

force. *See also* COMMUNES, p. 210; GREAT PROLETARIAN CULTURAL REVO-
LUTION, p. 156; MAOISM, p. 101.

Significance   In the Great Leap, Mao declared China's independence
from the Soviet Union, and in so doing, showed his supreme confidence
in China's own ability to accomplish the task of socialist construction in a
short period of time. Mao's strategy was to mobilize the masses for this
purpose. What was needed, he proclaimed, was human will and effort.
The Great Leap emphasized the theme of "politics takes command,"
that is, correct political consciousness as the best and only proper base
for social action. The Chinese Communist Party served as the vanguard
for the promotion of this nationwide movement. The peasants were
mobilized collectively and were forced to forsake their own material
possessions to the communal organization, and abandon their old habits
and customs. Moreover, they were to be self-supporting, thus emphasizing administrative decentralization and local initiatives. The Great Leap
Forward movement was never a concrete plan with consistent guidelines
or objectives, but rather a set of general policies put forward by Mao
Zedong in highly rhetorical terms. Very often, therefore, political zeal
was applied where concrete planning was needed. Local cadres often
used force to mobilize recalcitrant peasants.

The failure of the Great Leap Forward meant the modification of its
romantic zeal and optimistic forecasts, and since 1961 the communes
were allowed to make use of agricultural mechanization through
reintroduced incentive pay, and utilize more realistic contracts, thereby
enticing the peasants to increase their productivity. Also reintroduced
were personal plots for the peasants to work for their own consumption.
Organizationally, the size of the commune was made smaller and more
manageable. Because the Great Leap Forward was closely indentified
with the leadership of Mao Zedong, its failure caused division within the
Party leadership and the decline of Mao's influence in the Party. For
instance, Peng Dehuai (P'eng Te-huai), Politburo member and minister
of defense, challenged Mao on the Great Leap at the Lushan meeting of
the Party's Central Committee in July–August 1959. At the time, however, Mao charged Peng with "right opportunism" and purged him
from the Party. When Liu Shaoqi (Liu Shao-ch'i) replaced Mao as
chairman of the People's Republic of China (the head of state), Mao's
failure with the Great Leap Forward movement seemed to have been
fully acknowledged. In the Cultural Revolution (1966–69), however,
Mao was able to purge many of his political opponents, including Liu.

Development Strategy: Import Substitution   A policy of economic development pursued by developing nations, to foster domestic

industries by restricting the importation of specific foreign manufactured goods. Import substitution literally means substituting imported goods with domestically produced goods. By import substitution, domestic industries are protected from foreign competition, on the theory that the industries so protected will create jobs. By import substitution, foreign exchange earnings can be saved for capital formation and further industrialization. Import substitution is a nationalist strategy of development, in that it is designed to encourage self-help and reduce dependency on foreign made goods. *See also* DEVELOPMENT STRATEGY: FOREIGN TRADE REGIME, p. 302; NATIONALISM, p. 104.

Significance   In theory, import substitution is highly recommended as a strategy of development, but in practice it has proven too costly. Where the domestic market is small, the domestically manufactured goods become too expensive, and therefore not many people can afford to purchase them. This means that the protected industries are unable to grow. The foreign exchange savings also dissipates, partly due to the need to purchase machinery for the protected industries, and partly due to the black marketing of foreign made goods. Import substitution is often used in an early stage of development. However, it has gradually been abandoned by rapidly growing economies, such as in South Korea, Taiwan, and Singapore, thus exposing their industries to international competition, but also actively seeking foreign loans and foreign capital investment needed for industrial development.

Development Strategy: Saemaul Undong   A new community movement in South Korea designed to eradicate rural poverty and improve the livelihood of people through local initiative and mutual help. *Saemaul* stands for new community and *Undong* for movement. The Saemaul Undong also means rural modernization and revolutionary change in people's livelihood. More specifically, its three purposes are (1) to enlighten the rural populace; (2) to improve their living environment; and, (3) to increase their income through diligence, self-help, and voluntary cooperation. Under the leadership of President Park Chung Hee (Pak, Chŏng-hui), South Korea's Saemaul Undong was first conceived in 1970 as a nationwide movement. Each rural community was encouraged to devise its own developmental programs in order to secure aid from the central government. Each community was encouraged to plan cooperative projects, to be more agriculturally productive, and to engage in supplementary income-producing activities. Community leadership training was also emphasized. In 1974, the Saemaul Undong was applied to urban development. The success of South Korea's Saemaul Undong has received much attention from that part of the international community concerned with rural development and it has served as a model for such countries as the Philippines, Thailand, Malaysia, and Indonesia. *See also* CH'ŎNGSANRI METHOD, p. 301; DEVELOPMENT STRATEGY: MILITARY AUTHORITARIANISM, p. 289; SOFT STATE, p. 320.

Significance   Rural poverty has been a fixture of Korea's countryside. The basic motivation of the Saemaul Undong was to improve this situation with the leadership of the government. In the beginning, the movement was carried out on an experimental basis. The idea was to encourage the people to do something about their own poverty; however, as the movement gained momentum, it was integrated into South Korea's overall development plan for mobilizing the whole countryside. The basic strategy remained the same—local initiative and problem solving by better use of available resources. For instance, it was reported that during the period 1971–78, the government's financial aid and investment in various projects associated with the movement was a low 28 percent, with local village contributions making up the remainder of the cost.

Overall, the movement has been able to transform the physical appearance of Korea's countryside through the improvement of roads, housing, introduction of advanced and mechanized agricultural production facilities, nursery farms, better marketing, and transportation. The traditional Korean thatched roof has almost disappeared from the countryside, having been replaced by colorful tiles. TV antennas are visible everywhere. The movement has proven the capability for local self-improvement and greater productivity when enough economic incentives are available. It also indicates the critical developmental role of government and central leadership. The movement has not been without criticism, however, and it has been too closely identified with President Park's authoritarian regime and his mobilization of rural areas for political support. Leadership training camps have been set up throughout the country to which people from the various sectors of society have been sent. These training programs have become increasingly politically motivated. Since the death of President Park in 1979, the initial fanfares for the movement may have subsided, but the movement is still stressed by the new South Korean government.

Foreign Aid   Assistance provided by a foreign government or an international institution. Foreign aid is provided bilaterally, by regional organizations and by international agencies operating under the United Nations. It can be economic, social, and/or military aid. Economic aid includes such categories as technical assistance, capital grants, development loans, surplus goods disposal, public guarantees for private investments, and trade credits. Social aid includes assistance in the area of education, family planning, housing, health, urban development, and transportation and communications development. Military aid helps in modernizing and strengthening the military capability for national security, which usually involves transfers of military hardware, and assistance in training and financial support.

Major donor countries have been the United States, the Soviet Union, Communist China, West Germany, Japan, Britain, Switzerland, and the Scandinavian countries. Among the better known regional and international organizations that aid the Asian developing nations are the Asian Development Bank, the United Nations Development Program, the International Monetary Fund, the World Bank Group (IBRD, IFC, and IDA) and the United Nations Conference on Trade and Development. Foreign aid is used in supporting allies, rebuilding war-shattered economies, promoting socioeconomic development, gaining ideological support, obtaining strategic materials, preventing economic collapse, and helping the sick and the poor. *See also* THIRD WORLD, p. 40; NEO-COLONIALISM, p. 315.

Significance   Foreign aid comes in many different forms. Applied to the developing nations of the world, it is sought as a way of breaking the cycle of poverty. The poor countries remain poor because they lack the capital needed for investment for their development programs. According to the United Nations, an underdeveloped nation is one that requires external aid to finance its development. There is a growing sentiment within the poor regions of the world that the richer nations have a moral responsibility to provide this assistance. This line of argument insists that the rich nations have become rich at the expense of the poor nations who supplied, and continue to supply cheap labor and natural resources for them.

American aid to underdeveloped nations started with the Point IV Program of technical assistance in 1949, and it has expanded to include development grants, loans, and military aid. On the whole, however, the rich nations of the world have been reluctant to provide necessary aid for the development of the poor nations. In 1966, the United Nations General Assembly recommended foreign aid at one percent of the gross national product of possible donor nations. However, this target has not been met. Aid is often politically motivated, and has too many strings attached. Increasingly, aid has been given more for military purposes than for the purpose of economic development. Aid has also been associated with corruption and waste, and has not often reached the places where it was needed most.

Green Revolution   A dramatic increase in agricultural production in the Third World resulting from the propagation and use of new high-yield seeds. Led by the Nobel Prize-winning geneticist, Norman E. Borlaug, who pioneered in the development of new, high-yield seeds, the Green Revolution has spread to many poor nations of Asia and Africa to help feed people suffering from famine. The Green Revolution has also promoted greater research and experimental methods in food production techniques. The result has been a doubling and even tripling of food production in many countries of Asia and Africa during the 1960s. *See also* FOREIGN AID, p. 306; THIRD WORLD, p. 40.

Significance   The so-called "miracle" seeds did a great deal of good. In India and other places, wheat yields doubled between 1964 and 1972. The new rice seeds developed by the International Rice Institute at Los Banos in the Philippines have had a similar effect. However, the new seeds require a large amount of fertilizer and pesticide. In the 1970s and 1980s, when the cost of energy soared, the price of fertilizers and pesticides increased dramatically. By the time the developing nations had paid for their energy imports to produce fertilizers and to accommodate other uses, they had little capital left to buy the other chemicals and nutrients that were also required. The Green Revolution has had some negative effects, in that it has benefited the larger and richer farmers, but not the landless and small holders. Fertilizers, insecticides, and irrigation improvements cost extra cash which the poor farmers do not have. The Green Revolution in many places has widened the gap between the rich and the poor.

Juche (Chuch'e)   The guiding principle of North Korea, which has been variously translated as independence, self-reliance, or self-management. Since it was first announced by President Kim Il Sung (Kim, Il-sŏng) of North Korea in 1955, the *juche* principle has been promoted as President Kim's trademark and North Korea's unique identity. It has also been theorized as a revolutionary philosophical system. According to the 1972 revised constitution of North Korea: "The Democratic People's Republic of Korea is guided in its activity by the juche idea of the Workers' Party of Korea, which is a creative adaptation of Marxism-Leninism to our country's reality."

Applied to international relations, juche signifies independence from the Big Powers, whether they are Communist states or non-Communist "imperial" powers. It means not taking sides in the Sino-Soviet disputes and dealing with the Soviet Union and the People's Republic of China as North Korea's needs dictate. It also calls for expelling foreign "aggressors," such as the United States, from Korea and working for Korean reunification. Applied domestically, it means managing internal affairs and developmental problems with available human and material resources. Juche is practiced in North Korea in agriculture, industry, performing arts, and education, and it is embodied in North Korea's highly nationalistic public statements and behavior. As a philosophical system, North Korea maintains that the juche principle is based on Kim Il Sung's discovery of the true human nature. To Kim Il Sung, the essence of human nature is to be independent. Many books have been written on juche in North Korea and they have been translated into many languages for free distribution abroad. North Korea has been also promoting juche study centers in friendly Third World countries. *See also* DEPENDENCY THEORY, p. 297; KIMILSUNGISM, p. 95; MAOISM, p. 101.

Significance   The principle of *juche* is applied to every aspect of North Korea's activity. The people are encouraged to be proud of what they have accomplished in the spirit of juche. They seek uniqueness in their performance and maintain that their socialist construction observes unique Korean traditions epitomized by the spirit of juche. For instance, all the public buildings in North Korea are said to combine modern conveniences with traditional Korean architectural features; their music is composed by their own composers incorporating traditional forms and styles; their writing is exclusively in *hangul*, the phonetic alphabet of Korean invention in the fifteenth century; they avoid imported or foreign educational doctrines. These elements give the North Korean people an extremely self-righteous attitude, narrowing their outlook and limiting their foreign contacts. As North Korea's industrialization and development progress, however, the chauvinistic spirit of juche may require adjustment. Increasingly, North Korea is in need of the technology which it cannot improvise to sustain its growth. Emphasis on juche may have served the narrow purpose of nationbuilding in North Korea, but the obsession with it has become counterproductive to North Korea's relations with South Korea and the world outside. North Korea feels increasingly isolated and may even be envious of the newfound friendship of the People's Republic of China, its Communist neighbor, with the United States and Japan.

Mass Line   A fundamental principle of mass mobilization which has been closely identified with the Chinese Communist Party and

Maoism. In a directive written for the Central Committee of the Chinese Communist Party in June 1943, Mao Zedong (Mao Tse-tung) stated that: "In all the practical work of our Party, all correct leadership is necessarily 'from the masses, to the masses.'" This refers to the continuing process of (1) taking the scattered and unsystematic ideas of the masses; (2) transforming them into concrete ideas; (3) relating them to masses; and, (4) testing their validity in action. In other words, the masses are mobilized to express their concerns and interests to the Party which, in turn, systematizes these concerns and interests. The various techniques used over the years to operationalize the mass line principle include discussion groups, mass movements and meetings, mass organizations, and mass media. *See also* KIMILSUNGISM, p. 95; MAOISM, p. 101.

Significance   Closely identified with the Chinese Communist Party and Mao Zedong, the mass line is a principle used for the mobilization of the masses for revolution and development. The Chinese Communist revolution could not have been successful without mass support. On its road to power, the Chinese Communist Party depended on the support of non-Party members for intelligence, food supplies, new recruits, and the performance of administrative duties. The mass line is a leadership principle which recognizes the importance of mass assistance in a revolutionary struggle. However, it is also used to control the bureaucrats and intellectuals, making them responsive to the needs of the people. The Chinese bureaucratic-intellectual tradition has been identified with excesses in, and abuses of, official power. The mass line insists that officials should have contact with the masses. In the Chinese context, the masses have included the peasants. The principle of mass line has emphasized peasant mobilization for, and participation in, socialist construction and development.

Meiji Restoration   The revolution which ended the Tokugawa *shogunate* (military government) in 1868 by anti-Tokugawa *samurai* (warriors), and which abolished Japan's traditional feudalism and structured a new government of Japan headed by the Meiji emperor. Earlier in 1854, Commodore Matthew C. Perry of the United States, leading his fleet of "black ships" and carrying a letter from President Fillmore, succeeded in opening Tokugawa Japan from the self-enforced seclusion of 215 years. At the time, the Tokugawa regime was in no position to go to war against the United States; thus, the conclusion of a treaty (the Treaty of Kanagawa), as dictated by the United States, was inevitable. However, the treaty exposed Tokugawa's weaknesses and when its opponents, mostly from the Satsuma and Choshu clans of south and southwest Japan, coalesced against Tokugawa rule with the double slogan,

"Honor the Emperor; Expel the barbarians," the Tokugawa were powerless to ward off the domestic opposition.

As the last shogun resigned peacefully, the restoration of power to the emperor was proclaimed on January 3, 1868. The emperor was then the fifteen-year old Mutsuhito, who assumed the reigning title of Meiji (Enlightened Rule). In his Charter Oath in April 1868, the Emperor Meiji proclaimed that he would seek "wisdom and knowledge from all over the world" and consult "public opinion" to promote the welfare of the empire, and he urged all people to unite. What followed was a hectic pace of modernization directed by Restoration leaders, mostly young former samurais. *See also* GENRO, p. 227; MODERNIZATION, p. 313; SCAP, p. 318; TOKUGAWA FEUDALISM, p. 123.

Significance   The Meiji Restoration symbolized the basic transformation of Japanese society from the feudal to the modern period. As a revolutionary movement, however, the Restoration was brought about in a relatively peaceful manner. It was not a result of a class struggle, since the leaders of the Restoration were from the traditionally ruling samurai class of feudal Japan. There were no mass uprisings or peasant movements. The Restoration was led mostly by samurais from the traditionally anti-Tokugawa regions of Satsuma and Choshu in south and southwest Japan. What followed during the Restoration was a model of national development purposively directed by the government. The leaders were former samurais; most of them young, ambitious, highly capable, and dedicated. In feudal Japan, they were born to lead, and they were determined to lead the people in the creation of a modern Japan which would be strong and wealthy. In order to modernize the country, they were willing to learn from the West. They provided leadership in the name of the emperor and the masses followed them, bearing the brunt of modernization expenses.

The major reforms which were planned and carried out over a wide range of political and socioeconomic areas included (1) abolition of the feudal political structure; (2) abolition of hereditary servitude, and of restraints on travel and choice of occupation; (3) consolidation of local, provincial, and national governments and their monetary functions; and, (4) establishment of universal education and military conscription. The government provided leadership in business and industry; fostered a select group of wealthy merchants to provide development capital; built model factories with public funds; constructed public roads; and set up telegraph and telephone systems. The political system that emerged out of the Restoration was authoritarian, led by a small group of former samurais, and highly centralized. The Meiji constitution of 1889, which concluded a long series of debates on the nature of constitutional government for Japan, made the emperor the ultimate source of power, vesting in him all of the appointive, executive, administrative, legislative, and judicial powers. The constitution also provided that the emperor, the successor to an unbroken line of divine ancestors, was a sacred personage. Modeled after the western constitutional practices of the time, the constitution made a small concession to liberal pressure for a parliamentary system and provided a two-house Diet, or legislative assembly, consisting of an appointive House of Peers and an elective House of Representatives.

During the so-called Taisho Democracy period in the 1920s, the House of Representatives became strong enough to select a prime minister from the majority party. However, the imperial power of appointment was exercised by a small group of oligarchs, intimately advising the emperor, and always present to befuddle the growth of an effective parliamentary system of government for Japan. The emperor had the power to appoint as prime minister whomever he wished, regardless of parliamentary party strength. Given his sacred personage, no one in prewar Japan would dare to challenge in public the exercise of his prerogatives. Japan as a full-fledged democracy has been strictly a post–World War II development.

Modern Societies   In their idealized versions, these societies are characterized as predominantly literate, urban, industrial, impersonal, and media-intensive in interpersonal communications. The social structure of modern societies is a highly differentiated network of specialized socioeconomic and political units. Furthermore, the state as the largest and the most comprehensive unit bears ultimate responsibility for meeting individual needs. Politically, these societies are characterized by complex, highly differentiated organizational structures for which achievement or merit is emphasized in personnel selection. Mass participation in the political process is intense.

Culturally, modern societies emphasize the values of political participation, achievement, creativity, nationalism, and personal qualities that are regarded as essential to the operation and perpetuation of modern economic and political systems. The above characteristics are idealized versions of modern societies, vis-à-vis traditional societies. In the real world, however, they exist in various combinations. Experience has shown that many traditional characteristics can be found in modern societies, and that modern characteristics are not always desirable, nor are all traditional ones undesirable. Certainly modern and traditional characteristics may complement one another in the achievement of development goals. *See also* DEVELOPMENT, p. 297; DEMOCRACY: JAPAN, p. 220; MODERNIZATION, p. 313.

Significance   Modern societies are those that have experienced the process of development toward modernity. According to prevailing contemporary thinking, being modern means being rational, scientific, secular, and politically capable. It also implies a successful economic conquest of the environment through industrialization and innovative application of scientific knowledge to production efforts. There may be other ways of being modern, but most Third World political leaders have emphasized industrialization as a way out of the poverty and deprivation of their nations. The question remains, however, how to industrialize and become modern. Some models are available, such as the capitalistic, socialistic, democratic, and totalitarian models, but these are often adapted to local situations and produce the mixed, syncratic model. Today, the countries that are clearly regarded as modern include the western nations, such as the United States, Great Britain, Canada, France, Germany, the Low Countries, and Scandinavia. Japan, the Soviet Union, and some Communist-bloc nations are also conditionally classified as modern.

Modernization   Literally, the process of becoming modern, an idealized state of development by which various social theorists characterize the modern states, such as the western democracies, some Communist bloc nations, and Japan. As a multi-dimensional concept, modernization could refer to political, economic, and social modernizations and their interrelationship. It is also a continuing process, progressing by degrees or stages, and any developing society that experiences the process of modernization finds within itself a variable mixture of traditional and modern cultural features. Modernization can be destabilizing especially when rapidly changing traditional and modern cultural features collide. *See also* DEVELOPMENT, p. 297; MODERN SOCIETIES, p. 312.

Significance   Modernity is the goal of modernization, but it is a timebound concept. What is modern today is not modern 50 years hence. In the contemporary context, however, modernization refers to a growth in rationality, particularly in the increasing use of science and technology for the betterment of human livelihood. It also refers to secular ways of thinking and behaving and their associated patterns of human interaction. The real world of the modern person is one of secular books, of concepts based on constant experimentation and observation, not one of superstition, magic, and dogmatic explanation. Moreover, the modern person considers him or herself to be a free agent, unbound by fetish, ritual, ceremony, or despotic political systems.

Modernization, as process, denotes the constant adjustment of people to their changing environment, in pursuit of their goals.

Multinational Corporation (MNC)   A large business organization with its headquarters in one country and subsidiary operations in other countries. MNCs have increasingly become worldwide phenomena and powerful political and economic influences. In 1971, more than one half of the MNCs were headquartered in the United States, with the remainder in western Europe, Japan, and Canada. In 1982, they were joined by the balance, headquartered in Argentina, Brazil, Colombia, Hong Kong, India, South Korea, Peru, the Philippines, Singapore, Taiwan and some OPEC countries. Among the world's largest MNCs are Exxon, General Motors, Royal Dutch/Shell, Ford Motor, Texaco, Mobil Oil, Standard Oil (Calif.), British Petroleum, Gulf Oil, and IBM. They produce as much revenue as many of the developing nations and often dictate the terms of business and investment. Whether or not MNCs help develop Third World nations is still debated. The developing Communist nations have either rejected them or restricted their operations. The non-Communist developing nations have welcomed them but feel ambivalent toward them. The developing nations feel that MNCs are out to make profits and seek monopolistic advantages. However, MNCs do bring in capital, new technology, management skills, new products, and increased efficiency and income. *See also* DEPENDENCY THEORY, p. 297; DEVELOPMENT STRATEGIES, p. 298; NEO-COLONIALISM, p. 315.

Significance   MNCs are new international forces. They operate transnationally, seeking to pursue their businesses where local conditions are favorable for profit-making operations. For MNCs, Third World nations provide natural resources, cheap labor, and political protection. MNCs can help the developing country to (1) finance a savings gap or balance of payments deficit; (2) acquire a specialized good or service essential for domestic production; (3) obtain foreign technology and management and entrepreneural skills; (4) provide employment opportunities for domestic skilled and unskilled workers; and, (5) generate tax revenue from income and corporate profit taxes. In recent years, however, critics of MNCs have maintained that their costs exceed their benefits. They have argued that MNCs (1) increase the dependence of the less developed nations on foreign sources for development, resulting in less local technological innovation and less local entrepreneural development; (2) introduce inappropriate products, technology, and consumption patterns; (3) create local big businesses which usually benefit only the richest 20 percent of the population; (4) require the subsidiary to purchase imports from the parent company regardless of cost disadvantages; (5) exert conservative political influence on the host government; and, (6) increase foreign intervention into the domestic political process. In the relationship between MNCs and Third World host governments, however, a growing trend has been a shift in bargaining power away from the MNCs to Third World governments, who have been able to increase their own economic and personnel resources. The number of joint ventures has also increased. The Third World host governments are now in a better position to maximize the benefits in their dealings with MNCs.

Neocolonialism   Term used by Third World nations to signify that western imperialism/colonialism has not receded. Neocolonialism points to the penetration of Third World nations by international capital. It centers on dependency relations between the developed and developing states, and it asserts that the Third World countries are controlled by the industrial states who dominate their economies. The principal neocolonial state is supposed to be the United States because its multinational corporations, as well as its grants and aid, influence policy, programs, and even the selection of governmental leaders in Third World nations. Japan is judged another important neocolonial state. According to some observers, its aggressive trading practices have succeeded where its armed forces failed in promoting Japan's Greater East Asia Co-Prosperity Sphere. *See also* COLONIALISM, p. 63; COLONIALISM: JAPAN, p. 66; COLONIALISM: USSR, p. 71; COLONIALISM: UNITED STATES, p. 69; DEPENDENCY RELATIONS, p. 335; GREATER EAST ASIA CO-PROSPERITY SPHERE, p. 15.

Significance   The Soviet Union has avoided being characterized as "neocolonial." The term is used more as a political epithet than as objective description. It uses a narrow interpretation of imperialism. Imperialism has come to be associated exclusively with capitalism, while other forms of imperialism are ignored or given less public attention. Racial considerations are also part of neocolonial perceptions, and the Soviet Union has avoided implication in racist policies. Moreover, Soviet technical and economic assistance to Third World nations is generally offered in return for commitment or barter, or both. The indebtedness of the Third World is a consequence of the industrial world's financial transactions, and the Soviets are perceived as alleviating that condition, not intensifying it. Finally, Lenin's interpretation of imperialism placed full responsibility on the capitalist nations, (viz., his 1916 treatise, "Imperialism: The Highest State of Capitalism"). That doctrine has been imbibed by a broad cross-section, especially young intellectuals, in the

Third World. It helps explain to them why they are underdeveloped, why they continue to be "exploited," and why they must suffer the leaders and the political systems that they find intolerable. The forces of revolution in the Third World, therefore, are fueled by this concept of neocolonialism.

Political Economy   A field of social science that emphasizes the interrelationship of political and economic processes. Political economy deals with questions of public choice or policy, and problems of allocation and exchange of scarce political, social, and economic resources. Political economy is also defined as the process of policy making for the enhancement of national and community wealth. Although these definitions stress the importance of politics in the economic process, political economy has often been regarded as more of a subfield of economics than of politics, and economists in the study of political economy have usually stressed its economic ramifications. A new interest in political economy by political scientists arises from the increasing role which government plays in national economies, particularly in the Third World. *See also* DEVELOPMENT STRATEGIES, p. 298; MILITARY AUTHORITARIANSHIP, p. 289.

Significance   Karl Marx's major work, *Das Kapital*, was subtitled "A Critique of Political Economy." Though long neglected by western political scientists, political economy as a field of study and as a set of analytical tools not only survives but shows renewed vigor. A new, realistic appreciation has emerged of the interrelation between the political and economic processes, especially since development in the Third World has come to entail a total, planned effort with much public funding channeled into it. Given a condition of scarce resources, development, whether economic or otherwise, becomes a question of public choice, and the study of political economy promises to help make that choice more relevant and efficacious.

Prismatic Society   A concept used by Fred Riggs (*Administration in Developing Countries: The Theory of Prismatic Society*. Boston: Houghton Mifflin Co., 1964) to characterize those societies that are in the process of development that lies between modern and traditional societies. A prismatic society is a transitional society. Using the characteristics of the prism, Riggs conceptualizes a traditional society as a fused society and a modern society as a diffracted society. As light passes through a prism, it diffracts and differentiates its component parts. When this process is halted in the transitional stage of development, Riggs describes such a stage as "captive." A traditional society in ideal form is characterized as ascriptive, particularistic, and diffuse (to use the Parsonian pattern variables) and a modern society as achievement-oriented, universalistic, and specific. A prismatic society is in the captive state, as is light when it is projected into a prism and is not yet diffracted. A prismatic society, therefore, remains in a confused state of animation. *See also* MODERN SOCIETIES, p. 312; TRADITIONAL SOCIETIES, p. 322; TRANSITIONAL SOCIETIES, p. 323.

Significance   In his theory of prismatic society, Riggs is particularly concerned with the structural configuration of developing societies, and his recharacterization of the prior conceptual terms (traditional, transitional, and modern) as fused, prismatic, and diffracted is said to be more descriptive. Not denying the contributions of Riggs, particularly in the field of comparative administration and the on-going discussion of politics and administration, the prismatic society model is not any more descriptive of transitional societies than prior models. In the prismatic society model, functions of light and prism must be universally agreed upon: light has the same characteristics everywhere and prisms perform the same function of diffraction and differentiation. What is implied here is, then, a universal pattern of development which is not necessarily an accurate description of reality. In addition, the prismatic society model does not explain what forces might be involved in bringing about change.

Red-Expert Controversy   A continuous controversy and policy shift in China involving the emphasis on ideological commitment on the one hand, and technological expertise on the other. The Chinese Communist Party, particularly under the leadership of Mao Zedong (Mao Tse-tung), has emphasized that people should strive to be both "red" and "expert," and that the ideal cadre should combine both characteristics. Ideological commitment entails endless meetings: about the Thought-of-Mao-Zedong and other Communist theoretical writings; about policy directives; about correct interpretation of the Party lines. Technological expertise, however, calls for specialized study and concentrated training. The more expert a person becomes, the less time he has to devote to ideological correctness.

In the larger world of Communist Chinese politics, the red-expert controversy has become a widely debated issue in the face of increasing bureaucratization of the Communist political process since the establishment of the People's Republic of China in 1949. The result has been a gradual loss of revolutionary fervor and initiative in, what Mao had called, "a sea of paper shuffling." Mao emphasized "redness," and while alive, he had the charisma and mass following to turn the tide of Chinese bureaucratic obsession by reinvigorating the revolutionary spirit of the Chinese Comnmunist Party. The so-called Cultural Revolution was, in a way, the last of Mao's campaigns against the increasingly problem-oriented strategy of Chinese development and the bureaucratization of revolutionary politics. *See also* GREAT PROLETARIAN CULTURAL REVOLUTION, p. 156; MAOISM, p. 101; MODERNIZATION, p. 313; ARMED FORCES: PEOPLE'S LIBERATION ARMY, p. 263.

Significance   The red-expert controversy addresses itself to one of the most fundamental questions in the conflict between revolution itself and the legitimization and administrative routine of political development and modernization. Since its victory in 1949, the Chinese Communist Party has increased its membership with new recruits having varied motivations, backgrounds, and skills. The Party has been charged with administering the gigantic socioeconomic transformation of the most populous nation in the world. The ideal situation for the new recruits and for the administration of development programs would have been a combination of "red" and "expert." Between the two, however, Mao's emphasis was on ideological correctness and loyalty to the Party, stressing mass mobilization over bureaucratic problem solving.

Mao was convinced that he was vindicated in his revolutionary emphasis by the unexpected outcome of the so-called Hundred Flowers Campaign (1957) which permitted the intellectuals to freely criticize the Communist government and its policies. Finding these criticisms deeply resentful of the Communist system and therefore not constructive, he attacked all critical intellectuals as being counterrevolutionaries and quickly ended the Hundred Flowers period by stopping all forms of criticism. Mao's overemphasis on ideological correctness and his hostility toward experts have unfortunately created an underutilization of China's intellectual resources, stifling their growth. The post-Mao leadership of Deng Xiaoping (Teng Hsiao-ping), however, has swung the pendulum in favor of the expert side, but it has been unable to end the controversy.

SCAP (Supreme Command for the Allied Powers)   The organization in charge of the Allied occupation of Japan following the conclusion of World War II in the Pacific theater. SCAP was created to implement the Potsdam Declaration of July 26, 1945, in which the Allied Powers defined the terms of Japanese surrender. Following the war, the Allied Powers established the Far Eastern Commission and the Allied Council as the controlling machinery for the occupation of Japan, but the post-war occupation of Japan was, in practice, an American occupation, since the U.S. government had maintained the exclusive right to communicate with SCAP under the command of General of the Army Douglas MacArchur, U.S.A. In April 1952, when the Peace Treaty with Japan and the Allied Powers became effective, SCAP was dissolved and the American troops remaining in Japan were transformed into security forces by an administrative agreement which had been reached earlier between Japan and the United States.

SCAP was guided in its operation by the U.S. Initial Post-Surrender Policy for Japan which had been formulated by the U.S. State, War, and Navy Coordinating Committee. SCAP was "(1) to ensure that Japan will not again become a menace to the U.S. or to the peace and security of the world . . ., and (2) to bring about the eventual establishment of a peaceful and responsible government which . . . should conform as closely as may be to principles of democratic self-government. . . ." To implement these broad guidelines, SCAP issued directives which were to be implemented by the Japanese government. The major areas of reform by SCAP included (1) execution of those convicted of war crimes and the purge of ultranationalists in designated public and private offices; (2) dissolution of the *zaibatsu* (giant business conglomerates) and a purge of their leaders; (3) encouragement of organized political activities and labor movements; (4) land reform; (5) social and educational reforms for the protection of equal educational and other opportunities; (6) enfranchisement of women and protection of their full legal equality; and, (7) abolition of the ministries of army, navy, and home affairs.

The purpose of the postwar Japanese constitution was to institutionalize the Occupation reforms on a permanent basis. When it was put into effect on May 3, 1947, it was regarded as one of the most democratic constitutions in the world. Under this constitution, Japan was able to transform itself into an operational parliamentary system of government. The emperor remained only as titular head of government. To protect the rights and liberties of the people, two-thirds of the constitution was devoted to their specific provisions. Article 9 of the constitution, furthermore, specifically stipulates that the Japanese people are "forever" to renounce "war as a sovereign right of the nation and the threat of use of force as a means of settling international disputes." *See also* DEMOCRACY: JAPAN, p. 220; PACIFIC WAR, p. 396; WARTIME CONFERENCES, p. 370.

Significance   The American occupation of Japan was a unique historical experiment in that a victorious power in a major war successfully carried out humane and democratic reforms for a defeated enemy nation. Only history will be able to show the ultimate success of SCAP's gigantic institution-building efforts in Japan. Appreciating Japan's modern and democratic potential, SCAP, in essence, attempted to remove hindrances to Japan's democratic growth, and encouraged changes conducive to such growth. SCAP did not attempt to impose the American system of government on the reluctant Japanese people. The willingness of the Japanese people to cooperate with the occupation was an additional asset. Not all the SCAP reforms were successful, however. As SCAP focused increased attention on economic recovery and the rebuilding of Japan as a major ally in Asia against world communism, it felt compelled to permit many of the old leaders to revive their activities, and acquiesced to the rise of new business leaders holding heavy concentrations of wealth and influence, reminiscent of the pre-war zaibatsu leaders. Another SCAP reform which experienced reversal involved local autonomy. The power of the national government to manage local affairs has been increasing in Japan. On the whole, however, SCAP's reform efforts must be regarded as a success.

Soft State   A characterization of many Third World nations that are weak and ineffective, and unwilling to execute programs needed for national development. The concept of soft state has been attributed to the Swedish social scientist Gunnar Myrdal (Myrdal, Gunnar. *Asian Drama*, 3 vols. New York: Random House, 1968). According to Myrdal, the government of a soft state lacks the will to develop. While it proclaims the need for radical social change, it emphasizes the need to preserve the traditional culture and maintain ethnic integrity. This conflict makes the government of a soft state unwilling to use its authority to enforce the necessary compliance to proposed policies for radical change. In the soft state, radical institutional reforms such as land redistribution are instituted, but often become watered down with numerous exceptions and loopholes to appease particular elites, thus seriously negating their original intent. *See also* MILITARY REGIME, p. 290; PRISMATIC SOCIETY, p. 316; TRANSITIONAL SOCIETIES, p. 323.

Significance   The theory of soft state maintains that the postcolonial states have often proven to be too weak for their much needed nation-building and development efforts, in part because of the existence of cultural diversity, the prevalence of traditional power groups, the lack of governmental legitimacy, and selfish factionalism. According to this line of argument, what is needed to implement serious national development programs is strong government. Due to the lack of a democratic tradition, however, a strong government often results in an authoritarian or totalitarian form of government. The question still remains on how best to both mobilize the people and exact the kind of obedience needed to ensure participation in the various development programs.

Taisho Democracy   The liberal period in prewar Japan which coincided with the reign of Emperor Taisho (1912–26). During the Taisho Democracy, the cabinet was made responsible to Diet majorities while party representation in the cabinet was substantially increased. In fact, this so-called "democracy" period extended beyond the reign of Emperor Taisho, lasting until 1932. The Meiji constitution (1889) provided a two-house Diet (legislature) and structurally provided for the cabinet or parliamentary form of government. Given the extensive imperial power of appointment, however, the emperor and his close personal counselors selected prime ministers regardless of their party strength in the Diet. In 1913, party members in the Diet refused the prime minister appointed by the emperor and succeeded in forming a cabinet which was representative of the Diet's majority party. At the time, the *Seiyukai* (Friends of Constitutional Government) and the *Kenseikai* (Association for Constitutional Government), renamed *Minseito* (People's Government Party), were most active and their leaders alternated as prime ministers.

There were other political changes during this period. The franchise was extended in 1925 to cover all adult males. Radical ideas and labor movements also spread. An expanding middle class and an urban population increase became significant factors in the political process. Through their financial support of the parties, business interests also became more politically influential. This was politically a hectic and uncertain period for Japan. Both liberal and ultranationalist political currents were at work, and the proponents of ultranationalist thought were as numerous and active as the liberals. An attempt was made at party government, but it was unable to control various power factions, and was powerless to meet both domestic and international challenges. Furthermore, most Japanese felt that the parties were ultimately controlled by the *zaibatsu* (big business combines) and were merely serving their interests. Eventually, it was the military that came to dictate the government and, culminating in January 1937, the cabinet of General Hayashi Senjuro was composed of all military men and professional bureaucrats. The depression of party politics further worsened during Japan's war with China later that year. Finally, in 1940, all the political parties dissolved themselves and joined the Imperial Rule Assistance Association, which was officially inaugurated on October 12. *See also* MEIJI RESTORATION, p. 310; MILITARISM: JAPAN, p. 284; SCAP, p. 318; ZAIBATSU, p. 258.

Significance   The Meiji constitution provided for a two-house legislature—the House of Peers and the House of Representatives. Because the former was appointive, the House of Representatives became the only constitutional organ where popular representation in the government was possible. Political parties were organized; representatives were elected by the voters. Within the Meiji constitution, however, the Diet was never meant to be an effective decision-making body.

The Taisho Democracy period was an interlude in prewar Japanese political development, but it reflected a myriad of socioeconomic and political changes which had taken place in Japan since the Meiji Restoration (1868), in part, reflecting the cumulative effects of the Meiji reforms. Compulsory education increased the literacy rate while mass communications and media flourished. Japan also made impressive progress in other areas of development, such as urbanization and industrialization. The Gross National Product increased from 1,997 million yen in 1900 to 11,845 million yen in 1920. The electorate was larger and more politically vigorous. Universal manhood suffrage was put into effect in 1925.

Internationally, Japan extricated itself from an unfavorable position in relation to the West and managed to rise to the status of an imperial power with its colonial possessions, including the island of Taiwan (Formosa), the Pescadores, and Sakhalin south of the fiftieth parallel, and the peninsula of Korea. Japan also enjoyed "most favored nation" status with China as did the western powers. During World War I, Japan fought on the side of the western allies and became closely related to these powers, welcoming western influence. Radical political ideas and labor movements spread. If it was a period of democracy in Japan, it was also a period of uncertainty, generating the rise of many ultranationalistic groups within the military and throughout the country as a whole. Young military officers, mostly from depressed rural families who had been severely affected by the Great World Depression, were most dissatisfied with the Democracy Period. They advocated business reforms and political reorganization, refusing to accept the second power status accorded Japan at the Washington and London disarmament conferences (1922, 1930). Their political agitations and their eventual rise to power terminated Japan's fragile experiment with the parliamentary system of government developed by the Meiji constitutional framework of the pre–World War II period.

Traditional Societies   Societies which in their idealized setting are structurally characterized as predominantly rural, agrarian, illiterate, familial, and primary in interpersonal relationship. In traditional societies, the social, economic, and political structures and dynamics are justified as either the will of God, or supernatural forces beyond the dictates of human endeavors. Therefore, traditional individuals are said to be passive, fatalistic, and conformist. Politically, transitional societies emphasize rudimentary organizational structures, in which roles are performed in a diffuse manner by ascriptively chosen individuals and their family members. These chieftains rule their politically dependent people as their own subjects. In reality, the idealized traditional society exists nowhere. However, traditional and modern characteristics exist together in varying proportions, depending upon the level of development and modernization present. Consequently, the more traditional a society is, the more predominant are values and practices associated with traditional society. *See also* DEVELOPMENT, p. 297; MODERNIZATION, p. 313; PARTYLESS GOVERNMENT: NEPAL, p. 249.

Significance   Traditional societies are non-modern societies. Beyond this general characterization, all similarities cease since such diverse societies are beyond simple definition. Among the societies that could be classified as traditional are: the tribes of camel herders in the Arabian desert; the remote villages of the Asian continent; and the imperial, highly sophisticated civilizations of Manchu China and Ottoman Turkey. Characteristics attributed to traditional societies are usually residual in that they are negatively defined. Just as modernity is perceived as dynamic, traditionalism is regarded as sluggish or inert. The fact, however, is that much change has taken place in traditional societies. Indeed, there are many accounts of the rise and fall of empires and civilizations, and of dynastic change. These changes in traditional societies, however, have not been able to produce qualitative, progressive transformations in the lives of people.

Transitional Societies   Societies in flux with changing demographic, economic, and political patterns as well as changing fundamental attitudes and values. For the purpose of classification, societies in the rapid, often revolutionary, process of development and modernization are called transitional societies, and all Third World countries, including those in Asia, are in this sense transitional societies. They are, in general, characterized by an uncertain or dysrhythmic mix of traditional and modern socioeconomic and political characteristics; their true identities are not yet securely established.

Politically, transitional societies are often structurally modern, but their various and often elaborate institutions, government or otherwise, have not performed the same functions that their counterparts in modern societies have. In these societies, legislative, judicial, and executive-administrative institutions are not adequately checked and balanced; they tend to be dominated by a supreme leader or an oligarchy. Institutions that aggregate and articulate political demands, such as political parties and interest groups, are most likely organized to serve the interests of a limited number of individuals. Popular input into decision making is highly limited, and transitional political systems have been characteristically unstable, showing an increasingly authoritarian tendency. Furthermore, the military has become the most dominant political group in these societies. *See also* DEVELOPMENT, p. 297; MILITARY AUTHORITARIANISM, p. 289; MODERNIZATION, p. 313; PRISMATIC SOCIETY, p. 316.

Significance   All the Third World Asian states can be classified as transitional societies in that they are in the transitional process from a pre-modern way of life. Because any transitional process is unsettling, people are inevitably dislocated from their traditional and accustomed way of life. Seldom is a transitional process systematic and harmonious. The process affects people differently and causes conflict between different people and groups—the old and young, the educated and uneducated, the rural and urban, the industrial and agricultural, the westernized and traditional, the rich and poor, and the elite and mass. Various new political and socioeconomic demands outpace the government's capability to meet them. The result of these many factors in simultaneous operation entails political instability, repression, and violent change in government, often leading to a military coup, and/or a communist assumption of power.

7. Diplomacy

Anzus   A treaty organization, officially named the Tripartite Security Treaty Between the Governments of Australia, New Zealand, and the United States. The ANZUS treaty was signed on September 1, 1951 and became effective April 29, 1952. The purpose of the ANZUS treaty was to provide for collective response to a threat in the Pacific area. ANZUS was concluded in combination with the peace settlement with Japan following World War II. It was meant to be part of a network of United States-supported mutual security arrangements in the Pacific. Unlike other security systems developed after World War II, ANZUS did not have a headquarters or permanent staff. Its only political body was the ANZUS Council, convened by its foreign ministers or their deputies. The Council was expected to meet at least once each year.

ANZUS illustrated the changing geopolitical character of the Southwestern Pacific and Southeast Asia. Prior to World War II, Great Britain would have been expected to protect Australia and New Zealand from foreign threat. In the postwar period, however, Britain no longer possessed capacity for such defense, and the burden devolved upon the United States. Australia and New Zealand acknowledged their commitment to the United States by joining with it in the formation of the Southeast Asia Treaty Organization in 1954. From a geostrategic vantage point, therefore, Australia and New Zealand were intimately related to events on the Asian rimland.

But events in the South Pacific were of more immediate interest to ANZUS in 1984–85. A radical and repressive regime in Tuvalu and violent disturbances in French-administered New Caledonia, posed potential threats to Australian national security. Moreover, Soviet naval activity in the region had increased, and Cuban advisors were reported operating on Tuvalu. The seriousness of the situation in New Caledonia precipitated the visit in January 1985 of France's President François Mitterrand. New consideration, therefore, was given to Australia's defense posture, and debate focused on the following areas: (1) Australia must establish air and naval superiority in the Eastern Indian Ocean, with bases stretching from Cockburn Sound to Northwest Australia (this would provide a link with American, French, and South African naval and air power); (2) Australia must assume reponsibility for Oceania, an expanse of the South Pacific from Papua New Guinea, through the Solomon Islands, Vanuatu, and Fiji down to New Zealand (this arrangement would link up with American military power in the Philippines); and (3) Australia must have intimate military, economic, and political relations with the ASEAN nations, especially Indonesia. *See also* ASSOCIATION OF SOUTHEAST ASIAN NATIONS (ASEAN), p. 326; DIEGO GARCIA, p. 12; INDIAN OCEAN, p. 22; SINO-VIETNAMESE CONFLICT, 1979– , p. 409.

Significance   Australians and New Zealanders need not be reminded how close the Japanese came to their shores in World War II. During that conflict the United States, not the British, aided in the defense of Oceania. ANZUS predated the establishment of the Southeast Asia Treaty Organization and the Central Treaty Organization. Those organizations were also concerned with the defense of the Asian rimland, but they did not fulfill expectations. Despite formal structures, permanent and skilled staffs, and the infusion of considerable resources, they lacked a harmony of interest. Differences between the U.S. and New Zealand in 1985 also seemed to threaten the integrity of ANZUS. U.S. nuclear naval forces have been denied the use of New Zealand ports.

Nevertheless, in the absence of a comprehensive Pacific security system, the ANZUS treaty still serves as a vehicle for political-strategic consultation. ANZUS members responded to American requests in the early stages of the Indochina War and sent symbolic contingents. More recently, the member states registered concern over growing Soviet naval presence in the South Pacific, and especially Moscow's use of the American-built base at Cam Ranh Bay in Vietnam. ANZUS members have also reacted in unison to Vietnam's invasion of Kampuchea (Cambodia), and have steadfastly refused to recognize the regime of Heng Samrin. On another front, ANZUS publicly condemned the Soviet invasion of Afghanistan, and called upon other rimland states, such as those in the Association of Southeast Asian Nations (ASEAN), to enhance their collective defense.

Association of Southeast Asian Nations (ASEAN)   A regional cooperative organization, established on August 9, 1967. Its members include Indonesia, Malaysia, Philippines, Singapore, Thailand, and Brunei. The purpose of ASEAN was primarily economic development and technical assistance. ASEAN was somewhat influenced by the performance of the European Common Market, organized in 1957, and it sought to promote collaboration, cooperation, and mutual assistance. ASEAN has developed projects and programs in a variety of fields, but stresses economic, social, cultural, scientific, and administrative activity. It continues to make progress in agriculture, industry, and trade, and it has encouraged schemes aimed at improving communication and transportation among the member states.

The principal organs of ASEAN are the ASEAN Heads of Government Council, the Ministerial Meeting, the Standing Committee, a variety of other permanent and ad hoc committees, and the Secretariat with its headquarters in Jakarta, Indonesia. ASEAN was the culmination of strenuous efforts by the noncommunist states of Southeast Asia to promote regional cooperation. The forerunner of ASEAN was the Association of Southeast Asia (ASA) which was created in 1961 by Thailand, the Philippines, and Malaya (Malaysia). Another organization known as MAPHILINDO was assembled in 1963 by the same three countries at the urging of Indonesia. Changes in the government of Indonesia in 1966, however, opened the way for a more expansive organization, and ASEAN was the direct result of all these efforts.

ASEAN permitted Japan, New Zealand, and Australia to sit in on the deliberations of the organization, but they were not invited to join. In 1975–76, following the North Vietnamese victory over South Vietnam, ASEAN members attempted to draw Vietnam as well as Cambodia (Kampuchea) into their association. Both communist states declined the invitation, and together with the Soviet Union, they condemned the organization as an instrument of the "imperialist" Americans. ASEAN, therefore, settled to the task of becoming a noncommunist organization, concerned not only with regional, but also intercontinental and global issues. Following the Vietnamese invasion of Kampuchea in 1979, and the establishment of a government there favorable to Hanoi, Vietnam modified its policy and sought a dialogue with ASEAN. In 1983–85, however, ASEAN decided to sustain the noncommunist world's semi-isolation of Vietnam. It also joined with a majority of the world's nations in refusing to recognize the Vietnamese-supported Kampuchean regime of Heng Samrin. *See also* ANZUS, p. 325; ONE PARTY VASSAL STATE: KAMPUCHEA (CAMBODIA), p. 242; SOUTHEAST ASIA TREATY ORGANIZATION, p. 360.

Significance On-going oversight of ASEAN projects is the responsibility of the Standing Committee, consisting of the foreign minister of the host country, the ambassadors accredited to that country from the member states, the ASEAN directors general, and the organization's secretary general, who serves a two-year term. ASEAN has also launched an ASEAN Finance Corporation which makes capital available for industrial projects. ASEAN, however, has been preoccupied with the Vietnamese occupation of Kampuchea. Members have called for the establishment of a UN presence in the country and for Vietnamese withdrawal. It later joined with China in supporting the Pol Pot/Khieu Samphan Khmer Rouge regime, over that of the Vietnamese-installed and Soviet-backed Heng Samrin. The United Nations International Conference on Kampuchea established a seven-country committee in 1981 which included ASEAN members Malaysia and Thailand. The Conference was empowered to begin discussions with all the parties.

In 1982, ASEAN foreign ministers condemned Vietnam for endangering regional peace and declared they would continue to pressure the Vietnamese to pull their troops out of Kampuchea. As in the Soviet invasion of Afghanistan, the Vietnamese ignored the demand. The continuing Vietnamese presence in Kampuchea and its direct impact on Thailand has turned ASEAN attention from development to politico-military concerns. The organization's "neutrality" therefore has ebbed and waned. Moreover, given the large Soviet naval presence at Vietnam's Cam Ranh Bay, the United States perceives ASEAN countries as vulnerable to Soviet/Vietnamese power. In 1984, Washington talked openly about the plight of Thailand as a front-line state; but it was even more concerned with the security of the Philippines, the site of major U.S. naval installations in the Western Pacific.

Bandung Conference   Otherwise known as the Asian-African Conference, this assembly was heralded as the first international meeting of nonwhite nations. The juxtaposition of white and nonwhite rekindled the memory of imperialism, and the subordination or outright enslavement of non-European people by Europeans. The post–World War II period witnessed the decline of western colonialism, and hope for its total abandonment. Regained cultural pride in the nonwhite nations intertwined with a strong sense of nationalism, and the heretofore subservient people of the world sensed a new and influential future. This was certainly the case when Ali Sastroamidjojo became prime minister of Indonesia.

At the first meeting of the newly formed Colombo powers, Sastroamidjojo proposed the holding of an international conference confined to nonwhite people. The idea was an instant success, and on April 18–24, 1955, 29 Asian and African states participated in this first-ever conference in Bandung, Indonesia. Southeast Asia was the best represented, with only Malaya and British Borneo absent. But the leaders of the important new Asian states were in attendance, including

Sukarno of Indonesia, Nehru of India, Zhou Enlai from China, Carlos Romulo from the Philippines, Pham Van Dong from North Vietnam, and Norodom Sihanouk from Cambodia. The Bandung Conference gave the Asians a voice in the contemporary world, and as an acute observer remarked, a "claim to a place in the counsels of the nations." Bandung marked the end of white superiority and set a course which Asians have pursued ever since. *See also* PANCH SILA, p. 109.

Significance   At the Bandung Conference, *Panch Sila,* or Five Principles of Peaceful Coexistence, were developed. A joint effort of the Indonesia, Chinese, and Indian delegations, it is best remembered for the positive relations projected between China and India. Peaceful coexistence between Afro-Asian countries signified non-interference in each others' domestic affairs as well as recognition of their independent status. Bandung made it possible to attempt the settlement of many old differences. Indonesia and China, for example, signed a Dual Nationality Agreement in which China waived an historic claim that argued all racial Chinese, irrespective of domicile, were national Chinese. Generally speaking, Asians realized a capacity to work together at Bandung, and by so doing, they were convinced that their security and prosperity could be guaranteed. India and China, therefore, proclaimed their brotherly relationship.

Other countries endeavored to build cooperative organizations, and most seemed to suggest that rivalry between Asian states was a thing of the past. It is striking to note how quickly the euphoria faded, however, and how intensely Asians battled one another. The Sino-Indian dispute which erupted in 1959 could not be contained, and the *Panch Sila* they spoke of so glowingly in Bandung, disappeared with their border war of 1962. Southeast Asia, especially Indochina, was plunged into even darker recesses in the 1960s. It would be simple to attribute Asians fighting Asians to something engineered by the western nations, particularly the United States. Although there is much to be said about European and American intervention in Asia after Bandung, it can also be said that Asians quickly lost, or ignored, the lessons experienced there.

Cabinet Mission   A British effort aimed at maintaining the unity of India. On February 19, 1946, Prime Minister Clement Attlee announced the formation of a high-level delegation that would proceed to India for the purpose of pressing the development of an Indian constitution that might sustain the unity of the country after British forces withdrew. The assignment became known as the Cabinet Mission and it included Lord Pethick Lawrence, secretary of state for India, Sir

Stafford Cripps, president of the Board of Trade, who had failed in a similar 1942 effort, and A. V. Alexander, first lord of the admiralty. The Cabinet Mission arrived in India on March 22, 1946 and immediately found a hostile environment. Nevertheless, it settled to its task, arranging interviews with all the key political leaders. Upon completing this phase, the Cabinet Mission began its discussions with the top Muslim League, Sikh, and Congress leaders. The Congress insisted it would not accept an independent Pakistan, or two constituent assemblies.

According to Mahatma Gandhi, the "two nation theory" of the Muslim League was absurd. No division of India could be contemplated, let alone discussed. The Sikh leaders told the Mission that they would support a united India, but if independence was granted the Muslims, they too would demand their own national state. The Muslim League, led by Mohammad Ali Jinnah, held to the Lahore Resolution of 1940, and its call for the establishment of an independent Muslim state or states. Frustrated, the Cabinet Mission decided to draw up its own plan, which it presented to the parties on a take-it-or-leave-it basis. After considerable bickering by all the principles, the Muslim League announced on June 6, 1946 that it accepted the Cabinet Mission scheme. However, in the event of a breakdown of the constitution-making process, it left itself the option of establishing Pakistan from the Muslim-dominant provinces. The Congress leaders reluctantly agreed to join the constituent assembly, but they refused to join the Interim Government because the Muslim League had been given a substantial role in it. The Cabinet Mission noted this failure before leaving for England on June 29, 1946. The Cabinet Mission's work was over, but the problems it sought to address continued to fester. *See also* KASHMIR DISPUTE, p. 386; LAHORE RESOLUTION, p. 97; TWO NATION THEORY, p. 128.

Significance   The Cabinet Mission was Great Britain's last effort at mediating the dispute between the Muslim League and Indian National Congress. The unity of India depended upon the capacity for compromise between the major parties. Their bitterness toward one another, however, intensified suspicions and accelerated the movement toward partition of the subcontinent. The British contributed to the collapse of the Mission when the Muslim League declared its willingness to form the Interim Government even if the Congress refused to join. Lord Wavell, the British viceroy in India, declined that offer and again asked the Congress to assume the responsibility. After protracted bickering, Jawaharlal Nehru assembled the government, and later, five Muslim Leaguers also joined the cabinet. Despite this apparent achievement, the work of the constituent assembly broke down when the Muslim League refused to participate. Thus on February 20, 1947 Prime Minister Atlee, noting the intransigence of the parties, declared his government's intention to take matters into its own hands. The British government would decide whether India would remain unified or be partitioned into separate sovereign states.

The Muslim League leadership followed with a call for Direct Action in the formation of Pakistan. Communal rioting among Hindus, Muslims, and Sikhs intensified, however, and the authorities were hard pressed to maintain law and order. Given their precarious situation between the hostile communities, the British decided to leave India a year earlier than forecast. Lord Louis Mountbatten replaced Wavell as viceroy, and he hastily arranged for the partition of the country. The Cabinet Mission, like those before it, had failed. Pakistan was now a certainty, but its future remained clouded. Moreover, the legacy of partition caused fears and enmities to harden. Denied their Khalistan, the Sikhs blamed the Muslims for their plight and sought their revenge against the Islamic community. Although India and Pakistan gained their separate independence, each perceived the other as its number one enemy.

Carter Doctrine   An American policy statement precipitated by the collapse of the Shah of Iran's regime, and the Soviet invasion of Afghanistan, both occurring in 1979. The abolition of the Iranian monarchy by the revolutionary government also brought the termination of Iranian-American relations. Washington had placed its confidence in the Shah's armed forces and their ability to defend the Persian Gulf, and its precious petroleum reserves. That confidence evaporated with the change in governments, and the United States considered the possibility of intruding its own forces into the area. United States naval forces from the Pacific and Mediterranean fleets were dispatched to the Indian Ocean in proximity to the Strait of Hormuz. The United States also began assembling a Rapid Deployment Force for ready assignment in the region if the occasion warranted such action.

The Soviet invasion of Afghanistan in December 1979 was believed to be related to the instability in Iran, in the wake of the revolution. Soviet land and air forces were strategically positioned only a few hundred miles from the entrance to the Persian Gulf. Moreover, Soviet presence in Afghanistan extended the Iranian-Soviet border to almost 2,000 miles (3,200 kilometers), making the Communist superpower Iran's most immediate neighbor. Observing the mounting threat to Western security interests, President Carter declared America's intention to resist a possible Soviet move against the oil fields of the Persian Gulf. In his State of the Union address on January 23, 1980, Carter noted: "An attempt by any outside force to gain control of the Persian Gulf region will be regarded as an assault on the vital interests of the United States of

America, and such an assault will be repelled by any means necessary, including military force."

Ayatollah Khomeini and his legions had dramatized American weakness in the area. The seizure of the American embassy and its staff had given new urgency to the situation. Moreover, the invasion of Afghanistan followed within weeks of the embassy takeover. Observers believed that Moscow's action was timed to coincide with that incident because so much American attention was diverted to the hostage situation. Carter, therefore, went on record warning the Soviets that their actions would not pass unnoticed. The Afghanistan operation was described as the most aggressive Soviet maneuver since World War II, and Carter said that it posed a serious threat to peace. Fear that Iran was also on the Soviet hit list, and that Iran could not defend itself, revived the notion of the American police role, even if the Iranians wanted nothing of American protection.

Although U.S. government officials claimed that the president was only reemphasizing established policy, the declaration involved new foreign and national security policies. To prove its determination, the American administration obtained the use of military installations in Oman, Somalia, Egypt, and Kenya. Efforts to convince the Saudis that American forces should also be located in their country were not successful. But American military personnel were already in Saudi Arabia in large numbers as technicians and trainers. They were bolstered by American-flown AWACS (early warning aircraft). Saudi Arabia did request and was sold its own AWACS aircraft, as well as the most sophisticated fight-bombers in the U.S. Air Force. The Reagan administration perpetuated the Carter Doctrine and stepped up the deployment of American forces in the Indian Ocean region. It also expanded and accelerated the transfer of weapons to allied and associated states. *See also* DIEGO GARCIA, p. 12; INDIAN OCEAN, p. 22; NIXON DOCTRINE, p. 345; PERSIAN GULF, p. 33.

Significance　　　The Carter Doctrine appeared to merge the Truman, Eisenhower, and Nixon Doctrines. The United States again saw the prime threat to the West as coming from the Soviet Union. Although the Soviets had the logistic advantage, the Persian Gulf was of such vital concern that the United States could not stand idly by. The Iraqi invasion of Iran in September 1980, and the threat that it posed to the Persian Gulf did not activate the Carter Doctrine, however. The United States was still in the process of negotiating the release of its hostages in Tehran, and concern for Iran among Americans was nil. In fact, many Americans displayed support for Iraq, even though the Arab state was the aggressor and had entered into a treaty of cooperation with the USSR in 1972. Washington saw no connection between the Iraqi invasion of Iran and Soviet machinations in the region. Thus, the war did not seem to pose the same threat to the Gulf as the Soviet invasion of Afghanistan.

For the first three years of the war, the Gulf remained open to international shipping, and oil continued to move from the Gulf states to outer markets. The U.S., therefore, did not become embroiled in the conflict. At the same time, it did not withdraw its fleet from the mouth of the Gulf. In 1984, however, Iraq announced its decision to destroy all shipping involved in transporting Iranian oil. Iran, in retaliation, declared it would close the Strait of Hormuz if the Iraqis carried through their threat. The destruction by both belligerents of vessels engaged in innocent passage heightened tensions in the area, and compelled the Reagan administration to improve Saudi Arabia's defenses. The Carter Doctrine had yet to be tested, but Washington's performance led some observers to believe the United States was preparing for a showdown. Because Saudi Arabia was aiding Iraq in its war against Iran, the United States was also leaning toward Iraq. The question raised by these crosscurrents was, to what extent would U.S. condemnation of Iran and "support" for Iraq eventually drive Iran closer to the Soviet Union, the country the Carter Doctrine seemed most concerned with protecting from the Red Army's position in Afghanistan? Moreover, assuming a Soviet-Iranian rapprochement, could Saudi Arabia's oil fields be protected? Indeed, could the Saudi monarchy be sustained?

China (PRC)-Japan Normalization of Relations

On September 29, 1972, Chinese Premier Zhou Enlai (Chou En-lai) and Japanese Prime Minister Tanaka Kakuei, signed in Beijing (Peking) a joint communique normalizing relations between their nations. The communique stated, among other points, that (1) "The Government of Japan recognizes the Government of the People's Republic of China as the sole legal Government of China"; (2) "The Government of the People's Republic of China reaffirms that Taiwan is an inalienable part of the territory of the People's Republic of China"; (3) "The Government of Japan fully understands and respects this stand of the Government of China and adheres to its stand of complying with Article 8 of the Potsdam Proclamation"; and (4) "To consolidate and develop the peaceful and friendly relations between the two countries, the Government of the People's Republic of China and the Government of Japan agree to hold negotiations aimed at the conclusion of a treaty of peace and friendship."

Subsequently, a treaty of peace and friendship between the PRC and Japan was signed in Beijing on August 12, 1978. The treaty was to be in force for ten years, during which time both countries pledged to adhere to the Five Principles of Peaceful Coexistence: respect for sovereignty and territorial integrity, mutual nonaggression, noninterference in internal affairs, equal and mutual benefit, and mutual respect. Furthermore, the treaty reaffirmed the principle of nonhegemony by any nation in the Asia-Pacific region. Both the normalization of relations and the subsequent conclusion of a peace treaty ended a long process of reapproachment between the two big powers in Asia, and heralded a new power alignment in East Asia. *See also* SHANGHAI COMMUNIQUE, p. 355; SINO-JAPANESE WAR, 1937–45, p. 407.

Significance   Following President Nixon's historical visit to China in 1972, China invited Japan to discuss normalization of their relations. Japan speedily responded. Given an opportunity, Japan showed her willingness to act on her own, independently of the United States, in her relationship with China. For Japan, China is valuable as a supplier of raw materials and as a potentially huge market. For China, Japan could be a useful ally in resisting Soviet expansionism in East Asia. China could also use Japan's financial and technological resources for much needed modernization. Since normalization of their relations, Japan has become China's most important trade partner. After the normalization of relations between the two, Japan withdrew her diplomatic recognition of Taiwan. Her embassy and consular services in Taiwan, however, have been replaced by the Japan Interchange Association, a semiprivate, incorporated entity for coordinating economic and trade relations with Taiwan. This so-called "Japan Formula" was later followed by the United States. Neither Japan nor the United States have diplomatic relations with Taiwan, but both have maintained significant economic and trade relations with the country.

Colombo Plan   An organization whose full name is the Colombo Plan for Cooperative Economic and Social Development in Asia and the Pacific. It was established in January 1950 and its headquarters were in Colombo, Sri Lanka. The Colombo Plan has 20 regional members and six major donor nations. The regional members are: Afghanistan, Bangladesh, Bhutan, Burma, Fiji, India, Indonesia, Iran, Kampuchea (Cambodia), South Korea, Laos, Malaysia, Maldives, Nepal, Pakistan, Papua New Guinea, Philippines, Singapore, Sri Lanka, and Thailand. The major donor nations are: Australia, Canada, Japan, New Zealand, United Kingdom, and the United States. When the Colombo Plan was first formed, it was called the Colombo Plan for Cooperative Economic Development in South and Southeast Asia. The current name was adopted in 1977 to reflect the organization's broader commitment and operations. The Colombo Plan is essentially nonpolitical, focusing on economic development and social change. Its highest deliberative body, the Consultative Committee, consists of ministers from the member governments and meets annually. The Plan Bureau oversees all assistance, distributes information, and prints an annual report. Activities are usually divided into two categories: (1) capital aid; and (2) technical assistance. The United States has provided the largest portion of the more than 60 billion dollars spent by the organization since its inception. The Colombo Plan also supports a Singapore-based Staff College for Technician Education. *See also* ASSOCIATION OF SOUTHEAST ASIAN NATIONS (ASEAN), p. 326; SOUTH ASIAN REGIONAL COOPERATION (SARC), p. 358.

Significance   The Colombo Plan has established its credentials as a nonpolitical organization, concerned exclusively with improving the wellbeing of its members. In the 1980s Afghanistan, Iran, and Kampuchea (Cambodia) virtually suspended their membership in the organization, but the Plan avoided focusing on their predicaments. Efforts have been made to improve the Plan's efficiency, however, and projects involving a variety of member states have been discussed. As presently administered, members receive financial and technical assistance from major donors on a bilateral basis. The overall plan, therefore, is multilateral in approach but not in operation. Arrangements for assistance are made by the individual countries not the organization as a whole. Moreover, the United States has cajoled Japan into playing a larger role in financing projects connected with the Colombo Plan. Tokyo has indicated an interest in raising its financial commitment, and the Colombo Plan appears assured of continued success through the 1980s.

Dependency Relations   India's dependence on the Soviet Union. Soviet economic assistance to India has been important in several crucial areas. Indian enterprises built with Soviet assistance account for 80 percent of all Indian metalware production, 60 percent of all India's heavy electrical equipment, 70 percent of its oil production, and one-third of its production of refined oil. The Soviet Union is also responsible for 35 percent of India's total steel production, and one-fifth of its energy production. The further development of Soviet-Indian economic cooperation has been provided for in the long-term Program of Economic Trade, Scientific and Technical Cooperation, signed in New Delhi in March 1979. Under terms of this program, the Soviet Union will help in the expansion and modernization of metallurgical works in Bhilai and Bokaro in order to bring their overall production up to 10.5 million tons. The two countries have also undertaken a third iron and steel works at Vishakhapatnam, as well as an aluminum factory which was to operate on a product-pay back basis. *See also* ARMED FORCES: SOUTH ASIA, p. 268; INDO-SOVIET TREATY (1971), p. 340; SOVIET COLLECTIVE SECURITY PROPOSAL FOR ASIA, p. 362.

Significance   India has repeatedly chastised Third World countries, especially Pakistan, for allowing themselves to become dependent on the United States. It is important to note that India seems no less dependent on the Soviet Union. Indeed, India's military capability and use of sophisticated weapons is due primarily to its association with the Soviet Union. Soviet transfers of weapons technology has enabled India to assemble late-model Soviet military paraphernalia domestically, including some of the latest MIG aircraft. Pakistan's intimacy with the United States between 1954 and 1962 enabled Washington to penetrate the public and private sectors of Pakistan, but that relationship was abruptly altered after the Sino-Indian border conflict of 1962, and the Pakistani-Indian War of 1965.

Between 1965 and 1975 Pakistan and the United States drifted apart. The Americans imposed an arms embargo on Pakistan in 1965 which was officially lifted ten years later. Military assistance to Pakistan was not renewed until 1981, and even then the arms package was far smaller than that received by India from the Soviet Union. Moreover, the United States never developed the economic leverage in Pakistan that the Soviet Union achieved in India. It is a matter of argument which South Asian country has the greater dependency on a superpower, but the record seems to portray India as a far larger beneficiary of Soviet assistance. Indo-Soviet relations have been sustained over a 30-year period, virtually without interruption. Except for a brief moment in 1977–79, when the Janata coalition controlled the New Delhi government, and Prime Minister Morarji Desai publicized his government's intention to steer a middle course between the Soviet Union and the United States, India has never wavered in its association with Moscow, or its criticism of Washington.

Farakka Barrage Agreement   A November 1977 agreement between India and Bangladesh on the use of Ganges river water. The dispute had plagued the two countries, and earlier Indo-Pakistani relations, since independence. Although the issue had not been totally resolved, the agreement underlined the willingness of the parties to find an acceptable compromise. The Farakka dispute surfaced in the days of British colonialism with the need to keep the port of Calcutta open to commercial navigation. The silting of the Hoogli threatened to destroy Calcutta's utility, and hydrological experts recommended the diversion of Ganges water to flush the Hoogli channel. Difficulties arose with the partition of British India into two sovereign states. India was concerned with Calcutta's future, while just across the border in East Pakistan, Ganges river water was used for irrigating crops during the dry season. Each country feared the other's project would deeply wound their economies and threaten their populations.

In 1951 India commenced construction on the Farakka Barrage. It was to be linked with a 26-mile-long canal which would direct water into the Hoogli channel, reducing tidal wave frequency and intensity. The plan offered protection against annual flooding, and made transportation more convenient. The Pakistan government, however, argued that the Indian authorities could not proceed without consulting them. India, already bitter toward Pakistan, rejected the Pakistani claim, insisting that the Farakka Barrage project was an internal matter. Frustrated, Pakistan sought the assistance of the United Nations, and requested the assembly of an international team of scientists to investigate the problem. Declaring India to be in violation of international law, Pakistan argued that Ganges water should be shared equitably between the two countries. Moreover, Pakistan was in the process of developing its Ganges-Kobadak project and planned to irrigate two million acres of land in East Pakistan. The Farakka Barrage would not only destroy that project's effectiveness, according to the Pakistanis, it would also increase the annual flood hazard and cause the salinization of the soil, thus destroying the land's ability to bear crops.

While each side proceeded with its independent scheme, talks between the parties were encouraged. India could not convince Pakistan that its irrigation system would not be disturbed. This conflict raged between the two neighbors up to the time of the Pakistan Civil War in 1971. When India entered that war in December 1971 in support of a Bangladesh government in exile, New Delhi expected an end to the diplomatic skirmishing over Farakka. A Joint Rivers Commission was established between India and Bangladesh in 1972, and in 1974, before the opening of the Farakka Barrage, New Delhi said it was interested in a river-sharing agreement. An interim agreement along these lines was signed in April 1975.

The assassination of Bangladesh leader, Shaykh Mujibur Rahman, in August 1975, however, brought a new government to power in Dhaka, and Bangladesh-Indian relations quickly deteriorated. So too, the agreement on the sharing of Ganges water. Bangladesh publicized its dispute with India in world forums from the United Nations to the Colombo Plan. India was angered by this, and its position became more intransigent. It was not until the Indian elections of 1977 swept Mrs. Gandhi from office that the issue was again addressed. Prime Minister Morarji Desai emphasized the need to improve Indo-Bangladesh relations, and serious discussions on Farakka were again instituted. High level ministers from Bangladesh and India met at one level, while experts on river control discussed the engineering requirements. Differences between the parties were quickly narrowed and in September 1977 the two countries concluded both a short-term river-sharing agreement and a long-term comprehensive agreement. The total package was officially signed on November 5, 1977 in Dhaka. *See also* GANGES AND BRAHMAPUTRA RIVERS, p. 13.

Significance Politics either facilitates or impedes solutions to socioeconomic, and especially environmental, questions. Farakka is a classic example of a dispute materializing because of political factors, festering for those same reasons, and ultimately being resolved when there is no longer a need to press one's objective at the expense of the other. Following Mrs. Gandhi's return to office in the 1980 elections, however, Indian-Bangladeshi relations again became strained.

The tension between the two countries was evident in the meeting of the Joint Rivers Commission which convened in New Delhi in February 1980. Both countries declared their dissatisfaction with the 1977 Farakka agreement. All the old issues reappeared, and Bangladesh, in part because it sensed weakness before India, argued that Nepal should also be admitted to the deliberations. Nepal's potential as a source of cheap hydroelectric power, better water storage, and irrigation development, was cited by Bangladesh officials. Dhaka also rejected an Indian proposal to build a canal through Bangladesh territory. Bangladesh demanded that Nepal be admitted to membership on the Joint River Commission before further deliberations on the use of the river system. At this point India insisted that the matter was a bilateral affair, and rejected broadening membership on the Commission. As a consequence, the talks failed and all the old issues resurfaced. In October 1982 the leaders of Bangladesh and India met in New Delhi and a Provisional Agreement on sharing Ganges water was signed. Interestingly, Mrs. Gandhi's chief nemesis in Bangladesh, General Ziaur Rahman, had been assassinated in 1981. His successor, General H. M. Ershad, apparently was more agreeable to the Indian prime minister, but it was clear the problem would continue to persist.

In 1983, the River Commission arrived at a temporary agreement, valid through 1985. It specified that India would release water from the Tista River for use in Bangladesh. Under the terms of the agreement, Bangladesh was to receive 36 percent of the water in the dry season. India was to receive 39 percent, with another 25 percent remaining unallocated. Bangladesh continued to urge the development of a system of reservoirs in Nepal from which both nations could draw water in the dry season. India, however, continued to press for a link canal 200 miles long and half a mile wide that would start in Assam and cut through Bangladesh territory to West Bengal. Dhaka voiced its concern that such a project would force the resettlement of several million people, cause considerable environmental damage, and do great harm to Bangladesh's economy.

Geneva Accords (1954)   Agreement terminating French involvement in Indochina. Specifically referred to as the Final Declaration of the Geneva Conference, July 21, 1954, it noted the termination of hostilities in Indochina, as well as the agreement to withdraw and not reintroduce foreign forces. The Geneva Accords followed the French defeat in Indochina and the Paris decision to give up its quest for empire in Southeast Asia. The principal participants were: Vietnam, Cambodia, Laos, France, China, the Soviet Union, and the United States. The United States, however, refused to sign the final document. According to the terms of the Accords, the military demarcation line between the northern and southern regions of Vietnam was judged provisional and in no way constituted "a political or territorial boundary." No foreign bases were permitted in the region and the settlement of outstanding political problems was to be effected on the basis of "respect for the principles of independence, unity and territorial integrity."

The Vietnamese people were free to live according to democratic principles and free, general elections were slated for July 1956 under the supervision of an international commission. The elections were aimed at dissolving the military demarcation line and unifying the country. Discussions on election procedures were authorized to begin on July 20, 1955. In the meantime, all Vietnamese were to be given the opportunity to decide for themselves where they would reside. The Accords also specified that each member of the Geneva conference would respect the sovereignty, the independence, the unity, and territorial integrity of Cambodia, Laos, and Vietnam. *See also* DIEN BIEN PHU, p. 380; PARIS ACCORDS (1973), p. 351; SEVENTEENTH PARALLEL, p. 37.

Significance   The months following the signing of the Geneva Accords were full of intrigue. Almost 1 million Vietnamese moved their domicile to the southern portion of the dividing line, whereas less than 100,000 went north of the seventeenth parallel. The prevailing western view was that the Vietnamese wanted to escape the repressive actions of the Hanoi government. Indeed, there were rebellions against Communist authority. These were crushed with heavy loss of life and it confirmed in the minds of the Vietnamese living in the south, and especially their American supporters, that the scheduled 1956 elections should not be held.

The United States had not been pleased with the Geneva Accords, and in contravention of the Accords it gave full support to the Saigon government of Ngo Dinh Diem. Diem, a Roman Catholic in a predominantly Buddhist country, had become prime minister of Vietnam two weeks before the Geneva Accords were negotiated. Although residing in Saigon after the Accords, he continued to believe he would become the ruler of a unified Vietnam. Diem, however, was an unpopular figure, without power even in the countryside south of the seventeenth parallel. He had to contend with the entrenched interests of the Buddhist religious orders as well as the Communists. His decision to destroy the Buddhist organizations weakened rather than strengthened his administration. Moreover, the use of violence against the Buddhists drove the southern Vietnamese to consort and conspire with their northern brethren. Hanoi agents that had moved south with the thousands fleeing the north, drew these noncommunist dissidents into their camp. The Geneva Accords of 1954 became a dead letter, and Vietnam and all of Indochina moved toward an epic struggle.

Indian Ocean Commission   An organization established in 1982 to promote closer collaboration between Mauritius, Madagascar, and the Seychelles, all southwest Indian Ocean islands. The commission is responsible for coordinating national development programs, improving trade, and lending technical and financial aid. It is also meant to dramatize the independence of the island states and their determination to avoid big power embraces. Commission members have displayed keen interest in creating a common tariff policy but do not seem to agree on whether it would be advisable to draw closer to the Organization of African Unity or the South Asian Regional Cooperation (SARC) organization. *See also* INDIAN OCEAN, p. 22; POLITICAL PARTIES: MAURITIUS, p. 187.

Significance   Small states are especially concerned with compensating for their weakness by joining with other states in common endeavor. They are also aware that alliances, associations, or pacts with larger, more powerful states could be counterproductive, and possibly dangerous. The Indian Ocean Commission brings together island states with limited military potential, who do not covet each other's territory. Mauritius, Madagascar, and the Seychelles all share similar goals, and identify with what is generally described as socialist, "progressive" forces.

Indo-Soviet Treaty (1971)   Formally known as the India-USSR Treaty of Friendship and Cooperation, it was signed in New Delhi on

August 9, 1971. Although never represented as a mutual security treaty, Article 9 specified that "in event that any of the Parties is attacked or threatened with attack, the High Contracting Parties will immediately start mutual consultations with a view to eliminating this threat and taking appropriate effective measures to ensure peace and security for their countries." Although the Indian president publicly declared that the treaty advanced India's policy of nonalignment, others were skeptical. Some of India's newspapers interpreted the treaty as affirming India's role in a Moscow-sponsored plan to establish a collective security system in Asia. At the very least, the treaty formalized the relationship between the two powers and intensified interaction between their military establishments. It is important to note that the United States had attempted a similar relationship but had been rebuffed by the Indian government. It was, therefore, the opinion of some observers that India had moved alongside, even if it had not joined, the Soviet bloc. *See also* DEPENDENCY RELATIONS, p. 335; NONALIGNED MOVEMENT, p. 348; PAKISTAN-INDIA WARS, p. 398.

Significance   India's sense of isolation, its fear of being an island in a Muslim sea, contributed to the decision to join the Soviet Union in signing the Treaty of Friendship and Cooperation. Also true to its peculiar interests, India's leaders seemed to concur that the country would be more secure by cementing friendly ties with Moscow. It saw no purpose in playing the American game of containing Soviet power and influence. Indeed, the latter approach, in the opinion of New Delhi, would have the reverse effect of assuring Moscow's bellicosity. In other words, India wanted to demonstrate to its near neighbor that it meant it no harm and that together they could establish an equilibrium in the region. Moreover, China was both an enemy of India and a friend to Pakistan, which was judged India's number one enemy.

Given Henry Kissinger's secret mission to China via Pakistan in 1971, New Delhi feared that the United States was about to form a Washington-Beijing-Islamabad Axis, and that India's security was jeopardized by these developments. Pakistan was also in an exposed position in 1971, bogged down in a bitter and costly civil war in East Pakistan. The Indian decision to intervene in that war on behalf of the Bengalis and against Islamabad, was obviously bolstered by the pledge of support from Moscow. India's invasion of East Pakistan and its attacks and bombardment of West Pakistan in December 1971, came less than five months after signing of the Indo-Soviet treaty. During debate in the United Nations Security Council, the Soviet Union supported India's invasion of East Pakistan, and cast a veto when that body voted to require New Delhi to withdraw its troops. With the UN unable to gain compliance, and the United States and other powers reluctant to intervene, India was successful in dismembering Pakistan.

Japan-Korea Normalization of Relations   Reestablishment of diplomatic and other relations between Japan and the Republic of Korea (South Korea) in February 1965, ending the thorny relations that had existed between them since the liberation of Korea from Japanese colonialism in August 1945. Japan and South Korea signed a draft treaty in February 1965 calling for (1) immediate establishment of diplomatic and consular relations; (2) nullification of all treaties and agreements concluded between the two nations on and prior to August 22, 1910 when Japan annexed Korea as a colony; (3) reaffirmation of the Government of the Republic of Korea (South Korea) as the only lawful government of Korea, as specified in the 1948 resolution of the UN General Assembly; (4) cooperation between the two countries for the promotion of common welfare and interests in conformity with the principles of the United Nations Charter; and (5) further negotiations on trade, navigation, commerce, civil aviation, and other matters at the earliest practical date.

This draft treaty, together with a set of agreements, was subsequently ratified by both governments in August 1965. The settlements which were agreed upon by both parties at the time included: property claims and economic cooperation; fishery problems; the legal status and treatment of Korean nationals residing in Japan; and return of the Korean cultural assets that had been illegally taken to Japan. In South Korea, the government of President Park Chung Hee (Pak, Chŏng-hui) faced widespread demonstrations by students and political opponents who were against both the treaty and related documents, regarded as undue compromises of the hard-line positions identified with previous administrations. North Korea denounced the treaty as unlawful, because the treaty denied North Korea's claims of legitimacy. *See also* COLONIALISM: JAPAN, p. 66; PACIFIC WAR, p. 396.

Significance   Japan and Korea are geographically close neighbors, yet their relationship has historically been laden with conflict. Japan's colonization of Korea from 1910 to 1945 is still vivid in the memories of many Korean people, and is a source of their ill feelings toward Japan. In order to reach an agreement with Japan, President Park of South Korea had to compromise several hard-line issues of earlier administrations, particularly that of President Syngman Rhee of the First Republic. President Park settled for a fraction of the compensation originally sought by President Rhee from Japan and also modified the Rhee line (the median line drawn between Korea and Japan) to provide that Japanese fishermen would be given greater access to South Korean waters.

As finally agreed, Japan was required to pay $300 million in goods and services over a 10-year period as a means of settling South Korea's property claims. Japan also promised $200 million in low interest loans (at an annual interest rate of 3.5 percent, repayable over 20 years with a 7-year grace period). The fishery agreements, the most detailed and the longest, set "the 12 nautical miles from the baseline along its coasts" as the area of each country's exclusive jurisdiction. It also established a Korea-Japan Joint Fisheries Commission to enforce the details of conservation in the joint fishing areas and to resolve possible fishing disputes.

By the terms of the agreements, some 600,000 Korean nationals, and their second and third generation descendants in Japan, were to enjoy fully the rights entitled to permanent residents of Japan. Lastly, the Japanese government agreed to return to Korea those cultural assets identified and listed in the South Korean document presented at the time of agreement. Though these agreements did not cover all the areas of conflict, and Japan's territorial claims over the Tokto Islands in the Sea of Japan remained unsettled, they were regarded as satisfactory by the Park government, who wanted the Japanese capital necessary for South Korea's industrial development, as well as trade opportunities with Japan. Currently, Japan and South Korea maintain close diplomatic and economic relations.

Japan-United States Security Treaty   A treaty signed between the United States and Japan initially on September 18, 1951, in which Japan, mindful of its security needs, set up a provisional arrangement for its defense with the United States, allowing the latter to maintain its armed forces in Japan. The United States and Japan Security Treaty of 1951 was signed on the same day as the Treaty of Peace which Japan concluded with its occupation forces for the restoration of its full sovereignty as an independent nation. Because Japan had been demilitarized as a nation after its capitulation in World War II, its national security posed a special problem. Article I of the Security Treaty stated: "Japan grants, and the United States of America accepts, the right, upon the coming into force of the Treaty of Peace and of this treaty, to dispose United States land, air and sea forces in and about Japan. Such forces may be utilized to contribute to the maintenance of international peace and security in the Far East, and to the security of Japan against armed attack from without, including assistance given at the express request of the Japanese government to put down large-scale internal riots and disturbances in Japan, caused through instigation or intervention by an outside power or powers." This arrangement was to last until Japan was able to assume responsibility for its own defense, and until both the United States and Japan agreed that other alternatives, individual or collective security dispositions, existed for Japan.

Following ratification, both governments further concluded a mutual defense assistance agreement in 1954. In 1960, the United States and

Japan also concluded a Mutual Cooperation and Security Treaty to replace the 1951 Security Treaty. This new treaty granted the use of Japan's "facilities and areas" to U.S. land, air, and naval forces. After ten years in force, however, the treaty could be terminated by either party giving prior notice to the other. Today, although security arrangements have been periodically reviewed, the treaty still remains in force. *See also* KOREAN WAR, p. 388; PACIFIC WAR, p. 396; ZENGAKUREN, p. 260.

Significance   Following the war, Japan was not only demilitarized, but was also disallowed any military establishments other than a small self-defense force. Mindful of its national security needs, therefore, Japan was desirous of U.S. military protection when it regained its sovereignty as an independent nation. Given its global role as the leader of the Allied Powers and in view of the worsening international situation in East Asia accentuated by the Communist victory in the Chinese mainland in 1949 and the Korean War (1950–53), the United States was willing to satisfy Japan's desire and maintain Japan as a dependable ally in East Asia under its security umbrella.

The radical student organization, *Zengakuren,* was active in the crisis. Organized labor joined, carrying out a nationwide protest strike. The situation at the time was so critical that the scheduled visit of U.S. President Eisenhower to Japan had to be cancelled. The Japanese government of Prime Minister Kishi of the ruling Liberal-Democratic Party was also forced to resign. The crisis was unprecedented although the Liberal-Democratic Party had enough votes to force the ratification of the treaty through the Japanese Diet (Parliament). Following the ratification and the resignation of the Kishi government, the agitation subsided. The whole incident, however, has served as a reminder of the critical importance in politics of Japan's antiwar and antimilitary sentiment.

Although dictated by mutual needs, the United States and Japan security arrangements have been increasingly questioned both by political opposition to the ruling conservative party in Japan and by Japan's critical public who feared active involvement in the Cold War, by serving as a military base for the United States. Especially, when it came to the ratification of the 1960 treaty, the Japanese Socialists and Communists were able to mobilize Japan's antiwar sentiment, bringing anti-treaty sympathizers into the streets of Tokyo and other places, and waging massive, violent demonstrations in May and June 1960, thus creating the so-called *Ampo* (Security) crisis.

Korea-U.S. Mutual Assistance Agreement   A treaty signed on October 1, 1953 between the governments of the Republic of Korea (South Korea) and the United States agreeing, among other things, that the United States would support South Korea militarily if South Korea is attacked by a hostile power. The Agreement recognized that "an armed attack in the Pacific Area on either of the Parties in territories now under their respective administrative control, or hereafter recognized by one of the Parties as lawfully brought under the administrative control of the other, would be dangerous to its own peace and safety and declares that it would act to meet the common danger in accordance with its constitutional processes" (Article 3). The Agreement also states that "This Treaty shall remain in force indefinitely," unless either party notifies the other party to terminate it. The United States saved South Korea from a military takeover by Communist North Korea during the Korean War (1950–53). Since the Korean War, the American perception of security in Northeast Asia has included not only the protection of the territorial integrity of Japan but also that of South Korea. In pursuance of the Treaty, the United States has provided massive defense assistance to South Korea. The United States has also maintained its troops in South Korea as a deterrence to North Korea launching another armed invasion. The Agreement is still in force. *See also* ARMED FORCES: NORTH AND SOUTH KOREA, p. 265; KOREAN WAR, p. 388.

Significance   The United States came to the defense of South Korea in the Korean War. Since the Korean War, the American perception of security in Northeast Asia has drastically changed. The South Korea-U.S. defense pact, and a similar pact, were signed with the Philippines, Australia, New Zealand, Taiwan, and the Southeast Asian nations. For South Korea, the Treaty has played a vital security role. The United States has helped South Korea become one of the most heavily armed nations in the world. President Carter had planned a phased withdrawal of about 40,000 American troops stationed there, but the plan was suspended after an initial pullout of some 3,500 troops in 1978. The withdrawal was halted due to opposition from South Korea, Japan, and other international and domestic forces.

Nixon Doctrine   Initially referred to as the "Guam Doctrine," it was a statement by President Richard M. Nixon in July 1969 that the United States expected "friendly" states threatened by foreign or foreign-assisted aggression to play a greater role in their own defense. This doctrine was described in greater detail in the president's 1970 annual foreign policy message to the Congress. It was reiterated in his 1971 report to the legislative branch of government.

The Nixon Doctrine was prompted by several factors and conditions. First, the United States had paid a heavy price in the Indochina War, and opposition to that war in the United States had reached sizable proportions. President Nixon sought a reduction in American military commitments, had begun to withdraw American forces from Indochina, and was seeking a peaceful solution to the conflict. Vocal elements of the American public, as well as the Congress, demanded sharp curtailment of U.S. operations abroad, and a pledge that the government would avoid future Vietnam-like wars. Second, in 1968, the British declared an "East of Suez" policy which meant removing British military personnel from their positions in Asia and the Indian Ocean. British interests were more narrowly defined in terms of Europe, the Mediterranean, and the North Atlantic, thus requiring a much smaller military establishment. Countries heretofore dependent on British protection, however, were required to find other means for their defense. Third, the world of nations had undergone significant change. The Soviet Union was a recognized superpower with global as well as continental interests, with offensive as well as defensive capabilities. Moreover, several score of less developed nations described as Third World, had achieved their independence, and they now sought to avoid major power pressures. The Third World, however, was characterized by political instability, intense regional rivalries, and competing ideologies. No single power had the capacity to control the others.

In light of western retreat and Third World weakness, the Soviet Union was perceived as meddling in the affairs of newly independent countries, and the question was raised about their proper and adequate defense. The American answer supposedly was the Nixon Doctrine. In 1971 Nixon noted: "The postwar order in international relations—the configuration of power that emerged from the Second World War—is gone. With it are gone the conditions which have determined the assumptions and practices of United States foreign policy since 1945." This statement clarified American perceptions of the world and influenced the American role. The Truman Doctrine of 1947, which spoke of containing international Communism and attempted to deny Soviet and Chinese Communist activity in the Third World, was no longer feasible or realistic. The United States reiterated its commitment to friendly governments, but it also tried to establish a more manageable foreign policy. The Truman Doctrine had been criticized as being too idealistic, and the United States government was viewed as having stretched American capacities too far to be effective. The Nixon Doctrine was concerned with avoiding neoisolationism on the one side, while encouraging the United States' allies and client states to assume greater responsibility for their individual and collective defense on the other. In this way the United States hoped to bring its commitments into line with its real capabilities and genuine interests. *See also* CARTER DOCTRINE, p. 331; DIEGO GARCIA, p. 12; INDIAN OCEAN, p. 22.

Significance   The Nixon Doctrine is usually attributed to Henry Kiss-inger, Nixon's national security advisor and later secretary of state. Kissinger apparently convinced Nixon that the problem with the Truman Doctrine was its idealistic character. The United States had overcommitted itself, stretched its forces too thin, and intervened in areas where U.S. national interests were not clearly defined. The Indo-china war had been a great mistake, and the primary cause for that involvement was believed to be the policy framework established by the Truman Doctrine. Kissinger argued the necessity for choice, to better identify countries and regions of high priority in the struggle against perceived Soviet aggression. A key feature of this thinking was the weaker states' capacity to respond to threats with their own power.

Although the logic appeared sound, operationalizing the shift to the Nixon Doctrine was an entirely different matter. The relationship between national and international events was not fully explored, and Iran became a classic example of how not to support a friendly govern-ment. No country received more attention in executing the Nixon Doc-trine, or was more receptive. Indeed, no country seemed more willing to play the role outlined by Washington, but the Americans did not ade-quately examine the nature of Iranian society, or take seriously the multidimensional opposition to the Shah. The Nixon Doctrine involved the transfer and sale of great stores of sophisticated weapons to Tehran. But the construction of a formidable Iranian armed force could not thwart the regime's internal opposition; nor could it be used for that purpose. The Shah, in spite of his vaunted power, fled his country in 1979, never to return.

The Iranian revolution did significant damage to the Nixon Doctrine before it could be fully tested. When Ronald Reagan assumed the American presidency, he chose to follow a modified Truman Doctrine. The United States decided it had to stem the Soviet advance with its own forces. Reagan dispatched advisors to Central America, and stepped up joint military exercises with friendly regional countries. He also autho-rized support to counterrevolutionaries in the struggle against the Sand-inistas of Nicaragua. Reagan sent a marine "peacekeeping" force to Beirut, and before its withdrawal in 1984, an American naval flotilla off Lebanon's coast several times bombarded the hills around the Lebanese capital. Reagan also ordered the invasion of the Caribbean island of Grenada in 1983, and forcibly removed the Marxist-military regime that had taken power earlier. The buildup of U.S. forces in the Indian Ocean, and the deployment of improved intermediate ballistic and cruise mis-siles in western Europe, all pointed to a new version of containment from that forecast by the Truman Doctrine. It was also significantly different from that conceived by the Nixon Doctrine.

Nonaligned Movement   Nonalignment refers to those countries wishing to avoid intimate entanglements with the Soviet Union or the United States. Nonalignment is considered to be different from neutrality, which suggests a state of belligerence. The nonaligned nations insist that their purpose is to avoid becoming parties to the rivalry between the superpowers, and hence to skirt what was called the "Cold War." The nonaligned were on record as supporting neither superpower against the other. They wanted to avoid becoming dependent on either Washington or Moscow. Indeed, if they were successful in establishing another center of power, the nonaligned believed they could help reduce the probabilities of war between the United States and the Soviet Union.

The first conference of nonaligned heads of state was convened in Yugoslavia in 1961. Yugoslavia's president, Josip Tito, presided over the meeting attended by 25 heads of state. Tito, along with Gamal Abdul Nasser of Egypt and Jawaharlal Nehru of India were considered the three most prominent personalities behind the movement. To some extent Sukarno of Indonesia was also a principal. After their initial meeting, the Nonaligned Movement added more sophistication and a formal structure took form. With more and more nations joining the organization, it held meetings in Egypt (1964), Zambia (1970), Algeria (1973), Sri Lanka (1976), Havana (1979), and India (1983). The principal organs of the Nonaligned Movement are the Conference of Heads of State, the Meeting of Foreign Ministers, the Political and Economic Committees, and the Coordinating Bureau. There were slightly more than one hundred members in the organization in the 1980s, and the movement's most recent presidents were Fidel Castro of Cuba and Indira Gandhi of India. *See also* BANDUNG CONFERENCE, p. 328.

Significance   From its birth the Nonaligned Movement assumed an anti-West posture. In Algiers in 1973, the world's poorer nations were called upon to join in common cause against the industrialized states. The debate which started there carried into the United Nations where it became a growing demand for a New International Economic Order (NIEO). This development produced the first Conference on International Economic Cooperation which convened in Paris in 1975. The Nonaligned Movement had demonstrated power and influence and some member states decided the organization could be used for a variety of purposes, especially to challenge United States foreign policy, trading practices, and overall deportment with Third World nations.

By 1976 the Nonaligned Movement was an aggressive, political aggregation determined to exploit western weaknesses. Those member states that refused to follow the lead of the majority, however, were left to fight a rearguard action without significant success. The organization was dominated by personalities who, in attacking the Americans and

West Europeans, appeared to favor the Soviet Union and the communist bloc. Colonel Muammar Qadaffi of Libya was one outspoken figure who insisted on hurling invectives at the Western nations, citing their past imperialisms and present neocolonialism. He urged the Nonaligned to develop producers' associations in bauxite, copper, and aluminum, much as OPEC and OAPEC had done in petroleum.

In the 1979 meeting of the Nonaligned in Havana, Cuba, Fidel Castro, a proclaimed communist and ally of the Soviet Union (with his troops actively engaged in Angola and Ethiopia), assumed the presidency of the Movement. Castro was accused of bending the organization toward the Soviet bloc. President Tito, the spokesman for those resisting such tactics, struggled with Castro and his supporters, and was able to include the "nonbloc nature" of the Movement in the Final Declaration of Havana. The document also noted the organization's equal disdain for "hegemony" (a term used to describe Soviet expansion), as well as all forms of imperialism, colonialism, and neocolonialism. Nevertheless, the Movement did approve an Arab-supported statement that "Zionism was equated with racism." It also demanded the withdrawal of Turkish troops from Cyprus and American troops from South Korea. In general, it came out in favor of selective popular movements such as the Palestinian, and condemned Egypt for its unilateral peace treaty with Israel.

The next meeting of the Nonaligned Movement was slated for Iraq in 1982. However, due to the Iraq-Iran War the site was moved to New Delhi, India, where it met in 1983. Although some of the same efforts were made to turn the meeting into a tirade against the West, Indira Gandhi's chairmanship of the meeting prevented much of the acrimony experienced in Havana. Nonetheless, the Movement repeated its attack on the West and particular targets, such as Israel, received almost total condemnation. The Nonaligned Movement had originally been established as a forum for countries wishing to avoid becoming victims of Soviet-U.S. rivalry. The Movement also hoped to play a moderating role between East and West. Events, however, seemed to make these objectives impossible. Distinguishing between the aligned and nonaligned proved to be little more than an exercise in semantics.

Pakistan-United States Mutual Defense Agreement   Officially described in two documents, the Mutual Defense Assistance Agreement of May 19, 1954 and the Pakistan-United States Bilateral Agreement of Cooperation, signed on March 5, 1959, they form the basis for American-Pakistani relations. The first treaty signaled the transfer of military supplies to Pakistan, and pledged American support in maintaining the independence, integrity, and security of Pakistan. In return, Pakistan promised to accept American personnel, including military, on its soil. It also agreed to cooperate with the United States in challenging nations "which threaten the maintenance of world peace." The 1959 treaty was made necessary by events following the signing of the initial document. Pakistan joined the American-sponsored Baghdad Pact in 1955 (in 1954 it became a member of the Southeast Asia Treaty Organization), but in 1958 a military coup in Iraq severed that country's connection to the alliance. The other members of the Baghdad Pact, Pakistan, Iran, Turkey, and Great Britain, along with the United States, which held associate status but was not a signatory, affirmed their intention to sustain the organization.

At United States insistence, the Baghdad Pact became the Central Treaty Organization (CENTO) and the member states pledged to continue their support for one another. Insofar as the United States was not an official member of CENTO it agreed to enter into separate agreements with each of the parties, especially with Iran and Pakistan which were not associated with the North Atlantic Treaty Organization (NATO). Thus Pakistan and the United States signed their bilateral agreement of cooperation which specified that Washington regarded "as vital to its national interest and to world peace the preservation of the independence and integrity of Pakistan" and that appropriate military assistance would be made available to the South Asian nation. *See also* KASHMIR DISPUTE, p. 386; PAKISTAN-INDIA WARS, p. 398.

Significance   The 1959 bilateral agreement of cooperation between the United States and Pakistan is considered Washington's most binding commitment to Pakistan's security. Although all the treaties sought to bolster Pakistan against international communist threats, the United States could not avoid assuming other roles, such as assisting Islamabad in its conflict with New Delhi. When the United States found it could not aid Pakistan in its war with India in 1965, treaty commitments were brought into question. In the 1971 Indo-Pakistani War, the United States was only slightly more supportive, but even in that case it did not transfer needed weapons to the Pakistani armed forces, nor did it indicate a desire to send its own forces into the battle.

The United States argued that its support for Pakistan was confined to communist aggression. The United States did not believe itself committed to Pakistan's quest for control of Kashmir, and it refused to be drawn into a physical controversy with India. Therefore, President Lyndon B. Johnson imposed an embargo on arms supplies to Pakistan during the 1965 war, despite treaty commitments to Islamabad. India was hardly placated by the American action. Meanwhile, anti-Americanism in Pakistan reached a new peak of intensity. Nevertheless, the 1959 commitment remained. In 1979, the Soviet Red Army invaded

Afghanistan, and Pakistan's security was again a major question in Washington. A proposal to resupply the Pakistani armed forces was at first rejected by Islamabad, but after Ronald Reagan assumed the American presidency in 1981, a deal was quickly assembled. Washington justified the sale and transfer of sophisticated aircraft and other military paraphernalia to Pakistan by citing the terms of the 1959 bilateral agreement of cooperation, and by again stating the importance of sustaining Pakistan's independence and territorial integrity.

When Pakistan was accused by New Delhi of conspiring with Sikh separatists, Rajiv Gandhi (before becoming prime minister) threatened Islamabad with war. Pakistani authorities denied any involvement in India's domestic affairs, claiming New Delhi was merely externalizing its internal problems. But the U.S. ambassador in Pakistan was quoted warning India that his government would stand by its security commitments with Islamabad. The publicity given to this statement added fuel to an explosive condition that President Zia tended to neutralize when he declared three days of national mourning in Pakistan over the death of Indira Gandhi, and personally attended the funeral rites for the assassinated Indian leader.

Paris Accords (1973)   A last-ditch effort on the part of the United States to prevent the realization of the objectives forecast in the Geneva Accords of 1954. The United States played a major role in drafting the 1973 agreement, even though it refused to accept the terms of the earlier one. American troops had fought a long and arduous war against Communist Vietnamese forces, but the latter refused to yield despite high losses. By 1971, the American commitment to South Vietnam began to diminish and a systematic withdrawal had begun. Washington reiterated its belief that the South Vietnamese could defend themselves as long as the United States continued to supply the country with arms and economic assistance, but other observers were less sanguine. They noted the increasing isolation of the Vietnamese government of General Nguyen Van Thieu, and comparisons were made between his situation and that of Ngo Dinh Diem prior to his overthrow and murder in 1963. Thieu, like Diem, had attempted to concentrate power in his own hands, and his "victory" in the 1971 elections did little to boost his popular appeal.

By 1972, it was obvious that all American forces were to be withdrawn from Vietnam. Negotiations were underway in Paris to bring an end to the war in Indochina, but Washington accused the North Vietnamese of stalling on a final settlement. After stepped-up U.S. bombing raids on North Vietnam, as well as the mining of important northern port facilities, Hanoi returned to the bargaining table. On January 27, 1973,

the United States, North Vietnam, South Vietnam, and representatives of the Communist Viet Cong put their signatures to an
"Agreement on Ending the War and Restoring Peace in Vietnam." A
separate protocol was signed with regard to Cambodia which became
a principal theater of conflict. The United States wished to believe,
however, that the independent status of South Veitnam was assured
by the Paris Accords of 1973. *See also* GENEVA ACCORDS (1954), p. 339;
KHMER ROUGE, p. 166; SECOND INDO-CHINA WAR (1964–75), p. 401; SEVEN-
TEENTH PARALLEL, p. 37.

Significance   The Paris Accords of 1973 did not end the war nor make
South Vietnam more secure. Although President Richard Nixon
described the agreement as "peace with honor," the North Vietnamese
had merely bought time before their final assault on the south. The
United States, true to the terms of the Accords, removed its forces from
Indochina. The seventeenth parallel was again identified as the official
and legal dividing line between North and South Vietnam, although
those areas of South Vietnam occupied by the North, or falling under
the control of the Viet Cong, were to be left undisturbed. No new forces
were to be introduced into South Vietnam, but provision was made for
the replacement of North Vietnamese troops. The agreement also stipu-
lated that no new arms could be brought into the country; however,
replacements for consumed supplies were sanctioned. The South Vietnamese government was especially displeased with the Accords. All that
had been done, they argued, was to permit the United States to withdraw its forces without being fired upon. The treaty in no way terminated the hostilities, nor were those clauses concerned with troop
deployment and weapons shipments enforceable.
    Henry Kissinger and Le Duc Tho, the principal negotiators at Paris,
were to receive the Nobel Peace Prize for their work, but the war
continued to take a frightful toll. The South Vietnamese lost tens of
thousands of frontline troops in 1973 and 1974, and the Paris agreement
had done nothing more than usher in a new military phase in the
conflict. Thieu attempted to sustain his government, but his administration only proved more repressive. The pro-Western Cambodian government of Lon Nol was the first to crack, however. Troops deserted en
masse and joined with the Khmer Rouge. Thieu understood that Cambodia's fall signaled the end of his administration, and he, like Lon Nol,
made plans to flee the country.
    In 1975, the North Vietnamese and Viet Cong opened a campaign
against South Vietnam that was reported to be larger than the 1968 Tet
Offensive. By April, South Vietnam had been split in half, and the main
force of the South Vietnamese army was cut off from resupply. With
Vietnamese refugees crowding the roads, Saigon's soldiers refused to

follow the orders of their commanders. They threw down their weapons, tore off their uniforms, and joined the civilian population pressing toward Saigon. South Vietnam's collapse was sudden and total. Panic seized virtually everyone, and there was no longer any chance of rallying troops for a counterattack. Saigon believed that the Paris Accords specified that the United States would reconsider its options if North Vietnam violated the terms of the agreement and pressed the war further south. Washington, however, hesitated and then decided to do nothing. Thieu accused the United States of failing in its pledge to defend the South, but the North Vietnamese repelled the last defenders and seized Saigon and the rest of the delta. Vietnam was unified under Hanoi leadership. Laos became a vassal state of the Vietnamese. And after a brief honeymoon, Vietnam invaded Cambodia in 1979, defeated the Khmer Rouge, and installed a government of its own choosing. The Paris Accords of 1973 had made it possible for Hanoi to realize the objectives forecast in the 1954 Geneva Accords.

Rann of Kutch Arbitration   A territorial dispute yielding to principles and procedures of diplomacy, and conventional international law, as in the case when bitter enemies, namely, India and Pakistan, agreed to submit their territorial dispute to an international tribunal for arbitration. The territory under dispute was known as the Rann of Kutch, a barren marshland in southeastern Pakistan separating it from India. Today, the Pakistani province of Sind and the Indian state of Gujarat border on this vast wasteland that spreads over approximately 8,400 square miles. In ancient times, the region was a navigable lake. Its current form is said to be the result of a severe earthquake that struck the area in 1819. This last recorded cataclysm cut and blocked the main channel with the Indus River, causing the lake to dry up. The Rann's swampy appearance is a consequence of the annual monsoon which inundates the Rann for several months each year. The evaporation of water in the Rann leaves a salty residue which makes it unfit for cultivation or habitation. The changeable character of the Rann of Kutch made boundary demarcation difficult. No border between India and Pakistan was defined in this region in 1947. The Indian government, therefore, argued that the entire Rann belonged to the princely state of Kutch, and given its accession, the territory came under Indian sovereignty. The Pakistan government contested this interpretation, insisting the Rann north of the twenty-fourth parallel had been part of the British administration in Sind. Thus Pakistan was the legal successor to the territory. Pakistan also used a second argument. It declared the area a landlocked sea, and under international law the boundary separating the two countries ran down the middle. India refuted this explanation, asserting the Rann was a swamp or marsh, not a lake; hence the middle line did not apply.

Because of enmities between the two states over this and other questions, skirmishes were fought in the Rann of Kutch in 1947, and because the border issue could not be resolved, intense fighting broke out again in April 1965. Each side accused the other of precipitating the conflict. Each side had built police and army posts in the Rann, in territory supposedly claimed by the other. Notes were exchanged, and demands were made to vacate the territory, but neither side showed any interest in yielding its position. Pakistan called for high level talks to settle the matter. India's Prime Minister Lal Bahadur Shastri, however, refused to discuss the subject until the Pakistanis withdrew. The conflict threatened to deepen as it spread over a 60-mile-long front. India readied a parachute brigade, a heavy bomber squadron, and other ground units for what appeared to be a large campaign. But it did not commit them to battle, and Pakistan held the advantage on the desolate battlefield. New Delhi apparently had an eye on China, which had attacked across India's northeastern sector in 1962 and had entered into intimate relations with Pakistan.

The Chinese were perceived to be encouraging the Pakistanis to sustain the struggle. The Soviets, on the other hand, refused to take a position, and the United States deplored the fighting but refused to support either belligerent. The United Nations failed to become involved. Almost by default, Great Britain played a pivotal diplomatic role. Sensing that neither side wanted a further escalation of hostilities, British Prime Minister Harold Wilson, despite rebuffs, persisted in offering good offices to the warring parties. On June 27, 1965, these efforts were successful. The parties agreed to a ceasefire, and after successful ministerial talks, Islamabad and New Delhi allowed their dispute to go to a board of arbitration. It is one of the ironies of history that at the time of the signing of the ceasefire agreement, Indian and Pakistani forces were preparing for a far more intense conflict over the disputed northern state of Kashmir. Nevertheless, the Indo-Pakistan Western Boundary Case Tribunal met in Geneva in February 1966, and began its reading of the Rann of Kutch dispute. The arbitration panel completed its work in July 1967. In February 1968 it rendered its decision, giving 10 percent of the Rann to Pakistan and the remainder to India. Although some opposition to the award developed in India, the new government of Prime Minister Indira Gandhi accepted the decision of the arbitration panel. *See also* KASHMIR DISPUTE, p. 386; PAKISTAN-INDIA WARS, p. 398.

Significance   The Rann of Kutch arbitration demonstrates the positive side of the diplomatic method. It also suggests that states are capable of reconciling rival moral claims if there is the will to reach a peaceful settlement. It cannot be overlooked, however, that the territory in dispute was of little consequence to either side. Neither India nor Pakistan wanted a major conflict over the Rann, in major part because each side was preparing for a larger war in a region of greater importance, namely Kashmir. The Rann encounter was a preliminary skirmish between two aggressive enemies. The success of Pakistani arms in the Rann influenced their later behavior. The Pakistanis assumed the Indians could not match their military expertise and insisted that one Pakistani was as good as six Indians. Their success in the Rann battle may well have confirmed Islamabad's decision to strike in Kashmir. Pakistan, however, deceived itself into believing it was militarily superior to India. The Indians committed only token forces to the Rann fighting. From the character of the war that unfolded in September 1965, it is clear the Indian high command was determined to bring the war into the heartland of Pakistan. Hostilities would not be confined to Kashmir, or as had been done earlier, to the Rann of Kutch. Pakistan, therefore, drew the wrong conclusion from the skirmish in the swampland. By the same token, if India had put up stiffer resistance in the Rann, it is possible the September war may have been postponed, or perhaps not started.

Shanghai Communique (1972): China   A communique issued jointly by the United States and the People's Republic of China (PRC) in Shanghai following talks between Premier Zhou Enlai (Chou En-lai) and President Richard M. Nixon at the conclusion of the latter's historic visit to China in February 1972. In the Shanghai Communique, which served as the basis for establishing formal diplomatic relations between the two nations in January 1979, the two sides recognized "essential differences" in their social and political systems and in their foreign policies. They did agree, however, to conduct their relations in the future on the basis of "Five Principles of Coexistence." More specifically, these principles included (1) respect for the sovereignty and territorial integrity of all states; (2) nonaggression against other states; (3) noninterference in the internal affairs of other states; (4) equality and mutual benefit; and (5) peaceful coexistence. Beyond these principles, both sides also pledged to develop contacts and exchanges in such fields as science, technology, culture, sports, and journalism; to facilitate the progressive development of bilateral trade; and to stay in contact through various channels for concrete consultations to further the normalization of relations.

Regarding the thorny issue of Taiwan and the Nationalist government within the island intending to replace the Communist government of the Chinese mainland, the PRC reaffirmed its position that Taiwan is a province of China and that the "liberation" of Taiwan is China's internal affair and, therefore, all U.S. forces and military installations must be withdrawn from Taiwan. For its part, the United States acknowledged the oneness of China and the fact that Taiwan is a part of it. The United States also pledged that it would progressively reduce its military presence in Taiwan as tension in the area diminished. *See also* SINO-SOVIET SPLIT, p. 356; TAIWAN QUESTION, p. 366.

Significance   The Shanghai Communique constitutes a historical transformation in Sino-U.S. relations. From the time of Communist victory in the Chinese mainland in 1949 up until 1971, China (PRC) and the United States regarded each other as implacable enemies. Compounding their misperceptions and hostilities were U.S. aid to the Nationalist government exiled in Taiwan, and the PRC's aid to North Korea during the Korean War (1950–53). If the United States was concerned with possible Chinese Communist expansionism throughout Asia, the PRC was fearful of the American intent in its alliance with anti-Communist forces around its periphery.

Despite these troubled historical and acrimonious relations, the newly found friendship between the United States and the PRC which began in 1971 has led to the near elimination of political invective throughout the 1970s, and has born fruit in the establishment of a formal diplomatic relationship between the two in 1979. In this new relationship, both could benefit from the growth of trade and peaceful participation in the regional and global balance of power. However, differences concerning the future of Taiwan remain a problem.

Sino-Soviet Split   Break-up of the close ties which the Soviet Union and the People's Republic of China (PRC) had maintained since 1949, over deep-seated and wide-ranging issues that are ideological, historical, and geopolitical in nature. The long border that China shares with the Soviet Union has been disputed ever since the Chinese Communists came into power in 1949. Highly nationalistic, the Chinese Communists, under the leadership of Mao Zedong (Mao Tse-tung), were never comfortable with the Soviet Union, but needing help from the Soviet Union for its post-revolutionary development, China concluded a friendship treaty with the Soviets in 1950. In return, the Soviet Union wanted China to accept Soviet leadership and recognize the primacy of the Soviet Communist Party in the world Communist movement. Eventually, China determined that the price it was paying to the Soviet Union was too expensive, and not in its national interests.

Deciding to go it alone in its development Mao mobilized the masses for the Great Leap Forward (1958), against Soviet advice. It frustrated the Soviet blueprint for China's development. Both sides differed further on how to appraise the nature of the American threat. Their differences were accentuated when the Soviet Union refused to aid China in its confrontation with the United States in the Taiwan Straits (1958). The Soviet Union withdrew its experts from China and stopped all aid in 1960, publicly opening the rift with the publication of the CCP's anti-Soviet editorial, "Long Live the Victory of Leninism." In the 1962 border dispute between India and China, the Soviet Union sided with India. Their final parting came when the Soviet Union signed the Test Ban Treaty, thereby, according to the Chinese government, joining the Americans in attempting to obstruct its nuclear development. In the 1960s, different roles in the Vietnamese conflict exacerbated Sino-Soviet relations. The 1970s were marked by a growing strategic realignment during which time the Sino-Soviet conflict was globalized, and China developed closer links and strategic understandings with the United States. *See also* MAOISM, p. 101.

Significance   Inasmuch as the Soviet Union and the People's Republic of China represent two Communist giants in the world arena, their split has had a profound impact on the world Communist movement and the global balance of power. Both of them continued to claim Marxism and Leninism as their ideological foundation, but their interpretations have differed with charges against each other of "revisionism" and "hegemonism" (PRC charges against the Soviet Union) and "dogmatism" (Soviet charges against the PRC). Their split, furthermore, reveals the importance of competing national interests. Their differences are accentuated by uncertainty regarding the world's longest frontier. Turkish minorities in central Asia and nomadic peoples such as the Kazakhs and Kirghiz, living on both sides of the border, represent conflicting national loyalties; thus the Soviet fear of Chinese fanaticism and expansionism in the 1960s led to armed border clashes along the Amur and Ussuri rivers in the northeast and also on the Zinjiang (Sinkiang) border in central Asia. Armed clashes on the Zhenbao Island on the River Ussuri on March 2 and March 15, 1969 were of significant proportions.

Since then, the Soviet Union has amassed its troops along the border and further fortified its military positions. According to one estimate, the Soviet Union has stationed along the Sino-Soviet borders some 400,000 troops (44 divisions), representing 25 percent of the entire Soviet ground forces, which are equipped with ultramodern military hardware. Whereas the Soviet Union has ideologically emphasized its own experience as the model for the world Communist movement to follow, China has opted for its own revolutionary experience and developmental priorities. Furthermore, what Soviet aid there was for China at the outset was not regarded as significant enough to dictate the PRC's developmental preference.

Following the death of Stalin in 1953, Mao Zedong became increasingly independent of Soviet leadership. To China, however, the Soviet Union is guilty of "revisionism." China also charged the Soviet Union with (1) unwillingness to assist China with nuclear weapon development; and (2) failure to side with China in her confrontation with the United States over Quemoy and Matsu, islands off the Chinese mainland held by the Nationalists in Taiwan. The Sino-Soviet split eventually led to the establishment of diplomatic and other friendly relations between the PRC and its former enemy, the United States. This was viewed by the PRC as a way of deterring Soviet expansionism in east Asia.

South Asian Regional Cooperation (SARC)   An organization assembled by South Asians, for South Asians. Although the antecedents for the arrangement can be found in the 1950s and 1960s, the impetus for SARC is traced to a May 1980 call by the president of Bangladesh, General Ziaur Rahman. Zia urged the holding of a summit conference between Bhutan, Bangladesh, India, Maldives, Nepal, Pakistan, and Sri Lanka. That call produced four conferences of foreign secretaries between 1981 and 1983. The final meeting in March 1983 designed the structure for South Asian Regional Cooperation. At the apex of the structure is the Foreign Ministerial Council, a policy-making body that was projected to meet on a regular basis. SARC members acknowledged India's preeminence when they agreed to hold the first ministerial meeting in New Delhi in August 1983. The next level of SARC was the Foreign Secretaries Committee, more formally known as the Standing Committee of Foreign Secretaries. This body was responsible for coordinating and monitoring the integrated program. Two lower levels, the Working Groups and the Study Groups or Technical Committees, completed the SARC structure.

The purpose of SARC was to engender cooperation among the regional states in the fields of agriculture, telecommunications, meteorology, health and population, transport, sports, art and culture, postal services, rural development, and science and technology. The total SARC program was named the Integrated Common Action Program for Regional Cooperation. General Zia's 1980 call for a summit meeting, however, was still in the offing in 1984. A February 1984 meeting of the foreign ministers, again in New Delhi, indicated SARC had passed from the conceptual into an active and functional phase. Despite apparent progress, and an invitation to Burma to join the organization, SARC continued to be hobbled by political and military questions raised by the individual states, especially India. *See also* COLOMBO PLAN, p. 334; INDIAN OCEAN, p. 22; SUBCONTINENT, p. 38.

Significance   South Asian Regional Cooperation was aimed at raising the standard of living in the area and, in so doing, alleviating tension and hostility among South Asian states. President Ziaur Rahman had discussed his idea with the Indian Prime Minister Morarji Desai in 1978, but the collapse of his Janata coalition negated efforts at holding an earlier meeting. Desai's policies had reduced tension between Bangladesh and India, and the Zia initiative was in reaction to the good will that the Janata leader generated in the region.

The return to office in January 1980 of Mrs. Gandhi, therefore, was not judged a good omen for regional cooperation. General Zia and Mrs. Gandhi were not on good terms. Moreover, Mrs. Gandhi let it be known she was unhappy with the 1978–79 Indo-Bangladesh Treaty on the Farakka Barrage question. Desai had agreed to the treaty in order to calm Bangladeshi fears over the distribution of Ganges water. Mrs. Gandhi indicated that her government was interested in modifying terms of the treaty. The Indian prime minister was not convinced that a regional organization was in her country's interest. Indian suspicions that the organization could be used to chastise India, to embarrass it, or to provide the smaller states with a vehicle to pressure New Delhi, worked against an enthusiastic Indian response.

In point of fact, Bangladesh had already drawn the governments of Nepal and Sri Lanka into the SARC project, and Pakistan gave its endorsement shortly thereafter. To New Delhi, the whole affair seemed threatening. As the major power in the region, India was accustomed to leading not following. Moreover, Pakistan assumed a posture that was oriented toward Southwest Asia and the Middle East; whereas Sri Lanka had expressed serious interest in joining the Association of Southeast Asian Nations (ASEAN). It therefore took more than a year to impress upon New Delhi that SARC was in its national interest.

The breakthrough came at a meeting of regional foreign secretaries in Colombo on April 8, 1981. Three additional meetings involving the foreign secretaries followed in Kathmandu (1981), Islamabad (1982), and Dhaka (1983). By the time the Foreign Secretaries met in February 1984, SARC was a going concern, but not without significant problems. Indian suspicions were aroused anew in 1984 with the rumor that the United States was seeking bases in Bangladesh, and that Dhaka was giving consideration to the request. Rioting and acts of terror in Sri Lanka perpetrated by Hindu Tamils against Buddhist Sinhalese seemed to bear an Indian connection, and the surfacing of the Kashmir problem following the assassination of an Indian diplomat in London also threatened the organization's operations. Nevertheless, SARC was the first serious effort at forming a regional organization in South Asia, and most observers believed it would survive.

Southeast Asia Treaty Organization (SEATO)   Sometimes referred to as the Manila Pact, this treaty organization was the outcome of deliberations entered into by the United States, Great Britain, France, Australia, New Zealand, Pakistan, the Philippines, and Thailand on September 8, 1954. The signatories agreed to assist one another in resisting either armed aggression or subversive activities. They also pledged their support in promoting economic development and in enhancing social well being. SEATO was organized against a background that included the victory of Communist forces in China (1949), the North Korean invasion of South Korea (1950–53), and the French collapse in Indochina (1953). The United States had prevented South Korea from falling into the Communist camp, had battled the Chinese Red Army as a consequence of that effort, and was concerned that the forces represented by Maoism would spread throughout Southeast Asia if not aggressively opposed. France's decision to abandon its role in Indochina appeared to set the scene for still another Communist thrust. Thus the United States urged the signatories to the SEATO treaty to defend non-Communist Cambodia (Kampuchea), Laos, and South Vietnam against Communist aggression. These countries, however, were never made members of the pact.

SEATO headquarters were established in Bangkok, the only continental Southeast Asian nation to join the organization. Geographically speaking, Pakistan was a part of South Asia, and the Philippines was an archipelago nation to the east of the Asian mainland. All the members, however, had geopolitical interests in the region. Moreover, SEATO seemed to provide opportunity for the members' foreign ministers or their deputies to meet on a regular basis. SEATO promoted multilateral discussions on a broad range of subjects from subversion to cultural and economic cooperation. The United States justified its involvement in the Indochina civil war on grounds that its SEATO commitments could not be ignored. Other SEATO members, however, did not assume such a commitment, arguing that South Vietnam was not a signatory to the alliance. Moreover, Article 4 of the treaty states that each member would counter an external threat "in accordance with its constitutional processes." In actual fact, nothing in the SEATO treaty required a member to automatically or unilaterally take action in defense of an ally, let alone a nonmember state.

Although the seeds of its destruction were sown early in its life, SEATO began to break up on the rocky shores of Indochina, and it came apart during the Pakistani civil war of 1971. India's decision to enter the struggle against Pakistan, and its role in the creation of the sovereign state of Bangladesh from what was formerly East Pakistan was not checked by SEATO. Pakistan's official break from the alliance in 1972, therefore, was expected. SEATO had failed to serve the interests of its members, and it lost all credibility when the United States withdrew from South Vietnam in 1973. Finally, the member states watched helplessly as North Vietnam overran and annexed South Vietnam in 1975, and cast its influence over Laos and Cambodia.

The United States assumed a somewhat different Asian posture in the post–1975 period. It inaugurated a policy of détente with Communist China in 1971–72, and unilaterally terminated its treaty with Taiwan on January 1, 1979. It showed little concern when the Central Treaty Organization (CENTO) was dissolved in September 1979. Little remained of Washington's late 1940s and 1950s efforts to contain international communism. SEATO, however, remained a paper organization and the United States continued to pay it lip service. In a special 1984 report, the American secretary general commented that the Manila Pact continued to express his country's commitment to "frontline" Southeast Asian nations such as Thailand. The United States commitment, however, may have had little to do with SEATO. Moreover, Moscow, not Washington, talked openly about constructing an Asian security alliance. *See also* NIXON DOCTRINE, p. 345.

Significance   SEATO was an extension of the United States containment policy in the post–World War II era. The alliance was supposed to emulate the North Atlantic Treaty Organization (NATO) which had been created in 1949. In major part, SEATO was the brainchild of the American Secretary of State, John Foster Dulles, a firm believer in United States capacity to confine international communism to the inner heartland of the Eurasian landmass. But the alliance never fulfilled the dreams of its inventor. The countries that became signatories to the pact were more concerned with immediate domestic questions, or external threats closer to home. Pakistan, for example, was far more concerned with Indian machinations and could not be expected to play an active role in the organization. Moreover, Pakistan had recognized Communist China in 1950 and had no reason to antagonize its giant neighbor. (It is interesting to note that when Washington decided it was time to deal directly with the Chinese, it was the Pakistanis who made it possible for President Nixon's National Security Advisor, Henry Kissinger, to make a secret visit to Beijing.)

On the other side, the French had paid a heavy price in blood and national wealth in a futile effort to sustain a colonial presence in Indochina. In 1954–55, their attention was riveted on Algeria, another colony in rebellion, closer to home and with more important prospects.

Moreover, President Lyndon B. Johnson's use of the SEATO treaty to commit American troops to the civil war in Vietnam in 1964 defied arguments against such deployment. In the final analysis, SEATO failed all its tests, and member states failed the organization.

Soviet Collective Security Proposal for Asia   A Soviet effort to establish dominance along the Asian rimland. In 1972 Leonid Brezhnev spoke of the need to develop an Asian collective security pact. Addressing the 15th Congress of Soviet Trade Unions, he declared the need for Asian countries to repudiate the "use of force . . ., to respect the sovereignty and inviolability of frontiers, noninterference in internal affairs, and broad development of economic and other cooperation on the basis of complete equality and mutual benefit. We advocate and shall continue to advocate such collective security in Asia and are ready to cooperate with all countries to make this idea a reality." The Soviet Union criticized efforts by the United States to develop "closed regional military-political groups," and insisted this was all part of an old "imperialist" plot to divide and rule the Asian nations. Moscow spoke of the "bitter legacy" of colonialism and how it perpetuated "economic backwardness, mutual distrust and suspicion, tribalism, and prejudice."

Kremlin spokesmen noted that two-thirds of the Soviet Union lay in Asia, and yet the United States, separated from the continent by thousands of miles, tried to deny the Soviet Union a role in the region. The Soviets insisted they were more conversant with the people of Asia than the Americans. In 1973, Brezhnev talked about a growing confidence in the countries of Asia which would allow them to pool their resources and consolidate their security. Bilateral relations between Moscow and neighboring Asian states was a starting point. The Indian Communist weekly, *Blitz*, wrote that if the principles underlying the Indian-Soviet treaty spread throughout Asia, they would ultimately lead to the creation of a system of collective security. The Soviets cited the convening of the International Conference for Security and Cooperation in Asia that was held in Bangladesh in May 1973, and the World Congress of Peace Forces, held in Moscow in October 1973. The Soviets reiterated their support for "progressive" nations at each of these conferences. *See also* AFGHAN-USSR CONFLICT (1979–), p. 373; INDO-SOVIET TREATY (1971), p. 340; NONALIGNED MOVEMENT, p. 348; SOVIET-VIETNAMESE TREATY OF PEACE AND FRIENDSHIP (1978), p. 364.

Significance   The Soviet Union exploited opportunities presented by the British withdrawal from Asia after World War II. It strengthened its position in Afghanistan between 1946 and 1954 and began to spread its influence among the emerging and re-emerging nations of Asia and

Africa in 1955. In the period 1955–64, Soviet leaders visited or hosted the officials of India, Pakistan, Indonesia, Burma, Afghanistan, the countries of Indochina, and others. Moscow's support for New Delhi in its Kashmir dispute with Pakistan in 1955 followed the latter's entry into a mutual assistance agreement with the United States in 1954. Most significant were the Sino-Soviet schism in 1957–58 and China's border incursion into India in 1962. Both India and the Soviet Union perceived enhancement of their individual security through a form of collective endeavor.

Moscow's closer alliances in Asia were reserved for India, Afghanistan, and North Vietnam. Fifteen percent of India's aggregate expenditures in foreign currency for its second five-year plan was covered by Soviet credits. Soviet credits to Afghanistan paid for more than one-third of the total investment in that country's national economy. Eighty percent of North Vietnam's military and economic needs were supplied by the Soviet Union. India, however, was a special case and it required a different form of wooing. For example, a Soviet-Indian agreement on the building of the Bhilai iron and steel plant was signed on February 2, 1955. The plant was put into operation in 1959, and a subsequent agreement called for more than doubling its capacity.

Given Soviet preoccupation with Western containment strategy, the Soviets countered the development of NATO by establishing their own Warsaw Pact. Moscow provided substantial assistance to North Korea and North Vietnam in their wars with the United States. But an Asian alliance similar to the Warsaw Pact was not envisaged until the late 1960s and early 1970s. In the meantime, Moscow's declaration of continuing support for wars of national liberation was instituted to weaken the West's containment program, while simultaneously promoting the Kremlin's version of détente. Moscow assisted Egypt in undermining the Baghdad Pact in Southwestern Asia. Following the 1958 military coup in Iraq, Moscow gave its support to the new Baghdad government which announced it had abandoned its Western alliance commitment. (Iraq signed a treaty of friendship and cooperation with the Soviet Union in 1972.) After the Baghdad Pact became the Central Treaty Organization (CENTO), the Soviets focused pressure on Iran and Pakistan.

The construction of the Southeast Asia Treaty Organization (SEATO) in 1954 was supposed to contain both the Soviet Union and China. Moscow and Beijing's assistance to the Communist regime in North Vietnam, and their attempts to draw closer to Indonesia during this same period, were meant to neutralize SEATO. The signing of the Indo-Soviet Treaty of Peace and Friendship in 1971, however, signaled a concerted attempt to formalize Soviet-Asian security needs. The 24th Congress of the Communist Party of the Soviet Union (March 30 to

April 9, 1971) established foreign policy guidelines for the next five years. They emphasized strengthening the unity of the Socialist countries and all "antiimperialist" forces, and the need to "pursue a policy of active defense of peace and international cooperation." The 1971 treaty with India, therefore, was meant to act as a catalyst for the creation of an Asian collective security pact. New Delhi was intrigued by the proposition but also believed a pact would compromise its nonaligned status. New Delhi declined the invitation to join such a pact, and other Asian states did likewise. Moscow continued to express the need for such an organization, but seemed satisfied with the reinforcement of its bilateral arrangements. The 25th Congress of the Communist Party of the Soviet Union (February 24 to March 5, 1976) repeated the call for an Asian collective security arrangement. In spite of the suspicion and fear aroused by the Soviet invasion of Afghanistan in 1979, the call for collective Asian defense was undiminished in the 26th Party Congress in 1981, and in 1985 the Kremlin sustained its patient pursuit of dominance on the Asian rimland.

Soviet-Vietnamese Treaty of Peace and Friendship (1978)   A treaty marking the formal separation of China from Vietnam, and Hanoi's decision to place exclusive confidence in Moscow. The treaty is somewhat similar to those the Soviet Union has entered into with India and Egypt (1971); Iraq (1972); Somalia (1974); Angola (1976); Mozambique (1977); Afghanistan (1978); South Yemen (1979); Syria (1980); and North Yemen (1984), although tailored to meet the special circumstances of the Vietnamese-Soviet relationship. The Vietnamese had avoided becoming embroiled in Sino-Soviet difficulties up to 1975. After that date, however, Vietnam was unified under Hanoi control, and guerrilla activities were put aside for conventional approaches, including the development of a sophisticated military institution. Mao's model of revolution no longer sufficed. The passing of Mao Zedong (Mao Tsetung), as well as the modification of his policies by his successors in China, opened old questions concerning Vietnam's role in Southeast Asia. Vietnam showed no interest in subordinating its power to that of the Chinese. Moreover, historic Chinese enmities surfaced. Beijing's open courting of the United States after 1972 was also perceived as a threat to long-term Vietnam interests. Hanoi therefore found itself moving away from China and into more intimate association with the Soviet Union. Moscow pledged military support to Vietnam and declared its intention to secure the country's borders. In return, Hanoi provided the Soviets with base rights at Cam Ranh Bay, one of the largest naval installations in Southeast Asia. Hanoi's request for association with ASEAN was ignored, in part because of its Moscow connection. Similarly, Vietnam's call for the creation of ZOPFAN, an acronym for zone of peace, freedom, and neutrality, fell on deaf ears because its Southeast Asian neighbors feared the combined military presence of the Communist states. Hanoi's request to join COMECON, the Communist Economic Community, organized and managed by the Soviet Union, was aimed at overcoming its somewhat self-imposed isolation. *See also* SINO-VIETNAMESE CONFLICT, 1979– , p. 409; SOVIET COLLECTIVE SECURITY PROPOSAL FOR ASIA, p. 362.

Significance   The Soviet-Vietnamese Treaty of 1978 committed Moscow to Hanoi's external defense. Vietnam's principal adversary was identified as Communist China. Some observers contend Vietnam entered into the treaty with the Soviet Union only after China massed an army on its northern frontier, but thwarting Chinese aggressive intentions can only be part of the story. Vietnam's massive invasion of Cambodia (Kampuchea) in 1979 does not reflect a country in a defensive posture. Moreover, the resemblance between this sequence of events and those between India and the Soviet Union in 1971 are striking. India entered into a similar treaty with Moscow, and several months later invaded East Pakistan and helped establish the new state and government of Bangladesh.

Vietnam's elimination of the Chinese-supported government in Phnom Penh and the institution of a government friendly to Hanoi had a familiar ring. Unlike Bangladesh where the Pakistan army had been defeated, however, the Vietnamese were encouraged to continue their occupation of Cambodia because the enemy had not been totally vanquished. Furthermore, Bangladesh was quickly recognized as an independent country. Vietnam's puppet regime in Phnom Penh was accepted only by the Soviet bloc. With the Soviet Union providing substantial economic and technical assistance, in addition to military aid, Vietnam sought to manage its significant debt. Moscow provided the funds necessary to sustain more than 150,000 Vietnamese soldiers in Cambodia and another 50,000 in Laos. The Soviets also advised Hanoi to resettle approximately half a million Vietnamese in western Cambodia. Despite the Chinese incursion into Vietnam in 1979–80, and continuing border incidents between the two Communist states, the Vietnamese refused to withdraw from Cambodia. Given Soviet support and traditional Vietnamese defiance, the Chinese did not prove any more successful than the French and Americans in influencing the Vietnamese to yield their gains.

By 1983, Hanoi held supremacy over Indochina, and a so-called summit was convened in Laos, attended by the Vietnamese leaders and their weaker counterparts in Cambodia and Laos. Hanoi began the process of formalizing activities between the three states, announcing it had created a ministerial position in the Vietnam government to coordinate the operations of the three administrations. The Soviet Union reinforced these actions and encouraged Hanoi to permit the French to reopen their cultural center in Saigon (Ho Chi Minh City). In 1983, the French foreign minister visited Vietnam and declared his country's intention to reschedule Vietnam's debt payments. Although Hanoi announced the withdrawal of some of its troops from Cambodia in 1983 and 1984, perhaps a gesture to the French and the extended world community, the bulk of the invasion army remained in place and in fact intensified its campaign against the Cambodian resistance on the Thai frontier in 1984–85.

Taiwan Question: China   A dispute surrounding an island off the southeast coast of the Chinese mainland, which has been controlled by the Chinese Nationalists since their retreat to it following their defeat by the Chinese Communists in mainland China in 1949. The island has been claimed by the Chinese Communist goverment in Beijing as their rightful territory, to be incorporated into the mainland through whatever means necessary and available. Both the Nationalists in Taiwan and the Communist government in the mainland regard Taiwan as part of China, but they disagree on each other's legitimacy as true representatives of the Chinese people. Further complicating the situation is the early decision of the United States to support the Nationalists and to challenge any use of force in settling the dispute. Since the improvement of relations between the United States and China in 1972, the United States has reduced its forces on and around Taiwan, and established diplomatic relations with China in 1979, thus terminating its security treaty with the Taiwan government and ending its 30-year commitment to the Nationalist regime. However, the United States still insists that the Taiwan question be settled peacefully. Final settlement of the question is still pending. *See also* SHANGHAI COMMUNIQUE, p. 355; NATIONALIST GOVERNMENT: TAIWAN, p. 238.

Significance   Taiwan, also identified as Formosa, lies about 120 miles off the south China coast and has an overall area of 14,000 square miles. Since Taiwan has its own history and identity, its future may not be dictated by the resolution of dispute between mainland China and the Nationalist regime in Taiwan. There is a strong sentiment among the Taiwanese for independence. The early history of Taiwan is not too well known. Given its strategic value, Europeans occupied the island in the fifteenth century. In 1662, Koxinga, the son of a famous pirate during China's Ming Dynasty, was able to expel the Europeans, making the island his personal kingdom. Twenty years later, his grandson surrendered the kingdom to a Ming emperor, thus bringing the island into the political control of mainland China. In 1895, however, Japan acquired it as a reward for her victory over China in the first Sino-Japanese War. By integrating the island to the Japanese economy and teaching the native Taiwanese the Japanese language, Japan built a prosperous colony.

Following Japan's defeat in World War II, the island reverted back to China as agreed by the Allied leaders. The Taiwanese, however, revolted against Chinese Nationalist rule in 1947 and expressed their desire to be independent. Charging Communist instigation of the revolt, the Nationalists practiced harsh repression, forcing the Taiwanese leaders to flee the island. Since their exile to the island in 1949, the Nationalists have turned the island into a military fortress with support from the United States. At the same time, they have concentrated on the economic development of the island with a great deal of success and have gradually left the responsibilities of local politics to the Taiwanese themselves. They have also co-opted the Taiwanese leaders into the Nationalist leadership structure. In this way, some measures of democracy have been introduced in Taiwan, but any movement for Taiwanese independence is harshly repressed. Although diplomatically abandoned by the United States and other powers who hold diplomatic relations with the mainland government, the Nationalist government in Taiwan maintains close economic and cultural ties with these countries.

Tydings-McDuffie Act, 1934   The American decision to give the Philippines self-determination. The United States seized the Philippine islands from Spain in the Spanish-American War of 1898. By 1907, American policy was concerned with bringing the Filipinos into key government operations. In 1916, the Jones Act declared that the Philippines would achieve full independence as soon as a stable government was assured. American educational and political reforms, however, did not alter the traditional landholding pattern or temper entrepreneurial control. Indigenous power remained in the hands of the wealthy who used the American presence to increase their power. Because the United States announced its intention to transfer authority to a Philippines government, nationalist movements were stunted and weak. The Filipinos were prepared to follow those leaders who counselled patience and restraint, rather than those demanding revolutionary change. The Tydings-McDuffie Act of 1934 authorized the United States government to convene a Philippines constituent assembly for the purpose of drafting a constitution for the soon-to-be-independent nation. The Americans established the guidelines for the constitution, which prescribed a republican system of government and a democratic orientation guaranteeing fundamental rights. It also provided for a high commissioner who would act as the representative of the American president until the country was completely independent. The Tydings-McDuffie Act specified a ten-year interim between the adoption of the constitution and the date of Philippines independence. *See also* HUK-BALAHAP UPRISING, p. 384; PACIFIC WAR: WORLD WAR II, p. 396; POLITI-CAL PARTIES: PHILIPPINES, p. 192.

Significance   The Tydings-McDuffie Act permitted the Filipino constituent assembly to complete its constitution-writing in February 1935. It was then submitted to President Franklin D. Roosevelt for his assent. The Filipino electorate ratified the document on May 14, 1935. Although still under American tutelage, the Filipinos put the constitution into effect and elected Manuel L. Quezon as their first president. Full independence was scheduled for July 4, 1946. Despite the onset of World War II, and the tragedy of the Japanese occupation from 1942 until 1945, the Filipinos showed remarkable stamina, courage, and perseverence. Despite a violent confrontation with the Hukbalahap Movement that first resisted the Japanese, and after the war, attempted to establish a quasi-communist system in the country, the Philippines held on their original inheritance. The Huks controlled a population of half a million in central Luzon and they were not defeated until Ramon Magsaysay organized a superior Filipino force, with American assistance. The Philippines anticipated the nurturing of their democratic experience, but entrenched vested interests proved to be a formidable obstacle. Those interests buttressed the rule of Ferdinand Marcos who assumed the presidency in 1965. Not content with his extraordinary powers, Marcos declared martial law in 1972, and even when it was lifted ten years later, his dictatorial behavior threatened to destroy what remained of Philippines democracy, as well as permanently alienate the Filipino people from the United States.

Unification Proposals: Korea   Various proposals advanced by both North and South Korea for peaceful reunification of their land, divided by the Allied Powers in World War II after Korea was liberated from Japanese colonialism in 1945. In 1945 the Allied Powers (the Soviet Union in North Korea and the United States in South Korea) were unable to establish a unified government for all of Korea as promised by the Cairo Declaration (1943), and instead two separate governments were established in 1948. Since the Korean War (1950–53), the division of the country has deepened, but both North and South have acknowledged need for national reunification and have presented various reunification proposals. Traditionally, South Korea's position has been that its government is the only legitimate government of all the Korean people, and that free elections must be held in North Korea under UN supervision in accordance with constitutional processes. Beginning in 1970, however, President Park (1963–79), dramatically departing from South Korea's position, emphasized peaceful coexistence and competition with the North and socioeconomic exchanges between the two Koreas. Revolutionary developments were (1) the meetings of 1971 and 1972, which were held between the two Koreas' Red Cross societies to discuss the problem of divided families; and (2) the establishment of a South-North Coordination Committee to prevent armed clashes, facilitate exchanges, expedite the Red Cross talks, and settle the reunification problem. All efforts, however, were unsuccessful.

Although North Korea participated in the Red Cross talks and the South-North Coordination Committee meetings, it has traditionally maintained that (1) foreign troops must be withdrawn from Korea (only then free elections would be held throughout Korea); and (2) a national congress of the Korean people would be convened by their elected representatives to work out details for a unified Korea. Then on August 14, 1960, North Korea's President Kim Il Sung (Kim, Il-sŏng) proposed a confederation of the fully autonomous North and South Korean governments. Finding his confederation plan salient and gaining support within and without Korea, President Kim has reiterated the proposal on various occasions. In 1980, he emphasized (1) the establishment of a supreme confederal assembly comprised of an equal number of representatives from the North and the South and an appropriate number of representatives from overseas nationals; (2) the establishment of a standing committee as a permanent organ of the assembly with the powers to discuss and decide on political affairs, national defense problems, foreign affairs, and other matters of common concern related to the interests of the country and the nation as a whole; and (3) the establishment of a "combined national army" under confederal jurisdiction, apart from the regional armed forces.

South Korea has rejected North Korea's confederation plan on the basis that it is too general and contains too many ambiguities, as well as being a device to force the withdrawal of U.S. troops from Korea. It is also viewed as a Communist scheme to instigate "national liberation" struggles in the South. In the latest round of proposals, however, President Chun Doo Hwan (Chŏn, Tu-hwan) of South Korea proposed on January 22, 1982, a consultative conference for national unification with representatives of the two Koreas, which would draft a constitution for a unified Korea. This constitution would be approved by a referendum in each area to make it legal, and general elections under the constitution would be held for the establishment of a unified legislature and government. North Korea, however, has refused to discuss the South Korean plan. *See also* KOREAN WAR, p. 388; THIRTY-EIGHTH PARALLEL, p. 41.

Significance   In the latest round of unification proposals by North and South Korea, the 1982 proposal of President Chun of South Korea is unprecedented in its bold departure from the earlier, more cautious South Korean proposals. There appears to be some common ground between North Korea's confederation plan and South Korea's constituent assembly plan. However, North Korea has refused to consider President Chun's proposal on the grounds that the South Korean government of President Chun is illegitimate since it is not based on popular will, and its use of force against the people is too blatant.

Meantime, no progress has been made toward Korean reunification. The urge for national unification is present in both North and South Korea, but its realization is continuously hampered by mutual distrust and deep enmity between the two. The bitter experience of the Korean War has not been forgotten. Furthermore, since the division, each regime has developed its own vested interests and has been fearful of their disruption. This fear is also shared by the Big Powers (the PRC, USSR, USA, and Japan) who all have what they consider a type of vested interest in the future of the Korean peninsula. Peaceful unification of Korea faces many insurmountable obstacles, made more difficult to overcome by the fact that, too often, unification proposals have been an instrument of progaganda warfare.

Wartime Conferences: Allied Powers   Significant among these conferences which dealt with the problems of Asia were the Quebec, the Moscow, the Cairo, the Teheran, the Yalta, and the Potsdam Conferences. The Quebec Conference was held in Quebec, Canada in the summer of 1943 among leaders of the Allied Powers, including President Franklin D. Roosevelt of the United States and Prime Minister Winston S. Churchill of Great Britain. At this conference, it was determined that greater aid to China would be a means of defeating Japan, a South Asian Command was created under Lord Mountbatten, and the question of Soviet entry into the Pacific War against Japan was discussed. The conference was followed in October 1943 by a meeting in Moscow of the foreign ministers of the United States, Great Britain, and the Soviet Union, which issued, with China's later approval, a declaration of general security, and which pledged to establish at the earliest practicable date a general international organization for the maintenance of world peace and security.

Next was the Cairo Conference, attended by President Roosevelt, Prime Minister Churchill, and Generalissimo Chiang. The conference dealt primarily with future military operations against Japan. Its communique, issued on December 1, 1943, stated in part that "Japan (following the war) shall be stripped of all the islands in the Pacific which she has seized or occupied since the beginning of the First World War in 1914 and . . . all the territories Japan has stolen from the Chinese, such as Manchuria, Formosa (Taiwan), and the Pescadores, shall be restored to the Republic of China." It also stated that "Japan will . . . be expelled from all other territories which she has taken by violence and greed. . . . The aforesaid three great powers, mindful of the enslavement of the people of Korea, are determined that in due course Korea shall become free and independent." This Cairo Conference was immediately followed by a meeting of President Roosevelt and Prime Minister Churchill with Josef Stalin of the Soviet Union in Teheran, Iran on November 28 through December 1. At this meeting, Marshal Stalin was briefed on the Cairo Conference. Marshal Stalin also showed his interest in entering war against Japan upon the final defeat of Germany. In February 1945, the Big Three Allied leaders of World War II met again at Yalta in the Russian Crimea, and dealt with various postwar problems, including the occupation of Germany, the future of East Europe, and the proposed United Nations organization. At this conference, the Soviet Union endorsed the agreement from the Cairo Conference. It was also agreed that the Soviet Union should join the United States in the war against Japan within three months after the end of the European war.

The last in the series of wartime summit conferences was held in Potsdam from July 17 to August 1, 1945 and was attended by President Harry Truman of the United States, Prime Minister Clement Atlee of Great Britain (assisted by Churchill), and Marshal Stalin of the Soviet Union. This conference defined the terms for Japanese surrender: surrender must be unconditional; Japan was to be occupied by the Allied Powers until a new order devoid of Japan's warmaking power was established; and Japanese sovereignty was to be limited to the islands of Honshu, Hokkaido, Kyushu, and Shikoku. The terms of the Cairo Declaration were also to be implemented fully. *See also* PACIFIC WAR, p. 396; THIRTY-EIGHTH PARALLEL, p. 41.

Significance   The Axis powers in World War II fought their wars more or less independently (for instance, Germany in Europe and Japan in Asia), each acting without prior consultation with the other. Thus, Japan was not aware of Germany's intention of attacking Poland or the Soviet Union, and Germany was not aware of Japan's plan to attack Pearl Harbor. The Allied Powers, on the other hand, held frequent summit confences in order to coordinate their activities and cooperate in the execution of their common objectives. They also endeavored to promote mutual friendship and trust. For example, during the war China was able to conclude treaties with the United States and Great Britain, abolishing their extraterritorial rights in China. Thus, at least on the diplomatic front, China became equal to the other members of the

Allied Powers. The United States Congress passed a law ending the longstanding, discriminatory immigration policy excluding the Chinese.

These positive influences of the wartime summit conferences did not eliminate deep-seated differences between the Soviet Union and the western Allied Powers. Furthermore, Allied efforts in the war to create rapport with the Soviet Union, through summit conferences as well as an emphasis on informality, may have created many postwar uncertainties and problems, such as the Korean division which was regarded as temporary but has become permanent, due to the development of the Cold War.

8. International Relations and Conflict

Afghan-USSR Conflict (1979–)   The Soviet Union invaded Afghanistan on December 27, 1979, and commenced a long, tedious campaign to transform the country into a chaste Marxist state, wholly dependent on Moscow. The Soviets enlisted what remained of the formal Afghan army in this endeavor. It also established a puppet government in Kabul that it insisted represented the popular wishes of the Afghan nation. The Afghan people, however, were almost totally opposed to Soviet intervention, and they wanted nothing to do with Marxism. Afghanistan lies in the shadow of the Soviet Union. A southern extension of Central Asia, it has long been coveted by the Imperial Russian as well as the Bolshevik state. Only the British presence in India prior to 1947 seemed to deny the Russians their quest. Britain made war on Afghanistan twice in the nineteenth century and once early in the twentieth century to ensure the operation of its "Forward Policy," a policy aimed at keeping the Russians from threatening India or the Persion Gulf states. Afghanistan was indifferent to British concerns and fought what it perceived to be English colonialism.

When the British withdrew from India after World War II, however, there was no counterforce to Russian interests in Afghanistan. The Soviet Union entered into military and economic agreements with Kabul in 1954 and 1956, and by the 1960s it was the preeminent power in the country. Afghanistan rejected all overtures by the United States that it join with its neighbors in collective defense of the region. In fact, Afghanistan considered Pakistan a far greater threat to its interests than the Soviet Union. Moreover, Afghanistan wanted an outlet to the sea, and the creation of Pakistan in 1947 denied that objective. Afghanistan turned its attention to undermining Pakistan's tenuous unity by encouraging the Pathans of Pakistan to press their claim for an independent

Pakhtunistan. Skirmishes between Pakistan and Afghanistan military units, therefore, were not infrequent occurrences along their mutual border. The sealing of the border by Pakistan in the 1960s tended to drive the Afghanis closer to the Soviet Union. This orientation was even more pronounced, given United States agreement to supply Pakistan's armed forces. Although in later years Pakistan somewhat reduced its American dependence, the Soviet Union was an ever-present force in Afghan domestic and international affairs.

In 1973, a cousin of the Afghan king, Mohammad Daud, a Soviet sympathizer, overthrew the monarchy with help from Marxist elements in the armed forces. Daud declared Afghanistan to be a republic and made himself the nation's first president. The Soviet-backed People's Democratic Party of Afghanistan (PDPA) increased its influence at this time. In 1978 the PDPA organized a coup with assistance from Marxist troops, murdered Daud, members of his family and government, and seized control of the government. The tribal Afghans, however, were not reconciled to the Marxist putsch and they commenced assaults on Afghan government officials, members of the Afghan armed forces, Soviet advisors, and collaborators. Stern measures by the PDPA government only deepened and spread the violence. When Moscow ordered the PDPA to placate the Afghans, to ease up on their reform program, the dominant figure in the Afghan revolution, Hafizullah Amin, refused to comply. The Kremlin ordered Amin's removal, but the Afghan leader sensed a threat to his life and reversed the tables by executing Moscow's Afghan agent, Nur Mohammad Taraki. This event signaled the Soviet Red Army to intervene in Afghanistan's affairs. Almost 100,000 Soviet troops entered the country, took control of the Afghan army and government, and quickly liquidated Hafizullah Amin. A new Afghan leader, Babrak Karmal, was dispatched from Moscow to take up the reins in Kabul.

Although Moscow controlled the Afghan government, it could not win the support of the tribal Afghans. The struggle against the Soviet Union became an act of faith as well as an attempt to maintain the independence of the country. The result was a protracted guerrilla war pitting regular Afghan and Soviet air and land units against an impoverished, fragmented, and desperate people. The Afghan *mujahiddin* tried to fight their enemy according to historic tradition, from hilltops and canyons, in small groups employing hit-and-run tactics. They never expected to win a major victory against the massed and better equipped army of the Soviets, but they had every intention of making the invaders pay a high price for their victories. In the spring offensive of 1984, the Soviets marshalled a large number of troops, many Afghan recruits, and attacked the mujahiddin in their stronghold in the Panjsher Valley. By June, the Afghan resistance had been broken.

It is estimated that more than a thousand guerrillas lay dead on the battlefield, and the Soviets occupied a primary base and sanctuary in proximity to the Pakistan frontier. Although the war was far from over, Soviet tactics had forced the resistance to fight a set battle on their own terrain, and the losses in men and supplies stored in the valley made the mujahiddin plight even more desperate in 1985. *See also* CENTRAL ASIA, p. 8; HINDU KUSH, p. 18; KARAKORUM HIGHWAY, p. 27; TRIBALISM, p. 125.

Significance   The consequences of the Afghan-Soviet conflict that began in 1979 are not yet perfectly clear. It can be speculated that the Soviet intention is to destroy the traditional, primitive, semifeudal life-style of the Afghan people. This drastic procedure is prelude to the metamorphosis of Afghanistan into a chaste Marxist state, wedded to the Soviet Union. But Afghanistan could also be geographically altered by its northern neighbor. Afghanistan's northern section might be severed and annexed by the Soviet Union. A new Afghanistan could emerge if the Soviet Union assisted the breakup of Pakistan and promoted the creation of an autonomous Pakhtunistan and Baluchistan. The latter might not only be carved out of Pakistan, but from Iranian Baluchistan as well.

Such long range plans are not to be treated lightly, given Soviet interest in Iran and the Persian Gulf. Mastery over this region could further reinforce the Soviet Union's association with India. Overall, the Soviets believe they are bringing civilization to a backward people. At the same time, they seek to bolster their security vis-à-vis the threat posed by the United States in the Indian Ocean. Neither the United States, nor Afghanistan's neighbors appear willing to risk spreading the conflict by offering massive direct assistance to the mujahiddin. The Soviet Union is therefore prepared to fight a patient, protracted war with limited means, for what appears to be a major objective. In the meantime, more than 20 percent of the Afghan population has fled to Pakistan, and a smaller percentage to Iran. With more than three million Afghan refugees in Pakistan alone, the burden imposed on Islamabad may prove more than it can bear.

Assam Massacre   An example of communal violence in India. Assam is an Indian state located in the northeastern segment of the subcontinent. It is a large territory, little developed, but rich in natural resources. It is also one of the least densely populated regions of India. The Assamese population is reported to be less than 20 million. Paradoxically, Assam borders on Bangladesh, one of the world's most densely populated countries (population estimated to be well in excess of 100 million). For almost a century Bengalis have been moving from the more crowded conditions at home to nearby Assam where they have settled and attempted to build new lives. Even during the British period in India the Assamese were fearful that colonial administrative policy could destroy their way of life.

Assamese-Bengali hostility was deep-seated, but the pent-up bitterness between the communities had not been displayed in such vivid detail until the Assam massacre of 1983. The violence which seized the region was precipitated by statewide elections. Mrs. Gandhi's government had insisted on the right of the Bengali immigrants to vote in the Assam election. The Assamese, however, were incensed by the directive. They argued that the elections gave the Bengalis an active voice in regional affairs. It was alleged that four million illegal Bangladeshis had entered Assam in the last ten years. Assamese leaders, therefore, called for a boycott of the election and for the removal of the Bengalis from the voting rolls. In a number of instances Bengalis were forcibly prevented from voting.

The Assamese protest quickly degenerated to random, indiscriminant, and gross acts of violence. Several thousand Bengalis were allegedly killed during the late winter and early spring of 1983. Included among the dead was a legislative assembly candidate from Mrs. Gandhi's party. The prime minister's party won the election, however, because most Assamese refused to cast their ballots. The government of Congress Chief Minister Hiteswar Saikia was extremely unpopular, and in one altercation involving dissidents, his nephew was killed. Although many Bengalis decided to return to Bangladesh, many remained, while others, undeterred by the widespread killing, continued to move into the country. New Delhi's efforts at halting the flow of illegal immigrants included the building of a barbed wire fence, but few believed that would bring an end to the migration or relieve Assamese bitterness toward the Bengalis and the government in New Delhi. *See also* CONSTITUTIONAL SECULARISM, p. 216.

Significance   Communal warfare is not uncommon in India. Despite the country's noble experiment with democratic processes, it remains subject to violent acts of revenge and intolerance. Many observers would argue that India's democratic objectives are often at odds with local tradition and that the quest for modernity imposes a heavy burden on the still largely illiterate, impoverished society. These same observers note that there are two Indias: the one identified with sophistication and progress and the other represented by the masses who have little if any opportunity to share in India's industrial and scientific achievements. Moreover, would-be leaders aim to arouse the masses and their demagogic behavior exploits the feelings of the uneducated and deprived.

Scapegoating is not an unusual occurrence, and the fact that it developed a violent character in Assam can be attributed to historic enmities and the capacity of local leaders to reap advantages from the fears of their constituents. The 1983 Assamese massacre of Bengalis was not so much a consequence of religious differences (the majority of the Bengalis were Muslim) as it was a reaction to sociopolitical and economic conditions prevailing in the state, and Assamese fear that the government in New Delhi was using the Bengalis to maintain their preeminence in the region. Intense Hindu-Muslim violence in and around Bombay, as well as in the southern city of Hyderabal in 1984, however, was attributed to religious questions.

Boxer Rebellion, 1900: China   A popular protest movement, especially in North China, directed against Manchu (Ch'ing, or Qing, Dynasty) misrule, foreign encroachment, and Christian missionaries and Chinese converts. During the 1890s, many anti-Manchu secret societies were formed in China. Toward the end of the century, however, these organizations, with the encouragement of local officials, shifted their enmity from the Manchu Dynasty to the foreigners. One of the most significant of these organizations was the *I Ho Chuan* (Yi He Zhuan) (meaning "Righteous and Harmonious Fists"). The Boxers had no binding ideology, they lacked sufficient weaponry, and they relied on ancient popular beliefs, practicing a martial exercise known as "Harmony Fists," hence the name "Boxer." The bravery of the Boxers in the face of overwhelming odds and deadly bullets also earned them the attribute of fanaticism.

In June 1900, the Empress Dowager Tzu Hsi (Cixi), who spearheaded the conservative force within the Ch'ing government, declared war on the West and ordered provincial authorities to organize the Boxers to fight an expected foreign invasion, bestowing legitimacy on the Boxers' attack on foreigners, including Japanese, throughout the country. In Beijing (Peking), the foreign community, which sought safety in the embassy compound, came under Boxer siege. To rescue them and protect their nationals, an international relief force was dispatched. Most of the western powers with an interest in China, including the United States and Great Britain, participated. Japan also contributed forces to this expedition. As a result, the Boxers were defeated, the Empress Dowager fled the capital and Beijing came under foreign occupation.

The Peace Protocol, signed September 7, 1900, provided that China would (1) pay some $334 million for the damages inflicted by the Boxers; (2) fix the tariff at 5 percent; (3) execute specified Chinese officials; and (4) allow permanently stationed foreign troops in the capital and other locations. The large area of the Inner City of Beijing protected by foreign troops became known as the Legation Quarter. *See also* OPIUM WAR, p. 394.

Significance   The Boxer Rebellion had far-reaching consequences. The tenacity and fanaticism with which the Chinese Boxers fought, coupled with rivalry and jealousy among the powers, helped to avert the partitioning of the country. However, the economic burden and the humiliation accompanying further infringements on sovereignty and interference in China's internal affairs, as provided in the Boxer Peace Protocol, almost sealed the fate of Manchu rule. The Protocol showed, once again, the willingness of the West to humiliate China. It permitted foreign troops to occupy important lines of communication and many strategic points.

Furthermore, the indemnity was so outrageously excessive that some foreign governments, notably the United States and Great Britain, volunteered to rechannel a portion of it to finance the education of Chinese students abroad. The United States also permitted China to use its share of the indemnity to build a college near Beijing. Following the Boxer Rebellion, the Manchu government again attempted to reform itself and strengthen the nation by abolishing the antiquated scholar-official examination system, by restructuring the government, and by proposing a constitutional government. The Ch'ing Dynasty proved hopelessly weak, however, in the face of increasingly chaotic situations in the country and the incessant encroachment of foreign enemies. The Boxer Rebellion was China's first anti-foreign nationalistic outbreak.

Confrontation Strategies   Indonesia's aggressive pursuit of its interests in the South Pacific. After achieving independence in 1949, it pressed the opportunity to include territories and islands in the archipelago which did not immediately fall within its sovereign power. Confrontation was the term used to press Indonesian claims against the Netherlands, Malaysia, and Portuguese Timor. The Dutch governed West New Guinea separately from its Indonesian colony, and the territory remained in European hands until Indonesia decided to seize it by force. The Netherlands government publicized its intention to fight to hold the region and sought assistance from some of its NATO allies in ferrying troops and supplies to the remote location.

When the United States refused to support the Dutch effort, the matter was transferred to the United Nations. In 1962, UN Secretary General U Thant intervened and called for an international peacekeeping force to prevent hostilities from erupting. In May 1963, Indonesia extended its rule over West New Guinea. However, the confrontation with Malaysia could not be resolved to the satisfaction of Indonesia. Indonesia controlled the major portion of Borneo, a former Dutch holding, but the northern coast had been the preserve of the British, and two of the three territories joined with Malaya to form the federation of Malaysia in 1963. Indonesia demanded Northern Borneo (Sabah), one of the federating units. (A less strident claim also had been made by the Philippines.) Malaysia, however, had no intention of giving up Sabah (the Indonesians called it North Kalimantan). The new federation called upon Britain to help defend the territory and the request was immediately complied with. Special contingents of the British army, predominantly Gurkas, took up positions in Sabah and were called upon to beat back repeated Indonesian assaults. The Indonesians exploited the dissident Azhari of Brunei and endeavored to sow seeds of dissension.

During this period of confrontation with Malaysia, Indonesia's Sukarno had become intimately associated with the Indonesia Communist Party (PKI), and the latter was intent on destroying the power of the commanding generals in the Indonesian army. The link-up of the PKI with the clandestine Communist Party of Sarawak, revealed "confrontation" was part of a Communist plot, not an heroic act of nationalism. The Communist plot against the Indonesian generals in 1965, and the murder of several members of the high command, necessitated counterblows. The surviving officers rallied their forces, thwarted the conspiracy, and launched an offensive to root out the PKI. In the carnage that followed, an estimated 600,000 to 800,000 Indonesians perished. Sukarno was eventually deposed in favor of General Suharto and the "Confrontation" with Malaysia was terminated.

The struggle for Portuguese East Timor commenced when Lisbon withdrew its claim to the colony. Indonesia proclaimed East Timor the twenty-seventh province of Indonesia in 1976, despite the absence of justifying criteria. The people of East Timor, however, insisted on their right to be independent, and they refused to submit to their powerful neighbor. A Front for the Liberation and Independence of East Timor (Fretilin) took up the challenge, and stubbornly fought the intruders. In the meantime, the matter was addressed in the United Nations. Indonesian efforts to get the UN to drop the issue failed, and in 1983 the UN Commission on Human Rights voted to affirm East Timor's right to self-determination. Indonesia, however, gave no indication of leaving the territory. *See also* POLITICAL PARTIES: PAPUA NEW GUINEA, p. 191.

Significance   Indonesia has been an ambitious state, and "confrontation" is a euphemism for "surrender or face the consequences." Nevertheless, the nation has been cautious in its selection of targets. Only in the case of Malaysia did it threaten, and even in that instance the threat was to its forces, not to the status of the country. Indonesia has expressed other interests which are disturbing to elements of the international community. Its declaration of sovereign control over the waters of the archipelago is another form of confrontation. A vast area of the South Pacific is involved, and important sealanes could be affected if the claim is aggressively policed. Indonesia's interest in Papua New Guinea is also a source of discomfort, and except for Australian support, that sovereign state might be under even greater pressure. Indonesia faced an insurrection on the island of Sumatra in the 1950s. Indonesia's leaders are aware of Moluccan aspirations for self-determination. The Moluccans dramatized their demands by engaging in sporadic acts of terror in the Netherlands, but Indonesia has not been troubled at home. Nevertheless, such demands from groups on the out-islands remind the Indonesians of the diversity of their country and the difficulties in sustaining unity.

Dien Bien Phu   A small town in the northeastern corner of Vietnam, near the Laotian border, that became the site for one of the decisive battles in post–World War II Asian history. Dien Bien Phu was called the "Seat of the Border County Prefecture" by the French, and because it was distant from the more important region of the Red River Delta, the French military command gave it little serious attention when the war began. The French Indochina War which commenced on December 19, 1946, and followed a bloody and painful route through the jungles of Indochina, came to an end when the garrison defending this remote village surrendered on May 8, 1954. Approximately 17,000 French defenders, many of them legionnaires from Germany and North Africa, faced a Viet Minh force of 49,500, with 55,000 support troops. Surrounded by a determined enemy, cut off from resupply, and denied air support (especially bomber capability), the French force held out for 56 days before surrendering to Vietnam's chief military strategist, General Vo Nguyen Giap.

Total French casualties were between 9,000 and 10,000, of which about 2,000 died during the battle. Some 7,000 were taken prisoner, however, and many of these died during the 500-mile march to the prison camps. The Viet Minh are estimated to have suffered more than 6,000 dead, and many more thousands wounded in the seige of Dien Bien Phu. Despite these higher losses, Hanoi was even more committed to its quest of unifying Vietnam under its leadership and of dominating all Indochina. Nevertheless, it sought respite from the fighting, and time to restore its battered armies, by agreeing to accept the seventeenth parallel as the temporary dividing line between its forces and those of the noncommunists in the south. France, however, acknowledged the futility of its campaign to reestablish authority in the region, and with the Geneva Accords of 1954, Paris withdrew all its forces from the area. *See also* GENEVA ACCORDS, 1954, p. 339; SECOND INDOCHINA WAR, p. 401; SEVENTEENTH PARALLEL, p. 37.

Significance   Dien Bien Phu terminated the First Indochina War, and set the stage for the Second. France had requested direct military assistance from its allies in the course of the battle, particularly air strikes against entrenched Vietnamese positions. Although the United States appeared ready to join in the conflict, Britain's negative response influenced President Dwight Eisenhower to deny the French plea. France never possessed the material or moral strength necessary to win a decisive victory in Indochina. French society, wearied by World War II, wanted a short-range solution. The French strategy, therefore, was the creation and support of national armies for the Associated States of Cambodia, Laos, and Vietnam. This force was supposed to fend off the Communist guerrilla challenge, once French forces had destroyed Hanoi's main battle formations.

France never achieved its stated objective. Paris was limited in the use of French conscripts by its own Budget Law of 1950, which specified that such troops could only be used in France, Algeria, and on German occupation duty. As a consequence, the main French force in Indochina was comprised of professional officers, noncommissioned enlisted men, and a variety of foreign recruits. But even this French army was never permitted to grow to full strength. On the other side, the Viet Minh grew in numbers on a daily basis. The French defeat was attributed in the United States to ineptitude and too few weapons. Washington ignored the intangibles that favored the indigenous force, such as Viet Minh organizing abilities, the degree of Vietnamese sacrifice, and the depth of their belief system. Nevertheless, it decided to pick up in Indochina where the French left off. It was inconceivable among the political and military planners in Washington that American forces would face the same misfortune as the French. Although Eisenhower had failed to aid the beleaguered French garrison at Dien Bien Phu, he was prepared to assist the non-Marxist Indochinese in warding off the threat of "international communism."

Guerrilla Warfare in Malaya, 1948–60   A campaign to transform Malaya into a Communist state in the aftermath of World War II. The population of Malaysia is divided between Malays, Indians, and Chinese, but the latter have traditionally been more politically and economically active as a group. During the British colonial period, the Chinese dominated the tin industry and were a major factor in the rubber trade. They also were responsible for the region's urban development where they played a primary role in banking, commerce, and construction. As the more aggressive and upward-bound community, the Chinese emphasized education in the Chinese language, and insisted on clinging to their unique culture and habits. During the period of British colonialism in Malaya, the Chinese continued to identify with their brethren in the homeland. Communism came to the region in the form of Chinese societies, organized for the purpose of influencing developments in the mother country. The Chinese Kuomintang of Sun Yat-sen opened its membership to Chinese Communists, and it surfaced in Malaya as an anticolonial party loyal to the interests of China. In 1927, however, Chiang Kai-shek expelled them from the party and the impact of that decision was felt all the way to Malaya. The Kuomintang had been banned in Malaya, but the British now removed objections to Malayan-based Chinese becoming members of the organization. The colonial authority scrutinized the visible side of the Chinese Malayan community, but it could not penetrate their secret societies. The British encouraged separate Chinese education as part of their divide and rule policy and sought to ingratiate themselves with the more aggressive community.

Communism in Malaya resurfaced in 1937 after Chiang entered into an agreement with the Communists, and the Japanese declared war on China. By this time the Chinese Communists, the most politically conscious element in Malaya, stood at the center of the Nationalist movement. Their anti-British activities had failed to attract the Malay population, but the Japanese invasion of Malaya gave them a new target. Japanese atrocities in China were replicated in Southeast Asia, and Chinese Malayans bore the brunt of the Japanese assault in 1941. The Chinese attempted to defend themselves against the onslaught but found many Malays indifferent to their plight. The Japanese in effect sought to use the divide-and-rule policy, but in reverse form from that of the British. The British, therefore, provided moral support to the Chinese-led Malayan Communist Party, and a guerrilla movement was organized which was the most successful of such operations against the Japanese occupation armies. When the war ended, the Chinese Communists in Malaya, having pursued the struggle against the Japanese virtually alone, on orders from Moscow took up arms against the British. But the British were not idle. Like the Japanese earlier, they threw their support to the Malays who held deep antipathies toward the Chinese community.

In 1948, the British replaced the Malayan Union with a Federation focusing on the Malay rulers. The Chinese reaction was to violently oppose the Federation and Malay preeminence. These developments precipitated a crisis, and a Communist insurgency began that not only brought British power to bear against the guerrillas, it also widened cleavages between the Malay and Chinese communities. In the latter instance, the Malayan Chinese community was itself divided between those following Chiang Kai-shek and those adhering to the teachings of Mao Zedong (Mao Tse-tung). The Malayan Communists were invigorated by Mao's victory on the mainland in October 1949, and their campaign against the British achieved its greatest success in that same year. The British, however, were provoked to launch a major effort and a state of emergency was proclaimed over all Malaya. The British labored to separate the Chinese Communists from the noncommunist Chinese of Malaya. They encouraged the assembling of a Malayan Chinese Association that worked closely with the authorities in repairing the damage done by the guerrillas. The British protected Chinese financial and commercial interests against Malay threats and, equally important, denied the Chinese Communists an important source of support.

The Malayan High Commissioner, General Sir Gerald Templer, was sent to the colony to suppress the guerrillas. He was also charged with preparing the transfer of power. His objectives were to isolate and confine the insurgents to the jungles, sustain the efficiency of government, and prevent a fall in the standard of living. His forces succeeded in achieving their first goal. The terrorists were denied food, ammunition, and new recruits. Although joined earlier by some Malays, the Communists remained a Chinese force, which even the Chinese community refused to associate with. Templer left Malaya in 1954, and although the insurgency continued through Malaya's independence in 1957, and up to 1960, its capacity to disrupt activities in the country had been effectively checked. *See also* HUKBALAHAP UPRISING, p. 384; MAOISM, p. 101; NATIONALIST PARTY (KUOMINTANG), p. 176.

Significance   Guerrilla warfare became the favored instrument of the Communists in the post–World War II era. Wars of national liberation were supported by the Soviet Union throughout the Third World, and they have been successful from Southeast Asia to Latin America. The United States has also attempted to employ insurgents against established governments, but its success rate is decidedly lower than that of its major adversary. Efforts to dislodge the Nicaraguan Sandinistas, for example, have not borne fruit; whereas the insurgency directed against El Salvador via Nicaragua, Cuba, and the Soviet Union, continues to spread. Contrasted with more direct aggressive acts, such as the North Korean invasion of South Korea in 1950, insurgencies have worn down resistance and prepared the scene for more sophisticated military performance. Vietnam is a prime illustration. Most insurgencies seem to be endowed with noble character, given the sacrifice of personal interest for collective gain. The pitting of relatively poor guerrillas against the affluence and vaunted power of authority usually invests the former with purpose denied the latter. This is why it is often impossible to counter an insurgency once it has begun.

Insurgency is a form of contemporary warfare. Counterinsurgency, the use of limited means, or insurgent techniques to counter another insurgency, does not usually work. Only a full wartime effort can eliminate an insurgency, it cannot be defeated piecemeal. This lesson, however, was not learned from the Malayan case. The success of the campaign against the Communist guerrillas in Malaya, and indeed in the Philippines against the Huks during the same period, was managed by engineering sociopolitical change, rather than by the aggressive action of authority. In other words, the insurgency in Malaya was not countered, it was prevented from developing. Despite their initial success, the Chinese Communists of Malaya did not benefit from their struggle with the Japanese. They failed to develop the leadership and the independence necessary to spread their influence among the communities of Malaya. Instead of attacking the retreating British, they would have been better served by joining with them in easing the transfer of power to indigenous hands. Moreover, they failed to make the appropriate connection with the Malay and Indian communities. But if the Chinese Communists misread their program of revolution, the Americans read too much into the British success against the insurgents.

The British experience in Malaya attracted the Americans who were searching for a formula in dealing with Third World insurgents. The Malayan antiguerrilla campaign became the prototype for United States counterinsurgency forces. Ramon Magsaysay's victory over the Huks in the Philippines reinforced these tactics. The United States hoped to achieve the same results with a similar approach in South Vietnam, where after 1954, the Viet Cong, supported by North Vietnam, had eroded the legitimacy of the Saigon government. American Special Forces and the Defense Intelligence Agency were organized with the purpose of developing the counterinsurgency instrument. Instructors, familiar with the Malayan experience, were brought to Washington and dispatched to counterinsurgency centers to assist in the training of American counterparts. But the lessons of Malaya were not applicable to conditions in South Vietnam, and fateful errors were made in designing and executing the program. Ultimately, the decision was made to bolster counterinsurgency with conventional warfare, but the latter was subordinated to the former, not vice versa. The Malayan insurgency failed for particular reasons. Although experiences could be drawn from the conflcit, they were not the experiences that soldiers are usually called upon to interpret.

Hukbalahap Uprising   During the war against Japan, a resistance movement was organized in the Philippines. The movement was known by its Tagalong name, Hukbalahap, or "People's Army against the Japanese." The organization was dominated by Filipino Communists and led by Luis Taruc and Casto Alejandrino. The Communists used the occasion of the war to strike at landlords and capital interests in the Philippines, as well as at the Japanese. The Huks claimed to represent the deprived, and after the war they commanded a broad peasant following in Central Luzon. The Huks also attacked the Americans upon their return to the islands and despite the arrest of the movement's leaders, the fighting intensified. The Huks were well armed and their numbers equalled those of the local constabulary. Taruc's release from prison, therefore, did not calm them, or temper their movement. Full independence came to the Philippines in 1946, and the Manila government felt compelled to ban the organization and arrest its leaders again. Later, the Huks were offered amnesty in return for their weapons, but this gesture was repudiated. The Huks hoped to reap advantage from the scandals afflicting Filipino government. Corruption was endemic, and the publicity it received undermined the legitimacy of those in power. Scandals caused widespread disaffection and helped swell the ranks of the Hukbalahap movement. In 1950 the Huks renamed their organization the Hukbong Mapagpalaya ng Bayan, or People's Liberation Army. Its stated objective was the violent overthrow of the government.

The Huks successfully occupied two provincial capitals on Luzon and caused Manila to take more concerted action. Ramon Magsaysay, a Filipino congressman of impeccable credentials, was named secretary of national defense. Magsaysay purged the military of corrupt officials and opened a campaign to destroy the Huks. Assisted by a United States economic aid program that targeted the rural poor, the dual campaign, along with Magsaysay's generalship, broke the back of the guerrilla movement in 1953. The Huks failed to mount another significant challenge in Luzon, but in the southern island of Mindanao where a Muslim insurgency developed in the 1970s, the New People's Army, a communist guerrilla group, joined the struggle against the Manila government of Ferdinand Marcos. The Moro National Liberation Front, a separatist Islamic group, like the Communists, claimed a popular following. In 1983, a major army sweep of Mindanao claimed to have killed more than 500 insurgents, but the conflict showed no indication of ending. *See also* KILUSANG BAGONG LIPUNAN (KBL), p. 167; POLITICAL PARTIES: PHILIPPINES, p. 192; TYDINGS-MCDUFFIE ACT, 1934, p. 367.

Significance   Magsaysay died in a plane crash in 1957, shortly after assuming the presidency of the Philippines. Earlier, Magsaysay had warned his people that it would be useless to go on killing Huks if the government "continues to foster and tolerate conditions which offer fertile soil to Communism." Magsaysay stood out from the other Filipino leaders. His honesty, integrity, and incorruptibility, separated him from the pack, and this was never better dramatized than during the presidency of Ferdinand Marcos. Marcos became president in 1956, declared martial law in 1972 rather than give up the office, and ruled the Philippines without effective constitutional safeguards. Despite massive displays of popular dissatisfaction, he steadfastly refused to yield power and forcibly represses his opposition. His authority is intertwined with the Filipino power elite who dominate the political and economic life of the nation. Meanwhile, United States military bases in the Philippines are the largest west of Hawaii, and geostrategically significant in balancing Soviet operations from Vietnam's Cam Ranh Bay. Continuing American presence is considered a principal support for the Marcos administration, and the 1983 renewal of U.S. use of the Subic Bay Naval Base and Clark Air Base has been roundly condemned from all sides of the Philippines opposition. The Huk movement had passed through a number of metamorphoses since it was organized in 1942, and yet another was in the offing in the mid-1980s.

Kashmir Dispute   A major cause of Indo-Pakistani conflict. The state of Jammu and Kashmir has been something of a battleground between India and Pakistan ever since they acquired independence in 1947. Kashmir is the contemporary description of the larger area. Kashmir is 86,024 square miles (138,412.62 kilometers) and is located in the heart of Central Asia. It has become India's northernmost territory and was officially proclaimed a state within the Indian Union in 1956. Kashmir is of considerable strategic importance to India. It is no less important to Pakistan, given its proximity to the vital Pakistani Punjab and the political and military nerve centers around Islamabad and Rawalpindi. It is important to note that Kashmir also borders on both the Soviet Union and China, and is located astride the old Central Asian trade routes between the Pakistani and Indian plains and the highlands of Central Asia. The population of Kashmir is estimated to be near or slightly more than 8 million, 75 percent of which is Muslim.

The Muslim character of the state is the central reason for the conflict that has long plagued Kashmir. The population of Kashmir can be divided between the Dogras of Jammu, both Hindu and Muslim; the Paharis of the so-called middle mountain region; the semi-nomadic Gujjars and Gaddis of the hills; and the valley people who are made up of the Kashmiri Brahmins or Pandits (believed to be the purest descendents of the Aryans), a small Sikh community, and the majority Muslim community. Jinnah tried to include Kashmir in the original partition of India but the British decided to leave the political future of the region in the hands of the Hindu maharaja, installed by the British and long sustained by them.

When India and Pakistan achieved their independence, the Maharaja opted for the independence of his kingdom. Muslim tribal elements from the North West Frontier, however, invaded the state and declared a jihad, or holy war, against the Hindu maharaja in an effort to free the majority Muslim population from his control. The maharaja called upon India for military assistance, and belatedly agreed to join the Indian Union, and New Delhi, believing Pakistan had encouraged and supplied the invaders, quickly joined the fray. Although Pakistan had minimal military capability at partition, it also sent forces into the state, and the first India-Pakistan War erupted. It was not quelled until action was taken by the United Nations, which arranged a ceasefire in 1949. The belligerents agreed to hold a plebiscite, but India backed away from its pledge and refused to permit the plebiscite. Several mediation missions mounted and sponsored by the UN also failed to bring about the desired international settlement.

India indicated by its actions that it was unwilling to run the risk of losing Kashmir in a plebiscite. Therefore the areas held by the two countries at the time of the ceasefire remained under their respective control. India controlled the major area of Jammu and Kashmir, particularly the vale or principal valley of Kashmir in which the majority population lived. Pakistan controlled a region to the west and northwest which it called Azad, or Free Kashmir. Although never formally incorporated within Pakistan, Azad Kashmir has been firmly under Pakistani administration.

The Kashmir dispute proved to be the most sensitive controversy between India and Pakistan and although Pakistan refrained from invading the state during India's 1962 border war with China, it did seek to wrest the territory from New Delhi's grasp in 1965. That effort, however, was frustrated by India's decision to strike a counterblow all along its frontier with West Pakistan, especially in the Pakistani Punjab. The Indian strategy forced Pakistan to use its limited military stores in defense of the home territory, and Islamabad was forced to accept the UN call for a ceasefire. Since the conclusion of the 1965 war, Pakistan has been unable to press its demand that the Kashmiri Muslims be permitted the right of self-determination. The India-Pakistan War of 1971 not only put the Kashmir dispute on a backburner, it allowed India to dismember Pakistan and play the role of midwife in the creation of Bangladesh. Since 1971 India has been recognized as the preponderant power in the subcontinent, and although Pakistan still propagandizes the cause of the Kashmiri Muslims, its support in the 1980s is far more distant, and its cries are less strident. Developments inside the state of Kashmir, however, could modify this scenario. Pakistan could find itself drawn into a conflict over Kashmir, if that conflict were precipitated by the Kashmiri Muslims themselves. *See also* NATIONAL CONFERENCE: INDIA, p. 174; PAKISTAN-INDIA WARS, p. 398.

Significance   India and Pakistan view one another as number one enemies in major part because of the bitter emotion generated by the Kashmir dispute. For India, the retention of Kashmir, although predominantly Muslim, is considered essential to India's national security and defense. It is also one of the keys to the continuance of the Indian Union. India prides itself on being a secular state. It is a congeries of peoples, different in cultural expression, ethnicity, and religious belief. Checking, but also satisfying cultural nationalisms is a constant imperative. The Muslims of Kashmir represent only a small portion of the Muslim minority of India (estimated to be between 70 and 90 million), and the integration of all the religious and ethnic communities is a sine qua non for the survival of India as a coherent, progressive state. If India had allowed the right of self-determination to the Kashmiris, a process would have been energized which, in the eyes of Hindu leadership, could lead to the unraveling of the national sociopolitical fabric.

India still sees Pakistan as its principal military threat. Pakistan's ties to the United States, which enable Pakistani armed forces to obtain modern implements of war, reinforce this perception. Rumors concerning Pakistan's future nuclear weapons capability further reinforce it. No less important, India is somewhat fearful of the Muslim world. Pakistan is identified with the worldwide community of Muslims, and India imagines itself an island in a vast "sea of Muslims." Indian strategists believe their country can be better protected with their armed forces entrenched in Kashmir. Pakistan, on the other hand, continues to emphasize the Muslim character of the Kashmir state, and although the issue does not possess the volatility of the Palestinian question, for some Pakistanis it is a similar matter. Pakistan's internal dilemmas, the threat posed to the country by the Soviet presence in Afghanistan, and the flight of three million Afghan refugees to Pakistan, have underlined the need to deal more diplomatically with India. Kashmir, realistically speaking, is not that significant either as fact or symbol. Although the Kashmir dispute is likely to linger, it will probably take a lesser position in Pakistani policy.

Korean War, 1950–53   A war between North and South Korea which broke out on June 25, 1950 when North Korean forces invaded South Korea (ROK) at several points across the thirty-eighth parallel. North Korea denied its invasion of South Korea, insisting that South Korea initiated the war. However, all the evidence seems to indicate that it was North Korea that launched a massive assault on South Korea, to oust the South Korean government then in power. In the initial weeks of the war, North Korea almost succeeded in its goal. Its aggression, however, encountered American intervention, and was condemned by the United Nations who created UN forces to assist South Korea. These forces were made up mostly of American troops, but also included troops from Great Britain, France, Australia, Belgium, Canada, Colombia, Ethiopia, Greece, Luxembourg, the Netherlands, New Zealand, the Philippines, South Africa, Thailand, and Turkey.

When the UN forces pursued North Korean forces deeply into North Korea to the Korean and Chinese border (the Yalu River), China (PRC) dispatched its "volunteer" forces to fight in aid of North Korea. The UN forces were forced to retreat to the south of Seoul, the South Korean capital, but were eventually successful in repelling Chinese forces across the thirty-eighth parallel. This UN action was interpreted by the South Korean government as a precursor to a forceful reunification of the country, but in reality the UN forces were only authorized for limited action to stop the aggression. A ceasefire was finally negotiated in 1953 along the current Demilitarized Zone (DMZ) which is generally drawn along the initial thirty-eighth parallel division of North and South Korea, and which was regarded as topographically more defensible by the UN forces. *See also* ARMED FORCES: NORTH AND SOUTH KOREA, p. 265; KOREA-U.S. MUTUAL ASSISTANCE AGREEMENT, p. 344; THIRTY-EIGHTH PARALLEL, p. 41.

Significance   The Korean War was more than a war between North and South Korea. It occasioned the first UN action against an armed invasion. Though the price of this action was high, both sides paying heavily in terms of casualties and destruction of properties, it was successful in frustrating North Korea's attempt to forcibly reunify the country. The Soviet Union did not send troops, but it supplied North Korea with weapons. China's entry into the war on the side of North Korea was with the obvious blessing of the Soviet Union.

The Korean War was an international war, the first of its kind following World War II, and it helped to aggravate the Cold War situation, forcing the United States to reevaluate its Asian policy. Earlier, the American defense perimeter in the Pacific was believed to be along the Aleutians through Japan and the Ryukus to the Philippines, excluding South Korea and Taiwan. This line was redefined in the course of the Korean War to include South Korea and Taiwan, evidenced by the fact that during the war, the U.S. Seventh Fleet was dispatched to protect Taiwan from possible Chinese invasion. Subsequently, the United States concluded a mutual defense treaty with South Korea in 1953, and with Taiwan in 1954.

For the United States, the Korean War was significant because in the course of that war, the concept of limited war was first applied, and political considerations were given priority, thus limiting the pursuit of ultimate military strategic necessities. South Korea today remains a strategic outpost of American presence in Northeast Asia against the expansion of world communism. Although UN forces have ended their presence in South Korea, leaving behind only the UN Armistice Commission to oversee the truce between North and South Korea, the United States maintains its troops in South Korea under the Combined Forces Command of the United States and South Korea which was established in 1978.

March First Movement: Korea   Peaceful anticolonial demonstrations of the Korean people in 1919 to show their desire for independence from Japan. The Korean people did not accept Japanese colonialism willingly and when American President Woodrow Wilson promised self-determination and independence of the colonial people at the end of World War I, they showed their determination for independence by waging street demonstrations throughout the country. The movement was secretly organized by Korean students in Japan along with Korean Christian and other religious leaders. On March 1, 1919, 29 of the 33 signatories of the Declaration of Korean Independence met at a restaurant in Seoul, read their Declaration, notified the Japanese Government-General of their action, and surrendered to the police. By that time, copies of the Declaration had already been posted throughout Seoul and other places in the country. The Declaration was the impetus for the massive demonstrations that resulted but which were quickly and systematically suppressed by Japanese authorities. *See also* COLONIALISM: JAPAN, p. 66.

Significance   Throughout the March First Movement, the Korean people showed their nationalistic desire for independence. They came to realize, however, that peaceful demonstrations alone would not regain their independence. The Japanese determination to stay in Korea was unshaken, and after 1919 the Japanese administration in Korea took special care to suppress Korean political activities. The Korean independence movement within Korea also suffered from a lack of leadership and organization due to localized and fragmented elements within the movement itself. One of the by-products of the movement was the creation of the Korean Provisional Government in Shanghai, China, which coalesced the various Korean anti-Japanese political activists, who had been forced to operate outside of Korea.

Ultimately, none of these anti-Japanese activities and incidents in or out of Korea, directly contributed to Korean liberation. Instead, Korean liberation resulted from Japan's loss in the Pacific War to the Allied Powers in 1945. This is not to say that the movement was without any significance. Rather, it became a source of inspiration for Korean nationalistic agitations. Since Korea's liberation from Japan, the signifi-cance of the movement for Korea's nationhood has become widely propagated both in North and South Korea. Each year, the First of March is celebrated as a national holiday in both Koreas.

Mukden (Manchurian or 9-18) Incident 1931: Japan   An inci-dent on the railway near Mukden, staged on September 18, 1931, by officers of the Japanese Kwantung Army as a pretext for taking over the whole of Manchuria. Japan had stationed its Kwantung Army in Man-churia since the Russo-Japanese War (1904–05) in order to guard its Southern Manchurian Railroad and other rights. Following the Mukden Incident, the Kwantung Army, known for its conservatism and advocacy of expansionist foreign policy, acted expeditiously, defeating Chinese troops, and taking control of Manchuria. The entire development was without prior consultation with the home government in Tokyo. The Tokyo government, powerless to act against the military, acquiesced in the military takeover of Manchuria, and justified the fait accompli before the rest of the world. When the League of Nations condemned Japan for its Manchurian action, Japan simply walked out of the League, thus discrediting the power of the League. Acting on its own, Japan organized the puppet state of Manchukuo in 1932 and set up as its titular head Henry Pu-yi, the last emperor of China's Manchu (Ch'ing or Qing) Dynasty, which had been overthrown in 1911 by Sun Yat-sen's revolutionary forces. In Manchukuo, real power was vested in the hands of the commander of the Kwantung Army. He also became governor-general of the Kwantung Territory and ambassador to Manchukuo, which became a virtual Japanese colony. *See also* MILITARISM: JAPAN, p. 284.

Significance   In the Mukden Incident, the Japanese military was reacting against the weakness of their civilian government in the face of many international and domestic problems which Japan had experi-enced in the late 1920s. Internationally, in the Washington (1921–22) and London (1930) naval disarmament conferences, Japan was relegated to a second rate power by the West. In China, the Nationalist govern-ment of Chiang Kai-shek also waged "rights recovery" campaigns to recover its own rights and territories from foreign control. Moreover, China was building its own railway system to rival the Japanese Southern Manchurian Railway system. By June 1931, Japanese negotiations to solve this railway dispute ended in failure. The Kwantung Army felt that the Tokyo government was too weak to act and that Japanese control over Manchuria might be compromised. Domestically, Japan was experienc-ing economic retrenchment as a result of the Great World Depression.

All these forces helped the Kwantung Army in its initiative to take over Manchuria and to expand the Japanese empire. Furthermore, the Japanese armed forces had never been properly controlled in the Meiji constitutional framework. The emperor was sovereign in the Meiji constitution and was the only source of power who might have controlled the military, but he was regarded as too sacred a personage to take an active part in government decision making. At the same time, no civilian leaders were politically strong enough to act against the military. The Mukden Incident further discredited the civilian government in Tokyo. The Japanese government's defense of their military action in Manchuria, despite condemnation by the League of Nations, and Japan's withdrawal from this international organization, eventually caused the demise of the League.

Mutiny of 1857   A turning point in British rule in India. In May 1857, troops of the British-officered Indian army mutinied in the Meerut cantonement, and killed a number of those in command. This event sent shockwaves throughout the colonial army and they did not subside until the following year, and after brutalities on both sides had taken a heavy toll of life. Both Indians and Pakistanis today refer to the Mutiny as the beginning of their war of independence from European imperialism. The reasons for the Mutiny are several. High on the list was the introduction of the Enfield rifle which used a greased cartridge that had to be torn with the teeth. The rumor that the cartridge was greased with pig-fat was absolutely repugnant to the Muslim soldier (*sepoy*), while the belief that it was smeared with cow fat angered the Hindu combatant. Both religious orders established absolute prohibitions in the matter of what could and could not be placed in the mouth, and the troops who refused to obey the command of their officers were summarily punished. Other troops came to their rescue and the Mutiny was on.

Given the escalation of the fighting between forces loyal and disloyal to the Crown, the mutineers rallied round the only political symbol they understood that could balance British power. This symbol was the aged Moghul emperor Bahadur Shah II, long a prisoner of the British, and ill equipped to mobilize the energies of the rebellious troops. The Muslims, it is argued, were also reacting to an order by the former British governor-general, the Marquess of Dalhousie, who desired to substitute European-style administration for that of the traditional rulers. The Muslim state of Oudh in present Uttar Pradesh (India), a surviving province of the Moghul empire, was poorly administered and given the absence of a male heir, Dalhousie annexed it. In fact, the governor-general had informed the powerless Moghul emperor that his royal title would lapse upon his death, and that his family would be moved out of the Red Fort in New Delhi to less pretentious quarters south of the capital. Indian Muslims, therefore, were forced to witness the elimination of their remaining empire. In these circumstances, their defense of the Moghuls was understandable. *See also* CABINET MISSION, p. 329; LAHORE RESOLUTION, p. 97; TWO NATION THEORY, p. 128.

Significance   The Mutiny of 1857 has been described as the most dramatic event to occur in India in the nineteenth century. It marked a period of unrest and reorganization. It gave the British new perspective on their Indian colony, and it raised to the surface deep-seated animosities about British rule and conduct. It elevated political consciousness to a new level, and for the first time serious thought as well as action turned toward finding a substitute for East India Company administration on the one side, and British rule on the other. It is important to note that the British were able to regain control of the army because the Punjab remained tranquil. Moreover, Punjabi and Pathan troops helped to hold the mutineers at bay long enough for a British expeditionary force to arrive in the winter of 1857–58.

The British were victorious because they had superior, unified leadership, and morale among the combined European and indigenous force was far higher than among the rebels. Although the mutineers fought valiantly, the absence of a central command and a clear cause undermined their effort. The British could offer stability and a solid alternative for those seeking an end to the violence. Indeed, the history of modern India began in the wake of the Mutiny when the East India Company was divested of its governing powers and administration was assumed by the Crown. A secretary of state for India, responsible to the British parliament, was created in London. A viceroy replaced the governor-general in India, and his legislative council was expanded to permit the inclusion of Indians. After the Mutiny, colonial administration in India would be more coherent, more predictable, and somewhat geared to the evolution of an open parliamentary process. For these reasons both Indians and Pakistanis believe the Mutiny was really their war of independence.

Naxalites   A rebellion in the West Bengal village of Naxalbari in the 1960s conferred upon the perpetrators the name Naxalites. The Naxalites were young Indian Marxists who followed the dictum that "power grew out of the barrel of a gun." These young revolutionaries unleashed a reign of terror in Indian West Bengal that spread to other areas of the country as far south as Andhra Pradesh and Kerala. The Indian government dealt harshly with the Naxalites who refused to yield to offers of amnesty. The Naxalites were linked with the thoughts and declarations of China's leader, Mao Zedong (Mao Tse-tung), in whose name they claimed the right to bring a peasant's revolution to India. They were largely drawn from alienated youth, and many were college and university students. All subscribed to the notion of rural revolution and their efforts were directed at inspiring the impoverished peasantry to commit acts of violence against all established order. In 1972, the Naxalite leader, Charu Mazumdar, was killed by the Indian army and the movement began to recede. In June 1975, however, Naxalites became active in West Bengal, Orissa, and Andhra Pradesh. Attacks on landowners by Naxalite tenant-peasants forced the military to take counter measures. Even the pro–Moscow Communist Party of India publicly described the Naxalites as a militant and primitive form of agrarian struggle and called for their destruction. After the assassination of the central government railway minister and an attempt on the life of the chief justice of the Indian Supreme Court, Prime Minister Gandhi stepped up the campaign against the Naxalites. Because many poor peasants began to see the Naxalites as heroes, the prime minister called upon the states to adhere to their land reform programs. Mrs. Gandhi and her advisors decided that this was still not enough to counteract the terror, and a state of emergency followed in 1975–77. *See also* COMMUNIST PARTY OF INDIA (MARXIST-LENINIST), p. 149; MAOISM, p. 101.

Significance   The Naxalite rebellions had a decided impact on Indian political life. They introduced into India the idea of peasant guerrilla warfare, and the government sensed the need for drastic action. The Naxalites spread their doctrine and tactics to East Pakistan. It is alleged that Indian Naxalite associations in Pakistani East Bengal acted as a catalyst for the civil war that consumed the country in 1971. Bangladesh, therefore, in some measure was inspired by the Naxalite Movement. Prime Minister Gandhi's decision to invade East Pakistan was no doubt influenced by India's desire to reduce Pakistani power. Another dimension of that intervention was the leverage it gave the Indian army to root out the Naxalites. The later state of emergency was also conceived to prevent a Bangladesh-type situation in India. In the final analysis, the Naxalite rebellions in India proved that Indian peasants were not passive, and that they could be mobilized for guerrilla warfare.

Opium War, 1839–42: China   A war between Great Britain and China (also called the first Anglo-Chinese War) between 1839 and 1842 over the traffic in opium, ending with the signing of the Treaty of Nanking (Nanjing) aboard the British ship *Cornwallis*. Great Britain was attracted by a potentially huge market in China but encountered persistent Chinese refusal to trade. When a British emissary was sent to negotiate a trade agreement with China's Ch'ing (Qing) government, he was asked to perform the "*kow-tow* (kou-tou)" (bowing on one's hands and knees). He did not comply and subsequently was denied audience with the emperor. No trade agreement was therefore reached. The Opium War resulted from this and other incidents that marked early British and Chinese contacts. The immediate cause of the war was the trafficking of opium which the British East India Company found lucrative, but which the Ch'ing government labeled economically damaging and harmful to the health of the people. When the ban was ignored, the Ch'ing official in charge of the port of Canton, Lin Tse-hsu (Lin Zexu), confiscated stocks of the drug found in Canton and dumped them into the sea. Britain immediately demanded compensation but the warning was not heeded. In response, the British parliament, in April 1840, decided to send a fleet to China for military action.

Thus began the Opium War. The British fleet, moving at will along the Chinese coast, took control of Shanghai and other cities and moved to capture Nanjing. The Chinese forces were too disorganized and ill equipped to prevent the British invasion. Their alarm was evident as they faced the British steamships: "They can fly across the water, without wind or tide, with the current or against it." At the end, the Ch'ing government was forced to meet the British demands and to sign the Treaty of Nanking in 1842, the first of the "unequal treaties" imposed on China by the West over the next 100 years. *See also* BOXER REBELLION, p. 377; TAIPING REBELLION, p. 410.

Significance   The Opium War was a crude display of western military prowess in Asia. The culprit was Britain, the most industrialized nation of the world at that time. Opium traffic was banned by the Ch'ing government of China but proved highly profitable for British traders and smugglers. Chinese efforts to squelch the opium traffic encountered British military reprisals, and ultimately China was subjected to humiliating treaties. The Treaty of Nanking resulted from the Opium War, and it was followed by others such as the U.S. Treaty of Wanghia, or the Cushing Treaty of 1844, the Franco-Chinese Treaty of 1844, and the Russian Treaty of Aigun of 1858, all extracting territorial, political, and/ or economic concessions.

All the treaty powers acquired "most favored nation" status and were accordingly treated as equal; that is, every right and privilege initially extended to any one treaty power was to be automatically extended to the rest. The treaty powers also enjoyed extra-territoriality in China. This system made a farce of Chinese sovereignty, since it permitted foreigners and their activities to be governed by foreign, not Chinese, law. The Treaty of Nanking in part stated: "His Majesty the Emperor of

China agrees that British subjects, with their families and establishments, shall be allowed to reside, for the purpose of carrying on their mercantile pursuits, without molestation or restraint at the cities and towns of Canton, Amoy, Foochow-fu, Ningpo, and Shanghai, ... His Majesty the Emperor of China cedes to Her Majesty the Queen of Great Britain ... the Island of Hongkong to be possessed in perpetuity ... The Emperor of China agrees to pay the sum of six millions of dollars as the value of opium which has been delivered at Canton in the month of March 1839. ..."

Pacific War: World War II   Early on December 7, 1941, the day which U.S. President Franklin D. Roosevelt labeled as "a date which will live in infamy," Japan carried out a surprise air and naval strike against Pearl Harbor, the U.S. naval base in Hawaii, almost demolishing the U.S. Pacific fleet. Ninety percent of U.S. air and surface strength in the area was immobilized or destroyed, including eight battleships and seven other vessels which were sunk or damaged. The Japanese memorandum to the United States, breaking off diplomatic relations, came later that day. The U.S. Congress also quickly approved President Roosevelt's war message on Japan on December 8, 1941.

World War II spread to the Pacific region, quickly involving all the countries in the area as Japanese troops fanned out in a wide arc from their bases in China, Indochina, Formosa (Taiwan), and the Pacific islands. After Pearl Harbor and the Japanese sinking of the British warships, the *Prince of Wales* and the *Repulse* on December 10, 1941, Anglo-American naval power in the Pacific was unable to stop the initial Japanese advances. Japanese troops were successful everywhere in destroying the Allied presence and their colonial possessions. In short order, Hong Kong fell on December 25, 1941, Malaya and Singapore on February 15, 1942, Burma in June 1942, the Netherlands Indies in March 1942, Manila (the Philippines) on January 2, 1942, Bataan on April 9, 1942, and Corregidor on May 6, 1942.

By the summer of 1942, the whole of Southeast Asia was under Japanese occupation and Japan was reaching southward toward Australia and eastward to Hawaii. Japan was, however, forced to halt these advances first at the Battle of Midway in June 1942, and then in New Guinea and the Solomons later in 1942. The Japanese war strategy was to seize Southeast Asia quickly and then seek a compromise peace in their advantage. They figured Germany's final victory in Europe but did not anticipate the American resolve and capability to mobilize resources, to strike back at their newly acquired territories in Southeast Asia, and to take the war to their homeland.

By February 1945, American forces under the command of General MacArthur had smashed their way up from New Guinea to Manila (the Philippines), and American planes were bombing targets in Japanese home islands. Also, Admiral C. W. Nimitz's Pacific island-hopping strategy against Japan was successful in defeating Japan in Guam, Saipan, and Iwo Jima in the central Pacific. When Okinawa was taken in April 1945, Japan was no longer capable of defending itself from Allied assaults. The atomic bombs dropped on Hiroshima on August 6, 1945 and on Nagasaki on August 9, 1945 hastened Japan's decision to surrender. Japan's surrender came on August 14, 1945 (August 15 in Japan). By that time, the Soviet Union had declared war on Japan on August 8, 1945 as agreed by the leaders of the three Great Allied Powers at Yalta in February 1945 that "in two or three months after Germany has surrendered and the war in Europe has terminated, the Soviet Union shall enter into the war against Japan on the side of the Allies. . . ."
See also GREATER EAST ASIA COPROSPERITY SPHERE, p. 15; SINO-JAPANESE WAR, 1937–45, p. 407; WARTIME CONFERENCES, p. 370.

Significance   Japan's surprise attack on Pearl Harbor, and full-scale war on the United States and the Allied Powers were an epoch-making development with immeasurable significance. Japan lost the war, but Japanese war efforts have revolutionized the Asian political landscape. Japan's war goals included (1) the establishment of a new order in East Asia by excluding the interests and influences of the western powers; (2) the erection of an impregnable East Asian defense system with strategic bases located on the perimeter of the Great East Asia Coprosperity Sphere under its dominant influence; (3) the creation of a self-sufficient economic community in the area; (4) the eventual formation of independent states out of the former western colonies; and (5) the Allied recognition and acceptance of peace terms embodying these objectives. At the outset of the war, Japanese invading forces freed the area from western control and encouraged the former colonial people to wrest their independence.

As a consequence of the war, all the western colonies in Southeast Asia became independent. The war, however, was a gross miscalculation for Japan. Japan lost the war and accepted in full the terms of surrender laid down in the Potsdam Declaration of July 26, 1945. The Instrument of Surrender was signed on September 2, 1945 on board the USS *Missouri*. As a defeated nation, Japan was to be subjected to military occupation until such time as the Allied Powers were convinced that Japan's war-making power was completely destroyed and that Japan was transformed into a peace-loving, democratic nation. The long-term effect of the war for the United States was to establish it as a Pacific power. The

United States also helped to initiate the post—World War II atomic age by developing the atomic bomb and dropping it on Hiroshima and Nagasaki.

Pakistan-India Wars, 1945—48, 1965, 1971   Pakistan and India have fought three wars against one another since obtaining their independence in 1947. The first two wars, in 1947—48, and 1965, involved the problem of Kashmir. The third focused on the dismemberment of Pakistan and the creation of the independent state of Bangladesh, formerly East Pakistan. The pattern of the three wars reveals an escalating intensity that makes a future limited war less probable. Pakistan precipitated the first two wars; India initiated the third. Pakistan won a token victory in the first war by occupying and retaining the western section of Kashmir. Its claim to the whole of Kashmir, or at least the right of the people of Kashmir to determine their own future, was rejected by India. Pakistan tried to force India to hold a plebiscite in Kashmir, but even United Nations pressure failed to get New Delhi to yield. Pakistan, therefore, was far from satisfied with its victory in Azad Kashmir (Free Kashmir), and in 1965 it attempted to seize by force what had been denied it by diplomacy.

The 1965 war, which was ignited in Kashmir, could not be contained there. India defended its position in its northernmost state, while striking diversionary blows against Pakistan's midsection in the Punjab and all along the India-Pakistan frontier. New Delhi even launched air raids against East Pakistan and threatened to move its troops into that distant eastern province. China, a friend of Pakistan and an enemy of India following their 1962 border war, also threatened involvement in the 1965 war. New Delhi had no reason to ignore the Chinese ultimatum, but it appears that Pakistan's president, Mohammad Ayub Khan, decided it was not in his country's long-term interest to allow Beijing to spread the conflict. Ayub's decision to accept the United Nations resolution for a ceasefire did not satisfy the Pakistani citizenry, but it brought the war to a swift close. The end result, however, was a stalemate and an escalation of bitterness on both sides.

The 1971 war began as an act of civil disobedience when the Pakistani Bengalis rebelled against the power of their West Pakistani brethren. After efforts at negotiating a settlement based upon the 1970 election results failed, the Pakistan army in East Pakistan was ordered to destroy the Awami League Party and leadership (the Awami League had won a majority of the seats in the national assembly). This unprecedented action galvanized the disgruntled Bengalis to join in a protracted struggle against the Pakistan army stationed in the province. After several months of vicious fighting, numerous atrocities, and the flight to India of millions of refugees, India decided to internationalize the struggle. When New Delhi's troops crossed the frontier into East Pakistan in December 1971, it marked a new level of combat. India's armed forces by this date were far superior in numbers and sophisticated weapons. Moreover, logistically they had the overwhelming advantage against the Pakistani garrison whose supply lines lay across India, or by way of a 3,000-mile sea journey from West to East Pakistan.

Although the UN Security Council voted to demand India's withdrawal from East Pakistan, the Soviet Union cast a veto making the action null and void. Unlike in 1965, China did not offer direct assistance to Pakistan, and the United States did not lift the embargo on arms to Pakistan that Washington had imposed at the outset of the 1965 war. In sum, Islamabad could not retain East Pakistan and was compelled to surrender and acknowledge the establishment of Bangladesh. India, however, did not confine the war to East Pakistan. It also struck deep blows against West Pakistan, destroying vital fuel dumps and port facilities in and around Karachi. Other Pakistani targets as far as Peshawar were also attacked. At sea, India sunk a number of Pakistani naval vessels, and although they fought gallantly, they were no match for the better-equipped Indians.

The 1971 war was the most conclusive of the three fought between the two countries. Pakistan lost one-sixth of its territory, more than half its population, and 90,000 Pakistani soldiers and airmen, as well as government personnel and their dependents were made prisoners of war. Economically speaking the country was near bankruptcy, and its public morale was never worse. The Pakistani military junta that had presided over this humiliating defeat quickly transferred power to the civilian government of Zulfikar Ali Bhutto, the first non-military administration since the first army coup in 1958. India fared far better as a consequence of the war. It claimed hegemony over the entire subcontinent and continued to expand its armed forces. India's leaders were emboldened to increase the nation's capability and to ensure the status that had been so aggressively crafted. *See also* ARMED FORCES: SOUTH ASIA, p. 268; AWAMI LEAGUE, p. 135; KASHMIR DISPUTE, p. 386.

Significance   Zulfikar Ali Bhutto wrote an end to the Kashmir question when he met with Prime Minister Indira Gandhi in Simla in 1972. Unlike 1966, when President Ayub Khan met with another Indian prime minister in Tashkent (Soviet Union) to iron out differences between their two countries, Bhutto's meeting was greeted with quiet resignation. Ayub's power waned after his discussions. Bhutto's appeared to blossom. Pakistanis were exhausted after the 1971 war, and the country did not have to be pressured into reconciling their differences with their bigger neighbor. India had demonstrated superior military performance and Pakistan was hard-put to simply sustain its integrity. It no longer voiced the view that one Pakistani soldier was the equal of six Indian soldiers. Islamabad no longer insisted on parity in military capabilities, and its claim to Kashmir was little more than a whisper. With the Simla Accords of 1972 providing a foundation, Bhutto anticipated normalizing relations with India. Diplomatic channels would be reopened, overflights of each other's territories would be reinstated, and trade restrictions and cultural barriers would be removed.

In the meantime, India behaved as a major power. In 1974 it detonated a nuclear device, and although denying it was building atomic weapons, its capability in this field was acknowledged throughout the world. Bhutto's call for an "Islamic bomb" to balance that of India's appeared out of character with his otherwise diplomatic overtures to New Delhi, but the Pakistani military establishment apparently insisted on a program of nuclear weapons procurement. The nuclear question blocked significant diplomatic breakthroughs based upon reconciliation, and when the army removed Bhutto from office in 1977, old fears between New Delhi and Islamabad resurfaced. The Soviet invasion of Afghanistan in 1979 and the United States decision to resupply the Pakistan armed forces in 1981 further aggravated relations between India and Pakistan. In 1983, India was accused of meddling in Pakistan's internal affairs and of supporting rebellious groups in Sind. In 1984 New Delhi accused Pakistan of supporting Sikh separatists in the Punjab. Despite efforts at improving commerce between the two countries, their relations remained severely strained.

Russo-Japanese War, 1904–05   A war between Imperial Russia and Japan for the control of the Korean peninsula and dominant influence in East Asia. Since the Sino-Japanese War (1894–95), tension continued to mount between Russia and Japan over the "Korean question." Russia was determined to proceed with her imperial scheme over Korea and Manchuria. Japan could not overlook Russia's southward advance. With support from Great Britain, Japan called on Russia to withdraw her Far Eastern armies stationed in Manchuria on the pretext of protecting the Trans-Siberian Railroad. In addition, Japan requested recognition of Japan's paramount interest in Korea. Upon Russian refusal to meet these demands, Japan broke off diplomatic relations in February 1904. Soon thereafter the Japanese navy initiated an attack on Port Arthur (Russia's Far Eastern naval base) and also sank a Russian warship in the Yellow Sea. The Japanese Imperial Rescript declaring war against Russia read in part: "The integrity of Korea is a matter of constant concern to this Empire," and Russia's occupation of Manchuria and its absorption of it "would render it impossible to maintain the integrity of Korea. . . ."

In the war Japan was victorious, but because she was unwilling to fight a long-drawn conflict with Russia she requested President Theodore Roosevelt of the United States to mediate for a peace settlement. Russia also found the war too costly and was willing to end hostilities. The Treaty of Portsmouth, which was signed on September 5, 1905, officially ended the Russo-Japanese War. Among other things, this treaty provided for Japan's "paramount political, military, and economic interests in Korea." Russia also agreed to cede to Japan (1) the lease of Port Arthur and Dalien (Dairen) and their adjacent territories, and the lease of the Changchun and Port Arthur Railroad (South Manchurian Railway) with all its branches; and (2) the southern part of the islands of Sakhalin and all the islands adjacent thereto. This treaty, together with the Taft-Katsura Agreement (between the United States and Japan) of July 1905 gave Japan a free hand to eventually annex Korea in 1910. *See also* COLONIALISM: JAPAN, p. 66; WARM WATER PORT POLICY, p. 47.

Significance   At the start of the Russo-Japanese War, the Korean government declared its neutrality, but Japan ignored this and deployed her troops as if Korea were already a Japanese colony. The more victorious Japan was against Russia, the tighter Japan's control over Korea became. Russia was beaten at Lushun in Manchuria, and her Baltic Fleet was destroyed in the battle of the Korean Strait. At the same time, her domestic political crises were mounting. In the fall of 1905, Russia was willing to make peace with Japan and retreat from the area and leave Japan with her controlling influence over Korea. Both Great Britain and the United States acquiesced to the rise of Japanese power in the area— Great Britain with the Anglo-Japanese Alliance (1902, 1904) and the United States with the Taft-Katsura Agreement of 1906. For his peacemaking efforts at the Portsmouth Conference, President Theodore Roosevelt received the Nobel Peace Prize in 1906. It was not long after the war that Japan formally annexed Korea (in 1910) and started expanding her influence over Manchuria.

Second Indochina War (1964–75)   An undeclared war fought by the United States in Indochina. The United States replaced the French in Indochina, but its stated purpose was to prevent the spread of aggressive international communism, not colonial conquest. Washington ignored its prior support for Ho Chi Minh, the Communist Viet Minh leader, during the war with Japan. It was familiar with Ho's lifelong quest to free Indochina from French colonialism. Washington gave France $954 million in military aid to fight the Viet Minh, but it also stood by helplessly in the final hours of the French agony at Dien Bien Phu. In spite of the French defeat in the First Indochina War (1946–54), the United States refused to sign the Geneva Accords of 1954. The accords recognized Ho and his associates as the ruling power north of the seventeenth parallel. Washington promoted the government of Ngo Dinh Diem south of the seventeenth parallel. The United States also advised Diem not to hold the elections called for in the 1954 agreement.

The United States assumed the role of chief protector and supplier for the administration in South Vietnam, and American economic and technical assistance poured into the country. Washington justified the transfer of developmental stores, and soon thereafter, military advisors and equipment, to South Vietnam on grounds that the loss of the country to the Communists would cause a chain reaction throughout Southeast Asia. Washington spoke of "falling dominoes" and insisted that Southeast Asian Treaty commitments (also developed in 1954) demanded maximum compliance. The United States underestimated the nature of the task it assumed in Indochina. It also underestimated the North Vietnamese and failed to understand the full meaning of the French defeat in 1954. Thus, the United States expanded its commitment to Indochina through Presidents Eisenhower, Kennedy, and Johnson.

At the time of President John Kennedy's assassination in November 1963 (Ngo Dinh Diem had been overthrown by his army chiefs and murdered several weeks earlier), the United States had approximately 16,000 "military advisors" in Indochina. The Vietnamese Communists, however, refused to be intimidated by the American presence, and attacks were launched against U.S. personnel. Washington ordered air strikes against Vietnamese military positions, but Hanoi refused to yield. In the summer of 1964, American naval vessels on patrol off the coast of Vietnam were attacked by North Vietnamese torpedo boats. It was Washington's position that the American destroyers were in international waters and that the attack was unprovoked. President Lyndon Johnson ordered retaliatory blows against Vietnamese fortifications. He also asked for and received a resolution from the American Congress condemning the Vietnamese act and authorizing him to make an appropriate response.

The Tonkin Gulf Resolution marked the formal beginning of the Second Indochina War. American troop levels escalated dramatically. At the height of the American involvement in Indochina more than 500,000 ground troops operated in the region, another 100,000 were aboard the naval armada offshore and in air bases in the South Pacific. The United States sought to accomplish what the French had failed to do, and they moved into the campaign with considerable confidence in their strategy and overall capability. The North Vietnamese and their Viet Cong allies in South Vietnam, however, remained steadfast. Despite high losses, the war became a protracted engagement in which the North Vietnamese leaders committed all their people and energy. The seemingly endless conflict, with its horrifying human cost, undermined American confidence and opened the American government to sustained criticism at home and abroad. U.S. body counts indicated a wearing down of the enemy, but they also dramatized the horrors of war. Military sweeps such as search and destroy missions were supposed to eliminate Viet Cong bases in the South. The enemy refused to fade away, however, and the repeated use of weapons of mass destruction against the villages of Vietnam produced incidents like "My Lai." My Lai became a code word for American atrocities against innocent civilians. Given the world media's coverage of the conflict, criticism was transformed into condemnation. Most importantly, the American government was verbally attacked by its friends and allies who counselled withdrawal from Indochina. The U.S. persisted despite this deepening opposition. Fortified hamlets were developed to protect the rural population from the Viet Cong guerrillas. But the guerrillas not only survived, they destroyed the effectiveness of the hamlets. Political instability in South Vietnam's government was another elusive problem.

After Diem, rule passed from one general to another until Nguyen Van Thieu consolidated his power, but his administration proved to be as repressive and corrupt as those preceding it. The government of South Vietnam had few friends in or outside the country. Moreover, the North Vietnamese "Tet Offensive" of 1968 left the Americans, as well as the South Vietnamese, disillusioned. Tet contrasted the overall weakness of the South Vietnam government with the substantial power and popular appeal of the North. American troops beat back the Communist drive, but the offensive demonstrated that the enemy was increasing in strength. Tet proved to be a turning point in the war. The United States realized it could not defeat the North Vietnamese without moving its army north of the seventeenth parallel and straight into Hanoi. This was judged an unacceptable risk because it would transform the limited war into a general one with the distinct possibility that China would enter the fray. President Johnson realized too late that his dream of quick victory has misled him, and he announced his decision not to seek another term. Johnson's departure opened the way for Richard Nixon, and he became president in January 1969. Nixon indicated his desire to end the war, and his National Security Advisor, Henry Kissinger, entered negotiations with the North Vietnamese. While the diplomats talked, the war continued and even intensified. Nixon ordered the saturation bombing of North Vietnam's cities and ports, the mining of its harbors, and in 1970, the crossing of the Cambodian frontier.

Cambodia had been bombed repeatedly by the United States in an effort to strike at Viet Cong sanctuaries in the country. Like Laos, Cambodia was drawn toward the center of conflict. Because he was perceived as aiding the Communists, Prince Sihanouk was overthrown in an American-engineered coup, and General Lon Nol, a loyal American supporter, took over the government in Phnom Penh. Cambodia's fortunes went from bad to worse after the American incursion. Indeed, the whole of Indochina was ablaze and the only opportunity to dampen the flames lay in the talks in Paris. Finally, in 1973, the United States, North and South Vietnam, and the Viet Cong signed an accord that was more aimed at permitting the United States government to withdraw its forces "with honor," than terminate the hostilities. The United States continued to emphasize the sovereignty of South Vietnam and it pledged to supply the aid necessary to sustain it against Communist encroachment. But the North Vietnamese did not come so far, or make such sacrifices, to stop there. The fighting continued through 1973 and 1974, and by the spring of 1975 Hanoi launched its final campaign. Crack South Vietnamese troops were cut off from resupply by the sudden North Vietnamese offensive. The population of the region panicked, as did the remaining forces, and a human sea of frightened people moved toward Saigon in front of the conquering army of the North. The Americans still in Vietnam, particularly the embassy staff, beat a hasty retreat to ships offshore as Hanoi moved into and occupied Saigon. The southern city was renamed Ho Chi Minh city, and the Second Indochina War drew to an end. *See also* DIEN BIEN PHU, p. 380; GENEVA ACCORDS, 1954, p. 339; KHMER ROUGE, p. 166; PARIS ACCORDS, 1973, p. 351; SEVENTEENTH PARALLEL, p. 37; SINO-VIETNAMESE CONFLICT, 1979, p. 409; TONKIN GULF, p. 43.

Significance   The Second Indochina War was the longest war ever fought by United States forces. It was also the only war it clearly did not win. After its conclusion, the United States Congress passed the War Powers Resolution (1973), restricting the president's use of troops in future undeclared wars. The government was generally reluctant to become embroiled in conflict distant from the United States, or where the country was not directly threatened. "No more Vietnams" was a common refrain and it prevented President Gerald Ford from assisting anticommunist forces in Angola. It also paralyzed the Carter administration, which was faced with the collapse of the Shah's regime in Iran, and later, with the seizure of the American embassy and its personnel in Tehran. Carter was left with little more than a wheat embargo and boycott of the 1980 Moscow Olympics when the Soviet Union invaded Afghanistan in 1979.

Ronald Reagan sought to reverse this situation on taking office in January 1981. His deployment of military advisors to El Salvador and military aid to Honduras, as well as the 1983 invasion of Grenada, seemed to signify the neutralization of the "Vietnam syndrome." In addition, the decision to station U.S. marines in Beirut was a bold step under questionable conditions. Despite the argument that the troops were defensive in nature, and in Lebanon, nothing more than "peace-keepers," the critics of the president's actions were numerous and vocal. After the tragic loss of more than 250 marines in Beirut, the majority killed by a single terrorist attack in October 1983, Reagan, under Congressional pressure, decided to remove the troops from Lebanon. But the question about his power to commit American forces to areas seized by internal warfare, continued to be debated in the Congress and American press.

The end of the Second Indochina War provided the Vietnamese Communists with the opportunity to consolidate their power and expand their influence. They were beneficiaries of a multitude of serviceable weapons that the United States had given to South Vietnam. Their army became the instrument of control, not only in unified Vietnam, but in Laos as well. Moreover, in 1979, Vietnam invaded Communist Cambodia, destroyed Chinese influence in Phnom Penh, and established a puppet regime in place of the ousted Pol Pot. Hanoi also opened the country to the Soviet Union, its primary benefactor. The Soviets pledged material support to Hanoi when China threatened invasion in 1979–80. Beijing declared it wanted Vietnam out of Cambodia, but the Vietnamese withstood a Chinese thrust across their border, and China withdrew its troops without achieving its objective. In the meantime, Hanoi provided the Soviet Union with a base at Cam Ranh Bay and eliminated pockets of resistance in the southern half of the country. Although Vietnam became the largest military power in Southeast Asia, it was also isolated from the region around it. Attempts to gain a voice in ASEAN were unsuccessful. Moreover, it was unable to inspire other states to recognize its client-government in Cambodia; and its trade with the outer world was largely restricted to East bloc countries. On occasion, the United States hinted that it was prepared to normalize relations with Vietnam, but Washington demanded a complete account of Americans still missing in action before diplomatic negotiations took place.

Sino-Indian War (1962)   Fighting broke out between Chinese and Indian forces on October 20, 1962 both on India's northeast frontier and in Ladakh. In India's North East Frontier Agency, the Chinese advanced over 100 miles south, threatening the plains of Assam. In Ladakh, they advanced to the line claimed by the Chinese as marking their territory. The Chinese showed their might in the fighting; the Indians proved unprepared. On November 21, however, the Chinese announced a unilateral ceasefire and the withdrawal of their troops. The immediate point of the dispute had been the boundary question between China and India. China (PRC) had wanted to have all the borders that had been imposed by the former imperial powers renegotiated. In addition, China's assertion of sovereignty over Tibet (Xizang) made the border question of the region important, as Tibet borders India and the Tibetans revolting against the oppressive Chinese rule were finding a haven in India.

As a way to better integrate Tibet to China proper, China built a road from Xinjiang (Sinkiang) to Lhasa (Tibetan capital) during 1955–58 and planned to build the first railway line by 1966 through Aksai-chin, which India inherited from the British Raj, who had occupied this frontier area during the height of their imperialistic expansion. China wanted a barter arrangement with India as had been done in the case of the China and Burma border. China would accommodate India's claim in the eastern sector provided that India did the same for China's claim in the western sector. However, India was against any territorial compromise and she was supported by both the USSR and the United States. The war did not settle the boundary question between China and India. China's diplomacy of violence did not bring about the hoped for result: bringing India to the negotiating table over the disputed boundaries. India refused to negotiate from a position of weakness. *See also* CHINA: AUTONOMOUS REGIONS, p. 10; INDO-SOVIET TREATY, p. 340; TIBET (XIANG), p. 42.

Significance   Uncertain boundaries exist around China's periphery, but the Sino-Indian War of 1962 was not merely over the boundary question. It was about China asserting its new international status and securing what it regarded as its rightful claim over Tibet. These reasons alone could not have brought about the war without the significant contribution of other factors. These factors include, in particular, the Soviet Union's relations with China and India. While the Soviet Union's relations with China had been worsening, her relations with India had become most amicable. While the Soviet Union terminated her aid to China, she agreed with India in 1962 to deliver Soviet Mig fighters for the Indian Air Force and to build a factory under license in India to make the aircraft, as if to support India in her border dispute with China.

In the war, China showed, in part, her displeasure with the Soviet-Indian military alliance. China's show of force, however, could not bring India to the negotiating table. India refused to compromise its national and strategic interests in the area. Furthermore, both claim leadership of the Third World and they are unwilling to accept any move that would tarnish their image. Any realistic compromise over the boundary problem between China and India is difficult for the moment, as each is jealously protective of its nationwide and international images.

Sino-Japanese War, 1894–95   A war between China and Japan for control of Korea, which ended in Japanese victory. The Japanese government declared war on China on August 1, 1894. This declaration was preceded by the sinking of the British steamer *Kowshing,* which was transporting Chinese troops from China to Korea. The Declaration read in part: "Corea (Korea) is an independent state. She was first introduced into the family of nations by the advice and guidance of Japan. It has, however, been China's habit to designate Corea as her dependency, and both openly and secretly to interfere with her domestic affairs. . . ." Within a month following the Declaration, the Japanese imperial navy was in control of the sea. By the end of the year, the Japanese army was also in control of Korea and the Manchurian Liao-dong peninsula. Japan even threatened to invade Beijing (Peking), the Chinese capital. China quickly sued for peace and sent its envoy to Japan. The Treaty of Shimonoseki, which terminated hostilities, was signed on April 17, 1895. According to the terms of this treaty, China was forced to abandon any claim for vassalage of Korea, to recognize the full and complete independence and autonomy of Korea, and to cede to Japan the following territories: (1) the southern portion of the provinces of Fengtien (Fengtian) (the Liaotung [Liaodong] Peninsula); (2) the island of Formosa (Taiwan); and (3) the Pescadore Islands. China also agreed to pay Japan, as a war indemnity, the sum of 200 million *kuping taels. See also* COLONIALISM: JAPAN, p. 66; TONGHAK REBELLION, p. 412.

Significance   The main issue of the Sino-Japanese War was control over Korea, but its impact reverberated far beyond Korea itself. Japan showed its military preparedness as a modern nation, and, by humbling China as easily as it did in the war, it inherited a dominant status over East Asia. The loss of the war was a sobering experience for many concerned Chinese. Many in China cried out for reform. Others advocated learning from Japan. In the eyes of the outside world, China was a sick giant who could not be trusted any longer as a counterveiling force against emergent Japan. Russia, in particular, felt her interests in East Asia threatened, and started reinforcing her presence in the area. Furthermore, Russia persuaded Germany and France to be part of a joint effort to force Japan to relinquish its claim over the Liaotung peninsula. In the face of possible joint Russo-German-French military action against her, Japan capitulated. Here, Japan encountered the first systematic western opposition to her newly assumed role in Asia.

Sino-Japanese War, 1937–45   A war between China and Japan which started on July 7, 1939 (Double Seven) over a Marco Polo Bridge incident near Beijing (Peking), when Chinese and Japanese forces clashed, and which lasted until Japan's surrender to the Allied Powers in

World War II. The details of the incident in which there was no formal declaration of war were never clarified. Following the incident, however, Japanese forces acted decisively, driving Chinese forces out of the entire Beijing-Tianjin area. By mid-August the war had spread to the Shanghai area, and Nanjing, the capital city of the Nationalist government, became the target of Japanese air attacks. Japan obviously sought an early Chinese surrender, but the war lingered on. Japanese forces pushed forward, but the Nationalist Chinese, with help from the United States, were secure in their wartime capital of Chongqing (Chungking). Meanwhile, Chinese Communist guerrillas fought Japanese troops and expanded their areas of operation, placing a large area of China under their control.

What Japan sought in China was the establishment of an autonomous north China region, in which a puppet government under Japan's control was to be set up. However, this design met with persistent Chinese resistance and worsened a widespread anti-Japanese feeling among the Chinese people.

In 1937, Japan was faced with the momentous decision of either waging war against a China divided due to the conflict between the Nationalists and the Communists, or waiting until the two groups formed a united front against Japan. Another option for Japan was to either abandon or temporize its design over China. Finally, using the Marco Polo Bridge incident as an excuse, Japan attacked China in its weakened state. The war dragged on, but Japan remained unshaken in its determination to stay in China. When the United States aided China and pressed Japan to withdraw from its conquest, the threat of direct conflict between Japan and the United States became increasingly evident. On December 7, 1941, Japan carried out a massive, surprise attack on the American fleet stationed at Pearl Harbor, Hawaii. *See also* MAOISM, p. 101; NATIONALIST PARTY: CHINA, p. 176; PACIFIC WAR, p. 396.

Significance   The Sino-Japanese War was the precursor of a bigger conflict between Japan and the United States in World War II. The United States could not overlook Japan's dominance in Asia and its adventurism in China. In Japan, the proponents of a strong China policy were in control of the government. Internationally, a strong anti-Japanese China, supported by the United States, was regarded as anathema to Japan's security. More significant was the impact of the Sino-Japanese War on the Chinese Communist movement, which successfully exploited the chaotic situation and transformed itself during the war from a small force almost at the verge of extermination into a force to be reckoned with in any balance of power consideration in China. Following the kidnapping incident of Chinese Nationalist leader, Chiang Kai-shek, in Xian (Sian), Chiang Kai-shek's anticommunist military campaign was halted and the Nationalists were forced to agree on a united front with the Communists against Japan.

During the Sino-Japanese war, the Communists obtained a respite from the long civil war and were supplied with Nationalist arms. Using their mobile guerrilla tactics effectively against the Japanese, they were able to further broaden their bases of operation and recruit mass followings, while Nationalist groups withdrew to the security of their Chongqing fortress. When Japan surrendered in 1945, the Communists were in control of 100 million men, and their so-called "people's militia" numbered about 2 million. Increasingly, the Communists, under the leadership of Mao Zedong (Mao Tse-tung), were able to present themselves as an attractive alternative to the Nationalist government. The Sino-Japanese War significantly helped the Chinese Communist cause in the Nationalist-Communist struggle for power in China.

Sino-Vietnamese Conflict, 1979–   A new conflict between historic antagonists that threatens Communist solidarity in Southeast Asia. The People's Republic of China (PRC) provided substantial assistance to North Vietnam in its wars with France and the United States and played an important role in Hanoi's ultimate conquest of South Vietnam in 1975. But Beijing's concern with Soviet influence in Vietnam and the PRC's conflict with Moscow revived old animosities and fears. Moreover, Vietnam's policies in Kampuchea (Cambodia) rivaled those of China. When Vietnamese forces attacked the Khmer Rouge in 1977, China believed it necessary to throw its weight behind Pol Pot's troops. The PRC terminated technical cooperation with Vietnam in December 1977 and all economic assistance in July 1978, only a month after Hanoi entered into a treaty of peace and friendship with Moscow. In December 1978 Vietnam sent a large invasion force into Kampuchea with the stated intention of destroying the Pol Pot regime. Moreover, Vietnam established a puppet government in Phnom Penh. Believing Vietnam and the Soviet Union threatened China's southern borders, Beijing ordered a "retalitory operation" into Vietnam. The PRC attacked Vietnam on February 17, 1979, sending 200,000 troops against the well-equipped, experienced army of Hanoi. The bulk of those confronting the Chinese, however, were militia, not regular army personnel. The entire campaign lasted 17 days, with Chinese forces moving approximately 25 miles inside Vietnam at certain points. But Vietnamese resistance was formidable, and the Chinese could not claim victory over their smaller but militarily adept neighbor. China announced the recall of its troops on March 5 and called upon Hanoi to enter into serious negotiations. Hanoi responded with a general mobilization of its population. Although China never completely withdrew from Vietnamese soil, talks between the two sides began in mid-April. But the Chinese had not achieved their anticipated victory. Vietnam refused to quit Kampuchea, and the talks between the belligerents were fruitless. *See also* KHMER ROUGE, p. 166; ONE PARTY VASSAL STATE: KAMPUCHEA, p. 242.

Significance   Hostilities between Vietnam and the PRC, increased Soviet support to the former, and especially Beijing's perception of the Soviet Union as a hegemonistic and imperial state contributed to an improvement in Sino-American relations. The Soviet invasion of Afghanistan in December 1979 reinforced Chinese perceptions of Moscow as aggressive and expansionistic. Thus when Vietnam mounted a new offensive against the Kampuchean resistance in 1984, China believed it necessary to increase its pressure on Hanoi. In March–April 1984 the two sides maneuvered more aggressively toward one another. Vietnam had been plagued by Kampuchean guerrillas operating near the Thailand frontier and it set out to destroy these resistance units by seizing their bases. In the meantime, the Soviets had transformed Vietnam's Cam Ranh Bay into a large naval base, home to 27 Soviet warships, including 6 attack submarines. Soviet bombers flew routine missions from the air base located at the facility. Furthermore, the first Soviet war games, including mock amphibious landings, were made along the Vietnamese coast in April 1984. Thailand protested the Soviet presence. China, however, reopened its limited military operations against Vietnamese forces in April, and clashes between the two communist armies continued sporadically into 1985. Vietnam let it be known it considered itself at war with China, but a formal pronouncement was avoided. More important, Vietnam intensified its operations in Kampuchea and displayed no inclination to withdraw to its own territory. Relations between China and Vietnam were programmed to remain conflicting.

Taiping Rebellion, 1850–64: China   A rebellion in China led by Hung Hsiu-ch'uan (Hong Xiuquan) to overthrow the Manchu (Ch'ing or Qing) Dynasty and establish *T'ai-p'ing T'ien-kuo* (Taiping Tianguo), the Heavenly Kingdom of Great Peace. Hung was born of a *hakka* farmer in 1814, in a village near Canton. The word "hakka," which means "stranger," found its origin in the century-old southern migration of the northern and central Han Chinese trying to escape from Manchu rule. Hung, as a youth, studied the Confucian classics to become a scholar-official, but his repeated failures at the state examinations left him greatly disappointed. Following the third attempt (1837), he fell gravely ill with a high fever and it was rumored that he remained in a coma for 40 days. During that time, he had a dream in which God called upon him to establish a theocracy called T'ai-p'ing Tien-kuo and to purge China of the alien Manchu Dynasty and the baneful teachings of Confucius. Hung rose from the dream as a changed man and began a new career as a teacher. Later he founded the Society of God.

Joining Hung in the formation of the Society was his friend, Feng Yun-shan, whose untiring efforts did much to contribute to the recruitment of the first converts, primarily in the district called Thistle Mountain in the Jiangxi (Kiangsi) province of south China. Feng was also active in carrying Hung's messages to other places. Hung taught that God was common to all people, and that in the world, as originally created, men and women were all brothers and sisters, and that societal corruption was the work of demons. His teachings, developed over several years, were a mixture of native Chinese and Christian concepts. While developing his thoughts, he befriended Christian missionaries and identified the God whom he had seen in his dream as Christ. Hung appealed to the poor peasants in south China, advocating land reform, abolition of private property, and equality of the sexes. In the winter of 1850, Hung's society came into open conflict with government authorities and a large-scale rebellion erupted in January 1851. It lasted until 1864 and encompassed much of south China, and seriously threatened the authority of the Manchu Dynasty. At the outset, government forces were unable to contain the Society's influence and suppress the rebellion. Aided by foreign officers such as Frederick Townsend Ward, an American, and Charles "Chinese" Gordon, a Briton, the rebellion was finally quelled in 1864. Hung died of illness during the siege of the rebel capital, Nanking (Nanjing), and most of his adherents were killed in their last battle. *See also* OPIUM WAR, p. 394.

Significance   At the height of the Taiping Rebellion, Hung and his rebel forces controlled much of South China and mobilized the anti-Manchu sentiment of the Han Chinese people. They labeled Nanking (Nanjing), an ancient capital along the Yangtze (Changjiang) River, as "Heavenly Capital" and later developed a complex political structure. Power was divided among "princes," each with a regional designation as well as an area of control and responsibility. Many reforms were decreed and enforced. Before long, Hung's Heavenly Kingdom was shaken by internal dissension among the princes, causing its eventual defeat and downfall. There were other causes attributed to the ultimate failure of the Rebellion: (1) poor leadership; (2) excessive fanaticism among the rebel followers; (3) strategic blunders during later military campaigns;

(4) radical reforms that alienated many possible supporters among China's elite class; (5) discrepancies between the theory and practice of Taiping life; and (6) the growing fear of Hung's eventual success among western nations.

Taiping Christianity, which seems to have died out as a spiritual force after 1864, was sufficiently eclectic to horrify western missionaries and diplomats, and alien enough to repel most of China's literate Confucian elite. As a matter of fact, leading Confucian scholar-officials like Tseng Kuo-fan (Zeng Guofan) and Li Hung-chang (Li Hongzhang) were successful in organizing local militia to fight the Taiping. Despite its failure, however, Hung's egalitarian and Christian ideas and his anti-Manchu emphasis found fertile ground for the revolutionary mobilization of the poor peasants of south China. The Taiping Rebellion also exposed the dilapidated state of the Ch'ing Dynasty to the world.

Tonghak Rebellion, 1894–95: Korea   A widespread anti-government rebellion by followers of the *Tonghak* religious movement in Korea in the last years of the traditional Yi Dynasty (1632–1910). Tonghak means "eastern learning." Its founder was Ch'oe Che-u. According to the Tonghak tradition, Ch'oe established a new religious order in 1860, following a revelation from God. His followers were mainly the alienated segment of the Yi Dynasty ruling class and the poverty-stricken people of Korea's rural areas. Ch'oe preached his precepts based on the four religious and philosophical orders then known in Korea—Confucianism, Buddhism, Taoism, and Catholicism—intermixing them with the native Shamanistic practices. Ch'oe called his teachings "eastern learning" in part because he was especially disturbed by the revolutionary preachings of Catholicism and by increasing western inroads in Korea.

Tonghak followers were promised a prosperous and egalitarian new world along with the magic power of healing. Their faith in these promises made them fearless and daring in the face of personal danger. They were, therefore, known for their fanaticism. In 1864, Ch'oe was accused of heretical teaching and was arrested and executed, but his followers continued his teachings, particularly among the depressed segments of rural Korea. By 1890, the movement became not only a religious but also a major political and social force, and when it led mass demonstrations and armed revolts in the early 1890s, the government, unable to suppress them, sought assistance from the Chinese government. Since the dispatching of Chinese troops to Korea meant greater Chinese influence over Korean affairs, neighboring Japan would not overlook this development on the Korean peninsula and so dispatched its own troops. In the end, the Tonghak rebellion was suppressed with the help of foreign troops, but the two intervening forces eventually clashed in the Sino-Japanese War of 1894–95. Tonghak was later renamed *Ch'ŏndogyo*. Though reduced in number and significance, its followers still exist in Korea. *See also* SINO-JAPANESE WAR, 1894–95, p. 000.

Significance   Largely developed among the peasants, the Tonghak Movement lacked the organization and leadership needed to become a major force in the transformation of traditional Korea. However, the anti-government rebellion of its followers in 1894 contributed to the downfall of the Yi Dynasty. The rebellion brought in Chinese and Japanese military intervention. These two forces clashed in Korea in the Sino-Japanese War (1894–95), and victorious Japan was able to eliminate Chinese influence in Korea and ease her eventual colonization of the Korean peninsula. The Tonghak followers, despite government persecution, persisted with their advocacy of social and political reforms, demanding expulsion of foreign influence (particularly Japanese) and improvement of the treatment of the so-called seven-vile-occupation groups, abolition of slavery, land redistribution, tax reform, and punishment of corrupt officials and arrogant *yangban* ruling class members. As rebel forces, they seized government granaries and returned tax grains to the peasants. Their final defeat came in the hands of combined Korean and Japanese forces. Subsequently, Korea was colonized by Japan in 1910. However, the Tonghak Movement has been able to survive the Japanese colonial period in Korea as a religious movement and as a source of anti-Japanese sentiment among its followers.

APPENDIX A: MAPS

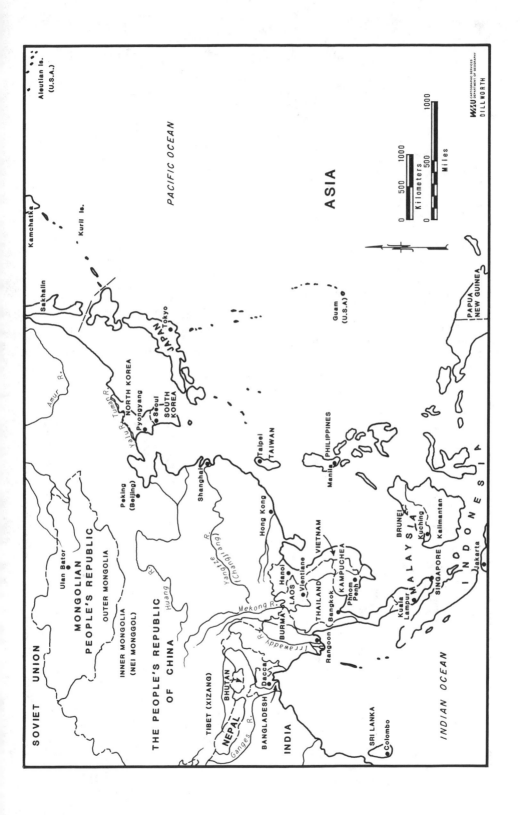

ASIA

PACIFIC OCEAN

INDIAN OCEAN

SOVIET UNION

MONGOLIAN PEOPLE'S REPUBLIC

OUTER MONGOLIA

INNER MONGOLIA
(NEI MONGGOL)

THE PEOPLE'S REPUBLIC
OF CHINA

TIBET (XIZANG)

NEPAL

BHUTAN

BANGLADESH

INDIA

SRI LANKA

Colombo

Dacca

Ganges R.

Huang R.

Yangtze R.
(Changjiang)

Mekong R.

Irrawaddy R.

Salween R.

BURMA

Rangoon

THAILAND

Bangkok

LAOS

Vientiane

Hanoi

VIETNAM

KAMPUCHEA

Phnom Penh

MALAYSIA

Kuala Lumpur

SINGAPORE

BRUNEI

Kuching

Kalimantan

INDONESIA

Jakarta

Hong Kong

Shanghai

Peking (Beijing)

Taipei

TAIWAN

PHILIPPINES

Manila

Guam (U.S.A.)

Amur R.

Yalu R.

Tumen R.

NORTH KOREA

Pyongyang

Seoul

SOUTH KOREA

JAPAN

Tokyo

Sakhalin

Kuril Is.

Kamchatka

Aleutian Is.
(U.S.A.)

PAPUA NEW GUINEA

Kilometers
0   500   1000

Miles
0   500   1000

WSU CARTOGRAPHIC SERVICES
DEPARTMENT OF GEOGRAPHY
DILLWORTH

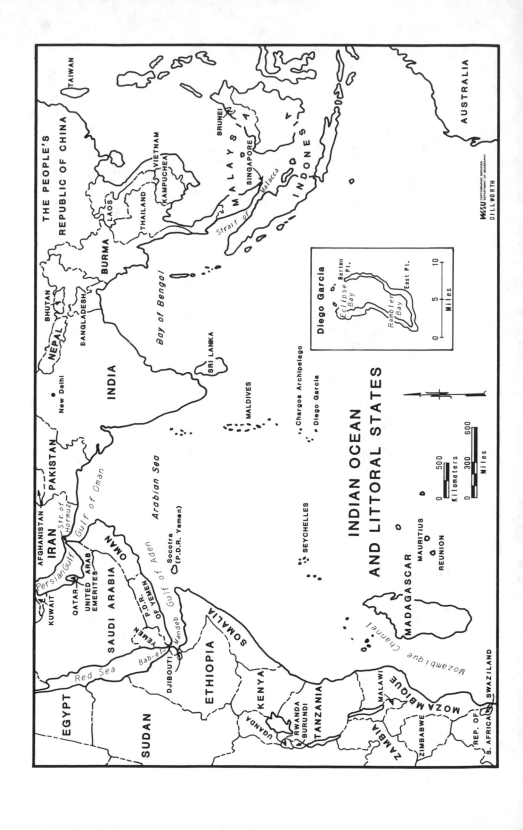

INDIAN OCEAN AND LITTORAL STATES

APPENDIX B: TABLES

419

TABLE B-1

Geographic, Demographic, and Economic Comparisons

Country	Post Colonial Independence Year	Capital	Area (1,000 sq. Kilometers)	Population Mid-1982 (Millions)	Population Annual Growth Rate 1980–2000 (Percent)	GNP Per Capita Dollars (1982)	GNP Per Capita Annual Growth Rate 1960–1982 (Percent)
Northeast Asia							
China (PRC)		Peking (Beijing)	9,561	1,008.2	1.0	310	5.0
China (Taiwan)	1949	Taipei	36	18.3	1.8	2,300	7.5
Japan		Tokyo	372	118.4	0.4	10,080	6.1
Korea, North (DPRK)	1948	Pyongyang	121	18.7	2.1	810	5.0
Korea, South (ROK)	1948	Seoul	98	39.3	1.4	1,910	8.0
Mongolia	1921	Ulan Bator	1,565	1.8	2.4		
Southeast Asia							
Brunei	1983	Bandar Seri Begawan	5.8	0.2	0.3	20,000	
Burma	1948	Rangoon	677	34.9	2.4	190	1.3
Indonesia	1945 (1949)	Jakarta (Djakarta)	1,919	152.6	1.9	580	4.2
Kampuchea (Cambodia)	1953	Phnom Penh	181	6.0	1.7		
Laos	1953	Vientiane	237	3.6	2.6		
Malaysia	1957	Kuala Lumpur	330	14.5	2.0	1,860	4.3
Papua New Guinea	1975	Port Moresby	462	3.1	2.2	820	2.1
Philippines	1946	Manila	300	50.7	2.1	820	2.8
Singapore	1965	Singapore City	1	2.5	1.0	5,910	7.4
Thailand		Bangkok	514	48.5	1.9	790	4.5
Vietnam (SRV, 1976)	1945	Hanoi	330	57.0	2.5	160	

Continued on next page

TABLE B-1—*Continued*

Geographic, Demographic, and Economic Comparisons

Country	Post Colonial Independence Year	Capital	Area (1,000 sq.) Kilometers)	Population		GNP Per Capita	
				Mid–1982 (Millions)	Annual Growth Rate 1980–2000 (Percent)	Dollars (1982)	Annual Growth Rate 1960–1982 (Percent)
South Asia (Indian Subcontinent)							
Bangladesh	1971	Dacca (Dhaka)	144	92.6	2.9	140	0.3
Bhutan		Thimpu	47	1.2	2.2	80	
India	1947	New Delhi	3,288	717.0	1.9	260	1.3
Nepal		Kathmandu	141	15.4	2.6	170	-0.1
Pakistan	1947	Islamabad	804	87.1	2.7	380	2.8
Sri Lanka	1948	Colombo	66	15.2	1.8	320	2.6

Sources: World Bank. *World Development Report, 1984.* New York: Oxford University Press. 1984.
Asia Yearbook, 1984. Hongkong: Far Eastern Economic Review. 1984.
Britannica Book of the Year, 1984. Chicago: Encyclopaedia Britannica, Inc. 1984.

TABLE B-2

Selected Comparative Information on Asia

Country	Literacy (Percent of Population Over Age 15)	Secondary Education 1981 (Percent of Age Group)	Urbanization 1982 (Percent of Total Population)	Labor Force in Agriculture 1980 (Percent)	Communist Regime	Military Coups (Successful)
Northeast Asia						
China (PRC)	34	44	21	69	Yes	
China (Taiwan)	86	80	66	30		
Japan	100	92	78	12		
Korea, North (DPRK)	95	87	46	49	Yes	
Korea, South (ROK)	94	85	65	34		Two
Mongolia		0	53	55	Yes	
Southeast Asia						
Brunei	0		59			
Burma	70	20	28	67		One
Indonesia	72	30	22	58		One
Kampuchea (Cambodia)					Yes	
Laos	41	18	14	75	Yes	
Malaysia	75	53	30	50		
Papua New Guinea	30	13	17	82		
Philippines	76	63	38	46		
Singapore	85	65	100	2		
Thailand	82	29	17	76		Four or more
Vietnam (SRV, 1976)		48	19	71	Yes	

Continued on next page

TABLE B-2—*Continued*

Selected Comparative Information on Asia

Country	Literacy (Percent of Population Over Age 15)	Secondary Education 1981 (Percent of Age Group)	Urbanization 1982 (Percent of Total Population)	Labor Force in Agriculture 1980 (Percent)	Communist Regime	Military Coups (Successful)
South Asia (Indian Subcontinent)						
Bangladesh	26	15	12	74		Two
Bhutan		3	4	93		
India	36	30	24	71		
Nepal	12	21	6	93		
Pakistan	27	17	29	57		Three
Sri Lanka	87	51	24	54		

Sources: World Bank. *World Development Report, 1984.* New York: Oxford University Press. 1984.
Asia Yearbook, 1984. Hongkong: Far Eastern Economic Review. 1984.
Britannica Book of the Year, 1984. Chicago: Encyclopaedia Britannica, Inc. 1984.

INDEX

Cross-references to dictionary entries are located in the text at the end of each definition paragraph. Page references in BOLD type indicate dictionary entries. For individual countries of Asia, consult the *Guide to Countries* on p. xv.

425